ENGLISH PHONETICS:
TWENTIETH CENTURY DEVELOPMENTS

ENGLISH PHONETICS: TWENTIETH CENTURY DEVELOPMENTS

Logos Studies in Language and Linguistics

Edited by
Beverley Collins, Inger M. Mees
and Paul Carley

Volume IV
English phonetics

LONDON AND NEW YORK

The Phonetics of English by Ida Ward reprinted from the
third edition published in 1939 by W. Heffer & Sons Ltd.

The Principle of English Phonetic Notation by Harold E. Palmer
reprinted from the second edition published in 1928 by The Institute
for Research in English Teaching, Tokyo.

Le Maître phonétique selections reprinted from
Le Maître phonétique, London: IPA, 1900-1970.

First published 2013
by Routledge
2 Park Square, Milton Park, Abingdon, Oxon OX14 4RN

Simultaneously published in the USA and Canada
by Routledge
711 Third Avenue, New York, NY 10017

Simultaneously published in Japan
by Edition Synapse
2-8-5 Uchikanda, Chiyoda-ku, Tokyo 101–0047

Routledge is an imprint of the Taylor & Francis Group, an informa business

Editorial material and selection © 2013 Beverley Collins, Inger M. Mees and Paul
Carley; individual owners retain copyright in their own material

All rights reserved. No part of this book may be reprinted or
reproduced or utilised in any form or by any electronic, mechanical,
or other means, now known or hereafter invented, including
photocopying and recording, or in any information storage or retrieval system,
without permission in writing from the publishers.

Trademark notice: Product or corporate names may be trademarks or registered
trademarks, and are used only for identification and explanation without intent
to infringe.

British Library Cataloguing in Publication Data
A catalogue record for this book is available from the British Library

Library of Congress Cataloging in Publication Data
A catalog record for this book has been requested

ISBN 13: 978-0-415-59054-9 (Set)
ISBN 13: 978-0-415-59058-7 (Volume IV)
ISBN 13: 978-4-86166-152-5 (Set: Japan)

Publisher's Note
The publisher has gone to great lengths to ensure the quality
of this reprint but points out that some imperfections in
the original documents may be apparent.

CONTENTS

VOLUME IV: ENGLISH PHONETICS

Acknowledgements   x

Introduction to Volume IV   1

12 *The Phonetics of English,* 3rd edn, Cambridge: Heffer, 1939, pp. 1–255   21
IDA C. WARD

13 *The Principles of English Phonetic Notation,* 2nd edn, Tokyo: Institute for Research in English Teaching, 1928, pp. 1–140   293
H. E. PALMER

14 Selection of articles on English 1900–70 from *le Maître phonétique,* London: IPA   433

   Dialects/Varieties

     1900 American English, pp. 72–3   437
     G. HEMPL

     1906 Scottish specimen, pp. 118–19 (and Erratum)   439
     D. JONES

     1908 Dialect of Whitby (Yorkshire), pp. 119–120   442
     G. NOËL-ARMFIELD

     1910 Some East London street cries, pp. 75–78   444
     G. NOËL-ARMFIELD

     1911 English Tyneside dialect (Northumberland), p. 184   448
     D. JONES

     1912 Some Aberdeenshire vowels, pp. 85–6   449
     J. L. WILSON

CONTENTS

1912 Specimen, London dialect (Cockney), p. 144   451
D. JONES

1913 Kentish dialect (Hythe), pp. 56–7   452
H. E. PALMER

1913 Dialect of North West Lancashire, p. 104   454
D. JONES

1913 Dialect of North West Lancashire (Torver, near Coniston), pp. 141–2   455
D. JONES

1923 Cornish dialect, p. 7   457
D. JONES

1927 American English, pp. 1–5   458
J. S. KENYON

1927 American English, pp. 40–2   463
L. BLOOMFIELD

1933 The Southern American drawl, pp. 69–71   466
C. M. WISE

1935 Dialect of Morebattle (Scotland), pp. 13–4   469
J. C. CATFORD

1939 East Devon dialect, p. 50   471
R. KINGDON

1946 ʌ and ə in British English, p. 2   472
D. JONES

1946 ʌ and ə in British English, p. 22   473
I. C. WARD AND D. ABERCROMBIE

1947 The phonetic system of a dialect of Newcastle-upon-Tyne, pp. 6–8   474
J. D. O'CONNOR

1954 A Scottish vowel, pp. 23–4   477
D. ABERCROMBIE

CONTENTS

1960 The glottalisation of voiceless plosives in London speech, pp. 14–15 — 479
L. A. ILES

1961 Some aspects of the phonetics of vowels in South African English, pp. 5–12 — 481
G. H. BRECKWOLDT

1962 Specimen of British English, pp. 2–5 — 489
J. C. WELLS

1963 Specimen of Black Country speech, pp. 30–3 — 493
C. PAINTER

1964 Specimen Cardiff, pp. 6–7 — 497
J. WINDSOR LEWIS

1965 Specimen passages of the speech of Gateshead-on-Tyne, pp. 6–7 — 499
W. VIERECK

1966 Specimen, English RP, as read by D. Abercrombie, p. 34 — 501
E. ULDALL

1966 The Stockport dialect, pp. 26–30 — 502
K. R. LODGE

1967 Specimen, Jamaican Creole, pp. 5–6 — 507
J. C. WELLS

1969 English: Cockney, pp. 41–43 — 509
J. R. HURFORD

1970 English: Cockney, pp. 38–9 — 512
J. R. HURFORD

Phonetic Transcription/Spelling

1906 Normalised phonetic spelling, pp. 71–3 — 517
H. SWEET

1906 Simplified phonetic spelling, pp. 125–7 — 520
H. SWEET

1910 The transcription of English vowels, pp. 102–7 — 523
H. E. PALMER

CONTENTS

1910 The transcription of English vowels, pp. 128–9   529
D. JONES

1911 Standard English speech and script, pp. 136–7   531
W. RIPPMANN

1913 Phonetic spelling of English, pp. 113–16   533
D. JONES

1923 A narrower transcription for English, pp. 17–19   537
L. A. ARMSTRONG

1925 Unstressed ɪ, pp. 23–5   540
H. E. PALMER

1926 Unstressed English ɪ, pp. 3–4   543
D. JONES

1931 Extra broad transcription (and response from Daniel Jones), correspondence, pp. 27–8   545
H. E. PALMER

1932 Extra broad transcription, correspondence, pp. 60–1   547
A. LLOYD JAMES AND D. JONES

1933 Review of H. Palmer, *The Principles of Romanization*, pp. 28–30   549
D. JONES

1935 Broad transcription of general American, pp. 7–10   552
B. BLOCH

1935, The transcription of English, pp. 10–13   556
G. L. TRAGER

1942 The letters ɪ and ʊ, pp. 14–15   560
D. JONES

1953 Phonetic transcriptions, pp. 32–4   562
D. ABERCROMBIE

Phonetic/Phonological Theory

1914 What is a syllable, p. 12, correspondence, with response by O. Jespersen, pp. 52–3   567
D. JONES

CONTENTS

1914 The affricates in English, pp. 53–4 570
P. H. DANNATT

1934 Breathed consonants, pp. 48–9 (with note by Daniel Jones) 572
E. KRUISINGA

1938 The weak form of *this*, p. 5 574
H. E. PALMER

1939 An experiment on stress perception, pp. 44–5 575
N. C. SCOTT

1952 Context in English intonation teaching, pp. 9–11 577
G. F. ARNOLD

1960 Strong and weak forms in southern British English, pp. 5–7 580
G. F. ARNOLD

1960 The instability of English alveolar articulations, pp. 7–10 583
A. C. GIMSON

1969 Describing assimilation, pp. 10–11 587
A. CRUTTENDEN

1969 Review of Andrésen, *Pre-glottalization in English standard pronunciation*, pp. 14–16 589
J. D. O'CONNOR

Phonetics in the Wider World

1905 Reminiscences of Melville Bell, pp. 107–09 595
D. MACRAE

1925 Broadcasting and phonetics, pp. 11–13 598
A. LLOYD JAMES

1926 The BBC committee on pronunciation, pp. 34–5 601
L. E. ARMSTRONG

1929 A test for telephone operators, pp. 13–15 603
A. LLOYD JAMES

1970 The last m.f., London: IPA, p. 28 606

ACKNOWLEDGEMENTS

The publishers would like to thank the following for permission to reprint their material:

Viki Angela for permission to reprint Harold E. Palmer, *The Principles of English Phonetic Notation*, 2nd edn (Tokyo: Institute for Research in English Teaching, 1928), pp. 1–140.

The International Phonetic Association for permission to reprint selections from *Le Maître phonétique* (London: IPA, 1900–70).

Disclaimer

The publishers have made every effort to contact copyright holders of the other works reprinted in the collection. This has not been possible, however, and we would welcome correspondence from those individuals/companies whom we have been unable to trace.

INTRODUCTION TO VOLUME IV

Ida C. Ward: *The Phonetics of English* (1939)

Life and career

Ida Caroline Ward (1880–1949) was perhaps the most gifted of all the many talented linguists whom Daniel Jones attracted to his University College London department in the interwar period. She was born in Yorkshire, the daughter of a Bradford wool merchant and, after some years at teacher training college, moved on to take her B Litt at the University of Durham. Ward then began a successful school teaching career, only later becoming interested in language study when in 1913 she enrolled as a part-time student at Daniel Jones's department of phonetics at UCL. In 1919 Jones, recognising her obvious talents, invited her to join his staff (Jones 1950a).

In her early university career, she concentrated her efforts on English phonetics (especially intonation) and speech pathology. Her published work included *Speech Defects* (1923) and – co-authored with her colleague Lilias Armstrong – the widely used *Handbook of English Intonation*, (Armstrong and Ward 1926). The present volume, *Phonetics of English*, followed in 1929. Like all his staff, Ward had been pressed by Jones into investigating 'exotic languages' (as non-European languages were dubbed at the time). Nevertheless, it was only relatively late in life, when she was approaching fifty, that she decided to focus on the languages of West Africa. It was on that basis that in 1932 she accepted a post in Arthur Lloyd James's department of phonetics at the University of London's School of Oriental Studies (later renamed the School of Oriental and African Studies, or SOAS). Then began a series of outstanding publications including a co-authored textbook on the study of West African languages (Westermann and Ward 1933), followed by two books on the Nigerian languages Efik (Ward 1933) and Ibo (Ward 1936). In these works, she pioneered research into crucial linguistic features such as tone and vowel harmony. She founded a department of West African languages at SOAS in 1937, for which she was granted a chair in 1944. In 1948 she retired, but continued her research up to her death just a year later. Her last book, on Yoruba, appeared posthumously in 1952.

She ended her career widely recognised as the world's leading authority on the phonology of African languages, and right up to her death was a driving force in establishing SOAS as a centre of excellence for African linguistics. It is truly remarkable that she only began to research in this area so late in life – long after most academics have produced their best work. Her personal character was perhaps best summed up in A. N. Tucker's obituary.

INTRODUCTION TO VOLUME IV

> The outstanding qualities of Ida Ward's character were her kindness and sympathetic understanding. She always put both staff and students at their ease, and the African members of the School found in her an understanding 'ma' to whom to take their problems [...] But those of us who knew 'Wardie' intimately will also remember with affection the little white-haired lady, living happily with her widowed sister in Golders Green, proud of her small garden and immensely proud of her great-nephew and niece (Tucker 1950: 544).

The Phonetics of English

Ward was not merely capable of undertaking groundbreaking research herself, including providing theoretical frameworks for others to build upon, but was also notable for an ability to explain her discoveries in lucid prose. This talent for clear-cut explanation of complicated ideas can also be seen in her more basic writing on English phonetics and in particular in her introductory textbook *The Phonetics of English* (henceforth *PE*). We have decided to reproduce the third edition (1939), since it contains much extra material, including chapters on the influence of broadcasting and the BBC on pronunciation, forming a link to the work of Lloyd James (see Vols II and III of this collection). In addition, she added a chapter comparing British and American English and transcriptions of speeches by King George V and President Franklin D. Roosevelt.

In her original preface to the 1929 first edition, Ward states that her book is aimed at the teacher who has to deal with 'indistinct or dialectal speech' (p. v), and emphasises the practical nature of her approach. *PE* is essentially concerned with elocution for native speakers, particularly those speaking basilectal forms of English – 'accent reduction', in modern parlance. The reader needs to bear in mind the general acceptance in this era of what today would be considered bigoted views of non-standard speech. It is also worthwhile remembering that Daniel Jones fought a personal battle against such opinions which were current in the 1920s, when *PE* was being written (Collins and Mees 2001). This difference in attitude accounts for Ward's overly prescriptive suggestions such as advocating defining 'the limits beyond which speech is considered markedly vulgar or dialectal' (p. 9) – there is most certainly no hint of anything resembling modern political correctness here. Ward concentrated on the dialectal features of the two English accents of which she had personal knowledge: Yorkshire, which she knew from birth, and Cockney, based on her living in London from her twenties onwards. It could well be that she was inspired in this work by her own experience of discrimination against her original northern accent – as is borne out by her anecdote of the training college student who, when asked if she came from Yorkshire, replied 'Yes [...] we're branded, aren't we?' (fn. p. 8). A recording is extant of Ida Ward's own speech which reveals her to have an accent which is remarkable for what can only be called artificiality, as has been observed by John Wells.[1]

> On the recording she sounds quite incredibly old-fashioned by today's standards [...]. Given her background, she may well have been a speaker of 'adoptive' RP rather than a native speaker like Jones. Perhaps she overdid things a little.

Chapter 1 is devoted to a long discussion on the vexed question of standard pronunciation and the role played by regional and social factors. She illustrates her argument that there is much greater variation in the speech of the working class population *vis-à-vis* that of higher social classes with the 'Variant Pronunciations' cone (p. 5, fig.1), which is the first published version of what Trudgill (1974: 42) later termed 'the sociolinguistic pyramid'. In fact, as Ward acknowledges, the idea for the cone is taken directly from Daniel Jones (see Collins and Mees 2003: Vol. VIII for the original rough sketch to be found in his lecture notes).[2]

Despite Ward's mentioning the possibilities of using phonetics in dealing with speech defects and the problems of the deaf, there is little attention to such matters in *PE* (she had of course already written *Speech Defects*, which had been well received). Chapter 3 on correction of pronunciation is concerned exclusively with dialect 'mistakes', and the technique for removing them to produce something closer to RP. She also mentions the dangers of teaching artificial pronunciations based on orthography, e.g. *fatal, carrot* and *cabbage* pronounced as /feɪtæl, kærɒt, kæbeɪdʒ/ (p. 27). She points out that to avoid such errors it is essential for the teacher to have good phonetic and linguistic training, and indicates how this could be achieved in teacher training colleges (ch. 4 and Appendix 1). It is noteworthy that Ward stresses throughout the importance of phonetic ear-training, including the use of nonsense words.

Ward's treatment of the classification of speech sounds is very similar to what can be found in comparable modern introductory textbooks on articulatory phonetics. The classification of vowels (pp. 66–73) draws heavily on Jones's cardinal vowel theory. Its appearance in the 1929 first edition is the very first explanation of the theory in a textbook on English – although Noël-Armfield (1919) and Trofimov and Jones (1923),[3] did so for general phonetics and Russian respectively. Only the primary cardinal vowels are mentioned here, although earlier in the book vowels with reversed lip positions, similar to secondary cardinals (rounded front vowels [y ø]) are offered for practice (p. 64). Similarly, the section on the phoneme (ch. 10), when it first appeared in 1929, would have been the first exposition of the theory in a textbook dealing with English, although Trofimov and Jones (1923) employed the concept in discussing the phonology of Russian. It was not until 1932 that Jones used the phoneme for his description of English in the third edition of the *Outline of English Phonetics* (Jones 1932a). Ward follows Jones's concept of the phoneme as a 'family of sounds' (p. 74), and differentiates between allophonic variation (although that term is not used) in a single idiolect from the variants occurring in the speech of different individuals – 'variphones' to use Jones's (1932b) later term. This anticipation by Ward of Jones's own (1932a) third edition of the *Outline* is one of the most striking features of *PE*.

Ward goes on to examine in detail the English vowels and diphthongs (chs 9 and 10) and consonants (ch. 14). The vowel descriptions are illustrated throughout using cardinal vowel diagrams. All the English vowels are indicated in red (a similar use of colour to the diagrams up till the last reprint of the tenth edition in Jones's *English Pronouncing Dictionary*, i.e. from Jones 1917 to 1955). Page 81, fig. 13, shows a representation of Ida Ward's estimate of her own English vowels placed on a cardinal vowel diagram. Figures 22 and 23 (p. 112) give the positions for the English diphthongs.

A consonant grid based on place and manner of articulation (p. 128) precedes Ward's detailed description of English consonants, which includes mention of features such as aspiration, voiceless plosives and devoicing of final voiced stops. The degree of phonetic accuracy here is due not only to good observation but also perhaps to data obtained from the kymographic research of Jones (1918: 168–82) and others. An interesting section is concerned with glottalisation of voiceless plosive consonants, which when it was published in the first edition could be considered the most thorough pre-1930 investigation of this phenomenon in non-standard British English speech.[4] Ward describes how often glottalisation occurs in non-standard accents, giving examples from Cockney and Yorkshire (pp. 135–6). Apart from reference to its use pre-vocalically for emphasis, its existence in RP goes unmentioned, but nevertheless a hidden indication of its occurrence might be found in her statement that in dialect 'before alveolar and labial consonants, where it occurs very frequently, the glottal stop is not so noticeable' (p. 135). However, her general advice to teachers is that glottal stop is 'unpleasant', 'makes for indistinctness' and 'teachers will have to wage vigorous war against it' (p. 136). That war has certainly been unsuccessful since it is now generally recognised that Daniel Jones's (1922) prediction that '[glottal stop] is noticeably spreading everywhere' has unquestionably been proved true; see Collins and Mees (1996) for further detail. Another interesting sociophonetic topic is the liaison forms 'linking and intrusive *r*' (p. 147). Ward, bravely for this era, acknowledges that stigmatised pronunciations such as /noʊ aɪdɪər əv ɪt/ for *no idea of it* are in fact frequent from educated speakers, although she claims that in educated speech intrusive *r* is confined to contexts following /ə/, and that *I saw it* as /aɪ sɔːər ɪt/ or /aɪ sɔːr ɪt/ is found only in basilectal varieties such as Cockney.

As might be expected, attention is also paid to h-dropping and h-epenthesis – the latter termed here 'intrusive *h*' (p. 150). Ward also mentions the absence of voiceless labial-velar fricative /ʍ/ in initial *wh*-words, noting that Wyld (1920: 311–12) states this has long been the case in standard English, even though /ʍ/ lives on in Scotland and parts of the North. The chapter concludes with a summary of the main differences between northern and London speech as compared with standard English. For the North, Ward highlights the use of the TRAP vowel in what would nowadays be termed the BATH words (Wells 1982: 133–5), conflation of NURSE and SQUARE, and the replacement of STRUT by FOOT, or a central vowel. For Cockney, she notes realisational variation in vowels, use of glottal stop and over-dark *l* (pp. 153–5).

In chapter 15, Ward discusses what she terms 'sound attributes', namely the supra-segmental features of stress and intonation and in addition length of individual segments. The treatment of intonation is largely taken over from her co-authored introductory textbook *A Handbook of English Intonation* (Armstrong and Ward 1926), which had been well received and, having found a gap in the market, had sold well. Ward continues in *PE* to use the same simple division into Tune I (falling) and Tune II (rising). The possibility of fall-rise patterns is briefly mentioned (p. 175) and the rise-fall has just one passing reference in a note (p. 234). Ward employs what is effectively an interlinear representation, although omitting the upper line. Dashes denote relatively prominent syllables whilst dots show non-prominent ones. In the in-text representation, stress is indicated by a vertical, whilst a double vertical is used for extra prominence, but there is no designation of a nuclear syllable, even though this had been clearly defined years earlier by Palmer (1922; see Vol. V of this collection). In considering stress, Ward notes the association of unstressed ('non-prominent') syllables with 'some kind of neutral vowel' (p. 160) – in particular [ə]. Such vowels are likely to be short and to lack obvious pitch change. She also distinguishes sentence stress and points out that there is a tendency for 'stressed syllables to occur at regular intervals of time' (p. 167) – what would today be termed stress-timing, cf. the perceptive comments of Lloyd James *Speech Signals in Telephony* (1940), reproduced in volume II of the present collection. Ward returns to stress in chapter 16, entitled 'Sounds in connected speech', where she also introduces strong and weak forms, providing a table spread over two pages (pp. 182–3). In this chapter, she also deals at length with assimilation, defined effectively as a modification of consonants as a result of phonetic conditioning resulting in phonemic change. Ward distinguishes this feature from similitude, where any such change is realisational, leaving unaffected the phonemic status of the consonants concerned. She introduces thereby a distinction developed by Daniel

Jones in his revised (1932a) *Outline*, and this is one obvious difference from the first edition of *PE*.

The first edition of *PE* ended at this point; the remaining chapters (chs 17–19) were added later. Chapter 17 covers what Ward regarded as recent developments in pronunciation, claiming them to be tendencies characteristic of those under 35, both male and female. Certain of her observations are to be found attested in present-day twenty-first century British non-regional pronunciation (Standard Southern British English), for example, labialisation of /r/ (p. 200) and the lack of labialisation with /ʊ/ and /oʊ/ (p. 202). Vowel lengthening is still to be heard today, in particular with /æ/, noted by Jones (1918), and more recently by Wells (1982: 289–90), for words like *bad, sad* as opposed to *lad, pad* – an effect which is sometimes nowadays termed the 'bad-lad split'. What Wells (1982: 238–9) calls 'smoothing' of vowel sequences /aɪə, aʊə/ was a notable feature of the speech of the 1930s, and continued for much later, even though it may possibly now be on the retreat. Ward misses out the increasing glottalisation of fortis stops – something clearly to be heard on audio recordings of this era (Collins and Mees 1996).

Ward's summary of differences between British and American English benefits from her having being provided with gramophone records of American English donated by an American speech department (p. 206); at this time, speech departments in the USA, dealing essentially with elocution and accent reduction, were flourishing. To back up her contrastive study, in chapter 19, Ward provides transcriptions together with intonation marking for two speeches by King George V and President Franklin D. Roosevelt. Although these speakers cannot be considered typical of the general population, and the material is prepared and formal in character, it must be remembered that recordings of informal speech were virtually unobtainable at this time. Ward covers the crucial areas – rhoticism, t-voicing and systemic differences in the vowels (pp. 210–12). She also mentions nasalisation as an ongoing voice quality feature, varying idiolectally (p. 213), and goes on to deal with intonation. At this time, thanks to the work of Jones, Palmer, Armstrong, and Ward herself, far more was known about British RP intonation than about its American counterpart. Her observations on Roosevelt's American intonation are somewhat vague, and she discovers little differentiation from British RP. This is probably because Roosevelt was not a typical speaker of General American; in fact he was regarded by Americans as having many British characteristics in his speech. He is often exemplified as being typical of the 'Mid-Atlantic accent', an artificial type of pronunciation with many RP features advocated by American elocutionists in the twenties and thirties. Her comments on differences in stress and rhythm are much more illuminating. The variance in vowel reduction to schwa and the effect on rhythm are well described, and the frequently heard American impression of British English as 'clipped' is noted (pp. 217–18). These transcriptions are a landmark in that – apart from Jones's remarkable early efforts on literary material in *Intonation Curves* (1909a) – they are probably the first such systematic and accurate representations of speech recordings ever made available in published form by a trained phonetician. Ward provides phonetic transcriptions for the two English dialects she had expert knowledge of (see above), using literary extracts: Bernard Shaw's *Pygmalion* for Cockney, and *The Good Companions* by Bradford-born J. B. Priestley for Yorkshire. The pronunciation represented is not based on actual speech but was devised by Ward herself; compare the phonetic transcriptions used by Jones (1909b) in the first edition of his *Pronunciation of English*.

The third edition of *PE* concludes with Appendices outlining a recommended course for speech training in teacher training colleges, in which she emphasises the importance of practical ear training (Appendix I). Appendix II features ear-training exercises, containing exclusively nonsense words of varying degrees of difficulty. The bibliography (pp. 246–8) is notable for the fact that it lists several volumes now available in Routledge *Major Works*, for example Lloyd James (*Our Spoken Language, The Broadcast Word*, volume II of this collection; *Broadcast English*, volume III of this collection), Jones (*An English Pronouncing Dictionary, The Pronunciation of English, An Outline of English Phonetics, Intonation Curves*, all reproduced in Collins and Mees 2003); Rip[p]man[n]'s *Sounds of Spoken English*, Viëtor/Ripman's *Elements of Phonetics* (both reproduced in Collins and Mees 2007), Coleman (1914) (reproduced in volume V of the present collection).

When it first appeared in 1929, *PE* anticipated in many respects Daniel Jones's 1932 radical revision of the *Outline of English Phonetics*. It is here, for instance, that we find the first detailed explanation of the phoneme, and also of the cardinal vowel system. Ward uses vowel quadrilateral diagrams consistently to explain features of English pronunciation – again this is the first textbook to do so. There is, for the time, a detailed examination of RP intonation. Although Ward might be criticised by a twenty-first century audience for her elocutionary approach and the use of what sounds to us like bigoted language, she is, for the era, very tolerant of basilectal regional variation. The most notable feature of the revised 1939 edition is the attention given to American English and the contrastive analysis of General American and British RP. In addition, Ward provides here transcriptions of authentic speech from audio recordings, together with intonation marking. Ward produced much more than just another phonetics textbook. She explained in lucid terms, and with excellent exemplification, new ideas and ways of thinking about speech that academic linguists had developed during the previous two decades, and showed how these could be applied in the real world. Finally, it is worth stating that the book sold well and was used extensively. Together with Lloyd James's publications and work for the BBC (see Vols II and III), Ida Ward ensured that from 1929 on phonetics became known in the British Isles to a far wider lay audience.

Harold E. Palmer: *The Principles of English Phonetic Notation* (1928)

Life and career

Harold Edward Palmer (1887–1949) was born in London, but brought up at Hythe in Kent, where his family had moved and his father ran the local newspaper. In his youth, Palmer was an outstanding scholar and 'carried off all possible prizes with apparently no difficulty' (Jones 1950b: 4), but left school at 15, and appears never to have been encouraged to go on to university. When young, he contributed to his father's newspaper, and was for a while its editor. In 1902, he moved to Verviers in Belgium, where he worked as a teacher in a language school using the Berlitz method, an experience which influenced him greatly. He soon established his own language school, originally called 'Institut des Langues Etrangères Palmer' (later abbreviated to 'Institut Palmer'), and ran it on his own much modified Berlitz lines, which he dubbed the 'Palmer method'. In 1907, he joined the International Phonetic Association and wrote several short pieces for *Le Maître phonétique* (e.g. Palmer 1925, see this volume). Palmer and Daniel Jones, who was at this point Assistant Secretary of the IPA, corresponded frequently from then onwards, but it was a chance meeting on the Dover-Ostend ferry in 1912 which cemented the relationship: 'We had a memorable talk on phonetics, and we struck up a friendship which it has been a privilege to me to enjoy ever since', wrote Jones (1950b: 5) on Palmer's death.

INTRODUCTION TO VOLUME IV

Advertisements in *Le Maître phonétique* reveal that from 1909 onwards Palmer was expanding his language teaching to include running summer holiday courses at Folkestone in Kent (Smith 1999: 43). 'There, every year we have the satisfactions [sic] of breaking up the old vicious habits and of inculcating the new ones by means of modern methods on a strictly phonetic basis.'[5] In 1913, he represented the Association Phonétique at the Ghent Congress of International Associations.[6] All this activity was soon to come to an end with the outbreak of World War I. Six weeks into the German occupation of Belgium, Palmer decided to flee the country with his wife and young child. Undertaking a hazardous journey, crossing the border hiding in a vegetable cart, they arrived safely in the Netherlands (which was neutral territory), and from there went back to Britain, eventually arriving penniless at the family home in Folkestone (Anderson 1969: 140). Palmer first took a temporary teaching job but lost little time in making his way to University College London, where he contacted Daniel Jones, who was now the head of the recently founded phonetics department. Jones, who never bothered about a lack of conventional educational qualifications if he thought a person had genuine talent, offered Palmer the chance to give a series of evening lectures. Jones said of him in a departmental report: 'his work has been most successful and his course of public lectures attracted large audiences',[7] and in 1916 made him a part-time member of his staff. Palmer continued to perform outstandingly well and, in addition to teaching, produced a remarkable series of books and articles on phonetics and language teaching, beginning with *What is Phonetics?* (1915), and followed by *A First Course of English Phonetics* (1917a), *The Scientific Study and Teaching of Languages* (1917b), *The Principles of Language-Study* (1921a), and *The Oral Method of Teaching Languages* (1921b). These works often reveal the extent to which Palmer had become an enthusiastic advocate of phonetics in general, and of its application to language teaching in particular. A book written towards the end of Palmer's time at Jones's department, *English Intonation with Systematic Exercises* (1922), has arguably had the longest lasting influence of any of his phonetic/phonological works. It is reproduced and discussed in volume V of the present collection. For details, summaries and commentary on these and Palmer's other publications, see Smith (1999) and also Tickoo (2008).

In 1921, Palmer received an invitation from the Japanese Ministry of Education to go to Japan as an advisor on English language teaching. He left London in 1922 and stayed in Japan for 14 years, founding the Institute for Research in English Teaching (also known as IRET) – the first centre of its kind in the world to be totally concerned with the teaching of English as a foreign language, and editing its *Bulletin*. A notable publication was the groundbreaking *Dictionary of English Pronunciation with American Variants (in Phonetic Transcription)* (Palmer, Blandford and Martin 1926) – the very first dictionary to list British and American pronunciation side by side (see Collins and Mees 2009). Palmer also produced a number of works on phonetics and pronunciation in the following years. *Concerning Pronunciation* (1928a) was a general discussion of the significance of pronunciation examined not only from the phonetic but also from the psychological viewpoint. *The Principles of Romanization* (1930) surveyed the possibilities for the reform of writing systems for Japanese. *A New Classification of English Tones* (1933) modified his earlier work on intonation, simplifying it for pedagogical reasons. For an overview of Palmer's period of time in Japan, and the crucial work on language teaching that he did for that country, see the excellent detailed survey in Smith (1999).

In June 1931, Palmer set out on a spectacular eight-month world tour, the like of which scarcely anyone would have been able to undertake in that era. He travelled first to Europe, and then crossed the Atlantic by ocean liner and stayed for some time in the USA. On his travels he met (amongst others) Otto Jespersen, Michael West, Edward Sapir, Leonard Bloomfield and (on board ship) the world-famous author H. G. Wells. A fascinating record of his experiences is to be found in his personal diary of the journey, portions of which have been made available in the Warwick ELT Archive.[8]

Palmer's daughter, Dorothée Anderson, notes that by the mid-1930s, after the 1931 Japanese occupation of Manchuria, the political situation in Japan was deteriorating, and there was 'increasing antipathy towards foreigners' (Anderson 1969). Consequently, as the non-Japanese head of an institute concerned with foreign languages, Palmer increasingly felt that he needed to leave Japan in order to have a chance to pursue his work 'in a more congenial atmosphere'. He was offered a post as a linguistic advisor for the publishers Longmans Green and, in 1936, shortly after receiving an honorary doctorate from the prestigious Tokyo Imperial University, Palmer returned to England. He bought a large house, set in a huge garden, at Felbridge in rural Sussex, where he was able to indulge his love of model railways by creating an outdoor system designed, intriguingly, to illustrate English sentence structure. We show Palmer's own diagram (Palmer 1938: 218–19) on p. 9. Japanese friends and colleagues had clubbed together to buy him a full size replica of a complete Japanese room, which was shipped over and erected in an extension to his Felbridge house. Palmer was in the habit of working in the room during the summer months, often wearing full Japanese dress. Despite bouts of ill health, he was able to continue his work on language teaching and applied linguistics and produced a number of books. The death of his son, Tristram, killed in action in 1942, affected him greatly, and with further deterioration in his health, Palmer largely withdrew from academic pursuits, dying aged 72 in 1949.

The Principles of English Phonetic Notation

The first edition of *The Principles of English Phonetic Notation* (henceforth *PEPN*) appeared in 1925. *PEPN* had its origins in earlier publications which are no longer in existence. Most notable among these is the 1925 booklet *A Few Documents in English Phonetic Notation*, mentioned in the (1925) IRET *Bulletin* 16 (July) as containing 'portions of the various sections of the larger book' (Smith 1999: 102–3). Another apparent forerunner is the 1923 *A Catalogue of the Weakenable Words of the English Language* (Smith 1999: 76). In the original 1925 version, although the individual items have page numbering, the book lacks continuous pagination. We have chosen to reproduce the enlarged and revised second edition with full pagination that came out three years later (Palmer 1928b).

When the first edition of *PEPN* appeared, Palmer had been in residence in Japan for three years, and he already had an impressive publishing record behind him. His attention was now firmly fixed on the needs of non-native learners of English, in particular on those of the Japanese students he was regularly meeting in his position as director of IRET. Like his mentor, Daniel Jones, Palmer saw phonetic observation, and the need to make a permanent record of observed features, as all-important both for foreign language teaching and for phonetic research. The contents of *PEPN* reinforce these opinions throughout, as stated in the introductory remarks (p. 3), where he claims that the book will 'serve as a textbook for study, as a means of propagating the use of phonetics and phonetic notation, and as a basis of discussion among technicians' (by which he appears to mean 'qualified phoneticians').

Palmer begins with an 'explanatory dialogue', that is to say a Socratic dialogue or mock conversation. This and similar 'question and answer' ploys, such as a mock exchange of letters, were a favourite writing technique of his. Palmer had used the letter exchange format

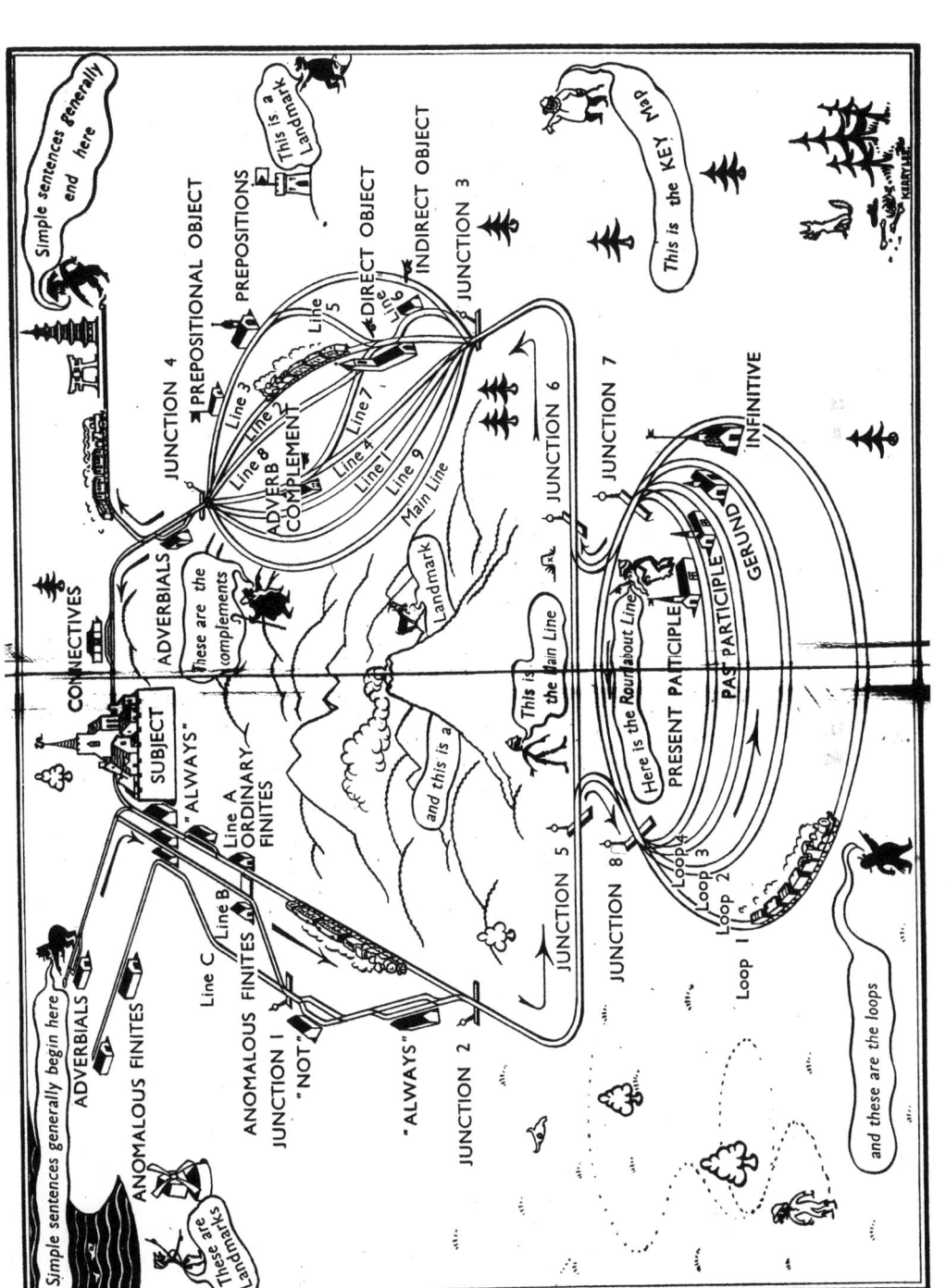

Illustrative diagram of Palmer's model railway demonstrating English sentence structure.

previously to good effect in *What is Phonetics?* (Palmer 1915), and was again to employ a dialogue in his co-authored *This Language Learning Business* (Palmer and Redman 1932). He now in *PEPN* uses questions and answers to explain basic phonetic and phonological concepts such as the different aims of orthography and phonetic transcription, and the need for different degrees of narrowness in phonetic notation. He goes on to discuss the significance of meaning for transcription but without actually employing the term 'phoneme'. Palmer continues with a brief history of the International Phonetic Association. It is worth noting that at the time such an historical survey did not exist elsewhere. He concludes this section with a mention of the reappearance of *Le Maître phonétique* and its use of the new type of phonetic notation, which he believed (wrongly) would become 'uniform and fixed' (p. 29). This last is the transcription system he describes in *PEPN*.

Palmer's next section, 'The impossibility of an "ideal" phonetic transcription' is a key portion of the book. He discusses at length what he considers to be the eight requirements for phonetic notation. His first point is that precision is not necessarily an advantage since it may overload the user with excessive detail. Symbol economy can be achieved by means of what Palmer terms 'broadening conventions' (p. 35). He concludes by stating that 'symbol economy is a very doubtful economy' (p. 39), and advocates using extra symbols if that procures gains in precision and simplicity. The section on 'phonemism' explains the phoneme in terms of meaning alternations. Curiously, for whatever reason, he avoids using the word 'phoneme' (it occurs just once on p. 42).

'Diaphonism' (p. 41) is a Jonesian concept which allows for a range of distinctions between phonemes in different language varieties, and the notational means of so doing (Jones 1932b). Palmer claims that few notation systems are completely consistent, and fears that 'too great attention to an ideal of consistency [...] will result in schematic artificiality' (p. 45); cf. previous statements about precision and symbol economy. 'Internationality' also involves a need for compromise in relation to the principle of symbol economy. By 'normativism' Palmer means the tendency for non-natives to interpret a phoneme in the target language in terms of a phoneme in the L1, and the need at times to employ a symbol to counteract this effect, and gives the example of the use of ɹ as 'a continual reminder that English *r* is an alveolar fricative' (p. 44). Lastly, Palmer points out that symbols need to have acceptability to the users, and that certain symbols may have to be avoided because of potential irritation. Palmer concludes on a quasi-Benthamite note saying that the best phonetic notation is one 'calculated to be of the greatest utility to the greatest number of users' (p. 47).

The following section provides a study of pronunciation models for English, taking as a starting-point H. C. Wyld's concept of 'Received Standard'. He compares the situation in Britain to that in Japan in terms of Wyld's classification of (1) Regional [pronunciation], (2) Received Standard, (3) Modified Standard (p. 51). He goes on to equate 'Received Standard' to Jones's (1917) definition of Public School Pronunciation (PSP). It is noteworthy that by the time the second edition of *PEPN* came out, Jones had changed his terminology from PSP to 'Received Pronunciation', and had coined the familiar abbreviation RP (Jones 1926). Palmer clearly did not feel it was worthwhile making the change. Palmer recommends Received Standard, making the point that at this time Americans often changed their speech to conform to British pronunciation norms, adding somewhat dubiously that the 'converse case is probably unknown' (p. 57).

The section 'The English Phonetic System' is another key portion of the book. Vowels are divided into five 'free' vowels vs. six 'checked' vowels, based on whether or not the vowel may occur word-finally (p. 61). Interestingly, as stated by Palmer (1925: 24), these terms were derived from the work of Kruisinga (1909, see Vol. VI of this collection). The vowels are further classified into 'kinetic' vowels, otherwise termed 'diphthongs' (p. 71), involving an obvious movement of the tongue during the articulation of the vowel. Finally, Palmer sets aside special symbols for two 'obscure vowels': (1) the final vowel in *happy* (cf. Wells 1982) and (2) the /ə/, including 'murmur diphthongs' terminating in [ə]. Consonant symbols are less problematical than vowels. However, for a number of consonants possible alternatives are mentioned, for example /θ ð ʃ ʒ tʃ dʒ/. The vowel and consonant inventories are presented in full on pp. 84–8, together with intonation tone marks. Palmer goes on to a chapter of '31 Chief Rules' for transcription of 'Received Standard', using his version of the International Phonetic Alphabet. As is true of *PEPN* as a whole, Palmer's rules are notable for their practicality and the avoidance of anything smacking of theoretical abstraction. Common sense instructions, such as not being 'influenced by traditional English spelling' (p. 91), avoiding capitalisation, using length marks and stress marks consistently or not at all, feature throughout.

Contrary to modern works on transcription (e.g. Lecumberri and Maidment 2000, Tench 2011), Palmer recommends the use of a full range of punctuation marks, but avoiding the apostrophe, which 'has no phonetic utility whatever' (p. 96) and the hyphen. It is notable that later Jones found a use for the hyphen as a marker of syllable division in otherwise identical representations (Jones 1956). Although Palmer clearly believes in the use of 'actual and normal pronunciation' (p. 91), few today would agree with his proscription of elided forms, such as /d/ in *kindness*, /t/ in *next week* (p. 100), or assimilations such as *of course* /f kɔˑs/, *has she* /hæʃ ʃi/ (p. 101). The section ends with a very full specification of suffixes and prefixes in transcription.

Another useful listing is the inventory of what Palmer labels 'weakenable words', the term Palmer uses for 'weak forms'. The list is divided into 'anomalous finites' (auxiliary verbs), pronouns and determinatives [sic], prepositions and 21 miscellaneous words. Some items are questionable (*saint, sir, so*), but for the most part Palmer's choice (similar to the list in Jones's *Outline*) is very much what would be chosen today. The book is rounded off by a number of model phonetic texts – interestingly, one of which was borrowed many years later by Abercrombie (1964) for his *English Phonetic Texts*. Palmer transcribes one passage in three versions: (1) according to his own system; (2) as it would have been rendered in the 1908 IPA transcription used in the *mf*; (3) in Mid-West American pronunciation. The last of these was supplied by J. Victor Martin, who had worked together with Palmer and Blandford on their 1926 *Dictionary of English Pronunciation with American Variants* mentioned above.

In his obituary of Palmer, Jones (1950b: 4–5) notes that Palmer had originally devised his own transcription system using accents to distinguish shades of vowel sound, but after having become a member of the IPA in 1907 he 'saw the superiority of the "new letter" system over the "diacritic" system, and very soon discarded his own transcription in favour of the IPA alphabet, which he thenceforward employed exclusively'. *PEPN* bears testimony to Palmer's enthusiasm for the IPA alphabet, and for his skills both as a theoretical and practical phonetician. It also shows that he managed to meet his own ambitions as stated at the beginning of the book (see above). Daniel Jones says of Palmer that he was 'a remarkable man', who 'had a most original and inventive mind' and 'possessed unusual talent for linguistic theory and pedagogy'. Jones's obituary forms a fitting tribute to one of the most creative thinkers in twentieth-century applied linguistics.

INTRODUCTION TO VOLUME IV

Selections from *Le Maître phonétique* (1900–70)
Origins and early history of the International Phonetic Association

The year 1886 witnessed a milestone in the history of phonetics with the founding of the International Phonetic Association (called originally 'dhi fonètik tîtcerz' asóciécon'). It started insignificantly, with a small group of 14 enthusiasts led by Paul Passy (1859–1940), Professor of Phonetics at the Ecole des Hautes Etudes at the University of Paris. Their numbers soon grew, with the association attracting well-known linguists from all over Europe: Henry Sweet (1845–1912), Johan Storm (1836–1920), Otto Jespersen (1860–1943) and Wilhelm Viëtor (1850–1918) were among early adherents. Just three years later, in 1889, membership had shown a remarkable increase to 321.[9] The name was changed in that year to the *Association Phonétique des Professeurs de Langues Vivantes*, to be altered finally once more in 1897 to the *Association Phonétique Internationale*. In English, it was called the 'International Phonetic Association', abbreviated more often than not to 'IPA'.

Up to this point, linguistic scholars had tended to work in whatever kind of transcription took their fancy, caring little for any overall uniformity. The importance of the IPA for the discipline of phonetics, and for linguistics as a whole, was that it produced a standard form of phonetic transcription. The IPA, chiefly inspired by Otto Jespersen, devised a set of symbols which could be used, in principle, to represent the sound of any language in the world. It became known as the International Phonetic Alphabet (also, somewhat confusingly, usually abbreviated to IPA). Based as it was on the latest contemporary phonetic knowledge, the alphabet soon attained international reputation and prestige. It enabled the pronunciation of major languages such as French, German and, notably, English to be transcribed phonetically in a manner which could be widely understood without difficulty. Progressive linguists had for many years been writing in Sweet's (1877: 105) 'Broad Romic', which was in essence a type of phonemic transcription, although the term 'phoneme' was as yet unknown in Western Europe, and the concept itself not clearly defined (Jones 1957). But now there was an official body promoting transcription systems of this type, and from 1904 onwards the IPA produced charts of its alphabet, regularly revised on the basis of IPA Council decisions; these charts provided a reference system which could be used worldwide. In this way, the IPA alphabet soon became an essential aid for anyone dealing with phonetics and phonology. (For further detail on the history of the International Phonetic Association, see MacMahon 1986.)

The IPA also produced a journal, entitled *Dhi Fonètik Tîtcer,* the entire content of which was printed in phonetic transcription. In 1889, the title was changed to *Le Maître phonétique* (in transcription [lə mɛːtrə fonetik], hence the abbreviation *mf*). It continued to be published under that title until 1971, when the commitment to publication in phonetic transcription was abandoned and the title changed to the *Journal of the International Phonetic Association* (or *JIPA*). In the early years of the twentieth century up to 1914, under the editorship of Paul Passy, assisted by Daniel Jones, the *mf* went from strength to strength. By 1911, it was coming out five times a year, with over 150 pages annually, not counting extra supplements containing longer articles in conventional orthography. At its peak, the membership of the IPA exceeded 1751 (MacMahon 1986: 31), all of whom received a copy of the *mf*. Such a circulation was astonishingly large for a journal of limited interest, printed (apart from supplements) exclusively in transcription, and in no fewer than five languages (even though most items appeared either in French or English, and, as time went by, increasingly in the latter). All this hectic publishing activity juddered to a halt when war broke out in

August 1914; although the IPA carried on through the war, its journal ceased publication for nine years.

When the decision was made to restart the *mf* in 1923, the editorial headquarters were effectively moved to University College London. A firm of printers was found, Stephen Austin, based in Hertford, which was prepared to take on the daunting task of producing a journal exclusively using phonetic symbols. Daniel Jones, now Professor of Phonetics at UCL, became the joint editor sharing billing on the cover with Paul Passy. In fact, it is clear that Jones was very much in control of both the IPA (he succeeded Passy as secretary in 1927) and its journal from this point on. He was assisted by Lilias Armstrong, a senior member of his staff, whose name appears as 'secrétaire de redaction' on the July 1923 issue, and who continued in that role up till her early death in 1937.

World War I had taken its toll on the IPA, and membership had fallen dramatically from pre-war days. Throughout the twenties, the *mf* appeared regularly several times a year, and the association made significant progress in returning to its former strength. By 1932, total membership had reached 552, with a large contingent resident in the USA. Paul Passy was ageing, suffering with health problems, and consequently providing Jones with little help. Nevertheless Passy remained a nominal joint-editor up till his death in 1940. On the outbreak of war in 1939, despite the obvious difficulties, Jones appears to have been determined to carry on producing the *mf*. Remarkably, he succeeded in this aim. After the war ended, he continued as editor until his retirement from his post at UCL in 1949, when he also resigned as secretary of the IPA, and handed the editorship of the *mf* over to A. C. Gimson, his young colleague at the phonetics department. Gimson continued in the editorial role for the next 20 years. Assisted latterly by John Wells in a joint editorship, he saw the *mf* through to the final issue of July–December 1970, and on to its reincarnation in 1971 as *JIPA*. Under the new title, the journal continues to be published to the present day.

The content of the mf

In the early days, under the editorship of Passy, the *mf* established a tradition of accepting contributions covering a wide range of topics. The basis of the journal was articulatory phonetics, and the emphasis was on observation rather than experimentation. In addition, attention was paid to the many practical applications of phonetics – in particular, to foreign language teaching, dialect description and spelling reform. The requirement for material to be submitted in transcription was enforced without exception. The editors and printers dealt well with the countless complications associated with problems of printing material in transcription, and typographical errors were remarkably infrequent. With some exceptions, most authors chose relatively broad transcription, which posed fewer difficulties to the reader. Whilst it was doubtless in many ways a self-imposed handicap, submission in transcription did have the hidden bonus of encouraging contributors to produce papers which were in general brief and to the point.

In choosing selected items from the vast amount of material which appeared in the *mf* over a period of 70 years, we have followed these guidelines.

(1) We have confined ourselves to pieces concerned with English and written in English.
(2) We have excluded any material of the following types: (a) items concerned with the administration or organisation of the IPA; (b) reports of congresses, summer schools, exhibitions or similar; (c) obituaries and other biographical material;[10] (d) exercises or practice material intended for aspiring students of phonetics.

In making a final selection, we have concentrated on four main areas as detailed below.

Descriptions of dialects and accent varieties

Samples and descriptions of varieties of English (and other languages) appeared regularly in the *mf*, many of which were published under the heading **spesimɛn** ('spécimen'). It is noticeable that the quality of these pieces increases greatly after the *mf* restarted in 1923, owing to two significant developments for both of which Daniel Jones can largely take the credit. Firstly, there was growing awareness in the western world of the phoneme concept, initiated by Jones in 1917, and promulgated by him and his followers in the twenties and thirties, which enabled descriptive work on dialect to be far more reliable and systematic. Secondly, an accurate reference system was made available for dealing with vowels thanks to the use of Daniel Jones's cardinal vowels, which he made public from 1916 onwards (see Collins and Mees 1995).

Phonetic transcription and spelling reform

Numerous articles trace the development of different transcription systems for English. Of particular interest is the decision to use narrower transcription in the *mf* after the restart in 1923, and the return to Jones's broader *EPD*-type transcription in later years. Abercrombie (1953) insightfully categorises the various issues to be taken into consideration when designing transcription systems; issues which had been the cause of many heated exchanges in the pages of the *mf* and which indeed continue to evoke strong feelings in internet blogs to this day. Once again the development of phoneme theory was a crucial factor. The *mf* also contained articles in support of spelling reform, a cause which was furthered by the establishment of the Simplified Spelling Society in 1908.

Phonetic/phonological theory

There is little to be found in the pages of the *mf* in the way of theoretical phonology. For the editors, a down-to-earth view of phonology sufficed for practical purposes. Post-1923, the *mf* focussed on phoneme theory, seeking to categorise the sounds of language and the potential for contrast between them. The emphasis was, as it had always been, on real-world applications and observations. In the 1960s, a number of articles appeared which dealt with suprasegmental features, such as intonation, stress, weak forms and assimilation.

Phonetics in the wider world

Contributions to the *mf* reflect the interest of phoneticians in disseminating knowledge of their discipline to the general public. In particular, the 1920s and 30s saw the emergence and development in Britain of national broadcasting, which brought phonetic issues into the homes of ordinary people up and down the country. The writings of Arthur Lloyd James (see also volumes II and III of this collection) are particularly worthy of note, especially in the light of his close connections with the BBC and his influence on the type of pronunciation which became known to the general public not as RP but 'BBC English'.

INTRODUCTION TO VOLUME IV

Brief details of authors

Basic biographical information is given below of the authors of the articles and other pieces selected from the *mf*. The information has been derived from a number of sources, but in particular Bronstein *et al.* (1977).

Abercrombie, David (1909–92). British phonetician. Professor of Phonetics at Edinburgh University (founder and head of phonetics department). Author of *Elements of General Phonetics* (1967). Member of IPA Council.

Armstrong, Lilias E. (1882–1937). British phonetician. Senior Lecturer at University College London phonetics department. Author of numerous works on English, French, and African languages, notably, *A Handbook of English Intonation* (with Ida C. Ward, 1926), *The Phonetics of French* (1932), *Studies in French Intonation* (with Hélène Coustenoble, 1934) and *The Phonetic and Tonal Structure of Kikuyu* (1940). Daniel Jones's editorial assistant on *Le Maître phonétique* 1923–37.

Arnold, G[ordon] F. (1920–99). British phonetician specialising in intonation. See volume V for further biographical detail.

Bell, Alexander Melville (1819–1905). Eminent Scottish phonetician and elocutionist. Author of *Visible Speech* (1867) and inventor of iconic transcription system of that name. Father of Alexander Graham Bell.

Bloch, Bernard (1907–65). American phonologist and dialectologist. Author of numerous articles, notably 'A set of postulates for phonemic analysis' (1948). Editor of the journal *Language* (1935–65).

Bloomfield, Leonard (1887–1949). Eminent American linguist. Main proponent of structural linguistics and author of the influential work *Language* (1933). Member of IPA Council.

Breckwoldt, Gerhard H. (1917–2001). Phonetician based at University of the Witwatersrand, South Africa.

Catford, J[ohn] C. (known as 'Ian') (1917–2009). Scottish-born phonetician and applied linguist. Director of School of Applied Linguistics, University of Edinburgh, later Professor of Linguistics at University of Michigan. Author of numerous books and articles, including *Fundamental Problems in Phonetics* (1977) and *A Practical Introduction to Phonetics* (1988). Member of IPA Council.

Cruttenden, Alan (1936–). British phonetician. Professor of Phonetics at Manchester University, specialising in child language and intonation. Has revised recent editions of Gimson's *Introduction to the Pronunciation of English*, the latest being the (2008) 7th edn.

Dannatt, Philip H. (1883–1947). British amateur phonetician. Daniel Jones's brother-in-law.

Gimson, A[lfred] C. (1917–85). British phonetician. Professor of Phonetics and head of University College London phonetics department. Author of influential *Introduction to the Pronunciation of English* (1962). Succeeded Daniel Jones in several roles: secretary of the IPA, editor of *Le Maître phonétique* (later *Journal of the International Phonetic Association*), editor (1964–1985) of *An English Pronouncing Dictionary*.

Hempl, George (1859–1921). American Germanist and dialectologist who undertook pioneering work on varieties of American English. Ardent spelling reformer. Author of *German Orthography and Phonology* (1903).

Hurford, James R. (1941–). British dialectologist and general linguist, educated at University College London. Professor of General Linguistics at Edinburgh University.

Iles, Laurence (1915–98). British phonetician. Lecturer at Edinburgh University, who pioneered work on synthetic speech.

Jespersen, Otto (1860–1943). Eminent Danish linguist and prolific author. Professor at Copenhagen University. Writer of numerous influential linguistic works including *Lehrbuch der Phonetik* (1904, original Danish version 1897) and *Language: its Nature, Development and Origin* (1922).

Jones, Daniel (1881–1967). Generally regarded as the leading British phonetician of the twentieth century. First professor of phonetics to be appointed at a British university (University College London). Secretary of the IPA, editor of *Le Maître phonétique*, author of numerous important publications, including *An English Pronouncing Dictionary* (1917), *An Outline of English Phonetics* (1918), and *The Phoneme* (1950c).

Kenyon, John S. (1874–1959). American phonetician. Co-editor (with Thomas A. Knott) of *A Pronouncing Dictionary of American English* (1944).

Kingdon, Roger (1891–1984). British phonetician, intonationist and language teacher. Educated at University College London and later based at Mexico City. Author of *Groundwork of English Stress* (1958) and *Groundwork of English Intonation* (1958). Member of IPA Council.

Kruisinga, Etsko (1875–1944). Dutch applied linguist and language teaching pioneer. See volume VI for further biographical details.

Lloyd James, Arthur (1884–1943). Welsh-born phonetician. Professor of Phonetics at London School of Oriental and African Studies. Influential in the 1930s through work for the BBC. See volume II for further biographical details.

Lodge, Ken[neth] R. (1943–). British phonologist. Emeritus Reader, University of East Anglia.

Macrae, D. (?–?). American clergyman. Personal friend of Alexander Melville Bell.

Noël-Armfield, G[eorge] (1868–1937). British phonetician. First lecturer ever to be appointed to Daniel Jones's phonetics department at University College London.

O'Connor, J. D[esmond] (known as 'Doc') (1919–98). British phonetician specialising in intonation and pronunciation training for non-natives. See volume V for further biographical details.

Painter, Colin (1933–2004). British-born phonetician educated at University College London. Specialising initially in dialect research, but later appointed Professor of Otolaryngology at Washington University, St Louis.

Palmer, Harold E. (1877–1949). British phonetician, applied linguist and language teaching pioneer. Lecturer at University College London, later based for many years in Japan. Prolific author of books and articles on phonetics and language acquisition. See this volume for further biographical details.

Rip[p]man[n], Walter (born Rippmann, later changed name to Ripman) (1869–1947). British applied linguist of German ancestry, author of *Elements of Phonetics* (1899) and *The Sounds of Spoken English* (1906/1907), and enthusiastic spelling reformer.

Scott, N[orman] C. (1899–1975). British linguist. Professor of Phonetics at the London School of Oriental and African Studies. Member of IPA Council.

Sweet, Henry (1845–1912). Eminent phonetician, philologist and all-round linguist, generally regarded as the leading British linguist of the nineteenth century. Prolific author of numerous influential works including *A Handbook of Phonetics* (1877), *The Practical Study of Languages* (1899) and *A Primer of Phonetics* (1890).

Trager, George L. (1906–1992). American structuralist linguist. Co-authored (with H. L. Smith) influential work *An Outline of English Structure* (1951). Professor of Linguistics at Yale, Georgetown and Buffalo universities.

Uldall, Elizabeth T. (known as 'Betsy'), née Anderson (1913–2004). American-born phonetician based at Edinburgh University. Member of IPA Council. Married to Danish linguist H.-J. Uldall.

Viereck, Wolfgang (1937–). German/Austrian dialectologist. Professor of English Linguistics, Bamberg University.

Ward, Ida C. (1880–1949). Eminent British phonetician and Africanist. Professor and head of African Languages Department at London School of Oriental and African Studies. See this volume for further biographical details.

Wells, John C. (1939–). Influential British phonetician. Professor of Phonetics at University College London. Author of the monumental *Accents of English* (1982) and of the *Longman Pronunciation Dictionary* (1990/2008).

Wilson, J. Leslie (?–?). Listed in 1913 *mf* (p. 10) as Dr J. Leslie Wilson, living in Newcastle-upon-Tyne.

Windsor Lewis, Jack (1926–). Welsh-born British phonetician specialising in intonation and language teaching. Taught at Oslo, Brussels and Leeds universities. For further biographical details see Vol. VI of this collection.

Wise, Claude M. (1887–1966). American phonetician, dialectologist and speech trainer. Author of *Applied Phonetics* (1957) and (with G. W. Gray) *Bases of Speech* (1934). Founder of the USA Southern Speech Association.

Notes

1. http://www.phon.ucl.ac.uk/home/wells/blog0804a.htm (7 April 2008). Accessed 18 December 2012.
2. Lecture 'Standard Pronunciation', first delivered by Daniel Jones to the English Association, Liverpool, on 11 March 1927.
3. Ward mistakenly lists the date of publication as 1924.
4. Note that it does not feature in our historiographical survey of glottalisation (Collins and Mees 1996), which deals essentially with glottalisation in Received Pronunciation.

INTRODUCTION TO VOLUME IV

5. *MPh* 1914 (2nd series) 29, p. 24.
6. *MPh* 1913 (2nd series) 28, p. 101.
7. University College London Phonetics Department, Report for 1915–16.
8. Warwick ELT archive: bit.ly/eltarchive
9. *MPh* (1900: 3), in a table giving the numbers of members of the IPA at the beginning of each year from 1886–1900. By 1900 there were 953 members.
10. See Collins and Mees (2003: Vol. VII) for a selection of the obituaries in the *mf* written by Daniel Jones.

References

Abercrombie, D. (1953) Phonetic transcriptions. *Le Maître phonétique* (3) 31: 32–4.
—— (1964) *English Phonetic Texts*. London: Faber.
—— (1967) *Elements of General Phonetics*. Edinburgh: Edinburgh University Press.
Anderson, D. (1969) Harold E. Palmer: a biographical essay. In H. E. Palmer and Redman, H. V. *This Language Learning Business*. (2nd edn). London: Harrap, pp. 133–66.
Armstrong, L. (1932) *The Phonetics of French*. London: Bell.
—— (1940) *The Phonetic and Tonal Structure of Kikuyu*. London: International African Institute.
Armstrong, L. and Ward, I. (1926) *A Handbook of English Intonation*. Leipzig & Berlin: Teubner; Cambridge: Heffer.
Bell, A. Melville (1867) *Visible Speech: The Science of Universal Alphabetics*. London: Simpkin Marshall. Reproduced in Collins and Mees (2007).
Bloch, B. (1948) A set of postulates for phonemic analysis. *Language* 24: 3–46.
Bloomfield, L. (1933) *Language*. New York: Holt.
Bronstein, A. J., Raphael, L. J. and Stevens, C. J. (eds) (1977) *A Biographical Dictionary of the Phonetic Sciences*. New York: Lehman College Press.
Catford, J. C. (1977) *Fundamental Problems in Phonetics*. Edinburgh: Edinburgh University Press.
—— (1988) *A Practical Introduction to Phonetics*. Oxford: Clarendon Press.
Coleman, H. O. (1914) Intonation and emphasis, *Miscellanea Phonetica* I, Bourg-la-Reine and London: IPA, pp. 6–26. Reproduced in volume V of the present collection.
Collins, B. and Mees, I. M. (1995) Daniel Jones, Paul Passy and the development of the cardinal vowel system, *Historiographia Linguistica*, 22 1/2, pp. 197–217.
—— (1996) Spreading everywhere? How recent a phenomenon is glottalisation in Received Pronunciation? *English World-Wide* 17.2: 175–87.
—— (2001) Daniel Jones, Prescriptivist, R.(I.)P. *English Studies* 82.1: 66–73.
—— (eds) (2003) *Daniel Jones: Selected Works*. 8 vols. London: Routledge.
—— (eds) (2007) *Phonetics of English in the Nineteenth Century*. 7 vols. London: Routledge.
—— (2009) Pronouncing dictionaries: mid-nineteenth century to the present day. In A. Cowie (ed.). *Oxford History of English Lexicography*. Oxford: Oxford University Press, pp. 176–218.
Coustenoble, H. N. and Armstrong, L. (1934) *Studies in French Intonation*. Cambridge: Heffer.
Cruttenden, A. (2008) *Gimson's Introduction to the Pronunciation of English*. (7th edn). London: Hodder Education.
Gimson, A. C. (1962) *Introduction to the Pronunciation of English*. London: Arnold.
Gray, G. W. and Wise, C. M. (1934) *Bases of Speech*. New York: Harper.
Hempl, G. (1903) *German Orthography and Phonology*. Boston: Ginn.
Jespersen, O. (1904) *Lehrbuch der Phonetik*. Leipzig & Berlin: Teubner. (Original Danish version *Fonetik, en systematisk fremstilling af læren om sproglyd*, Copenhagen: Gyldendal 1897.)
—— (1922) *Language: Its Nature, Development and Origin*. London: Allen & Unwin.
Jones, D. (1909a) *Intonation Curves*. Leipzig and Berlin: Teubner. Reproduced in Collins and Mees (2003).
—— (1909b) *The Pronunciation of English*. Cambridge: Cambridge University Press. Reproduced in Collins and Mees (2003).

—— (1917/1926/1949) *An English Pronouncing Dictionary*. London: Dent (3rd edn 1926; 10th edn 1949). First edn reproduced in Collins and Mees (2003).
—— (1918/1932a) *An Outline of English Phonetics*. (3rd edn 1932). Leipzig: Teubner. (First edn, 1918, reproduced in Collins and Mees 2003).
—— (1922) Why we are bad linguists. (London) *Evening News*, 13 December 1922.
—— (1932b) The theory of phonemes, and its importance in practical phonetics. *Proceedings of the [1st] International Congress of Phonetic Sciences*, Amsterdam, 23–4.
—— (1950a) Ida Ward (obituary). *Le Maître phonétique* (3) 28: 2–3.
—— (1950b) Harold Palmer (obituary). *Le Maître phonétique* (3) 28: 4–7.
—— (1950c) *The Phoneme: Its Nature and Use*. Cambridge: Heffer.
—— (1956) The hyphen as a phonetic sign. *Zeitschrift für Phonetik* 9: 99–107.
—— (1957) *History and Meaning of the Term 'Phoneme'*. London: International Phonetic Association.
Kenyon, J. S. and Knott, T. A. (1944) *A Pronouncing Dictionary of American English*. Springfield, MA: Merriam-Webster.
Kingdon, R. (1958) *Groundwork of English Stress*. London: Longman.
—— (1958) *Groundwork of English Intonation*. London: Longman.
Kruisinga, E. (1909) *A Grammar Present-day English*. Vol. 1 *English Sounds*. Utrecht: Kemink.
Lecumberri, L. G. and Maidment, J. A. (2000) *English Transcription Course*. London: Hodder.
Lloyd James, A. (1940) *Speech Signals in Telephony*. London: Pitman.
MacMahon, M. K. C. (1986) The International Phonetic Association: the first 100 years. *Journal of the International Phonetic Association* 16: 30–38.
Noël-Armfield, G. (1919) *General Phonetics: for Missionaries and Students of Languages*. (2nd edn). Cambridge: Heffer.
Palmer, H. E. (1915) *What is Phonetics? An Answer to this Question in the Form of 12 Letters from a Phonetician to a Non-phonetic Friend*. Bourg-la-Reine & London: IPA.
—— (1917a) *A First Course of English Phonetics*. Cambridge: Heffer.
—— (1917b) *The Scientific Study and Teaching of Languages*. London: Harrap. Reprinted (1968) Oxford: Oxford University Press.
—— (1921a) *The Principles of Language Study*. London: Harrap.
—— (1921b) *The Oral Method of Teaching Languages*. Cambridge: Heffer.
—— (1922) *English Intonation with Systematic Exercises*. Cambridge: Heffer.
—— (1925) Unstressed ɪ. *Le Maître phonétique* (3) 3: 23–5.
—— (1928a) *Concerning Pronunciation*. Tokyo: Institute for Research in English Teaching.
—— (1925/1928b) *The Principles of English Phonetic Notation*. (2nd edn 1928). Tokyo: Institute for Research in English Teaching.
—— (1930) *The Principles of Romanization*. Tokyo: Maruzen.
—— (1933) *A New Classification of English Tones*. Tokyo: Institute for Research in English Teaching.
—— (1938) *The New Method Grammar*. London: Longmans Green.
Palmer, H. E., Blandford, F. G. and Martin, J. V. (1926) *Dictionary of English Pronunciation with American Variants (in Phonetic Transcription)*. Cambridge: Heffer.
Palmer, H. E. and Redman, H. V. (1932) *This Language Learning Business*. London: Harrap. Reprinted (1969) Oxford: Oxford University Press.
Rippmann, W. (1899) *Elements of Phonetics: English, French and German*. London: Dent. (Translated and adapted from Viëtor, W. (1897) *Kleine Phonetik*. Leipzig: Reisland.) Reproduced in Collins and Mees (2007).
—— (1906/1907) *The Sounds of Spoken English: A Manual of Ear Training for English Students*. London: Dent. 2nd edn 1907, reproduced in Collins and Mees (2007).
Smith, R. C. (1999) *The Writings of Harold E. Palmer: An Overview*. Tokyo: Hon-No-Tomosha.
Sweet, H. (1877) *A Handbook of Phonetics*. Oxford: Clarendon Press.
—— (1899) *The Practical Study of Languages: A Guide for Teachers and Learners*. London: Dent.
—— (1890) *A Primer of Phonetics*. Oxford: Clarendon Press.

Tench, P. (2011) *Transcribing the Sound of English*. Cambridge: Cambridge University Press.

Tickoo, M. L. (2008) *Harold E. Palmer: From Learner-Teacher to Legend*. New Delhi: Orient Longman.

Trager, G. L. and Smith, H. L. (1951) *An Outline of English Structure*. Washington: American Council of Learned Studies.

Trofimov, M. and Jones, D. (1923) *The Pronunciation of Russian*. Cambridge: Cambridge University Press. Reproduced in Collins and Mees (2003).

Trudgill, P. (1974) *Sociolinguistics: An Introduction to Language and Society*. Harmondsworth: Penguin.

Tucker, A. N. (1950) Ida Caroline Ward (obituary). *Bulletin of the School of Oriental and African Studies*. University of London, 13. 2, pp. 542–76.

Ward, I. C. (1923) *Speech Defects: their Nature and Cure*. London: Dent.

—— (1929/1939) *The Phonetics of English*. (3rd edn 1939). Cambridge: Heffer.

—— (1933) *The Phonetic and Tonal Structure of Efik*. Cambridge: Heffer.

—— (1936) *An Introduction to the Ibo Language*. Cambridge: Heffer.

—— (1952) *An Introduction to the Yoruba Language*. Cambridge: Heffer.

Wells, J. C. (1982) *Accents of English*. Cambridge: Cambridge University Press.

—— (1990/2008) *Longman Pronunciation Dictionary*. Harlow: Longman. (3rd edn 2008, Harlow: Pearson Education).

Westermann, D. and Ward, I. C. (1933) *Practical Phonetics for Students of African Languages*. London: Oxford University Press.

Wise, C. M. (1957) *Applied Phonetics*. Englewood Cliffs, NJ: Prentice-Hall.

Wyld, H. C. (1920) *History of Modern Colloquial English*. London: T. Fisher Unwin.

12

THE PHONETICS OF ENGLISH, 3rd edn

THE PHONETICS OF ENGLISH

BY

IDA C. WARD, D.Lit.

University of London
School of Oriental and African Studies

CAMBRIDGE
W. HEFFER & SONS LTD
1939

First published 1929
New Edition.. 1931
Third Edition (entirely revised, with additional chapters) 1939

PRINTED AND BOUND IN GREAT BRITAIN
AT THE WORKS OF
W. HEFFER AND SONS LTD., CAMBRIDGE, ENGLAND

PREFACE

THE aim of this book is to present the main facts of English pronunciation of to-day. The writer has had in mind the teacher who is expected to deal with indistinct or dialectal speech, and for this reason, she has made the book as practical as possible. It is hoped that the teacher or student may make his own observations on local and individual usages and develop for himself the hints given on correction. These suggestions are based on many years of practical experience in lecturing to teachers and teaching in school.

If dialectal speech is illustrated from Yorkshire and Cockney more than from other dialects, the writer's excuse is that she knows these dialects much better than any others; moreover, many of the peculiarities of Cockney speech which are discussed, can stand for those of other Southern dialects, and those of Yorkshire for many Northern dialects.

The writer wishes to acknowledge her indebtedness to Mr. A. K. Maxwell for the drawings of the open mouth and the vocal chords, and to Mr. T. L. Poulton for the remaining diagrams of tongue positions.

UNIVERSITY COLLEGE,
    LONDON.

September, 1928

PREFACE TO THE SECOND EDITION

A FEW pages of phonetic transcription have been added to this edition. Since Cockney and Yorkshire have been used considerably as examples of dialect speech, extracts have been chosen which illustrate these two dialects.

I am very much indebted to Mr. Bernard Shaw for his permission to use a passage from *Pygmalion*, and to Mr. J. B. Priestley for allowing me to take an extract from *The Good Companions* for this purpose.

I. C. W.

PREFACE TO THE THIRD EDITION

THE book has been entirely revised and additional chapters have been added on Broadcasting and Spoken English, on British and American English and on Recent Developments in English Pronunciation. Two new phonetic texts are also included, one of the Christmas message to the Empire of His late Majesty, King George V, in 1935, which has been transcribed from a gramophone record made by H.M.V. Gramophone Co., and the other of President Roosevelt's broadcast speech on the occasion of the special convocation of Congress on October 13th, 1937, which has been transcribed from a recording made by the B.B.C.

I have to acknowledge with gratitude the gracious permission accorded by His Majesty the King to make use of the record of King George V's 1935 Christmas Broadcast, and to H.M.V. Gramophone Company for their consent.

I. C. W.

December, 1938.

CONTENTS

		PAGE
Preface		v
Preface to Second Edition		vi
Preface to Third Edition		vii
Illustrations		xi
List of Symbols		xiii

CHAP.		
I.	Standard Pronunciation	1
II.	Broadcasting and Spoken English	11
III.	Correction of Pronunciation	23
IV.	Qualifications of the Teacher	28
V.	Phonetic Transcription	32
VI.	Use of Phonetics in the Teaching of English	36
VII.	Spelling Pronunciations	38
VIII.	Organs of Speech	48
IX.	Vowels and Consonants: Classification of Vowels	65
X.	Phonemes	74
XI.	English Vowels in Detail	79
XII.	English Diphthongs	111

CHAP.		PAGE
XIII.	NASALISATION OF VOWELS	125
XIV.	CLASSIFICATION OF CONSONANTS: ENGLISH CONSONANTS IN DETAIL	127
XV.	SOUND ATTRIBUTES: LENGTH, STRESS, INTONATION	156
XVI.	SOUNDS IN CONNECTED SPEECH	180
XVII.	RECENT DEVELOPMENTS IN ENGLISH PRONUNCIATION	199
XVIII.	BRITISH ENGLISH AND AMERICAN ENGLISH	206
XIX.	PHONETIC TRANSCRIPTIONS	220
APPENDIX I.	SUGGESTED COURSE FOR TRAINING COLLEGES	241
,, II.	EXERCISES IN EAR TRAINING	243
BIBLIOGRAPHY		246
INDEX		249
PHONETIC INDEX		252

ILLUSTRATIONS

Fig.		Chap.	Page.
1.	Variant Pronunciations	I	5
2.	Organs of Speech	VIII	49
3.	Open Mouth	,,	51
4.	Vocal Cords in Four Positions	,,	52
5.	Soft Palate Raised and Lowered	,,	57
6.	Open Mouth with Palate Raised	,,	58
7.	Photograph of Tongue Spreading and Contraction	,,	60
8.	Tongue Positions of Cardinal Vowels i, a, ɑ, u	IX ,,	69
9.	Tongue Positions of the Eight Primary Cardinal Vowels	,,	70
10.	Cardinal Vowel Diagram	,,	70, 71
11.	Photographs of Lip Positions	,,	72
12.	Illustrating Principles of Correction	XI	80
13.	English Vowels	,,	81
14.	Varieties of i Vowel	,,	82
15.	,, ,, ɪ ,,	,,	86
16.	,, ,, ɛ ,,	,,	88
17.	,, ,, æ ,,	,,	90
18.	The u Phoneme	,,	100
19.	Varieties of u Vowel	,,	101
20.	,, ,, ʌ ,,	,,	104
21.	Semi-weak Vowels	,,	109

xi

Fig.		Chap.	Page.
22.	English Diphthongs (a)	XII	112
23.	,, ,, (b)	,,	112
24.	Varieties of ei Diphthong	,,	113
25.	,, ,, ou	,,	115
26.	,, ,, aɪ	,,	117
27.	,, ,, au	,,	118
28.	Triphthongs	,,	123
29.	English Plosive Consonants	XIV	130
30.	Illustrating Nasal Plosion	,,	132
31.	Illustrating the Starting Position for tθ, ts, tʃ, tʒ	,,	137
32.	Nasal Consonants	,,	139
33.	Primary Articulation of l	,,	140
34.	Clear and Dark l	,,	141
35.	Over-dark l	,,	143
36.	Rolled r	,,	144
37.	Fricative r	,,	145
38.	Inverted r	,,	145
39.	Uvular Rolled r	,,	146
40.	English Fricative Consonants	,,	148
41.	Semi-Vowels	,,	151
42.	Illustrating Assimilation	XVI	191

LIST OF SYMBOLS

THE alphabet used is that of the International Phonetic Association in its "narrow" form. For the benefit of those students who are used to the "broad" form, the differences between the two are here set out.

Narrow.	Broad.
i	iː
ɪ	i
u	uː
ʊ	u
ɑ	ɑː
ɔ	ɔː
ɒ	ɔ
ɜ	əː

ː placed after a vowel indicates full length.

ˑ   ,,   ,,   ,,   ,,   ,,   half ,,

ˌ placed underneath a symbol indicates that the sound is syllabic: e.g. **pɑˑsn̩ɪdʒ**—three syllables (parsonage).

ˈ placed before a symbol shows that the syllable is stressed.

Secondary stress is marked thus ˌ, e.g. pɪˌkjulɪˈærɪtɪ (*peculiarity*).

₀ placed underneath a symbol indicates that the sound is pronounced without voice: e.g. n̥.

English Vowels.			English Diphthongs.		
i	as in	*see*	eɪ	as in	*play*
ɪ	,, ,,	*sit*	oʊ	,, ,,	*go*
ɛ	,, ,,	*set*	aɪ	,, ,,	*my*
æ	,, ,,	*sat*	aʊ	,, ,,	*now*
ɑ	,ˑ ,,	*calm*	ɔɪ	,, ,,	*boy*

xiii

LIST OF SYMBOLS

English Vowels

ɒ	as in	*not*
ɔ	,, ,,	*bought*
ʊ	,, ,,	*put*
u	,, ,,	*soon*
ʌ	,, ,,	*but*
ɜ	,, ,,	*bird*
ə	,, ,,	*about*

English Diphthongs.

ɪə	as in	*here*
ɛə	,, ,,	*there*
ɔə	,, ,,	*more*
ʊə	,, ,,	*poor*

English Consonants.

p	as in	*put*
b	,, ,,	*but*
t	,, ,,	*ten*
d	,, ,,	*den*
k	,, ,,	*come*
g	,, ,,	*go*
tʃ	,, ,,	*church*
dʒ	,, ,,	*judge*
m	,, ,,	*make*
n	,, ,,	*not*
ŋ	,, ,,	*long*
l	,, ,,	*like*
ɫ	,, ,,	*well*

f	as in	*full*
v	,, ,,	*very*
θ	,, ,,	*thin*
ð	,, ,,	*then*
s	,, ,,	*some*
z	,, ,,	*zeal*
ʃ	,, ,,	*ship*
ʒ	,, ,,	*pleasure*
r (or ɹ)	,,	*run*
h	,, ,,	*hat*
w	,, ,,	*went*
ʍ	,, ,,	*white*
j	,, ,,	*yet*

OTHER SYMBOLS.

Vowels.

y Front close rounded vowel, similar to the French vowel in *rue* (see § 83).

ø Half-close front rounded vowel, similar to the French vowel in *peu* (see § 83).

œ Half-open front rounded vowel, similar to the French vowel in *sœur* (see § 83).

ɯ Close back unrounded vowel (see § 361 (v)).
ɤ Half-close back unrounded vowel (see §§ 167, 175c).
ï Centralised i (see § 171).
ü ,, u ,, § 171, 172).
ë ,, e ,, § 200).
ö ,, o ,, § 200).

The symbols i, e, ɛ, a, ɑ, ɔ, o, u are used to denote the eight primary cardinal vowels (see § 99).

Consonants.

ɸ Bi-labial fricative, voiceless (see § 84 c).
β ,,   ,,   voiced ,, § 84 c)
ɹ Fricative r (see § 271 iii).
ɾ One-tap r (see § 271 ii).
R Uvular rolled r (see § 271 v).
ʁ ,,   fricative r (see § 271 v).
ç Palatal fricative, voiceless (see §§ 282 c, 334).
x Velar fricative, voiceless (see § 242).
l̥ Voiceless l (see §§ 77 d, 266 c, 334).
m̥, n̥, ŋ̊ Voiceless m, n, ŋ respectively (see §§ 77d, 334).
ɱ Labio-dental nasal (see § 353).
ɦ Voiced h (see § 278 vi).
ʔ Glottal stop (see §§ 75d, 250e, 250 (e) (f), 251.

CHAPTER I.

STANDARD PRONUNCIATION.

1. It is necessary at the outset of a book such as this to discuss the vexed question of " standard pronunciation," since teachers are being told—in the daily press and elsewhere—that the English language is degenerating into mere unintelligible jargon, and that it is their responsibility to preserve a standard, and turn out their pupils able to express themselves in correct and vigorous English, spoken in a clear and pleasing manner.

2. What *is* Standard Pronunciation? No one can adequately define it, because such a thing does not exist; yet every one knows what is meant when one speaks of Standard English, and the Committee on the Teaching of English in England, without entering into the question in any detail, describes it as one free from vulgarisms and provincialisms.[1] The term " Standard English " implies one type of speech which is used by the educated population of the country, and which has received the approval of some authoritative body. But an examination of facts proves that no two people, even of the same district and upbringing, speak exactly alike. Different generations have not the same habits in speech sounds or in vocabulary. Nor is there at present any body of experts which has the authority to state what standard pronunciation is and to insist on its introduction into the schools.

3. There are many divergencies in the speech of educated people of different districts. The educated Northerner may use the sound a or æ in words like

[1] See *Report on the Teaching of English in England*, p. 66.

dance, grass, etc., where a Southerner would use ɑ; an educated Westerner may pronounce what is called a *retroflex* " *r* " in words like *farm, port* (fɑɹm, pɔɹt), where other people would use no *r* at all; not all educated Londoners use the same diphthong in words like *go* and *cold*; and the speech of educated Australians, Canadians, South Africans, and Americans differs in many respects from that of Englishmen. It may be argued, however, that although these divergencies among educated people exist, they are comparatively small, and can be ignored. This is, to a certain extent, true; but before any pronouncement is made on the subject, the state of English pronunciation at the present day should be thoroughly examined and understood, and all the arguments for and against the establishment of a standard speech in the country, and for the teaching of such a pronunciation in the schools, should be plainly stated.

4. The type of speech used by an individual depends chiefly on the region in which he is brought up and the social class to which he belongs. These two factors give rise to what may be called Local and Class Dialects, dialects which have a long and interesting history. Is there any argument to be used for the replacing of these dialects by a standard pronunciation (which means, in time, abolishing the dialects), or, while not discouraging the use of the dialect, for advocating the acquirement of a standard pronunciation as an auxiliary language?

5. The student should, first of all, disabuse his mind of the idea, which is very common, that one dialect—class or local—is intrinsically better, or more beautiful, or more " historically correct " than another. All the dialects are developments of English in different

directions, or at different rates. Cockney is one form of English, as Yorkshire and Devonshire are other forms. One may have more sonorous sounds, a more varied intonation than another, and in this way, may strike the ear as more musical. But the general principle upon which people unconsciously judge a pronunciation is that of the associations which it calls up. If we are accustomed to hearing one type of pronunciation used by people of vulgar and uncouth habits, with harsh and discordant voices, we consider that dialect ugly. One often hears it said that the Cockney pronunciation of the word *paint* (paɪnt) is ugly because aɪ is an ugly diphthong; whereas the same diphthong is used in *pint* (paɪnt) by non-Cockney speakers, and is considered beautiful. In the same way a Northerner's pronunciation of *but* as bʊt is called "broad," while there is no question of criticising the same vowel in *put* (pʊt). Moreover the dialect of a distant part of the country may be thought "quaint" and romantic, while that nearest is looked on as a debased form of English. Country dialects are said to be good and pure, while town dialects are considered bad and slipshod English. Again, these judgments depend largely on association: the simpler country life appeals to the aesthetic sense, and the country speech is included in this appeal; while the speech of the town receives part of the condemnation which is directed against the rush and bustle of a more complex life. There is, however, one reason which has some justification behind it for considering town dialects bad and country dialects good. Owing to the influx into the towns of people from different parts of the country, the original local dialect has come under many and varying influences, and is, in consequence, not so pure as the country dialect. The kind of person, too, who uses a dialect is likely to influence our judgment of his speech; if he is slipshod in appearance and impolite in manners, we are inclined to think his speech is bad. In so far as any speech is the result of continued lazy habits of articulation, it is to be deplored and condemned. A slovenly pronunciation, however, which is lacking in precision and difficult to understand, is not confined to any one part of the country, nor to one class of people, but may be heard often enough from lecturers and preachers, as well as from loungers at the street corners of any town or of any country village. There is, indeed, a refinement of voice and manner and a precision of speech associated with good breeding, and often accompanying a " standard " pronunciation, which, of course, should be encouraged, since speech is a form of social behaviour, and like other kinds of social behaviour, e.g. table manners, dress, general behaviour in public places, it has its rules and customs. The lack of this is often put down to " accent," under which general term all the factors which go to make up speech are judged. In this book, however, we are concerned mainly with actual speech sounds and their use, and not with voice production or manners, but it should be remembered that pronunciation alone is not enough; idiom, usage and the social behaviour accompanying "good speech" are part and parcel of the whole.

6. The preceding paragraph is not intended to support any and all kinds of dialectal speech, nor does the writer wish to put on one side the aesthetic point of view in the judgment of speech. It is merely an appeal

to the reader to consider carefully, before he condemns one type of speech and praises another, the true reasons which lie behind his dislikes and his preferences.

7. There are good reasons why it may be thought advisable to attempt to teach in the schools some kind of pronunciation which would be acceptable in any part of the country, and in any class of society. The chief argument is one of mutual intelligibility. It is obvious that in a country the size of the British Isles, any one speaker should be capable of understanding any other when he is talking English. At the present moment, such is not the case: a Cockney speaker would not be understood by a dialect speaker of Edinburgh or Leeds or Truro, and dialect speakers of much nearer districts than these would have difficulty in understanding each other. The following diagram, devised by Professor D. Jones, illustrates graphically the position of affairs as they actually are. The base of the cone represents a map of England, and the lines joining various points on its base to the apex, the different types of speech used at each place, the apex A representing a kind of pronunciation which bears no signs of any particular district. Thus the line joining L and A would represent all the different kinds of pronunciation used by London speakers, from the extreme Cockney at the base through varying degrees of Cockney, till the apex is reached, when all distinctive signs of a London dialect have been shed. The

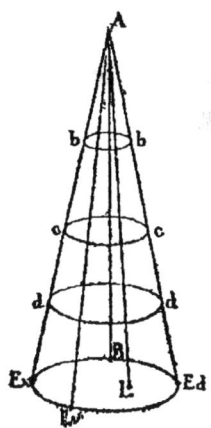

FIG. 1. Variant Pronunciations

line joining B and A would show the same for Bradford speakers, and so on for all parts of the country.¹

8. If a section be taken across the cone at any point between the base and the apex, the differences at this point between the dialects of various places will be fewer than they are at the base, i.e. some of the most outstanding peculiarities will not be found: at a section further towards the apex, the differences will be still less and the types of pronunciation of the different localities will more nearly resemble each other; and as we near the apex, the divergencies which still exist have become so small as to be noticed only by a finely trained ear. These, for all practical purposes, may be neglected. Let us assume that at the section marked *d* such dissimilarities as would make for lack of understanding have dropped—i.e. a speaker from any part of the country using the type of speech represented here, would be understood by any other. This may be called the limit of intelligibility. For the sake of mutual understanding it can be argued that a pronunciation should be taught in the schools which lies above the line assumed at *d*. That would not necessarily, however, be a pronunciation used by educated speakers, and would contain many marked dialectal peculiarities; but it *would* be understandable, and thus

---

[1] The speech represented at the base of the cone is assumed to be that which would be used in reading English not containing dialect words and constructions, i.e. we are concerned with pronunciation, not grammar and vocabulary.

Note to Third Edition.—The cogency of this argument is greater now than when the book was first published. (See Chapter on Broadcasting.)

one object of pronunciation teaching would be secured. If the aim is to approach nearer to *one* type and to teach an *educated* pronunciation, we should have to choose a section nearer the apex of the cone. Let us assume such a section at *c*. This would represent a number of types of speech used by educated people from different parts of the country. It is still not *one* standard pronunciation, but it approaches thereto. At a section still nearer the apex (at *b*), the pronunciation will have lost all easily noticeable local differences. This type of speech may be considered as that most generally understood throughout the English-speaking world and may be called Received Pronunciation.

9. A second argument in favour of encouraging a more uniform type of pronunciation throughout the country lies in the prestige of the English language in other countries. English is the most universally used of all European languages, and from this point of view, it is desirable that something approaching a standard should be set up which would be recognised as the type to be recommended to foreigners.[1]

10. There is also the argument of convenience or expediency. The regional dialects may suffice for those people who have no need to move from their own districts; but few people nowadays remain all their lives in their native town or village without having occasion to leave it for one purpose or another. That language which serves for his own district will not easily serve for a more distant one, and the dialect speaker will find himself at a disadvantage in his travels, or in his ambition to improve his position, if he is unable

---

[1] See *Report on Teaching of English*, p. 67.

to use any other but his own local form of speech.[1] Closely bound up with this point is the fact that certain types of speech are considered as belonging to the lower social classes, and if it is desired to break down class barriers in this democratic age, an attempt at setting up a more uniform pronunciation will lessen the feeling of linguistic inferiority and will go far to overcome what is at present one of the few remaining class distinctions.

11. In face of these arguments in favour of some kind of standard pronunciation, we come to two practical questions: first of all, what is it advisable to teach in the schools, and secondly, how far is such a scheme of pronunciation teaching possible? A consideration of the wide divergencies in regional and class dialects and even the pronunciation of educated speakers, leads us to think that to aim at *one* standard speech—either the apex of the cone or one chosen type, e.g. educated London pronunciation,[2] or the speech of one man— would be useless and unnecessary; useless, because it would be impossible to carry out, and unnecessary because several types of educated speech do exist which would be acceptable anywhere. These recognised types are not only mutually understandable, but vary from each other only in slight details. A plan which seems natural and feasible would be to teach the educated

[1] "Do you come from Yorkshire?" asked one Training College student of another. "Yes," answered the other cheerfully, "we're branded, aren't we?"

[2] Sir Mark Hunter put forward a plea for educated London pronunciation to be considered as a standard, and based his arguments on the history of English pronunciation. He would allow, however, that a number of divergencies from this would be found in educated provincial speech, and need not be discouraged.

speech of the district in which the school is situated, a pronunciation represented by any part of the cone above the section we have assumed to be at (c). This plan has the advantage that the children have opportunities of hearing such a pronunciation, whereas if *one* type of speech were chosen, it would be familiar only to the children in the part of the country where that type was used; children in other parts of the country would *feel* this to be an affectation, and it would be looked on as such by their families, while the other might easily become natural. This would amount to setting up a number of modified received pronunciations, varying from Received Pronunciation in certain details in which they are influenced by the local dialects. There is likelihood of disagreement at first, as to what is to be accepted and what rejected in these local received pronunciations, but it should not be difficult in the long run to come to some agreement as to the limits beyond which speech is considered markedly vulgar or dialectal.

12. The second practical question, how far such a scheme is possible, depends partly on the importance which the head and staff of the schools attach to good speech, and partly on the skill of the teacher in tackling the difficulties of "curing" indistinct and slipshod speech and dialectal peculiarities. It is obvious that the teacher himself should use one of these local received pronunciations or one which lies above this section across the cone, and he should know the local received pronunciation of the district in which he is teaching. This is the first step towards establishing an educated speech throughout the country,[1] and it is in the Training

[1] *See Report*, p. 176.

Colleges that this work must be begun. The question of how these pronunciation difficulties are to be tackled is treated in the chapters on "Correction of Pronunciation" and "Qualifications of the Teacher" and in Appendix No. I ("Suggested Course of Speech Training for Training Colleges").

13. It should be possible to teach a pronunciation which is clear and distinct, which is free from slovenliness and from the outstanding peculiarities of the local dialect. It should be possible to encourage a pleasing voice and manner of speech. But teachers, in order to do anything at all, will have to think it worth while. The work will take time and much patience, besides skill and a rigorous training; some other part of school instruction will probably have to be sacrificed and the results will be slow in showing themselves. The local speech will not disappear, but the children will gradually become bi-lingual, using their dialect with its familiar associations at home, and learning an auxiliary language which they will use in school, and which they will have at their command, if they wish to use it in after life.

14. *Note.*—The influence of broadcasting on the speech of the country is likely to make itself felt in the near future. Interest is taken in the Mother Tongue such as has probably not been known before, and broadcasting is a prominent factor in this interest. The B.B.C. has set up a committee on pronunciation, which decides on the pronunciation of doubtful words, and to whose rulings the announcers are expected to conform. It is a significant fact that, as the present writer has been informed, those announcers and speakers whose speech shows the influence of local dialect least are the most popular with the general public.

CHAPTER II.

BROADCASTING AND SPOKEN ENGLISH.

15. Since this book was first published in 1929, a new factor, at that time in its infancy, has taken an important place in the field of speech. That broadcasting would have considerable influence on the study and practice of English pronunciation was then predicted. It is now time to examine, in the light of the experience of the last nine years, what that influence has been and how it is likely to develop. It will be necessary to examine the kinds of English which are acceptable in broadcasting, not only to the various social and regional groups of this country, but also to the millions of listeners in the Dominions, in the Colonies and in America. Thus the question of standard pronunciation dealt with in Chapter I is in a very wide sense concerned in the matter. It will be necessary also to discuss the frequent objections to what is popularly called B.B.C. English, to analyse those characteristics which make for good broadcast speech—and conversely, what is bad—and to consider how all these affect the teaching of spoken English in the schools and colleges of this country.

16. It is obvious that only the fringe of the subject can be touched upon in this short chapter. The reader who wishes to pursue further the innumerable tracks which lead to interesting and diverse problems, is advised to read *The Broadcast Word*, by Professor A. Lloyd James, and the booklets issued by the B.B.C.

entitled *Broadcast English*[1]: he will be certain of good hunting. Here we must somewhat rigidly limit ourselves to the points enumerated in the preceding paragraph, after the examination of a few general principles.

17. The British nation has become speech conscious—self-conscious in many cases—and comment and criticism are heard from all sides. Much of this criticism is uninformed and without any basis of scientific knowledge; in the matter of speech, everyone who speaks, thinks that by this feat alone, he has the right, the power and the knowledge to criticise other people's performance in this art. Since speech so intimately concerns each one of us, however, these personal reactions, due to the background of geographical and social life and education, even if they are illogical, must be allowed for and reckoned with. It is, indeed, difficult to obtain an impartial and objective opinion from anyone, and we must stress once again the fact that in judging speech, the subjective is the point of view from which most people regard it.

18. Perhaps the most outstanding general contribution which broadcast speech has made to the world is in directing attention to the spoken as opposed to the written word and in stressing the need for a definite conception of the differences between these two types of language. Never since the period before the invention of printing has the spoken word played such an important role in the life of the world as it does to-day. The printing press had ruled our language for so many centuries that we had ceased to realise its tyranny and accepted its criteria unquestioningly. The new means

[1] See Bibliography.

of communication in broadcasting, by which the spoken word takes an honourable place again after centuries of neglect, causes us to examine with greater exactitude what are the essential differences between spoken English and written English, what we can legitimately expect from each of these, and more important still, what each cannot provide.

19. If we examine the two forms of language, eye-language and ear-language, we find they have little in common except intelligibility: the one conveys meaning through the eye, the other through the ear. Because of the work of the printing presses and the standardisation of spelling, the visual language is practically the same over the whole of the English-speaking world. Not so the spoken language. But because we have been conditioned to the written word by long tradition and by the processes of our education, we find it difficult to separate the two and are apt to think what is written in the black and white of the printed page is by some alchemy transformed exactly into the noises we make and recognise as the spoken language, and that *vice versa*, the ephemeral thing called speech is capable of accurate and standardised representation on paper. This confusion of sounds and letters is a frequent cause of the attitude of many to "standard" and "correct" pronunciation, viz. that it should conform in some way to the printed word. At the best, conventions must be made to show the relation of the auditory to the written language, and English is pre-eminently a language which defies all efforts at making such conventions. Moreover, it is impossible to record in an ordinary orthography those subtle elements of speech, such as degrees of stress

and emphasis, relative length of syllables, pitch, the type of voice used, slight variations in pronunciation, all of which contribute to the general effect of the spoken word and to "accent" as a whole. It is necessary to remind ourselves of this frequently, as it is to remember that the spoken word is always changing while the written language remains static.[1]

20. The main criterion in judging speech is intelligibility. The requirements for intelligibility with our immediate neighbours are low, since context of situation, community of interests and surroundings supply much of the necessary material for understanding. A wider circle, however, is reached to-day through the greater mobility of all classes and especially through broadcasting.[2] The requirements for intelligibility in broadcast speech are, therefore, stricter, since where little context of situation is provided, and (until television becomes common) the eye gives no help, the lack of this has to be supplied by the spoken word itself. But intelligibility is not all. Broadcast speech, to be acceptable to the majority of English speakers in the world should be some form of speech which is not too far removed from the various standards of educated English in the different parts of the country and of the Empire; indeed America may also be included. That is to say, it must not be too "precious" nor too vulgar, but

[1] See Chapter XVII, p. 199.

[2] "So long as the oral language was restricted in its currency, nothing mattered, but when it was called upon to serve as a national and international medium of communication over the ether, there were bound to arise national and international questions of standard."—Prof. A. Lloyd James "The Art of Announcing."

a mean with no outstanding peculiarities in the way of vowel and consonant sound, of stress and intonation.

21. We should be reminded, however, and reminded frequently, that it would be impossible to please all listeners all the time. A "standard" acceptable to all could never be achieved, and indeed one of the criticisms hurled at the B.B.C. is that it is attempting to level, up or down according to the individual critic, the pronunciation of English and to impose on the country the speech of the men who form the body of its speaking officials. Such criticism is without foundation, since it is no part of the B.B.C or of its Advisory Committee on Spoken English to lay down principles for the speech of the general public.[1] How far the speech of announcers and other wireless talkers is likely to influence the speech of the country is discussed later in this chapter. But there is no doubt that certain characteristics of the type of pronunciation used by the majority of B.B.C. speaking officials rouse unfavourable reactions in many listeners, and it will be useful to investigate the reasons for this. The fundamental reason for this antagonism is the fact that these men, who belong to the younger generation of Englishmen educated mainly at the older universities, exhibit the "advance guard" of change in the speech of our time and therefore theirs is a minority speech; their speech habits, which to them are natural and not, as many critics say, "affected," are, like other habits of the younger generation, deplored by their elders.

22. The main characteristics of this type of speech are set out in Chapter XVII, where the changes which have been taking place in recent years are analysed. It

[1] See § 33 for the work of this Committee.

will be well to sum up here some of these which are not acceptable to many listeners. The chief ones are

- (a) the flattening of diphthongs and triphthongs;
- (b) the centralising of vowels, which makes all vowels nearer together in tongue position and in quality;
- (c) the unrounding of vowels and diphthongs which have had lip-rounding; this removes some of the definite characteristics of such vowels.
- (d) the "clipping" effect of weak vowels, where listeners expect strong ones;
- (e) the non-pronunciation of *r* in post-vocalic positions. This is a characteristic of a large number of English people of all generations, and is not a recent tendency; note also, that this criticism is generally based upon spelling;
- (f) the occasional use of intrusive "*r*".

23. The writer feels that she must make plain her own attitude to the question. While not one of the younger generation and not using many of their newer pronunciations, she feels that the announcers perform a difficult task with the utmost skill; their reading of news and announcing of items in the programmes is clear and business-like. When one realises the amount of material they get through in one news bulletin and how this would pall if the delivery were at all laboured, one must admit that these officials would be hard to beat at their somewhat thankless task.[1]

[1] See *The Broadcast Word*, p. 147, for what is expected of the announcer. See also the leading article in the *Listener* of Sept. 22nd, 1938, on "Reading the News," which stresses the weight of responsibility on the announcer who has news of a serious character to read.

24. The question of the use of dialect must again be touched on here. Along with the accusation of imposing a dead level of uniformity of speech on the country, the B.B.C is arraigned as the prime criminal in the death of dialect speech. The dialects as general speech currency, were doomed before the advent of broadcasting, though probably the process has been hastened by the wireless word. Whether announcing in varieties of modified dialects would be more generally acceptable than the present régime is doubtful; in any case, only trial could prove this. It should be noted that most of those who deplore the loss of our dialects are people who do not use them; nor do they bring up their children using them. Thus their wish to preserve dialect speech is from an aesthetic, historical or sentimental point of view. This is a perfectly legitimate point of view and indeed there is no reason why local patriotism should not foster a feeling of pride in the dialect and its historical background, so long as this does not interfere with the acquirement of a more general type of speech by those who may need it.

25. One other factor in the dialect question is the use that is made of it for comic entertainment. Such treatment is likely to militate against the natural use of dialect, while on the other hand, the bringing to the microphone (as, for example, in the "In Town To-night" series) of dialect speakers who have something of interest to say and whose speech rings true and sincere, gives dialect a pleasing dignity and reality.

26. We now come to an analysis of what makes good broadcast speech. There is no doubt that a new technique for the microphone has had to be developed,

different from that of all other kinds of public speaking, from lecturing, preaching or declaiming. This is largely due to the intimate situation in which radio talk is received. It is inconceivable that we should sit in an easy chair by the fireside to be "preached at"; declamation is out of place and makes us feel uncomfortable, and the first reaction to pomposity is to switch off.

27. The best broadcast speech is natural; it is talk and not the recording of literary or journalistic prose. Here it will be seen that matter and its arrangement enters into the question as well as manner. It is manner, however, that concerns us most in this book, but no one can use a natural speaking manner if he has to read aloud material which has been written—probably unconsciously—for the eye and not for the ear, and which contains constructions or uses a word order such as would never in the ordinary course of affairs be *spoken*.[1] As far as speaking is concerned, however, by natural, we mean there must be no undue exaggeration of stress or intonation and no over-carefulness which makes itself observed. We are all familiar with the speaker who reads his script in the wooden fashion typical of a not too intelligent school-boy reading aloud; and even more unpleasant to listen to is the broadcaster, who, under the impression that he must be very distinct, uses "strong" forms of unimportant words and syllables, and in this way destroys the rhythm of the spoken language. For, if naturalness is the first virtue of broadcast-speech, it is evident that the rhythms and intonations of the ordinary spoken language must be preserved.

28. Since, however, the subject-matter of many wireless talks is of such a nature that the speaker must

[1] See *The Tongues of Men*, by J. R. Firth, pp. 57–8.

go slowly in order that the ideas should reach the minds of his hearers, he must in some way modify this natural technique. This is also true of a speaker in a big hall where his words have to reach the most distant member of a large audience. How can he preserve the naturalness which we consider essential? A slowing up of the whole speech is the most telling way of producing the desired effect, i.e. breaking the sentences into small sense-groups, making slightly longer pauses between the sense-groups than is usual in familiar speech, and taking each at a slower pace. But—and this is important—not destroying the natural rhythm by unnatural exaggeration of pronunciation or of stress, nor by giving undue prominence to unimportant words and syllables. It is, in fact, the slow motion picture translated into sound, i.e. no separate element is exaggerated and the normal proportion is not destroyed. One of the most successful exponents of this method of public speaking suitable for broadcasting, if perhaps too slow for normal occasions, was His late Majesty, King George V. A note on his excellent technique is added to the phonetic transcription of the record of his 1935 Christmas broadcast to the Empire in § 380.[1]

29. A further factor in the naturalness which is the main quality necessary in broadcast speech lies in the use of an ordinary voice and intonation. Until the advent of broadcasting, reading aloud or speaking for public purposes was confined to a few classes, the clergy, lawyers, the elocutionist and the political orator. Each had its own technique. Nowadays, the clerical voice

[1] Incidentally this method is recommended for the teaching of reading in school, in order to do away with the wooden word-by-word reading which is sometimes heard.

and manner, the oratorical devices of the public speaker and the tricks of the elocutionist move us no longer; and broadcasting is partly responsible for this. They are out of place at the microphone and a natural voice and intonation is demanded.

30. How do these varied questions affect the teaching of spoken English in England? First of all, broadcasting gives a new prestige to the spoken word and should eventually range the oral at least on a level with the literary language in the work of schools and colleges. As far as standard pronunciation is concerned, it should reinforce the efforts of those who wish to give our school children the possibility of acquiring some form of "standard" speech, as an auxiliary language. The speed with which such a change may be anticipated should not be over-estimated, however. In the early days of broadcasting it was thought that reform would be rapid, but results of this kind are slow to show themselves. The teacher, however, can train the child to listen, to observe differences of pronunciation, to realise why he likes certain kinds more than others, to be tolerant of a type of speech which is other than that with which he is familiar. He can apply some of the principles of good broadcast speech to his own class-room work and that of his pupils, introducing naturalness, ease, good rhythm, pleasant manner into the work of all oral lessons, and thus do his share in the reinstatement of the spoken word to an honourable place in English education.

31. The B.B.C. arranged for the broadcasting of speech-training lessons over a period of years. During this time an experiment was undertaken to test the value of the lessons. Gramophone records were made of the speech of a class of children in a Central School in

London before the course began and again at the end. A second class, not following the lessons, used as control, was also recorded. The results have been analysed and set out in a publication of the B.B.C. entitled *Evidence regarding Broadcast Speech Training*.[1] The second records showed evidence of change in pronunciation which compared favourably with the untaught class. But one could not expect that the whole speech habits of the children should be changed by a lesson a week over nine months. Broadcast speech-training lessons were given up in England in 1933, on a majority vote of the Central Council for School Broadcasting, mainly because of the objections which were raised to the imposition of a "standard" and to the lack of definition of what the "standard English" sounds are. It is interesting to note that a successful speech-training course has been given in Scotland since 1935 definitely to teach "standard Scottish": in this case the "standard" has been very carefully worked out by a special investigation committee formed on a national basis.[2]

32. Broadcasting gives to the student of English phonetics unlimited opportunity of hearing varieties of English pronunciation, and this should be a valuable adjunct to the ear-training which is so necessary a part of such work. This chapter is introduced here to encourage students to use the listening end of broadcasting and to bring an unbiassed mind to the many still unsettled problems of spoken English.

[1] Enquiry Pamphlet No. 3: Central Council for School Broadcasting.

[2] This information is from the report (in *Good Speech*, Jan., 1938) of a lecture by Miss Mary Somerville, B.B.C. Director of School Broadcasts, at the Speech Fellowship Conference in London, 1937.

33. *The B.B.C. Advisory Committee on Spoken English.* —The B.B.C. Advisory Committee on Spoken English as at present constituted, consists of a large and representative body of people, the chair of which is held in rotation, and goes up for election every two years; nobody may hold it three years in succession, but a man may be re-elected after he has been out of office for two years. The present chairman (1938) is Professor G. Gordon, of Magdalen College, Oxford. The research work is carried out by a sub-committee of four experts, Professor H. C. Wyld, of Merton College, Oxford; Professor Daniel Jones, of University College, London; Mr. H. Orton, of the University of Durham; and Professor A. Lloyd James, of the School of Oriental Studies, University of London (Hon. Sec.). This committee draws up the recommendations which are submitted to the big committee. Their work is varied and covers a wide field, as can be seen from the titles of the publications issued by the B.B.C. under the editorship of Professor Lloyd James (see Bibliography, p. 246). They deal with all the problems of pronunciation of doubtful words for announcing, of words with more than one accepted pronunciation; of personal and place names in England; of the "anglification" of Scottish and Welsh place names which is necessary for the understanding of English listeners; of the pronunciation of foreign terms in general use; of foreign personal and place names, etc. Some of their decisions, as is inevitable, meet with a certain opposition. It should be stated, however, that the committee does not attempt to set up a standard of general pronunciation either for the announcers or for the country.

Chapter III.

CORRECTION OF PRONUNCIATION.

34. Differences of speech fall into several clearly differentiated categories.

(1) A dialect speaker may use *words* which are not known in other parts of the country: e.g. in the West Riding of Yorkshire, the sentence *He's lakin at taws up a ginnel* [i z lɛːkɪn ət tɔːz ʊp ə gɪnɪl, He's playing at marbles in a passage] could not be understood, however it was pronounced, if the words *lakin, taws* and *ginnel* were not known.

(2) He may employ unusual constructions, ungrammatical or otherwise: e.g. *Wait while Monday* for *Wait till Monday* (Yorks.); *He come in the house and play with me every day* (East Anglia); *That belongs to I* (West Country).

(3) He may stress words differently: e.g. *mis-ˈchievous* instead of *ˈmischievous*.

(4) He may have an unusual rise and fall of the voice.

(5) He may use *sounds* which are not found in educated speech: e.g. kʊm for kʌm (Yorks. and Lancs.); nʌʊ for noʊ (Cockney); lɑŋ for lɒŋ (East Anglia and West Country).

(6) He may omit or insert normal sounds or substitute one sound for another: e.g. mɪsˈtʃiːvɪəs for ˈmɪstʃɪvəs, wɛstˈmɪnɪstə for ˈwɛstmɪnstə, ˈgʌvəmənt for ˈgʌvənmənt, etc.

23

35. A consideration of dialect speech in general would include a study of all these factors. In this book, however, we are concerned mainly with pronunciation, and for our purpose, the last two points must be discussed thoroughly. The question of stress and intonation (points 3 and 4) is touched on in a later chapter.

36. The two main mistakes, therefore, with which we are concerned are the use of sounds not found in educated speech—wrongly formed sounds—and the insertion, omission or substitution of sounds which do occur in educated speech. In the first class come such pronunciations as the Cockney tsïü ən tsïü ə fɔːwə for tu ən tu ə fɔː (or fɔə), nʌʊ or næʊ for noʊ, tsəi for tiː, kɛʔl for kɛtl (this last is not confined to Cockney); the Northern pronunciation kʊm, lʊv for kʌm, lʌv, mɔːtə for moʊtə, and the Midland pronunciation of sɪŋgɪŋg for sɪŋɪŋ.[1]

37. In the second class, i.e. the use of normal sounds in wrong places, or the insertion or omission of sounds, are the pronunciations haitθ (haɪt), ɒpəsait (ɒpəzɪt), gʌvəmənt (gʌvənmənt), ɛərɪeɪtɪd (ɛəreɪtɪd), wɛstmɪnɪstə (wɛstmɪnstə), ɛərɪəpleɪn (ɛəropleɪn), rɛkənaɪz (rɛkəgnaɪz), sɛkətrɪ (sɛkrətrɪ), klɜ·k (klɑ·k), kjuˑpɒn (kuˑpɒn), etc.

38. The first kind of mistake is by far the more difficult to correct, and the teacher's work should be mainly concerned with this—the teaching of new sounds that the pupil does not possess. The Cockney child says tïü because he cannot say tuː, and generally cannot imitate the teacher's pronunciation; the Yorkshire child

---

[1] These dialectal pronunciations will be better understood after the chapters on vowels and consonants have been read.

says kʊm because the vowel ʌ does not exist in his speech; the Midlander says sɪŋgɪŋg because he cannot say the sound ŋ followed by a vowel or finally: he always adds a g sound. It is the business of the teacher, therefore, if he is going to attempt the task of teaching pronunciation, to find, when imitation fails, some other means of making his pupil pronounce the sounds which he thinks desirable.

39. In modern language teaching the old idea that one could " pick up " a good pronunciation is exploded, and the best modern language teachers now realise that pronunciation, like every other branch of language work, has to be taught, and taught scientifically. The problem of teaching a new pronunciation of the Mother Tongue is almost the same as that of teaching a foreign language; the pupil cannot make certain sounds which the teacher wishes him to make. It is, in fact, more difficult than teaching the pronunciation of a foreign language, since the pupil has acquired fluency in " incorrect " usages, and his " bad " habits must be broken. These pronunciation difficulties must be analysed and the most suitable method of treatment applied.

40. The phonetically trained teacher will be able to do this best, as he will realise not only what the right sound is which he is going to teach, but what the wrong sound is that his pupil is using, and the relation of the one to the other. Having this knowledge, he is able to invent exercises which will produce the required sound and help the pupil to get rid of the wrong one. In this book, suggestions for exercises of this type will be given in the detailed description of the vowels and consonants.

41. The correction of the second class of mistake, the misplacing of existing sounds, sounds the pupil already knows, is of little difficulty compared with the first kind. These mistakes are not made because the pupil is unable to say the normal sound—he can say klɑˑk as easily as klɜˑk—but because he has been accustomed to hear and use these pronunciations. Many of the mistakes are due to false analogy with other words; he says haɪtθ and deɪtθ and wɛstmɪnɪstə because he says lɛŋθ and brɛdθ and mɪnɪstə; and if he is told the correct pronunciation he can use it without difficulty.

42. It is generally found that the teacher who has had no scientific training in the analysis of English speech either does not realise or cannot tackle the first type of these mistakes; and unless the children can imitate with ease, he leaves them alone, concentrating entirely upon mistakes of the second type. Indeed, he often lays himself open to the charge of making wrong corrections on these lines, and of teaching an artificial pronunciation which is never heard outside a classroom. Thus he will insist on the word *sailor* being pronounced ˈseɪlɔː; *captain* is taught as ˈkæpteɪn, *oval* as ˈoʊvæl, *movement* as ˈmuˑvmɛnt, and *conduct* (verb) as kɒnˈdʌkt, *parliament* as pɑˑlɪəmənt, etc. This is because he has not the power of analysing exactly what people say, and, in spite of the inconsistencies of English spelling, he imagines the spoken word has a close resemblance to the written word. Such people consider speech as made up of a number of syllables, each pronounced in connected speech as it would be if said in isolation: *o-r* spells ɔː, therefore *s-a-i-l-o-r* spells seɪlɔː. They ignore entirely the changes which sounds undergo in connected speech

CORRECTION OF PRONUNCIATION

under the influence of stress and rhythm, and try to teach not what is a good current pronunciation of certain words, but what they think the pronunciation ought to be. This point is dealt with in the chapters on "Spelling Pronunciations" (Chap. VII) and on "Sounds in Connected Speech" (Chap. XVI, §§ 324-8).

Note.—To illustrate this fact, an extract is given here from a speech-training scheme for elementary school children which was submitted to the present writer.

"Distinction must be made between the final syllables of the following pairs of words:

leopard, shepherd   parrot, garret
fatal, battle   cousin, cozen
porridge, college   carrot, carat
bacon, taken

-age must be pronounced, not				*-ige* in	*cabbage, village,* etc.
-ent	,,	,,	,,	,, *-unt* ,,	*excellent, benevolent*
-ence	,,	,,	,,	,, *-unce* ,,	*patience, silence*
-et	,,	,,	,,	,, *-ut* ,,	*wicket, basket*
-ness	,,	,,	,,	,, *-niss* ,,	*witness, kindness,* etc."

Does anyone say feɪtæl, kærɒt, kæbeɪdʒ, bɑskɛt, saɪlɛns? The scheme was in reality no speech-training scheme, but a list of hints for the teacher for the dictation lesson to ensure correct spelling,—of little value also in the teaching of spelling.

Chapter IV.

QUALIFICATIONS OF THE TEACHER.

43. A consideration of the different types of mistake in pronunciation and the problem of dealing with them, brings us to the question as to what qualifications are necessary for the teacher who is going to attempt this difficult task.

Ear-Training.

44. The basis of all speech-training is ear-training. A teacher who can hear only the most outstanding divergencies of pronunciation is at a loss when he wants to deal with subtler differences. He knows, but vaguely only, that something is not quite right, instead of being able immediately to put his finger on the spot and say *exactly what is wrong*. It is essential, then, for a teacher to have an ear trained to recognise fine distinctions in speech sounds if he is going to correct pronunciation.

45. To train his ear for speech sounds, the student must accustom himself to listening to sounds, not only in the ordinary speech of different people but in systematic exercises devised for the purpose. Such practice is given by the teacher of phonetics, who dictates meaningless words which the student writes down in phonetic script. The reason for the choice of meaningless words for ear-training is that by this method, the student has no other preoccupation than with the sounds themselves; he is not thinking of the associations which real-words would call up, the ordinary spelling, his own or the teacher's pronunciation, or the meaning; he concentrates on the sounds alone, and in this way is able

28

to train himself to observe even minute differences in pronunciation. The teacher can see by the written exercise if the student has heard correctly or not, and if he has made a mistake, the teacher can further help him by repeating alternately the sounds which the student thought he heard, i.e. the ones he has written down, and the ones which were actually said. In this way, he will gradually come to perceive the acoustic differences between the sounds which he has confused. Such a training, if carried out systematically and for a considerable period of time, should enable a student to recognise exactly the differences between his pupils' pronunciation and the one he is trying to teach.[1]

TRAINING FOR CONTROL OF THE ORGANS OF SPEECH.

46. The student of pronunciation who is going to attempt to correct wrong sounds, must not only be able to recognise the wrong sounds when he hears them, but he must also be able to *make* them. This is a matter of mouth gymnastics, which will enable him to use his speech organs in a way to which he has been hitherto unaccustomed. Such training involves considerable practice in making speech sounds of all kinds, not only those of normal English, but also many dialectal and individual variants, and the sounds of foreign languages. In this way the student will gain such control of the speech organs as will enable him to make at will any sound he wants, i.e. he will be able to imitate correctly the wrong sounds his pupil makes, and will consequently know *how* they are made. This training, obviously, cannot be obtained from books or lectures, although, as in the

[1] Ear-training exercises are added in Appendix II.

present book, exercises can be suggested; it is best obtained by careful study with a competent teacher, who will tell the student what to do with his organs of speech, and give him exercises to help him to carry out these instructions.[1]

Knowledge of Theory.

47. The third qualification of a teacher, who is going to use phonetics to teach pronunciation, is that he shall know how the sounds of English are made, i.e. what position the organs of speech take up in the formation of all the sounds of the language, and how they are used in connected speech. This knowledge of theory can be obtained from books and lectures, in which the sounds of English are described, and a study of the theory, together with a careful observation of his own speech habits will give a student a good working knowledge of how English speech sounds are made.

48. In the first two requirements, however, books play a secondary rôle; they may describe certain types of mistake, and suggest methods of dealing with them, but they can do no more. The teacher must analyse for himself the pronunciation of the pupil he is dealing with, and for this he must rely on his own trained ear.

49. When the student has these three qualifications, viz. the knowledge of the formation of the correct sound, the power to recognise the wrong sound and the ability to make it, he is in an excellent position to use phonetics in the teaching of pronunciation, i.e. to attempt to cure any mispronunciation he may come across. His theoretical knowledge and practical skill will enable

[1] Certain exercises are added in Chapters VIII and IX for the student to practise.

him to devise exercises to get rid of wrong and teach correct sounds in the quickest way possible.

50. A few words of warning should be given here. It is not advocated that phonetic theory should be taught in schools. The aim of the teacher is, presumably, to teach a good pronunciation, and in the quickest time possible. Phonetics is a science *for the teacher to know and apply in a practical fashion in the teaching of pronunciation*. In some cases, it may be interesting and profitable to introduce a certain amount of phonetic theory, where time allows; children like to know what they do in their mouths when they talk and they like to hear about other speech habits than their own, and to compare pronunciations, but this is not essential to the teacher's primary purpose. Also it cannot be too strongly stated that a knowledge of the formation of speech sounds on the part of a student does not necessarily mean that he can make the sounds correctly, nor does detailed information about the functions of the organs of speech imply that he has control over these organs. Moreover, the idea that to know a phonetic alphabet is either to know phonetics or to possess a "correct" pronunciation, or be able to teach it—an idea common enough, though perhaps not actually stated—should not be allowed currency. Knowledge of a phonetic alphabet is no guarantee whatever of the pronunciation of the user of it. Phonetic transcription is a useful adjunct to phonetics,[1] but it does not *teach* sounds. Phonetics is a science of great practical value in linguistics, and a theoretical knowledge only of the subject is of little use.

[1] See next Chapter.

CHAPTER V.

PHONETIC TRANSCRIPTION.

51. Phonetics is the science which analyses and records sounds and other elements of speech, and their use and distribution in connected sentences. For the purpose of *recording* speech sounds, without fear of ambiguity, it is necessary to make use of a phonetic alphabet, i.e. an alphabet based on the principle of " one letter per phoneme " (for Phonemes, see Ch. IX). Without such an alphabet, an accurate description and record of speech usages would be clumsy and awkward, and liable to misinterpretation. It should be remembered, however, that a phonetic alphabet is not phonetics, nor does it *teach* sounds; it is a most useful, in fact, almost indispensable accompaniment of phonetics, in that by means of it, a ready way is found of writing down the pronunciation of individual words, and of showing with fair accuracy and without ambiguity how sounds are used in connected speech. A phonetic dictionary can show the pronunciation of individual words, can even give alternative pronunciations, strong and weak forms, etc. (see Ch. XVI), and can show how words are stressed, but it cannot indicate *when to use* the strong and weak forms in connected speech; nor can it show how the normal word stress is changed under the influence of sentence stress. This is possible only in a phonetic transcription.

52 The student is advised to learn to recognise and make the English sounds in isolation and in words,

and the symbols which represent these sounds, and then to practise writing down his own speech in sentences by means of a phonetic alphabet. He will find in this way that a phonetic transcription is a valuable aid to the study of pronunciation. It will help him, in the first place, to get rid of the natural idea that the conventional spelling represents pronunciation; we are still very much the slave to the written word. Secondly, it will enable him, as no other method could, to realise his own speech habits; he will find that he uses far more "weak forms" and that he drops more consonants and makes more assimilations than he is aware of, and does not pronounce every syllable in connected speech as he would do if it were said in isolation.

53. In this connection, it should be remembered that the *interpretation* of a phonetic transcription requires an understanding of phonetics. Critics of the subject are apt to criticise the whole science adversely on seeing and attempting to read a phonetic transcription without the necessary knowledge; they judge that it represents a slipshod speech. This is generally due to either or both of two reasons; the reader not trained in speech analysis does not realise his own speech habits, he still thinks the spelling more or less represents the pronunciation; he does not realise, for example, that he pronounces no vowel in the second syllable of *mutton*, or that he does not pronounce the second syllables of *mountain* and *attain* alike. Or, as he is unfamiliar with a phonetic transcription, he deciphers it word by word, or even syllable by syllable, when it was written to represent natural quick connected speech. When this occurs, he sees the word *was* written as wəz,

i.e. *unstressed*, and he gives it undue prominence, and turns it into wɜz, which, of course, does not occur in the English language in anyone's speech. In this way, because of his ignorance of the subject, he condemns phonetics, by misusing a phonetic transcription.

54. Just as a phonetic transcription can show a student with fair accuracy his own speech habits, so it can serve to represent the similarities and differences in the pronunciation of individuals and of dialects: e.g. the difference between N. and S. pronunciation of words like *plant, after* (N. plænt, æftə, or plant, aftə; S. plant, aftə), the Cockney diphthong in *lady* (lɑɪdɪ) as compared with the Received pronunciation leɪdɪ; the difference, not dialectal but individual, between the two pronunciations of the word *associate* (əsouʃɪeɪt and əsousɪeɪt), etc. The student of dialects will find an accurate knowledge of a phonetic alphabet invaluable for recording dialect speech of any kind.

55. In Chapter IV, on the training of the teacher of pronunciation, the importance of *ear-training* was stressed; in order to do adequate ear-training, a phonetic alphabet is necessary; without it only the simplest form of ear-training is possible.

56. In this book the phonetic transcription used is that known as the "narrow" transcription. The differences between "broad" and "narrow" are set out on p. xiii. Many phoneticians make use of the "broad" transcription of English,[1] in which length marks (ː) are used to show a difference in quality as well as in length. This can be justified as adequate for representing, with certain well-defined conventions, the

[1] Prof. D. Jones uses it in his *Outline of English Phonetics*.

normal pronunciation of English. Here, however, where we are comparing somewhat fine dialectal and personal differences, it has been thought better to use the "narrow" transcription, and to make length marks represent length only and not quality also.

Note.—A phonetic orthography based upon the principles of the International Phonetic Association has been established for the writing of many African languages. The name "Africa" script is given to this. (See Memorandum on Orthography published by the International Institute of African Languages and Cultures). There is a movement to extend this as a "World Orthography."

Chapter VI

APPLICATION OF A KNOWLEDGE OF PHONETICS TO THE TEACHING OF ENGLISH.

57. In Chapter V of this book, phonetics is defined as the science which analyses and records speech. This analysis is the work of the phonetician, who is an observer with an ear trained to fine distinctions of sound. When such analyses and records have been made by the phonetician, there are several uses to which this knowledge may be put. In the present book we are concerned with its use in the teaching of English. It was assumed at the outset that teachers wish to teach a clear and distinct articulation and a pronunciation free from outstanding dialectal peculiarities, i.e. to "cure" an accent. This is, of course the most obvious use of phonetics to the English teacher, —and in this book it takes the chief place. The differences and similarities between articulation in speech and in song, between every-day speech and what is popularly known as "elocution," can be dealt with by phonetics, which should be used in teaching both elocution and singing.

58. Besides attempting to change an accent, the teacher can apply phonetics to the cure of specific speech defects, such as lisping of various kinds, inability to pronounce various consonants, such as r, k, etc. Children who have defects of this kind can generally be taught by phonetic methods to get rid of them: those children whose speech is slow in development can be helped, and those who have had cleft-palate successfully

36

APPLICATION OF A KNOWLEDGE OF PHONETICS

operated on can be taught to speak much better by a phonetically trained teacher.[1]

59. Teachers of the deaf have generally to undergo a phonetic training of some kind: this use of phonetics—the teaching of speech to the deaf—is one of the most useful applications of phonetic science.[2] A few experiments have been made in the teaching of reading in its initial stages by phonetics. A description of such an experiment is published by the International Phonetic Association (University College, London), under the title of *Phonetics and Phonetic Texts in the Teaching of Reading*, by R. Jackson, M.A.

60. A further use of phonetics lies in its application to the study of philology. Existing dialects can be analysed and recorded with great precision by a student with a trained ear and a knowledge of good phonetic notation, and the pronunciation of previous ages can be reconstructed and the development of modern pronunciation from Early English can be traced with considerable accuracy. In fact, without an exact and scientific knowledge of phonetics, philology becomes a mere history of the written word.[3]

---

[1] This side of the work is dealt with in the writer's *Defects of Speech: their Nature and Cure*. Dent & Co. Third Edition, 1936. 2s. 6d.

[2] Miss Iza Thompson, Hugh Myddelton School for the Deaf, London, has written on work of this kind in various magazines on the teaching of the deaf. See *Volta Review*, July, 1927.

[3] Sweet, Preface to *Handbook of Phonetics*: "Without a knowledge of the laws of sound change, scientific philology—whether comparative or historical—is impossible, and without phonetics, their study degenerates into a mere mechanical enumeration of letter-changes."

Chapter VII.

SPELLING PRONUNCIATIONS.

61. A comparison of the pronunciation of certain words at the present day with that of other periods throws interesting light on tendencies and developments that have shown themselves in the history of English speech. Pronunciation changes are of two kinds: (*a*) Those gradual changes, which have taken centuries to develop, and which have changed Early English into the speech of to-day; and (*b*) those changes which are somewhat sudden, and which are, in the first place, a *deliberate* alteration of the established pronunciation for some purpose or other. In this book, it is not possible to deal with the first class, but the second class it will be advisable to examine, as this habit of deliberate alteration of an established pronunciation, which has shown itself for some generations, is still active to-day.

62. The main purpose of such alterations has been the desire to bring pronunciation more into line with the spelling, and for this reason the term " Spelling Pronunciations " is given to them.

63. Spelling pronunciations arise through some person who deliberately adopts a new pronunciation because he thinks it better; it is an affectation on his part. At first it is probably regarded as a false refinement by those who do not use it, but gradually by frequent repetition, the new pronunciation spreads, and a succeeding generation acquires it as its natural pronunciation. This tendency to change is marked at

38

SPELLING PRONUNCIATIONS 39

the present day, but it is by no means of recent development; it probably began with the grammarians and purists of the early eighteenth century. Until then people had written more or less as they spoke, and had certainly not let the written word affect their pronunciation. Since that time the tendency seems to have grown and an examination of modern speech shows it to be still going on.

64. Those who are interested in this aspect of pronunciation should consult Professor Wyld's *A History of Modern Colloquial English*, Chapter VIII, and *Studies in English Rhymes from Surrey to Pope*, and the sources he quotes. Most of the examples given here are collected from these books or from seventeenth and eighteenth century writers on English grammar and pronunciation.

EXAMPLES OF SPELLING PRONUNCIATIONS.

65. I. *Consonant sounds introduced*.

(a) The pronunciation of k in *perfect, verdict* (pɜˑfɪkt, vɜˑdɪkt) is a spelling pronunciation. The word *perfect* as introduced into English from Norman French was *parfet* or *parfit* ; the c was re-introduced into the spelling in order to show the derivation of the word from Latin, and the pronunciation was altered to fit the spelling. Elphinston,[1] writing in 1790, says that c is not pronounced in *perfect, verdict, indict*. In the last-named it is still silent; we say ɪndaɪt; cf. also *victual* (vɪtl), in which it is also silent. In the same way the d was introduced into *adventure*, which was originally *aventure*; in *language*

[1] Elphinston, *Inglish Orthography Epittomized*.

(from *langage*) the *u* was introduced under the influence of the Latin *lingua*, and was afterwards pronounced as the semi-vowel w (læŋgwɪdʒ); *equal*, written as *egal*, acquired its w in a similar fashion.

(b) The habit of dropping *t*'s and *d*'s is not altogether a modern one; indeed, examples go to show that *t*'s and *d*'s dropped regularly in the seventeenth and eighteenth centuries have been re-introduced into the pronunciation in a number of words under the influence of spelling. Jones,[1] writing in 1701, gives a list of words in which he says *t* or *d* is not pronounced: *often, Christmas, costly, ghostly, mostly, roast beef, husband, pageant, Wednesday, wristband, Wiltshire, friendly, handmaid, fondle, candle, handle, children*. In some of these it has been restored, and in others it is still not pronounced. (In the Yorkshire dialect *fondle, candle, handle, kindle*, are pronounced fɒnl, kanl, hanl, kɪnl.) In *Wednesday* and *often* the process of " restoration " is seen at work, some people pronouncing wɛnzdɪ, ɒfn, and others wɛdnzdɪ, ɒftn (or even ɒftən); but we have not yet attempted to restore *t* in *castle, listen*, etc., though the writer *has* heard *apostle* and *epistle* pronounced əpɒstl and ɪpɪstl in the pulpit, and *pestle* is often pronounced pestl.

(c) *p* is said to have been silent in *prompt, tempt*, etc., and *b* in *tumbling, Cambridge, chamber, humble* (cf. Yorks. dialect tʊml for *tumble* and tʃɛːmə for *chamber*). The *p* in *corpse* is intrusive: *corse* (kɔrs), which was the normal spelling and pronunciation in Tudor times, is still found in poetry.

[1] Jones, *The Expert Orthographer*.

SPELLING PRONUNCIATIONS 41

(d) The present *th* of *theatre, anthem, author, Catherine,* has replaced a previous *t*; the spelling was first altered and later the pronunciation.

(e) The words *woman, Edward, forward, backward, inward,* were formerly pronounced ʊmən (written *'ooman*), ɛdəd (*Ed'ard*), fɒrəd, bækəd, ɪnəd; the *w* is now pronounced in these words (cf. *towards,* tɔːdz and tʊwɔːdz). But *Greenwich* and *Norwich* remain grɪnɪʤ and nɒrɪʤ; cf. also *answer* ɑːnsə, *pennyworth* pɛnəθ, *hussy* hʌsɪ or hʌzi (from *housewife*), and the so-called vulgar pronunciation sʌmət for *somewhat.*

(f) The l sound in *fault, falter, vault, Walter, falcon, almanac, cauldron, falchion, Talbot, St. Albans,* is a spelling pronunciation. The word *fault* was *faute* when it came into English; the *l* was introduced in the spelling and then into the pronunciation. Jones (1701) says that the *l* in most of these words, and in *almost, Falmouth,* and *Chelmsford* is not pronounced; cf. *chalk, calf, almond, alms,* where it is still silent, and the name *Ralph,* which some people pronounce rælf, some as rɑːf, and others as reɪf. The *l* in the pronunciation of *soldier* is of comparatively recent introduction, the spelling *soger,* found frequently in the seventeenth century, indicating the pronunciation soʤə or sɒʤə, a pronunciation heard probably well on in the nineteenth century.

(g) The pronunciation of *h* in *habit, horror, homage,* and in *herb, hospital, humour,* is due to the influence of spelling, all these words having lost their *h*-sound in French before they came into English. In the first three the *h* was re-introduced somewhat early; in the last three it is comparatively recent, and *humour* is still pronounced by some of the older generation as juːmə. *Hermit, horizon, hostler, heretic, hypocrite* are given by the seventeenth century writers as pronounced without *h*.

(*h*) Initial *h*, in words of other than French origin, seems also to have been frequently omitted, as the spellings *Amton Court,. alff, at ome*, show. Its regular pronunciation nowadays in all but uneducated speech is probably due to the influence of spelling; the phrase *at home* may still be heard as ə toʊm from a number of educated speakers.

(*i*) Professor Wyld finds words like *white, when, wheat* spelt as *wite, wen, wete* as early as the fifteenth century, indicating the pronunciation w not ʍ. The pronunciation ʍaɪt, etc., is due to the influence of spelling in Southern and Midland English (but not in Scottish or Northern English, where *wh* has always been pronounced ʍ). Writers on pronunciation in the eighteenth century (as to-day) deplore the omission of *h* in such words, and say that it should be pronounced, a fact which seems to prove that both pronunciations were heard, and that the use of w for ʍ is not, as many are inclined to think, a recent degenerate tendency.

(*j*) The pronunciation of the termination *ing* is interesting. In words like *running fishing, hunting*, etc., the pronunciation ɪn seems to have been common as early as the fourteenth century. The pronunciation ɪŋ is probably due to the spelling, and is now generally considered correct, the use of ɪn, like the dropping of the h being thought to be a vulgarism. There are, however, a number of educated people of the older generation who still use ɪn for the termination *ing*. Poet's rhymes go to prove that *ing* was pronounced ɪn: Pope rhymes *garden* and *farthing*; Swift *garden* and *Harding*; and Cooper, a grammarian. writing in 1685, says that the final syllables of *coming* and *cummin, coffin* and *coughing*, are pronounced alike.

66. · II. *Words in which assimilations were made and later dissimilation, under the influence of spelling, has taken place.*

The spellings *emedgetly, teges, ojus, hijjus, perfyjus* (found by Wyld in diaries and letters), indicate the pronunciations ɪmiːʤətlɪ, tiːʤəs, oʊʤəs, hɪʤəs, pəfɪʤəs. These pronunciations, probably good colloquial usage at the time when they were so written, are nowadays considered vulgar and slipshod; the influence of spelling reversed the process of assimilation which had led to these forms, and the result is the present pronunciations of ɪmiːdjətlɪ, tiːdjəs, oʊdɪəs, hɪdɪəs, pəfɪdɪəs. For modern tendencies in this direction see Chapter XVI, §§ 344-5 on Assimilation.

67. III. *Changes in vowel pronunciation due to the influence of spelling.*

(a) Words written with *er* are interesting, for some of these have retained their original pronunciation of ɑː, though still spelt with *er*, e.g. *clerk, Derby, Berkshire, sergeant, Hertford* (cf. *University* and

'Varsity). But *servant, person, learn, vermin, deserve, earn, universal,* and others, which must at some time have been pronounced with ɑː (and still are in some dialects), are now pronounced with ɜː. The present writer has come across the surname *Learner* in Norfolk which is pronounced by most people lɑːnə.

(b) Words written with *au* such as *taunt, launch, staunch, laundry,* and the place names *Launceston, Taunton,* were formerly pronounced with ɑː; some people still consider lɑːndri and lɑːnʃ correct, and *Launceston* and *Taunton* are pronounced lɑːnstən and tɑːntən by natives of these places.

(c) In words like *grovel, hovel, Coventry, Bromley, Honiton,* the vowel was probably ʌ, but the spelling pronunciation ɒ seems gradually to be replacing this. Both pronunciations are heard of *accomplish, Coventry,* and *Bromley,* while *accompany* is always, and *constable* generally, pronounced with ʌ.

(d) The word *bowls*—the game of bowls—from the French *boule*, like all other *ou* words, should have developed into aʊ. Its present pronunciation, oʊ, is probably due to the fact that it was spelt like *bowl*, a basin, and has developed the same pronunciation. In the Yorkshire dialect a bowling green is still called a baʊlɪŋ griːn.

(e) The sounds ju in certain words must be due to the influence of spelling, for the words *nephews, monument, reputation* are found written as *nevys, moniment, repetation,* obviously indicating the pronunciation nɛvɪz, mɒnɪmənt, rɛpɪteɪʃn.[1]

---

[1] See Luick, *Historische Grammatik der englischen sprachen,* §§ 466, 597, 608.

SPELLING PRONUNCIATIONS

68. IV. *Spelling pronunciations due to words being* seen *written and not heard.*

Place and family names (like foreign words) which are seen and not heard are naturally pronounced as they are spelt. Thus anyone unfamiliar with London would pronounce *Holborn* as hoʊlbɔːn or hɒlbɔːn, *Marylebone* as mɛərɪləboʊn, not knowing that these names have in the course of time developed into hoʊbən, mærɪbən (or mɑːlɪbən), pronunciations that are well established.[1] Place names ending in *-ham* are frequently given a spelling pronunciation which violates the original form of the first part of the word. Thus *Merstham* may be heard as mɜːsθəm and *Streatham* as strɛθəm (not by Londoners, however). *North Walsham*, in Norfolk, is pronounced by non-inhabitants wɒlʃəm, but by inhabitants wɒlsəm, the former being a spelling pronunciation. Note also the pronunciation of *Southampton*, saʊθhæm(p)tən, as if it were South-hampton. In recent years the B.B.C. Advisory Committee has had to consider the question of spelling pronunciations with respect to certain place names. *Daventry*, which had developed into deɪntrɪ during centuries of use, has by the force of spelling returned to dævntrɪ, since to large numbers of people who do not know the local pronunciation and who read the name daily in the papers, the old pronunciation would be unrecognisable. A fierce newspaper correspondence followed the B.B.C. pronunciation of the word *conduit* (*Conduit St.*). Here the purists insisted on kʌndɪt; the ordinary man in the street pronounces it kɒndjuɪt. What is the wisest line

---

[1] Marylebone seems, however, to be very frequently pronounced mærɪləbən.

to take in such a case? Surely here is a place for tolerance of a spelling pronunciation and for the purist few not to object to a pronunciation they themselves do not use.

69. V. *Modern tendencies in Spelling Pronunciations.*

There are two main ways in which the tendency towards Spelling Pronunciations shows itself to-day; the first is in reversing the assimilations that have been made by previous generations, and the second is in giving the strong vowel pronunciation in syllables where the weak vowel has been established for long years. The pronunciation əpriˑsɪeɪt instead of əpriˑʃɪeɪt is an example of the first, and kɒnsɛnt, weɪstkoʊt, pɑːlɪəmənt, instead of kənsɛnt, wɛskət, pɑːləmənt, are examples of the second. Individuals who themselves imitate such pronunciations, however, are seldom consistent, using the careful spelling pronunciation form in some words and not in others. For the most part, such speakers use these pronunciations with the idea that they are making their speech more distinct. Both these tendencies are dealt with in the Chapter on " Sounds in Connected Speech," where Assimilation, Dissimilation, and the influence of stress and rhythm on the pronunciation of sounds are considered.

70. What attitude is the teacher to take in the matter of spelling pronunciations? Spelling pronunciations which are well established in the language will, of course, be accepted, but what must he do about fresh innovations? The main thing for the teacher to avoid is a false idea of the value of spelling in spoken language, an idea which will lead him to teach artificial pronunciations under the impression that he is teaching

"careful" speech. If he is trained to observe what are the actual usages in the spoken language, he will be less likely to fall into this mistake. Whether the tendency towards re-establishing a pronunciation that has long passed away is to be encouraged or not is a question upon which every person is entitled to his own opinion. But it is the safer and wiser plan for the individual teacher to confine himself to teaching good modern usages, rather than to set himself up as a maker of a new standard of correctness.

Chapter VIII.

ORGANS OF SPEECH.

71. The student should have an elementary knowledge of the construction of the speech organs and how they are used in the formation of speech sounds. The diagrams in this chapter show all that it is *essential* to know; the student who is interested in physiology and anatomy will find further information in books on these subjects.

72. In the following diagram, the main organs of speech are shown and named. The student should familiarise himself with these terms and should examine as far as he can with the aid of a mirror the inside of his mouth, and try to realise the movements he makes. To do this last easily will take some time, but he will gradually acquire the power of feeling what he is doing and of being able to describe it.

- L.L.   Lips.
- T.T.   Teeth.
- T.R.   Teeth (ridge alveolar) or gums: convex part of the roof of the mouth, immediately behind the teeth.
- H.P.   Hard palate: concave part of the roof of the mouth.
- S.P.   Soft palate (velum): membranous curtain.
- U.   Uvula: pendulous end of the soft palate.
- N.P.   Nasal pharynx: space between the soft palate and the back wall of the throat.
- P.   Pharynx: space between the back of the tongue and the back wall of the throat.

48

ORGANS OF SPEECH

Bl. Blade of tongue, including tip; that part which lies opposite the teeth ridge when the tongue is in a position of rest.

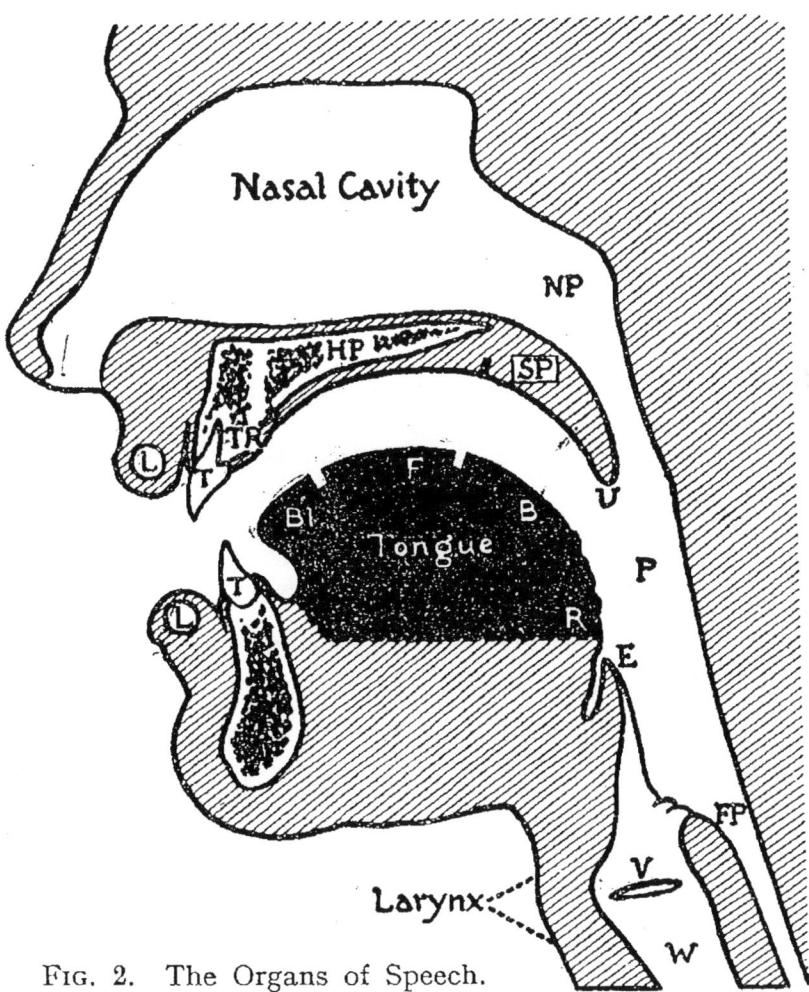

Fig. 2. The Organs of Speech.

F. Front of tongue: that part which lies opposite the hard palate when the tongue is in a position of rest.

B. Back of tongue; that part which lies opposite the soft palate when the tongue is in a position of rest.

R. Root of tongue.

E. Epiglottis: this is drawn over the windpipe when swallowing.

W. Windpipe.

F.P. Gullet or food passage.

V. Vocal cords or lips[1]: membranes stretched from front to back across the larynx.

La. Larynx: the upper extremity of the windpipe (popularly called Adam's apple) which contains and protects the vocal cords.

Glottis: space between the vocal cords.

MOVABLE ORGANS OF SPEECH.

73. The vocal cords, the soft palate, the tongue and the lips are movable: the other organs of speech are fixed. The movable organs of speech can act independently of each other and their movements can be combined in different ways: consequently it is possible to make a very large number of different speech sounds. In any one language, however, the number of combinations is not very large. [See Section on voiced and voiceless sounds, where the action of the vocal cords is combined with movements of tongue, lips, palate, etc.]

HOW SPEECH SOUNDS ARE MADE.

74. The breath in passing from the lungs to the outer air is modified on its way by one or more of the

---

[1] "The vocal cords form a membranous reed-instrument, consisting of two elastic plates, stretched so as to leave a narrow fissure between them, so that when the current of air streams through the fissure, they are thrown into vibration."—C. H. von Meyer, *The Organs of Speech*.

ORGANS OF SPEECH

movable organs of speech; and this gives rise to the various sounds of speech. In the following paragraphs the modification of the breath stream by each of the organs of speech will be examined in turn, and exercises suggested to enable the student to obtain full control over his speech mechanism.

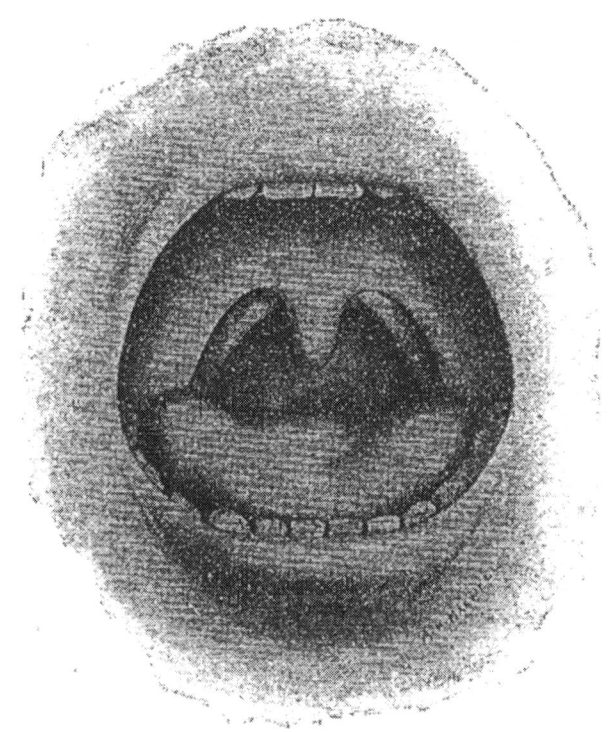

Fig. 3. Open Mouth.

THE VOCAL CORDS.

75. The vocal cords or vocal lips, as they may be called, for they resemble lips rather than cords, are stretched across the larynx from front to back. These cords can take up several positions, and in this way affect speech sounds.

52 THE PHONETICS OF ENGLISH

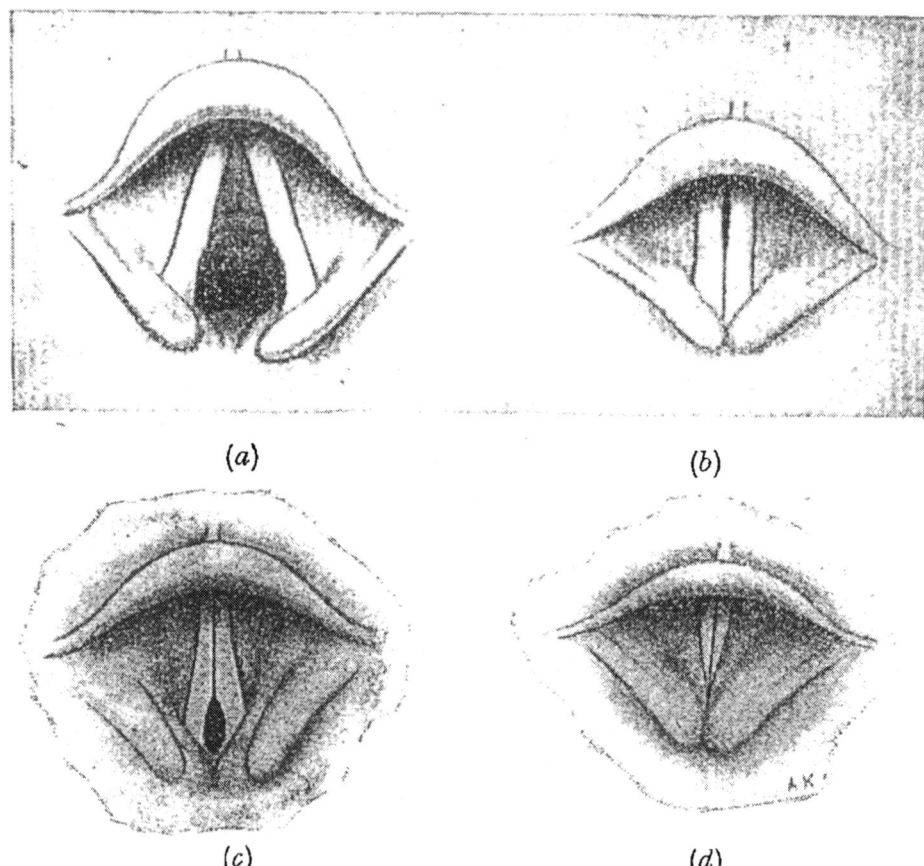

(a)   (b)
(c)   (d)

FIG. 4. Drawings of Vocal Cords.
[Drawings of the vocal cords of Mr. Stephen Jones, made by Mr. A. K. Maxwell.]

(a) Vocal cords in position for breath.
(b) ,,   ,,   during formation of a chest-note.
(c) ,,   ,,   during whisper.
(d) ,,   ,,   in position for a vigorous glottal stop.

(a) The vocal lips can be apart, leaving space for the breath to pass through without any obstruction of any kind. This gives rise to what is known as *breath* (heard purely in the English sound h). Fig. 4(a) above. The vocal cords are in this position for the consonant sounds p, t, k, f, θ, s, ʃ.

ORGANS OF SPEECH

(b) The vocal lips can be brought together in such a way that the air, forcing its way through them in rhythmical puffs, opens and closes them regularly and very rapidly. This, commonly called vibration of the vocal cords, gives rise to a musical note, which may vary in pitch and intensity according to the number and extent of the rhythmical movements, and the note is called voice. Fig. 4(b) shows the position of the vocal cords while a chest note is being sung. All speech sounds which have this musical accompaniment are said to be voiced. All vowels are produced with this action of the vocal cords; and the consonants b, d, ɡ, m, n, ŋ, l, v, ð, z, ʒ, r are voiced.

(c) In Fig. 4(c) the position of the vocal cords is shown which gives rise to whisper.

(d) The vocal lips can be brought into complete contact so that the air is entirely stopped for a moment. This is the position taken up when one holds one's breath, and is known as *closed glottis* (Fig. 4(d)). On the sudden separation of the vocal cords an explosion is heard, when the air, which has been compressed behind the stop, escapes. This sound is called the glottal stop [phonetic symbol ʔ]. In an exaggerated form it is heard as a little cough (ʔəhə, ʔəhə). The glottal stop is a common speech sound in many varieties of English pronunciation (see Ch. XIV, § 250), but, as it has no letter in English orthography to represent it, its existence is not generally realised.

Voiced and Voiceless Sounds.

76. It has been observed that the actions of the movable organs of speech are independent of each other, and their movements can be combined in a large number of ways, and thus give rise to a large variety of speech sounds. The commonest combination is that of the action of the vocal cords with movements of the tongue, soft palate, and lips: i.e. when the lips, tongue and soft palate are in certain positions, articulating certain sounds, the vocal cords can be open or in vibration. Thus we speak of voiced and voiceless sounds; voiced sounds are those which are accompanied by the vibration of the vocal cords, while all the sounds in which the vocal cords are apart, as in Fig. 4(a), are said to be voiceless. All vowels are voiced sounds. Every consonant can be made with or without voice, e.g. f is voiceless, v is voiced; both are articulated in the same way, the difference between them being due to the action of the vocal cords. ʃ and ʒ, θ and ð are other pairs of consonants articulated in the same way; for the first of each pair, the vocal cords are open, allowing a free passage of the air, and for the second they are close together and open and close rhythmically and very rapidly. The student is advised to practise distinguishing the presence or absence of voice; he can do so by saying the sounds alternately, at the same time covering the ears with his hands, or placing the hand on the top of the head, or feeling the outside of the larynx. For the voiced sounds a vibration can be felt. Not all English consonants are found in pairs, however; l, m, n, ŋ, r have voice, and their voiceless counterparts are not

ORGANS OF SPEECH

considered normal English sounds. (They are sometimes heard in combination with other consonants; see Ch. XVI, § 334.) But it is possible to make a voiceless l, m, n, ŋ, and r, and the student is advised to practise making these sounds, as a good exercise for control of the vocal cords. The term "breathed" is sometimes given to those sounds in which the vocal cords are open; it is convenient to use this term for continuant sounds and "voiceless" for the plosive consonants—the latter because there cannot be a current of air passing between the vocal cords during the stop of a plosive, as would be implied by the term "breathed." Both, however, can be called "voiceless." Note that voiced and voiceless consonants differ not only in the presence or absence of voice, but in vigour of articulation and breath force; the voiced consonants are weaker in articulation and less breath force is used.

77. EXERCISES FOR CONTROL OF THE VOCAL CORDS.

(a) For pupils who have difficulty in voicing consonants. The pupil should pronounce the vowel ɜ (the vowel sound in *bird*), and while saying this, bring the bottom lip against the top teeth, making ɜːv. The voice should continue throughout; if the pupil thinks of the *vowel* all the time, the voice will go on through the consonant as well. If necessary he should sing it. The contact of lip and teeth may be light to begin with, but it should gradually become stronger.

(b) Similar exercises can be performed with z, ʒ, ð. When the pupil can carry on the voice into the consonant, he should try to pronounce the voiced consonant without the preceding vowel.

(c) The exercise of alternating breathed and voiced consonants is of great value—

 sz sz sz   θð θð θð
 fv fv fv   ʃʒ ʃʒ ʃʒ.

Each of these pairs of consonants should be repeated several times without a break.

(d) When the vocal cords are sufficiently under control to do these familiar pairs of sounds, the same exercise should be practised with other pairs of consonants, of which the voiced one only occurs in English, e.g. the pupil should say l, and then say it without voice; this gives l̥, the sound of Welsh *ll*. These two should then be alternated— l l̥ l l̥ l l̥. Similar exercises can be made with the nasal consonants m, n, ŋ; m m̥; n n̥; ŋ ŋ̥. (The sign ₀ placed below any symbol—or above in the case of letters with tails—indicates that it is pronounced without voice.)

The Soft Palate.

78. The soft palate can take up two positions; it can be in the position marked (*a*) in the Figure below, when the passage to the nose is open, or in the position marked (*b*) where it is raised to touch the back wall of the pharynx. When the palate is raised, all the air from the windpipe escapes through the mouth, giving rise to *oral* sounds; when the palate is lowered and the passage to the nose is open, the air can escape either entirely through the nose (if the mouth passage is closed), or through the nose and mouth. The lowering of the soft palate gives

rise to nasal, or nasalised sounds. Its function, therefore, is to close or open the passage to the nose, to close it for the production of those sounds which are not nasal, and to open it for the nasal sounds.

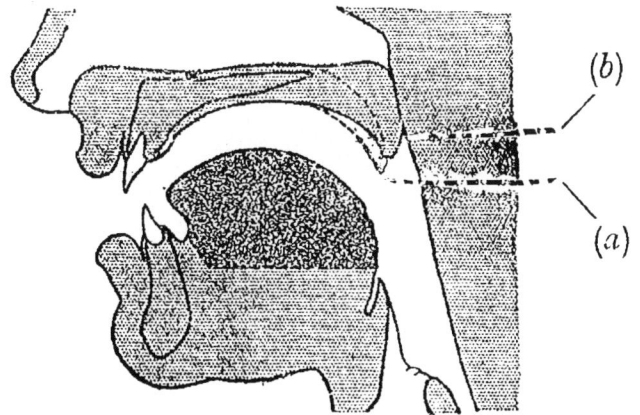

Fig. 5. Soft Palate raised and lowered.

79. The student of phonetics, especially if he is going to use his knowledge in the teaching of pronunciation, should be able consciously to control the movements of the soft palate. He should look into his mouth, say a very back variety of a with considerable vigour, trying to lower the back of his tongue, and see how the palate rises. If he cannot do this at once, he should depress the back of the tongue with a tongue spatula (or a spoon handle) and watch the movement of his palate; then he should practise until he can do this at will, without the tongue being pressed down. Compare the two illustrations of the inside of the mouth (pp. 51 and 58). In the first the palate is lowered; in the second it is raised as high as possible. If the student cannot raise the palate easily, he should try the following exercise. Open the mouth wide, keeping the

tip of the tongue pressed against the bottom teeth; then yawn vigorously. The palate will be seen to rise.

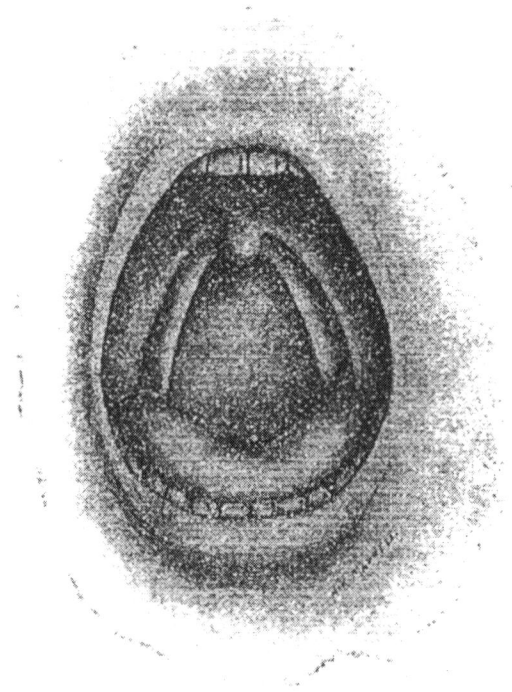

FIG. 6. Open Mouth with Palate raised.

Relax the muscles thus stretched and the palate drops. A repetition of these two movements will help towards the control of the soft palate. Another way of realising the movement of the palate will be found in pronouncing the word *mutton* (mʌtn) with considerable force. The student must take care that he puts no vowel between the *t* and *n*; the explosion he can feel and hear is made as the soft palate leaves the back wall of the pharynx, and the air compressed below that place escapes through the nose. A repetition of **tn tn tn** will help him to realise the movement of the palate and in time to control it. [He should be quite sure that he is saying **tn** and not ʔn.] Similarly, he should practise dn dn dn, as in *sudden* (sʌdn), kŋ kŋ kŋ, gŋ gŋ gŋ, in each case without moving the tongue, and pm pm pm and bm bm bm without moving the lips. He should try to realise the position of the soft palate *before* the explosion is heard, i.e. when it is touching the back wall of the pharynx. A more difficult exercise is to alternate oral and nasal vowels, e.g. ɑã ɑã ɑã. This should be done without any appreciable movement of the tongue, and care must be taken not to add the nasal consonant ŋ to the vowel ɑ.

THE TONGUE.

80. The tongue is, perhaps, the most important of the organs of speech, for it is capable of making many movements, and consequently of modifying the breath stream in numerous ways. It plays the chief part in the formation of vowel sounds, when its different positions alter the shape of the resonating chamber of the mouth and give rise to vowel sounds of various acoustic qualities. It is used in the articulation of many of the consonants, when it either blocks the air passage through the mouth at some point or other, or narrows it so that friction is heard. These movements will be dealt with in the chapters on vowels and consonants. Here it is necessary only to give a few exercises for the control of the tongue.

EXERCISES FOR CONTROL OF THE TONGUE.

81. The pupil should take a mirror, and where the mouth is sufficiently open to permit of it, he should watch the movements of his tongue while he does the following exercises.

60 THE PHONETICS OF ENGLISH

(a) Touch with the tip of the tongue the top lip, the bottom lip, the left corner, the right corner of the mouth. Repeat this many times until it can be done very quickly and with great precision.[1]

(b) Open the mouth; alternately spread and point the tongue.

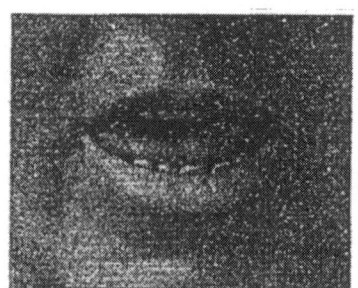 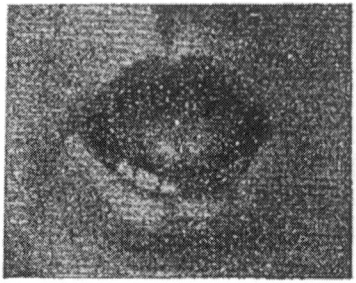

Fig. 7a   Fig. 7b

Photograph of Tongue spreading and contraction.

(c) For precision in consonant formation, repeat the following exercises many times, in whisper and in ordinary voice, concentrating on the movements of the tongue.

pɑ tɑ kɑ	kɑ tɑ pɑ	tɑ kɑ pɑ
bɑ dɑ gɑ	gɑ dɑ bɑ	dɑ gɑ bɑ
kɑ pɑ tɑ	pɑ kɑ tɑ	tɑ pɑ kɑ
gɑ bɑ dɑ	bɑ gɑ dɑ	dɑ bɑ gɑ
mɑ nɑ ŋɑ	ŋɑ nɑ mɑ	nɑ mɑ ŋɑ
nɑ ŋɑ mɑ	mɑ ŋɑ nɑ	ŋɑ mɑ nɑ

[1] This sounds a very childish exercise; but the writer has found many people unable to perform it.

ORGANS OF SPEECH

sa ʃa sa ʃa	ʃa sa ʃa sa	sa ʃa sa	ʃa sa ʃa
za ʒa za ʒa	ʒa za ʒa za	za ʒa za	ʒa za ʒa
fa θa fa θa	θa fa θa fa	fa θa fa	θa fa θa
va ða va ða	ða va ða va	va ða va	ða va ða
fa sa fa sa	sa fa sa fa	fa sa fa	sa fa sa
va za va za	za va za va	va za va	za va za
θa sa θa sa	sa θa sa θa	θa ʃa θa	ʃa θa ʃa
ða za ða za	za ða za ða	ða ʒa ða	ʒa ða ʒa
la ra ma	ra la ma	ma la ra	
ra ma la	la ma ra	ma ra la	

82. These exercises should be pronounced with a vigorous articulation of the consonants; in this way they will prove useful to counteract a tendency to indistinct speech, as well as in giving quick control of the movements of the tongue. The teacher can vary them with different vowels, and can invent other combinations of consonants. It is well to do preliminary practice of this kind on meaningless syllables rather than on real words, so that the attention is not diverted from the main purpose, i.e. precise movements of the tongue.

83. For tongue control in the formation of vowel sounds, the following exercises should prove useful. The student should pronounce the vowel iː (the sound in *see*); while continuing the sound, he should round his lips without moving the tongue. This will give rise to a new vowel, not used in English (similar to French vowel in *rue*, phonetic symbol **y**). A useful exercise can now be made by alternating these two sounds, **iy iy iy**; the student will find it difficult at first to keep

the tongue still, and he will want to pronounce his familiar u sound instead of y. If he finds difficulty in obtaining this new sound, he can reach it in another way, by first rounding the lips, and, while keeping them in this position, trying to say the vowel i. Similar exercises can be made from other vowels. Pronounce the vowel e; while continuing this sound, round the lips, and the new sound ø (similar to French vowel in *peu*), is produced; then eø eø eø can be practised. In the same way ɛœ ɛœ ɛœ gives a further exercise for control of the tongue.

Note.—In these and all similar exercises the student should practise on *one* note without any break: if he uses a different tone for each vowel, he may think he is making a change in the *quality* of the vowel, whereas the change may be one of *note* only. It would be advisable for the student to postpone the practice of these last exercises until the chapter on cardinal vowels has been studied.

THE LIPS.

84. The remaining organs of speech to be dealt with are the lips. The lips can articulate sounds themselves, and their movement can be combined with that of other organs of speech in the formation of both consonants and vowels. Like the vocal cords, the lips can take up four positions.

(*a*) They can be wide open, as in the sounds ɑ or h.

(*b*) They can be brought into contact so that the air is completely stopped for a moment and then released. This gives the sound p (with addition of voice, b).

ORGANS OF SPEECH

(c) They can be brought close together, so that the air pushes itself through, making friction. This is the sound we make in blowing out a candle and is called *bi-labial f* (phonetic symbol ɸ); it exists as a speech sound in many languages, as does the voiced equivalent, bi-labial *v* (β). The student should practise these sounds, although they are not English, as such an exercise helps in the control of the lips. Care should be taken not to round the lips or raise the back of the tongue as for the English ʍ or **w**.

(d) They can be made to vibrate. This is the sound that babies are fond of making, and in some countries it is used to encourage a horse to go quickly. In Bavaria and Sweden it is used to command a horse to stop.

85. In addition to these positions, the lips come into play in the formation of vowel sounds. It has been shown in § 83 that rounding the lips alters the quality of vowels. Most English back vowels have a certain amount of lip-rounding, and most English front vowels are pronounced with neutrally open lips. (See photograph of lips in Ch. IX, p. 72). When the front vowels are articulated with great vigour, the lips may be spread. Foreigners generally accuse English people of talking with closed mouth, and with very little lip movement, and although we dislike the exaggerated " mouthing " that is sometimes seen in recitation, it is well to encourage pupils to make a sufficient amount of lip movement to ensure that their speech is as clear and distinct as it can be.

86. Exercises for the Control of the Lips.

(*a*) The student should practise with the aid of a small mirror the four positions described in § 84.

(*b*) For the sake of practice, he should make exaggerated movements in rounding and pushing out the lips and in spreading them. Alternate the following pairs of vowels with vigorous lip and jaw movement.

uːiː uːiː	ɑːuː ɑːuː	uːeː uːeː
ɛːoː ɛːoː	iːɑː iːɑː	ɑːiː ɑːiː
ɛːuː ɛːuː	ɔːiː ɔːiː	iːɛː iːɛː

(*c*) To keep the lips still, while the tongue moves, the student should say the sound uː (as in *soon*), and while keeping the lips in this rounded position, he should try to say the sound iː. The result will be the sound **y**, which has already been obtained in another way (see § 83). The two vowels can now be alternated **uy uy uy**. Similar exercises can be made from other vowels. If the student pronounces o, and with the lips in this position, he tries to say e, he will pronounce ø (see § 83). Now **oø oø oø** can be alternated, the student taking care that the lips do not move. Similarly if he pronounces ɔ, and with the lips in this position tries to say ɛ, he will pronounce œ. Now ɔœ ɔœ ɔœ can be alternated.

These exercises and those suggested in § 83 can be considered as exercises for both lips and tongue. In the one case the lips must be held still and the tongue must move, and in the other the tongue is still and the lips move.

CHAPTER IX.

CLASSIFICATION OF SPEECH SOUNDS. VOWELS AND CONSONANTS. CARDINAL VOWELS.

87. It is necessary for the purposes of phonetics to be able to describe all speech sounds of a language, and in order to do this accurately some method of classification must be adopted. Speech sounds are generally divided into *vowels* and *consonants*. The main difference between a vowel and a consonant is one of sonority; vowels are those sounds which have most carrying power; but certain consonants such as *l* and *m* also have considerable carrying power, so that a definition of a vowel must be such that it does not include these sonorous consonants.

88. In ordinary speech a *vowel* is a voiced sound in the pronunciation of which the air passes through the mouth in a continuous stream, there being no obstruction and no narrowing such as would produce audible friction. All other sounds are consonants.

89. A *consonant* is a sound accompanied or unaccompanied by voice, in which there is either a complete or partial obstruction which prevents the air from issuing freely from the mouth.

90. The old definition of a consonant as a sound which cannot be pronounced without a vowel is wrong. It is quite easy to pronounce a consonant, in fact, in many languages there are words consisting entirely of

consonants; **tz**, in Chinese, **f**, in Czech, **krk**, in Croatian, are words; and in English we say ʃ when we want someone to be quiet, the word *from* often becomes **frm** in quick speech (aɪ kʌm frm lʌndən), and we speak of **snt pɔːlz**. For the classification of consonants see Chapter XIV.

Classification of Vowels.

91. The difference in quality between one vowel and another is caused by the movements of the tongue and lips, which alter the shape of the resonance chamber of the mouth. For the sake of describing and identifying vowels, we classify them according to the position of the tongue. The student is advised to look into his mouth and watch his tongue as he pronounces ɑ - - iː; then, i - - ɛ - - ɜ - - ɑ - - ɔ, keeping the mouth open as wide as possible. He will see that for iː, the *front* part of the tongue is raised to a considerable height, for ɛ it is lower, for ɑ and ɔ it is the *back* which is mainly concerned, while for ɜ a part is raised that is *intermediate* between front and back.[1] Consequently, vowels are classified as *front*, *back*, and *central*, according to the *part of the tongue* that is raised, and as *close, half-close half-open*, and *open*, according to the *degree* of raising which takes place. Thus i in *see* is a front close vowel, æ as in *man* is a front half-open vowel, ɑ as in *half* is a back open vowel, ɔ as in *all* is a back half-open

---

[1] See diagram on p. 49. The reader is reminded that the *front* of the tongue lies opposite the hard palate and does not include the blade and tip. The blade and tip play little part in the production of vowel sounds except in the case of the retroflex vowels of American speech and of certain English dialects. For the formation of these, see p. 210.

vowel, ʊ as in *book* is a close back vowel, and ɜ as in *bird* is a central half-open vowel. It is not easy to know what one is doing with one's tongue in the formation of vowel sounds, and the student is advised to practise all the vowels he can say—his own natural ones, any others he can imitate, or any foreign ones he knows—and at the same time try to realize what part of the tongue is mainly concerned, how he is moving it, and what the vowel sounds like. In this way, he will learn to recognise from his own muscular sensations and from the acoustic effect, whether a vowel is back, front, or central, whether open or close.

92. English vowels, according to this scheme of classification, can easily be put into one of these categories, but the classification does not allow for the existence of several varieties of i, of ɛ, of ɔ, of ɑ, etc. It would, of course, be possible to say that one person's pronunciation of the vowel sound in *get*, for example, is more close or more open than another's, and if the two speakers are together, the difference between the two types of pronunciation can be heard. But if, in a book on phonetics, a writer refers to the vowel sound in the word *get*, the reader does not know which of the many varieties is meant.[1] Something else, therefore, is needed. If a vowel, in addition to being classified as a front, back or central vowel, close or open, can be compared to some known, unchangeable vowel, the student is in a much better position to realize exactly what the sound is. In most books on pronunciation,

[1] The close and experienced observer of pronunciation readily recognises that there are many varieties of most vowel sounds, even in educated speech. See Chapter XI.

whether of the Mother Tongue or of a foreign language, a list of key words is given. But as there are many varieties of pronunciation in one language, these key words, though possibly indicating roughly what a sound is like, are valueless for exact study, as the reader is likely to interpret them in a different way from that in which the writer intended. (Moreover, in the case of a foreign language, it is impossible to describe the pronunciation of one language in terms of another.)

93. To avoid this difficulty, it is necessary therefore, to have some *standard* vowels, which shall act as a kind of scale or measure, with which to compare all other vowel sounds, and which shall be constant. It was with this end in view that Professor Daniel Jones devised a scheme of *cardinal vowels*. These vowels do not belong to any one language; they have been chosen arbitrarily to represent certain well-defined tongue-positions, and have a definite acoustic quality. X-ray photographs have been taken of the tongue positions of most of them, and gramophone records have been made of them.[1] They form an acoustic sequence such that the intervals between any two consecutive ones shall be as nearly as possible equal.

94. It is obvious that if these cardinal vowels are going to be used at all, the student must know them; he must be able to identify and say each one with accuracy. The best way to do this is to work with a trained teacher who knows them. If such a teacher is not available, the next best thing is to try to imitate

---

[1] The cardinal vowel record is obtainable from the Phonetics Department, University College, London, W.C.1. Price 6s. + cost of packing and postage.

the gramophone. They should be pronounced with the tip of the tongue against the lower front teeth throughout, with tense muscles, with the extreme of the appropriate lip position (except for Nos. 4 and 5), and all on the same pitch. Once the cardinal vowels are learnt the work of the comparison of vowels can begin. The scheme is invaluable for the identifying and describing of the vowel sounds of a foreign language, for the comparison of the vowel sounds of two or more languages, and can be used with equal success in the comparison of variant pronunciations of the Mother Tongue, whether dialectal or individual differences.[1]

CARDINAL VOWEL FIGURE.

95. The cardinal vowel figure is made up from the accompanying diagrams of tongue-positions (Figs. 8 and 9).

– – – – Vowel limit: the tongue moved beyond this limit, with normal breath force, would cause friction, and the resulting sound would be a consonant.
——— Tongue position of the most forward and the closest vowel sound possible.
–•–•–• Tongue position of the lowest and most retracted vowel sound possible.
–•••– Tongue position of the furthest-back close vowel sound possible.
–•■•■– Tongue position of the lowest and most forward vowel sound possible.
× Highest point of the tongue in each case.

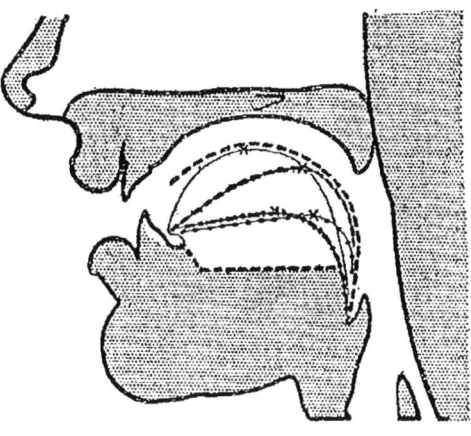

FIG. 8.

Tongue positions of Cardinal Vowels

i, a, ɑ, u.

[1] The cardinal vowel figure is now almost universally used.

These four positions give the four " corners " of the cardinal vowel figure. Two intermediate tongue positions between i and a and between u and ɑ are chosen, giving e and ɛ as half-close and half-open *front* vowels respectively, and o and ɔ as half-close and half-open *back* vowels respectively.

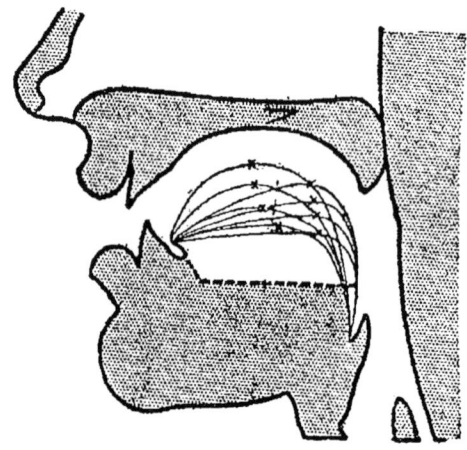

Fig. 9.
Tongue positions of the Eight Primary Cardinal Vowels.

96. The relation of these tongue positions can be more easily realised in diagrammatic form than in a drawing like the one given above. The true shape of such a diagram should be Fig. 10 (a) which is made by a line joining the highest point of the tongue of each vowel position, but for practical reasons it has been found better to conventionalise it into the form represented in Fig. 10 (b)

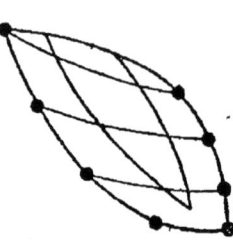

Fig. 10 (a).

97. This gives a rough indication of the relative tongue positions of the *eight primary cardinal* vowels.

CLASSIFICATION OF VOWELS

There are others, the learning of which it will be convenient to defer to a later time. When the cardinal vowels are known, any vowel can be placed on the figure and thus its relation to the nearest cardinal vowels can be shown. To do this accurately

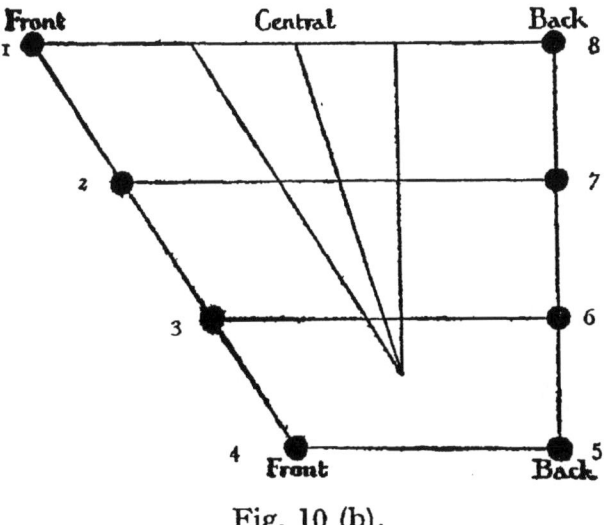

Fig. 10 (b).

requires a finely trained ear and much practice, but once such skill is gained, it is possible to show and interpret the relation of any vowel to any other with considerable precision.

98. In Chapter XI of this book the writer's English vowels are placed showing their relation to the cardinal vowels. The student should first master the cardinal vowels and then try to place his own vowels on the figure. English readers should note that the cardinal vowels are *pure* vowels, not diphthongs, i.e. the organs of speech remain in *one* position during the whole of the time that the sound is being made. They will need to watch particularly Nos. 2 and 7, in which a tendency to diphthongise is likely to show itself.

99. It is convenient for reference to number the eight primary cardinal vowels.

1.	2.	3.	4.	5.	6.	7.	8.
i	e	ɛ	a	ɑ	ɔ	o	u

100. In addition to the tongue, the lips are also concerned in the production of vowel sounds. The lips can be either rounded or spread or in a neutral position.

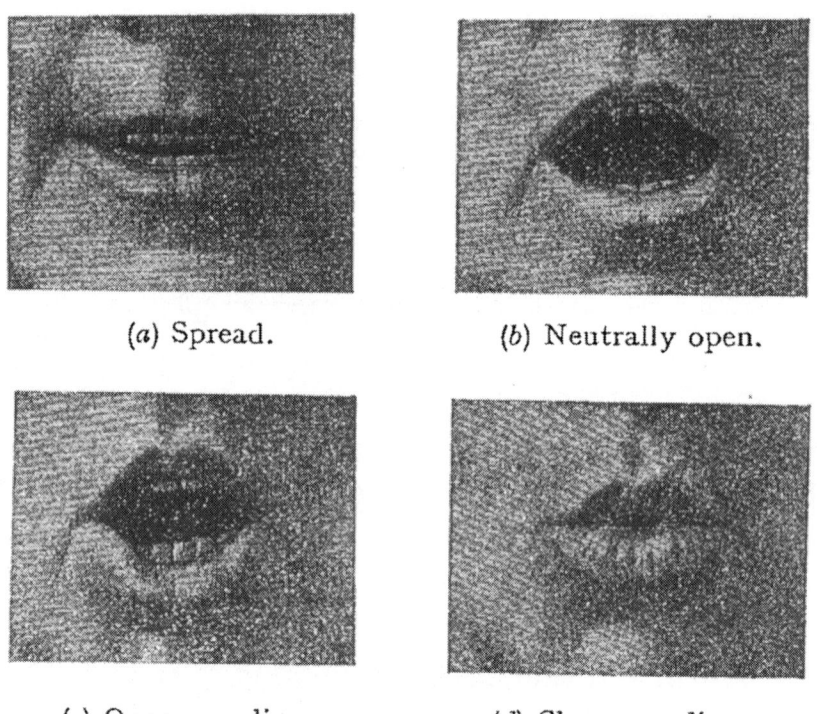

(a) Spread. (b) Neutrally open.

(c) Open rounding. (d) Close rounding.

Fig. 11. Photographs of Four Lip Positions.

For i they are spread; for u they are close-rounded; for ɔ open-rounded and for a and ɑ and for ɜ they are neutrally open.

101. In the cardinal vowels the four front vowels are pronounced with spread lips; cardinal ɑ has neutrally open lips, and the back vowels ɔ, o and u have varying degrees of lip-rounding. The lip-position of the English vowels will be given in the detailed descriptions of each one. (See Chapter XI.)

102. Some phoneticians consider the tenseness or laxness of the muscles of the tongue as being of importance in the production of vowel sounds. For instance, i is often described as a tense vowel, and ɪ as the corresponding lax one; u is said to be tense, while ʊ is lax. But the tenseness or laxness of vowels has not yet been sufficiently well demonstrated for it to be of primary importance in the description of English vowels.

CHAPTER X.
PHONEMES.

103. The scientific study of pronunciation has revealed the fact that any language contains far more speech sounds than is usually recognised. It is often stated that English possesses thirty-nine speech sounds, but an examination of facts shows that if the term speech sound is understood in its accurate sense, the English language has very many more than thirty-nine. For this purpose, the difference between a speech sound proper and what is termed a phoneme must be explained. " A speech sound proper is a sound of definite organic formation, and definite acoustic quality which is incapable of variation."[1] It is found that the sounds of a language group themselves into a number of families, that, for instance, a speaker does not use *one* ɪ sound and one only, one ɛ, one t, one l sound, but several varieties of ɪ, of ɛ, of t, and of l, etc. To these families of sounds the name *Phoneme* has been given. A phoneme is a family of sounds in a given language which are related in character and are such that no one of them ever occurs in the same phonetic context in a word as any other. By language in this connection is understood one person's pronunciation, and by phonetic context is meant surrounded by the same sounds and under the same conditions of length, stress and intonation.[2]

[1] *The Pronunciation of Russian*, D. Jones and M. Trofimov, 1924. (Cambridge University Press.)

[2] Definition given by Prof. D. Jones in *Outline of English Phonetics*, 3rd Edn.

74

104. Examples will make this clearer. In the word *little* (lɪtl) the two *l*-sounds are of different formation (see Chapter XIV, §§ 262–3, on "clear" and "dark" *l*); the tongue position for **k** in *key* is different from that of **k** in *call*; in the pronunciation of many people the two vowel sounds in *city* (sɪtɪ) are different, the ɛ in *get* is different from ɛ in *well*; the u in *music* is different from the u in *cool*; the actual point of contact in making the **t** sound varies in the words *each* (iˑtʃ), *eats* (iˑts), and *eighth* (eɪtθ) (see diagram, p. 137). That is to say, we must speak not of the English **k**, the English ɪ, the English **t** *sound*, since from these examples it is obvious that there is more than one **k**, one ɪ, one **t**, but of the English **k, ɪ, t** phoneme or family, meaning all the varieties of **k, ɪ, t**, etc., which are used in different combinations of sounds by one speaker.

105. Care must be taken not to confuse the various members of the phoneme with the different pronunciations heard from different people. The latter may be termed *variant pronunciations*; the different sounds constituting a phoneme occur in *one* person's pronunciation.

106. It is impossible to trace the history of all these groups of sounds, but many of the varieties are due to the influence of surrounding sounds and to the position in the sound group. Thus the second ɪ in *city* is often more open than the first because it is final; the **k** in *key* is made in a more forward position than that in *cool*, because of the following *close, front* vowel iː; the **t** in *eighth* (eɪtθ) is made against the edge of the top teeth, and not against the teeth-ridge (which is the commonest variety, and therefore the main member of the

phoneme) in order to be ready for the following θ sound; the u in *music* (mju·zɪk) is often more forward than the u in *cool* (kuːl) under the influence of the preceding j.

107. The native speaker of English, because he always uses the members of the phoneme in the same positions and never varies them, is generally unaware of these differences in pronunciation, even when, as sometimes happens, they are in actual formation far removed from each other. There is a considerable difference in tongue-position and in the acoustic quality between the various *l*-sounds which form one phoneme in English (see Chapter XIV, § 263-4), but because an Englishman uses a "clear" *l* before vowels and a "dark" *l* before consonants and finally, he finds it hard to realise that there *is* any difference.

108. For the purposes of language study, it is interesting and useful to note the existence of phonemes— a phenomenon that occurs in all languages. It is most important considered from the point of view of recording languages phonetically. The smallest number of symbols required for writing down a language unambiguously is the number of phonemes in that language. For the native speaker no more are needed, as he will generally use the subsidiary members in their right place naturally; and to have a separate symbol for even the important members of every phoneme would add unnecessarily to the alphabet and make it unwieldy. The student of English phonetics should know the habits of English people in the use of the subsidiary members of the phonemes, and be ready to observe them in his own pronunciation and in that of other people.

PHONEMES

109. In the study of foreign languages a knowledge of the phoneme theory is extremely important. The sounds grouped into one phoneme in one language may belong to two or more phonemes in another language, and a speaker must be aware of this fact, or in keeping the phoneme usage of his own language, he may be be misunderstood; for the test of whether two or more sounds belong to one phoneme or to more, is that of significance. If the substitution of one sound for another makes a change in meaning, they belong to different phonemes. For example, to substitute "clear" *l* for "dark" *l*, or *vice versa*, in English, would not change the meaning, as they are members of one phoneme; such a pronunciation would only sound unusual. [Try it in the word little!] But in Russian, the substitution of "clear" *l* for "dark" *l* would change the meaning of some words, for in that language these two sounds belong to different phonemes.

110. But the present book is not concerned with the pronunciation of foreign languages. A knowledge of the ordinary usage in the matter of English phonemes is, however, important for the student of English pronunciation. In the first place, his ear should be sufficiently fine to distinguish the various members of the different phonemes, and to note their use by the people whose pronunciation he is studying. Secondly, if he is unaware of the existence of phonemes as opposed to speech sounds, he may try to teach a wrong member of the phoneme under a mistaken idea that he is teaching "the correct English sound." (The very frequent occurrence in elocution of "clear" *l* where "dark" *l* is usual may be due to this.) And thirdly, he will find it useful in the

correction of pronunciation, as he may have pupils whose phoneme usage is unusual and gives rise to certain peculiarities of pronunciation and even to misunderstanding. For instance, some speakers (particularly Cockney) use an ɪ vowel before dark *l* in words like *field* (fiːld), i.e. they substitute the ɪ for the i phoneme in this position. In this way they are likely to be misunderstood, as confusion arises between the words *field* (fiːld) and *filled* (fɪld), which are both pronounced fɪld. The present writer has been told that London elementary school children often confuse these two words in pronunciation and in spelling.

111. It should be noted here that some people consider i and ɪ, u and ʊ, ɔ and ɒ, respectively, to belong to one phoneme. This can be justified by treating a certain degree of length as belonging to a particular member of the phoneme, i.e. going with a particular quality. They can only be so considered in the case of those whose speech shows a consistent relationship of length and quality, i.e. if i is always longer than ɪ under the same set of circumstances, ɔ longer than ɒ, u than ʊ. For those speakers who lengthen the so-called short vowels ɪ, ɒ, ʊ (who say, for instance: bɪːg, fɒːg, guːd,[1] etc.) i and ɪ belong to different phonemes. In Scottish pronunciation i and ɪ are separate phonemes; i occurs short and long, e.g. *agreed* is əgriːd and *greed* is grid.

112. In Chapters XI, XII, XIV of this book the usages in the matter of English vowel and consonant phonemes are described.

[1] See Ch XVII, § 361 (vi), for this habit.

Chapter XI.

ENGLISH VOWELS IN DETAIL.

113. With the majority of English speakers, there are twelve pure vowel and nine diphthong phonemes. The symbols for these are numbered, as shown below, for convenience of reference.

1.	2.	3.	4.	5.	6.	7.	8.	9.	10.	11.	12.
i	ɪ	ɛ	æ	ɑ	ɒ	ɔ	ʊ	u	ʌ	ɜ	ə

13.	14.	15.	16.	17.	18.	19.	20.	21.
eɪ	oʊ	aɪ	aʊ	ɔɪ	eə	ɛə	ɔə	ʊə

114. METHOD TO BE OBSERVED IN CONSIDERING EACH SOUND.

(a) Each vowel sound and diphthong will be described and placed on the vowel figure.

(b) The members of the phoneme will be noted.

(c) The principal variants in the pronunciation heard in different parts of the country and from different speakers will be discussed.

(d) Methods of teaching the sound will be suggested.

115. In this chapter a paragraph is given under each vowel, suggesting methods of teaching the vowel and correcting dialectal peculiarities. It may be stated that these methods are based on a principle which can be illustrated at the outset. When a pupil pronounces one vowel and the teacher wishes him to say another, the latter uses his knowledge of the relative positions of (a) the pupil's wrong sound, (b) the sound he wishes to teach, and (c) any other sound which the pupil possesses

79

near to the desired sound. He can also use the method of exaggeration, i.e. the pupil says sound No. 1, the teacher wishes him to say sound No. 2, so he tries to make him say sound No. 3, which lies beyond 2, in the hope that he will say 2.

116. Both methods can be illustrated from the accompanying diagram. A pupil says the sound at A (ɛ); the teacher wishes him to say the sound at B (æ); he tells him to try to say the sound at C (a); the pupil probably produces a sound near to B, and with a little practice can

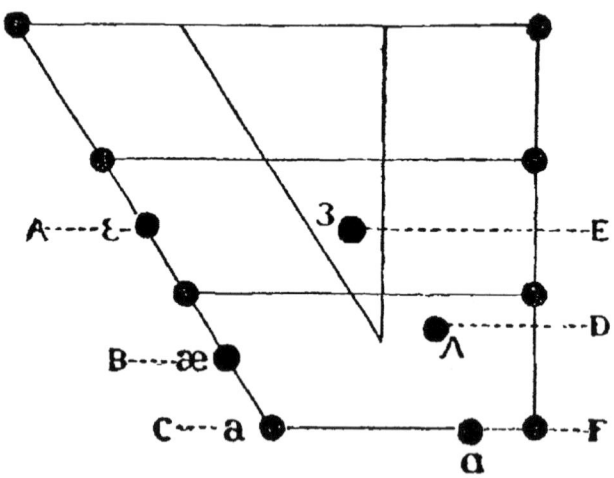

Fig. 12. Diagram illustrating Principles of Correction.

manage the correct one. The teacher wishes to teach the sound at D (ʌ) to a pupil who does not possess it; he possesses sounds at E and F, however (ɜ and ɑ); the teacher makes the pupil say ɜ and ɑ alternately and try to produce a sound between; or he tells him to make his ɜ sound more like ɑ. Thus the pupil arrives at a sound between the two. It may also be said that the methods suggested in this chapter are based on experience; but not every method fits every pupil—the teacher

ENGLISH VOWELS IN DETAIL

must try exercises on the lines suggested, and modify them to suit individual needs.

ENGLISH VOWELS PLACED IN THE CARDINAL FIGURE.

117. The writer's English vowels are shown in the following diagram in relation to the cardinal vowels.

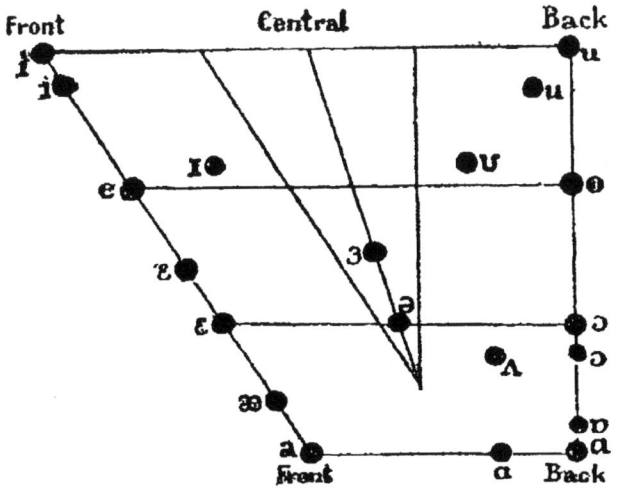

FIG. 13. Diagram illustrating English Vowels.

Note.—One pronunciation only can be shown here; other variants will be discussed under heading of each vowel. The student should practise placing his own and other people's vowels on the vowel figure.

118. *No. 1.* i, the sound in *sea, feel, read.*

Description.

(a) Front of tongue raised towards hard palate.
(b) Tongue raised almost to close position (near to Cardinal No. 1).
(c) Lips spread to neutral.

119. In the pronunciation of some people when the sound occurs finally, it is diphthongised, but not in a closed syllable, i.e. *see* becomes sɪi (see next §), but *read* is riːd.

120. Many people diphthongise this vowel to a greater or less extent in all positions; it is not a pure vowel, but the tongue starts from a somewhat lower position than the one marked on the figure, and moves up to a higher position. The commonest variety—a variety often used by educated speakers is ɪi (sɪi). In many dialects, however, the diphthong is more noticeable, the first element being retracted towards a central position, i.e. the diphthong becomes əi.

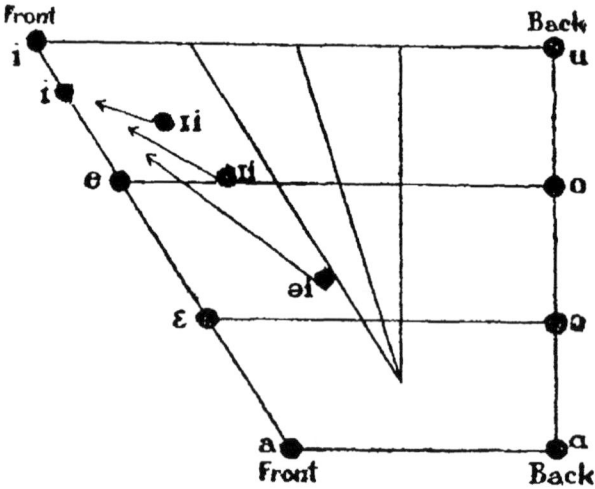

Fig. 14. Varieties of the i Vowel.

This is a marked characteristic of Cockney speech, especially in a stressed position (e.g. gɪv ɪt tə ˈməi), and is heard, in a less pronounced form, in the Northern, Midland and Eastern counties.

121. To correct this marked diphthongisation, the pupil should be told to say the sound i with considerable vigour. A second method is to let him make a fricative

ENGLISH VOWELS IN DETAIL

consonant corresponding to i, i.e. a fricative j; in this way he raises his tongue high enough, and he can easily get rid of the friction.

122. The student should notice that many words which are pronounced with i when said alone, often have an alternative pronunciation with the vowel ɪ or ə when they occur in unstressed positions. Such words are *he, she, we, be, the, been*.

E.g. ˈwɒt dɪd (h)ɪ ˈseɪ?   wɪ ʃl ˈsuːn bɪ ˈðɛə.
ˈdʌz ʃɪ (or dʌʒ ʃɪ).   ðə ˈbʊk.
ˈʃæl wɪ ˈɡoʊ?
aɪ v bɪn ˈwɜːkɪŋ ˈleɪt.

wɛər əv jʊ ˈbɪn (bɪn for *been* is often used both in stressed and unstressed syllables).

With some speakers the sound used in such positions is a very short i.

123. In Cockney pronunciation the vowel i is regularly replaced by ɪ before a "*dark l*," e.g.: stiːɫ is pronounced stɪɫ. To cure this, it is necessary not only to raise the ɪ to i, as shown in § 100, but to alter the resonance of the *dark l*. (See Chapter XIV, § 268.)

124. *No. 2.* ɪ, the sound in *fit, did, little*.

Description.

(a) Front of tongue raised towards hard palate, the highest point of raising being towards the central position; i.e. it is considerably retracted from a fully front vowel position.

(b) Tongue raised slightly higher than half-close position (above Cardinal 2 line).

(c) Lips somewhat spread.

(d) Many people think that lax muscles are necessary for the production of ɪ.

125. Two or three varieties of ɪ sound can be distinguished in the pronunciation of most people, e.g. the ɪ in hɪl is more open than that in hɪt, and a final ɪ is generally of a low variety. This is particularly noticeable in words like *busy, smithy, pretty, chimney* (bɪzɪ, smɪðɪ, prɪtɪ, tʃɪmnɪ), where the two ɪ sounds occur in the same word.

126. In words of this type, however, i.e. when ɪ is final, there are several variant pronunciations.

(a) The commonest is the one noted above, where the final unstressed ɪ is lower than that in the stressed syllable.

(b) Some speakers, notably S. Africans, Scots, Northumbrians, use a No. 1 vowel finally, and say bɪzi (or bizi).

(c) Some speakers make no appreciable difference between the two vowels.

(d) Some speakers use such an open variety of vowel that it approaches to e or even ɛ, e.g. bɪze or bɪzɛ.

127. Note those words in which three ɪ sounds occur, e.g. *willingly, explicitly, probability*. With the speakers under (a) and (d), the final ɪ would be the lowest of all; with those under (b) the final vowel would be i. Note also an alternative pronunciation with ə, for some (but not all) of these words, e.g. ɪnfɪnɪtɪ or ɪnfɪnətɪ, sɪmplɪsɪtɪ or sɪmplɪsətɪ.

128. A low variety of ɪ is heard in such words as *ticket* ('tɪkɪt), *visit* ('vɪzɪt), *pocket* ('pɒkɪt), *market* ('maˑkɪt), *message* ('mɛsɪdʒ), *frigid* ('frɪdʒɪd), *modest* ('mɒdɪst),

fearless (ˈfɪəlɪs), *savage* (ˈsævɪʤ), *knowledge* (ˈnɒlɪʤ), *audible* (ˈɔːdɪbl).

129. For many of these words, however, there is an alternative pronunciation with ə, e.g. ˈpɒkɪt or ˈpɒkət, ˈpraɪvɪt or ˈpraɪvət, ˈfɪəlɪs or ˈfɪələs, ˈɔːdɪbl or ˈɔːdəbl. Some people use a vowel lying between ɪ and ə. Students should note also that, though many words written with *e* or *a* are pronounced with ɪ or ə, not all words of this type follow the same rules: e.g. *modest* may be pronounced mɒdɪst or mɒdəst (the vowel in the last syllable being a kind of neutral vowel in both cases; see § 184), but *contest, inquest, manifest* would generally have a strong vowel in this syllable, ˈkɒntɛst, ˈɪnkwɛst, ˈmænɪfɛst; *voyage* is vɔɪʤ, *savage* is ˈsævɪʤ, but *outrage* is generally ˈaʊtreɪʤ; *perfect* may be ˈpɜːfɪkt, but *prefect* is ˈpriːfɛkt. This is not a question of the influence of stress, such as the difference between ˈsʌbʤɪkt (noun) and səbˈʤɛkt (verb), nor of differentiation of function as in ˈɛstɪmeɪt (verb) and ˈɛstɪmət (noun), in ˈdjuːplɪkeɪt (verb) and ˈdjuːplɪkət (adj.), ˈmɒdəreɪt (verb) and ˈmɒdərət (adj.). It may be noted that those words in which the strong vowel is used are less common than those in which ɪ is used.[1] Note also that in the use of ɪ in words such as *fearless* and *subject* is not common in Northern speech (see Chapter XVI, § 327); they are generally pronounced ˈfɪələs, ˈsʌbʤɛkt.

130. The pronunciation of *pencil* as ˈpɛnsɪl or ˈpɛnsl, of *pupil* as ˈpjuːpɪl or ˈpjuːpl, *April* as ˈeɪprɪl or ˈeɪprl, *passenger* as ˈpæsɪnʤə or ˈpæsnʤə, seems to

[1] For explanation of this see Luick, *Historische Grammatik der englischen Sprache*, §§ 595, 605.

86   THE PHONETICS OF ENGLISH

show that unstressed ɪ tends to drop out before an alveolar consonant, particularly when preceded by another alveolar continuant consonant.

131. In addition to the preceding differences in subsidiary members of the ɪ phoneme, there are several variant pronunciations.

(a) In London speech another phoneme is substituted for final ɪ in words like *busy*; this is pronounced bɪzəi, i.e. for final unstressed ɪ, the London pronunciation of No. 1 vowel is used: e.g. twɛntəi, prɪtəi, etc.

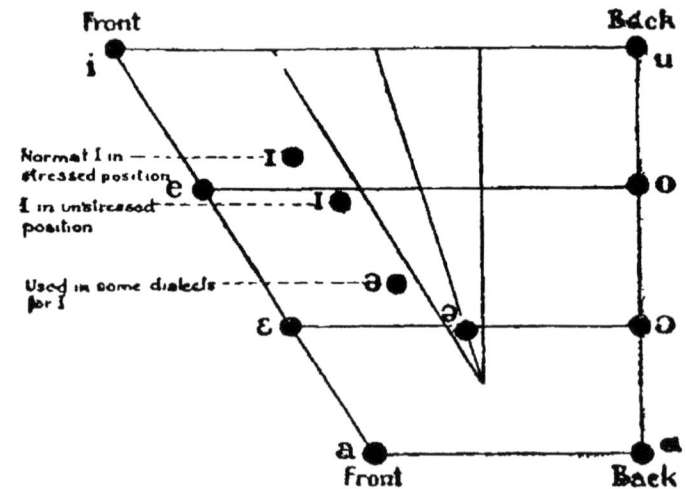

Fig. 15. Varieties of the ɪ Vowel.

(b) In some dialects ə is used regularly by educated speakers where S. England has unstressed ɪ, e.g. ɔˑdəbl, krɛdəbl, mɛsədʒ, mɒdərət, wɜˑθləs, bəfɔə, bəniˑθ.

(c) In many dialects, including Scottish, Irish, American, and West Country (I have heard it also in the West Riding of Yorks., and in Norfolk), a very retracted and lowered ɪ, approaching towards ə,

ENGLISH VOWELS IN DETAIL

is used in stressed as well as unstressed positions, e.g. *timid* is təmən, *bit* is bət. This form appears to be spreading in the speech of the younger generation in S. England. See § 361 (i).

(d) In some types of South African speech ɪ is a close variety, approaching i.

132. To cure the pronunciation indicated under (a) above should not be difficult, as the pupil already possesses an ɪ sound which he uses in words like *fit* (fɪt). The teacher should try to make him say this sound in isolation (which is not always an easy thing to accomplish, however), and use it at the end of a word. Sometimes it is only necessary to tell him to make the final sound very short. If it is desired to correct the pronunciation təmən, the pupil must be told to make a sound more nearly resembling his i sound, but it must be very short.

133. *No. 3.* ɛ, the sound in *bet, egg, bell.*

Description.

(a) Front of tongue raised.
(b) Tongue raised about half the distance between close and open (half-way between Cardinal e and ɛ).
(c) Lips neutral to spread.

134. If the three words given above are compared, it will generally be found that the vowel varies in each word; the ɛ in *bet* is somewhat closer than that in *egg*, and the ɛ in *bell* is more open than either of the other two. The phoneme varies, therefore, between a point just below Cardinal No. 2, and another one slightly higher than Cardinal No. 3. It should be noted again that the dark 1 of *bell* has the effect of lowering the vowel which precedes it.

135. Many variant pronunciations, ranging from e to ɛ, are heard. The Northerner uses an open variety, while the Cockney speaker uses a sound near to Cardinal e; in Hampshire a cardinal ɛ is often used, and in Devonshire and the West a diphthong eɪ is sometimes heard (eɪg, beɪd), while in many parts of the country a retracted and lowered variety of ɛ is heard. This

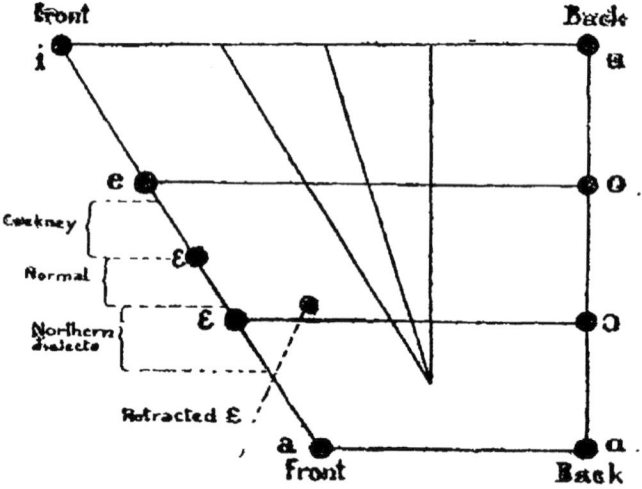

Fig. 16. Varieties of the ɛ Vowel.

is common in the West of England, in Yorks., and Lancs., and in the Eastern counties.[1] It is particularly noticeable before *r* in words like *very*, which often sounds like vɜrɪ. One type of American ɛ is also considerably retracted. Many Americans say gɛᵊt for *get*, but do not use a diphthong in all words of this type. (See Ch. XVIII, § 368.) In Cockney speech ɛ followed

[1] Note the pronunciations of the word *breakfast*: **brɛkfəst, breɪkfəst** and **briːkfəst**. The last can be heard in Lancashire and Yorkshire, as can also **stiːk** for **steɪk** (*steak*). For explanation of this see Wyld, *History of Modern Colloquial English*, pp. 209 and 212.

by dark l is retracted to such a degree that it resembles ɔ (and the l disappears), e.g. the London bus-conductor says sɔˈfrɪdʒɪz or sɛɔfrɪdʒɪz for *Selfridges* (sɛlfrɪdʒɪz).

136. The correction of an ɛ will generally consist in modifying an extreme variety—either close or open, or of getting rid of a retracted variety. The first correction is not difficult to make; it is generally only necessary to make the pupil exaggerate in the other direction. The correction of a retracted ɛ is more difficult, and it is essential to attempt this, as retraction of the tongue makes for vowels of an obscure and indistinct quality. Many people find it difficult to isolate an ɛ sound; in trying to pronounce it they say something approaching ə.

137. In order to correct this tendency and to teach a wholly front ɛ, it is well to begin with the diphthong eɪ, in which the pupil probably pronounces a front e or ɛ as the first element. The first element should be lengthened e - - - ɪ, and the second part gradually dropped. If the resulting e sound is too close, it is not difficult then to teach a more open variety. A good general exercise for obtaining a front vowel is to begin with i, which most people can make well forward, and then try to get the same quality of "frontness" into e and ɛ.

138. *No. 4.* æ, the sound in *bad, catch*, etc.

Description.

(*a*) Front of tongue raised.

(*b*) Tongue raised approximately one-sixth of distance from open to close: i.e. about half-way between Cardinal 3 and 4.

90 THE PHONETICS OF ENGLISH

(c) Lips neutral to spread.

(d) Some people consider this vowel lax, but sufficient investigation to prove this has not yet been made.

139. In addition to the above details describing æ, there seems to be another factor in its articulation, namely, a certain amount of pharyngal contraction. It is a noteworthy fact that singers do not use this sound, as the quality of the voice is rarely so good in singing æ as in other vowels.[1]

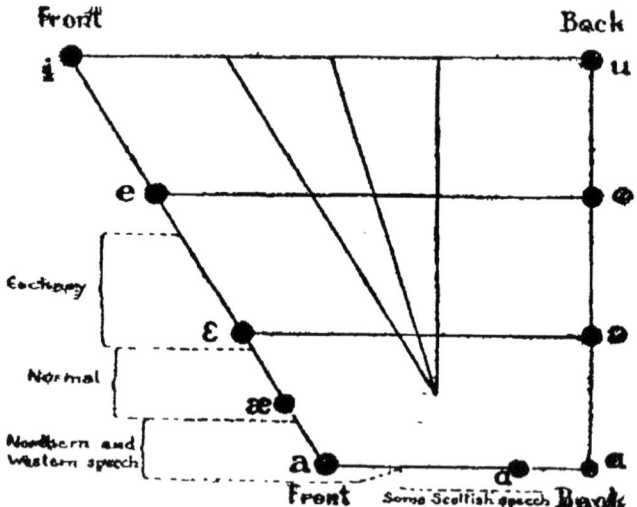

FIG. 17. Varieties of the æ Vowel.

140. The only subsidiary member of the æ-phoneme is a somewhat lower variety, nearer to ə when a "dark" l follows; compare *shall* and *shally*; æ in the former followed by "dark" l is lower than in *shally*, which has a "clear" l. The difference, however, is not very great.

[1] Another reason for the avoidance of æ by singers may be the fact that Italian singing masters were unable to pronounce this sound and substituted their own ɑ vowel for it: and in this way, the tradition of using ɑ or a for æ has grown up.

141. Variant pronunciations between a very close æ verging on ɛ, and a or even ɑ are heard. The use of some kind of a, a sound round about Cardinal No. 4, is very widespread; it is an easily recognised characteristic of Northern, Midland, and, to a certain extent, of Western speech. In Scotland the sound ɑ is often heard, while in some types of Scottish town speech—sometimes called "Kelvinside" or "High English," an attempt has been made to imitate the S. English æ, with the result that the closeness of the vowel has been exaggerated and the pronunciation is practically ɛ, e.g. dʒɛks ə bɛd lɛd. In London dialect, the sound is much closer than the normal, reaching ɛ or even e in some cases, e.g. kɛb bɛŋk, kɛtʃ, bɛːd.

A tendency to diphthongise æ towards ə is observed to-day, particularly before alveolar consonants: thus *bad* is frequently pronounced bæəd. This is an American variant and is also one of the newer developments of to-day. See Chs. XVII, XVIII.

142. For teaching, it is generally advisable to choose a middle variety of æ; in the North where a is heard from many educated speakers, it is wise to allow a variety that is not too open or too retracted towards ɑ. The pupil who uses ɛ or e should be made to keep his mouth wider open when he says the vowel, and should be told to modify his sound slightly in the direction of ɑ in *father*. The pupil who uses a retracted a or ɑ should be told to make the sound more like ɛ.

143. *No. 5.* ɑ, the sound in *father, calm, half*.

Description.
   (a) Back of the tongue concerned in the formation of this vowel.

(b) Tongue quite low down in the mouth; an open vowel.

(c) Lips neutrally open.

144. There are no subsidiary members of the phoneme differing to any marked extent from the main one.

145. In the educated and semi-educated speech of different parts of the country, there is little variety in the pronunciation of this vowel. In some Northern dialects, however, a forward variety of a is heard, faːðə or faðə (short), and in the extreme dialect fɛːðə is heard. In some forms of Scottish and in South African pronunciation a vowel near Cardinal ɑ is found. In London a very retracted ɑ used to be common, though at present a more forward a (faːðə) is frequently heard; ɑ is replaced by æ or a in some dialects, in words like *can't, half* (kænt, kæːnt, kant, or kaːnt). This is common in some types of Irish and some American speech. In those dialects (W. and S.W. English and American[1] chiefly) where r is pronounced (see Chapter XIV, § 271, iv) the quality of the vowel is affected and it becomes a front a, e.g. *harm* is pronounced haɹm. It has been noted that in semi-educated speech in South Devon, a very retracted ɑ is used which sounds to a Londoner like ɒ. When r follows in spelling this *may* be an attempt to avoid an advanced a.

[1] The analysis of one American's pronunciation showed that he had three sounds of the letter *a*, viz.: æ (a low variety), as in *bad*, a (about one-third of the way between cardinals a and ɑ), for some words such as *can't, harm*, and ɑ (as in normal Southern English), for others like *calm, father*, etc. See, however, Chap. XVIII, § 371.

ENGLISH VOWELS IN DETAIL

146. In order to correct a too retracted form of ɑ, tell the pupil to spread his lips and to modify his sound in the direction of æ. The opposite fault, a too forward a, can be corrected by telling the pupil to aim at ɒ, and to lengthen the sound.

147. There are certain words in which many Northern speakers use a or æ, which in the South are pronounced with ɑ. Such words are *last, grass, after, dance, ask, plant*. Certain words, however, do not follow this rule: e.g. *lass* and *crass* are pronounced by Northerners and Southerners alike as læs, kræs (or in the N., las, kras); and a few words have two pronunciations with some speakers, indicating different meanings: e.g. *mass*, mæs, *heap*; mɑˑs, the religious service[1]; *ass*, æs, the animal; and ɑˑs, a term of friendly abuse. The pronunciation ɑˑfrikə has been reported from South Devon; the present writer has heard it from a Scot (whose work was in Africa).

148. In Northern and Midland schools it would be unwise to try and insist on the pronunciation ɑ in such words as have been mentioned, for many educated people use æ or a, although it may be pointed out that this pronunciation is one of the obvious marks of a Northern or Midland pronunciation which anyone can recognise.

149. *No. 6.* ɒ, the sound in *not, long, box*.

Description.

(a) Back of tongue raised.

---

[1] See *Broadcast Word*, p. 104, for a note on the pronunciation of the words *mass* and *catholic*.

(b) Raising is very slight; a little higher than Cardinal ɑ; an open vowel.

(c) Slight open lip-rounding.

150. There are no subsidiary members of the phoneme worth noting.

151 In some parts of the country, particularly in Scotland, a vowel with a higher tongue position and more lip-rounding is used: i.e. the vowel resembles Cardinal No. 6,[1] and there are varieties between the two. Compare nɒt lɒŋ and nɔt lɔŋ. This is particularly noticeable in words written with *wa*, e.g. *watch, was, want*, which are pronounced wɔˑtʃ, wɔz, wɔnt. In the Midlands and some parts of S.W. England a vowel with the same tongue position, but with neutrally open lips, is used. The vowel then resembles Cardinal No. 5, hɑt, lɑŋ, ɑn ðə tɑp for hɒt, lɒŋ, ɒn ðə tɒp. This is one variety of American speech. In some dialects ɒ is replaced by ʌ: e.g. *not* is pronounced nʌt, *was* wʌz.[2]

152. If the unrounded variety ɑ is considered objectionable, it is easy to cure. To tell the pupil to round his lips while pronouncing the vowel is generally sufficient.

153. There are a good many words in which some people substitute for ɒ the vowel ɔ. Such usage is somewhat parallel to the use of æ and ɑ (see §147, p. 93), but in this case the division is not entirely a local one. The most important of these words are *cross, lost, off,*

---

[1] Grant (*Pronunciation of English in Scotland*) uses the symbol ɔ for this sound.

[2] The writer has been told that this is often taught in Edinburgh schools, probably as a correction of wɔˑz.

soft, often; probably ɒ is used by the majority, but a considerable number of people, including many educated speakers, use ɔ. The latter is not found in Northern pronunciation, and it is not at all general in the South. By those who do not use it, such a pronunciation is often considered vulgar.

154. There is no doubt that the use of the vowel ɔ in these words is dying out gradually[1]; the use of ɒ seems to have been a spelling pronunciation in Southern English in the first case, and it is extremely likely that eventually krɒs, etc., will be the only form. Educated speakers who use ɔ at the present day are mainly middle-aged, or conservative speakers. It is to be noticed that this alternation occurs in words where *s* or *f* follow the vowel, and not in all these: *moss, boss,*[2] *scoff,* are rarely pronounced with ɔ, and tɔˑf for *toff* is considered Cockney; there are also people who would say krɔˑs but tɒs. At the present day it would be a waste of time to insist in schools on the pronunciation krɒs, since many educated speakers still use the form krɔˑs.

155. Occasionally a similar alternation is found when the letter *o* occurs before other consonants, e.g. *gone, dog, God*. The pronunciation dɔˑg used to be fairly frequent, but it is rarely heard now, and is considered decidedly vulgar; gɔˑd (*God*) is occasionally heard, sometimes as a particularly pious way of saying the word, but like dɔˑg, it is generally considered vulgar; gɔˑn is still heard from educated speakers. Of these

---

[1] "I was astonished to find recently, in a Council Central School in London (Marylebone), that the pronunciation krɔːs was laughed at by the children." *Broadcast English,* p. 161.

[2] bɔˑs is heard in American speech.

three, it would certainly be advisable to correct dɔ·g and gɔ·d.

156. A similar alternative pronunciation is found in words which are spelt with *aus, ault, als, alt*. The pronunciation ɔ in such words as *auspices, fault, false, alter, Austria,* belongs to the South and ɒ to the North, but here again the distinction is not entirely local. Note the pronunciation of *because* (bɪkɒz and bɪkɔːz). (Some Irish speakers say bəkʌz.)

157. *No. 7.* ɔ, the sound in *saw, caught, all.*
Description.
- (*a*) Back of tongue raised.
- (*b*) Tongue raised to near the Cardinal 6 position: a half open vowel.
- (*c*) Lips considerably rounded. This vowel is sometimes said to be *over-rounded,* i.e. the degree of rounding is greater than is usual in a vowel having such a tongue position.

158. In educated speech there are no notable subsidiary members of the phoneme.

159. The main variants in the pronunciation of this vowel lie in the degree of lip-rounding used; the tongue position does not seem to vary much. In London pronunciation there is considerable lip-rounding, so that the vowel strikes the ear as being of an o-type: e.g. *fall* becomes foːl, *caught* becomes ko·t, and *saw* so·ə. This tendency of using close lip-rounding appears to be spreading among educated speakers in the South. The other extreme is heard in some parts of the country, i.e. the sound is pronounced with very open lip-rounding. For the Scottish pronunciation of words such as those given above, see Grant, *Pronunciation of English in Scotland.*

ENGLISH VOWELS IN DETAIL

160. It is not difficult to correct either of these tendencies; for the London pronunciation, if the pupil is told to open his mouth more, he will soon make the more normal sound; and the other extreme is corrected by rounding the lips more.

161. The words written with *or, ore, oar, oor, our* must be considered under the heading of this vowel, for many speakers in S.E. England use the vowel ɔ in all such words, e.g. *for, more, hoar, door, pour, fort, hoard, course,* etc. Speakers from other parts of the country, however, do not pronounce them all alike; the words fall into two distinct classes:

(a) Those words which have *or, ore, oar, oor, our* final and *oar, our,* followed by a consonant (e.g. *hoarse, court*), together with *some* words with *or* followed by a consonant (e.g. *fort*).

(b) Other words with *or* followed by a consonant (e.g. *corn*).

162. These classes have variant pronunciations. The main variants heard are:

When no *r* is pronounced—

(1) As stated above, both classes pronounced with ɔ in S.E. England.

(2) The first class pronounced ɔə and the second ɔ; this is heard from many English speakers from different parts of the country.

(3) The first class pronounced oə and the second ɔə or ɔ in many parts of the country.

When *r* is pronounced—

(1) The first class pronounced or and the second ɔr; this occurs in Scottish pronunciation.

(2) The first class pronounced oɹ, the second ɔər or ɔːɹ. (For the retroflex *r*, see Chapter XIV (§ 271 iv).) This is common in S.W. England.

163. The words written with *or* + a consonant present an interesting problem, for there is nothing in the modern form of the words themselves to indicate to which class they belong,[1] but where any distinction at all is made in these words, it is made, with very few exceptions, in the same words by speakers from N., N.W., W., S.W. England, from Scotland, Ireland and Wales. Thus *port*, with its derivative, *report*, etc., *sport, ford, sword, sworn, forge*, belong to Class 1, and *cord, record, order, accord, short, adorn, morn, horn*, belong to Class 2. A complete list of all the words under consideration is to be found in Grant's *Pronunciation of English in Scotland*.[2]

164. In London dialect those words, particularly where *or* is final, are pronounced with a marked oə diphthong. Sometimes the two vowels o, ə form two syllables with a kind of w between them, e.g. *door* becomes doːwə, *four* becomes foːwə, and *more* becomes moːwə. Other words in which there is no *r*, and which are normally pronounced with ɔ, are by false analogy pronounced in the same way. So that *saw* and *paw* become soːwə and poːwə. Two things are necessary to correct this; the pupil must be told to pronounce the vowel with his mouth more widely open. This will bring him near to ɔ; and to get rid of the diphthongisation,

---

[1] See, however, Jespersen's *Modern English Grammar*, Vol. I. (Allen & Unwin), and Luick, *Historische Grammatik der englischen sprache*, §§ 567–8.

[2] Cambridge University Press.

he must keep his mouth in one position and not move it during the pronunciation of the sound.

165. *No. 8.* ʊ, the sound in *put, book.*

Description.

(*a*) Back of tongue raised towards soft palate; the raising is slightly advanced from the full back position.

(*b*) Tongue raised to a little above half-close position.

(*c*) Lips generally close rounded.

(*d*) This vowel is considered by many to be lax.

166. There do not seem to be many important subsidiary members of the phoneme. With some speakers, however, ʊ followed by dark *l* has a lower and further back tongue position than when it precedes other consonants. Cf. *put, pull.*

167. This sound is sometimes replaced by an unrounded vowel with a similar tongue position (phonetic symbol ɤ). It is especially noticeable in the word *good*, which is pronounced gɤd or gɤːd by a number of people; this is an individual not a local pronunciation, and is often considered affected.[1] I have heard ɤ, however, as a regular sound from American speakers for all words which in normal English have ʊ. One variety of Yorkshire and Lancashire speech has a low type of ʊ sound, slightly unrounded in words like *put*. In Cockney the ʊ, followed by dark l in words like *pull*, *full*, resembles an o, i.e. it is markedly retracted and lowered from the normal.

168. In Scotland, words which in English are pronounced with ʊ have a short u sound, e.g. *put* is pronounced

---

[1] See Ch. II, § 22 (c) and Ch. XVII, § 361 (v).

put, *foot*, fut. Such words as these do not differ in their vowel sounds from *food, rude*, except perhaps very slightly in length. Compare the Scottish pronunciation of *full* and *fool, foot* and *food* (ful, ful, fut, fud). In the north of England ʊ in words like *cook, book, look*, is regularly replaced by u, often fairly long, giving ku·k, bu·k, lu·k (or kʊuk, bʊuk, lʊuk). Note also the two pronunciations of the word *room*, ruːm and rʊm; these are not purely local, though rʊm does not normally occur in Northern dialects. In the S.W., *boots, soup, hoop, cooper* may be bʊts, sʊp, hʊp, kʊpə.

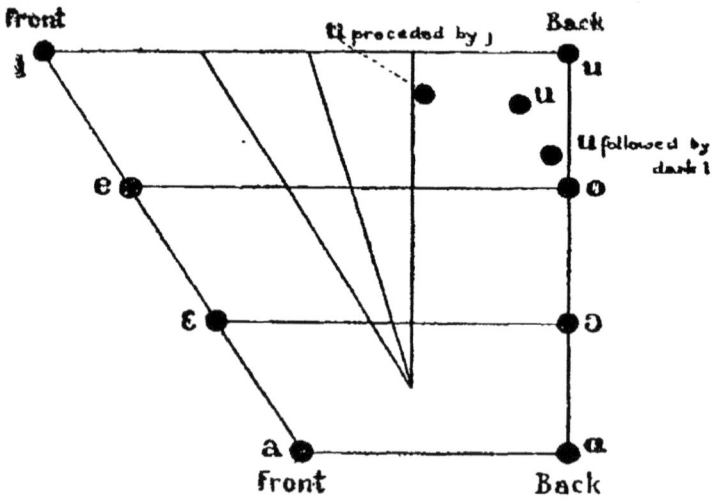

Fig. 18. The u Phoneme.

169. *No.* 9. u, the sound in *rude, fool*.
Description.
 (*a*) Back of tongue raised towards soft palate.
 (*b*) Tongue raised almost to close position.
 (*c*) Lips close rounded.

170. In words where u is preceded by j, e.g. *music* (mju·zɪk), u has a more forward position; where it is

ENGLISH VOWELS IN DETAIL 101

followed by dark *l* as in *fool*, fuːl, a lower variety is heard. This is especially the case with Southern dialect speakers (see § 171). Many speakers would have one sound only in the words *music, rude, fool*, i.e. their phoneme consists of one member only. When the vowel occurs in a final position, it is often diphthongised: e.g. *do* is pronounced duu. (Compare sɪi, § 119.)

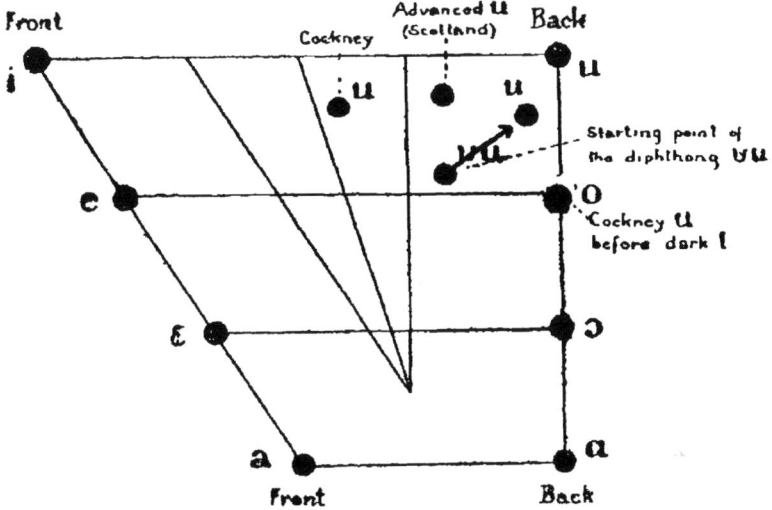

Fig. 19. Varieties of the u Vowel.

171. Many people diphthongise this vowel to a considerable extent, i.e. the tongue begins at a position near to ʊ and glides up to u (ʊu). Compare ɪi. In Scottish pronunciation the u is generally very much shorter and closer than in English; in some parts the u is of an "advanced" type, i.e. the tongue raising is further forward than a full back position. In Southern English and to a marked extent in Cockney pronunciation, the u is of a very "advanced" character, the raising being as far forward as half-way between i and u, i.e. it is a central vowel (represented here by ü). Generally words like *boots, shoes, moon, food*, are pronounced with the diphthong ïü, ï being a retracted i very nearly half-way between i and u, and ü a similar, though probably slightly further back tongue position, with slight lip-rounding. But when this sound occurs before dark l, the tongue position goes back almost to o. Compare in Cockney speech the words *food, fool* (fïüd, foːl).[1]

172. The Cockney ü is not easy to cure. Slight evidences of this sound remain in speech that has lost almost all other signs of Cockney origin. Three methods may be tried.

(1) Let the pupil aim at o, i.e. tell him to say **moːn, boːts**; then let him modify this towards **u**.

(2) Hold down the front of the tongue with the finger or a tongue-guide (a small paper-knife, or a glass rod). This forces the back up into the correct position when he tries to say his u sound.

(3) Let the pupil whistle a low note. This gives the tongue position for u, and it should not be difficult after a time to pass from the whistled note to the spoken vowel. Sometimes a pupil can *sing* u when he cannot say it, and this can be used to get the spoken vowel.[2]

[1] Note, however, that *fooling* is pronounced fïülɪŋ.

[2] But an advanced u is frequently heard in the "crooning" songs of dance bands!

ENGLISH VOWELS IN DETAIL

173. *No. 10.* ʌ, the sound in *but, mother*.

Description.

(a) Back of tongue raised, but not fully back; somewhat advanced towards a central position.

(b) Tongue raised not quite one-third of the total distance from open to close; near the Cardinal ɔ line.

(c) Lips neutral.

174. In educated speech there do not seem to be any outstanding subsidiary members of the ʌ phoneme. For London speech, however, see next paragraph.

175. Many variant pronunciations of this vowel are heard:

(a) In London pronunciation (and in Devonshire), it tends to become a kind of a vowel, somewhat approaching Cardinal No. 4, except before dark l, when the vowel is generally a kind of ɒ or ɔ, e.g. bʌlb, rɪzʌlt, mʌltɪplaɪ, become bɔlb, rɪzɔlt, mɔltɪplaɪ.

(b) In some parts of the country the tongue position is advanced towards the central vowel ɜ; I have heard the pronunciation lɜˑv, kɜˑm in Bristol and the S.W., and lɜv, kɜm from Northern speakers, where, however, it may be due to the avoidance of a typical Northern vowel. With some American speakers it is also somewhat more central. (See Ch. XVIII.)

(c) In the North of England, particularly in Yorks. and Lancs., and to a certain extent in the Midlands, the sound ʌ does not exist. In the broad dialect, it is replaced by ʊ, but in a more "refined" dialect, the sound used is one lying between ʊ and ʌ, a kind of ɤ partially rounded. Most words in which ʌ is now used were originally pronounced with ʊ; in the South, the vowel ʊ has changed gradually from ʊ to ʌ, going through many intermediate stages as far as tongue position is concerned, and also in losing lip-rounding. In the North this change has not gone so far as ʌ, and the sound now heard is generally some type

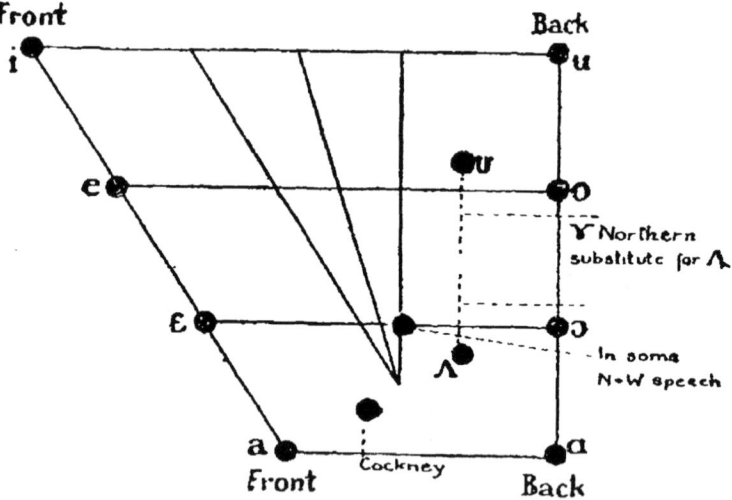

FIG. 20. Varieties of the ʌ Vowel.

lying between ʊ and ʌ in tongue and in lip position. But not in all words which were formerly pronounced with ʊ has the vowel changed to ʌ, cf. *put, but*, pʊt, bʌt. Consequently speakers who use ɤ where normal English has ʌ, confuse the vowel in words such as *but, put, butcher, sugar, hunt*. Many Northerners and Midlanders have difficulty in pronouncing ʌ before *r*, in words like *hurry* (hʌrɪ); they use a kind of short ɜ vowel in such positions (hɜrɪ).

ENGLISH VOWELS IN DETAIL

Note.—Speakers who have no difficulty in distinguishing between *but* and *put, bull* and *cull,* are apt to think that the Northerners invert the two vowels and say **bʊt** and **pʌt**. It is the writer's opinion, but this has not been verified sufficiently well yet for it to be a certainty, that practically one sound is used in all these words, viz. the one between ʊ and ʌ, marked ɤ on the diagram, and that when one expects to hear ʌ, and the speaker uses ɤ, the hearer thinks he hears ʊ, and when ʊ is expected and ɤ occurs, he thinks he hears ʌ; so that *Mr. Butler, the butcher* pronounced **mɪstə bɤtlə ðə bɤtʃə** sounds like **mɪstə bʊtlə ðə bʌtʃə**. There are some Northern speakers, however, who *do* invert the two vowels; it is often those people who have learnt that *two* vowels are used in these words and not *one*, and have not yet learnt in which words they occur.[1]

176. In order to get rid of the Cockney a sound, let the pupil make the sound more like ɔ without any lip-rounding. The pupil who makes the vowel like ɜ must be told to make it resemble ɑ. To teach the sound ʌ to Northern speakers who do not possess it, it is well to begin with ɔ, to make this without any lip-rounding and then to modify it—but not too far—towards ɜ. It is sometimes sufficient to make him say his own sound with exaggerated opening of the mouth. This is the first step towards getting rid of the confusion between ʊ and ʌ. When the pupil can make ʌ, then comes the second stage; he must learn in which words ʊ occurs, and which have the ʌ vowel. This latter stage is a question of memory.

[1] I have heard the word *woman* pronounced **wʌmən**.

177. *No. 11.* ɜ, the sound in *bird, fur, learn*.

Description.

(*a*) Central part of the tongue raised.

(*b*) Tongue raised about half-way between open and close.

(*c*) Lips neutral.

178. There do not seem to be any subsidiary members of the phoneme to be noted.

179. The commonest variants in the pronunciation of this vowel occur with those people who make some attempt to pronounce the following *r*. In some parts of Scotland where the *r* is rolled, ɜ is often replaced by ʌ, *bird* (bɜːd) is pronounced bʌrd. In the N.W., W. and S.W. of England the r is pronounced with the tip of the tongue curled up (see § 271 iv), bɜɹd, and here the ɜ is of a closer variety than the one marked on the diagram. It is also frequently found that, while the vowel is being pronounced, the tip of the tongue is curled up, not sufficiently to make a fricative consonant, but enough to modify the vowel sound. Some types of American speech have a pronunciation similar to this. In S. Lancashire and Cheshire and the Midlands generally, the ɜ has a more forward position, approaching towards ɛ, i.e. *fur* (fɜː) is pronounced rather like fɛː; *Birmingham* is pronounced bɛːmɪŋɡəm.

180. If it is wished to teach ɜ without the inversion, it is only necessary to tell the pupil to press the tip of his tongue against the bottom teeth and keep it there. If he cannot do this without help, his tongue should be held down with a spatula or tongue-guide. To correct

ENGLISH VOWELS IN DETAIL

the Lancashire tendency towards a too front vowel, the pupil should be told to make his sound ɜ more like ʌ, and to lengthen it.

181. *No. 12.* ə, the first vowel in *alone* and the last in *butter*.

Description.

(a) Central part of the tongue raised.

(b) Tongue raised about one-third of the way from open to close.

(c) Lips neutral.

(d) The vowel is always very short.

182. The phoneme varies from a vowel of a half-close tongue position between two velar consonants, as in bæk əgeɪn, where the ə is distinctly close, to a position well below the Cardinal ɛ - - - ɔ line in final positions.

183. Like ɜ, this vowel is often pronounced in the W., N.W. and S.W. with the tip of the tongue inverted when *r* occurs in the spelling. Some speakers use a very much more open sound in final positions, a kind of ʌ, or even ɑ, e.g. bʌtʌ; and there are speakers who make a difference between words ending in *er* and those ending in *a* (where no *r* is pronounced), who say, for example, oʊvə, but tʃaɪnʌ, soʊfɑ or soʊfʌ.

184. The vowel ə is interesting because it replaces almost all other vowels and diphthongs in unstressed positions: i and ɪ, however, are exceptions to this: i is generally replaced by ɪ in unstressed positions, and ɪ remains the same: e.g. ˈre-ˈname, ˈriːˈneɪm, but *reˈmain*, rɪˈmeɪn, *finish*, fɪnɪʃ (ɪ in stressed and unstressed syllables in this word). The strong form ði is replaced by

ðə before a consonant, ðə bʊk, and the termination *ible* is sometimes pronounced əbl, though ɪbl is probably more frequently used. Such pronunciations as bəˈliˑv, ˈsætən are occasionally heard.

185. *Examples of the Neutral Vowel ə Replacing Strong Forms.*

ɛ in *pence* (pɛns), but ə in *sixpence* (sikspəns)
æ ,, *valid* (ˈvælɪd) ,, ə ,, *validity* (vəˈlɪdɪtɪ)
ɑ ,, *particle* (pɑˑtikl) ,, ə ,, *particular* (pəˈtɪkjʊlə)
ɒ ,, *conduct* (ˈkɒndəkt) ,, ə ,, *conduct* (kənˈdʌkt)
ɔ ,, *ward* (wɔːd) ,, ə ,, *backward* (ˈbækwəd)
u ,, *to* (as in *set to* (tuː) ,, ə or ʊ in *today* (təˈdeɪ or tʊˈdeɪ)
ʌ ,, *some* (sʌm) ,, ə ,, *handsome* (ˈhænsəm)
ɜ ,, *Bert* (bɜˑt) ,, ə ,, *Herbert* (ˈhɜˑbət)
eɪ ,, *face* (feɪs) ,, ə ,, *preface* (ˈprɛfəs)
oʊ ,, *most* (moʊst) ,, ə ,, *topmost* (ˈtɒpməst)
aʊ ,, *mouth* (maʊθ) ,, ə ,, *Plymouth* (plɪməθ)
ɛə ,, *there* (ðɛə) ,, ə ,, *there isn't any* (ðərˈɪznt ɛnɪ)
aɪə ,, *shire* (ʃaɪə) ,, ə ,, *Yorkshire* (ˈjɔˑkʃə)

186. These weak forms occur in conversational speech; in careful speech, however, it is customary not to reduce the strong vowels completely to the neutral vowel, but to use something more nearly approaching the original vowel. If the speaker in his efforts to be very clear and careful, uses the strong vowel in unstressed positions, the result is very unpleasant. Such a habit gives the effect of stressing unimportant words. For example, a clergyman who says hu ɑˑt ðɪ ɔˑθər ɒv piˑs ænd lʌvər ɒv kɒŋkɔˑd, sounds as if he were stressing

ENGLISH VOWELS IN DETAIL

the unimportant words ði, ɒv, ænd. I have heard such a preacher who also tried to say *sympathy* very carefully, with the result that he said sɪmpɜ·θɪ.[1]

187. The best method of getting over the difficulty is to say a vowel that lies in an intermediate position between the strong vowels and the neutral ə.

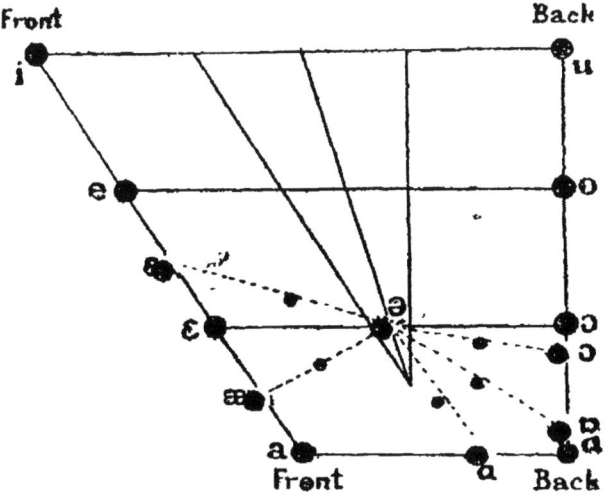

FIG. 21. Semi-weak Vowels.

188. The semi-weak forms of u and oʊ are generally ʊ and o: thus *do* pronounced in its weakest form would be də or d, as in wɒt d jʊ wɒnt: a more careful pronunciation would be dʊ. Similarly the words *obey, November, protest, phonetics*, can be pronounced ə'beɪ, nə'vɛmbə, prə'tɛst, fə'nɛtɪks (very weak), o'beɪ, no'vɛmbə, pro'tɛst, fo'nɛtɪks (semi-weak), and oʊ'beɪ, noʊ'vɛmbə, proʊ'tɛst, foʊ'nɛtɪks (very careful style). The middle variety is probably the commonest.

189. It should be noted that those diphthongs which can be reduced to ə in very quick speech, e.g.

[1] See Chapters XV., XVI.

ðɛə, baɪ, which can be ðə, bə or bɪ, should have their full value in more careful speech. In Professor Jones' Pronouncing Dictionary *my, myself* are given with two forms: maɪ, maɪsɛlf and mɪ, mɪsɛlf; *by* with the form baɪ, and as an *occasional* weak form bɪ. mɪ, bɪ were traditional stage pronunciations at one time, but their use has now died out; one example, however, remains in mɪlɔːd (*my lord*). mɪ, mɪsɛlf are still heard in colloquial speech, though perhaps less frequently than maɪ, maɪsɛlf.[1]

190. On pp. 152 ff. a summary is given of the main differences in vowel pronunciation between Northern speech and Southern English and between London pronunciation and Standard English.

---

[1] Note that in some dialects—as far apart as Yorkshire and Devon—*night* is pronounced naɪt, but *fortnight* as fɔˈtnɪt (fɔ(ɹ)tnɪt).

Chapter XII.

DIPHTHONGS.

191. It is customary to consider a diphthong as a combination of two vowel sounds, so pronounced as to form one syllable. In reality it is a gliding sound. The tongue starts in one vowel position and glides towards another vowel position by the most direct route. A diphthong is made by one impulse of the breath, i.e. there is no diminuendo—crescendo of breath force. This can be realised best by pronouncing slowly the English diphthong aɪ, a----ɪ----, and then pronouncing the two vowels á - í, with a fresh impulse of the breath on ɪ. (Take care not to insert a glottal stop.) The first will be felt as one syllable, the second as two; the first is a diphthong and the second is not.

192. English diphthongs, like those of most languages, are of the " falling " type, i.e. they have their greater prominence at the beginning; they are decrescendo diphthongs. English diphthongs are usually written phonetically with two letters, the first representing the starting point of the tongue, and the second the *direction* in which it moves. In the diphthong aɪ, for example, the tongue starts at the position of a, and moves towards, but does not actually reach, the ɪ position.

193. Diphthongs can be made by beginning at any one vowel and going in the direction of any other, so that the number of possible diphthongs is very large.

112   THE PHONETICS OF ENGLISH

In English the majority of speakers possess nine diphthongs, which are represented by the symbols

13.　14.　15.　16.　17.　18.　19.　20.　21.
eɪ　　oʊ　　aɪ　　aʊ　　ɔɪ　　ɪə　　ɛə　　ɔə　　ʊə

194. They can be shown on the Cardinal vowel figure as is indicated in the accompanying diagrams.

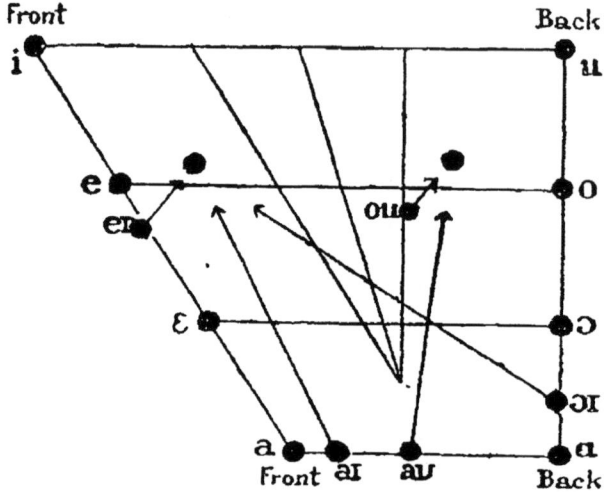

FIG. 22. English Diphthongs (a).

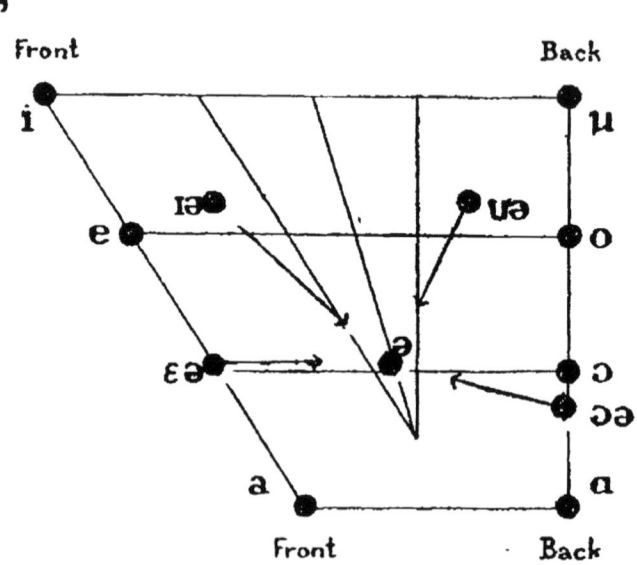

FIG. 23. English Diphthongs (b).

ENGLISH DIPHTHONGS

195. *No. 13.* eɪ, the sound in *lady, make*.

Description.

The tongue starts in the position of a vowel somewhat below Cardinal No. 2, and moves towards the position of ɪ. As the movement is through a very small distance, this diphthong is said to be narrow.

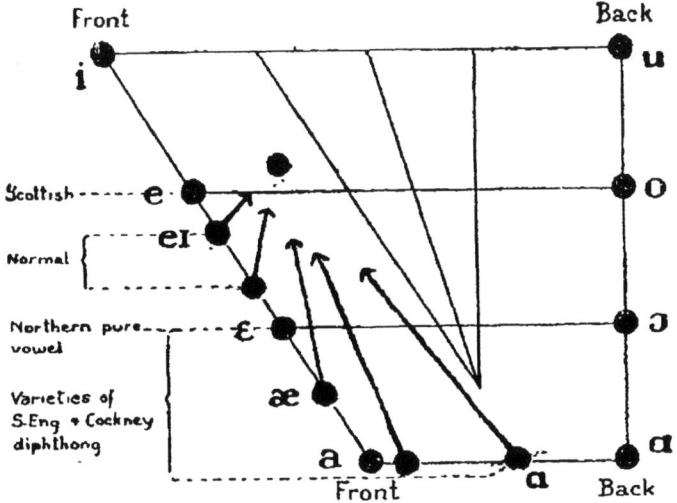

FIG. 24. Varieties of the eɪ diphthong.

196. In Scotland and many parts of the North of England, this diphthong is replaced by a pure vowel eː or ɛː. (The former is Scottish and Northumbrian, and the latter Yorks. and Lancs.). Thus the word *day* (deɪ) is pronounced deː or dɛː.[1] Another Northern pronunciation is an extremely narrow diphthong eɪ, where the starting point is a very close e vowel and the movement very slight. In the S. Midlands, S., S.W., and Eastern Counties, many varieties of wider diphthongs, ranging from ɛɪ to ɑɪ (through æɪ and aɪ), are heard. Thus the word *lady* is pronounced as leɪdɪ, lɛɪdɪ, læɪdɪ, laɪdɪ, lɑɪdɪ. The first two are generally

[1] See Ch. XVII for the modern pronunciation of words like *day*.

considered correct and the last three are looked on as markedly dialectal. A diphthong with the first element retracted towards ə, e.g. ləɪdɪ, pləɪs, is common in the Eastern counties, in the West of England, and with individual speakers.

197. The wider varieties of this diphthong can be corrected by exaggerating in the opposite direction, i.e. a pupil who says laɪdɪ must be told to make his sound more like leːdɪ, and the attempt will probably lead him to say a very good leɪdɪ or lɛɪdɪ.

198. The effect of a "dark *l*" following this diphthong, particularly the Cockney æɪ and aɪ, is to make the second element more like ə, so that a word such as *tale* is pronounced tæəl and taəl (with a very dark *l*). To correct this tendency the diphthong must be taught separately, and the 1 must be produced with a less "dark" quality, i.e. lᵘ or lᵊ, not lᵞ. (See Chapter XIV, § 268).

199. *No. 14.* oʊ, the sound in *go, home.*
Description.

The first element of this diphthong is somewhat advanced from a fully back o, and there is not much movement of the tongue; hence it is, like eɪ, a narrow diphthong.

200. Many variant pronunciations of this diphthong occur in different parts of the country, the difference being due chiefly to the tongue position of the first element. In Scotland and in parts of the North of England a pure vowel is substituted for the diphthong, *I don't know* being pronounced aɪ doːnt·noː. In the N. Riding of Yorkshire an open ɔ is used : aɪ dɔˑnt nɔː. (In the W. Riding broad dialect this would be a dʊənt nɔː.) A

very narrow ou diphthong is heard in educated Northern speech: in a less educated type of Northern speech, ɔu occurs in some words: e.g. nɔu (*know*). In Midland, Southern and Eastern pronunciation many varieties are found, ranging from ɔu and ʌu, in both of which the tongue starts in a much lower and further back position than in ou, to əu, æu, œu, and au, where the starting position is further forward, sometimes almost reaching that of a front vowel. Of these perhaps ɔu and ʌu are the commonest, while öü and ëü, which are made with a fronted position of each element, ëü, having the first vowel unrounded, are found in what is often called affected speech.[1] The difference between this pronunciation and one form of Cockney lies almost entirely in the quality of voice of the speaker; the diphthongs are practically of the same formation. In some dialects (e.g. Norfolk) the word *wholly* is pronounced hʌlɪ.

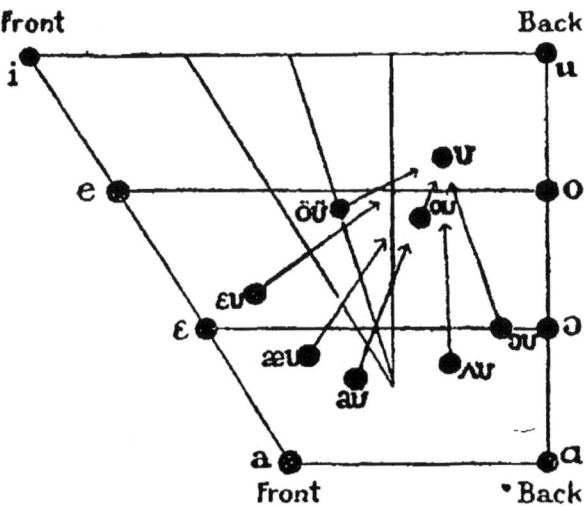

FIG. 25. Varieties of the ou Diphthong.

[1] In some forms of "modern" pronunciation there is no lip-rounding whatever. See Ch. XVII, p. 361 (v).

201. If the teacher wishes to get rid of ʌu or ɔu, the best way is to begin from ɜ. Let the pupil make this sound, then pronounce it with lip-rounding and pass to u, gradually modifying the first element towards o. To get rid of a first element that is too far forward, make the pupil aim at a pure o, and then make a slight movement towards u.

202. In certain words where ou occurs in an unstressed position, it is reduced to o; thus, *obey, November, going, phonetics, protest*, by some people are pronounced obeɪ, novɛmbə, goɪŋ, fonɛtɪks, pro'tɛst (alternative pronunciations əbeɪ, nəvɛmbə, fənɛtiks, prə'tɛst; oubeɪ, nouvɛmbə, gouɪŋ, founɛtiks, prou'tɛst).

203. *No. 15.* aɪ, the sound in *my, time*.

Description.

The tongue starts somewhere near the position of Cardinal a and moves towards ɪ; as the movement is considerable, aɪ is said to be a wide diphthong.

204. The main differences in the pronunciation of this diphthong lie in the starting point of the first element. This varies from æ, through various types of a, to ɑ and even ɒ, so that æɪ, aɪ, ɑɪ, ɑːɪ, ɒɪ are heard in addition to əɪ, where the first tongue position approaches that of a central vowel. æɪ is often considered affected, while ɑɪ, ɑːɪ, and ɒɪ are generally associated with Cockney pronunciation; and it is to be noted that this diphthong is often nasalised in London speech. In Yorkshire and Lancashire a diphthong beginning with a cardinal a rather lengthened is heard: aːɪ. In Southern speech the variant ɑɪ seems likely to become the commonest one, and it is heard

ENGLISH DIPHTHONGS

very regularly on the stage. It differs from one Cockney variety in length, and in the fact that it is not nasalised, but it is of practically the same tongue articulation. Another variety of London diphthong is æɪ, which is considered ultra " refaned " by many people, and it is possible that ɑɪ is a reaction against this pronunciation.

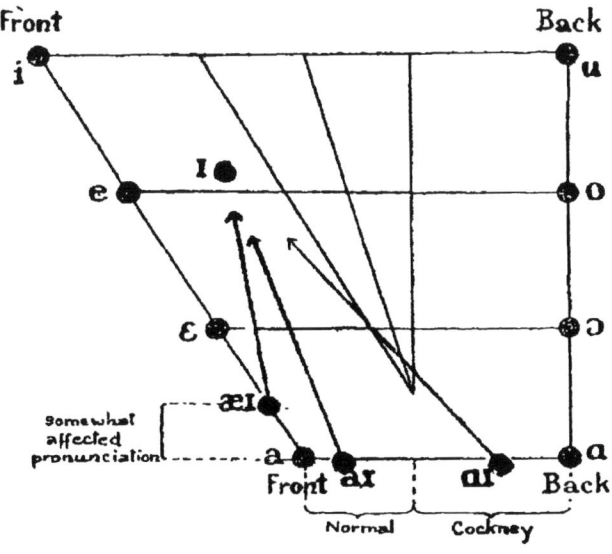

FIG. 26. Varieties of the aɪ Diphthong.

205. It is to be noted that aɪ followed by " dark l," as in words like *I'll, while, mile*, tends to become the pure vowel ɑː, ɑːl gou ɪn ə lɪtl wɑːl. The London bus conductor calls out " tʃɑːlz ɪl " for *Child's Hill*.

206. This pronunciation is found particularly in Southern speech, and is heard from speakers who have no other outstanding marks of Southern speech.

207. It is generally considered desirable to modify the pronunciations of a too-retracted ɑɪ, ɑːɪ and ɒɪ in the direction of aɪ, and this can easily be done by making the pupil exaggerate in the front direction; by attempting to say æɪ, he will probably say aɪ.

118 THE PHONETICS OF ENGLISH

208. *No.* 16. aʊ, the sound in *now, round*.

Description.

This diphthong might well be written as ɑʊ, since the first element lies between a and ɑ, and is often near to the English ɑ as in *father*. The tongue starts at a point about half-way between Cardinal No. 4 and No. 5, and moves towards ʊ; it is a wide diphthong.

209. The diphthong varies in the starting position of the tongue, Northern speakers, especially Scottish, using a decided ɑ, Southern speakers tending towards Cardinal a and Cockney to æ, so that æʊ, aʊ, and ɑʊ are heard. In addition to these varieties, in the Eastern counties, a diphthong beginning with a centralised vowel is heard, something approaching əʊ, and in the West of England the second element becomes a front instead of a back rounded vowel, e.g. ay, wɪðayt, graynd. In the broad Yorkshire dialect the diphthong becomes Cardinal a long, e.g. *now* is naː.

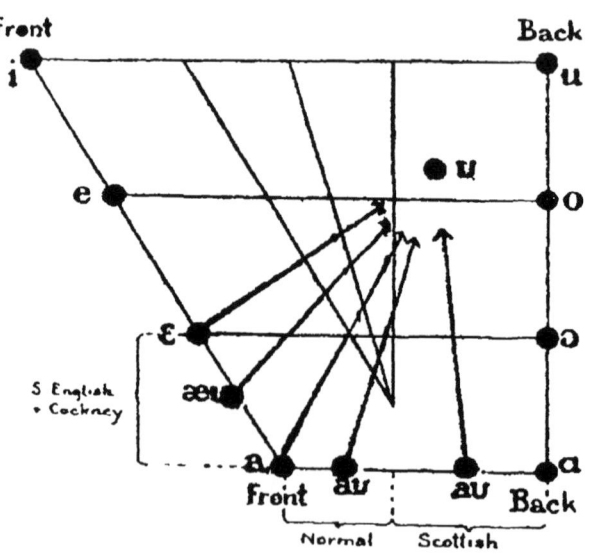

Fig. 27. Varieties of the aʊ Diphthong.

ENGLISH DIPHTHONGS

210. In Cockney, certain words in which æʊ would be expected, have the pronunciation a, or ɑː: e.g. *about* (əbaʊt) becomes əbaːt, wɒt əbaːt ɪt or wɒr əbaː? ɪ?, *how* becomes aː, *out* becomes aːt, *cow* becomes kaː (kæʊ is a "refined" Cockney).

211. If these extreme pronunciations are to be corrected, the usual principle of making the pupil exaggerate in the opposite direction may be applied; if he says æʊ, make him try to say ɑʊ. If he says aː, after getting a further back a, make him add ʊ, a - - ʊ, making two syllables; gradually reduce the space between the two elements and let him glide quickly to the ʊ position.

212. *No. 17.* ɔɪ, the sound in *boy, noise*.

Description.

The tongue position of the first element is a little higher than that of the English ɒ sound, and the movement is towards ɪ.

213. The different pronunciations of this vowel are due to the differences in the starting position of the tongue, and in some cases to the position of the lips. The varieties range from ɑɪ, where the first element is unrounded, a pronunciation which is heard in the Eastern counties, and, to a certain extent, in the West of England, to oːɪ, where the first position is closer and over-rounded. This pronunciation is found in London. bʌɪ (for *boy*) is said to exist in Devonshire and bwɔ or bɔ (spelt *bor*) in Suffolk.

214. If it is desired to teach ɔɪ instead of oːɪ, all that is necessary is to tell the pupil to open his mouth more at beginning the word, while ɔɪ can be obtained by telling the pupil who says ɑɪ or ʌɪ to round his lips. This also produces the necessary tongue adjustment.

215. *No. 18.* ɪə, the sound in *here, beard, idea*.
Description.

The tongue starts in the position of ɪ and moves towards the neutral vowel ə.

216. Many varieties of this diphthong are found. In Cockney the first element is very close, i, and it is often separated from the ə by the semi-vowel j. " Darlin' Dora " in *Fanny's First Play* says ʌʊl diːjə, and the London flower sellers say vãːlɪʔs diːjə. ɪə is heard in many parts of the country, and eə, ɪʌ, or ɪɑ, in the last two of which the tongue moves beyond the ə position, are met with in what is sometimes called affected pronunciation. In those parts of the country where final *r* is pronounced, the following variants occur: iːr (in Scotland), ɪər (in many parts of N. England), ɪəɹ and ɪə (in N.W. and W.) with the tongue-tip curled up. The two pronunciations of the word *year* should be noted, jɪə and jɜː.[1]

217. To teach ɪə instead of iːjə, make the pupil begin with a lower tongue position, i.e. let him aim at e, and glide gently towards the ə.

218. *No. 19.* ɛə, the sound in *fair, scarce*.
Description.

The starting point of the tongue is near to Cardinal ɛ position, the movement of the tongue in this case being chiefly from front to back, towards the central position.

---

[1] I have heard a lecturer pronounce *this era* as ðɪs jɜˑrə.

ENGLISH DIPHTHONGS

219. All varieties from iə to æə are heard. In the broad Yorks. dialect *there* is pronounced ðiə; Cockney pronunciation is ðeə, sometimes ðeːjə. In Southern English a more open first position is heard.[1] In addition to this, we find the varieties where some kind of *r* is pronounced, ðeːr, in Scotland, ðɛəɹ or ðɛə (with the tongue-tip curled up) in the N. and N.W., and in S. Lancashire and in Cheshire, particularly in Liverpool and Birkenhead the pronunciation ɜ is heard, e.g. skɜˑslɪ, kɜˑfʊl.[2] The words *fur, hair*, in this part of the country are often pronounced fɛː, hɜː. It is probable, however, that a sound intermediate between the two is used for both, and that the hearer who is not accustomed to this pronunciation thinks the speaker is using ɜ in place of ɛ, and ɛ in place of ɜ. (Cf. note on p. 105.)

220. To teach ɛə to pupils who say ejə or ɜ, begin with an open ɛ sound, or with a sound resembling æ, and glide to the ə sound from that.

221. *No. 20.* ɔə, the sound in *more, board*.

Description.

The tongue starts a little below Cardinal ɔ position and moves towards the neutral ə.

222. A large number of South-eastern English speakers do not use this diphthong at all; for it, they use the pure vowel ɔ. The many different pronunciations of words in which this diphthong can occur were dealt with under the English vowel No. 7, ɔ §§ 161–163.

223. *No. 21.* ʊə, the sound in *pure, your*.

---

[1] This is the pronunciation indicated in *A Phonetic Reader*, by Mackenzie and Drew (Manchester University Press).

[2] It is reported also from Devonshire.

Description.

The tongue starts from the ʊ position and moves to ə.

224. Pronunciations vary from uːə, heard in the North, through ʊə, oə, ɔə, to ɔ, and there are also varieties where either an r is pronounced, e.g. puːr (Scotland), pʊər, pʊəɹ, or the vowel is made with inversion of the tip of the tongue. oə and ɔə and ɔ are heard in educated London speech, particularly in the word *poor*, while in *your*, perhaps jɔ is the commonest Southern pronunciation. A Cockney speaker pronounces these two words as pɔːwə and jɔːwə.

225. To teach ʊə to a Cockney who says pɔːwə it is necessary to isolate the ʊ sound in the word pʊt, and make the pupil glide from that to ə; there should be no exaggerated lip movement, such as would give the semi-vowel w.

226. It should be noted that in Cockney and other dialects in different parts of the country, there is a tendency to drawl the diphthongs. This is often a marked characteristic of dialectal speech, and should be corrected. A Cockney says nʌ - - - ʊ or mɑː - - - ɪn, and a Yorkshire speaker says mɑː - - - ɪt, in which he differs from an educated speaker only in the "drawl," and probably voice quality. To correct this tendency should not be difficult; the speaker can be told to glide quickly from the first element, or it is often sufficient to tell him to say the sound vigorously.

TRIPHTHONGS.

227. The groups of vowel sounds aɪə and aʊə, as in certain pronunciations of the words *fire* and *power* are often considered triphthongs. They are not, however,

ENGLISH DIPHTHONGS

true triphthongs, for the first and last sounds in each group are more sonorous than the middle one, that is, they belong to different syllables, having a diminution of prominence between them. They often strike the ear, however, as one syllable, and are treated as such in poetry.

228. The diagram illustrates approximately the movements of the tongue in making these two groups

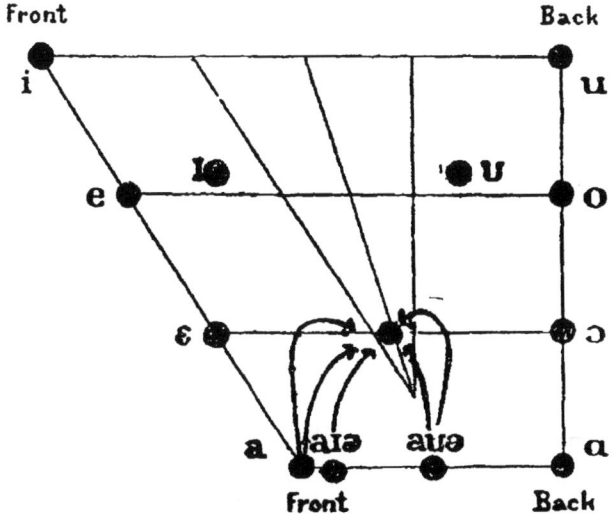

FIG. 28. Triphthongs.

of sounds. It will be noted that the starting position is known, that the tongue moves towards the ɪ and the ʊ positions, but does not nearly reach them, and then moves towards ə; aeə and aoə would be a closer representation of the sounds.

229. It is often found that these two triphthongs are reduced to diphthongs, that the words *fire* and *power* are pronounced faə and paə (the a in the latter being further back than the former: it could be represented as ɑə). Sometimes they are even reduced to a

pure vowels aː and ɑː. Speakers who use this pronunciation for *fire*, distinguish between it and *far* (fɑː), the tongue position in the former being a little further forward than in *far*, and a suspicion of two syllables is added by a slight diminution and reinforcement of the breath force. It is in the word *our* that this reduction is most noticeable: *our own*, often being pronounced aːr oʊn. The pronunciation faː for *fire*, taː for *tire*, tɑː for *tower*, etc., is used by the younger generation in the south, and is criticised severely by people who do not use this type of pronunciation. See Ch. II, § 22, and Ch. XVII, § 361 (iv).

NOTE.—The combinations of sounds written as eɪə, ɔɪə, and oʊə, as in *player*, *employer*, and *mower* can also be considered as triphthongs of a kind. These groups, however, constitute two syllables in the pronunciation of many people. The pronunciation vɔɪlɪn (vaɪəlɪn), vɔɪlɪt (vaɪələt) may be a mistaken spelling pronunciation due to a confusion of *oi* and *io*.

230. On pp. 152 ff. a summary is given of the main differences in the pronunciation of diphthongs in Northern and Southern English, and in London and Standard pronunciation.

Chapter XIII.

NASALISATION OF VOWELS.

231. Nasalised vowels are not found in normal English speech, although there is no doubt that vowels which occur in the neighbourhood of nasal consonants are partially nasalised: e.g. in the word *man* (mæn), the soft palate is lowered for m and for n, and between these two sounds, it makes a movement towards closure for the vowel. But the time is so short that a complete closure is not possible; and in pronouncing the vowel some of the breath escapes through the nose as well as through the mouth. If this nasalisation is too great, it becomes noticeable and is considered disagreeable.

232. Nasalisation (which is not due to physical defect) is often the result of bad habit, and is found in certain dialects and in some individuals. Cockney speakers add strong nasalisation to vowels in the neighbourhood of nasal consonants and sometimes where no nasal consonant occurs.

There aren't any becomes ðər ãĩʔ ɛnĩ.
I don't think so ,, ãɪ dʌ̃ʊ̃ θĩʔ soʊ.

(Note the n of *aren't, don't* and the ŋ of *think* have disappeared; the nasalisation of the vowel takes their place.)

233. To cure nasality is not an easy task.[1] The teacher must try and work from sounds which are not

[1] See chapter on "Nasal Twang" in the writer's *Speech Defects*, pub. by J. M. Dent & Co., Third Edition, 1936.

125

nasalised. Sometimes the vowels are nasalised when not near nasal consonants. The open vowels lend themselves to nasalisation more readily than the close ones, and it is often found that i and u are free from nasalisation. If so, it is possible to work from these and gradually to get from i to ɪ and eɪ, from u to ʊ and oʊ, and so on to the more open vowels. ɑ is most subject to nasalisation, and should therefore be left till the last. Exercises for the control of the soft palate are useful, as they induce a more vigorous movement of the palate.

234. If all the vowels are nasalised, the teacher may begin with the consonant z, which loses its characteristic buzz if it is nasalised—which is a rare occurrence. Let the pupil practise zi, zi, zi; zu, zu, zu; then go on to ze, zɛ, zɔ, etc. When nasalisation beings to appear, it will be necessary to go back to a vowel which is not nasalised.

235. The vowels should be practised in isolation before there is any attempt made to use them in words. When they can be pronounced as purely oral vowels, they may be introduced into words. Words in which a nasal consonant occurs should be left to the last, and even then, the vowel should at first be separated from the nasal consonant by a complete break æ—nd, n—aɪs, the pause being gradually reduced until there is no break.

Chapter XIV.
ENGLISH CONSONANTS IN DETAIL.

236. Consonants are classified according to the *organs* articulating them and according to the *manner* of their articulation. This double classification lends itself to a useful diagrammatic form, the terms along the top of the diagram giving the *organs* by which they are articulated, and those down the side the *manner* in which they are articulated.

237. TABLE OF ENGLISH CONSONANTS.
See page 128.

Note.—Symbols which occur twice indicate sounds which have a double articulation, the secondary articulation being shown in brackets, thus ( ).

VOICED AND VOICELESS CONSONANTS.

238. In Chapter VIII, § 76, it was shown that it is possible to combine the movements of the vocal cords with the articulation of any consonant: i.e. consonants can be voiced (z, ʒ, b, g, l, m, etc.), or they can be voiceless (s, ʃ, p, k, etc.). In most languages there occur numbers of pairs of consonants, articulated by lips, tongue, teeth, etc., in exactly the same way, and differing in the presence or absence of voice (p b, f v, θ ð, s z, etc.). In the following table, where these pairs are shown, the first is voiceless, the second voiced. Many consonants (such as m, n, ŋ, r, l) have only their voiced form as usual speech sounds of English. These can be pronounced, however, without voice, and the student is advised to practise this as a good phonetic exercise. (See Chapter VIII, § 77 d.) It should also be noticed that voiceless consonants require more force

127

	Labial		Dental Alveolar		Palatal			
	Bi-labial	Labio-Dental	Pre-dental	Post-dental or Alveolar	Palato-Alveolar	Palatal	Velar	Glottal
Plosive	p b			t d			k g	ʔ
Affricative			tθ dθ	ts dz tʃ̬ dɹ	tʃ dʒ			
Nasal	m			n			ŋ	
Lateral				l			(ɬ)	
Rolled				r				
Fricative		f v	θ ð	s z ɹ	ʃ ʒ			h
Semi-vowel	ʍ w					j	(w)	

164

of exhalation than voiced consonants and are articulated with greater vigour; there is a tighter closure for the plosives and a sharper release, and for the fricatives a smaller opening. To test the difference in breath force hold the hand before the mouth while θ and ð (or f and v, p and b) are pronounced alternately.

239. The voiced consonants in English in initial and final positions are not fully voiced: i.e. in initial position the vibrations of the vocal cords do not begin immediately the consonant is formed, but some way through the articulation; in final positions, the vibrations cease before the consonant is finished. Thus in *dog* (dɒg), the voice does not begin until perhaps half-way through the d, and it ceases before the articulation of the g comes to an end, i.e. it resembles t͡dɒg͡k in pronunciation. It is important for teachers to realise this, as some are apt to waste time in making children voice fully English consonants in final positions, under the impression that it is an essential of English speech. Thus they will insist on a voiced off-glide to a b, d, g, rɒbᵊ, sædᵊ, bɪgᵊ, which is not desirable even for very careful speech.

Plosive Consonants.

240. Plosive consonants are made by the stoppage of the air passage at some point. The air compressed behind the stop rushes out with a slight explosion when the stop is released. Thus a plosive consists of (*a*) a stop, (*b*) a release, and (*c*) some sound which follows the release. In forming p and b, the stop is made by the two lips; in t and d by the tip of the tongue against the teeth ridge; in k and g by the back of the tongue against the soft palate.

K

130   THE PHONETICS OF ENGLISH

Voiceless Plosives.

241. The English voiceless plosives are said to be aspirated, i.e. on the release of the stop a slight h is heard before the following vowel, e.g. *park* is pʰɑ·k, *too* is tʰuː, *come* is kʰʌm. This aspiration is marked in *stressed*, but not in *unstressed* positions: thus, *ten* is

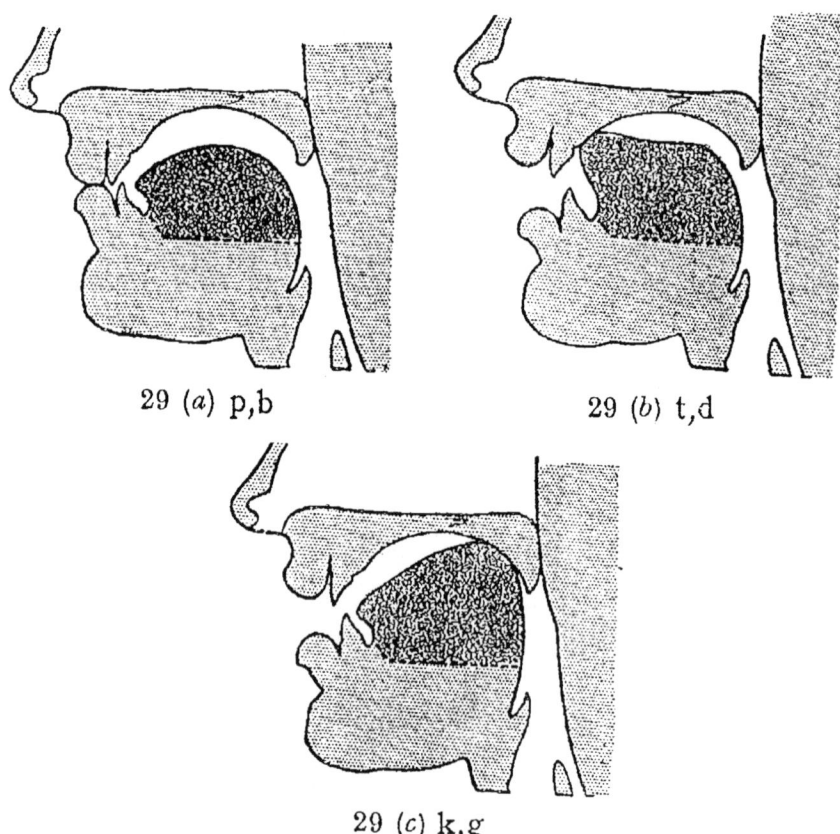

29 (a) p,b   29 (b) t,d

29 (c) k,g

Fig. 29.   English Plosive Consonants.

tʰɛn, but in *letter* (lɛtə), the aspiration is very slight. Compare the French and Italian voiceless plosives where the vowel sound begins immediately on the release of the stop; these are said to be *unaspirated*.

242. In Cockney speech, the consonants p, t, k are said to be over-aspirated; the puff of breath before

ENGLISH CONSONANTS IN DETAIL

the vowel sound is so great as to be noticeable, and such a pronunciation is thought undesirable. This is particularly the case with t, where strong aspiration, added to a lazy articulation of the stop and a slow release, results in ts, the s being heard as the tongue is removed slowly from the t position. Similarly the aspiration of k together with a a slow release results in the affricative kx, the velar fricative x being heard as the back of the tongue is removed slowly from the k position. Thus a Cockney will say ə kxap əv tsəi for ə kʌp əv tiː. In Northern English, particularly in Lancashire and Yorkshire, aspiration of p, t, k even in stressed positions is either very slight or absent altogether.

243. In order to cure over-aspiration, it is necessary to tell the pupil to make the contact firm and the release vigorous. If after a vigorous pronunciation the aspiration is still too noticeable, he should be told to make his p more like b, his t more like d, and his k more like g.

244. Teachers of singing try to combat aspiration of p, t, k as it lets out a great quantity of breath, leaving little behind with which to sing the succeeding voiced sounds.

INCOMPLETE PLOSIVES.

245. In § 240 a plosive is shown to have three parts; but in English there are some cases in which all the three parts are not made, when the *stop* alone is formed, but no release. This occurs when two plosive consonants follow each other: in *act, stopped, doctor* (ækt, stɒpt, dɒktə), the first plosive in each pair is not exploded, we do not say ækʰt, stɒpʰt, dɒkʰtə. The same thing happens when the first plosive is at the end of one word

and the second at the beginning of another, e.g. tɒp bɔɪ, lɒg kæbɪn, bæd gɜːl, hɒt pɒt, stɒp tɔˑkɪŋ, etc. When the two consonants are the same, as in blæk kæt, gʊd dɒg, ðæt taɪm, stɒp pliːz, they form a long stop with one release. To explode the first plosive in such combinations does not add to distinctness even in slow speech; in fact it detracts from clarity by the addition of an extra sound which does not belong to normal speech.

246. When three plosives follow each other, in conversational speech, it is possible for the last one only to receive its full plosion: e.g. ə beɪkt tɑˑt, ækt tuː, ə lɒkt dɔə, ən æpt pjuˑpɪl, ə lɒpt triː, ə rɛkt trɔˑlə, tʊ ækt kaɪndlɪ.

Faucal or Nasal Plosion.

247. In the pronunciation of such words as *button, hidden, shopman, oatmeal,* the plosive consonant is immediately followed by a nasal consonant, bʌtn, hɪdn, ʃɒpmən, oʊtmiˑl, and the plosive is not exploded in the normal way. While the tongue or lips remain in the position for the plosive the soft palate is lowered to allow the air to pass through the nose for the following nasal consonant. (See accompanying diagram, Fig. 30.) The explosion that is heard and felt is made by the air rushing out through the nose, on the lowering of the soft palate. This is called faucal or nasal plosion.

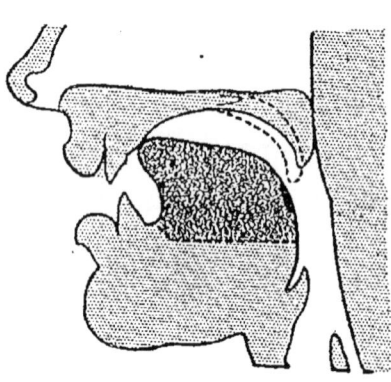

FIG. 30.
Illustrating Nasal Plosion.

ENGLISH CONSONANTS IN DETAIL

248. Examples of nasal plosion are found in the following words: sɪdnɪ, heɪpnɪ, beɪkŋ (alternative pronunciations beɪkn, beɪkən), ɔˑgŋ graɪndə (alternative pronunciation ɔgən graɪndə), oʊpm (alternative pronunciations oʊpn, oʊpən).

LATERAL PLOSION.

249. When a plosive is followed by an l sound, the explosion is made by the sides of the tongue leaving the upper teeth and the air rushing out along the sides of the tongue: e.g. lɪtl, mʌdl, rætl. This is called lateral plosion.

250. NOTES ON THE PLOSIVE CONSONANTS.

(a) t and d before r are articulated on the teeth, not on the teeth-ridge, in some types of Irish pronunciation and in North Yorkshire. Thus *true* has a dental t and a rolled r. This gives the impression of tθruː. (This word is often written *thrue* to indicate an Irish pronunciation.) (For dental t and d see Fig. 31a.)

(b) The substitution of d for t between two vowels is occasionally heard: e.g. sædədɪ for sætədɪ. Such a d tends to become a semi-rolled r; thus sædədɪ weakens into særədɪ, bɛtə becomes bɛdə and then bɛrə. This tendency is seen in the vulgar speech of many dialects in the phrase gɛr əweɪ for gɛt əweɪ. It is also a marked characteristic of American speech: e.g. lɛrə for *letter*, kaˑrɪdʒ for *cottage*. Compare *porridge* (pɒrɪdʒ), which has come from *potage*. The London bus-conductor often calls *Swiss Cottage* swɪs kɒrɪdʒ.

(c) A voiceless fricative r (ɹ) is used for final or intervocalic *t* by some Irish speakers: e.g. *better, sit* are pronounced bɛɹə, sɪɹ.

(d) *The Glottal Stop.*—The glottal stop (for description and diagram see § 75 d, p. 53) is a regular speech sound in English in the pronunciation of many people. It is used normally in the following cases:

i. For the sake of emphasis, when a stressed syllable begins with a vowel, a glottal stop is introduced before it, e.g.

ɪt wəz ðɪ ǁʔoʊnlɪ ˈθɪŋ tə ˈduː.

ɪt s əz ǁʔiːzɪ əz kən ˈbiː.

[ǁIndicates extra emphasis.]

It is generally at the beginning of words that the glottal stop is used in this way, but particularly emphatic speakers use it in words like traɪʔʌmfənt, ɛkstrəʔɔˈdɪmərɪ, krɪʔeɪʃn, ʔiːlɪ daɪʔɒsɪsn əsoʊsɪʔeɪʃn. This sound is not essential for English speech either for meaning or for emphasis, as it is possible to emphasize sufficiently by using extra force of breath without making a glottal stop.

ii. To avoid a hiatus between two vowels, e.g.

pʊt ə kɒmə ʔɑˑftər ɪt.

liːnə ʔæʃwɛl (Lena Ashwell).

Some speakers use it instead of r in phrases like *better and better*, bɛtə ʔən bɛtə, *Westminster Abbey*, wɛstmɪnstə ʔæbɪ. It is possible, however, to make a smooth passage from one vowel to the next without either the glottal stop or r. (See §§ 273-4 for linking *r* and for intrusive *r*.)

ENGLISH CONSONANTS IN DETAIL 135

(*e*) The glottal stop is used in all parts of the country to replace other plosive consonants. This tendency, probably of long standing, seems to be growing. It is found to a marked extent in Scotland, Yorkshire and Lancashire, in the Eastern counties, in the Home Counties and in London. Most people are familiar with the Scottish wɔːʔər or wɒʔər for *water*, with the Cockney lɛʔə for *letter*, and tɒʔnəm koːʔ rʌʊd; in *Stockport* the town is often called stɒʔpɔːʔ, *Bradford* is called braʔfəd, and all over the country *little* is pronounced lıʔl, *lately* leıʔli, *exactly* ɛgzæʔli, and *mutton* mʌʔn. The Cockney newsboy calls out paıʔə for *paper*; in London I heard iːz biːn toːʔın əbaːʔ ıʔ əbaːʔ ɛıʔiːn mʌ̃ʔs (He's been talking about it about eighteen months); in Yorkshire I have heard bıʔwiˑṅ; and in the Eastern Counties aı toʊld ðə pɔˑʔə tə pʊʔ ıʔ ın ðə væn; ðeı ə kʌmıŋ hıə ʔəmɒrou; mɛʔm; (*make him*); ðæʔ dəṹʔ mæʔəs lɒŋ z jə gɒʔ ə tıʔıʔ, *That doesn't matter, so long as you've got a ticket*; ðıs hɒʔ wɛðə meıʔs pıˑʔl θĩʔ əbaʊʔ teıʔn hɒlıdız (*This hot weather makes people think about taking holidays*). Here the glottal stop replaces p, t, k). It is easily recognised in the above examples, but before alveolar and labial consonants, where it occurs very frequently, the glottal stop is not so noticeable, e.g. ðæʔ sɔˑʔ əv θıŋ, skɒʔlənd, ı doʊnʔ nou, doʊnʔ lɛʔ mi kiˑp ju, nɒʔ bıfɔə tuː, ðæʔ wʌn, pʌʔnı, mʌʔn.

(*f*) Many London speakers insert a glottal stop before a voiceless plosive in certain words: e.g. njuʔtrəl (*neutral*), pɒʔpjʊlə (*popular*), mæʔtrıs (*mattress*), rɛʔklɪs (*reckless*), pɛʔtrəl (*petrol*). This often gives the impression of a long stop on the p, t or k, i.e. njuˑttrəl, pɒppjʊlə, etc., but the glottal closure is almost always there in such pronunciations.

251. If the glottal stop is to be got rid of—and it certainly makes for indistinctness—teachers will have to wage vigorous war against it. It ought not to be difficult to eliminate, for the pupil *can* pronounce the correct consonant, and always does so in stressed positions; he says bʌʔə for *butter*, but never ʔɛn for *ten*. In actual practice, however, to get rid of the glottal stop is not easy. It is not a question of teaching a new sound, but of getting the pupil to remember to use a sound he already possesses, in unfamiliar positions, i.e. to lose an old habit and create a new one. Careful, slow reading in the first instance, paying particular attention to the articulation of the plosive consonants should make it possible for the pupil to cure himself.[1] The *over correction* of a glottal stop, however, i.e. the insistence of an off-glide to the t (e.g. sit[h] stɪl) is as unpleasant as the glottal stop itself. Where the glottal stop is inter-vocalic it is useful, as a preliminary step, to break up the words in this way: pʊ - - - tɪ - - - tɒn ðə teɪbl.

Affricative Consonants.

252. A plosive consonant can be pronounced with either quick or slow separation of the articulating organs. If a slow separation is made, there is no noticeable explosion, but on the release of the stop a fricative

---

[1] See Ch. II, § 28 for the technique of "slowing up," which could be used here to get rid of the glottal stop.

consonant is heard. Such a method of articulating plosives gives rise to what are called *affricative* consonants.

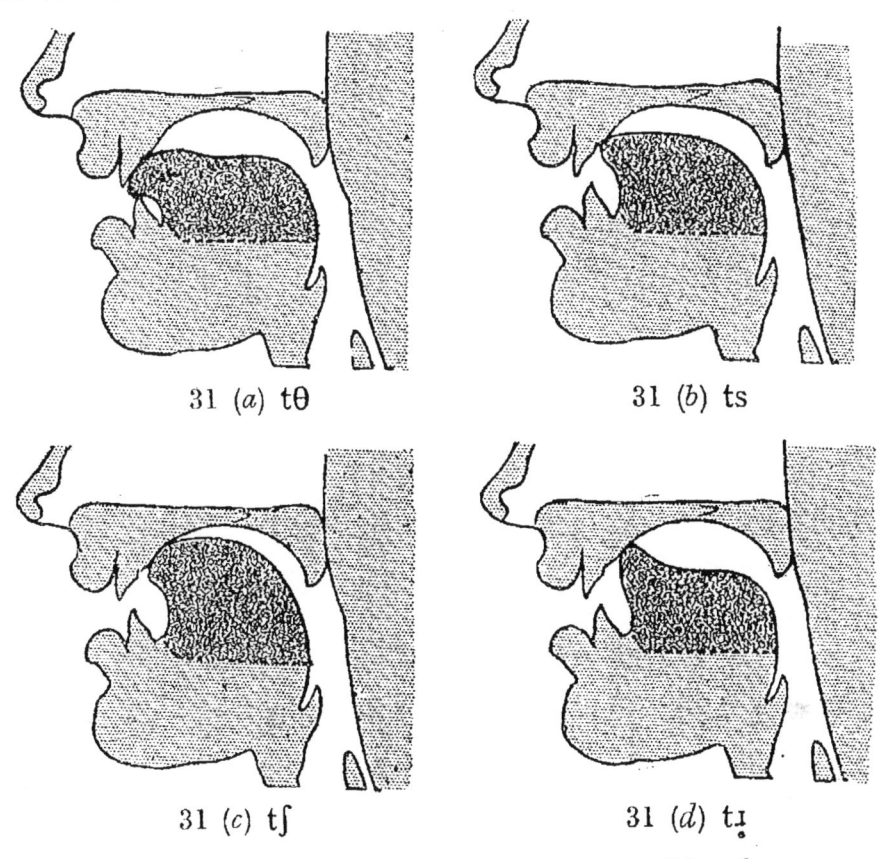

FIG. 31. Illustrating the starting position for tθ, ts, tʃ and tɹ̥.

253. An affricate is a plosive consonant in which the articulating organs are separated less quickly than in the case of normal plosives, with the result that the corresponding fricative is heard momentarily as the organs separate.

254. To every plosive a corresponding affricate can be made, and the student is recommended to try to pronounce as many as he can. In English, however,

those given on the table on p. 128 are the only ones that occur normally. E.g.

eighth, eɪtθ; *width*, wɪdθ; *eats*, iˑts; *beds*, bɛdz; *lunch*, lʌntʃ (alternative pronunciation lʌnʃ); *church*, tʃɜˑtʃ, *jump*, dʒʌmp; *German*, dʒɜˑmən; *bridge*, brɪdʒ. tɹ and dɹ, as in the words *tree* and *draw*, may also be considered affricatives, the t and d made in this case with the tip of the tongue slightly curled up in readiness for the ɹ. [See Fig. 31 (d)].

Nasal Consonants.

255. Nasal consonants are formed by closing the mouth passage at some point, and at the same time lowering the soft palate, so that the air can escape through the nose. In English there are normally three nasal consonants, m, n and ŋ.

256. The connection between nasal and plosive consonants can be seen by comparing the foregoing diagrams with those for p.b, t.d, k.g on p. 130, the difference being in the position of the soft palate, which is lowered for the nasal consonants and raised for the plosives. When for any reason—cold or adenoid growths—it is impossible for the breath to escape through the nose, something like the corresponding plosive is heard instead of the nasal consonant, e.g. *morning* (mɔːnɪŋ) is pronounced almost as bɔˑdɪg, a *strong man* (ə strɒŋ mæn) becomes almost ə strɒg bæd.

257. In the table on p. 128, the nasal consonants are given without their voiceless equivalents, m̥, n̥, ŋ̊. The student is recommended to practise these (see exercises in §77 d). They occur occasionally in words like *ahem, humph* (ʔm̥m, m̥mm̥), and in mm̥m (*yes*).

ENGLISH CONSONANTS IN DETAIL 139

258. The nasal consonants are often "syllabic," i.e. they form the most sonorous element of a syllable, e.g. mʌtn, hɛvn, iːvn, spoʊkn or spoʊkŋ, neɪʃn, prɪzm, oʊpm, klæpm, beɪkn or beɪkŋ. Some of these forms occur only in quick speech, oʊpən, beɪkən, klæpəm, etc., being a more careful form.

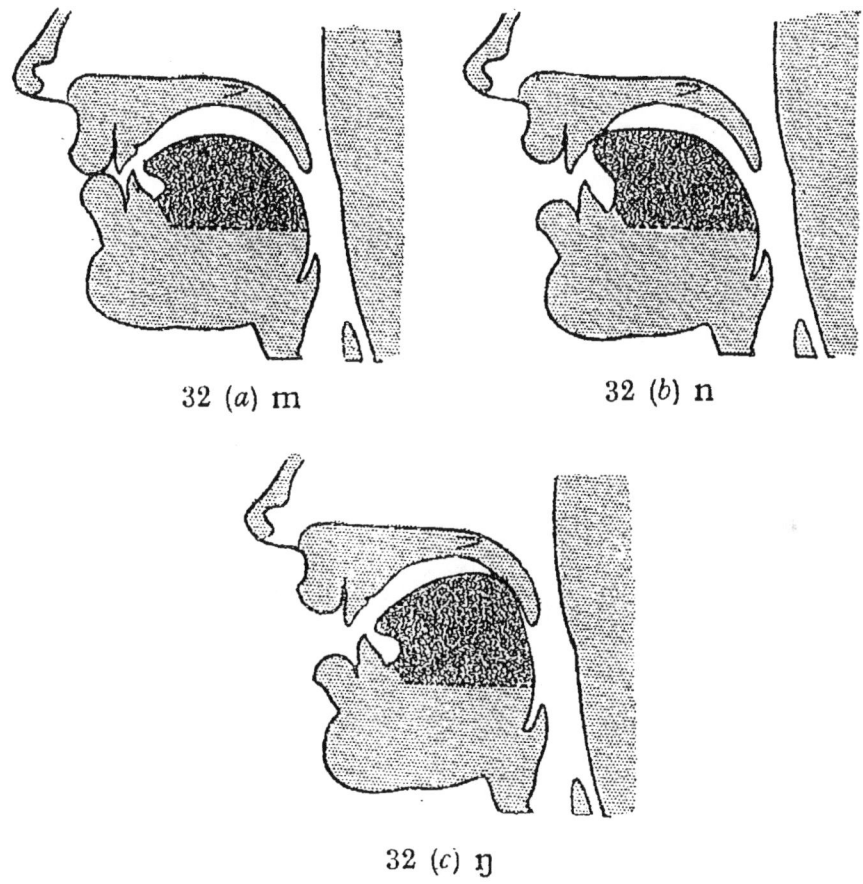

32 (a) m   32 (b) n

32 (c) ŋ

Fig. 32. Nasal Consonants.

259. The nasal consonants are extremely susceptible to the influence of other neighbouring sounds. For the changes which m, n, ŋ undergo, see the Chapter on Sounds in Connected Speech, §§ 335, 340—348.

140 THE PHONETICS OF ENGLISH

260. The letters *ng*, pronounced as ŋ in words like *singer*, *singing* (sɪŋə, sɪŋɪŋ) are pronounced ŋg (sɪŋgə, sɪŋgɪŋ) in the Midlands. Words like *longer*, *finger*, *single*, normally pronounced lɒŋgə, fɪŋgə, sɪŋgl, become lɒŋə, fɪŋə, sɪŋl in some parts of Scotland, Yorkshire and the North Midlands. In Cockney speech *nothing* and *anything* have by false analogy become nafɪŋk, ɛnɪfɪŋk, and *kitchen* has become kɪtʃɪŋ; maʊntɪŋ and faʊntɪŋ pɛn can also be heard. What is known as *"dropping one's g's"* is replacing ŋ by n, e.g. goʊɪn, teɪkɪn. This practice is very widespread and is not confined to dialect speakers only. (See Chapter on Spelling Pronunciations, § 65 (j).)

LATERAL CONSONANTS.

261. The English *l* is termed a lateral consonant because the air passage is stopped in the centre by the tip of the tongue against the teeth-ridge, the air escaping along one or both sides of the tongue.

262. In English there are two well-defined types of *l* sounds; in both, the main articulation is that described above, i.e. the tip of the tongue against the teeth-ridge.

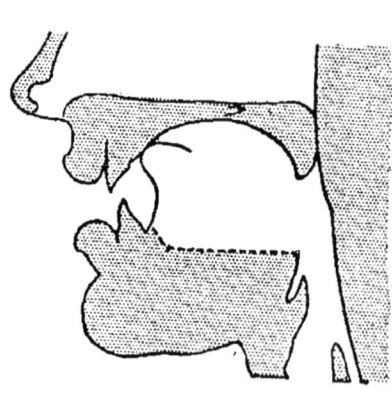

FIG. 33.
Primary Articulation of *l*.

263. They differ from each other in the position of the rest of the tongue. Where *l* occurs before vowels, the front of the tongue is raised towards the hard palate; when it occurs finally or before consonants, the front is slightly hollowed, and the back is raised towards the soft palate. The

ENGLISH CONSONANTS IN DETAIL 141

former is called "*clear l*," and the latter, which has a somewhat obscure quality, is called the "*dark l*." Some writers say that in "*dark l*" the contact of the tip of the tongue is further back than in "*clear l*." This *may* be so with individual speakers, but it is not *necessarily* so; the difference in quality is chiefly due to the difference in the position of the main body of the tongue, not in that of the tip. The terms "clear" and "dark" are descriptive of the accoustic effect of the sounds and not a technical or scientific name; the correct phonetic terms are "palatalised" and "velarised,"

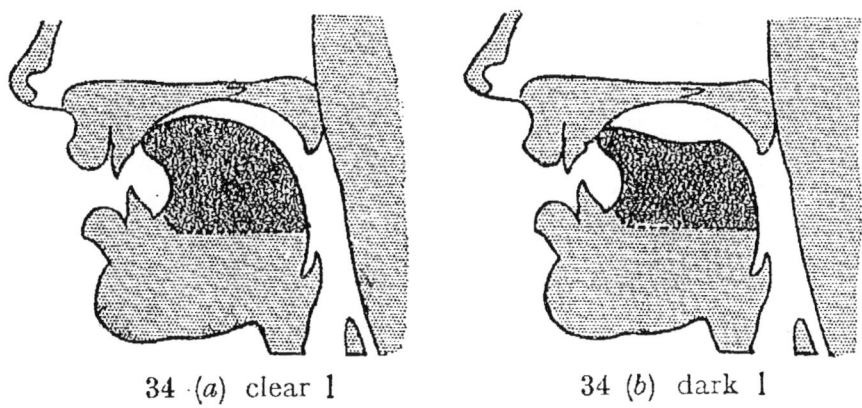

34 (a) clear l   34 (b) dark l

Fig. 34. Clear and Dark *l*.

i.e. palatalised means that the front of the tongue is raised towards the hard palate, velarised the back of the tongue raised towards the soft palate; in both cases this modification is a secondary articulation, the primary one being the tip of the tongue against the teeth ridge.

264. It is possible to make *l* which is the most sonorous of all the consonants with the resonance of any vowel. The English *clear l* has an ə resonance tending towards i, the *dark l* has an ʊ resonance. Many speakers use a kind of *mid l* instead of a *dark l*, i.e.

with an ɜ instead of an ʊ resonance. This is particularly noticeable in Northerners. Students should practise as a phonetic exercise, the making of *l* with the resonance of each Cardinal vowel in turn: lⁱ, lᵉ, lᵋ, lᵃ, lᵅ, lᵓ, lᵒ, lᵘ.

265. Like the nasal consonants m and n, l is often syllabic: e.g. lɪtl, ræbl, fɪkl, θɪmbl, etc. If it is required to mark l as syllabic, the symbol ļ is used, but it is unnecessary to use this symbol in a phonetic transcription, unless it is possible to make l either syllabic or non-syllabic: e.g. in bɒtl the l must be syllabic, while in bɒtlɪŋ it could be pronounced either bɒtlɪŋ (two syllables), or bɒt|ɪŋ (three syllables).

266. Voiceless *l* (ḷ) does not occur as a speech sound of normal English. It is the sound of Welsh *ll*, and as a speech defect, is one of the common substitutions for s.

267. In Ireland and some parts of the North of England, a *clear l* is used in all positions, teɪblⁱ, piːplⁱ, bɛl'z. In Scotland and in some types of American and West Country speech, *dark l* is often found initially ɫeɪt, ɫɒŋ.¹ In London dialect, the *dark l*, instead of having an ʊ resonance, has that of o or ɔ, i.e. the vowel quality is that of a lower and more retracted vowel than ʊ. With this drawing back of the back of the tongue, there is a tendency for the tip to leave the teeth ridge; in such cases *l* is replaced by a vowel. E.g.

 milk is pronounced mɪlᵒk (with a very dark *l*) or mɪɔk
 while ,, waːlᵓ or waːɔ, (with no l),

¹ I have been told by a competent authority that *clear l* occurs in Galloway, even finally.

ENGLISH CONSONANTS IN DETAIL

Bill is pronounced bɪɔ or bɪo,
sale ,, sɛɪɔ or sɛɪo.

268. The "*dark* 1" has a marked influence on vowel sounds which precede it. This is especially noticeable in London speech, and teachers should be aware of this fact, for often what is considered an incorrect vowel sound is due, not to inability to say a correct vowel, but to the influence of too dark an *l*, and if the 1 is put right, the vowel is generally easy to correct. This point is noted in Chapter XI under the head-

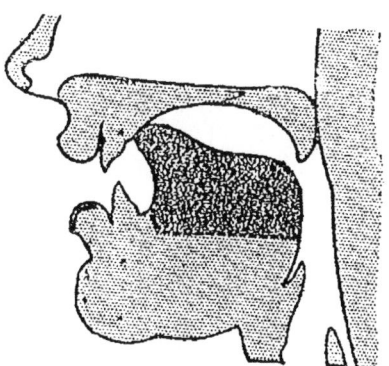

FIG. 35. Over-dark 1.

ings of the particular vowels. To correct the over dark 1, it is essential, in the first place, to insist on a firm contact with the tip of the tongue. Then tell the pupil to try and say 1 and ʊ at the same time; this should give the correct resonance for normal dark 1; it may, however, be necessary to exaggerate a little towards a more clear 1, i.e. to say 1 with an ɜ resonance, or to aim at something approaching the pupil's sound of 1, which he uses before vowels. When the "over-dark" 1 is corrected, then comes the teaching of the use of it after vowels, so that the vowel quality is not too much altered. It is well to separate vowel and consonant, e.g. bɛ.., 1, fi...1, as a first stage, insisting on the correct pronunciation of both. Then the pupil can gradually reduce the pause between the two.

Rolled Sounds.

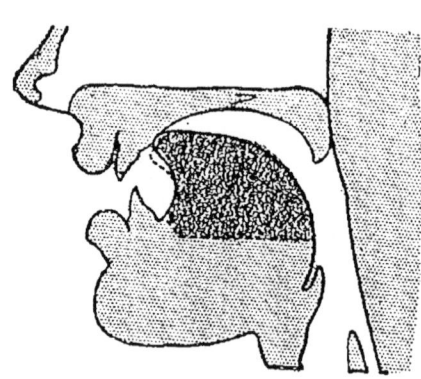

Fig. 36. Rolled *r*.

269. The rolled r is made by a rapid succession of taps of the tongue-tip against the teeth-ridge.

270. This sound is not common in Southern English, the letter *r* being more usually pronounced as a fricative consonant. In many parts of the country, *r* is not pronounced finally, e.g. hɜː, ðɛə, or before consonants, hɑːd, gɜːl.

271. **Different Kinds of *r* Sounds.**

i. The rolled *r* described above is used in Scotland in all positions, even before consonants and finally, e.g. hɑrd, gɛrl or gʌrl. In North Yorks., where it is used after *t* and *d,* the *t* and *d* are dental, truː, draɪ. (To roll an *r* after an alveolar consonant is very difficult for English people.)

ii. A semi-rolled or one-tap *r* (special symbol ɾ), consisting of one tap of the tongue, is commonly used between voiced sounds, e.g. vɛɾɪ, kwɒɾl and frequently after the pre-dental fricatives, θ and ð, e.g. θɾuː, brɛðɾɪn.

iii. A fricative *r* (special symbol ɹ) is used in many parts of the country in positions where an *r* is sounded at all. It is the usual *initial r* in all parts of the country except Scotland.

ENGLISH CONSONANTS IN DETAIL

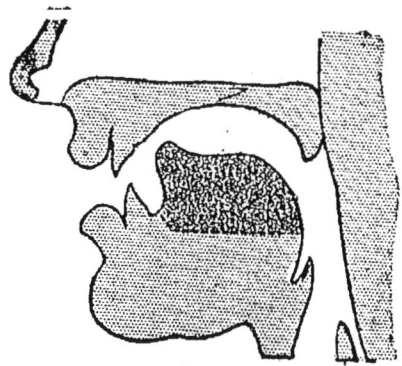

Fig. 37. Fricative *r*.

iv. An "inverted" *r*, i.e. a fricative made with the tongue-tip curled up considerably, is used finally and before consonants in many parts of the West Country (N. and S.), in the South as far east as Surrey, and in Ireland and America (hɑɹd, gɜɹl). It is heard in the pronunciation of many educated speakers in these districts. The inversion of the tip of the tongue may, and often does, take place while the preceding vowel is being pronounced, so that the vowel quality is affected. If the space between the tip of the tongue and the palate is not narrow enough to justify the sound being called a consonant, the effect of the inversion can still be heard in the vowel. Recent experiments carried out in a Phonetics Laboratory prove that in some American speech, what sounds like an inverted *r* is in reality not a consonant at all—i.e. the space between the tongue and the roof of the mouth is too wide to allow any friction—but a vowel made with the tip of the tongue slightly curled up.[1]

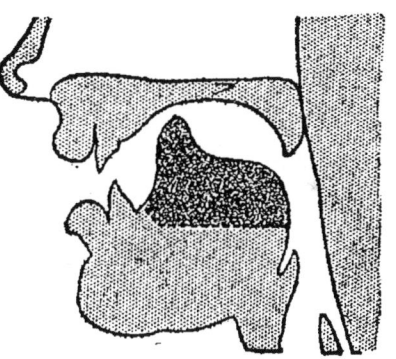

Fig. 38. Inverted *r*.

---

[1] See Kenyon, *American Pronunciation*, p. 63, § 87.

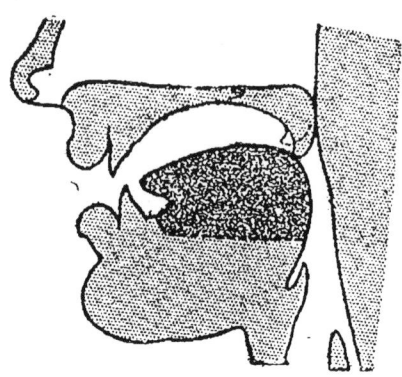

Fig. 39. Uvular Rolled *r*.

v. In Northumberland and Durham a uvular variety of *r* is heard: this is formed either by the vibration of the uvula against the back of the tongue (special symbol ʀ), or by a narrowing between the back of the tongue and the uvula (special symbol ʁ): e.g. dɒʀəm or dɒʁəm (for dʌrəm, *Durham*).

272. Those students who cannot roll an r should practise the following exercise. Pronounce tədɑtədɑ, the t articulated against the *teeth* and the d against the *teeth ridge*. When these sounds are said very quickly, a one-tap r takes the place of d. This can be developed gradually into a fully rolled r; but a rolled r is not easy to acquire and takes long and patient practice.

"Linking r."

273. When *r* in spelling occurs at the end of a word or phrase, it is generally not pronounced in Southern English: e.g. gɪv mi səm mɔə, hɪə nɒt ðɛə. But when such a word is followed by another word in close connection with it, beginning with a vowel, the r is introduced by many speakers.

E.g. gɪv mi səm mɔər əv ɪt.
hɪər ən ðɛə.

Westminster is pronounced wɛstmɪnstə, but wɛstmɪnstər æbɪ is often heard. (Some people insert a glottal stop

ENGLISH CONSONANTS IN DETAIL

instead of r in such combinations, wɛstmɪnstə ʔæbɪ.) The linking r is generally omitted when the syllable begins as well as ends with an r:

E.g. nɪərə ənd nɪərə, not nɪərər ənd nɪərə.[1]

"Intrusive r."

274. An "*intrusive* r" where none exists in spelling is very frequently inserted between two words, the one ending and the next beginning with a vowel, in order to avoid what is felt to be an awkward hiatus. This is partly due to a false analogy with the linking r: compare aɪ v nou fɪər əv ɪt and aɪ v nou aɪdɪər əv ɪt. It is in this phrase, "*the idea of it*," and other similar ones, that the intrusive r shows itself most frequently; this pronunciation is heard among educated speakers who are quite unaware that they use it, and who would be horrified to learn it. I have heard from the pulpit or the stage:

nɔər ənd hɪz fæmɪlɪ.
ɪz sɪlvɪər ət houm.
put ə kɒmər aˑftər ɪt.

There is no doubt that the intrusive r is spreading; even in districts and among classes where it has not been known, the younger generation is using it. In Cockney speech the phrase "*I saw it*" is often pronounced aɪ sɔər ɪt or aɪ sɔːr ɪt. In this context, however, note that the preceding vowel is ɔː not ə, and in such a position intrusive r would not be used by the educated speaker.

---

[1] I heard recently on the radio, however, ðɪ ɛərɪər əv ɪt (*the area of it*), where intrusive r in this position was used.

FRICATIVE CONSONANTS.

275. Fricative consonants are formed by narrowing the mouth passage at some point, so that the air, forcing its way through, makes a rubbing sound. It is possible to make fricative consonants with the same articulating organs as the plosives; a glance at the table on p. 128 will show that there are more fricatives than plosives in English

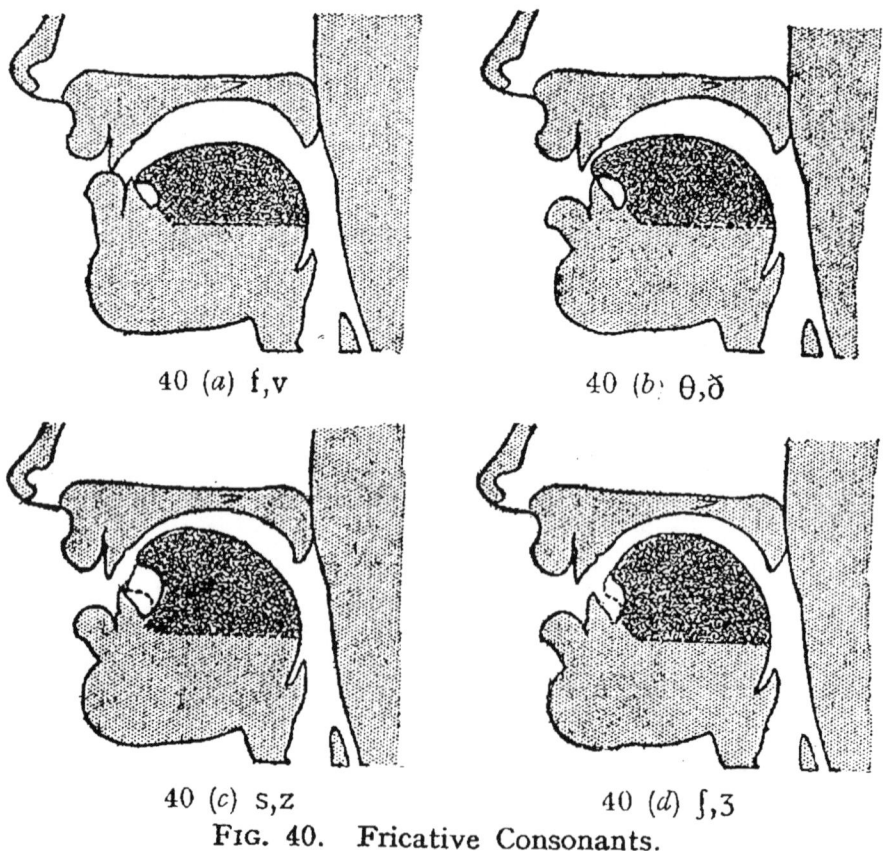

40 (a) f,v 40 (b) θ,ð

40 (c) s,z 40 (d) ʃ,ʒ

FIG. 40. Fricative Consonants.

276. In the voiced consonants of this class it is sometimes difficult to recognise their fricative character; this is due to the fact that less breath force is used than

ENGLISH CONSONANTS IN DETAIL

for the voiceless fricatives, and that the passage is not very narrow, hence there may be no audible friction.

277. The English fricative consonants are:
f, v; θ, ð; s, z; ʃ, ʒ; ɹ; h.

278. NOTES ON THE FRICATIVE CONSONANTS.

i. In Somerset, initial voiceless fricatives are replaced by voiced fricatives: e.g. vʊt, ðɪŋ, zʌm.

ii. The v of *of* (ɒv) often disappears in London and other dialects in familiar phrases such as ə glɑˑs ə bɪə, ə pɛər ə glʌvz.

iii. In Scotland and parts of N. England, *with* (wɪð) and *though* (ðoʊ) are pronounced wɪθ, θoʊ.

iv. In London dialect θ and ð are replaced by f and v, friː (θriː), ˌmʌvə (mʌðə); θ is sometimes replaced by t in *months*—mʌnts (mʌnθs).

v. There is a tendency even among educated speakers to drop θ and ð in quick speech, when followed by s or z: e.g. kloʊz (kloʊðz), sɪkss (sɪksθs), mʌns (mʌnθs).

vi. h is a glottal fricative, i.e. the air passes through the glottis, and slight friction occurs between the open vocal cords. A further element in its articulation is the sudden expulsion of the air from the lungs, and frequently some friction can be heard in the mouth after the sudden "jerk." h varies according to the vowel which follows it, i.e.

for the word hard (hɑːd), the tongue is in the position of ɑː while the h is being pronounced, for hʊd it is in the position of ʊ, for hiːd in the position of iː: i.e. the h in these words is similar to the unvoiced vowels (а̥, u̥, i̥.) h can be voiced (phonetic symbol ɦ). Many people use a voiced *h* between two vowels: e.g. əɦɑː (*ahɑ!*), pəɦæps, ə ɦaʊs. This sometimes sounds as if the h were dropped. Voiced *h* is used more by men than by women.

vii. "*Dropping one's h's* has been looked upon as a sign of lack of education, and the *h* is being re-introduced under the influence of spelling even in local dialects where it had quite disappeared. In words like *he, his, her, have*, occurring in unstressed positions, however, the " *h* " is actually dropped in conversational speech by educated people. For instance, no one would pronounce all the *h's* in *he put his hat on his head*, hi pʊt hɪs hæt ɒn hɪz hɛd; *I should have thought so* becomes aɪ ʃʊd əv θɔːt soʊ. In slow deliberate speech, however, the *h's* are generally pronounced even in unstressed unimportant words.

viii. "Intrusive *h*." The pronunciation of *h* where there is no *h* in the spelling is perhaps not so frequent among the younger generation even of semi-educated or dialect speakers as it used to be and as it still is among older people in some parts of the country. Such use is due to lack of knowledge of the *distribution* of this sound and occurs mostly in those areas where the true dialect does not possess an *h*.

ENGLISH CONSONANTS IN DETAIL 151

SEMI-VOWELS OR VOWEL GLIDES.

279. A semi-vowel may be defined as a gliding sound in which the tongue starts in the position of a close or half-close vowel and immediately leaves that position to take up one belonging to a more open vowel. There are two semi-vowels in English, w and j.

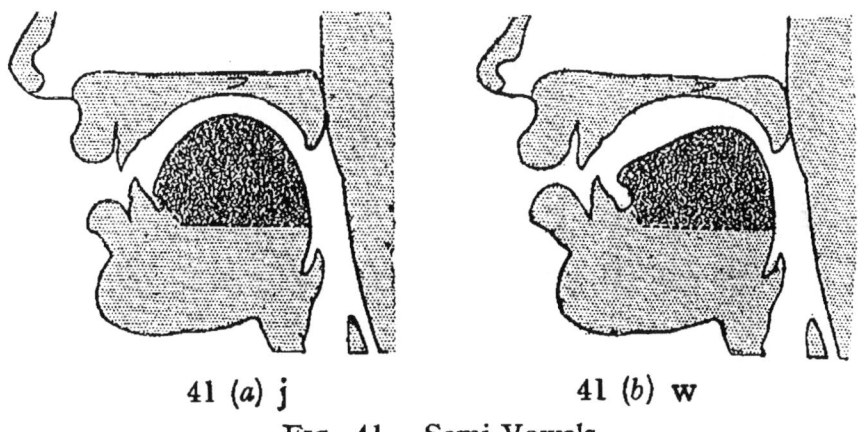

41 (a) j   41 (b) w
FIG. 41. Semi-Vowels.

280. w has a double articulation; the primary formation is that the lips are rounded and pushed forward; at the same time the back of the tongue is raised towards the u position.

281. Voiceless w (phonetic symbol ʍ) is used by many people who distinguish w from wh in words like *witch* and *which*. Another method of pronouncing wh is to prefix h, i.e. hw. In Scotland and many parts of the North this distinction is regularly made, and by individual speakers in all parts of the country. Professor Wyld states that wɛn, wɒt, etc., have been established in S. English for hundreds of years, and says that the pronunciations ʍɛn, ʍɒt, are spelling pronunciations. (See Chapter VII, § 65 i.)

282. For the semi-vowel j the front of the tongue is raised towards the hard palate, and immediately leaves this position to take up that of the vowel which follows it. The voiceless glide corresponding to j is often heard in the pronunciation of words like *human, huge, Hugh*, which are pronounced çuˑmən, çuːʤ, çuː; instead of hjuˑmən, hjuˑʤ, hjuː. The acoustic difference between these two pronunciations is very slight: in the former the fricative element is heard more strongly. Note that in the word *ear* (iə) and other words with the group iə, some people use jɜː; thus *ear* may be jɜː, and *hear* and *here* are pronounced hjɜː by many people.

SUMMARY OF THE MAIN DIFFERENCES BETWEEN NORTHERN SPEECH AND SOUTHERN ENGLISH AND BETWEEN LONDON PRONUNCIATION AND STANDARD ENGLISH.

283. In this brief summary the main differences between these two types of speech and a more general standard are indicated. Most of the points will be found in the chapters immediately preceding, together with hints for the teaching of the recognised standard sounds. It is not the broadest dialect pronunciations that are noted here, but the slighter differences occurring in the speech of those who still show regional influences, which are not so easy to detect and which are even more difficult to correct. Many of the observations made on Northern speech apply to the Midlands and to the West, but the present writer is not competent to sum up the chief characteristics of these areas so well as those of the North and of London with which she is familiar.

ENGLISH CONSONANTS IN DETAIL

284. *Northern Pronunciation.*

(i) *Vowels.*

ɛ and æ : Very open ; æ is replaced by a.

ɑ : Not used in certain words where Southerners use it ; a takes its place. Not very important to attempt to alter this unless the speaker definitely wants to adopt a Southern pronunciation.

ʌ : Replaced by a vowel between ʊ and ʌ or by a central vowel near to ɜ (but short).

ɜː and ɛə : Confused in South Lancashire and Cheshire ; a sound between the two is used for both.

eɪ, oʊ : Pure vowels e and o[1] are used instead of these, often long eː, oː, or for oʊ a wider diphthong (ɔʊ : nɔʊ for *know*).

The diphthongs ɪə, ɛə, ɔə, ʊə are wider than in Southern English ; there is considerably more tongue movement. Similarly in aɪə, aʊə all the elements are heard. This is not important ; indeed, it is good, if they are not slowed up too much and the first element not too long.

(ii) *Consonants.*

Use of the glottal stop before alveolar consonants and finally; nɒʔ raɪʔ for *not right*.

In the Midlands ŋg is used for ŋ in words like *singer*, sɪŋgə.

---

[1] The pure vowel replacing eɪ is not that which is noted as coming into use in Southern English pronunciation, but a closer type. (See Ch. XII, §§195-6.)

h is frequently dropped in Yorkshire (except in the North Riding) and in Lancashire.

r: The Northumberland "burr" is the use of uvular r.

(iii) *Other characteristics.*

The speech is often rather slow and gives the impression of lack of precision.[1] Unimportant words and syllables frequently have "strong" forms which sound as if they are stressed, and with this characteristic, the rhythm changes. Voice quality is often different; some Northern voices are hard and metallic or lacking in resonance in some way; this sounds to be the result of pharyngal contraction and of forcing. For the main differences in intonation see §§ 319—20.

285. *London Pronunciation.*

(i) *Vowels.*

ε and æ: Closer than standard.

ɔ: Very close, tending to o.

u: Centralised. Even in the less broad Cockney this tendency is strongly marked.

eɪ: Low starting point of the diphthong, approaching ε.

ai: Not unlike modern educated Southern English, but is frequently drawled and nasalised.

oʊ: Open starting point, ɔ or ʌ.

---

[1] This in Lancashire in spite of a considerable amount of jaw movement.

ENGLISH CONSONANTS IN DETAIL 155

aʊ : Too forward a starting point, approaching æ.

In the type of speech considered here there is little nasalisation but sometimes undue lengthening of vowels and diphthongs.

(ii) *Consonants.*

Use of the glottal stop in many positions, including intervocalic.

"Intrusive" r is common, often after the vowel ɔ: aɪ sɔːr ɪt (*I saw it*).

Over dark l is common and is especially noticeable after the diphthongs eɪ and aɪ. Note that it affects vowel quality to a considerable degree: eɪl is pronounced ɛəl and aɪl is pronounced ɑːl: affricated t's and d's in stressed positions.

(iii) *Other characteristics.*[1]

Voice is frequently produced with contraction of the pharynx and is often "husky," with little resonance; it tends also to be adenoidal. Drawling somewhat affects rhythm and to a certain extent intonation patterns.

---

[1] See §§ 319-20, p. 177, for notes on the main differences between Northern and Southern speech in intonation.

Chapter XV.

SOUND ATTRIBUTES: LENGTH, STRESS, INTONATION.

286. When one hears English spoken or read aloud, one realises that a number of words or syllables stand out from the rest of the sentence. This standing out may be termed *prominence*. Recent investigations go to show that the effect of prominence is produced by the very intimate combination of length, stress, pitch, and inherent sonority of sounds, i.e. a sound or syllable has prominence when it stands out from its neighbours because (1) it is more sonorous, (2) it is longer, (3) it is louder, because of greater breath force, or (4) it has a different pitch. It is often extremely difficult to disentangle these elements and to say which is most important: the general effect of *accent* is often due to a combination of two or more of them.

287. An attempt is made here to show the recurrence of the prominent syllables in a number of sentences and to analyse what constitutes this prominence. The mark ˈ (the conventional stress mark) is used to denote prominence, while ˈˈ shows *special* prominence or extra emphasis. The notation to indicate intonation [1] is as follows:—Lines denote prominent,

---

[1] This is the notation used in *A Handbook of English Intonation*, by Armstrong and Ward.

156

SOUND ATTRIBUTES

and dots non-prominent syllables; a straight line ‾ shows that the pitch of the syllable so marked is level, and ＼ and ／ that the pitch in these syllables falls or rises respectively.[1]

288. The intonation[2] of the sentences should be very carefully studied first. In the majority of the sentences, one typical intonation has been given; there may, of course, be others; there certainly would be other varieties if emphasis were intended and *special* prominence given to one part of the sentence.

(1) ˈgɪv ɪt tə ˈˈhɜː.

(2) ˈdɪd jʊ ˈgɪv ɪt tə hɜ.

(3) ˈðæt s wɒt aɪ ˈsɔː.

(4) aɪ sɔ ˈnʌθɪŋ əv ðəm.

(5) ˈwɛər əv jʊ ˈbiːn?

(6) aɪ v bin tə ˈtaʊn.

(7) ˈwɒt ə jʊ ˈgoɪŋ tə ˈduː əbaʊt ɪt?

(8) ˈwɒt djʊ ˈwɒnt?

    ˈwɒt dəjʊ ˈwɒnt?

    ˈwɒt dʊ jʊ ˈwɒnt?

(9) aɪ d noʊ aɪˈˈdɪə jʊ wər ɛnɪwɛə nɪə ˈˈhɪə.

---

[1] If a non-prominent syllable rises, as sometimes happens, it must also be indicated by ／, as it would be impossible to show a rise by a dot.

[2] See later §§ 301–18 for a summary of the intonation patterns of English.

(10) aɪ ˈdaʊnt maɪnd kənˈfɛsɪŋ ˈˈmaɪ ʃɛər ɪn ðə mætə. ‾ ·· — . ↘ ....

(11) aɪ ˈwɪʃ hi ˈˈwʊd. · ‾ ·⌒ or ·↘·⌒

(12) ˈwɒt wʊd jʊ əv ˈsɛd tə ˈðæt? ‾ ··· — . ↘

289. Examine the sentences from these aspects—the intonation of the prominent syllables, the breath force used in saying them, and the length and quality of the vowels used in them.

(1) It will be seen that the prominent syllables all have a different pitch from that of the neighbouring prominent syllables. Alter the pitch of these syllables and note the effect. E.g.

(a) ˈwɛər əv jʊ ˈbiːn?   ‾ ·· ↘   *where* and *been* are prominent.

(b) ˈwɛər əv ˈjuː bin?   ‾ · ↘.   *where* and *you* are prominent

(c) ˈwɛər əv jʊ bin?   ↘ .. ↗   *where* only is prominent

(d) wɛə ˈhæv jʊ ˈbin?   · — · ↘   *have* and *been* are prominent

(2) Try to say all these sentences with varying intonations, with as *even* breath force as possible. It will be noticed that the lack of strong breath force does not affect the general result: the right effect is produced by the intonation. This seems to prove that pitch is an essential part of prominence. In fact if these sentences are pronounced with extra breath force on

the *non-prominent* syllables, so long as the typical intonation is preserved, there is very little change in meaning. If, for instance, one pronounces *Heroes and Hero Worship* (ˈhɪərouz ənd ˈhɪərou wɜˈʃɪp) with the intonation ‾ ·· \\ ..., it matters little if one puts extra breath force on wɜˈʃɪp (‾ ·· \\ . __ .) so long as the same " tune " is kept.

(3) Although, as has just been stated, the right effect of prominence *can* be obtained without extra breath force if the intonation is right, this is not the normal usage and such effect is not dependent wholly upon intonation. All the syllables of a sentence are not pronounced with the same amount of breath, and those which are most important are pronounced generally with more breath force than the others. Thus stress or breath force seems to be a component part of prominence. It is customary in dictionaries to mark the stress of individual words of more than one syllable, and in phonetic texts to mark what is called sentence stress. The sentences given as examples should be said quite naturally and the breath force noted; the strongest force will generally be found to fall on the syllables marked as stressed.

(4) Now note the length of the vowels in the prominent syllables. In the sentences ˈgɪv ɪt tə ˈˈhɜː and ˈdɪd jʊ ˈgɪv ɪt tʊ hɜ? the word *her* occurs twice, both times at the end of the sentence. The vowel in the first *her* is much longer than in the second. In the sentences ˈwɛər əv jʊ ˈbiːn and aɪ v bin tə ˈtaʊn note the difference in the length of the vowel in the two words *been*. In ˈwɒt ə jʊ ˈgoɪŋ tə ˈduː əbaʊt ɪt?

and ˈwɒt djʊ ˈwɒnt? note the words *do*: in the first, the vowel is long; in the second, the vowel has disappeared and the word consists of d. In aɪ ˈdoʊnt maɪnd kənˈfɛsɪŋ ˈˈmaɪ ʃɛər ɪn ðə mætə, compare the length of the diphthong aɪ in *mind* and the extra prominent word *my*. Compare the diphthong ɪə in *near* and *here*, in the sentence aɪ d ˈnoʊ aɪˈdɪə jʊ wər ˈɛnɪwɛə nɪə ˈhɪə. In the sentences aɪ ˈˈwɪʃ hi ˈˈwʊd and ˈwɒt wʊd jʊ əv ˈsɛd tə ˈðæt? compare the two words *would*. These examples show that vowel sounds in the prominent syllables are generally longer than those in non-prominent syllables.

(5) In English speech there is a well-established tendency for the vowel sounds in non-prominent syllables to be some kind of neutral vowel. Examine, in the sentences given, some of the words which are used in both prominent and non-prominent syllables e.g. the vowel in *do* in sentence No. 7 has its full value u, whereas in No. 8 it is reduced to dʊ, də or d. In sentence No. 5 pronounced with *have* prominent, wɛə ˈhæv jʊ ˈbiːn? the word has its strong vowel æ, whereas in ˈwɛər əv jʊ ˈbiːn? it is reduced to əv. Note in sentence No. 10 the word *confessing* (kənˈfɛsɪŋ). If the first syllable *con* is pronounced kɒn, the strong vowel ɒ gives the impression of prominence. The present writer has heard people, in criticising Northern speech, say that northern speakers stress the first syllable in words like *confess, success* instead of the second. This is not true, i.e. they do not use noticeably more breath force on the first syllable than on the second, but the pronunciation kɒnˈfɛs, sʌkˈsɛs, instead of kənˈfɛs, səkˈsɛs, gives the *impression* of stress on the

first syllable, i.e. the use of the strong vowel adds prominence. This seems to prove that vowel quality plays some part in prominence.

290. These examples illustrate briefly that prominence is produced by a combination of certain elements of speech, viz. pitch, stress, length and vowel quality. Which is most important it is difficult to say. The conventional method of marking breath force or stress seems to answer well, especially for English people studying their own language, as, with additional breath force, they naturally alter the pitch, lengthen the vowel and consonant sounds, and use " strong " vowels.

291. In considering English speech as a series of "peaks" of prominence separated by "valleys," it is perhaps useful to associate the positive elements of outstanding stress and pitch as contributing to the "peaks," and the negative weakening and shortening of vowels as contributing to the "valleys." If the syllables normally occurring in the "valleys" are made stronger or longer, the valleys are raised somewhat and the difference between them and the peaks is smaller, i.e. the elements we may consider as subordinate are given undue prominence; this in its turn detracts from the importance of those words and syllables which normally stand out, i.e. the "undulations" are less steep. The teacher should be fully aware of this, lest he insist on an undue strength being given to unimportant elements. (See further, § 326–8, p. 183.)

292. Length, stress and intonation are generally called *sound attributes*. The teacher of English should be able to make his own observations on these elements

of speech. For convenience, the main rules governing their use are summed up here.

293. *Length.*—(1) All vowels can be pronounced long or short: the vowels i, ɑ, ɔ, u, ɜ, however, under similar circumstances of stress and surrounding sounds are longer than the remaining vowels, ɪ, ɛ, æ, ɒ, ʊ, ʌ, ə. It is customary to mark length only in the case of the long vowels i, ɑ, ɔ, u, ɜ in phonetic transcriptions, because the varying degrees of length are difficult to detect in the short vowels. The vowels æ and ɛ in the pronunciation of some people may be considered long, especially in a few odd words: e.g. æ in *bad* is often pronounced long, bæːd, and ɛ in *yes* pronounced in a hesitating fashion is long jɛːs.[1] Diphthongs are generally considered long, though these also vary according to the surrounding sounds and the stress. (See Sentences 9 and 10 in § 288.)

(2) Several degrees of length can be noted by the trained observer; it is necessary, however, to show only three degrees, viz. short, half-long and long. (Long vowels are marked with ː, and half-long vowels with · following them.)

(3) As has been shown above in §289 (4), vowels are generally longer when stressed than when unstressed.

(4) A vowel in a final position is longer than in a non-final position: e.g. ˈwɒt dɪd jʊ ˈsiː?; aɪ ˈsi· jɔər ˈpɔɪnt; ɪt ˈɪznt ˈfɑː; ɪt s ˈnɒt ˈfɑ·r əˈweɪ; ˈðæt s wɒt aɪ ˈsɔː; aɪ ˈsɔ· hɪm ˈjɛstədɪ; ɪt s ˈkwaɪt ˈnjuː; aɪ ˈnju· hɪm ət ˈwʌns.

See Ch. XVII, p. 199 for modern tendencies in this respect.

SOUND ATTRIBUTES

(5) Vowels are longer when followed by a voiced consonant than when followed by a voiceless consonant.

In	liːv	the vowel	i	is longer than in				liˑf.
,,	hɑːv	,, ,,	ɑ	,,	,,	,,	,,	hɑˑf.
,,	nɔːd	,, ,,	ɔ	,,	,,	,,	,,	nɔˑt.
,,	ruːd	,, ,,	u	,,	,,	,,	,,	ruˑt.
,,	hɜːd	,, ,,	ɜ	,,	,,	,,	,,	hɜˑt.
,,	meɪd	,, diphthong	eɪ	,,	,,	,,	,.	meɪt.
,,	goʊd	,, ,,	oʊ	,,	,,	,,	,,	goʊt.
,,	laɪv	,, ,,	aɪ	,,	,,	,,	,,	laɪf.
,,	maʊð	,, ,,	aʊ	,,	,,	,,	,,	maʊθ.
,,	bɪd	,, vowel	ɪ	,,	,,	,,	,,	bɪt.
,,	bɛd	,, ,,	ɛ	,,	,,	,,	,,	bɛt.
,,	bæd	,, ,,	æ	,,	,,	,,	,,	bæt.
,,	bʌd	,, ,,	ʌ	,,	,,	,,	,,	bʌt.

Note also that ɜ is longer in bɜːnd than in bɜˑnt, and oʊ is longer in boʊld than in boʊlt.

(6) The oʊ in goʊ is longer than in goʊɪŋ (often pronounced, and therefore written, gɔɪŋ), the i in biːn is longer than in biɪŋ, i.e. when a vowel or diphthong is immediately followed by another vowel, it is shortened somewhat. The ɜ in bɜːn is longer than in bɜˑnɪŋ, the ɔ in mɔːn is longer than in mɔˑnɪŋ, i.e. when the syllable in which a long vowel or diphthong occurs is followed by one or more unstressed syllables, the vowel becomes shorter. This is illustrated also in (4).

(7) Consonants may be pronounced short or long. They are longer when preceded by a short vowel than when preceded by a long vowel, e.g.

In bɪn the final consonant is longer than in biːn.

,, fɪl ,, ,, ,, ,, ,, ,, ,, fiːl.

Note also that:

In bɜːnd the n is longer than in bɜˑnt.
„ fɛld „ l „ „ „ „ fɛlt.

(8) Consonants are often lengthened for the sake of emphasis, e.g.

hiːz ə ⁞nnɔˑtɪ ˈbɔɪ.
ɪt s ⁞ʔɔːffɫɪ ˈgʊd əv jʊ.
aɪ ʃl ⁞nnɛvə ˈdu ɪt.
ɪt s ə⁞vvɛrɪ ˈlɒŋˈwɛɪ.
ðə wəz ə trɪ⁞mmɛndəs ˈbʌsl.

Note.—There are individual speakers who habitually lengthen most of their consonants in initial positions in prominent words, e.g. ɪt wəz ttʌtʃ ən ggoʊ, haʊ ffʌnɪ, etc. This gives rather a deliberate effect to the speech. Some Northern and Midland speakers pronounce a long *t* in the numbers ɛɪtɪ, ɛɪtiːn (ɛɪttɪ, ɛɪttiːn or ɛɪʔtɪ, ɛɪʔtiːn).

294. The teacher should make himself aware of differences in length, for he may find among his pupils some who do not observe these usages, and who thus have a pronunciation which is not normal. An undue lengthening of the vowels and diphthongs gives rise to what is usually termed " drawling," and a drawling pronunciation lacks precision and vigour. It is often accompanied by a gliding or " portamento " intonation: e.g. nö - - - ʊ. Cockney pronunciation is known by its drawled vowels and diphthongs: e.g. nã - - - ɪs, sə - - - i, gɪv ɪt tə mə - - i ; and this habit is found in other parts of the country: e.g. Yorks. ha - - - ʊs, la - - - ɪk, ˈdʊu jə ˈla - - - ɪk ɪt? a ˈdoˑnt ˈnɔ - - - ʊ.

295. Such drawling speech can be improved by making the pupil move quickly to the second element of the diphthong; he may even, with advantage, exaggerate the second element, as a stage in working to the right length: e.g. nai - - - s, hau - - s, plei - - -.

296. *Stress.*—Every word of more than one syllable has its own *word stress*: e.g. ˈcountry, aˈbroad, emˈphatically, recoˈllect,[1] etc., but when words are combined into sentences, the word stress is often modified under the influence of sentence stress. This depends chiefly on the relative importance of the words in a sentence, and also on rhythm. It is impossible to do more than give a few examples of sentence stress here. English students, with practice, will be able to analyse their own speech from this point of view. Teachers will find it a useful exercise and of considerable help in the teaching of reading and recitation. Children like to find out the stress of new words; and the correct pronunciation of words which are commonly wrongly stressed become a matter of interest: e.g. ˈlamentable, ˈvehement, etc., ˈlæməntəbl, ˈvɪəmənt.

297. Certain English words differ in meaning according to stress: in some, the change in stress alters the vowels (see Chapter XVI, §§ 324–7), others differ in stress and to a slight extent in vowel length, e.g.

ˈincrease	ˈɪnkriˑs	inˈcrease	ɪnˈkriːs
ˈcompact	ˈkɒmpækt	comˈpact	kəmˈpækt
ˈconduct	ˈkɒndʌkt	conˈduct	kənˈdʌkt
ˈsubject	ˈsʌbdʒɪkt	subˈject	səbˈdʒekt

[1] In some long words another syllable bears considerable stress, and is said to have secondary stress, e.g. pɪˌkjulɪˈærɪtɪ aˌbɒmɪˈneɪʃn.

298. The following observations on sentence stress, with examples, should be sufficient to put the student on the right lines to analyse his own stress. Word stress is marked in any good dictionary.

(a) In an ordinary statement, the most important words of the sentence are stressed, viz. nouns, principal verbs, adjectives, demonstrative and interrogative pronouns, and adverbs, e.g.

> He 'told his 'story 'quickly and with 'great en'joyment.
> They 'called to 'see him 'early in the 'day.
> 'Where are you 'going?
> 'This won't 'do.
> 'How do you 'like my 'new 'hat?

(b) Where it is desired to emphasize one idea above others in a sentence, the word expressing that idea receives an extra amount of stress, and the surrounding words lose a good deal of their stress.

> I 'don't know 'what he 'wants. (Normal stress.)
>
> ''I don't know what he wants. (Implying someone else may know.)
>
> I 'don't know ''what he wants. (I've tried everything I can think of.)
>
> I 'don't know what he ''wants. (Impatience.)

SOUND ATTRIBUTES

I ˈdon't ˈˈknow what he wants. (I've tried to find out and cannot.)

⸱ ‾ ⟍ ⸱⸱

Note the varying intonation in this sentence, and compare the sentences in §§ 288 and 289.

(c) When compound words which normally bear a double stress, e.g. ˈhome-ˈmade, ˈunˈknown, ˈbad-ˈtempered, occur in a sentence preceded or followed by a stressed syllable, one of the two stresses may disappear under the influence of the rhythm of the sentence.

ən ˈʌnnoʊn ˈwɒrɪə; hiˑz ˈkwaɪt ʌnˈnoʊn;
ˈhoʊm meɪd ˈdʒæm; ɪt s ˈɔːl hoʊm ˈmeɪd;
ə ˈbæd tɛmpəd ˈdɒg; hi wəz ˈɔˑlweɪz bæd ˈtɛmpəd.

(d) Contrast between two ideas expressed or un-expressed may be shown by varying the normal stress, e.g.

ˈraɪs ˈpʊdɪŋ but aɪ wɒnt ˈraɪs pʊdɪŋ (not plum pudding).
ˈdaʊn ˈhɪl but hi wɛnt ˈdaʊn hɪl (not up).

This may be compared with (b), where the special emphasis given to one word in the sentence often implies contrast. Note also that the intonation changes.

(e) English is a language of strongly marked rhythm, and there is a tendency for stressed syllables to occur at regular intervals of time.

ˈðɛər aɪ ˈfʌndəˈmɛntəlɪ dɪsəˈgriː wɪð ju. | waɪlst ədˈmɪtɪŋ ðət ɪndɪˈvɪdjʊəlz ˈvɛərɪ ɪn kəˈpæsɪtɪ, | aɪ bɪˈliːv ðət ˈiˑtʃ ˈwʌn | hæz ðə ˈpaʊər əv meɪkɪŋ ʌn'lɪmɪtɪd 'proʊgrɛs, | ɪntɪ'lɛktjʊəl ənd 'spɪrɪtjʊəl. | ðə 'tuː 'stʌmblɪŋ blɒks | ɪn ðə 'weɪ əv 'moʊst piːpl | ɑ ðɛər 'ɜˑlɪ 'mɪs-ɛdjʊ'keɪʃn | ənd ðɪ 'ʌnɪn-'spaɪərɪŋ ɛn'vaɪərnmənt | ɪn 'wɪtʃ ðeɪ hæv tə 'pɑːs | 'moʊst əv ðɛə 'laɪvz.

In this sentence, the stressed syllables within the breath groups occur at almost regular intervals of time, and however many or few unstressed syllables there may be between the stresses, they seem to fit in to the time allowed. Many examples can be found to illustrate this tendency, and the skilled teacher will know how to apply this fact to the rhythmic reading of prose, and also to obtain variety of expression in the reading of both prose and poetry.

299. The reader is advised to note carefully the sentence stress marked in any phonetic reader, and to compare this rendering with his own. For the manner of stressing may vary to a certain extent from individual to individual. There is, for example, considerable divergence in the stressing of certain compound words, e.g. *Christmas present* is stressed as 'krɪsməs 'prɛznt by some, and as 'krɪsməs prɛznt by others.

Plum-cake is either 'plʌm'keɪk (‾ ⟍) or 'plʌm keɪk (⟍.).

Shirt-sleeves is either 'ʃɜˑt 'sliːvz (‾ ⟍) or 'ʃɜˑt sliˑvz (⟍.).

Hide and seek is either 'haɪd n 'siˑk (‾ ⟍) or 'haɪd n siˑk (⟍..).

[Note the intonation which goes with these different stresses.]

300. As far as the present writer's experience goes, Northerners and Southerners have different habits in some compound words of this type (but nǫt of all compound words, e.g. *blackbird* is always ˈblækbɜˑd (⌒.), and *North Sea* is ˈnɔˑθˈsiː (‾ \)), but a sufficient number of examples has not yet been collected to justify any authoritative statement being made about these varying usages.

301. *Intonation.*—Intonation is the term given to the rise and fall in the pitch of the voice in speech. Change in pitch is due to differing rates of vibration of the vocal chords.

302. Intonation varies somewhat from individual to individual, and considerably from district to district, each part of the country having its distinctive speech melody—a melody which often remains in the speech when all other signs of local dialect are absent. Students should practise analysing their own intonation and that of other people, and note how different kinds of feeling can be expressed by the " tune " of a sentence.

303. The different intonations used in various parts of the country have not been sufficiently well investigated to give examples here. The analysis of a typical Southern intonation has been attempted, however, in *A Handbook of English Intonation*. This book, although originally intended for foreign students of English, forms a basis on which to work for a further comparative study of English Intonation. Students are advised to read it, and see if the simple rules formulated and illustrated in it fit with their own habits in the matter of speech melody, and where there are

differences, to see in what these differences consist, and if any reason can be given for them. A brief note on some of the differences between Northern and Southern intonation is given in §§ 319–20.

304. It will perhaps be useful to summarise very briefly the main intonations used in English, which are treated more fully in the *Handbook of English Intonation*. What have come to be known as the two fundamental "tunes" of English speech can be illustrated by the following sentence:

ɪf ju ˈdoʊnt bɪˈliːv mi │ aɪ ˈkɑˑnt ˈhɛlp ɪt

The first clause has the tune of an unfinished group (which we call Tune II), and the second that of a definite statement (Tune I). It is convenient to consider first sentences which are not unduly emphatic.

305. Normal Tune I consists of a series of stressed syllables forming a descending scale, the last of these having a fall in pitch. Unstressed syllables preceding the first stressed syllable are usually low; those between the stressed syllables are generally not far removed in pitch from that of the preceding stressed syllable[1]; final unstressed syllables are on a low level.

306. *Examples.*

ɪt ˈɔːl ˈstɑˑtɪd ˈjɛstədɪ [. ‾‾ ‾ ˑ \ . .]
ɪt ˈsiːmd ˈhoʊpləs [. ‾ \ .]
aɪ ˈkʊdnt ˈseɪ, s₃ [. ‾ ˑ \ .]
aɪ ˈsɔː ˈtuː ə ˈθriː əv ðəm [. ‾ ‾ ˑ \ . .]

[1] See D. Jones, *Outline of English Phonetics*, §§ 1025–6.

SOUND ATTRIBUTES 171

ɪt wəz ˈkwaɪt ɪmˈpɒsɪbl [..‾·\..]
ˈhuː z ˈðɛə [‾ \]
ˈwɒts ðə ˈmætə [‾· \.]
wɛər ə juː gɔɪŋ [‾·· \.]
ˈteɪk ɪt ˈɒf [‾· \]
ˈʃʌt ðə ˈdɔː pliːz [‾· \.]
ət ˈwʌns [. \]
ˈhaʊ [\]

307. It will be seen that the tune can be spread over a considerable number of syllables or compressed into a small space; that the sentences given above are not very long; that definite statements, questions which begin with an interrogative word (and which cannot be answered by "yes" or "no"), and commands take this type of intonation.

When a group requiring Tune I is somewhat long, it is modified by raising the pitch of one of the stressed syllables before descending to the end of the sentence.[1]

ɪt ˈrɪəli ˈstɑːtɪd ˈfɔː ˈjɪəz əgoʊ [.‾·‾·‾ \..]
aɪm ˈsɛndɪŋ juː ˈtuː ˈtɪkɪts fə ðə ˈθɪətə [.‾··‾··· \.]

308. Tune II, like Tune I, consists of a descending scale of stressed syllables with a rise from a low pitch at the end. The last stressed syllable is the lowest and if it is the last syllable of the group, it has a rise in itself; if not, any unstressed syllables which follow carry the rise. This tune is used, as illustrated above in § 304, in an unfinished sense group; it is also used in questions

---

[1] Note that the rise is generally on a more or less emphatic word, and frequently the sentences could be divided at this point into two groups, the first having Tune II.

of the type which can be answered by "yes" or "no,"
in requests, and in certain types of statement where
something is implied but left unexpressed in words.

309. *Examples.*

(i) In unfinished groups.

ˈwɛn jʊ ə ˈrɛdɪ | ˈkʌm ən ˈkɔːl mi
[⁻ ·· __ · | ⁻ · \ .]

ə ˈfjuː ˈjɑːdz ˈfɜˑðər ˈɒn | ðə ˈpɑːθ ˈwaɪdnd
[· ⁻ — · ⁄ | · ⁻ \ .]

tə ˈtɛl ðə ˈtruːθ | ɪts ˈdʒʌst ˈtɛmpə
[· ⁻ · ⁄ | · ⁻ \ .]

ɪn ˈðæt keɪs | aɪ ˈʃɑːnt ˈkʌm [· ⁻ · ⁄ | · ⁻ \ ]

ðə ˈjɪə ðət ɪz ˈpɑˑsɪŋ | həz ˈbiːn tə ˈmiː | ˈmoʊst ˈmɛmərəbl [· ⁻ ·· __ · | · ⁻ · ⁄ | ⁻ \ ··]
(See p. 220.)

(ii) In questions requiring the answer "yes" or "no."

ˈɑː jʊ ˈrɛdɪ [⁻ · __ ·]
wɪl jʊ kʌm wɪθ əs [⁻ · __ ··]
ˈdjʊ ˈθɪŋk soʊ [⁻ __ ·]
ˈhæv jʊ ˈbiːn hɪə ˈlɒŋ [⁻ · — · ⁄]
ˈdʌz ɪt ˈmiːn ɛnɪθɪŋ [⁻ · __ ··]
ˈwɪl jʊ [__ ·]
ˈdʌznt hi [__ ··]

(iii) In requests.

ˈlɛt mi ˈnoʊ ˈsuːn [⁻ · — ⁄]
ˈdoʊnt ˈtrʌbl tʊ ˈɑˑnsər ɪt [⁻ — ·· __ ··]
ɪksˈkjuːz mi ˈwʌn ˈmoʊmənt [· ⁻ · — __ ·]

Note that requests can also be said with Tune I.

ˈkʌm ən ˈsiː mi [⁻ · \ .]
ˈlɛt mi ˈnoʊ ˈsuːn [⁻ · — \ ]

(iv) In statements in which something is implied.

ɪt ˈwoʊnt ˈteɪk ˈlɒŋ [. ‾ — ╱]
ðæts ˈɔːl, ʤɒn [‾ __ ·]
aɪ səˈpoʊz ɪts ˈtruː [. . ‾ · ╱]

310. Note that in this type of sentence (iv), emphatic stress and its accompanying change of intonation is more usual than the unemphatic Tune II. If said with little emphasis and the intonation as indicated above, these sentences give the impression of casualness.

311. *Emphatic Intonation.*

Emphasis, an all-round increase of effort on the part of the speaker to express

(i) some added meaning or intensity;

(ii) some extra prominence which he wishes to attach to a particular idea is shown in part by intonation.[1]

312. *Emphasis for Intensity.*

Emphasis for intensity expresses in a higher degree the quality inherent in the word or phrase.[2] This is usually effected by widening the range of pitch.

ðə ˈmæn wəz ɪn ə ˈsteɪt əv ˈˈbɔɪlɪŋ ɪndɪgˈneɪʃn
[. ‾ · · · ─ · ‾ · · · ╲ .]

---

[1] Note that means of emphasising other than by stress and intonation frequently accompany these two elements; different type of voice, use of pauses, use of glottal stop, lengthening of vowels and consonants, gesture and facial expression.

[2] Note that only words expressing measurable quality can have this type of emphasis. See D. Jones, *Outline of English Phonetics*, § 1046 and footnotes.

‖sɜːtnlɪ ‖nɒt [¯ ·· \ ]

ɪt wəz ə ‖mɑːvələs ˈdeɪ [.. · ¯ ·· \ ]

An abnormal narrowing of the range of intonation can also be used to show intensity.

ˈpʊər ˈoʊld ˈθɪŋ [— — \ ]

ɪts ˈpɜːfɪklɪ əbˈsɜːd [. ¯ ·· \ ]

313. *Emphasis for Prominence or Contrast.*

An examination of the following sentences will illustrate the changes in intonation which are used to show contrast.

ˈðæt ɪznt ˈwɒt aɪ ˈment [¯ ·· — · \ ],
 tune of the normal statement.

ˈðæt ɪznt wɒt aɪ ‖ment [¯ ··\ ] *or* [. ···\ ],
 "meant" with extra emphasis for contrast.

‖ðæt ɪznt wɒt aɪ ‖ment [\ ··\ ],
 "that" and "meant" with extra emphasis for contrast.

‖ðæt ɪznt wɒt ‖aɪ ment [\ ··\.],
 "that" and "I" with extra emphasis for contrast.

ðæt ‖ɪznt wɒt aɪ ment [. \ ....],
 the negative idea emphasised—a contradiction.

ˈðæt ɪznt wɒt aɪ ˈment [\ .... ⌣]
 an implication here, but no extra emphasis.

ðæt ɪznt wɒt aɪ ‖ment [\ .... ∩],
 though I may have given the impression that it was.

314. It will be seen that the word to be strongly emphasised always has a fall in pitch from high to low; the greater the fall, the greater the emphasis as a rule. The emphasis is stronger if the stress of the remaining

SOUND ATTRIBUTES 175

stressed syllables is reduced somewhat, or if they are treated, as far as the intonation pattern goes, as unstressed syllables.

Tune II with contrast emphasis on the final stressed word has the fall belonging to that emphasis, followed by the rise which is inherent in this tune. The fall-rise may be spread over a number of syllables or compressed into one, as will be seen from some of the examples below.

315. *Further Examples.*

aɪm ⁱsɒrɪ aɪ ˈkɑːnt goʊ ˈwɪð ju [. ╲ . . ▬ . ▬ .]
ɪts ⁱvɛrɪ ⁱsɪərɪəs [. ╲ . ╲╱]
ju ⁱniːdnt meɪk soʊ mʌtʃ ⁱnɔɪz əbaʊt ɪt
   [· ╲ . . . . ╲ . . ·]
ˈwɒts ðə ⁱmætə [▬ · ╲ .], cf. [▔ · ╲ .]
ⁱɛvrɪbɒdɪ ˈwɒnts ɪt [╲ . . ▬], cf. [▔ · · ╲ .]
aɪ ˈdoʊnt θɪŋk ɪts ⁱraɪt [. ▬ · · ╲], cf. [. ▔ · · ╲]
aɪ ⁱθɪŋk soʊ [· ╲ ╱]
aɪ ⁱwɪʃ hi ⁱwʊd [· ╲ . ∩]
aɪ ⁱhoʊp aɪ hævnt kɛpt ju ⁱweɪtɪŋ [· ╲ . . . . ╲ ╱]
ɪts ⁱsoʊ naɪs tə ⁱsiː ju əgeɪn [· ╲ . . ╲ . . ╱]

316. Note that the use of Tune II in sentences with an implication or reservation is very common in English when emphasis is added. By this means we can express many things which in other languages must be put into words.

317. The intonation of King George V recorded in the Christmas broadcast (see p. 220) is typical of normal unemphatic speech with a purposely slow delivery. The student is advised to study this and analyse his

own intonation of material of the same kind. President Roosevelt's speech (see p. 226) shows a considerable number of points of similarity in intonation, but some variations which have been pointed out. A short passage is added here which shows a mixture of emphatic and non-emphatic intonation.

318. æz ðeɪ ˈstɛəd ˈæŋgrɪlɪ ət wʌn ənʌðə, ðæt

mɪsˈtɪərɪəs ˈsɪmpəθɪ əv ðə ˈflɛʃ wɪtʃ wi kɔːl ˈfæmɪlɪ

ˈlaɪknɪs, ˈspræŋ ˈaʊt frəm ɪts ˈhaɪdɪŋ pleɪs, ˈstæmpɪŋ

ðɛə ˈtoʊtəlɪ dɪˈsɪmɪlə ˈfiːtʃəz wɪð ən ˈɛlfɪʃ ɪˈfɛkt əv

ˈmjuːtʃʊəl ˈkærɪkətjʊə. ɪt wəz əz ˈðoʊ ˈiːtʃ ˈsɔː hɪmsɛlf

ɪn ə dɪsˈtɔːtɪŋ ˈmɪrə, waɪl ðə ˈvɔɪsɪz maɪt əv biːn

ˈwʌn vɔɪs wɪð ɪts ˈɛkoʊ.

"ˈlʊk ˈhɪər oʊld ˈtʃæp," sɛd ˈpiːtə, rɪˈkʌvrɪŋ

hɪmsɛlf, "aɪm ˈfraɪtflɪ ˈsɔrɪ. aɪ ˈdɪdnt ˈmiːn

tə ˈlɛt maɪsɛlf ˈgoʊ laɪk ˈˈðæt. ɪf juː ˈˈwoʊnt ˈˈseɪ ɛnɪθɪŋ

juː ˈˈwoʊnt. ˈɛnɪhaʊ wɪər ˈɔːl ˈwɜːˈkɪŋ laɪk ˈˈbleɪzɪz,

ənd wɪə ˈˈʃʊə tə faɪnd ðə ˈˈraɪt ˈmæn | bɪfɔː vɛrɪ ˈˈlɒŋ."

319. A few notes on the main differences between Northern and Southern intonation are given below.

(1) The range of voice is generally greater in the north than in the south. Thus ˈðætsˈraɪt [— ⌣] would have the pitch [— ⌣]; the rise and the interval are also probably greater in such a sentence.

(2) The Southern English descent of stressed syllables illustrated in the sentence (on p. 157) wɒt ə juː goɪŋ tə duː əbaʊt ɪt? [— ·· — · ⟍...] is frequently replaced by a series of syllables on a high level tone with a big fall in the last [— ·· — · ⟍...].

 aɪ ˈdoʊnt θɪŋk aɪ ˈkæn [· — ·· ⟍]
         instead of [. — ·· ⟍]
 ˈwɛər əv juː ˈbiːn [— ·· ⟍] instead of [— ·· ⟍]
 ɪt wəz ˈɔːl əbaʊt ˈsʌmθɪŋ ən ˈnʌθɪŋ [.. — ·· — ⟍ .]
        instead of [.. — ·· — ·· ⟍ .]
 hi ˈdɪdnt tɛl mi ˈwɒt hi wəz ˈduˈɪŋ [. — ·· — ⟍ .]
 ˈdoʊnt teɪk ɛnɪ ˈnoʊtɪs ɒv ɪm [— ·· ⟍ ...]

(3) Another alternative to this type of "tune" (used in a statement or in a question beginning with an

interrogative word) has frequent falls from the high level which often give the impression of emphasis.

ˈwɒts ðə ˈneɪm əv ðɪs ˈstriˑt [‾‾ ˑ ╲ ˑ ‾‾ ╲]
ɪt wəz mɪstɪ ən frɒstɪ ən əz blæk əz pitʃ
[ˑˑ ╲ ˑˑ ╲ ˑˑ ‾‾ ˑ ╲]

Again the same note is hit several times, and the range is wide.

(4) Similarly in the "tune" of an unfinished group and of a question requiring the answer "yes" or "no," a wide range is used and a high level pitch maintained until the last important word, when there is a sudden drop to the bottom limit of the voice before the rise which belongs to this tune.

ˈkæn ju ˈtɛl mɪ ˈɛnɪθɪŋ əˈbaʊt ɪt [‾‾ ˑ ‾‾ ˑ ‾‾ ˑˑ __ ˑ]
ˈwɪl ju lɛt mɪ ˈhæv ɪt ɪn ðə ˈmɔːnɪŋ [‾‾ ˑˑ ‾‾ ˑˑ __ ˑ]
djə ˈθɪŋk ɪt ˈmætəz [ˑ ‾‾ ˑ __ ˑ]

(5) The use of "Tune II" (the tune of an unfinished group) with a rise at the end, is frequently used in North and South for a statement with some reservation in the speaker's mind.

ðər ɪznt ˈtaɪm tə goʊ ˈbæk [ˑˑ ╲ ˑˑ ╱],

the difference between the two being only in the range of pitch. But some northerners use this tune when one expects a more direct statement with the falling intonation of "Tune I," and this gives the impression of a reservation, particularly if it is some expression of opinion. I have frequently heard ˈjɛs, ɪts ˈvɛrɪ ˈnaɪs [╲ ˑ __ ˑ ╱], when on other evidence there was no reservation in the mind of the speaker, though to a listener who would not use this tune in this place, it distinctly conveys an idea of a "but," or of a grudging approval. It should be noted that this intonation in some sentences is frequently an encouraging one: e.g. kʌm əˈlɒŋ [‾· ⌒] or [__ · ⌒].

320. The above observations refer mainly to Lancashire and Yorkshire speech. In North Yorkshire, County Durham and Tyneside, an intonation pattern which does not occur in the South is heard. This is a variation of Tune II which ends on a falling pitch from high to mid-level. Thus:

hæz ˈɛnɪwʌn ˈsiːn ˈmɛərɪ ˈmɑˑtɪn [. __ · · __ __ . ⌒ ·]
ˈwɒt djə ˈkɔːl ˈðɪs ˈθɪŋ [__ . __ ‾‾‾ __]
ˈhav djə ˈθɪŋk hiˑz ˈlʊkɪŋ [__ . __ . ‾‾ ·]

321. These brief notes are only intended to draw the reader's attention to some differences in intonation he may find in his investigations and to warn him that what is called an "accent" is not merely a matter of sound but is frequently due to variations from the normal in intonation patterns. Moreover, an unexpected intonation conveys to the hearer an impression which the speaker does not intend (as under (5) above). Intonation is frequently the cause of real misunderstanding of attitude, since we interpret it as the expression of feelings we should have if we used that pattern.[1]

[1] See *The Broadcast Word*, pp. 8, 9, where the question is treated from the point of view of foreign languages.

Chapter XVI.

SOUNDS IN CONNECTED SPEECH.

322   Our habit of reading written words is apt to make us think that the unit of speech is the word. From a grammatical and orthographic point of view, a sentence may consist of a number of separate words, but in the spoken language such is not the case; the word is not the unit of speech, nor are spoken words separated from each other by pauses, as the written words are by spaces. A short spoken sentence is continuous: "*It's a very fine day,*" is as continuous as the single words *peculiarity* or *sympathetically*. A long sentence can easily be broken up into "sense-groups," and the number and complexity of these will vary according to the character of the sentence and the circumstances under which it is uttered. In somewhat careful and deliberate speech, such as one would use in reading aloud or in addressing a number of people, the sense-groups would probably be shorter and the pauses more frequent than in familiar conversation.[1]

323.   The grouping of speech sounds in connected sentences brings them under the influence of new factors, and leads to modifications and changes which must be considered. In the chapter on Phonemes and in the description of the individual sounds of the language, the

---

[1] See the transcription of the speech of King George V, p. 220.

SOUNDS IN CONNECTED SPEECH

influence of the juxtaposition of one sound with another has already been noted. Further changes may now be considered.

THE INFLUENCE OF STRESS.

324. English is a language of widely differing degrees of stress; strongly marked stresses occur at more or less regular intervals of time separated by syllables bearing little stress. It is in these unstressed syllables that we must look for change. In the sentence, " 'What are you 'going to 'do to-'day," there are four stressed and five unstressed syllables; the unstressed words pronounced separately would be ɑː, juː, tuː, but the sentence is pronounced 'wɒt ə ju 'ɡɔiŋ tə 'duː tə'dei, i.e. *are* becomes ə, *you* becomes ju, and *to* becomes tu or tə in the word *to* and in the first syllable of *to-day*. The vowels in these unimportant words are reduced to a kind of neutral vowel under the influence of the stress and rhythm of the connected sentence. In the following extract, note the unstressed syllables where the original vowel has been replaced by the neutral ə (or ɪ in the case where the "strong" vowel was i, and ʊ where it was u).

'let ðə 'mænɪdʒmənts 'fɜːst əv 'ɔːl dɪ'praiv 'leit-'kʌməz əv wɒt ɪz 'nau ðɛə 'best ɪks'kjuːs—'neimlɪ, ðə 'kʌstəmərɪ 'leitnəs əv 'kɜːtn raiz. ðei 'kʌm 'leit bɪ'kɒz, ðei sei, ðə 'plei 'ɔːlwəz bɪ'ɡɪnz leit. 'if ðə 'θiətəz wə junɪ'vɜːsəlɪ əz 'pʌŋktjʊəl əz ðə dɪ'pɑːtʃəz əv ɪks'pres 'treinz, 'nou wʌn wud bɪ 'temtɪd ɪntu 'ouvər-'estɪmeitɪŋ ə 'fjuː 'mɪnɪts 'ɡreis. ə'nʌðə remɪdɪ ɪz tə prə'vaid 'leit-'kʌməz wið 'stuːlz əv rɪ'pentəns ənd tu ɪn'sɪst əpɒn ðɛər 'ɒkjʊpaiɪŋ ðəm.

Strong and Weak Forms.

325. The following words have strong and weak forms: the strong forms are used in stressed, and the weak forms in unstressed positions.

Word.	Strong Form.	Weak Form.
am	æm	əm, m
be	biː	bɪ
been	biːn, bɪn	bɪn
is	ɪz	z, s
are	ɑː	ə
was	wɒz	wəz
were	wɜː	wə
have (aux. vb.)	hæv	həv, əv, v
has ,,	hæz	həz, əz, z, s
had ,,	hæd	həd, əd, d
do	duː	dʊ, də, d
does	dʌz	dəz, dz
shall	ʃæl	ʃəl, ʃl
should	ʃʊd	ʃəd, ʃd
will	wɪl	l
would	wʊd	wəd, d
can (vb.)	kæn	kən, kn (rarely kŋ)
could	kʊd	kəd
must	mʌst	məst, məs, mst, ms
you	ju	jʊ, jə
your	jɔː	jə, jo
he	hiː	hɪ, ɪ
she	ʃiː	ʃɪ
we	wiː	wɪ
me	miː	mɪ
him	hɪm	ɪm

Word.	Strong Form.	Weak Form.
her	hɜː	hə, ə
his	hɪz	ɪz
us	ʌs	əs
them	ðɛm	ðəm, ðm
who	huː	hʊ
some	sʌm	səm, sm
and	ænd	ənd, ən, n
a	eɪ	ə
an	æn	ən
the	ði	ðɪ, ðə
not	nɒt	nt
or	ɔː	ə
at	æt	ət
for	fɔ	fə
from	frɒm	frəm, frm
of	ɒv	əv, v
to	tu	tʊ, tə
upon	əpɒn	əpən
but	bʌt	bət
as	æz	əz
than	ðæn	ðən, ðn
that	ðæt	ðət
there	ðɛə	ðə
my	maɪ	mɪ
by	baɪ	bɪ

326. The importance of considering the question of strong and weak forms lies in the fact that the speaker untrained in speech analysis does not realise that he makes any difference in these words. When he sees the word *was* written, he thinks he always pronounces it wɒz,

as he does when he says it in isolation. Such a person is often shocked to find the number of neutral vowels in a phonetic transcription, and judges it as representing a slipshod and degenerate manner of speaking, the real fact of the matter being, that the transcription is an accurate representation of colloquial—and quite good—speech. The student will find when he begins to analyse and write down his own pronunciation that the number of neutral vowels he uses is considerably greater than he at first realised. This fact would be brought home to him if he heard a passage read, as it sometimes is, with all the unstressed vowels given their original "strong" forms, which creates the effect of emphasising unimportant words and syllables, and in its turn this weakens the important words. I have heard such pronunciation in schools in the reading lesson, where the teacher encourages his pupils to "speak each word and syllable distinctly, and not to slur them" thus giving rise to a wooden and unintelligent reading in which all the syllables have equal value.

327. It is difficult to say how long this habit of weakening the unstressed vowel into ə or ɪ has been in existence—Professor Wyld thinks for many centuries; at present it is well-established. In the North of England, however, particularly in Yorks., and Lancs., the use of the strong form in unstressed syllables is very common, in the small, unimportant words, and in the unstressed syllables of longer words. Thus one hears kɒnˈsɪdə, sʌkˈsɛs, ˈɒbdʒɛkt, ˈpɜˈfɛkt, ˈæksɛnt, ˈspɛktɛklz, ˈwɒt wɒz hi ˈduɪŋ?, where in the South we should hear kənˈsɪdə, səkˈsɛs, ˈkɛəlɪs (or kɛələs),

ˈɒbdʒɪkt, ˈpɜˑfɪkt, ˈæks(ə)nt, ˈspɛktəklz, ˈwɒt wəz hi ˈduɪŋ ?¹

328. If this method of speaking is very marked, the effect, contrary to what one might expect, is not of a somewhat over-careful speech, but of a speech lacking in precision and finish. This the writer believes to be due to the fact that the important words and syllables are not given sufficient prominence and the characteristic rhythm of the sentence is lost.

Assimilation and Similitude.

329. The organs of speech moving in connected speech from one position to another are apt, because of the rapidity of these movements, to take "short cuts"— i.e. to drop out consonants or to modify their articulation. This phenomenon, which is common to all languages, is called *assimilation*. Assimilation is interesting to study because it is an important factor in the historical development of a language and is responsible for many changes in pronunciation.

330. Assimilation may be defined as the process of replacing a sound by another sound under the influence

---

¹ Many Southerners have said to me, "Northerners stress the first syllable in *success*, they say ˈsʌksɛs [╲ .]." As a matter of fact they do not stress the first syllable nor give the intonation which would accompany such stressing; they pronounce sʌkˈsɛs [. ╲], but the use of the strong vowel plus the extra length this has in comparison with the neutral ə, gives the impression of prominence which the hearer associates with stress. (See Ch. XV, §289 (5.)

of a third sound which is near to it in a word or sentence; the coalescing of two sounds into a single sound may also come under the heading of assimilation.[1]

331. There are two clearly defined kinds of assimilation, viz. historical and juxtapositional. Historical assimilation is that which has taken place in the course of the development of the language. We know, for instance, from various kinds of evidence, that the word *nature* was once pronounced næːˈtiur; its present-day pronunciation ˈneɪtʃə is due, as far as the consonant tʃ is concerned, to this process of assimilation.

332. Juxtapositional assimilation is an assimilation which occurs when words are juxtaposed in a sentence or in the formation of compounds, and by this juxtaposition, a word comes to have a pronunciation which is different from that used when the word is said in isolation. An example of juxtapositional assimilation is found in the pronunciation of the words *does she* as dʌʃʃi or dʌʒʃi, where the pronunciation of the word dʌz has been changed to dʌʒ or dʌʃ under the influence of the neighbouring ʃ.

333. Many examples of this kind of assimilation occur in conversational English and the teacher will do well to observe these and note how far such changes may or may not impair intelligibility. He should beware of a too meticulous avoidance or correction of current assimilations of this kind, lest his pronunciation

---

[1] See D. Jones, *Outline of English Phonetics*, Third Edition, 1932, p. 202.

or that of his pupils should have that over precision which draws undue attention to itself, and which is not in line with accepted usage.

334. It has been customary to consider other phenomena of similarity in the articulation of neighbouring sounds as examples of assimilation, but this term is better reserved for the two types of *change* of pronunciation illustrated above, i.e. to define assimilation proper as a process. The other similarity, to which the name similitude is given, describes an existing fact.[1] Thus in English when s, p, t, k are followed by m, n, l, r, j, w, e.g. in *small, please, slow, try, pew, queen, curiosity*, the second of the pair is partially devoiced. These words are pronounced smo‧l, sl̥oʊ, pl̥iːz, tr̥aɪ, pçuː,[2] kwi‧n, kçʊərɪɒsɪtɪ. (It is easiest to hear in tr̥aɪ, pçuː, pl̥iːz.) In these cases a subsidiary member of the m, n, l, r, j, w phoneme is used (the voiceless equivalent of each consonant) which has a greater resemblance to the preceding consonant (in its voicelessness) than the main member of these phonemes. There is no evidence to show that these sounds were ever pronounced in any other way than voiceless, hence it is not correct to say that they are due to assimilation, "When the sequence of two phonemes requires that a subsidiary member of one of them should be used, which has a greater resemblance to the neighbouring sound than

---

[1] Professor D. Jones is responsible for this division of what has previously been grouped under the one term assimilation. There is no doubt that the separation makes for exactitude and clarity. See *Outline of English Phonetics*, pp. 203-4.

[2] ç represents the sound of j pronounced without any voice. See Chap. XIV, p. 152, § 282.

the principal member has, there is said to be similitude between them."[1] Similitude has been illustrated fairly fully in the chapter on phonemes, where the use of the various members of the phoneme was shown to depend mainly on the proximity of some other sound: e.g. the use of a special kind of t (made on the teeth) before the θ-sound of *eighth*, and of another kind of t (made with the tongue-tip curled up) before the r of *tree*.

335. A still further similarity in neighbouring sounds which is neither assimilation nor similitude occurs in words like *conquer, congregation, concrete, concord*, which are pronounced kɒŋkə, ˈkɒŋgrɪˈgeɪʃn, ˈkɒŋkeɪv, ˈkɒŋkriːt, ˈkɒŋkɔːd, i.e. the neighbouring nasal and plosive consonants are both articulated at the same place. Many writers have given the name of assimilation to this fact, but again there is no evidence to show that the *con*-prefix was ever pronounced as kɒn under the same set of circumstances of neighbouring consonants and stress. Nor can this fact be explained as similitude, according to the definition given above, since n and ŋ are not members of the same phoneme in English.[2] Note that in all these words, either primary or secondary stress occurs on the first syllable. In the words *conˈcur, conˈcussion, conˈcretion, conˈcordance*, when the stressed syllable follows the prefix, the latter is pronounced kən, kənˈkɜː, kənˈkʌʃn, kənˈkriːʃn, kənˈkɔːdns.[3]

---

[1] D. Jones, *op. cit.*, p. 202.

[2] In Italian they are members of one phoneme and the pronunciation of *in casa* as ɪŋ kasa is an example of juxtapositional assimilation in this language.

[3] Some people would use ŋ in these positions too.

SOUNDS IN CONNECTED SPEECH 189

336. A further example of similarity in neighbouring sounds occurs in Northern pronunciation in words like *climb, glow*, which are pronounced tlaɪm, dloʊ, i.e. t and d are articulated in the same place as l and replace the normal k and g. Such pronunciations as dlæd, tlɒk, intluːd are very common,[1] and the difference between them and the usual glæd, klɒk, inkluːd is not very easy to hear.

337. The points illustrated in the two previous paragraphs, though not examples of assimilation or similitude, are treated here because they have been considered as exemplifying assimilation, and because some of this type of similarity in neighbouring sounds may possibly be due to assimilations which can no longer be traced.

338. *Examples of Assimilation.*

Assimilation (and similitude) can be concerned with any of the organs of speech.

339. *Vocal Cords.*

(a) Voiced sounds have been replaced by voiceless sounds under the influence of a neighbouring voiceless sound; the v in faɪv is replaced by f in faɪfpəns because the voiceless p follows; the z of njuːz is replaced by s in njuˈspeɪpə; in quick speech the phrase aɪ juːzd tʊ becomes aɪ juːst tʊ; with some speakers, particularly in the North, the d of *width* and *breadth* is pronounced t, wɪtθ, brɛtθ. *Bradford* is often pronounced bræt͡ʃəd (or braʔfəd).

---

[1] I have heard strʌdl, for *struggle*.

(b) A change from a voiceless to a voiced sound is seen in words like *raspberry* and *gooseberry* (rɑˑzbrɪ, gʊzbrɪ). The p has been lost in the b and the b has resulted in s being replaced by z. In some parts of the country, the North particularly, raspbɛrɪ, gu·sbɛrɪ, are still heard. In the plural of words like *bed*, *dog* (bɛdz, dɒgz),[1] the final sound is voiced owing to the influence of the previous voiced consonant.[2]

340. *Soft Palate.*—Nasal consonants often influence the plosives articulated in the same place, e.g. in *kindness*, kaɪndnəs, generally pronounced kaɪnṇəs, the d, influenced by the preceding and following n, becomes n and then readily disappears; grænmʌðə is another example of the same thing, and in hænsəm, the d has been dropped under the influence of the preceding n.

341. *Tongue.*—There are a large number of words in which the tongue-position of a consonant is changed.

(a) The pronunciation in quick speech of beɪkŋ, broʊkŋ, tʃɪkŋ (*bacon, broken, chicken*) is an assimilation due to the dropping of the vowel and the bringing together of the two consonants; in careful speech these words would normally be beɪkən, broʊkən, tʃɪkɪn.

---

[1] The Early English plural *dogs* was probably *dogges*, dɒgəs; with the dropping of the vowel the two consonants have come together, and the s has been replaced by z; this is a case of historical assimilation.

[2] But note that although transcribed with z, like all final voiced consonants, the sound is only partially voiced. See § 239.

SOUNDS IN CONNECTED SPEECH 191

(b) A regular series of assimilations has been made in the language in words which were originally pronounced with s or z, or t or d, followed by i or j; these combinations have been changed into ʃ, ʒ and tʃ, dʒ respectively; e.g. *nation* pronounced as næːsion in Shakespeare's day, has become neɪʃn; *occasion* is now əkeɪʒn from ɒkæˈzjon; *nature*, pronounced formerly as nætiʊr, has become neɪtʃə; *verdure*, from vɜˑdjur, has become vɜˑdʒə.

342. How easy and natural this transition is will be seen from the accompanying diagram. In the word *nation* (næːsjon), the s followed by j has resulted in the sound ʃ, the tongue position of which lies between the two original sounds; while in *nature*, the t, under the influence of j, is pulled back to a point of articulation (see Fig. 31 c, p. 137), which makes the transition to ʃ extremely easy. It is to be noted that such assimilation has been made in unstressed syllables only; in stressed syllables it should be avoided: e.g. ˈneɪtʃə but məˈtjuə.

343. In the two words *sure* and *sugar*, however, formerly (and still in some dialects) pronounced sɪʊr, sɪʊgər, the assimilation has been made in a stressed syllable. In Cockney speech it is made in words like *Duke, Tuesday, tube* (dʒuˑk, tʃuˑzdɪ, tʃuːb); these pronunciations are still considered examples of uneducated speech. (I have heard dʒʊerɪŋ

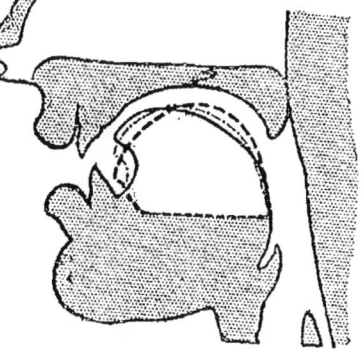

— Tongue position for s
--- Tongue position for j
····· Tongue position for ʃ

FIG. 42.
Illustrating Assimilation.

or dʒuˑrɪŋ for *during*, and ɪnˈdʒuər or ɪnˈdʒuːr foɪ *endure* from educated Scottish speakers.) There are, however, large numbers of words in which the assimilation is made by some educated speakers and not by others, and in these words the process of assimilation is seen working. For example, literature is pronounced by some as lɪtrətjuə, and by others as lɪtrətʃə,

education	as	ɛdjukeɪʃn	and	ɛdʒukeɪʃn
associate	,,	əsousɪeɪt	,,	əsouʃɪeɪt
immediately	,,	ɪmiˑdjətlɪ	,,	ɪmiˑdʒətlɪ
issue	,,	ɪsjuː	,,	ɪʃuː
appreciate	,,	əpriˑsɪeɪt	,,	əpriˑʃɪeɪt
individual	,,	ɪndɪvɪdjuəl	,,	ɪndɪvɪdʒuəl.

344. Many of the assimilated forms here given would by many people be considered slipshod pronunciation, and by most would be avoided in careful speech, but opinion would be by no means unanimous on all the words, nor would one person necessarily be consistent in using either all the careful forms or all the assimilated forms. Fashion accounts for some of these: for example, əsouʃɪeɪt is heard almost always from older educated people, and əsousɪeɪt from a younger generation, while əpriˑsɪeɪt would be considered an affectation by many who would say lɪtrətjuə; and one person will say tɪʃu peɪpə, and speak of the bodily tɪsjuːz.

345. In the pronunciations əpriˑsɪeɪt and əsousɪeɪt a process the reverse of assimilation, viz. *dissimilation*, is showing itself. There is no doubt that əsouʃɪeɪt and əpriˑʃɪeɪt have been well-established, good colloquial forms of the language and the newer pronunciation is a somewhat pedantic effort to make a spelling pronunciation, conscious on the part of the first users of it, but becoming unconscious and natural in others who follow. Such *dissimilation* has already taken place in certain words, the newer forms have become well-established again, and the assimilated forms are considered vulgar. (See Chapter VII on Spelling Pronunciations.)

346. *The Lips.*—Assimilation affects the lips as well as the other organs of speech, particularly in quick speech. Words like *open, ribbon, tenpence* (oʊpən, rɪbən, tɛnpəns) sometimes become oʊpm, rɪbm, tɛmpəns, i.e. the alveolar consonant n is replaced by the labial m under the influence of the preceding or following labial p or b. (I have heard rɒbmsn for *Robinson* and sʌm?m for *something*.)

347. Vowels may also be subject to assimilation, the influence being either that of a neighbouring consonant or of a vowel in a neighbouring syllable. Thus the pronunciation tʃʊldrən, prʊtɪ may be due to the influence of the l and r which have an ʊ-quality together with some lip-rounding. The plural of *man* and *mouse*, mɛn, maɪs, is a case of historical assimilation; the old plurals were manɪz, myːs[1] (from an earlier muːsɪz); thus the influence of the ɪ of the second syllable resulted in the replacing of a by ɛ, of u by y. This type of vowel assimilation is often termed vowel harmony. There are not a large number of examples of it in English.

[1] The change from myːs to maɪs took place after the y was established and followed the natural line of development of the language, viz. myːs > miːs > meɪs > mɛɪs > maɪs. Note that once it had become miːs it fell in with other words of this type and followed the same course.

348. *Assimilation in Phrases.* (Juxtapositional Assimilation.)

Assimilations resembling those already described are often made in phrases, when a sound ending one word is changed under the influence of the first sound in the next word.

E.g. *Goodge Street* (guːdʒ striːt) is pronounced by the bus-conductor as guːʒ ʃtrit, or guːʃ ʃtrit;

I should think so (aɪ ʃʊd θɪŋk soʊ) is pronounced aɪ ʃt θɪŋk soʊ;

please shut the door (pliːz ʃʌt ðə dɔə) is pronounced pliːʒ ʃʌt ðə dɔə;

I can't go (aɪ kɑːnt goʊ) is pronounced aɪ kɑːŋ goʊ, or aɪ kɑŋk goʊ.

I can get it (aɪ kən gɛt ɪt) is pronounced aɪ kŋ gɛt ɪt.

In ten minutes (ɪn tɛn mɪnɪts) is pronounced ɪn tɛm mɪnɪts.

In bed is pronounced ɪmbɛd.

Cup and saucer (kʌp ən sɔːsə) is pronounced kʌpmsɔːsə.

Bag and baggage (bæg ən bægɪdʒ) is pronounced bəgŋbægɪdʒ.

Such assimilations as these, which may pass unnoticed in familiar conversation, are generally considered unsuitable for any other type of speech.

349. *Examples of Similitude.*

Similitudes show the same kind of varieties as assimilation.

SOUNDS IN CONNECTED SPEECH

350. *Voice and Breath.* (Vocal cords.)

The examples given under § 334 illustrate this type of similitude. A further example is provided in the pronunciation of voiced h (ɦ) in intervocalic positions, e.g. bɪɦaɪnd, ə ɦæt, etc. (See p. 150, § 279 h.)

351. *Soft Palate.* (Nasalisation.)

The chief example of this type of similitude occurs in the slight nasalisation of vowels in the neighbourhood of consonants. The soft palate lowered for the nasal consonant, remains lowered during the production of the following vowel for part or all the time; where the nasal consonant follows the vowel the palate is lowered before the end of the vowel sound to be ready for the nasal consonant, e.g. lɔ̃ŋ, mãɪt.

352. *Tongue Position.*

The different members of the consonant phonemes described in the chapters on consonants and on phonemes illustrate similitudes affecting tongue position. The different t-sounds have been given as an example; the various kinds of h, k sounds provide other illustrations. (See Chs. X, XIV.)

353. *Lips.*

In the pronunciation of words like *queer, quite, quest, quick,* k is made with lip-rounding; similarly, g followed by w: e.g. *Gwendoline, language.* When f or v follows m or n the nasal consonant is often made with the bottom lip against the top teeth, to be ready for the f or v, giving rise to a labio-dental nasal consonant (phonetic symbol ɱ). This is seen in the pronunciation of some people in words like *conversation* (ˈkɒɱvəseɪʃn), *convenience* (kəɱˈviːnɪəns), *triumph* (ˈtraɪəɱf), *circumference* (sɜˈkʌɱfərəns), and occasionally when the *m* ends one word and the *f* begins another, as in *come forward* (kʌɱ fɔˑwəd). A similar change from bi-labial to labio-dental consonant is found in one pronunciation of *obvious*, where the b is replaced by a labio-dental stop.[1]

354. *Vowel Similitude.*

Vowel similitude is illustrated by the examples given of a front vowel followed by a "dark" 1; here the vowel and consonant approximate in vowel quality and that quality is not the same as the vowel has in other positions. Thus in *fill* (fɪl) the vowel is lower and more retracted than in *fit*, i.e. it approximates more to the ʊ-quality of the dark 1. Similarly the fronting of u preceded by j as in mjuːzɪk is another illustration.

Dropping of Consonants.

355. Closely allied to the process of assimilation is the simplifying of groups of consonants in single words or phrases. The ease with which a consonant in a group is dropped is partly due to the fact that it generally bears some relation in articulation to one of the neighbouring consonants, either in the place or the manner in which it is made; for this reason, too, the loss of it is not so easily noticed by the ear.

356. The English language is full of examples of this process: here it will be possible to give only a few, but the student should add to this list from his own observations.

---

[1] Note that this pronunciation is regularly used by people who have prominent upper front teeth, and who consequently find it difficult to bring the lips together.

(a) *In Words.*

d has been dropped in *handkerchief* (hæŋkətʃɪf),
kindness (kaɪnnɪs),
grandfather (grænfɑˑðə),
Wednesday (wɛnzdɪ),
t has been dropped in *castle* (kɑˑsl),
epistle (ɪpɪsl),
bustle (bʌsl), etc., and by a large number of people in
often (ɒfn or ɔfn),
soften (sɒfn or sɔfn),
postman (poʊsmən),
Christmas (krɪsməs), etc.,
p is often not pronounced in
empty (ɛmtɪ), *tempt* (tɛmt),
k is often omitted from
anxious (æŋʃəs),
thanked (θæŋt),
and always from
blackguard (blægɑˑd),
p is omitted in *cupboard* (kʌbəd).

Note that in *recognise, Arctic, secretary, government*, the pronunciations rɛkənaɪz, ɑˑtɪk, sɜkətrɪ, gʌvəmənt are generally considered as uneducated pronunciations.[1] In these cases the dropped consonant is not articulated in the same place as the next one.

[1] I have heard sɛkətrɪ and gʌvəmənt from educated speakers. Note the dropping of occasional consonants in King George V's speech on p. 225; e.g. moʊs mɛmərəbl.

(b) *In Phrases.*

The same dropping of consonants occurs in phrases, under similar conditions, in colloquial speech, especially where the phrases are very familiar ones: e.g.

I don't believe it may be pronounced aɪ doʊmbɪliːv ɪt,

I don't know is pronounced aɪ doʊn noʊ, or aɪ doʊnoʊ, or even aɪ dənoʊ,

Bread and butter is pronounced brɛd n bʌtə,

Next Monday is pronounced nɛks mʌndɪ,

Breakfast time is pronounced brɛkfəs taɪm,

I must go is pronounced aɪ məs goʊ,

I've almost finished is pronounced aɪ v ɔˑlmoʊs fɪnɪʃt,

Last night is pronounced lɑˑs naɪt.

357. The student should note the assimilations and simplifications made in his own and other people's quick speech, and compare them with those he finds recorded in texts which represent colloquial speech. Note that in a slower and more careful type of speech, assimilation and the simplification of consonant groups is much rarer than in quick colloquial speech.

Chapter XVII.

RECENT DEVELOPMENTS IN ENGLISH PRONUNCIATION.

"English, like all living languages, changes from generation to generation: slight and imperceptible as the differences in the pronunciation of father and son may appear to be, there is always some change under ordinary normal conditions. Hence pronunciations which are vulgar in one century may become fashionable in the next, sounds which are distinct in one generation may be confounded in another, and new distinctions may be made, new sounds may arise."
—Sweet: *The Sounds of English.*

358. Readers of this book will have realised from the chapters on Standard Pronunciation, on Spelling Pronunciations and on Assimilation, that many changes have taken place in the pronunciation of our language. But it is not always easy to realise that changes are going on in our own time and generation. During the last 20 years or so, a considerable number of changes have been noted which it will be well to sum up here.

359. The younger generation of educated Southerners together with many of the products of the Universities of Oxford, Cambridge and London show certain well-marked tendencies in pronunciation. Generally speaking, these are confined to persons—of both sexes—under the age of 35, though I have heard them from occasional people up to 45 or thereabouts.

360. *Consonants.*

(i) The treatment of the consonant **r** is interesting. While intrusive **r** is spreading in areas and among

199

classes where formerly it was not used, there is also a tendency, in the type of speech we are dealing with, for the *"linking r"* not to be used.[1] Thus

our own	is pronounced	aʊə oʊn and aə oʊn
moreover	,, ,,	mɔːoʊvə
wherever	is pronounced	wɛəɛvə
Sir Edgar Ede	,, ,,	sɛ ɛdgə iːd
Westminster Abbey	,, ,,	wɛsmɪnstə æbɪ
more and more	,, ,,	mɔː ən mɔː
anywhere else	,, ,,	ɛnɪwɛə ɛls

(ii) r is strongly labialised, i.e. pronounced with considerable lip-rounding. This may be due to the fact that r has little or no friction; it is a very weak consonant and the labialisation may be added unconsciously to strengthen it.

(iii) A kind of s which has a double articulation, viz. the lower lip against the upper teeth in addition to a tongue articulation is common. This gives the effect of a slight whistling lisp. The tongue articulation is not that illustrated in § 275 (p. 148), as can be proved by holding the lower lip free from the teeth, when the resulting sound resembles θ, not s, i.e. the slight friction heard is made between the tip of the tongue and the front teeth; there is no narrow passage between the blade and the teeth-ridge.

---

[1] Such pronunciation used to be considered a womanish affectation.

RECENT DEVELOPMENTS IN ENGLISH PRONUNCIATION

361. *Vowels and Diphthongs.*

(i) The front vowels, ɪ, ɛ, æ tend to be retracted in tongue position, in words like *bit, big, bed, bad*, etc. In *yes* this retraction has long been common, and it is heard in all types of speech. (See (iv) below for lengthening of vowels.)

(ii) The vowel ʌ is fronted and lowered in many cases, so that it is near to cardinal a.[1]

(iii) There is a general tendency to replace the diphthong eɪ by a pure vowel ɛ: thus *pain* is pronounced pɛ·n, the ɛ being more open and retracted than ɛ in *pen*, from which it is clearly differentiated. This tendency is especially noticeable where the sound occurs in a final position: e.g. *play* is plɛ (the vowel is not long here).

(iv) The aɪ diphthong has a back type of a as its first element, i.e. it is the ɑɪ such as is described in § 203 (p. 116), (without the nasalisation belonging to the Cockney ɑɪ, however), and, like other diphthongs it tends to become narrower or flattened out as it were. Thus with little movement of the tongue ɑɪ sounds like ɑe. Similarly, aʊ sounds like aʌ (see below for lack of lip-rounding). The triphthongs aɪə, aʊə are regularly flattened as described in § 229 (p. 123). I have heard in a recent lecture *liability* pronounced lɑɑbɪlɪtɛ (with a slight re-inforcement of

---

[1] It has been suggested that this sound should be written phonetically with the letter a

breath between the two ɑ's, and a retracted ε in the final syllable), *environment* as ɪnvɑːrnmənt, *desire* as dɪzɑɑ (again with a little push of breath in the middle of the long ɑ). The same speaker used ε³ in *sphere, experience, period,* which he pronounced sfε³, ɪkspε³rɪəns, pε³rɪəd, the vowel ε being very much retracted and lowered.

(v) The vowel ʊ and the diphthong oʊ have very little lip-rounding: *good* is pronounced gɯːd or gɤːd and *go* resembles gəɯ or gʌɯ.[1]

(vi) Perhaps one of the most noticeable features of change in English pronunciation in recent years is the lengthening of some of the vowels which have usually been considered short. This tendency has long been noted in the case of æ, which is regularly pronounced long in words like *bad, man,* etc., especially when extra emphasis is given to them. In *dog, fog, long, bed, said, men, this, bit,* the vowel is frequently lengthened and we have dɒːg (not dɔːg, which is now confined to uneducated speech), fɒːg, lɒːŋ, bɛːd, sɛːd (when stressed), ðiːs, bɪːt. The lengthening and unrounding of ʊ in *good* has been noted above. Some of these vowels (the front ones) are diphthongised somewhat, towards ə, as in certain types of American speech, but it would appear that the tendency to lengthening had begun before the influence of American speech of the moving pictures could have been felt: the diphthongisation *may* be due to America influence.

[1] ɯ represents unrounded u, ɤ unrounded o.

362. The lengthening of the traditionally short vowels and the monophthongisation of diphthongs, if these continue, are likely to introduce problems of phonetic transcription which we have not had to consider up to the present. The "broad" transcription (see Ch. V, § 56) in use in many books on English phonetics cannot represent all the variations of length and quality used by the younger generation of to-day, nor indeed, would the present "narrow" transcription used in this book be entirely adequate; a still narrower one may be necessary.

363. It must not be thought in the summing up of modern tendencies in pronunciation attempted here that all Southern English speakers of the younger generation make use of all of them. The conditions under which lengthening takes place are rather obscure; considerable investigations would have to be made to discover the rules, and the speech of a large number of typical people would have to be analysed. Nor should it be thought that these changes are all in the normal line of development of English pronunciation, and are certain to spread and be generally adopted. Some are doubtless due to an unexplainable fashion, and may change as unaccountably as they have developed.

364. *Intonation.*

It has not been possible up to the present to make accurate observations on any changes in intonation which may have taken place in the speech of the younger generation. The present writer has noted three intonation habits which are not familiar, however. One, observed mainly on the stage, is a tendency to use Tune II (see § 308, p. 171) in questions beginning with an interrogative word: e.g. ′What's your ′husband's ′name? (heard in *Eden End*, by J. B. Priestley) had the pattern [‾ · — . ╱]. This occurs in a quarrel and gives the impression of a challenge, and as such would have the implication belonging to this pattern. The second, heard mainly in the broadcasting of news, is the habit of stressing the last word of a phrase, and with this stress is heard the accompanying high-fall in pitch. Thus: "*This was decided at a Cabinet meeting*" frequently has the intonation [‾ ·· — ··· ― ·· ╲ .] where the normal "tune" of the last two words would be [‾ ·· ╲ .]. It is most likely due to the desire to clinch some definite final statement, but there is no doubt that it plays tricks with the expected tune and often gives the impression of contrast stress and intonation, which actually is not meant or needed.

The following phrases were noted recently during the reading of a news bulletin, all of them final in a sentence.

···The keystone of our policy [. ‾ ·· ╲ ..]

It would be dangerous to European peace
[··· ‾ ·· — ··· ╲]

·· ′for the next twenty-four hours [.. ‾ ··· ╲]

··· copyright reserved [— ··· ╲]

He will describe it in to-night's 10 o'clock news
[··· ‾ ·· — ··· ╲]

·— Where they were given a warm welcome
[··· ‾ ·· — ╲ .]

·— the Madrid front [.. ╲╲]

RECENT DEVELOPMENTS IN ENGLISH PRONUNCIATION

Finally, a very monotonous intonation is used by commentators on news films (*not* in broadcasting) which consists mostly of Tune I, repeated many times with little variation in the range used, i.e. each group begins at the same height and descends in regular steps to a fall in the last syllable.

'Here is the 'bridge a'cross Ni'agara [⁻· ⁻· — · ↘ ..]
as it 'was before the 'recent 'storms
[.. ⁻· — ·· ↘]
and 'now you 'see what it 'looks like [. ⁻ ···· ↘ .]
when the 'rush of 'waters has 'done its 'worst
[.. ⁻· — ··· ↘].

This habit is probably due to the effort to squeeze a great amount of comment into little time.

Chapter XVIII.

BRITISH ENGLISH AND AMERICAN ENGLISH.

365. An attempt is made in this chapter to summarise briefly some of the general differences between British English and American English. It must not be taken as an analysis of American pronunciation, since this obviously could not be undertaken within the limits of a short chapter nor without considerably more investigation of the many types of American speech on the part of the writer. American phoneticians who are best qualified for the purpose have made complete phonetic analyses of American pronunciation.[1] The points set out here are the result of personal observation of Americans in England and of the examination of gramophone records; they have been submitted to American phoneticians of note for confirmation. Records made in the Speech Department of Teachers' College, Columbia, by 17 students of Mrs. J. Dorsey Zimmerman[2] are used to illustrate the general comparisons and contrasts which it is the aim of this chapter to outline. It is impossible to print all the phonetic transcriptions of these records here; nor would it serve a useful purpose, since they illustrate many variant pronunciations of American speech which are outside the scope of this enquiry.

[1] See Bibliography, p. 246.

[2] These were put at my disposal by Mrs. Zimmerman in August, 1937.

206

BRITISH ENGLISH AND AMERICAN ENGLISH

366. The sentences recorded have been taken from *A Handbook of English Intonation*[1] (2nd edition, p. 36, Nos. 1, 2, 4, 5, and pp. 49–59, Examples IIa), and are given below in the phonetic form found in that book with the intonation marks.[2]

(1) hi ˈfɛlt ɪn hɪz ˈpɒkɪt ənd wəz glæd tə faɪnd hɪz lætʃki ənd hɪz mʌnɪ — fɔ wɪð ðiːz tuː ə ˈmæn kəmˈɑːndz ðə ˈwɜːld.

(2) ðə ˈskɒtʃ ˈdaɪəlɛkt ɪz ˈrɪtʃ ɪn ˈtɜːmz əv rɪˈproutʃ əgeɪnst ðə ˈwɪntə ˈwɪnd. ðeɪ ər ˈɔːl ˈwɜːdz ðət ˈkærɪ ə ˈʃɪvə wɪð ðəm.

(4) hi ɪz ðə ˈdʒɒlɪəst əv ˈkəmpænjənz ən ðə ˈstɛdɪəst əv

---

[1] *A Handbook of English Intonation*, Armstrong and Ward (W. Heffer & Sons Ltd).

[2] These sentences form part of the gramophone records which were made to illustrate the book and were spoken by Miss Armstrong. The intonation marked is that of the record.

ˈfrɛndz ənd pəhæps ðə moʊst ˈdʒɛnjʊɪn ˈbʊk-lʌvər

in ˈlʌndən.

(5) hi ˈnɛvə ˈrɛd ðə ˈpeɪpəz tɪl ðɪ ˈiˑvnɪŋ ˈpɑˑtlɪ

bɪkɒz i ˈhædnt ˈtaim ənd ˈpɑˑtlɪ bɪkɒz hi soʊ

sɛldəm faʊnd ˈɛnɪθɪŋ ˈɪn ðəm.

GENERAL OBSERVATIONS.

367. (1) The quality of vowels and consonants is influenced by a tendency to draw back the whole of the tongue somewhat and to raise the back towards the soft palate; in many cases too, the back of the tongue appears to be hollowed, i.e. it has a furrow down the middle and the sides are raised a little.[1] As a result of this tendency, consonants articulated at or near the alveolar ridge have a secondary articulation; they are velarised or "dark." Dark 1 is common in final positions and before consonants in most varieties of English. In American English it is also used in initial positions, as it is in Scottish. The exact quality of initial 1 varies with the following vowel and from individual to individual, but, generally speaking, "clear" 1 is not used in this position. The American velarisation of other alveolar consonants is not so easy to note, but it is

[1] "Sulcalised" is the phonetic term given to this tongue position.

recognisable in post-vocalic n, and the other consonants such as s, z, ʃ, ʒ, r, t, d, are often made with some raising of the back of the tongue or a general backward pull, which contributes something to the effect of American as compared with British English. In the records, "dark" 1 is noticeable in words like *glad, latchkey, jolliest, London*.[1]

368. Vowel sounds are affected also by this action of the tongue, particularly the front vowels. Many of these are definitely more retracted in American speech than in English,[2] and some of them frequently are pronounced with an ə-glide before the following alveolar

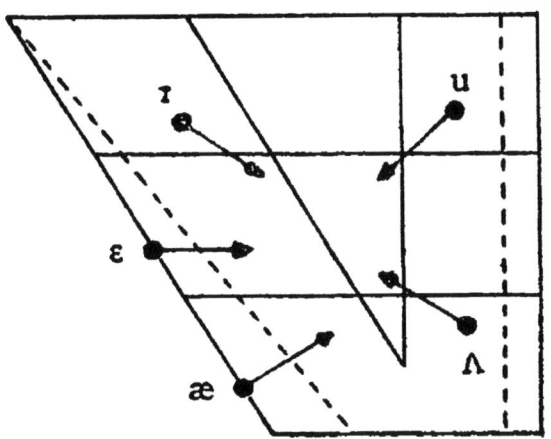

(*Dots*, represent normal British English vowel positions; *arrows*, the direction towards the position in which the American vowels tend to be pronounced; the *dotted line*, roughly the front and back limit of American vowels.)

[1] The whole word *London* sounds velarised and sulcalised.

[2] See, however, § 361 for a modern tendency towards this in England. See also the note on the President Roosevelt record. I heard recently in a broadcast of the speech by the President of Harvard the words *minimise* and *within* pronounced with a very much lowered and centralised vowel: these words sounded like mənəmaɪz, wəðən, the ə having somewhat of an ɛ quality.

P

consonant. Thus ɪ, ɛ, æ are frequently pronounced ɪᵊ, ɛᵊ, æᵊ. The vowel i, however, does not appear to be affected in this way, and is often very close. This is illustrated in the majority of the records, where *wind, friend, command* are pronounced wɪᵊnd, frɛᵊnd, komæᵊnd with a marked glide. The retraction of the front vowels, together with an advancing of some of the back vowels makes the vowel area smaller than in normal British English.

369. (2) When the letter *r* follows a vowel in spelling, the consonant is usually pronounced either with the tongue-tip curled up or with a "bunching" up of the front of the tongue.¹ This takes place during the pronunciation of the vowel and affects the vowel quality by adding to it something of the quality of a central vowel (ɜ). Thus in the records the word *partly* is almost pɜɹtlɪ. It is noticeable that with several speakers, post-vocalic r is very lightly pronounced; in some cases it is scarcely perceptible.²

370. (3) Generally speaking, American English has a weaker consonant articulation than that of British English, a less vigorous contact and release. An intervocalic consonant which is voiceless in British English, in American speech has the weaker articulation which normally belongs to a voiced consonant, and frequently *is* voiced. Intervocalic t is so short as to be a very rapid

---

[1] See p. 145 for diagram and explanation of retroflex r. There is often little or no friction, so that the pronunciation of vowel + r is vowel with retroflexion or bunching up of the tongue and not consonant. See Kenyon, p. 62.

[2] President Roosevelt does not use it except as a linking r before a word beginning with another vowel. See p. 385.

BRITISH ENGLISH AND AMERICAN ENGLISH 211

"tap" or touch of the tongue-tip on the teeth ridge, and the voice goes on through this "vestigial" t. Thus *letter* is pronounced lɛtə in British English and lɛt̬r[1] in American. The difference between the two is not only in the voice introduced into the American type, but in the use of the weaker articulation which belongs to voiced consonants.

Examples: bɛt̬ɪ (*Betty*), θɜɹt̬ɪ (*thirty*), lɪt̬l̩ (*little*), wɪnt̬ɹ (*winter*),[2] ɔːt̬əm (*autumn*), ðæt̬ ɪt̬ ɪs (*that it is*).

To English ears, intervocalic t pronounced in this way sounds like a one-tap r; *Betty* pronounced bɛt̬ɪ sounds like bɛrɪ (*berry*), the r being a single tap and not the fricative variety. The consonants p and k, though pronounced with weak articulation in similar positions, are not so noticeably different from English p and k.

371. (4) While it is impossible to treat American vowel sounds systematically in this short chapter, there are one or two points to which attention is drawn. One of the outstanding difficulties of the British phonetician dealing with American speech is that of classifying the distribution of the vowels æ, a, ɑ, ɒ, ɔ. Many Americans use three sounds of the letter *a*, viz. æ, a, ɑ; the use of these, however, varies considerably from British custom. Thus *man* and *can't* are both pronounced with æ; *father* has frequently a more forward position than in English (faːðɹ) while ɑ is used in words in which Englishmen use

---

[1] t̬ = t with some voice.
[2] The contact for t in this word in some of the records is so weak that it gives the impression that it isn't there: wɪnɹ.

ɒ: nɒt (*not*). Again, ɔ occurs with many speakers where ɒ is used in England: *long* (lɒŋ) is frequently pronounced lɔːŋ. In the experience of the present writer, however, there are many variations in the use of these vowels among American speakers, and it is no part of this work to attempt a classification of their use, but merely to draw attention to this point.[1] In the records, *glad, latch* are pronounced by several speakers with a distinctly low and retracted variety of a (glad, latʃ), due probably to the influence of the initial dark "l," and the same speakers use æ in *man* (mæᵊn) and *commands* (kəmæᵊndz); *pocket, Scotch, jolliest* are pronounced pɑkət, skɑtʃ, dʒɑlıəst by many, and *wrong* is rɔːŋ. But it should be stressed once more that there is by no means uniformity in these pronunciations.

372. (5) American usage in the matter of vowel length varies from that of British English. Certain vowels, which by the majority of English people[2] are considered short, are pronounced considerably longer in America, and some of the long vowels and diphthongs are also longer.[3] The diphthongisation of the front vowels ɪ, ɛ, æ, which are considered short vowels in English, illustrates this point; in American speech these are noticeably longer than in that of most English people. The question of length is also closely linked with that of rhythm and intonation. Examples of the differences in

---

[1] See Kenyon, *American Pronunciation*, pp. 94–104, 114–118, for a very full analysis of these vowels and their distribution.

[2] See, however, § 361 (vı).

[3] See Vowel Length ın "American Speech," April, 1937. (Professor Heffner).

BRITISH ENGLISH AND AMERICAN ENGLISH 213

this respect between the two types of English are given below.

373. (6) In all speech, vowels in the immediate neighbourhood of nasal consonants are nasalised to some degree; in some kinds of American speech, nasality in this position is more noticeable than in British English. This is one of the characteristics of American speech that the non-trained observer notes, but it should be pointed out that the degree of nasalisation varies widely, and that what is usually considered by Americans as the best type of speech is no more nasalised than the best British variety. In the records examined, nasality is not marked in the majority of the speakers, nor is it noticeable in the Roosevelt record.

374. (7) It is perhaps in intonation, stress and rhythm that the greatest general differences are found between British and American English, and these are often subtle and difficult to analyse and to explain on paper without audible illustrations.

INTONATION.

375. (a) In American speech a falling intonation in a succession of stressed syllables appears to be common. This usually denotes emphasis in British English, so that a non-emphatic statement with these frequent falls gives the impression of an emphatic speech. Thus:

ənd wəz glæd tə faɪnd hɪz lætʃki ənd hiz mʌnɪ

214

```
 .   \   .   \   .   \
```
ə mæn kəmændz ðə wɜrld

```
 .  .  \  .  .  \  .  \  .
```
ɪn ə truːlɪ dɛməkræˈtɪk kʌntrɪ.

(*President of Harvard's broadcast*, Mar. 29, 1938.)

Curiously enough, however, emphatic speech sounds less vigorously stressed. American speakers on their side feel British English to be less stressed. The explanation of this difference lies, as far as the present writer has been able to ascertain, in the different methods of the two sets of people in applying stress. In British English, one way in which emphasis shows itself is by a more vigorous articulation of the consonants, i.e. a tighter and longer contact (or, in the case of fricatives, a narrower opening) and a sharper release; this, of course, with increased breath force. The American who feels that he uses considerable effort, expends it rather on the vowel than on the consonant, i.e. it would appear that he has a stronger diaphragm movement and he lengthens his vowels, but the incidence of this extra force expended affects his consonants little. Thus the judgment on each side is subjective; since he does not find the type of emphasis he uses himself, with its acoustic effect, each thinks that it is absent in the other. It should be possible to analyse by experimental methods these two types of producing emphasis, and confirm—or otherwise—what is put down here as a tentative suggestion, the result of careful observations and discussion with an American phonetician.

(b) It will be seen from the first sentences set out on p. 170 that a succession of stressed syllables in a descending scale, with a fall on the last one, is typical of an unemphatic statement in British English; it is rare to find these syllables on the same note. In American English, however, the same pitch is struck frequently, as is shown by the intonation given under (a) above, with, of course, the fall within the syllable. To English ears this gives the impression of monotony; the fall evidently gives the necessary variety to Americans. In the records examined, the men speakers particularly show this tendency; the limits of the voice within which they speak also are narrow, and the bottom limit in some cases is reached only at the end of a sentence.

(c) As far as intonation alone is concerned, the records illustrate the foregoing points. They also show that in the emphatic sentences the intonation of the two types of speech are not unlike. There are naturally variants where the speaker has made one idea more prominent than was done in the original recording. Thus: *How do you know it's wrong* has the intonation [·ˑ⌐. ⎯], making *know* prominent and not *wrong* (which implies that the fact of it's being wrong has already been stated). This is a normal reading of the sentence, and would be used by both Americans and English alike. Similarly, one speaker gives the sentence *It's not my business* the intonation [.. ⎯ ..] with extra stress on *my*, and using Tune II with its implication, which is quite as usual as [. ⎯ ⎯ ˎ.]¹. The use of Tune II in

¹ I have been told that this sentence is not American English. An American would express the same idea by "That's none of my business."

statements is perhaps not quite so frequent in American speech as in English, and as far as the present writer has observed the pattern

I know what you mean [· ___ ..‿] is used rather than [.⁻ ·· ‿].

There is no material in the records, however, which can illustrate this habit. The following variations in the tune of an unfinished group which are not common in British English were heard in a broadcast from America:

eɪ ˈmɔːr əˈtræktɪv ˈproɡræ·m [.⁻ · — .⁻ ·]

hu du ‖nɒt ɡoʊ tʊ ˈkɒlɪdʒ [.. ↘ ·· — ·]

ə weɪst əv ˈprɛʃəs ˈfʌndz [.⁻ · — . ⁓]

eɪ ˈmænjʊəl ˈwɜːkər [.⁻ · — ·] (the two last in a series).

One further point should be mentioned. The use of the two speech tunes varies. What is perfectly polite to American ears may sound somewhat casual to British ears, while a normal British tune may give the impression of a dogmatic or even rude utterance to the American.[1] In this connection it would be interesting to make a careful study of the intonation of the small change of greetings, farewells, familiar questions and sentences in the two types of speech.[2]

[1] See *The Broadcast Word*, by Professor A. Lloyd James, pp. 7–9, for the misunderstandings that may arise from differences in this particular bit of speech behaviour.

[2] The intonation [__ ⁓] for the word "Goodbye" at the end of a business interview gave to the present writer an impression of a casualness which was decidedly out of place. She has been told by Americans that it was in point of fact probably intended to be extra friendly and polite.

BRITISH ENGLISH AND AMERICAN ENGLISH

STRESS AND RHYTHM.

376. One of the main contributory factors to the difference between English and American rhythm is the fact that the American makes use of fewer "weak forms" and neutral vowels than the Englishman. This changes the rhythmic patterns entirely. The pronunciation of the words *vacation, necessarily, romance* illustrates this point as far as words are concerned. In British English they are pronounced və'keɪʃn, 'nɛsɪsərɪlɪ (or 'nɛsəsərɪlɪ), ro'mæns (rə'mæns), while in most types of American English they are veɪ'keɪʃn, 'nɛsɪ'sɛərəlɪ (or nɛsə'sɛrɪlɪ), rou'mæns (or 'roumæns). There may or may not be secondary stress on the syllable which is unstressed in English, but in any case the use of the diphthongs eɪ, ɛə, ou in place of the short neutral vowel gives greater prominence to the syllables in which they occur, since they are longer and of a stronger quality. Thus the rhythm of the word and the relative length of the syllables is altered. When this habit is carried over into the sentence, and words which in British English have weak forms with the minimum of stress are pronounced with a stronger form and at greater length, it is easily seen how different the rhythmic patterns become. At the same time, the American usage of relatively long vowels where British English has short ones, and the greater length of long vowels and diphthongs also contributes to the variations in rhythm between the two types of speech. It should be noted that to the American the reduction of so many vowels to the neutral, and the occurrence of a succession of unstressed syllables with a neutral vowel gives the impression of "clipped" speech, of the swallowing of

syllables and of distortion of the word,[1] while the more deliberate American pronunciation sounds to the Englishman as if undue importance were given to unimportant words and syllables.

377. A considerable number of examples occur in the few sentences of the records under examination.[2] In unstressed syllables of single words, the only differences of this kind are *reproach*, pronounced rɪproʊtʃ, instead of rɪproʊtʃ, *genuine* as dʒɛnjuain,[3] and *partly* as paɹtli (with final i) by two or three speakers. Of the unimportant words, *of* is never anything but əv, except in one case where *the joliest of friends* is pronounced ði dʒɑlɪəst ɒv frɛ°ndz, where *the* is also pronounced ði. The women speakers mostly use h in unstressed *his*, but not the men: *you* is often ju and not jʊ as in the question *How many times have you been there?*, where *have* also has its strong form (but *been* is usually bɪn, where English usage would probably give fifty per cent. saying biːn): *with them* is almost always pronounced wɪððɛm and not wɪððəm; *and* is frequently ænd, and the article *a* is sometimes pronounced eɪ: eɪ mæ°n komæ°ndz ðə wɜɹld. The words *winter wind* illustrate a different rhythmic pattern from British English; in the latter the two words take up the same time and have even stress; most of the records give the impression of a stronger stress on *wind* because (*a*) the vowel in it is longer, and the vowel in

---

[1] Several types of English dialect speech share, to some extent, this characteristic of American. See §§ 284 (iii) and 327. See also § 20 where the reaction of Colonials to this type of speech is mentioned.

[2] They are not all alike, however, in this respect.

[3] This is said to be an emphatic form and somewhat "rustic."

winter is shorter, and (*b*) there is a different relation of the pitch of the two syllables; as far as time is concerned, the one can be represented as ♩.♪♩ and the other as ♪♪♩..

378. In this brief chapter general differences between British and American English have been illustrated. Further illustrations of these points are given in the notes on the pronunciation of President Roosevelt's record, of which a phonetic transcription is given on p. 226–31. The writer would like to point out once more, however, that these are not to be considered as exhaustive nor of universal application. Moreover, it must be stated that in the great body of English pronunciation there are many more points of similarity than of variation between the two types of speech. A close comparison of the two would reveal subtleties difficult in the first place to analyse and in the second to record, and requiring a major work in which to do justice to the problem. It is to be hoped that such a work may sometime be forthcoming.

Chapter XIX.

PHONETIC TRANSCRIPTIONS.

The intonation given for the first two texts has been noted down from the records and is shown above each line.

379. King George V's Message to the Empire, Christmas, 1935.

aɪ ˈwɪʃ ju ˈɔːl, maɪ ˈdɪə ˈfrɛndz, ə ˈhæpɪ ˈkrɪsməs.

aɪ v biˑn ˈdiˑplɪ ˈtʌtʃt bə ðə ˈgriˑtɪŋs wɪtʃ ɪn ðə ˈlɑˑst

ˈfjuˑ ˈmənɪts hæv ˈriˑtʃt mi frəm ˈɔːl ˈpɑˑts əv ðɪ

ˈɛmpaɪə. lɛt ˈmiː ɪn rəsˈpɒnts sɛnd tə ˈʔiˑtʃ əv ˈju

ə ˈgriˑtɪŋ frəm maɪˈsɛlf. maɪ ˈwɜːdz wɪl bɪ ˈvɛrɪ ˈsɪmpl,

bʌt ˈspoʊkən frm ðə ˈhɑˑt, ɒn ðɪs ˈfæmɪlɪ ˈfɛstəvl ɒv

ˈkrɪsməs. ðə ˈjɪə ðət ɪz ˈpɑˑsɪŋ, ðə ˈtwɛntɪ-ˈfɪθ ˈsɪns

220

maɪ ækˈsɛʃn həz ˈbiːn tə ˈmiː ˈmoʊs ˈmɛmrəbl ɪt

ˈkɔːld ˈfɔˑθ ə ˌspɒnˈteɪnɪəs ˈɒfrɪŋ ɒv ˈlɔɪəltɪ ən aɪ

ˈmeɪ ˈseɪ, əv ˈlʌv, wɪtʃ ðə ˈkwiːn ən ˈaɪ kən ˈnɛvə

ˈfəgɛt. ˈhaʊ kʊd aɪ ˈfeɪl tə ˈnoʊt ɪn ˈɔːl ðə rəˈdʒɔɪsɪŋz,

ˈnɒt ˈmɪəlɪ rəsˈpɛkt fə ðə ˈθroʊn, bət ə ˈwɔːm ænd

ˈdʒɛnərəs rɪˈmɛmbrəns əv ðə ˈmæn hɪmˈsɛlf, ˈhuː,

meɪ ˈgɒd ˈhɛlp ɪm, hæz biːn ˈpleɪst əpɒn ɪt. ɪt ˈɪz ˈðɪs

ˈpɜˑsnəl ˈlɪŋk bətwiːn ˈmiː æn maɪ ˈpiˑpl wɪtʃ aɪ

ˈvælju ˈmɔː ðən aɪ kən ˈseɪ. ɪt ˈbaɪndz əs təˈgɛðə

ɪn ˈɔːl aʊə ˈkɒmən ˈdʒɔɪz ˈænd ˈsɒroʊz, æz ˈwɛn ˈðɪs.

ˈjɪə ju ˈʃoʊd jɔː ˈhæpɪnəs ɪn ðə ˈmærɪdʒ əv maɪ ˈsʌn,

æn jɔː ˈsɪmpəθɪ ɪn ðə ˈdeθ əv maɪ bəˈlʌvəd ˈsɪstə.

aɪ ˈfiːl ðɪs ˈlɪŋk ˈnaʊ, əz aɪ ˈspiˑk tə ju fər aɪ m

ˈθɪŋkɪŋ ˈnɒt so ˈmʌtʃ əv ði ˈɛmpaɪə ɪtˈsɛlf, əz ɒv ði,

ˈɪndəˈvɪdɪʊəl ˈmɛn, ˈwɪmɪn ˈænd ˈtʃɪldrən hu ˈlɪv

wɪˈðɪn ɪt, ˈweðə ðeɪ ə ˈdwɛlɪŋ ˈhɪə ət ˈhoʊm ɔː ɪn

sʌm ˈdɪstənt ˈaʊtpoʊst ɒv ði ˈɛmpaɪə. ɪn ˈjʊərəp ən

ˈmɛnɪ ˈpɑˑts əv ðə ˈwɜːld æŋˈzaɪətɪz səˈraʊnd əs. ɪt

ɪz ˈgʊd tə ˈθɪŋk ðət aʊə ˈʔoʊn ˈfæmɪlɪ əv ˈpiˑplz ɪz

æt ˈpiˑs ɪn ɪtˈsɛlf æn juˈnaɪtɪd ɪn ˈwʌn dəˈzaɪə tə

bi ət ˈpiˑs wɪð ˈʌðə ˈneɪʃnz, ðə ˈfrɛnd əv ˈɔːl, ði ˈʔɛnɪmɪ

ɒv ˈnʌn. ˈmeɪ ðə ˈspɪrɪt əv ˈgʊdˈwɪl æn ˈmjuˑtʃʊəl

'hɛlpfʊlnɪs 'grou, 'ænd 'sprɛd. 'ðɛn ɪt wɪl 'brɪŋ 'nɒt

'ounlɪ ðə 'blɛsɪŋ əv 'piˑs bət ə sə'luːʃn əv ðɪ ˌiˑkɪ'nɒmɪk

'trʌblz wɪtʃ 'stɪl bɪ'sɛt əs. tə 'ðouz hu ə 'sʌfrɪŋ ɔˑ

ɪn dɪ'strɛs 'wɛðə ɪn 'ðɪs 'kʌntrɪ ɔˑ ɪn 'ɛnɪ 'paˑt əv ðɪ

'ɛmpaɪə, aɪ 'ɒfə maɪ 'diˑpəs 'sɪmpəθɪ. 'bʌt aɪ wʊd

'ɔˑlsou gɪv ə 'krɪsməs 'mɛsɪdʒ əv 'houp ænd 'tʃɪə.

ju'naɪtɪd baɪ ðə 'bɒnd əv 'wɪlɪŋ 'sɜˑvɪs, 'lɛt əs 'pruːv

auəsɛlvz bouθ 'strɒŋ tʊ ɪn'djuə ən 'rɛzəluˑt tʊ

ouvə'kʌm. 'wʌns ə'geɪn əz aɪ 'klouz, aɪ 'sɛnd ju

'ɔːl æn 'nɒt 'liːst tə ðə 'tʃɪldrən hu 'meɪ bɪ 'lɪsnɪŋ

tə 'miː, maɪ 'truˑəst 'krɪsməs 'wɪʃɪz, ənd 'ðouz əv

maɪ ˈdɪə ˈwaɪf, maɪ ˈtʃɪldrən ænd ˈgræntʃɪldrən hu ɑ

ˈwɪð mi təˈdeɪ. aɪ ˈæd ə ˈhɑˑtfɛlt ˈprɛə ðət wɛəˈɛvə

ju ˈɑː gɒd meɪ ˈblɛs ænd ˈkiˑp jʊ ˈɔˑlweɪz.

NOTES.

380. (1) The speech is deliberately slow; the sense groups are smaller and the pauses longer than in ordinary speech, but the normal rhythm is very little disturbed by this, nor is there much exaggeration of sound or any undue stressing. The slowing-up is in proportion. (See Ch. II, p. 119.)

(2) Certain of the unimportant words which in quicker speech would have a weak form have the full vowel here. These occur frequently after a pause and occasionally within the group when the slow speed would mean too great a length for the neutral vowel:

    bʌt ˈspoʊkən frm ðə ˈhɑˑt.
    hæz biːn ˈpleɪst əˈpɒn ɪt.
    ə ˈwɔːm ænd ˈdʒɛnərəs rɪˈmɛmbrəns.

(3) The range of voice and intonation patterns are also without exaggeration and this in its turn strengthens the impression of sincerity. The intonations used illustrate the normal patterns of English unemphatic speech. Note, however, two examples of a character-

istic of public speaking, viz. a rather high-pitch ending to a Tune II group:

wɛðə ðeɪ ə dwɛlɪŋ hɪə,

and a low level ending of a similar group:

bouθ strɒŋ tu ɪndjuə.

(4) The following details of pronunciation may be noted.

(i) The frequent use of ə where many people use ɪ: rədʒɔɪsɪŋz, rəspɛkt, bəlʌvəd, mənɪt.

(ii) The ou is near to ɔu in many words: spɔukən but nout.

(iii) A voiced h is used in *help* in gɒd hɛlp ɪm.

(iv) "Linking r" is generally not used (but it occurs in fər aɪ m θɪŋkɪŋ): ɔ ɪn dɪstrɛs, wɛə ɛvə juˑ ɑ, ɔ ɪn ɛnɪ pɑˑt əv ðɪ ɛmpaɪə. This is the only characteristic of those noted in Ch. XVII as belonging to the modern type of Southern English. In one place a glottal stop is used: auə ʔoun fæmɪlɪ əv piˑplz.

(v) The occasional dropping of the d of *and*, and of t: mous mɛmərəbl, diˑpəs sɪmpəθɪ, and of h in unstressed positions. It should be noted that the record had to be played over a considerable number of times to decide whether these consonants were pronounced or not; the omissions are not noticeable without very careful attention. This is another illustration of the naturalness of the speech.

President Roosevelt's Speech: "Fireside Chat"

381. *Survey at the time of the special convocation of Congress, Oct. 13, 1937. First side of Record.*

maɪ ˈfrɛnz, ðɪs ˈæˑftəˈnuːn aɪ əv ˈɪsjuːd ə ˈprɒkləˈmeɪʃn

ˈkɔːlɪŋ eɪ ˈspɛʃl ˈsɛʃn əv ðə ˈkɒŋgrəs tʊ kənˈviːn ɒn

ˈmʌndɪ, noʊˈvɛmbə ˈfɪfˈtiːnθ, ˈnaɪntiˑn ˈθɜˑtɪ ˈsɛvn.

a ˈduˑ ˈðɪs ɪn ˈɔˑdə tʊ ˈgɪv tʊ ðə ˈkɒŋgrəs ən ɒpəˈtjuˑnətɪ

tʊ kənˈsɪdə ɪmˈpɔˑtnt lɛdʒɪsˈleɪʃn bəˈfɔˑ ðə ˈrɛgjʊlə ˈsɛʃn

ɪn ˈdʒænjʊərɪ, ˈænd tʊ əˈneɪbl ðə ˈkɒŋgrəs tʊ əˈvɔɪd

eɪ ˈlɛŋθɪ ˈsɛʃən ˈnɛkst ˑjɪə ɛksˈtɛndɪŋ ˈθruː ðə ˈsʌmə.

aɪ ˈnoʊ ðət ˈmɛnɪ ˈɛnəmɪz əv dəˈmɒˑkɹəsɪ wɪl ˈseɪ

ðət ɪt ɪz ˈbæˑd fə ˈbɪznəs, ˈbæˑd fə ðə træŋˈkwɪlətɪ əv

ðə ˈkʌntɹɪ tə hæv ə speʃl seʃn ˈiːvn ˈwʌn bɪˈgɪnɪŋ

ounlɪ ˈsɪks ˈwiːks bəfɔː ðə ˈregjʊlə seʃn, bət ˈaɪ həv

ˈnevə ˈhæd ˈsɪmpəθɪ wɪð ðə ˈpɔɪn̯t əv ˈvjuː ðət ə ˈseʃn

əv ðə ˈkɒŋgrəs ɪz ən ˈʌnˈfɔːtʃənət ɪnˈtɹuːʒn əv ˈhwɒt

ðeɪ kɔːl ˈpɒˑlətɪks ɪntʊ aʊə ˈnæʃnəl (ə)ˈfɛəz. ˈðouz hu

ˈdu nɒt ˈlaɪk dəˈmɒkrəsɪ ˈwɔːnt tə ˈkiˑp ˈledʒɪsleɪtɔːz

ət ˈfiɔːm. bət ðə ˈkɒˑŋgrəs ɪz ən əˈsenʃl ˈʔɪnstrəmənt

əv ˈdeməkrætɪk ˈgʌvənmənt, ˈænd ˈdeməkrætɪk ˈgʌvən-

mənt kən ˈnevə bi kənˈsɪdəd ən ɪnˈtruːdə ɪntʊ ðɪ əˈfɛəz

əv ə ˈdeməkrætɪk ˈneɪʃn. aɪ ʃl ˈæˑsk ðɪs ˈspeʃl ˈseʃən

tʊ kənˈsɪdəɹ əˈmiˑdɪətlɪ ˈsɜːtn ɪmˈpɔˑtnt ledʒɪsˈleɪʃn wɪtʃ

'ɒn maɪ 'riˑsnt 'trɪp θru ðə 'neɪʃn kən'vɪnsɪz 'mi ðɪ

ə'mɛɹɪkən 'piˑpl ə'miːdɪətlɪ 'niːd. 'ðɪs 'dʌz 'nɒt 'miːn

ðət 'ʌðə lɛdʒɪsleɪʃn tu 'wɪtʃ aɪ əm 'nɑu rɪ'fɜɹɪŋ tə'naɪt

ɪz 'nɒt ən ɪm'pɔˑtnt paˑt əv auə 'næʃnl wɛl-'biˑɪŋ, bət

'?ʌðə lɛdʒɪsleɪʃn kæn bi mɔ 'ɹɛdəlɪ dɪs'kʌst æt ðə 'rɛgjulə

'sɛʃn. 'ɛnɪwʌn 'tʃɑːdʒd wɪð prə'pouzɪŋ ɔ 'dʒʌdʒɪŋ

'næʃnəl 'pɒˑləsɪz 'ʃud hæˑv 'fɜˑst-hænd 'nɒlɪdʒ əv ðə

'neɪʃn əz ə 'houl. 'ðæt ɪz 'hwaɪ ə'geɪn 'ðɪs 'jiəɹ aɪ əv

'teɪkən 'tɹɪps tu 'ɔːl 'paˑts əv ðə 'kʌntrɪ. 'læˑst 'sprɪŋ

aɪ 'vɪzɪtɪd ðə 'sauθ-'wɛˑst: 'ðɪs 'sʌməɹ aɪ meɪd 'sɛvrəl

'trɪps ɪn ðə '?iːst: 'nau aɪ əm 'dʒʌst 'bæk frəm ə 'trɪp

PHONETIC TRANSCRIPTIONS

ˈɔːl ðə ˈweɪ əˈkrɒs ðə ˈkɒntɪnənt ənd ˈleɪtə ðɪs ˈɔːtəm aɪ

ˈhoʊp tə ˈpeɪ maɪ ˈʔænjʊəl ˈvɪzɪt tə ðə ˈsaʊθ-iˑst. tʊ ə

ˈprɛzədənt əsˈpɛʃəlɪ, ɪt ɪz eɪ ˈdjuˑtɪ tʊ ˈθɪŋk ɪn ˈnæʃnəl

ˈtɜˑmz. hiˑ məst ˈθɪŋk ˈnɒt oʊnlɪ əv ˈðɪs jiə, bət əv

ˈfjuˑtʃə jiəz wɛn ˈsʌmwʌn ˈɛlts wɪl bi ˈprɛzədnt. hi

məst ˈlʊk bɪjɒnd ðɪ ˈævɹɪʤ əv ðə pɹɒsˈpɜɹətɪ ənd ˈwɛl-

ˈbiˑɪŋ əv ðə ˈkʌntɹɪ bɪkɒz ˈævəɹɪʤɪz ˈiːzəlɪ ˈkʌvəɹ ˈʌp

ˈdeɪnʤə spɒˑts əv ˈpɒvətɪ ənd ˈɪnstəˈbɪlətɪ. hi ˈmʌst

ˈnɒt ˈlɛt ðə ˈkʌntɹɪ bi dəˈsiːvd baɪ ə ˈmɪəlɪ ˈtɛmpəɹəɹɪ

prɒsˈpɛɹətɪ wɪtʃ dəˈpɛndz ɒn ˈweɪstfʊl ɛksplɔɪˈteɪʃn əv

rɪˈsɔːsɪz wɪtʃ kænɒt ˈlæːst. hi ˈmʌst ˈθɪŋk ˈnɒt oʊnlɪ

əv ˈkiːpiŋ ʌs aʊt əv ˈwɔː tuˈdeɪ, bət ˈɔːlsoʊ əv ˈkiːpiŋ

əs aʊt əv ˈwɔːə ɪn ˈdʒenəreɪʃnz tə ˈkʌm. ði ˈkaɪnd əv

pɪəsˈpərəti wi ˈwɔːnt ɪz ðə ˈsaʊnd ənd ˈpɜːmənənt kaɪnd

wɪtʃ ɪz ˈnɒt ˈbɪlt ˈʌp tempəˈrærəli ət ði ekˈspens əv enɪ

ˈsekʃn ɔ ˈgruːp, ænd ðə ˈkaɪnd əv ˈpiːs wi wɔːənt ɪz ðə

ˈsaʊnd ənd ˈpɜːmənənt kaɪnd wɪtʃ ɪz ˈbɪlt ʔɒn ðə ˈkoʊ-

ɒpəreɪtɪd ˈsɜːtʃ fə ˈpiːs baɪ ɔːl ðə ˈneɪʃnz hwɪtʃ ˈwɔːnt

piːs. ði ˈʌðə ˈdeɪ aɪ wəz ˈaːst tʊ ˈsteɪt maɪ ˈaʊtˈstændɪŋ

ɪmˈpreʃn ˈgeɪnd ɒn ðɪs ˈriːsnt ˈtrɪp tə ðə pəˈsɪfɪk ˈkoʊst

ən bæk, ən ˈaɪ ˈsed ðət ɪt ˈsiːmd tə ˈmiː tə ˈbi ðə ˈdʒenərəl

ʌndəˈstændɪŋ ɒn ðə ˈpaːt əv ði ˈʔævərɪdʒ ˈsɪtəzn ʌndə-

stændɪŋ əv ðə ˈbrɔːd əbˈdʒektɪvz ənd ˈpɒləsɪz wɪtʃ aɪ əv

PHONETIC TRANSCRIPTIONS 231

ˈdʒʌst ˈaʊtlaɪnd. ˈfaɪv ˈjiəz əv ˈfrəs dɪsˈkʌʃn ənd dəˈbeɪt:

ˈfaɪv ˈjiəz əv ɪnfəˈmeɪʃn θru ðə ˈreɪdɪoʊ and ðə ˈmuːvɪŋ

ˈpɪktʃə hæv ˈteɪkən ðə ˈhoʊl ˈneɪʃn tʊ ˈskuːl ɪn ðə

ˈneɪʃnz ˈbɪznəs.

NOTES ON THE PRONUNCIATION: INTERPRETATION OF THE PHONETIC TRANSCRIPTION.

382. *Vowels and Diphthongs.*

ɪ A low variety is used; it is difficult to say whether unstressed ɪ or the neutral vowel ə is used in words like *because, citizen*, which sound near to bəkɔːz, sətəzən. Final ɪ is closer than is usual in British English; it is between ɪ and i.

ɛ A fairly open variety is used; in the word *west* it is lengthened and diphthongised, wɛːᵊst. When followed by r, e.g. in the word *American* it is very much centralised, nearing ɜ, and liable to English ears to be confused with ɜ + r. Comparison of the two words *American* and *referring*, however, shows them to be different, the former having a distinct ɛ quality and the latter being a rather close central vowel.

æ A little lower than Southern English æ. It is often long and is diphthongised in the word *last* (læᵊst). Note its use in *temporarily* (tɛmpəræərəlɪ).

ɒ   This symbol has been used throughout the text, but must be taken to represent a sound somewhat like cardinal ɑ (cf. § 371, p. 211). It gives the impression of some slight lip-rounding, however. In stressed positions it is considerably longer than the corresponding sound in British English.

ɔ   A fairly close variety, with more lip-rounding than cardinal No. 6; it is very similar to British English ɔ. In the word *war* (the second time it is used when it has emphatic stress and a fall-rise intonation) it sounds diphthongised.[1]

ʌ   More central than the normal Southern English variety, nearing ɜ.

ɜ   A close variety, near the e–o-line.

ə   The neutral vowel is used very frequently where many English people use ɪ.

oʊ The first element is verging on ɔ[2]; in the word *home*, a pure vowel is used, between o and ɔ.

ɑʊ The first element is further back than in normal Southern English: in the word *outstanding* it is almost ɔʊ.

ɪə In strongly stressed positions, where lengthening of the diphthong is a sign of emphasis, iə is frequently used: e.g. *five years*.

There is no noticeable nasalisation.

---

[1] There may also be retroflexion of the tongue, giving slight impression of ɹ.

[2] This wide diphthong ɔu was also noted in the speech of the President of Harvard, which was broadcast on 29th March, 1938, when the words *ago, both, only* were pronounced əgɔ̊u, bɔuθ, ɔunlˈ.

383. *Consonants.*

(a) The letter **r** is not pronounced after consonants or finally except as a linking **r**.

(b) **r** is the retroflex fricative; the inversion of the tongue is noticeable between vowels, but not in the groups **tr, pr, kr, gr**, etc.

(c) **t** is generally voiced (**t̬**) between vowels unless there is a pause. In one or two places, however, it sounds voiceless.

(d) **l** is dark in all positions.

(e) **ʃ** is dark; it is noticeable in the word *impression*.

384. *Stress and Rhythm.*

(a) Much of the stress and rhythm is very close to that of British English.

(b) The "push" on the vowels for emphasis (see § 375 a, p. 214) is noticeable.

(c) Strong forms are used frequently: *does, not, to*, generally have the forms **dʌz, nɒt, tʊ**, or **tu**, *and* is usually **ænd** (or **æn**) whenever it follows a pause, but in closely related phrases it is **ən**: e.g. **əkrɒs ðə pəsɪfɪk ən bæ·k**; *a* in two places occurs as **eɪ**. In the word *legislators*, the last syllable is pronounced **tɔːz**; *November* is **noʊvɛmbə**.

(d) A number of unimportant words are given importance by a high pitch: e.g. *I* and *and* at the beginning of sentences.

(e) Where the rhythm differs from that of many British English speakers, it is due to

    (i) The use of strong forms as described under (c) together with the spacing out of and slight

234 THE PHONETICS OF ENGLISH

stressing of short and what might be considered unimportant words: e.g. ˈðɪs ˈdʌz ˈnɒt ˈmiːn. This is not, of course, an invariable characteristic of American speech: the record is much more deliberate than conversation would be.

(ii) The use of longer forms of individual words: e.g. *immediately* is pronounced əmiˑdɪətlɪ, whereas in British English it would probably be ɪmiˑdjətlɪ; *January* is ʤænjuərɪ as against djænjʊrɪ; *temporarily* is tɛmpəˈrærɪlɪ as against ˈtɛmpərərəlɪ; and *resources* is rɪsɔːsɪz as compared with rɪsɔːsɪz.

385. *Intonation.*

(1) The groupings and distribution of Tunes I and II are very similar to those of normal British English.

(2) Many of the intonation patterns are the same.

(3) The typical fall on a number of stressed syllables in one group is frequent (see § 375, p. 213).

(4) Note the rise-fall or rise-level intonation for emphasis (see *Handbook of English Intonation*).

FROM *Pygmalion*, BY G. BERNARD SHAW, ACT II, p. 119.
386. NOTES ON THE PRONUNCIATION OF COCKNEY.

In one type of Cockney, the *t*'s and *d*'s in stressed positions would probably be affricated, i.e. pronounced as tˢ and dᶻ: this is marked in one case only where there is extra stress. The diphthong in the word *pay* (normal peɪ) is represented here by aɪ: the first element should be pronounced somewhat retracted and centralised, i.e. between cardinal No. 4 and ʌ.

387. *Mrs. Pearce.* ə ˈjʌŋ ˈwumən wɒnts tə ˈsiː ju, sɜˑ.

Higgins. ə ˈjʌŋ ˈwumən! ˈwɒt dəz ʃɪ ˈwɒnt?

Mrs. Pearce. ˈwɛl, sɜˑ, ʃɪ ˈsəz juˑl bɪ ˈglæd tə ˈsiː hɜ wɛn ju ˈnou wɒt ʃiˑ z ˈkʌm əbaut. ʃiːz ˈkwaɪt ə ˈkɒmən gɜːl, sɜˑ, ˈvɛrɪ kɒmən ɪnˈdiːd. aɪ ʃud əv ˈsɛnt hɜr əˈweɪ, ounlɪ aɪ ˈθɔˑt pəhæps ju ˈwɒntɪd hɜ tə ˈtɔˑk ɪntə ˈwʌn ə jɔə məˈʃiːnz. aɪ ˈhoup aɪ v ˈnɒt dʌn ˈrɒŋ; bət ˈrɪəlɪ ju ˈsiˑ sʌtʃ ˈkwɪə ˈpiˑpl səmˈtaɪmz— juˑl ɪksˈkjuːz mi, aɪ m ˈʃuə, sɜˑ—

Higgins. ou ˈðæts ɔˑl raɪt, mɪsɪz pɪəs. ˈhæz ʃɪ nɪ ˈɪntrəstɪŋ ˈæksnt?

Mrs. Pearce. ˈou, ˈsʌmθɪŋ ˈdrɛdful, sɜˑ, ˈrɪəlɪ. aɪ ˈdount ˈnou hau ju kən ˈteɪk ən ˈɪntrəst ɪn ɪt.

Higgins. ˈlɛts hæv ər ˈʌp. ˈʃou ər ˈʌp, mɪsɪz pɪəs.

Mrs. Pearce. ˈvɛrɪ ˈwɛl, sɜˑ, ɪts fə ˈjuː tə ˈseɪ.

Higgins. ðɪs ɪz ˈrɑˑðər ə ˈbɪt əv ˈlʌk. aɪ l ˈʃou ju hau aɪ ˈmeɪk ˈrɛkɔˑdz. wiːl ˈsɛt hɜ ˈtɔˑkɪŋ; ˈaɪl teɪk ɪt ˈdaun ˈfɜˑst ɪn ˈbɛlz ˈvɪzɪbl ˈspiˑtʃ; ˈðɛn ɪn ˈbrɔːd ˈroumɪk; ən ˈðɛn wiːl ˈgɛt hɜr ɒn ðə ˈfounəgrɑˑf sou ðət ju kən ˈtɜːn hɜr ˈɒn əz ˈɒfn əz ju ˈlaɪk wɪð ðə ˈrɪtn ˈtrɑˑnskrɪpt bɪˈfɔˑ ju.

Mrs. Pearce. ˈðɪs ɪz ðə jʌŋ wumən, sɜˑ.

Higgins. ˈwaɪ, ˈðɪs ɪz ðə ˈgɜːl aɪ ˈdʒɒtɪd ˈdaun ˈlɑˑs ˈnaɪt. ˈʃiːz nou juˑs: aɪv ˈgɒt ɔˑl ðə ˈrɛkɔˑdz aɪ ˈwɒnt əv ðə ˈlɪsn ˈgrouv lɪŋgou; ənd aɪm ˈnɒt goɪŋ tə ˈweɪst əˈnʌðə ˈsɪlɪndər ɒn ɪt. bɪ ˈɒf wɪð ju: aɪ ˈdount ˈwɒnt ju.

The Flower Girl. ˈdã͡ũ? ˈjɨː ˈbəi ˈsʌu ˈsɔːsɪ. jɨː ˈã͡ĩ? ˈɜˑd wɒ? aɪ ˈkam fɔː ˈjɪ?. dɪdʒə ˈtel ɪm aɪ ˈkam ɪn ə ˈtɛksəi?

236 THE PHONETICS OF ENGLISH

Mrs. Pearce. ˈnɒnsns, gɜ·l! ˈwɒt dju ˈθɪŋk ə ˈgɛntlmən laɪk ˈmɪstə ˈhɪgɪnz ˈkɛəz ˈwɒt ju keɪm ɪn?

The Flower Girl. ˈʌʊ, wɪ ˈɑː ˈpraːd! ˈãĩʔ əˈbav ˈgɪvɪn ˈlesnz ˈnɒʔ ˈɪm: aɪ ˈɜ·d mɪ ˈsaɪ sʌʊ. ˈweɔ, aɪ ˈãĩʔ kam ˈijə tə ˈɑ·s fər eni ˈkɒmplɪmənʔ; ən ɪf ˈmɑːɪ ˈmanɪz ˈnɒʔ ˈgʊd ɪnaf, aɪ kŋ ˈgʌʊ eɔsˈweə.

Higgins. ˈgʊd ɪnʌf fə ˈwɒt?

The Flower Girl. ˈgʊd ɪnaf fə ˈjiːʉ· ˈˈnaː jə ˈnʌʊ, ˈdãʊntʃə? aɪ m ˈkam tə ɛv ˈlesnz ˈɑːɪ ɛm, ən ˈpaɪ fər əm ˈˈtˢi̶ʉ; ˈmaɪʔ. nʌʊ mɪsˈtaɪʔ.

Higgins. ˈwɛl!!! ˈwɒt dju ɪkˈspɛkt mɪ tə ˈseɪ tə jʊ?

The Flower Girl. ˈweɔ, ɪf jə wəz ə ˈdʒɛʔɔmən, jə mãĩʔ ˈɑ·s mɪ tə ˈsɪ ˈdæʊn, ˈaɪ θɪʔ. ˈdʌʊn aɪ ˈtel jə aɪ m ˈbrɪŋɪn jə ˈbɪznɪsʔ.

Higgins. ˈpɪkərɪŋ, ˈʃæl wɪ ˈɑ·sk ðɪs ˈbægɪdʒ tə ˈsɪt ˈdaʊn, ɔ ˈʃæl wɪ ˈθrou ər ˈaʊt əv ðə ˈwɪndoʊ?

The Flower Girl. ˈˈʌʌʌ ... ʊʊʊ ... aɪˈ wãũʔbɪ ˈkoːd ə ˈbɛgɪdʒ wen aɪ v ˈɒfəd tə ˈpaɪ laɪk ˈenɪ ˈlaɪdɪ.

Pickering. ˈwɒt ɪz ɪt jʊ ˈwɒnt, maɪ gɜːl?

The Flower Girl. aɪ ˈwɒ̃ʔ tə bəi ə ˈlaɪdɪ ɪn ə ˈflaːʃɒp ˈsted ə ˈselɪn əʔ ðə ˈko·nər ə ˈtɒʔnəm ˈko·ʔ ˈrʌʊd, bət ðɛɪ ˈwãũʔ ˈtaɪʔ mɪ anˈles aɪ kŋ ˈto·k mo· dʒenˈtɪɔ. ˈəi sed ɪ kʊd ˈtəɪtʃ mɪ. ˈweɔ, ˈijər aɪ ˈɛm ˈredɪ tə ˈpaɪ ɪm—ˈnɒʔ ˈɑ·stɪn enɪ ˈfaɪvə—ən ɪ ˈtrəɪʔs mɪ əz ɪf ɑ wəz ˈdɜ·ʔ.

Mrs. Pearce. ˈhaʊ kən ju bi sʌtʃ ə ˈfuˑlɪʃ ˈɪgnərənt ˈgɜːl əz tə ˈθɪŋk ju kʊd əˈfɔːd tə ˈpeɪ mɪstə ˈhɪgɪnz?

The Flower Girl. waɪ ˈʃʊdn aɪʔ aɪ ˈnʌʊ wɒʔ ˈlesnz ˈkoːst əz ˈwel əz ˈjiʉ diʉ; ən aɪm ˈredɪ tə ˈpaɪ.

PHONETIC TRANSCRIPTIONS

Higgins. ˈhaʊ ˈmʌtʃ.
The Flower Girl. ˈnæʊ jə ˈtoːkɪn. aɪ ˈθoˑʔ jəd kam
 ˈɔːf ɪʔ wen jə ˈsoˑr ə ˈtʃɑːns ə ˈgeʔɪn ˈbɛʔ ə ˈbɪʔ ə ˈwɒʔ
 jə ˈtʃaʔt əʔ məi ˈlaˑs ˈnãĩʔ. jəd ˈɛd ə ˈdrɒp ˈɪn,
 ˈɛntʃə?
Higgins. ˈsɪt ˈdaʊn.
The Flower Girl. ˈʌʊ, ɪf jə ˈgʌɪnə maɪʔ ə ˈkɒmplɪmənʔ
 ɒv ɪʔ—
Higgins. ˈsɪt ˈdaʊn.
Mrs. Pearce. ˈsɪt ˈdaʊn, gɜːl, ˈduː əz jʊə ˈtoʊld.
The Flower Girl. ˈʌʌʌ . . . ʊʊʊ . . .
Pickering. ˈwo̯ʊnt jʊ sɪt ˈdaʊn?
The Flower Girl. ˈdãỗʔ ˈmãĩn ɪf ɑɪ ˈdɨɫ.
Higgins. ˈwɒts jɔ ˈneɪm?
The Flower Girl. ˈlaɪzə ˈdɨɫɪʔɔ.

FROM *The Good Companions*, BY J. B. PRIESTLEY, p. 32.

388. NOTE ON THE PRONUNCIATION OF YORKSHIRE.

The transcriber has endeavoured to represent a type of Yorkshire (Bruddersford) pronunciation which would be used by a man like Jess Oakroyd, but it is not the only possible pronunciation: it is probably one degree removed from the broadest dialect of that part of Yorkshire both in pronunciation and vocabulary.

389. ðə ˈnɛkst ˈmoʊmənt hi ˈwɒz ðɛə, ə ˈgraɪmɪ, ˈhɒt ənd
ˈæŋgrɪ ˈmæn hu ˈflʌŋ hɪz ˈkæp ənd hɪz ˈbæg əv ˈdʒɔɪnəz
ˈtuːlz ˈdaʊn ɒn ðə ˈsoʊfə, ˈðɛn ˈkloʊzd ðɪ ˈaʊtə ˈdɔə wɪð
ə ˈbæŋ. " ˈwɪər ɪ ðə ˈneɪm ə ˈgʊdnəs əv jə ˈbɪɪn? " hɪz
ˈwaɪf dɪˈmɑːndɪd. " ən jə ˈtrɪ ˈweɪtɪn ˈɪər ə ˈfʊl ˈaːr ən
ə ˈaːf ! "

" 'bɪin ɒn tə t 'ɪunɪən ɒfɪs," hi 'ɑˑnsəd 'ʃɔːtlɪ. ʃi 'glɑˑnst ət hɪz 'feɪs ən 'ðɛn 'mɒdəreɪtɪd hə 'toʊn. " 'wɒˀ djə wɒnt tə goˑ 'ðɪə fɔr ət 'ðɪs taɪm? "

" kɒz av bɪin 'stɒpt." hi 'bɛnt 'daʊn ən bɪ'gæn tʊ 'ʌn'leɪs hɪz 'hɛvɪ 'wɜˑkɪŋ 'buˑts.

" jəv bɪin 'wɒt? " hɪz 'waɪf 'ʃriˑkt.

" 'stɒpt, 'sakt, 'peːd 'ɒf, wɒ'tɪvə jə 'wɒnt tə 'kɔːl ɪt." hi 'streɪtnd hɪmsɛlf ən 'θruː ən ɪn'ʃʊərəns kɑːd ən səm 'manɪ ɒn ðə 'teɪbl. " am 'nʊt iiˑvn ʊndə 'noˑtɪs. 'ɪgdɪnz əz 'fɪnɪʃt wɪ mə, ən 'aɪv 'fɪnɪʃt wɪ 'ðɛm. ðəz ə 'wɪiks 'mʊnɪ 'ðɪə." hi bɪ'gæn tʊ ʌn'leɪs ðɪ 'ʌðə buˑt.

" 'wɛl a 'nɪvə 'dɪd l" 'kraɪd mɪsɪz 'oʊkrɔɪd. ʃi 'flɒpt 'daʊn ɪntʊ ə 'tʃɛə ənd rɪ'gɑˑdɪd hɪm wɪð ðɪ 'ʌtmoʊst əs'tɒnɪʃmənt. " 'wɒt ə jə bɪin 'dʊuɪn?"

" al 'tɛl jə ɔːl ə'baːt ɪt ɪn ə 'mɪnɪt. a 'wɒnt ə 'wɛʃ ən 'sʊmət tə 'ɛɪt." hi 'matʃt ɪn hɪz 'stɒkɪŋd 'fiˑt tɔːdz ðə 'skʌlərɪ. " 'gɛˀ mɪ 'trɪ rɛdɪ ən ðɛn jəl 'sʊɪn 'nɔː wɒt av bɪin dʊuɪn," hi 'ædɪd 'grɪmlɪ.

ɪn 'brʌdəsfəd 'waɪvz 'doʊnt 'stænd ɒn 'sɛrɪmənɪ ət sʌtʃ 'moʊmənts əv 'kraɪsɪs, ən 'mɪsɪz 'oʊkrɔɪd, wɪðaʊt ə 'wɜˑd əv 'proʊtɛst, 'meɪd ðə 'tiː ənd rɪ'liˑst ðə 'kɪpə frəm ɪts 'lɒŋ ɔˑ'dɪəl.

" ɪf 'ðɪs iə 'fɪʃ əd ə bɪin bɪ t 'faɪər ə 'mɪnɪt 'lɒŋə," sɛd 'mɪstər 'oʊkrɔɪd, 'naʊ 'siˑtɪd ət ðə 'teɪbl, " ɪt əd ə 'stɑˑtɪd 'waˑpɪn. ɪts 'laɪk ə 'bɪt ə 'bʌrnˀ 'wʊd."

" 'apm ɪts 'last jəl 'sii fər ə bɪt," hɪz 'waɪf rɪ'tɔːtɪd, hævɪŋ biˑn 'raʊzd baɪ ðɪs grəˈtjuɪtəs 'sælɪ. " 'nɛvə 'maɪnd əbaˑˀ 'ðaˀ. 'wɒt av jə 'gɒˀn 'stɒpt fɒ?"

" fə 'nɔʊt, 'dʒʊs 'nɔʊt," hi bɪgæn, "ər ɪf jə 'laˑɪk fə 'brɪin ə 'man ən 'nʊt ə 'damd 'mʊŋkɪ." hi 'stɒpt tə 'teɪk ə 'drɪŋk əv 'tiː, 'ðɛn, 'pɔɪntɪŋ hɪz 'fɔˑk ət mɪsɪz 'oʊkrɔɪd, hi rɪ'zjuːmd: " 'ðɪs 'mɔˑnɪn a 'adnt ə 'wagən

ɪn, ən sɔː wə ˈdouɪn nɔut fər ə bɪt. ˈsɪmsn, t ˈʊndə-
manɪdʒə, ˈkʊmz ˈʊp ən ˈsɛz, ' ˈwɒt ə jə ˈɒn wɪð, oˑkrɔɪd?'
ən a ˈtɛlz ɪm ' ˈnoʊʔ dʒʊs ˈnɑː.' ðɐ ˈpʊtɪn ʊp ə ˈtɛmpərɪ
ˈʃɛd fɔʔ t ˈwagənz, ən so ˈsɪmsn ˈsɛz ' ˈwɛl, ˈɛlp wɪ t ˈʃɛd.
jə kŋ ˈstaˑt bɪ ˈgɛtɪn ˈðɪs ɪntə ʃɛːp.' ən ɪ ˈpɔɪnts tʊ ə
ˈbiəm ðe ˈpʊld aˑt ət t ˈɔʊd ʃɛd, ən ɪ ˈfɪnz t ˈmɛʒəments
fɒ mɪ. so a ˈbɒrəz ə ˈaks, ən ə ˈbɪg ˈkrɒs kʊt ˈsɔː ən
ˈgɛʔs tə ˈwɜːk ə ˈðɪs iə ˈbiəm. a ˈavnt bɪɪn ˈat ɪt mʊə
nə ˈtɛn ˈmɪnɪts wɛn ə ˈtʃap ˈtaps mə ɒnt ˈbak. a ˈdoᵊnt
ˈnɔː ɪm bʊd a ˈnɔː ɪz ˈwʊn ə t ˈʃɒp-strɪuədz. 'ən ˈwɛn
dɪd ˈjʊuː dʒɔɪn t ˈkaˑpɪntəz ˈɪunɪən, ˈkʊmreːd?' ɪ sɛz,
ˈvərɪ ˈnastɪ. ' ˈwɒʔ djə ˈmiən,' a sɛz ðoʊ a ˈnɪu wɒʔ wəz
ˈkʊmɪn. ɪ ˈpɔɪntɪd tə t ˈbiəm: "ðats ə ˈkaˑpɪntəz dʒɒb!"
ɪ sɛz, ' ən ˈjʊu kɪip ˈɒf ɪt, ˈkʊmreːd.' a ˈgɪv ɪm ə ˈlʊuk.
' ˈkʊmreːd!' a sɛz, "maˑɪ ˈgɒd!' ' av ˈnoˑtɪst ˈjɪu ˈwʊns
ə ˈtwaɪs,' ɪ sɛz, ' ən ɪts ˈstrʊk mɪ jəv gɒʔ t ˈmɛkɪnz əv ə
ˈblaklɛg,' ɪ sɛz. ' ən ˈsʊmət ˈɛls l straɪk jə ɪn ə ˈmɪnɪt,
meːt, ɪf jə ˈsteː ˈiə ˈkoˑlɪn ˈmɪɪ ˈneːmz, a sɛz. ' wɛl ˈlɪɪv
ˈðaʔ ˈdʒɒb əˈlɔːn,' ɪ sɛz, ən ˈwɔˑks ˈɒf. ən əv ˈkʊəs a
ˈad tʊu."

hi ˈpɔːzd fə rɪˈfrɛʃmənt, ənd hɪz ˈwaɪf ˈstɛəd ət hɪm
ən ˈsɛd ðət ʃi ˈdɪdnt ˈnoʊ wɒtˈɛvə ˈθɪŋz wə ˈkʌmɪŋ tʊː.

" ˈwɛl, ˈlɛʔ mə ˈfɪnɪʃ," sɛd mɪstər oʊkrɔɪd, əz ɪf ʃi əd
bɪːn prɪvɛntɪŋ hɪm. " so ad ˈnɔʊt tə ˈdʊu əgiən. ˈbaɪ
ən ˈbaɪ ˈsɪmsn kʊmz ˈraːnd əgiən, ˈðɪs taɪm wɪʔ t ˈmanɪdʒə
ɪsˈsɛn, ˈɔʊd ˈθɔˑlɪ. ðə ˈtakɪn ə ˈkwɪk ˈlɪʊk ˈraːnd ən
ˈsɪɪm ə ˈbɪt ˈflʊstəd. ˈθɔˑlɪ ˈsɪɪz ˈmɪɪ. ' ˈwɒʔs ˈðɪs man
ˈdouɪn,' ɪ asks. ' ˈɛɪ, oˑkrɔɪd,' ˈsɪmsn ˈʃaːts əˈkrɒs,
' ˈgɛr ɒn wɪ ˈðaʔ ˈdʒɒb ən ˈʃaˑp əˈbaːt ɪt.' ' a ˈkãˑk gɛr ɒn
wɪ ɪt,' a ʃaˑts bak, ən ˈmʊuvz əˈkrɒs tə ˈtɛl əm. ' ˈgo
ˈɒn, man, ˈgo ˈɒn, man, ˈgo ˈɒn!' sɛz ɔʊd θɔˑlɪ, ˈweˑvɪn
ɪz ˈand at mɪ, ən ˈaːt ðe ˈgoːz. ət ˈdɪnə taˑɪm, a ˈiəz

ðat t ˈgreːt ˈman ɪsˈsɛlf, ˈsɜː ˈdʒoːzɪf ˈɪgdɪn, baːt,—ən ɪz ˈfaðə wə ˈnɒbət ə ˈweɪvɪn ˈɔʊəlʊʊkə laɪk ˈmaːɪn—ɪz ˈɒn t ˈprɛmɪsɪz. a ˈnɪu ˈnaː waɪ t ˈmanɪdʒəz wə sə ˈflʊstəd. ˈ al ˈbɛʔ ðə ˈkʊtɪn ˈsʊmət ˈdaːn,' a sɛz. əbaˑʔ ˈθrɪi əˈtɪɒk ðe ˈlanz ɪ ˈaː dɪpaˑtmənt, ˈsɜː ˈdʒoˑzɪf ən ˈθɔˑlɪ, wɪ ˈsɪmsn bɪˈaɪnd. a ˈsɪi ˈsɜː ˈdʒoˑsɪf ˈweˑv ɪz ˈand. ðən ˈθɔˑlɪ ˈlʊuks ˈraːnd, ən a ˈsɪi ɪm ˈlʊuk əʔ ˈmɪi ən ðɛn ˈseˑ sʊmət tə ˈsɪmsn. ɪn ə ˈmɪnɪt ə tʊu, ˈsɪmsn ˈkʊmz ˈʊp ən ˈsɛz, ˈ am ˈsɒrɪ oˈkrɔɪd, bʊt jəl ˈɛ tə ˈtak ə ˈwɪiks ˈnoˑtɪs.' ˈ ˈwɒʔ ˈfɒ?' a sɛz, ˈ ˈwɒt av a ˈdʊn?' ˈ ɪts jər ˈɔːn ˈfɒlt,' ɪ sɛz, ˈ ðəz ˈsoː mɒnɪ tə bɪ ˈstɒpt, ən jə ˈsʊdnt əˈlɛʔ mɪstə ˈθɔˑlɪ ˈsɪi jə ðɪs ˈmɔˑnɪn.' ˈ ɪʔ wə ˈnoˑ ˈfɒlt ə ˈmaːɪn,' a sɛz, ˈ ən aˑm ˈgoɪŋ tə av ə ˈwɜːd wɪ mɪstə θɔˑlɪ.' ən a ˈdɪd av ə wɜːd wɪ ɪm, ən ə ˈfaʔ ˈlɒt ə ˈgʊd ɪʔ ˈdɪd mə. a bɪˈgɪnz tə ˈtɛl ɪm ˈaː ˈlɒŋ ad ˈbɪin ðɪə, ən ɪ ˈkʊts mɪ ˈʃɔˑt ən sɛz ˈsʊm əv ʊz ˈɔʊdə ˈmɛn ɪz əz ˈaɪdl əz t ˈjʊŋ ənz ɪsˈtɛd ə ˈsɛtɪn ə ɛgˈzampl. ˈðaʔ wər ɪˈnʊf fə ˈmɪi, ən a ˈsɛz sʊmət a ˈsʊdnt ə sɛd. ˈ ˈpeː ɪm ˈɒf ən ˈgɪv ɪm ɪz ˈkaːd,' ɪ sɛz. ˈ ˈðɪs ˈman z ˈfɪnɪʃt wɪ ˈɪgdɪnz fə ˈgʊd ən ˈɔːl.' "

APPENDIX I.

SUGGESTED COURSE OF SPEECH TRAINING IN TRAINING COLLEGES.

This scheme is drawn up on the basis of sixty hours work spread over two years, the amount recommended in the Report on the Teaching of English in England. It is possible to give lectures and ear-training to a fairly large number of students at once, but the practical work should be done in groups of not more than fifteen.

The work should consist of:

(a) VOICE TRAINING, particularly for those who need it. The simplest outline only of the vocal mechanism is necessary. Exercises on breath control, on relaxation, on the cultivation of clear and pleasing tone, on the avoidance of a high-pitched voice.

(b) PHONETIC THEORY. An outline of the formation of English sounds and their distribution in ordinary speech: chief dialectal sounds; how to teach normal sounds, clear articulation, etc., how to get rid of particular defects of speech. If time is to be economised, some parts of the theory can be studied by the students from books.

(c) EAR TRAINING. This is most important: each student should have a short ear-training class a week, in which, at first, ordinary English sounds only are used, in meaningless words (such as those given in Appendix II). Later dialectal variants can be introduced, and non-English sounds.

(d) PRACTICAL WORK. Exercises for the control of the organs of speech, the making of sounds by the students themselves, sounds of all kinds, those of standard English, of the modified standards, of dialects, of foreign languages. Exercises in usual and unusual combinations of consonants.

Analysis and comparison of the pronunciation of the students; this is again a most valuable form of ear-training, and if approached in the right spirit, is not likely to be misunderstood or resented by the students themselves.[1]

Discussions of questions of theory and methods of teaching: what is to be taught in different parts of the country, and corrected in individuals.

The students should do regular exercises—which need not be long—in transcribing phonetically their own pronunciation, particularly in colloquial speech.

SUGGESTED ARRANGEMENT OF THE WORK.

FIRST AND SECOND TERMS: TWO HOURS PER WEEK.
- 40 min.   Lecture.
- 20 min.   Ear Training.   40 *hours*.
- 40 min.   Practical Work.
- 20 min.   Voice Exercises.

THIRD TERM.
- 30 min.   Practical Work.   10 *hours*.
- 30 min.   Ear Training

FOURTH TERM.
- 40 min.   Practical Work, including some Reading.   10 *hours*.
- 20 min.   Ear Training.

[1] Note to 3rd Edition. It will be realised that broadcast speech provides an excellent field for the study and comparison of variant pronunciations, and for ear training.

Appendix II.

Ear-Training Exercises.

I. Containing English Sounds Only.

(a) *Simple.*

ˈbɑˈgʌnət	ˈθuglnaɪt	ˈflouzˈdʒʌgpæt
ˈteɪblouˈnæp	ˈnoumˈbɛtl	ˈvwɔgˈjʌn
blɛtʃk	ˈbeɪˈnɪdʒnɔ	ˈblætlɛtˈjɔg
ˈfrudʒˈdɜvz	ˈbʌdɪˈðændaɪg	ˈlɔɪˈvɜnɪ
ˈfkuðɔ	ˈflaɪtˈsɪtʃkri	ˈpeɪˈmouθ
ʌbˈlɪtkɑ	ˈglounɪəˈlaɪkɜ	ˈbaɪgŋpʌtʃ
ˈætʃˈgɔvɪg	ˈθeɪˈnɒp	ˈsifθglɜə
ˈvruəˈtsɛk	ˈfugrɒʃʌð	ˈʃteɪklˈpoutʃ
ˈpɒŋkˈtɪədaɪb	θrɔtsk	ˈbɜlɪˈfustə
ˈɪngaɪθˈbɔɪtn	ʃkutʃˈtlɪə	ˈʃtɛgliˈgɒtʃ
ˈplɑgənaɪf	ˈfɒzˈbɒnɪ	ˈkɔdʌntˈblægz
ˈfɑˈnʌtpaɪð	ˈjɪdˈnouv	ˈnaɪˈðɛtɪpɜ
puˈbaɪtl	ˈdʒɔɪˈflʌndə	ˈpænˈgrɒmɪtus
ˈfɑθˈtrɔɪb		

(b) *More difficult.*

ʃpʃæsps	ˈlaɪprˈðɛəgʌn	ˈθsnɪpɪtθs
ˈpfɛtˈgɑvɪgʌdʒ	gŋaɪŋg	ˈsɜndouˈvɔkɒk
ˈjɛntsɪˈpæʃndɔʃ	ˈnɛvɪˈpauðəˈduə	ˈʃkrudəˈnɪbtu.
ˈrɔtˈmɑgənæŋ	ˈtsvaubʃɪə	ˈdʒæfkˈsougæ
ˈtɛpɑkˈnaub	ˈflætɪˈŋauˈfɛðz	ʃfeɪðpi
ˈpætɪˈŋɔvmu	ˈflɛgɪˈbætəpul	ˈdɒnɪˈaɪkə

243

244   APPENDIX II

'ɪdn'keɪtəʃk   'θkɛks'tʃaʊndʒ   'tnærɪpm
'grgl'ðaɪvz   'fklaɪps'plʊdʒ   kʃ'pʊðə'vɪə
'boʊnɪ'ɒt'gaɪðə   'zɔlaŋ'boʊrɪə'gæt   'æθɪ'ðəvətɒf
'pʊθ'klɛəbətɒfk   'knaɪ'pfɛkʃɪə   'θɛsts'pʌ
'bloʊnɪ'aʊvɪ'ɔɪ   fɪsθs   'θpɪd'vɛstθs
'ʒnɪl'meɪŋəsoʊf   'groʊgl'pʃɒk   'aʃp'dreɪbzku
pʃguf   'dlɪə'ʃɛksʌz   'klɪəgeə'vraɪbm
'tɔ'paʊəfl   'gʊdn'fɪəʒ   'pʃkætʃ'kɒflkaʊg
'sθpɪkəlɛt   'bɒkə'nɔtʃɛə   'θraʊf'rɪəp
'krɪk'tæθɪdɔp   'ŋɪdlʌt'fɛəθbru   'prʌt'θɑ'ðɔkl

(c) *Still more difficult, including some dialectal diphthongs.*

'neɪlpʃɛtʃ'kʃaɪv   'dzɔʊvɒdʒʌdz   'gŋɔvn'pæʔudʒ
'ʒnaʊgl'mʒgŋ   'ʃuʒ'pʌskʃəi   'ʃklɛʔəpɪkənɪb
pʊθ'klɛəbəˀtɒfkʃ   'ŋgaɪn'dɒʔinbʌ   ɜʒ'ŋɛkfθ
'wɛlɪoʊ'jaɪnə   ststaɪŋs   'dlʌʔ'nɪəgəmeɪʔ
'ʒleɪgŋ'bɑvɪdɛk   fʃɛ'katʃɪ'kɒpf   gŋɔgŋ
'oʊlɪ'ɒdʒɪ'naɪʃn   'khurɪ'ʃəʊpskŋ   knɪl'jɛbɪtʃkʃ
'mæntrɪuklɔr   əb'sʌnvɪg   'bzmjaɪ'fʌʃl
'ɛəðpʌk'ŋɪleɪ   'tnɛɪz'tʃatrʌnst   łʊbʃ'kraʊŋɛʃ
'pjuʃmæk'waʊðg   'ŋɒl'pmaɪðŋ   'zgʊnt'nɔʊljə'raɪ
'tʌnɪ'lætəf'latnbaʊə   'ŋgu'phinaθ'lɪə   'ðɪθwʒð'pðɪθ
'tnɔʊf'klɛə'boʊʒ   łɛɪbʌtɪθæŋ   'blaɪ'fʊtnoi
'æɪdʌ'nɔʊ   'ʒɪθɪks'pɔɪ   'skiu'gɛtəmei

II. CONTAINING A FEW NON-ENGLISH CONSONANTS AND CARDINAL VOWELS, IN ADDITION TO ENGLISH SOUNDS.

[*For the values of the non-English symbols, see List of Symbols.*]

l̦ɪknaɪfθ   ŋaɪçpɔrɪvʒnɛk   ŋaɪpm̥kakŋ̍
eglpɔtʃkɛ   łɛpɛɪtɛʃkæ   lɔvɛʒɑpoç

njuzvatʃjeklɑ	noblfʃekspʃ	zgyntwoʊbm
ʃnuglfɛədlnɒt	tjuneçabux	l̥ybiteçop
goxəçaɪl̥u	nobkɑpm̥pʌŋk	ŋgaɪgŋfaɪç
ŋoʊvpeʔldɑ	bøniʃlygatʃ	ŋopmɔʊθ
çɛəbɪktibøʔ	ʃaθɛspɪç	ɑheogəʔut
lɔxkn̥pɑt	ɑxɑlepotʃ	zmaɪtəpeɪpsjun
flaʊnɛl̥y	laɲipʊtlbʌʔ	dn̥ʌtlɛətn̥
anfijɛx	nʃærɛmpm̥	ŋgəriaʃexi
dɬɪbðʌʔlbzwaʊn	faʔʊllibetɑx	mlytʃvrki

BIBLIOGRAPHY.

GENERAL PHONETICS.

NOEL-ARMFIELD, G. *General Phonetics* (Heffer).
DUMVIL'E, B. *The Science of Speech* (Clive & Co.).
JESPERSEN, O. *Lehrbuch der Phonetik* (Teubner).
VIETOR and RIPMAN. *Elements of Phonetics* (Dent & Co.).
JONES, D. *Pronunciation of Russian* [First 50 pages]. (Cambridge Univ. Press).
WESTERMANN, D., and WARD, I. C. *Practical Phonetics for Students of African Languages* (Oxford University Press).

ENGLISH PHONETICS.

SWEET, H. *Primer of Phonetics* (Oxford Univ. Press).
JONES, D. *A Pronouncing Dictionary* (Dent & Co.). *The Pronunciation of English* (Cambridge Univ. Press). *Outline of English Phonetics*, Third Edition (Heffer & Sons).
LLOYD JAMES, A. *Our Spoken Language* (Nelson). *Exercises on our Spoken Language*. (See also Publications of the B.B.C. Committee below.)
RIPMAN, W. *Good Speech* (Dent & Co.). *The Sounds of Spoken English* (Dent & Co.).
DUMVILLE, B. *The Science of Speech*, Second Edition, 1927 (University Tutorial Press).
ALLISON, L. H. *The Sounds of the Mother Tongue, for the Use of Children* (Black).
GRANT and ROBSON. *Speech Training for Scottish Students* (Cambridge Univ. Press).
GRANT and DIXON. *Manual of Modern Scots*.
LLOYD, R. J. *Northern English* (Teubner).
MACDONALD, G. *English Speech To-day* (Allen & Unwin).
REANEY, P. H. *Elements of Speech Training* (Methuen).
STOREY, BARBARA. *The Way to Good Speech* (Nelson).
PALMER, MARTIN and BLANDFORD. *A Dictionary of English Pronunciation, with American Variants* (Heffer).
KRAPP, G. P. *The Pronunciation of Standard English in America* (Oxford Univ. Press).
KENYON, J. S. *American Pronunciation* (Wahr, Ann Arber, Mich.).

BIBLIOGRAPHY

PUBLICATIONS OF THE B.B.C. ADVISORY COMMITTEE ON SPOKEN ENGLISH (A. LLOYD JAMES).

Broadcast English I. *Regarding Certain Words of Doubtful Pronunciation.*
,, ,, II. *The Pronunciation of English Place Names.*
,, ,, III. *The Pronunciation of Scottish Place Names.*
,, ,, IV. *The Pronunciation of Welsh Place Names.*
,, ,, V. *The Pronunciation of Northern Irish Place Names.*
,, ,, VI. *The Pronunciation of Foreign Place Names.*
,, ,, VII. *The Pronunciation of Foreign Personal Names* (in preparation).
,, VIII. *The Pronunciation of English Personal Names* (in preparation).

PHONETIC READERS.

JONES, D. *Phonetic Transcriptions of English Prose* (Oxford Univ. Press). *Phonetic Readings in English* (Winter, Heidelberg).

RIPMAN, W. *Specimens of English* (Dent & Co.).

ARMSTRONG, L. E. *An English Phonetic Reader* (London Univ. Press).

NOEL-ARMFIELD, G. 100 *Poems for Children* (Teubner). *English Humour in Phonetic Transcription* (Heffer).

MACKENZIE and DREW. *A Phonetic Reader* (Manchester Univ. Press).

GRANT, W. *A Phonetic Reader, for use in Scottish Schools* (W. Smith & Sons, Aberdeen).

LLOYD JAMES, A. *A Basic Reader* (Kegan Paul).

INTONATION.

JONES, D. *Intonation Curves* (Teubner).

PALMER, H. E. *English Intonation with Systematic Exercises* (Heffer).

ARMSTRONG and WARD. *A Handbook of English Intonation* (Heffer).

SCHUBIGER, MARIA. *The Rôle of Intonation in Spoken English* (Heffer & Sons).

COLEMAN, H. O. *Intonation and Emphasis* (Miscellanea Phonetica 1912: published by the Association Phonétique Internationale).

MISCELLANEOUS.

LLOYD JAMES, A. *The Broadcast Word* (Kegan Paul & Co.).

FIRTH, J. R. *Speech* (Benn & Co.). *The Tongues of Men* (Watts & Co.).

WARD, I. C. *Defects of Speech: Their Nature and Cure* (Dent & Co.).

AIKEN, W. A. *The Voice: An Introduction to Practical Phonology* (Longmans).

FOGERTY, E. *The Speaking of Verse* (Dent & Co.).

GULLAN, M. *Spoken Poetry in the Schools* (Methuen).

RICE, C. M. *Voice Production with the Aid of Phonetics* (Heffer)

JESPERSEN. *Modern English Grammar* (Allen & Unwin).

WYLD, H. C. *History of Modern Colloquial English. English Rhymes from Surrey to Pope.*

REANEY, P. H. *Grammar of the Dialect of Penrith* (Manchester Univ. Press).

ANNAKIN, M. L. *Notes on the Dialect of Nidderdale, Yorks.* (Association Phonétique Internationale).

COWLING, G. H. *The Dialect of Hackness, N.E. Yorks.* (Cambridge Univ. Press).

Transactions of the Scottish Dialect Committee, Grant (Training College, Aberdeen).

Transactions of the Yorkshire Dialect Society

"*Le Maître Phonétique,*" *Organ of Association Phonétique Internationale* (Phonetics Department, University College, London).

"*Speech,*" *Quarterly Journal of the Society of Speech Therapists* (Pitman & Co.).

"*Good Speech,*" *Quarterly Journal of the Speech Fellowship* (56, Gordon Square, W.C.1.).

INDEX

The Index is in two parts, (*a*) subjects, (*b*) phonetic. The phonetic symbols are given in the order shown in the list of symbols at the beginning of the book.

The numbers indicate paragraphs.

Accent, 5, 321
"Africa" script, note on, p. 35.
Affricative Consonants: formation, 252–3; diagrams of, 252; English, 254
Analogy: false, 41
Assimilation: 66; modern tendencies in, 66, 69, 329; definition, 330; illustrations of, 338–48; affecting vocal chords, 339; affecting soft palate, 340; affecting tongue, 341; diagram illustrating, 343; affecting lips, 346; in phrases, 348; juxtapositional, 331; historical, 331–3

Bi-labial *f* and *v*, 84(*c*).
Bilingualism, 13
Breath, 74, 75.
Broadcasting: influence of, 14; Committee on Pron., 33; intonation in, 364.
Broadcast Speech Lessons, 31; in Scotland, 31

Cardinal Vowels, 93; gramophone records of, 93; books in which used, 94; tongue positions of, 95; diagram of, 95; use of, 97; and English vowels, 98; numbers of, 99.

Class distinctions, 10; dialect, 4
Clear l (and dark), 107, 109, 262–4, 268
Cockney Speech: illustration of, 306; *see also* description of vowels and consonants
Consonants: insertion of, 65; dropping of, 65, 355–6; definition of, 89; English consonants in detail, 236–85; classification of, 236; diagram of, 238; voiced and voiceless, 238; voiced cons. in initial and final positions, 239; plosive, 240–51; affricative, 252–4; nasal, 255–9; lateral, 261–8; rolled, 269, 271–2; fricative, 275–8; American, 367–70, 383
Correction: of pronunciation, 12; wrong, 23; method of, 115–6; principles of, 115–6

Dark l: 107, 109; 262–4; 268
Dialect: local, 4, 11; class, 4; pronunciation (see under headings of each sound), 24–5

249

Diphthongs: definition, 191; falling, 192; representation of, 192; English diphthongs numbered, 193; on Cardinal figure, 194; drawling of, 226
Dissimiliation, 66, 69, 345
Drawling, 226, 294; cure of, 295
Dropping one's g's, 260
Dropping one's h's, 65, 278, vii

Ear Training: Use of, 25; method of, 26; exercises in, 20, Appendix II, App. I(c)
Eighteenth Century Grammarians, 63
Elphinston: *English Orthography Epittomized*, 65
Emphasis: 288, 298, 310-6
English Language: prestige of, 9

Faucal or Nasal Plosion, 247-8
Fricative Consonants: formation, 275-6; English, 277; notes on, 278

Glottal stop: drawing of, 75; use of, 250(d); in dialectal speech, 250(d); to avoid, 251
Glottis, 72
Grant: *Pronunciation of English in Scotland*, 163, 151, 159
Gullet, 72

h: dropping of, 65, 278(vii)
His Majesty King George V, 28, 317; Broadcast Message to the Empire, 379-80

Intelligibility: mutual, 7; limit of, 8, 20
Intonation: 301-21; definition, 301; varieties of, 302-3, 319-20; "Tunes," 304; Tune I, 304-7; Tune II, 304, 308-10; Emphatic, 311-5; for Intensity, 312; of King George V, 317; American, 374, 376-8; of President Roosevelt, 385; changes in, 364; Northern and Southern compared, 319
Jespersen: *Modern English Grammar*, 163
Jones, Daniel: pronunciation cone, 7; cardinal vowels, 93
Jones: *Expert Orthographer*, 65

Labio-dental nasal, 353
Language: auxiliary, 4
Larynx, 72, 75
Lateral Consonants: formation, 261; English, 262-3; syllabic, 265; voiceless, 266, 334
Lateral Plosion, 249
Laxness, 102
Length: of sounds, 293; rules of, 293; of American vowels, 372; modern tendencies, 361(vi), 362
Lips, 72; use in formation of speech sounds, 84, 85; exercises for control of, 86; use of in formation of vowels, 100-1; photographs of, 100

Microphone Technique, 26
Mistakes of Pronunciation: type of, 17

INDEX

Nasal Consonants: formation, 255-6; voiceless, 257; syllabic, 258
Nasal, or Faucal Plosion, 247-8
Nasal sounds, 78
Nasal vowels, 231-2; cure of, 233-4; in American speech, 373, 382
Nasalised sounds, 78
Nasality: cure of 233-4
Northern speech: ɑ and æ in N. speech, 142; strong forms in, 327-8
Northern and Southern Speech: summary of main differences, 283-5

Organs of speech: training of, 46; use in formation of sounds, 71; movable, 73

Palate: hard, 72; soft, 72, 78
Pharynx, 72; nasal, 72
Phoneme: 103; definition of, 103; illustration of, 104; existence of, 108; importance of knowledge of, 108.
Phonetician: work of, 57
Phonetics: use of, in teaching of English, 57; in teaching of elocution and singing, 57; in curing speech defects, 58; in teaching the deaf, 59; in teaching of reading, 59; in study of Philology, 60
Phonetic Alphabet, 51; use of, 52; use of in study of dialects, 55; use of for ear-training, 56

Phonetic Dictionary: use of, 52; limitations of, 52
Phonetic Theory: Use of, 48; limitations of, 50; App. I (b)
Phonetic Transcription: use of, 51; interpretation of, 53; criticism of, 53
Pitch: 289, 290, 301
Plosive consonants: formation, 240; voiceless, 241; aspiration of, voiceless plosives, 241; over-aspiration of, 242; cure of over-aspiration, 243; incomplete, 245-6; notes on, 250
Practical work: App. I (d)
President Roosevelt: Broadcast speech, 381-5
Prominence: 286-7, 290-1; special, 288; and intonation, 289-90; and neutral vowels, 289 (5), 290
Pronunciation: standard, 1, 20-1, 30; slovenly, 5; cone, 7; educated, 8; Received, 8, 11; correction of, 12; B.B.C. committee on, 14, 33; spelling, 61-70; changes in, 61, 358ff.; variant, 105 (see also under headings of each sound); American, 365ff.; of announcers, 21, 23

r sounds: 264-74; different kinds of, 271; rolled r, 269, 271; semi-rolled r, 271 (ii); fricative r, 271 (iii); inverted r, 271 (iv); uvular r, 271 (v); linking r, 273; intrusive r, 274, 360

Rhythm: 28; 285; 296, 298; 328; American, 374, 376–8

Rolled consonants: formation of, 269; lingual rolled r, 271; uvular, 271 (v); teaching of rolled r, 272

Semi-vowels: 279–82

Semi-weak vowels: 186–8

Sense-group, 28, 322

Similitude: 334, 337; examples of, 349–54

Soft palate: two positions of, 78; functions of, 78; exercises for control of, 79

Sonority, 87

Sound attributes, 286ff.

Sounds and letters, 19

Sounds: use of sounds not found in educated speech, 34; insertion of, 34; omission of, 34; use of wrongly formed, 36; use of normal sounds in wrong places, 37; classification of, 87–90

Speech: differences of, 34; organs of, 71ff.; unit of, 322

Speech sounds, formation of, 74; classification of, 87–90; definition of, 103

Speech Training: suggested course of, 12; App. I

Spelling Pronunciations, 61–70; modern tendencies in, 69

Spoken word, 18, 19, 30

Standard: Pronunciation, 1; English, 2, 5, 15

Stress: 286, 289–91; word stress, 296–7; sentence stress, 296–300; meaning, 297; of compound words, 299–300; and rhythm, 298(e); influence of, 324–5

Strong forms: 325–7; misuse of, 326; in Northern speech, 327–8

Strong and weak forms, 42, 184–6, 286 (5), 324–6

Teacher: work of, 38; the phonetically trained, 40

Teaching of English in England: Committee on, 2; Report on, 2

Teeth: 72; ridge, 72

Tenseness, 102

Tongue: blade of, 72; front of, 72; back of, 72; root of, 72; use in formation of speech sounds, 80; exercises for control of, 81, 82; spreading and contraction of, 81; tenseness and laxness of, 82

Training Colleges, 12; App. I

Triphthongs, 227

Unvoiced vowels, 278 (vi)

Uvula, 72

Uvular r, 271 (v)

Vocal cords: 72; description of, 75; drawings of, 75; exercises for control of, 76

Voice: 75; training, App. I ( )

Voiced consonants: in initial and final positions, 239

Voiced and voiceless consonants, 76, 238

INDEX

Voiceless l, m, n, ŋ, r: 76, 77, 238; w, 281

Vowel quality, 91, 289 (5)

Vowels: change of pronunciation due to spelling, 67; nasal, 79; definition of, 88; classification of 91; front, 91; back, 91; central, 91; close, 91; half-close, 91; half-open, 91; open, 91; cardinal 93-101; comparison of, 94; English vowels in detail, 113-90

Vowels: English vowels numbered, 113; English vowels placed on Cardinal figure, 117; semi-weak, 187-8; nasalisation of, 31-35; neutral, 181-6, 324-6

Whisper, 75

Windpipe, 72

"World Orthography," note on p. 35.

Written word, 18, 19

Wyld: *History of Modern Colloquial English*, 64; *Studies in English Rhymes*, 64; on spelling pron., 64; on weak vowels, 327

Yorkshire speech: illustration of, 388; *see also* description of vowels and consonants.

PHONETIC INDEX

iː: phoneme, 118–19; variant pron. of, 120; teaching of, 121; in unstressed positions, 122

ɪ: phoneme, 124–5, 131; final, 126–7; in final closed syllable, 128; alternative pron. of unstressed ɪ; teaching of, 132

ɛ: phoneme, 133–4; variant pron. 135; teaching of, 136–7

æ: phoneme, 138–40; variant pron. of, 141; teaching of, 142

ɑ: phoneme, 141–2; variant pron. of, 143; teaching of, 144; ɑ–æ is N and S pron., 145

ɒ: phoneme, 149-50; variant pron. of, 151; teaching of, 152; ɒ and ɔ, alternative pron. of, 153–4

ɔ: phoneme, 157–8; variant pron. 159-164; teaching of, 160; in *or*, *ore*, *oar*, *oor*, *our* words, 161; variants of these, 162–3

ʊ: phoneme, 165–6; variant pron. of, 167–8

u: phoneme, 169–70; variant pron. of, 171; teaching of, 172

ʌ: phoneme 173–4; variant pron. of, 175; northern pron. of 175 (note); teaching of, 176

ɜ: phoneme, 177–8; variant pron. of, 179; teaching of, 180

ə: phoneme, 181–2; variant pron. of, 183; in weak forms, 184–6

eɪ: phoneme, 195; variant pron. of, 196; teaching of, 197

oʊ: phoneme, 199; variant pron. of, 200; teaching of, 201; unstressed, alternative pron. 202

aɪ: phoneme, 203; variant pron. of, 204; teaching of, 207

aʊ: phoneme, 208; variant pron. of, 209-10, teaching of, 211

ɔɪ: phoneme, 212; variant pron. of, 213; teaching of, 214

ɪə: phoneme, 215; variant pron. of, 216; teaching of, 217

ɛə: phoneme, 218; variant pron. of, 219; teaching of, 220

ɔə: phoneme, 221; variant pron. of, 161–2

ʊə: phoneme, 223; variant pron. of, 224; teaching of, 225

aɪə: 227–8

aʊə: 227–8

p: formation, 240–42; aspiration of, 241–3; unexploded, 245

b: formation, 240–2; unexploded, 245

t: formation, 240; aspiration of, 241–3; unexploded, 245; dental, 250 (a); dropping of 65 (b); used instead of k, 336

254

PHONETIC INDEX

d: formation, 240; unexploded, 245; dental, 250 (a); substitution for t, 250 (b); dropping of 45 (b); used instead of g, 336 (b).

k: formation, 240; aspiration of, 241–2; unexploded 245; dropping of, 65 (a).

g: formation, 240.

tʃ: formation, 252; 254

dʒ: formation, 252; 254

m: formation, 255; voiceless, 76; 77 (d); 257; syllabic, 258

n: formation, 255 voiceless, 76, 77 (d); syllabic, 258

ŋ, formation, 255; syllabic, 258; substitution of n, 260; in Midland pronunciation, 260

l: clear, 107; formation of, 261–64; 268; dark, 107; overdark l, 267; influence of, 268; correction of overdark l, 268, voiceless, 76, 77, 266; with other vowel resonances, 264; syllabic, 265

r: rolled, 269; semi-rolled, 271(b), 271(ii); fricative, 271 (iii); inverted, 271 (iv); uvular, 271(v); linking, 273; intrusive, 274

f: formation, 275; replaced by v, 278(i).

v: formation, 275

θ: formation, 275, replaced by f, 278(iv); dropping of, 278 (v)

ð: formation, 275; replaced by v, 278(iv); dropping of, 278(v)

s: formation, 275

z: formation, 275

ʃ: formation, 275

ʒ: formative, 275

h: insertion of, 65(g); dropping of, 65, 278(v i); formation, 278(vi); voiced, 278(vi)

w: formation, 280; voiceless, 281

ʍ: use of, 65, 281

j: formation, 282; voiceless, 282

ʔ: diagram, 75; use of, 250(d); in dialectal speech, 250(e); to avoid, 251

13

THE PRINCIPLES OF ENGLISH PHONETIC NOTATION, 2nd edn

THE PRINCIPLES OF ENGLISH PHONETIC NOTATION

By

Harold E. Palmer

Linguistic Adviser to the Department of Education, Director of the Institute for Research in English Teaching.

TOKYO
THE INSTITUTE FOR RESEARCH IN ENGLISH TEACHING
1928

First Edition .... August, 1925
Second (Révised) Edition .... April,   1928

[All rights reserved]

PRINTED AT
THE HERALD OF ASIA PRESS, TOKYO.

Introduction

The various memoranda and documents contained in this book have been compiled for the benefit of

(1) those who wish for a rapid initiation into the principles of English Phonetic Notation;

(2) those who wish to become acquainted with the history of English Phonetic Notation;

(3) those who wish to know the reasons for the adoption of the present scheme of notation.

It may therefore serve as a textbook for study, as a means of propagating the use of phonetics and phonetic notation, and as a basis of discussion among technicians.

CONTENTS

	PAGE
Introduction	3
Phonetics and Phonetic Notation. An Explanatory Dialogue	9
A Short History of English Phonetic Notation	25
The Impossibility of an "Ideal" Phonetic Notation	33
Received Standard Pronunciation	51
The English Phonetic System	61
The Phonetic Alphabet	84
The 31 Chief Rules for Transcribing "Received Standard" English	91
The 70 Weakenable Words	115
A Model English Text	127
Specimens of English Phonetic Transcription	133

PHONETICS AND PHONETIC NOTATION.

AN EXPLANATORY DIALOGUE.

Question. What is Phonetics?

Answer. Broadly speaking, it is that science which is concerned with all the phenomena relating to the sounds made by the vocal organs for the purposes of speech.

Question. Might we call it the science of pronunciation?

Answer. Yes, provided that you use the term *pronunciation* in its widest sense, including length, stress, intonation, etc.

Question. Is it not true that phonetics is such a difficult science that it requires many years of study?

Answer. It is true that like mathematics, physics and other sciences, it is a never-ending study, but as in the case of those other sciences, the elements of the theory may be mastered in a few days.

Question. Is not phonetics primarily concerned with the correcting of faulty pronunciations, such as vulgar or local dialects, foreigner's pronunciation, etc?

Answer. No, not primarily. Its primary purpose is to ascertain the facts concerning pronunciation, to ascertain what sounds exist in the languages and dialects of the world, to find out how they are formed and in what cases they are used, to classify them and to observe the differences between them.

Question. I have heard some people say that phonetics is a sort of new alphabet with a large number of strange letters in it. Is that true?

Answer. It is not true that phonetics is an alphabet; phonetics is a science, but like other sciences, it requires a notation. We have the notations of arithmetic, mathematics, chemistry, music, etc. and we have also the notation of phonetics.

Question. Has phonetics any practical utility?

Answer. Certainly. In addition to being the base of all linguistic study, it furnishes the teacher with exact information concerning the pronunciation-system of any language. A knowledge of phonetics dissipates all those superstitions and false notions concerning pronunciation and the teaching of pronunciation.

Question. Will you give me an example of such false notions?

Answer. Willingly. The average person imagines

[10]

that his language is built up of a small number of distinct sounds, each of which is accurately provided for in his alphabet by one letter or sign. As for the languages of foreigners, he generally feels that the sounds they use are the same as those he is familiar with but that there is a mysterious "accent" that gives them their air of strangeness. This naive feeling is largely illusory on both scores.

Question. But do such illusions really matter?

Answer. Yes, they matter very much. If a teacher with such illusions talks about or teaches pronunciation, he does not know what he is talking about, and does not understand what he is teaching. A person who thinks that the earth is flat would be a very poor teacher of geography.

Question. Am I right in presuming that the teacher who is a phonetician strives to inculcate the one true pronunciation of a language and to fight against dialectal pronunciations? For instance, I suppose that an English phonetician will do his best to protect his language from American or Scottish pronunciations, and will declare them to be vicious.

Answer. On the contrary, it is precisely the English phonetician who does not do so. In fact he usually declares that the various pronunciations used by educated native speakers are all good. It is

[11]

precisely the phonetician whose views on the subject are the most liberal and broad, and it is usually the person ignorant of phonetics who is dogmatic. The idea that every language possesses one and only one form of pronunciation intrinsically correct is another of the illusions I mentioned just now.

Question. Tell me more about the phonetic notation. In what way does it differ from an ordinary alphabet? And why does it contain strange letters instead of familiar ones?

Answer. The basic idea of a phonetic notation is this: to provide for each independent sound a specific letter, so that the same letter will always stand for the same sound, and the same sound always stand for the same letter. As the English alphabet contains only 26 letters, and as the English language contains about 44 independent sounds, it becomes necessary to invent new letters.

Question. I have been told that when you write English with a phonetic alphabet, you have to write *yes* with a *j* instead of with a *y*. How is this? A *y* surely is a *y* and a *j* a *j*.

Answer. The phonetic alphabet is as far as possible international, and is intended for international usage. Now English is about the only language which gives to the letter *j* the value of the first

[12]

sound of *joy*. The French give this letter quite a different value; the Spaniards give it another, but in German, Dutch, Polish, Swedish, Norwegian, Danish, Czech, Hungarian and other languages, the letter *j* stands for the sound of *y* in *yes*.

Question. Is that really so? I fancied that each letter must have a fixed value.

Answer. That is precisely the first of the illusions I quoted. Do you know that *Don Quixote* is written in Spanish as *Don Quijote*, that the sound *sh* of *ship* is written *ch* in French, *sch* in German, *sc* in Italian, *s* in Hungarian, *sz* in Polish, and *sj* in Swedish? A letter has only the value that is attributed to it by those who devise national spellings. The fundamental idea of an international phonetic notation is to give a fixed international value to each letter.

Question. And has this idea been carried out?

Answer. Partly. There is more than one type of phonetic notation. One type aims at the greatest possible accuracy, and to represent each shade of sound by one special sign. This "narrow" notation, as we call it, is used in phonetic research, and the number of its signs increases every time a new language is analyzed. But for ordinary purposes less exact types of notation are used, according to circumstances and requirements. Thus the *o* of the

[13]

French word *or* is not the same sound as the *o* of the English word *or*, but the sign [ɔ·] is used for both.

Question. I don't quite understand. Is the phonetic notation international or not? Is it accurate or not? It can't be both.

Answer. For certain purposes and in certain cases it tends to be as international and as accurate as possible. For other purposes and in other cases it tends to be less international and less accurate. The principles of phonetic notation are conveniently elastic, and therefore are practicable.

Question. I heard recently that an English teacher once, in giving a pronunciation lesson to a Japanese pupil, used an artificial palate to teach him to make the difference between an *l* and an *r*. Is this sort of thing common among phoneticians? It struck me as being rather absurd, because people do not usually speak with machines in their mouths.

Answer. That is an example of experimental and demonstrative phonetics. An artificial palate is useful for demonstrating, for instance, the difference between the physical formation of *l* and *r*. Probably in the case you mention the teacher dusted a coating of chalk over a black metal palate, inserted it in his mouth, pronounced the sound *l*, removed the palate, and showed that the tongue contact removed a patch

[14]

of chalk from the front just behind the teeth. Then probably he repeated the operation for the *r*-sound, in which case the tongue contact removed patches of chalk on the extreme back left and right. Well, I should say it was an excellent method of demonstration.

Question. It seems rather bewildering to me. Does phonetics replace imitation by suchlike demonstrations? As "imitation is the sincerest flattery" it seems to me that "imitation is the soundest training in pronunciation."

Answer. It is. To imitate the sounds made by the teacher is the fundamental process in learning pronunciation, but this process may be quickened by various devices. You can help anybody to pronounce a Japanese [F] by blowing out a candle; you can help him to understand the English *ng* sound by suddenly pinching his nose, and the mouthpiece of a Shikishima cigarette is a fine little piece of apparatus for demonstrating how the French *u* is made.

Question. There is one point upon which I am not quite satisfied. Very few foreigners, if any, ever succeed in getting more than an approximation to English pronunciation. We have to face facts as they are. To get the mass of foreign students to pronounce English as it is really pronounced is an impossible ideal. Since, then, we have to content ourselves with approximations, why should we take the trouble to employ such a scientific procedure as to use such an exact instrument as phonetic notation? Is it not like using a razor to cut butter?

Answer. Your term "approximation" is very vague. I prefer to use such terms as "a 5% pronunciation," "a 50% pronunciation" or "a 100% pronunciation." Every one falling short of the "100% mark" is an "approximation." But it is the *degree* of approximation that is important. I consider a 25% degree as wholly and needlessly inadequate; I also consider the 100% degree as unnecessarily perfect. Personally I favour the 75%—90% as a reasonable range; it is easily attainable by those who from lack of understanding content themselves with the 25% ideal. To cut butter with a razor is not a "scientific procedure" if we use the term scientific in its right sense. In teaching, a "scientific procedure" is not to use the most *accurate* instruments but to use the most *appropriate* instruments.

Question. But your special signs, your upside-down letters, your invented letters — each one of these is a device to show the 100% standard! You use, I understand, the sign [æ] for the vowel of *cat*, and the sign [ɔ·] for the vowel of *bald*. You do this, I

[16]

presume, because you require a 100% correctness in the pronunciation of these words.

Answer. You cannot ensure a 100% correctness in pronunciation (nor any other degree of correctness) merely by inventing a new symbol. No phonetician suffers from the delusion that a strange symbol will ever ensure a good pronunciation. The chief use of phonetic symbols is to demonstrate the *distribution* of sounds.

Question. What do you mean by that?

Answer. I mean this. It is immaterial whether the foreigner pronounces *cat* as [kat] or as [kæt] so long as he does not give us the impression that he is talking about a *cut*. It is immaterial whether he pronounces the vowel of *bald* correctly or incorrectly so long as he does not make us think that he is talking about a *bold* man instead of about a *bald* man!

Question. Are not these fine distinctions?

Answer. Personally I think that the distinction between a *cat* and a *cut* or between a *bald* man and a *bold* man are not "fine distinctions." And when the average Frenchman or Japanese says something to me which is intermediate between "I want to go" and "I won't go," or "I can go" and "I can't go," it causes trouble and misunderstanding on his

[17]

side and mine. Believe me, but what is a "fine distinction" to a foreigner is as the difference between black and white to a native. On the authority of my friend Noel-Armfield I am told that there is a case on record of a lady informing Chinese children that American soldiers ride on cats. The misunderstanding is due to the fact that she did not realize that the word *ma* meant *horse* with one tone and *cat* with another. In Uganda, I have heard from the same source, we may order a man to be *killed* [kuta] instead of *released* [kutha], the two verbs differing only in the aspiration of the *t*.

Question. But is it necessary to have recourse to a phonetic alphabet to indicate such obvious distinctions?

Answer. A phonetic alphabet (or phonetic notation — the two terms are almost identical) does help us to note such distinctions. The $l-r$ distinction is indicated even in ordinary English traditional spelling, but distinctions equally important can be shown only in phonetic spelling.

Question. You have just said something which tends to prove my point. You have said that the $l-r$ distinction is indicated "even in ordinary English traditional spelling," but I would ask you: how many Japanese observe this distinction indicated "even in ordinary English traditional spelling"?

[18]

Answer. Very few, I admit. Deplorably few.

Question. Very well. That is my point. If, for example, the Japanese do not observe a distinction indicated "even in ordinary spelling," how many will observe distinctions which have to be indicated in phonetic transcription?

Answer. I see your point. Remember however that the $l-r$ distinction is peculiarly and exceptionally difficult for the average Japanese. Other distinctions are not so difficult. The difference between "in Norway" and "in no way" is comparatively easy to demonstrate, as is also the difference between "I live here" and "I leave here."

Question. Well, but what bearing has this on the question of phonetic notation?

Answer. It has a most important bearing. In all this confusion of ideas and notions concerning difficult and easy distinctions, concerning native sounds and foreign sounds, concerning illusory spellings and actual pronunciations, concerning approximations and realities, concerning a 25% and a 75% standard, one thing stands out clearly; that a phonetic transcription, set down in actual type and based on correct and scientific observation, does actually show concretely and intelligibly what are the facts.

[19]

Question. Do we not obtain the same facts by means of the new Funk and Wagnall notation?

Answer. The new Funk and Wagnall notation *is* a phonetic transcription. Any system, Funk and Wagnall, Webster, or other which replaces conventional spelling by a series of symbols intended to show sign for sign the actual pronunciation values of the component sounds of English (or of any other language) is a system of phonetic notation. Personally I prefer the system of the International Phonetic Association.

Question. Why?

Answer. Because it is international, and is therefore utilizable for all languages for purposes of comparison, and also because this particular notation is used almost universally by all whose business it is to investigate the nature of speech-sounds and to raise the standard of foreigner's pronunciation of any language to the 75% or the 90% degree.

Question. I think I understand you, and I think I am convinced of the value of phonetic theory and notation. In what book can I find a simple and concise description of the most practical notation of English?

Answer. In this present booklet. It has been designed to furnish to beginners an outline of the

[20]

application of the elementary principles of the phonetic notation of English. There are many other books, of course, treating the same subject. The *Institute for Research in English Teaching* is publishing a series of volumes designed specifically for Japanese students. Heffer's of Cambridge (England), among other publishers, have produced many books dealing with the phonetics of English and other languages.

A SHORT HISTORY OF ENGLISH PHONETIC NOTATION.

A SHORT HISTORY OF ENGLISH PHONETIC NOTATION

from 1877.

From the time of the appearance of Sweet's *Handbook of Phonetics* in 1877 to the present day, the form of English phonetic notation has never been definitely fixed, nor has there ever been any common agreement to adopt any one standard form. For various reasons (e. g. typographical exigencies, expediency, considerations of theory, conformity with the dialect to be represented, or special requirements), the tendency has been for each phonetician either to compose his own notation or to introduce personal modifications into an existing notation. Or again, certain phoneticians have adopted successively various forms of notation, each deemed to be an improvement upon the former. Thus the notation of Sweet's *Handbook* (1877) differs very greatly from that of his *Primer of Phonetics* (1890).

An important step towards unification was made when in 1886 the International Phonetic Association was founded and, in 1888, drew up an international phonetic alphabet. It was however made clear that

[25]

this alphabet was designed as tentative and subject to future modification, for in the 1904 edition of the *Aims and Principles* of the association, we read:
"It must be understood however that the Association is in no way bound to its alphabet; not only are its members at liberty to use any other phonetic system they may prefer (except in "Le Maître Phonétique), but they frequently suggest such alterations and improvements as they think proper. A member of the Association, Mr. Robert Stein (of the United States Geological Survey), has lately suggested the idea of an international conference of linguists, teachers and dictionary-makers, to settle on a definite phonetic alphabet for all purposes; the Association, by its most prominent officials, has endorsed the plan, and declared itself ready to give up its own system if any other should be adopted by the conference."

The conference, unfortunately, never came into being, but on the other hand the International Phonetic Association has maintained its existence to the present day and is still considered as the most authoritative body of phoneticians in the world.

The following points are worthy of note by those who are especially interested in the history of phonetic notation:

1. The International Phonetic Alphabet consists of an almost unlimited number of symbols, each corresponding more or less to a single speech-sound.

2. As each language or dialect comes to be analyzed phonetically for the first time, an appropriate

[26]

new symbol is chosen to represent each new sound discovered.

3. Each language (or dialect) uses only those symbols which are required to represent its sounds, thus to write Received Standard English we require 46 symbols only out of the total; to write one variety of Standard Scottish pronunciation, we require 49 symbols (many of these differing from those used for Received Standard English); for French we require 38 symbols only (many of these differing from those used in any English pronunciation), for Received Standard Japanese, 26 symbols will suffice (many of these differing from those used in any English or French pronunciation), and so on.

4. The principles of the International Phonetic Association provide "broadening" conventions and "narrowing" conventions. The principle of "broadening" is that by which we reduce to the minimum the number of symbols used for writing a given language or dialect. Thus although the vowel of the English word *pen* is not the same as the first vowel heard in the word *care*, the symbol ɛ may serve to represent them both. In the same way, although the *l* of *let* is not pronounced in the same way as the *l* of *told*, the symbol l may serve to represent them both. The principle of "narrowing" is that by

[27]

which we devise new symbols to represent the finer shades of pronunciation. Thus we may use the symbols ϵ and ε respectively to indicate the difference between the vowel of *pen* and that of the first vowel heard in *care*.

5. The International Phonetic Association holds a very tolerant attitude towards the introduction of new symbols or the modification of existing symbols. In the pages of its organ, Le Maître Phonétique, however, the needless introduction of a new symbol or the use of a symbol in a way contrary to the fundamental principles of the Association would not be sanctioned.

6. The history of the notation used for transcribing Received Standard English in the official organ of the Association may be divided roughly into four periods :

i. Up to about the end of the last century there was a marked lack of uniformity; each contributor used his own style of notation but within the limits imposed by the compilers of the International Phonetic Alphabet.

ii. From about the beginning of the century up to 1914, a type of "broader" transcription was in vogue. [ij], [uw], [I] and [ʊ] went out of fashion, and were replaced respectively by [iː], [uː], [i], and

[u]. On account of the particularly large output of phonetic textbooks and dictionaries during this period, this style of notation has become better known than those which preceded it and those which have followed it.

iii. From 1914 to 1923 the publication of Le Maître Phonétique was suspended. In 1921, however, a new edition (in French) of the *Aims and Principles* appeared. The specimen of English transcription showed three important modifications of the notation. In the meantime individual members of the Association were writing texts in notations differing considerably from that of the 1900 — 1914 period. This third period was a period of transition during which the notation was in a state of flux, the tendency however being towards a type likely to bring about a high degree of uniformity and stability.

iv. The fourth and last phase may be said to have started with the reappearance of Le Maître Phonétique, for since then the new type of notation seems to have become uniform and fixed; it is now used in the editorial pages and by the majority of its contributors. This is the form of notation which is set forth and described in the following pages.

[29]

THE IMPOSSIBILITY OF AN "IDEAL" PHONETIC NOTATION.

THE IMPOSSIBILITY OF AN "IDEAL" PHONETIC NOTATION.

In weighing the comparative advantages of this or that system of spelling or of phonetic notation, we must take into consideration the various uses to which it may be put, and the various (and often contradictory) requirements of its users.

Those who are engaged in phonetic research require, above all, a notation of a high degree of precision and accuracy; for them the greater the number of symbols the better. But for those who are interested solely in a working national system of spelling (e. g. the Rōmajists, Kanaists, "Simplified Spellers", etc.), phonetic precision is comparatively needless, and the minimum number of symbols is a positive requirement.

There is a similar divergency of requirements between those who use phonetic notation for transcribing various languages or various dialects, and those whose interest is confined to one language or to one dialect.

In a system of rational simplified spelling for English, for instance, the vowel of *boat. toe* or *go*

[33]

might conveniently be represented by the simple and almost universal letter [o]. But those who wish to express in writing with the maximum of precision the quality of this vowel as used in Received Standard English (as compared with that of Scottish, American Middle West, etc. English) would have to use a special and unfamiliar symbol, such as [oᵘ]. Similarly, for most purposes the symbol [r] suffices to represent the first sound of the word *red*; but in a particularly precise notation, we should have to use for this sound such a symbol as [ɹ].

No system of phonetic notation can ever satisfy all possible requirements, consequently we must resign ourselves to using the one which seems to be in sufficient conformity with the greatest number of desiderata without too obvious inconsistencies or too great sacrifices of principle.

Among the various requirements of those who use phonetic notation the following eight seem to be of practical importance.

1. Precision.
2. Symbol Economy.
3. Phonemism.
4. Diaphonism.
5. Consistency.
6. Internationality.

[34]

7. Normativism.
8. Acceptability.

1. Precision.

The only notation that may represent an absolute degree of precision is that which is the enlargement of the tracing of a gramophone record, for it registers automatically every shade of sound, and is, so to speak, the photograph of the voice that made the record.

But such a degree of precision is far beyond the range of practical phonetic notation, and indeed would be a positive disadvantage rather than an advantage from the point of view of learning a foreign pronunciation.

Sweet's "Organic Alphabet" is perhaps the nearest working notation embodying the highest practicable degree of precision.

2. Symbol Economy.

There are at least 7 conventions adopted or adoptable with a view to economizing symbols, to reduce the number of symbols or to avoid the use of non-familiar symbols. These are sometimes called "broadening conventions." Most of these correspond to what the International Phonetic Association has termed "principles of simplification." They consist for the most part in replacing separate symbols by *conventions* to be learnt once for all.

Convention 1. "In settling for any language the form of transcription best suited for practical pusposes (as distinguished from scientific purposes), the language should be regarded by itself without reference to other languages."

This may mean, for instance, that English [ɹ] or French [ʀ] may both be written with the symbol [r]; that English [p' t' k'] may be written as [p t k], and that Japanese ウ may be written as [u].

Convention 2. According to this convention, the length-mark [ː] may be utilized to indicate phenomena other than phenomena of *length*; its presence or absence may serve to determine vowel-*quality*. Thus while [iː] represents the vowel of *seat*, [i] may represent the vowel of *sit*; while [uː] represents the vowel of *fool*, [u] may represent the vowel of *full*; while [ɔː] represents the vowel of *caught*, [ɔ] may represent the vowel of *cot*; while [əː] represents the vowel of *bird*, [ə] may represent the obscure *a* of *ago*.

But this convention has an obvious disadvantage. The student may be left in doubt as to whether [i] stands for the *i* of *sit* or for the true shortened [iː]

[36]

(as Japanese イ, or as the *i* of French *site*); as to whether [u] stands for the *u* of *full* or for the true shortened [uː] (as the French *ou* of *foule*); as to whether [ɔ] stands for the *o* of *cot* or for the true shortened [ɔː] (as the *a* of *although*); as to whether [ə] stands for the *a* of *China* or for the true shortened [əː] (as the *ur* of *suburb*).

The half-length-mark [˙] may be used to show phenomena other than half-length.

For instance

the symbol i˙ may be used to show optional iː or i,
ɔ˙ may be used to show optional ɔː or ɔ,
u˙ may be used to show optional uː or u.

Convention 3. The stress-mark [ˈ] may be used to mark phenomena other than stress-proper (either word-stress or sentence-stress). By using the stress-mark in əˈgou, ɪˈlevn, etc. it may not be necessary to specify the obscure vowels [ə] [ɪ] by special symbols (we must distinguish between *obscure* and *unstressed* vowels. The [ə] of *China* is unstressed and obscure. The [ou] of *window* is unstressed but not obscure).

Convention 4. Single symbols may be used instead of digraphs. Conceivably [e] may stand for [eɪ]; [o] may stand for [ou]; [ns] may stand for [nts]; and, in Japanese, [ʒ] may stand for [dʒ], and [z] may stand for [dz].

[37]

Convention 5. Digraphs may be used instead of new symbols.

tʃ may be used instead of ʧ

dʒ may be used instead of ʤ

kn „ „ „ „ „ ƙn

tn „ „ „ „ „ ƭn

hw „ „ „ „ „ ʍ

Convention 6. Familiar symbols may be used instead of unfamiliar symbols:

g for ɡ

a for ʌ or for ɑ

è or e for ɛ

l for ɬ

å for ɔ

Other Conventions.

a. Absence of stress-mark when the stress falls on the first syllable of a word.

b. Final *l* and *n* are syllabic in English when not preceded by a vowel.

c. Two successive vowels form a diphthong (or kinetic vowel).

d. The first of two successive stops is not exploded.

e. ʃ in tʃ is not necessarily identical with ʃ.

[38]

f. {
  y in *happy* is not necessarily identical with the *i* of *give*.
  e in *expect* is not necessarily identical with the *i* of *give*.
}

Conventions such as these do have the effect of economizing symbols, but they also have the effect of making a transcription more difficult for foreigners to read with a correct pronunciation.

As we see from the above, symbol economy is a very doubtful economy. If we can reduce the number of conventions by the use of a few extra symbols, the notation gains both in precision and in simplicity.

3. Phonemism.

Two sounds which are organically and acoustically different but which mark no significative difference in a given language or dialect may be represented by one and the same symbol.

Thus, the first element of ラリルレロ may be represented by [r], and not necessarily by [l] or [d];

the varying values of the *ee* of *see* may be represented by [iː], and not necessarily by [ij] or by [ɪi];

the varying values of the *oo* of *moon* may be

represented by [uː], and not necessarily by [uw] or by [ʊu].

We know that the consonant element of ラリルレロ is pronounced almost indifferently by Japanese as [r,] [l] (or even in some cases as [d]), but as these divergencies correspond to no significative difference, these three "phonemic members" may be written indifferently as [r], or (in a more precise notation), as [ɹ].

We know that the vowel of *see* may be pronounced indifferently as [iː], as [ij] or as [ɪi], but as these divergencies correspond to no significative difference, we may in all cases represent them by the symbol [iː].

We know that the vowel of *pen* may vary between the two extremes of cardinal [e] and cardinal [ɛ], but as such divergencies correspond to no significative difference, we may make an exclusive use either of [e] or of [ɛ].

We know that the sound *k* of *keep* differs very much in quality from the sound *k* of *cool*, but as, in English, this divergency does not correspond to any significative difference, we may in both cases use the symbol [k].

On the other hand, if we were to exaggerate the claims of "phonemism," we should make no distinc-

[40]

tion in phonetic transcription between the s of *vision* and the s of *poison*.

4. Diaphonism.

A notation may be designed in such a way as to be applicable to one dialect and to one dialect only, ignoring all others. Or it may be designed in such a way as to be utilizable for two or more dialects. The latter type of transcription may be termed (according to Professor Jones) *diaphonic*. Conditions in Japan, where 80 per cent of the foreign teachers do not use Received Standard, seem to point to the desirability of accepting in some measure the principles of diaphonism, especially when such principles offer no obstacle to the needs of those who are teaching Received Standard.

The following are the chief diaphonic conventions:

1. The use of *italic symbols* may cover not merely personal divergencies, but may be extended to cover diaphonic values, such as [*h*w], which may mean optional [w] or [hw]; [ɔˑə] which may stand for optional [ɔː] or [ɔə]; [*h*iˑ] which may stand for [hiˑ] or [iˑ].

2. *A broad interpretation of values.* Thus the symbol ə may stand for the *ir* of *bird* in its Received

[41]

Standard, Northern States American or Southern States American values.

3. Certain *conventional diacritics* may be used to show optional divergencies, diaphonic or other. Example: [ə, ɔ, ɑ] may indicate susceptibility of adding or including some sort of r-element.

4. As ɛə and eə form one single phoneme in some American dialects, it is immaterial which symbol is used as the first element.

5. Consistency.

Probably few notations are ideally consistent. In the introduction to the Jones Dictionary reasons are given why absolute consistency is incompatible with considerations of absolute precision or of practicability. At the same time, there is no necessity for diverging needlessly from convenient consistency. Thus if the two vowels of *further* are distinguished by the respective use of [ɜ] and [ə], the two vowels of *city* should be distinguished by the respective use of [i] and [ɪ]. On grounds of parallelism also, the [iʴ] [ɪ] distinction should correspond to an [uʴ] [ʊ] and to an [ɔʴ] [ɒ] distinction. On the other hand, if it is considered needless to distinguish between the *e* of *demand* and the *y* of *happy*, it seems needless to distinguish between the initial *a* of *again* and the *a* of *China*.

Too great attention to an ideal of consistency, however, will result in schematic artificiality, just as too little attention to it will result in needless anarchy.

6. Internationality.

The ideal of an international notation is contrary to convention 1 of the symbol-economy conventions. The letter *r* differs in phonetic value according to whether it is used in Received Standard English, Scottish, Northern United States, Southern United States, Parisian French, Regional French, Danish, Italian, Spanish or Japanese. A truly international notation will take these varied values into consideration, and provide for each a separate symbol. The degree in which separate symbols are to be provided depends upon to what extent two or more separate phonetic systems are to be compared or contrasted by the student. If the same symbol is used to represent different values according to the language in which it occurs, it will tend to confusion of ideas. On the other hand, a multiplicity of symbols may tend to make phonetic study needlessly complicated. Much depends upon the mother-tongue of the student. For all ordinary purposes, the symbol [k] may suffice for representing the *k* of *key*, the *c* of *car*, the *k* of キ and the *k* of カ; but students of Arabic will find it necessary to distinguish between them. These considerations open up a wide field of discussion, and cannot be entirely ignored when determining the ideal system of notation to be used in Japan.

7. Normativism.

In certain special cases it is considered desirable to take into consideration the normative function of a phonetic notation.

French and German students tend to interpret the *o* of *come* as French *eu* or German *ö*. The symbol [ʌ] does not help them to overcome the tendency, but the symbol [a] does have this effect, therefore it may occasionally be desirable to replace [ʌ] by [a].

The use of the symbol [r] in English is likely to cause French and German students to give to it the value of French or German *r*. It is therefore occasionally expedient to use an unfamiliar symbol such as [ɹ] as a continual reminder that English *r* is an alveolar fricative.

The symbol [f] in Japanese tends to cause Europeans to give to the consonant element of フ the value of *f*. It is therefore desirable in a normative course to replace [f] by [ꜰ] or even by [h].

[44]

Japanese students, however, are helped by such devices in a lesser degree than those whose own language uses Roman spelling as the normal writing system.

At the same time normativism has its claims even in Japan. In view of the widespread tendency to over-strengthen the obscure vowels of a foreign language, it is expedient to reserve special symbols for the obscurer vowels such as the second *a* of *magazine* or the initial *e* of *eleven,* and not to use for these the symbols representing the *ir* of *first* or the *i* of *give*.

8. Acceptability.

If, on the one hand, we ignore the claims of acceptability, and make no concessions to popular prejudices, a phonetic notation is likely to arouse needless opposition, and this will tend to hinder the scope of its utility.

If, on the other hand, we lay too much stress on acceptability, and make too many concessions to popular prejudice, our notation will tend to become stultified, imperfect and non-international.

Certain symbols or certain phonetic conventions may act as irritants to the uninitiated. If we can remove the cause of irritation without impairing the

[45]

value of the notation we shall do wisely.

The symbol [j] for the *y* of *yes* is likely to be unpopular in England, America, France and Japan on account of its cross-associations with the traditional English, French and Japanese values of the letter *j*. For this reason some prefer the symbol [y], and use it in their transcription, but this concession strikes at the very root of the idea of an international system of spelling. Indeed the most "acceptable" or "popular" notation will be that which most nearly coincides with the traditional spelling of the language.

We have to consider not only the degree of acceptability on the part of the students, but also that on the part of the teacher whose native tongue is the language he is teaching.

Conclusion.

From the above considerations it will be seen that no off-hand solutions to the problems of phonetic notation are desirable or possible. Every practicable system ever devised of denoting pronunciation by means of written symbols must be in the nature of a compromise, for no system can ever be in full conformity with the various desiderata of an "ideal" notation. Every scheme of notation suggested becomes

[46]

therefore the target of criticism (legitimate and illegitimate), for each scheme must necessarily offend against one or more of the various desiderata treated above.

We may conclude by suggesting that the most desirable phonetic notation is that which is calculated to be of the greatest utility to the greatest number of users.

RECEIVED STANDARD PRONUNCIATION.

"RECEIVED STANDARD PRONUNCIATION."

In accordance with the theory of Wyld, there would seem to be three types of English pronunciation-dialects:

1. Regional,
2. Received Standard,
3. Modified Standard.

The Regional pronunciations are those which are associated with geographical districts, thus we may speak of the Yorkshire, the Devonshire, the Kentish, the London, the Edinburgh, the Midland etc. pronunciations, each found in its own particular region and not extending beyond it.

The Received Standard pronunciation, although originating in the South of England (particularly London), is not a local pronunciation, but rather a class (or social) pronunciation-dialect. It is practically the only pronunciation that is independent of locality. It may be found existing side by side with the regional pronunciations all over the English-speaking world. Although the majority of Scots, Americans, Canadians, Devonians, Yorkshire folk etc. use pronunciations other than this, a minority

[51]

of such people do use it. Putting the subject in other words, we may note that many Americans, Scots etc. may speak with Received Standard pronunciation, but that no English people speak with any American, Scottish etc. pronunciation.

Modified Standard pronunciations. These are varieties of Received Standard modified by the Regional pronunciations. Thus we may find in a given district of (let us say) Scotland the three types. Speaker A may use his "broad Scots," the pronunciation of the district; Speaker B may use Received Standard (and thereby make his speech indistinguishable from that of many Londoners or Americans), and Speaker C may use a pronunciation approximating to Received Standard but in which we readily detect certain Scottish characteristics.

Applied to Japanese, the Wyld theory would work out somewhat in the following way:

Regional pronunciations. The purely local pronunciations of Kagoshima, Tosa, Osaka, Sendai, Niigata, etc. (including the popular pronunciation of Tokyo).

Received Standard pronunciation. The "Kanto Samurai" pronunciation, particularly characteristic of Tokyo aristocracy, but heard all over Japan.

Modified Standard pronunciation. The "Kanto

[52]

Samurai" pronunciation modified more or less strongly by local peculiarities.

The type of English pronunciation to which Jones applies the term P.S.P. (Public School Pronunciation) corresponds on the whole to Wyld's Received Standard. In his dictionary Jones decribes it in the following terms:

"That pronunciation most usually heard in every-
"day speech in the families of Southern English
"persons whose men-folk have been educated at the
"great public boarding-schools. This pronunciation
"is also used by a considerable proportion of those
"who do not come from the South of England, but
"who have been educated at these schools. The
"pronunciation may also be heard, to an extent
"which is considerable though difficult to specify,
"from persons of education in the South of England
"who have not been educated at these schools. It
"is probably accurate to say that a majority of
"those members of London society who have had a
"university education, use either this pronunciation
"or a pronunciation not differing very greatly from
"it. Having stated what the pronunciation is, it
"may be as well, in order to avoid possible
"misunderstandings, to state what it is not. It
"is not the pronunciation commonly used in

[53]

"declamation, still less is it that used in singing.
"It is not as a rule heard from Americans, South
"Africans, or Australians; it is not as a rule used
"by those who have been educated at day schools
"in Scotland, Ireland or the North of England, and
"it is not used by a considerable proportion of
"those educated at day schools in the South of
"England. Least of all is it a product of the
"delusion under which many lexicographers appear
"to have laboured, viz. that all educated people
"pronounce alike."

Jones proceeds to explain: "The fact that the
"scope of this [dictionary] has been limited to the
"speech af the persons referred to [above] does not
"mean that I consider their pronunciation intrinsi-
"cally superior to any other. On the contrary, it is
"clear to me that if we consider this type of speech
"on its intrinsic merits (i. e. without regard to
"external considerations, such as the social position
"of the persons who use it), it will be found in no
"way 'better' than any other type. I have thought
"it desirable to record this pronunciation for two
"reasons, (1) because such a record has certain
"practical uses detailed elsewhere, (2) because it
"happens to be the only type of English about
"which I am in a position to obtain full and

[54]

"accurate information. The record would be worth
" publishing for the latter reason, even if it dealt
" with a dialect only used by few speakers, since all
" accurate linguistic information is of value. To
" those who think reforms or standards are necessary
" must be left the invidious task of deciding what
" is to be approved and what is to be condemned.
" This book will provide them with a small fraction
" of the materials they will require as a basis to
" work upon."

In a special message written by Jones to the *Institute for Research in English Teaching* (in Japan), he emphasizes still further the fact that Public School Pronunciation is not necessarily the ideal, and suggests West of England pronunciation or that of some recognized American standard as being more suitable.

In the *Bulletin* of the Institute (New Series No. 2, December, 1923), appeared the opinions of those who have a certain competence in the matter under discussion. Probably the most strongly-worded arguments against the adoption of any American Standard was written by an American. Other contributors declared British dialects other than the Received Standard Dialect to be obsolescent.

If the "Public-School Pronunciation" of the Jones

[55]

dictionary should be considered the most suitable as a standard for Japan, the chief reasons in favour of it are:

1. That it is the one pronunciation-dialect of English that has been fully analyzed by competent observers, therefore more is known about it than about other pronunciation-dialects;

2. It is the pronunciation forming part of that dialect (Received Standard) which is used to the exclusion of all others by writers throughout the whole of the English-using world. Exception is of course made in the case of such writers as Burns, "Mr. Dooley," or Ring W. Lardner, who, for special and obvious reasons, use dialects other than Received Standard;

3. That more textbooks using this pronunciation have been published and are far more widely-known than any other textbooks;

4. That this pronunciation (in theory at least) has already been tacitly accepted by the mass of Japanese teachers and students;

5. That this pronunciation, containing, as it does, fewer sound-distinctions than do other pronunciations, is easier for foreign students than other pronunciations;

6. That users of this pronunciation are generally

[56]

less liable to criticism or censure than users of other pronunciations. Native Americans and Scots in large numbers do deliberately and from choice use and recommend this pronunciation, whereas the converse case is probably unknown.

On the other hand, over 80% of English teachers in Japan use (and consequently serve as models for) pronunciations other than Received Standard.

THE ENGLISH PHONETIC SYSTEM.

THE ENGLISH PHONETIC SYSTEM.

DETAILED EXAMINATION OF THE INDIVIDUAL PHONES AND THE MANNER OF REPRESENTING EACH.

1. The vowel of "key."

The symbols [i], [iː], [iˑ], [ii], [ij], [ɪi], and others, have at various times been proposed for this vowel.

In the present scheme the symbol [i] has been selected. This symbol (with the length-mark) has been used by the International Phonetic Association since 1908 specifically to represent the vowel of "key." The use of the half-length mark [ˑ] or of the full-length mark [ː] is optional, and depends upon considerations of precision or of expediency. In general the use of the half-length mark is to be recommended.

[i] is one of the five English "free vowels;" in other terms, it may occur at the end of an English word.

	1908 Notation.	Present Notation.
key	kiː	ki, kiˑ, kiː
see	siː	si, siˑ, siː
eat	iːt	it, iˑt, iːt
feet	fiːt	fit, fiˑt, fiːt

This symbol may be used in such words as *twentieth* [twɛntiɩθ], *create* [kriɑt].

2. The vowel of "star" or "calm."

The symbols [ɑ], [ɑ·], [ɑː], [ɑɑ], [aː], [aa], [aə], and others, have at various times been proposed for this vowel.

In the present scheme the symbol [ɑ] has been selected. This symbol (with the length mark) has been used by the International Phonetic Association since 1888 specifically to represent the vowel of "star" or "calm" in Received Standard Pronunciation. The use of the half-length mark [·] or of the full-length mark [ː] is optional, and depends upon considerations of precision or expediency. In general the use of the half-length mark is to be recommended.

[ɑ] is one of the five English "free vowels;" in other terms, it may occur at the end of an English word.

	1908 Notation.	Present Notation.
star	stɑː	stɑ, stɑ·, stɑː
calm	kɑːm	kɑm, kɑ·m, kɑːm
far	fɑː	fɑ, fɑ·, fɑː
laugh	lɑːf	lɑf, lɑ·f, lɑːf

[62]

Optional divergency for the *ar* of *star* etc.

In order to indicate the susceptibility of [ɑ] to become [ɑr] (or in other ways to suggest an *r*-like sound), the symbol [ɑ] may be used, especially when transcribing pronunciations other than Received Standard.

	1908 Notation.	Present Notation (optional).
star	stɑː	stɐ, stɐˑ, stɐː
far	fɑː	fɐ, fɐˑ, fɐː
harm	hɑːm	hɐm, hɐˑm, hɐːm

3. The vowel of "horse" or "ball."

The symbols [ɔ], [ɔˑ], [ɔː], [ɔɔ], [å], [å̊å̊], and others, have at various times been proposed for this vowel.

In this present scheme the symbol [ɔ] has been selected. This symbol (with the length-mark) has been used by the International Phonetic Association since 1888 specifically to represent the vowel of "horse." The use of the half-length mark [ˑ] or of the full-length mark [ː] is optional, and depends upon considerations of precision or expediency. In general the use of the half-length mark is to be recommended.

[ɔ] is one of the five English "free vowels;" in other terms, it may occur at the end of an English word.

[63]

	1908 Notation.	Present Notation.
ball	bɔːl	bɔl, bɔ·l, bɔːl
caught	kɔːt	kɔt, kɔ·t, kɔːt
horse	hɔːs	hɔs, hɔ·s, hɔːs
off	ɔːf	ɔf, ɔ·f, ɔːf

Optional divergency for the *or* of *horse* etc.

In order to indicate the susceptibility of the [ɔ] to become [ɔr] (or in other ways to suggest an *r*-like sound) the symbol [ɔ] may be used, especially when transcribing pronunciations other than Received Standard.

	1908 Notation.	Present Notation (optional).
horse	hɔːs	hɔs, hɔ·s, hɔːs
fourth	fɔːθ	fɔθ, fɔ·θ, fɔːθ
mourn	mɔːn	mɔn, mɔ·n, mɔːn

Words of this class may also be transcribed (according to the dialect of the user) with the symbols [ɔə], [ɔə]. (See "The vowel of *door*").

4. The vowel of "moon."

The symbols [u], [uː], [u·], [uu], [uw], [ʊu], and others, have at various times been proposed for this vowel.

In the present scheme the symbol [u] has been selected. This symbol (with the length-mark) has

[64]

been used by the International Phonetic Association since 1908 specifically to represent the vowel of "moon." The use of the half-length mark [ˑ] or of the full-length mark [ː] is optional, and depends upon considerations of precision or of expediency. In general the use of the half-length mark is to be recommended.

[u] is one of the five English "free vowels;" in other terms, it may occur at the end of an English word.

	1908 Notation.	Present Notation.
moon	muːn	mun, muˑn, muːn
too	tuː	tu, tuˑ, tuː
tooth	tuːθ	tuθ, tuˑθ, tuːθ
move	muːv	muv, muˑv, muːv

5. The vowel of "bird."

The symbols [əː], [əˑ], [əə], [ʌː], [ɔˑ], [ʊː], [ɜˑ], and others, have at various times been proposed for this vowel.

In the present scheme the symbol [ə] has been selected. This symbol was first used in the French edition of the *Aims and Principles of the International Phonetic Association*, 1921. The use of the half-length mark [ˑ] or the full-length mark [ː] is

[65]

optional, and depends upon considerations of precision or expediency. In general the use of the half-length mark is to be recommended.

[ə] is one of the five English "free vowels;" in other terms, it may occur at the end of an English word.

	1908 Notation.	Present Notation.
bird	bəːd	bəd, bəˑd, bəːd
learn	ləːn	lən, ləˑn, ləːn
word	wəːd	wəd, wəˑd, wəːd
year	jəː	jə, jəˑ, jəː

As this sound is in every case susceptible (in certain conditions) to become [ər] (or in other ways to suggest an *r*-like sound), it is not necessary to provide a special symbol parallel to [ɑ] and [ɔ]. The symbol [ə] may stand for the vowel of "bird" irrespective of its various phonetic values. In other terms, [ə] may be considered as a diaphonic symbol.

6. The vowel of "fish."

The symbols [i], [ɪ], [ɨ], and others, have at various times been proposed for this vowel.

In the present scheme the symbol [ɪ] has been selected. This symbol has been used for an open

[66]

variety of the [i]-class of vowels since the earliest days of the International Phonetic Association, and since 1923 has been used specifically in *Le Maître Phonétique* to represent the vowel of "fish." In order to avoid any confusion between [ɪn] and [m], the upper bar is slightly reduced: [ɪ]. In handwriting this symbol may be a single upright stroke: [ɪ].

[ɪ] is one of the six English "checked vowels;" in other terms, it never occurs at the end of a word.

	1908 Notation.	Present Notation.
fish	fiʃ	fɪʃ
give	giv	gɪv
big	big	bɪg
ill	il	ɪl

7. The vowel of "pen."

The symbols [e], [ɛ], [ɛ], [è], [e], and others, have at various times been proposed for this vowel.

As the tendency among the English-speaking peoples is towards Cardinal Vowel 3 rather than towards Cardinal Vowel 2. In the present scheme the symbol [ɛ] has been selected. This symbol has been used for an open variety of the [e]-class of vowels since the earliest days of the International Phonetic Association. In the 1912 edition of the *Aims and Principles*

[67]

it was used specifically to represent the vowel of "pen," and since 1921 the Association has reverted to this usage.

[ɛ] is one of the six English "checked vowels;" in other terms, it never occurs at the end of an English word.

	1908 Notation.	Present Notation.
pen	pen	pɛn
get	get	gɛt
tell	tel	tɛl
red	red	rɛd

8. The vowel of "cat."

No other symbol than [æ] has apparently ever been proposed for this vowel, and so in the present scheme this symbol is retained.

For some reason not yet determined, in certain words this vowel is considerably longer than in others. In these cases the half-length mark may be added.

	1908 Notation.	Present Notation.
cat	kæt	kæt
have	hæv	hæv
man	mæn, mæːn	mæn, mæˑn
bad	bæd, bæːd	bæd, bæˑd

[68]

9. The vowel of "duck."

The symbols [ʌ], [a], [ɐ], and others, have at various times been proposed for this vowel.

In the present scheme the symbol [ʌ] has been selected. It has been in constant use since its introduction by the International Phonetic Association in 1888.

[ʌ] is one of the six English "checked vowels;" in other terms, it never occurs at the end of a word.

	1908 Notation.	Present Notation.
duck	dʌk	dʌk
cut	kʌt	kʌt
come	kʌm	kʌm
up	ʌp	ʌp

10. The vowel of "box."

The symbols [ɔ], [ɔ̇], [o], [*o*], [å], [ɒ], and others, have at various times been proposed for this vowel.

In the present scheme the symbol [ɒ] has been selected. This symbol was suggested for the first time in Jones' *Outline of Phonetics* (1914), and was used for the first time in Mackenzie and Drew's *Phonetic Reader* (1919).

[ɒ] is one of the six English "checked vowels;"

in other terms, it never occurs at the end of a word.

	1908 Notation.	Present Notation.
box	bɔks	bɒks
hot	hɔt	hɒt
stop	stɔp	stɒp
dog	dɔg	dɒg

11. The vowel of "book."

The symbols [u], [ʊ], [ù], and others have at various times been proposed for this vowel.

In the present scheme the symbol [ʊ] has been selected. This symbol has been used for an open variety of the [u]-class of vowels since the earliest days of the International Phonetic Association, and since 1923 has been used specifically to represent the vowel of "book." The exact shape of this symbol has varied in details, but has always been centered about the shape of a small capital [ʊ]. In handwriting this symbol may be written as [ʊ].

[ʊ] is one of the six English "checked vowels;" in other terms, it never occurs at the end of a word.

	1908 Notation.	Present Notation.
book	buk	bʊk
good	gud	gʊd
put	put	pʊt
pull	pul	pʊl

[70]

12. The vowel of "gate."

The symbols [ei], [eɪ], [eˡ], [ɛe], [èi], and others have at various times been proposed for this vowel.

With a view to uniformity, and to effecting a conciliation between the various conflicting manners of representing this vowel, in the present scheme the symbol [ɐ] has been adopted.

[ɐ] is one of the five chief "Kinetic Vowels" (or "Diphthongs").

	1908 Notation.	Present Notation.
gate	geit	gɐt
take	teik	tɐk
day	dei	dɐ
same	seim	sɐm

13. The vowel of "eye."

The symbols [ai], [aɪ], [æ], [aì], and others have at various times been proposed for this vowel.

With a view to uniformity, and to effecting a conciliation between the various conflicting manners of representing this vowel, in the present scheme the symbol [ɑ] has been selected.

[ɑ] is one of the five chief "Kinetic Vowels" (or "Diphthongs").

[71]

	1908 Notation.	Present Notation.
eye	ai	aɪ
time	taim	taɪm
high	hai	haɪ
tie	tai	taɪ

14. The vowel of "cow."

The symbols [au], [aʊ], [ao], [aù], and others have at various times been proposed for this vowel.

In the present scheme the symbol [aʊ] has been selected. This symbol (or a close approximation to it) has been used in the organ of the International Phonetic Association since 1923 specifically to represent the vowel of "cow."

[aʊ] is one of the five chief "Kinetic Vowels" (or "Diphthongs").

	1908 Notation.	Present Notation.
cow	kau	kaʊ
now	nau	naʊ
town	taun	taʊn
out	aut	aʊt

15. The vowel of "boy."

The symbols [oi], [ɔi], [ɔɪ], [ɔe], and others have at various times been proposed for this vowel.

[72]

With a view to uniformity, and to effecting a conciliation between the various conflicting manners of representing this vowel, in the present scheme the symbol [ɔɪ] has been selected.

[ɔɪ] is one of the five chief "Kinetic Vowels" (or "Diphthongs".

	1908 Notation.	Present Notation.
boy	bɔi	bɔɪ
oil	ɔil	ɔɪl·
join	dʒɔin	dʒɔɪn
noise	nɔiz	nɔɪz

16. The vowel of "nose."

The symbols [où], [ou], [oᵘ], [ɔo], and others have at various times been proposed for this vowel.

In the present scheme the symbol [ɔu] has been selected. This symbol has been used since 1923 in *Le Maître Phonétique* specifically to represent the vowel of "nose." This digraph is however more or less arbitrary, as the first element differs considerably from "cardinal [o]," and seems to be intermediate between this and a vowel in the [ə]-position. In London (or "Cockney") pronunciation (as distinguished from "Received Standard") the vowel is almost [əu] or [ʌu].

[73]

In unstressable position, it is permissible to abbreviate the vowel as [o].

[ou] is one of the five chief "Kinetic Vowels" (or "Diphthongs").

	1908 Notation.	Present Notation.
nose	nouz	nouz
coat	kout	kout
go	gou	gou
no, know	nou	nou

17. The final vowel of "happy," "houses," or the initial vowel of "immense," "emotion."

In examining the various symbols that have been proposed at various times to represent this obscure vowel, in discussing the suitability or unsuitability of each, or in selecting the one which seems most appropriate, we must remember that this obscure vowel is the result of a process by which two distinct vowels have come to be "levelled" or nearly so. Originally the *y* of *happy* was entirely distinct from the *e* of *houses*; and the *i* of *immense* was entirely distinct from the *e* of *emotion*. Even to-day many speakers either make the distinction, tend to make it, or imagine they make it. From the earliest days

[74]

of the phonetics movement, it has been recognized unanimously by competent observers that the vowel of *emotion, eleven, expect, houses, goodness, wanted, Sunday*, etc., is, to all intents and purposes, identical in ordinary speech to the vowel of *immense, inquire, happy, money*, etc. Admitting the theoretical possibility of these being distinguished in speech, the fact that both vowels occur only in unstressed position and have an "obscure" (or weakly-articulated) quality makes it highly desirable for them to be levelled and to share one common symbol.

The symbols [i], [ɪ], [i], [e] and others have at various times been proposed for this vowel. some have identified it with the *i* of *give*, others with the first *e* of *create*; in fact the divergent usages of these various symbols has been responsible for much confusion of thought and frequent misunderstandings. With a view to uniformity, and to effecting a conciliation between the various conflicting manners of representing this vowel, in the present scheme the symbol [ɿ] has been selected. The absence of a dot distinguishes it sufficiently from the vowel of *see*, and the slight differences between it and [ɪ] serve to distinguish it from the vowel of *give*.

[ɿ], then, is one of the two "obscure" vowels (the other being [ə]).

[75]

	1908 Notation.	Present Notation.
happy	hæpi	hæpɪ
money	mʌni	mʌnɪ
houses	hauziz	haʊzɪz
wanted	wɔntid	wɒntɪd
goodness	gudnis	gʊdnɪs
Sunday	sʌndi	sʌndɪ
immense	imens	ɪmens
inquire	iŋkwaiə	ɪŋkaɪə
eleven	ilevn	ɪlɛvn
expect	ikspekt	ɪkspekt

18. The final vowel of "china" or the initial vowel of "ago."

Practically the only symbol ever suggested for this vowel since the earliest days of the International Phonetic Association has been [ə], and in the present scheme this symbol remains with its usual value.

[ə] is one of the two "obscure vowels." Phonologically speaking, it constitutes the "weak" form of many vowels, and the Received Standard pronunciation of such spellings as -*er*, -*ir*, -*or*, -*ar*, -*our*, -*re*, etc.

	1908 Notation.	Present Notation.
china	tʃainə	tʃaɪnə
ago	əgou	əgoʊ
aeroplane	ɛərəplein	ɛərəplæn

[76]

Optional divergency. In order to indicate the susceptibility of [ə] to become [ər] (or in other ways to suggest an *r*-like sound), the symbol [ɐ] may be used.

	1908 Notation.	Present Notation.
better	betə	betɐ (*or* betə)
doctor	dɔktə	dɒktɐ (*or* dɒktə)
collar	kɔlə	kɒlɐ (*or* kɒlə)
honour	ɔnə	ɒnɐ (*or* ɒnə)
theatre	θiətə	θɪətɐ (*or* θɪətə)

Note. In order to represent English pronunciations other than that of the Received Standard Dialect, the symbol [ɐ] may frequently be used even when followed by a consonant.

	1908 Notation.	Present Notation. (Received Standard.)	(Not Received Standard.)
understand	ʌndəstænd	ʌndəstænd	ʌndɐstænd
Saturday	sætədi	sætədɪ	sætɐdɪ
forget	fəget	fəget	fɐget

19. The vowel of "ear."

The symbols [iːə], [iə], [ɪə], and others have at various times been proposed for this vowel.

In the present scheme the symbol [ɪə] has been selected. Since 1923 this symbol has been used

[77]

specifically in *Le Maître Phonétique* to represent the vowel of " ear."

[ɪə] is one of the four " Kinetic Murmur-Vowels " (or " Murmur-Diphthongs).

	1908 Notation.	Present Notation.
ear	iə	ɐ
deer	diə	dɐ
here	hiə	hɐ
near	niə	nɐ

Optional divergency. In order to indicate the susceptibility of [ɐ] to become [ɐr] (or in other ways to suggest an *r*-like conclusion) the symbol [ɪə] may be used, especially in transcribing pronunciations other than Received Standard.

	1908 Notation.	Present Notation.
ear	iə	ɐ (*or* ɪə)
deer	diə	dɐ (*or* dɪə)
here	hiə	hɐ (*or* hɪə)
near	niə	nɐ (*or* nɪə)

20. The vowel of " chair."

The symbols [ɛɹə], [ɛə], [eə], and others have at various times been proposed for this vowel.

In the present scheme the symbol [ɛə] has been selected. Since 1888 this symbol has been in constant

[78]

use in *Le Maître Phonétique* to represent the vowel of "chair."

[ɛə] is one of the four "Kinetic Murmur-Vowels" (or "Murmur-Diphthongs").

Optional divergency. In order to indicate the susceptibility of [ɛə] to become [ɛər] (or in other ways to suggest an *r*-like conclusion), the symbol [ɛə] may be used, especially in transcribing pronunciations other than Received Standard.

	1908 Notation.	Present Notation.
chair	tʃɛə	tʃɛə (*or* tʃɛə)
care	kɛə	kɛə (*or* kɛə)
there	ðɛə	ðɛə (*or* ðɛə)
pear	pɛə	pɛə (*or* pɛə)

21. The vowel of "door."

The symbols [ɔ], [ɔː], [ɔə], [ɔˑə], [å̊ə], [oə], and others have at various times been proposed for this vowel.

In the present scheme the symbol [ɔə] has been selected.

[ɔə] is one of the four "Kinetic Murmur-Vowels" (or "Murmur-Diphthongs").

The fact that in Received Standard English usage varies between [ɔˑ] and [ɔə] has made it exceptionally

[79]

difficult to arrive at a definite decision concerning the symbol to be adopted. It may be noted also that Received Standard (or P. S. P.) pronunciation has levelled the distinction (observed in other dialects) between such pairs of words as *morning* and *mourning*.

Optional divergency. In order to indicate the susceptibility of [ɔɐ] to become [ɔər], [ɔr], etc. (or in other ways to suggest an *r*-like conclusion), the symbol [ɔə] may be used, especially in transcribing pronunciations other than Received Standard.

	1908 Notation.	Present Notation.
door	dɔɐ	dɔɐ (*or* dɔə)
four	fɔɐ	fɔɐ (*or* fɔə)
more	mɔɐ	mɔɐ (*or* mɔə)
oar	ɔɐ	ɔɐ (*or* ɔə)

22. The vowel of " moor."

The symbols [uːə], [uə], [ʊə], and others have at various times been proposed for this vowel.

In the present scheme the symbol [ʊə] has been selected. Since 1923 this symbol has been used in *Le Maître Phonétique*, to represent the vowel of "moor."

[ʊə] is one of the four " Kinetic Murmur-Vowels " (or " Murmur-Diphthongs ").

[80]

Many users of Received Standard (or P. S. P.) pronunciation level the distinction between [ʊə] and [ɔə], thereby making homonyms of such pairs of words as *moor* and *more*. Indeed, [ʊə] is often replaced by [ɔ·] thereby rendering indistinguishable such words as *poor, pour, pore* and *paw* ; or *sure, shore* and *shaw*.

Optional divergency. In order to indicate the susceptibility of [ʊə] to become [ʊər] (or in other ways to suggest an *r*-like conclusion), the symbol [ᴜə] may be used, especially in transcribing pronunciations other than Received Standard.

	1908 Notation.	Present Notation.
moor	muə	mᴜə (*or* mʊə)
tour	tuə	tᴜə (*or* tʊə)
poor	puə	pᴜə (*or* pʊə)
cure	kjuə	kjᴜə (*or* kjʊə)

Consonants.

Unlike the vowel-symbols, the consonant-symbols present few divergencies. The following, however, may be noted:

The *th* of *thing*.

[θ] is used by the International Phonetic Association.

[81]

[p] is used by Jespersen, Sweet, Kruisinga, Wyld and others.

The *sh* of *ship*.

[ʃ] is used by the International Phonetic Association.

[š] is used by Kruisinga.

The *ch* of *chin*.

[tʃ] or [t͡ʃ] are used by the International Phonetic Association.

[tš] is used by Kruisinga and others.

The *s* of *measure*.

[ʒ] is used by the I. P. A.

[ž] is used by Wyld, Kruisinga and others.

The *j* of *joy*.

[dʒ] or [d͡ʒ] are used by the I. P. A.

[dž] is used by Wyld, Kruisinga and others.

The *g* of *go*.

[g] is used by the I. P. A.

[g] is used by Jespersen, Sweet, Kruisinga, Wyld, Krapp, Kenyon and others.

[82]

The *r* of *red*.

[ɹ]. This is the symbol used by the International Phonetic Association when contrasting this sound with such sounds as the front-trilled-*r* [r] as used in Italian, Russian and other languages. In the usual notation of the Association, however, the symbol [r] is used.

[r] is used by the majority of phoneticians. We may note that Krapp uses the symbol [ɹ] to represent the vowel-like retroflex *r* "commonly heard in American speech before consonants and finally."

The *wh* of *which*.

[w] is used by those who make no distinction between the *wh* of *which* and the *w* of *which*.

[ʍ] is the symbol representing the true voiceless [w], but

[hw] is generally used by those who do make the distinction referred to above.

[*h*w] may be used as a "diaphonic" symbol; i. e. to show optional [w] or [hw].

The *ll* of *tell*.

[l] is the symbol generally used for this.

[ɫ] is used in order to contrast this so-called "dark" *l* with the "clear" initial *l*.

[83]

THE PHONETIC ALPHABET,

according to the system of notation now in use and as applied to Received Standard Pronunciation.

Vowels.

Five "Free" Vowels.

1. [iˑ]   key   [kiˑ]
2. [ɑˑ]   star   [stɑˑ]
3. [ɔˑ]   horse   [hɔˑs]
4. [uˑ]   moon   [muˑn]
5. [əˑ]   bird   [bəˑd]

Six "Checked" Vowels.

6. [ɪ]   fish   [fɪʃ]
7. [ɛ]   pen   [pɛn]
8. [æ]   cat   [kæt]
9. [ʌ]   duck   [dʌk]
10. [ɒ]   box   [bɒks]
11. [ʊ]   book   [bʊk]

Five "Kinetic Vowels" (or "Diphthongs").

12. [eɪ]   gate   [geɪt]
13. [aɪ]   eye   [aɪ]
14. [aʊ]   cow   [kaʊ]
15. [ɔɪ]   boy   [bɔɪ]
16. [oʊ]   nose   [noʊz]

Two "Obscure" Vowels.

17. [ɪ]   chimney   ['tʃɪmnɪ]
           eleven   [ɪ'levn]
           elephant   ['elɪfənt]
18. [ə]   collar   ['kɒlə]
           potato   [pə'teɪtoʊ]
           aeroplane   ['ɛərəpleɪn]

Four "Murmur-Diphthongs" (or "Murmur Kinetic Vowels").

19. [ɪə]   ear   [ɪə]
20. [ɛə]   chair   [tʃɛə]
21. [ɔə]   door   [dɔə]
22. [ʊə]   moor   [mʊə]

[85]

Consonants.

Six " Plosives " or " Stops."

23. [p] *put*   [pʊt]
24. [b] *bee*   [biˑ]
25. [t] *take* [teɪk]
26. [d] *do*   [duˑ]
27. [k] *come* [kʌm]
28. [g] *go*   [goʊ]

Three " Nasals."

29. [m] *my*   [maɪ]
30. [n] *no*   [noʊ]
31. [ŋ] *king* [kɪŋ]

One " Lateral."

32. [l] *like* [laɪk]
         tell [tɛl]

Ten " Fricatives."

33. [f] *five* [faɪv]
34. [v] *very* [ˈvɛrɪ]
35. [θ] *thin* [θɪn]
36. [ð] *then* [ðɛn]

[86]

37.	[s]	*so*	[sou]
38.	[z]	*zinc*	[zɪŋk]
39.	[ʃ]	*shut*	[ʃʌt]
40.	[ʒ]	*measure*	[ˈmɛʒə]
41.	[r]	*rose*	[rouz]
42.	[h]	*hat*	[hæt]

Two "Affricates."

43.	[tʃ]	*church*	[tʃəˑtʃ]
44.	[dʒ]	*judge*	[dʒʌdʒ]

Two "Semi-Vowels."

45.	[j]	*you*	[juˑ]
46.	[w]	*wait*	[weɪt]

Miscellaneous Signs.

47. [ˈ] The Stress-mark.
48. [ː] The Length-mark.
49. [ˑ] The Half-length mark.
50. [.] The mark placed under a consonant to give it a syllabic value.

[87]

51. [ɑ˞] = [ɑ] with susceptibility of adding an *r*-like sound.

52. [ɔ˞] = [ɔ] with susceptibility of adding an *r*-like sound.

53. [ɘ˞] = [ə] with susceptibility of adding an *r*-like sound.

54. [⌐] The High Level Tone-mark.

55. [—] The Mid Level Tone-mark.

56. [\] The Falling Tone-mark.

57. [↘] The Falling Tone-mark, when preceded by a High Level tone.

58. [⌐\] The Intensified Falling tone-mark.

59. [/] The High Rising Tone-mark.

60. [⌣] The Falling-Rising Tone-mark.

61. [⌄] The Low Rising Tone-mark.

THE 31 CHIEF RULES

FOR TRANSCRIBING "RECEIVED STANDARD" ENGLISH.

THE 31 CHIEF RULES

FOR TRANSCRIBING "RECEIVED STANDARD" ENGLISH WITH THE PRESENT NOTATION OF THE INTERNATIONAL PHONETIC ASSOCIATION.

IGNORE TRADITIONAL SPELLING.

Rule 1. Do not be influenced by traditional English spelling, but write down the words and sentences phone by phone in accordance with what seems to you to be the actual and normal pronunciation of those who use Received Standard pronunciation.

Do not write the *h* of *hour*, the *b* of *lamb*, the *w* of *write*, the *n* of *autumn*, the *r* of *forget*, etc.

NATURAL PRONUNCIATION.

Rule 2. Do not be influenced by any fictitious standard of correctness. What people *ought* or *ought not* to pronounce does not concern the student or teacher of phonetics and phonetic transcription; the only thing that concerns them is what the average educated person *does* pronounce when using Received Standard dialect and when not on his guard against possible critics.

[91]

If you are convinced that the two vowels of *except* are pronounced alike by such speakers in such conditions, then transcribe the word as [ɛksɛpt]; if however you consider that the first vowel is identical (or nearly so) with the first vowel of *intend*, then transcribe the word as [ɪksɛpt].

LETTER-SYMBOLS.

Rule 3. Use only those letter-symbols that are set forth in the accompanying *Catalogue of English Phones*.

(a) Use no capital letters:

Mr. John Brown = [mɪstə dʒɒn braʊn].

(b) Do not use the letters *c, q, x, y*; they are not required when transcribing English.

nice [naɪs], *quite* [kwaɪt], *next* [nɛkst], *examine* [ɪgzæmɪn], *yet* [jɛt].

(c) Make your writing conform as far as possible to the simple printed forms, avoiding loops when writing *b, f, g, h, j, l* and *y*; avoiding curves when writing *v* and *w*, and using *r* in preference to ɹ.

Rule 4. Give to each phonetic symbol the value indicated in the accompanying *Catalogue of English Phones*.

[92]

(a) Do not use [a] for [ɑ], [e] for [ɛ], [i] for [ɪ] or [ɪ], [u] for [ʊ], [z] for [ʒ], or vice versa.

(b) Do not use the symbol [s] when you wish to represent the sound of [z].

(c) Do not use [sh] for [ʃ], [th] for [θ] or [ð], [ng] for [ŋ] or [ŋg], etc.

(d) Do not use [a] or [o] as isolated symbols. They occur only in the digraphs [aɪ], [aʊ] and [oʊ].*

Rule 5. Use only those digraphs provided in the accompanying *Catalogue of English Phones*. Such combinations as [ɔo], [ɔʊ], [ɛɪ], [aʊ], etc. may be used by phoneticians for special purposes, but they are not used in the conventional transcription of Received Standard English.

SYMBOLS OTHER THAN LETTER-SYMBOLS.

Rule 6. When [n], [l] or (more rarely) [m] and [ŋ] constitute syllables without an accompanying vowel, the syllabic mark [ˌ] may be placed beneath the symbol. E. g. *given* [gɪvn] or [gɪvn̩], *people* [piˑpl] or [piˑpl̩].

---

* [o] however is permissable as a variant of unstressed [oʊ]; e. g. [wɪndo] for [wɪndoʊ], [novɛmbə] for [noʊvɛmbə], etc.

[93]

Rule 7. Use the length-marks [ˑ] and [ː] consistently or omit them entirely.

(a) In no other case can either mark be used than after the five "free vowels" [i], [ɑ], [ɔ], [u] and [ə] and, in certain cases, the "checked vowel" [æ].

(b) Omit the length-mark for the following words. Unstressed *you, who, whom, whose*: [ju], [hu], [hum], [huz];

That variety of unstressed *to* which is not pronounced [tə]: [tu];

That variety of unstressed *into* which is not pronounced [ɪntə] or [ɪntə]: [ɪntu] or [ɪntu];

Unstressed *he, she, we, me, be*: [hi], [ʃi], [wi], [mi], [bi];

That variety of unstressed *the* which is not pronounced [ðə]: [ði];

Unstressed *her* may be [hə] or [hɜ];

(c) In unstressed syllables the length-mark may be omitted, e. g. *although*: [ɔlðou] or [ɔˑlðou]; *already*: [ɔlrɛdɪ] or [ɔˑlrɛdɪ]; *rewrite*: [rɪraɪt] or [riˑraɪt]; *survey* (verb): [səveɪ] or [səˑveɪ]; *July*: [dʒulaɪ] or [dʒuˑlaɪ].

(d) The transcriber may use the full-length-mark [ː] in cases where the vowel is exceptionally long (e. g. when final in the word or sentence), reserving the half-length-mark [ˑ] for other cases, thus:

[94]

I can't see: [aɪ kɑˑnt siː];

I can't see it: [aɪ kɑˑnt siˑ ɪt] or [aɪ kɑˑnt si ɪt];

I have seen it: [aɪ v siˑn ɪt];

or he may make an exclusive use of the half-length-mark, or he may ignore both length-marks.

Rule 8. Use the stress-mark ['] consistently or not at all.

It may be used either

(a) to show which syllable in a plurisyllabic word is stressed or stressable (i. e. to mark *word-stress*)

(b) or to show which word or word (of one or of more syllables) in the sentence is or are of logical importance (i. e. to mark *sentence-stress*.)

Thus the use of the stress-mark for isolated words indicates word-stress:

window: ['wɪndəʊ], *machine:* [məˈʃiˑn].

but in a connected text indicates *sentence-stress* (in which case it coincides practically with the "nucleus-tone"):

[hi wəz 'hɪə lɑˑst 'wiˑk]

[hi wəz 'hɪə jestədɪ ɑˑftəˈnuˑn].

Although no absolute rule may be formulated, it is advisable not to make a double use of the stress-mark in a connected text, such as

[95]

['mistə 'braʊn wəz ə'weɪ fə 'sevərəl 'deɪz ɪn sep'tembə],

Sentence-stress may be indicated by means of the nucleus-tone symbols [\], [ˆ], [/], [ˇ], [↲], in accordance with the rules suggested in works specifically treating the phenomena of intonation.

PUNCTUATION, ETC.

Rule 9. Observe the traditional usage of the full stop, comma, semi-colon, marks of interrogation and exclamation, dash, quotation-marks and parentheses.

Rule 10. Make sufficient distinction between the colon and full-length-mark by writing the latter close up to the vowel, and the former with a slight space in between.

Rule 11. Avoid as far as possible the use of the hyphen, as this is of little utility from the point of view of phonetics.

Rule 12. Do not use the apostrophe, for this has no phonetic utility whatever.

WEAKENING.

Rule 13. In the case of the words set forth in the accompanying *Catalogue of Weakenable Words*, do not use the strong form when the weak form should be used, and vice versa.

E. g. do not use [kæn] for [kən], [mʌst], for [məst], [æm] for [m], etc. or vice versa.

Rule 14. Avoid making needless additions to the *Catalogue of Weakenable Words*. The word *on*, for instance, is never pronounced by native English speakers as [ən]. In Received Standard pronunciation, *too* is always [tuˑ], and never [tə].

Rule 15. When the strong and weak forms, or two weak forms, differ from each other by the presence or absence of [h], the symbol [h] may be enclosed in parentheses or, in printed texts, may be italicized. Such variations commonly occur in the following seven cases: Unstressed *he, him, himself, who, whose, her, herself*.

Rule 16. When two weak forms differ from each other by the presence or absence of [ə], the symbol [ə] may be enclosed in parentheses or, in printed texts, may be italicized. Such variations commonly occur in the following 21 cases: unstressed *am, was, have, has, had, does, shall, should, would, can, could, must, them, from, of, than, that, and, such, as, some.*

[97]

DIVERGENCIES.

Rule 17. In the case of words varying in (Received Standard) pronunciation between a possible [ɔə] and [ɔˑ], the vowel may be written as [ɔə], as [ɔˑ] or as [ɔ(ə)]. In printed texts the parenthetical [ə] is usually italicized. Such variation may occur in all those words which in Jones' Pronouncing Dictionary are shown with both pronunciations. E. g. *before* : [biˈfɔː], [biˈfɔə].

Thus *lord* may be written as [lɔˑd], [lɔəd] or [lɔəd], but laud is written as [lɔˑd].

Rule 18. Certain other divergencies occurring in Received Standard Pronunciation may be treated by an appropriate use of parentheses or italicized letters. Thus [*h*wɒt] indicates that the word *what* may not or need not be aspirated, [kɛəf(ʊ)l] indicates that the [ʊ] may be or need not be sounded. On the whole, however, it is generally preferable to select a given pronunciation and to ignore any divergencies.

Rule 19. It is practically impossible to write a phonetic transcription in such a way as to show the more important diaphonic divergencies, i. e. the divergencies between one dialect and another. We may represent more or less faithfully such dialects as

[98]

Received Standard, Edinburgh Scottish, Dublin or Belfast Irish, New York, Middle West or Southern States American, etc. but not in one and the same transcription. Do not therefore unduly strain the resources of phonetic notation in striving to reconcile the irreconcilable, but use for each dialect the appropriate transcription. We may note that Professor Daniel Jones has devised a system of "spelling" (not "phonetic notation") which is admirably adapted for the purposes of a scientific orthography covering all English dialects.

SOUND-JUNCTION AND ASSIMILATION.

Rule 20. Do not transcribe the letter *r* by the symbol [r] unless the sound immediately following is a vowel. Conversely, do not omit the symbol [r] when the sound immediately following (without any pause) is a vowel.

It's better: [ɪt s betə].

It's getting better and better: [ɪt s getɪŋ betər ənd betə].

There's another one there: [ðə z ənʌðə wʌn ðɛə].

There are no others there at present: [ðər ə nou ʌðəz ðɛər ət preznt.]

Rule 21. Two successive consonants *in one syllable*

[99]

must be either both voiced or both voiceless. Do not therefore write [tz] or [ds]; the pronunciation you wish to indicate is either [ts] or [dz]; do not write [fz] or [vs]; the pronunciation you wish to indicate is either [fs] or [vz], etc.

The consonants [r], [l], [m], [n], [ŋ], being voiced or voiceless according to context, may combine freely with voiced or with voiceless consonants.

Rule 22. Do not exaggerate the principle of phonetic writing. In ordinary fluent speech, certain sounds tend to become inaudible on account of their juxtaposition with other sounds. Thus

kindness	may be heard as	[kaınnıs]
French	" " " "	[frɛnʃ]
friends	" " " "	[frɛnz]
next week	" " " "	[nɛks wi·k]
some more	" " " "	[sə mɔə]
allow	" " " "	[l̩laʊ]

It is however generally considered inadvisable to indicate such omissions in the course of ordinary transcription work, especially when an absolute fidelity to actual pronunciations would make transcription unnecessarily complicated. Many speech phenomena, such as the above, may be covered by conventions; consequently the beginner may write the above

[100]

words as [kɑndnıs], frentʃ], [frɛndz], [nɛkst wɪ·k], [səm mɔə], [əlaʊ].

For the same reason it is unnecessary (for the beginner at least) to write *as far* as [əs fɑ·], *of course* as [f kɔ·s], *last year* as [lɑ·st ʃə·], *has she* as [hæʒ ʃi] or [hæʃ ʃi] etc. He may write the more conventional [əz fɑ·], [əv kɔ·s], [lɑ·st jə·], [hæz ʃi·] etc.

INFLECTIONS.

Rule 23. The regular plural of nouns (*s* or *es* in in traditional spelling) is written phonetically as

[s] after the voiceless consonants [p], [t], [k], [f], [θ]: *cups* [kʌps], *cats* [kæts], *months* [mʌnθs] etc.

[ız] after [s], [z], [ʃ], [ʒ]: *horses* [hɔ·sız], *sizes* [saızız], *churches* [tʃə·tʃız], *judges* [dʒʌdʒız].

[z] in all other cases: *tables* [tæblz], *chairs* [tʃɛəz], *pens* [pɛnz] etc.

Rule 24. The regular inflection for the 3rd person singular of the present tense (*s* or *es* in traditional spelling) is transcribed phonetically in exactly the same manner as that of the regular plural of nouns (see Rule 23):

breaks [brɛks], *wishes* [wıʃız], *knows* [noʊz], *carries* [kærız].

[101]

Rule 25. The inflection for the possessive of nouns ('s or ' in traditional spelling) is transcribed phonetically in exactly the same manner as that of the regular plural of nouns (see Rule 23):

cat's [kæts], *James'* [dʒeɪmzɪz], *George's* [dʒɔˑdʒɪz], *friend's* [frɛndz], *friends'* [frɛndz].

Rule 26. The regular inflection for the preterite or past participle of verbs (*d* or *ed* in traditional spelling) is transcribed phonetically as

[t] after the voiceless consonants [p], [k], [f], [s], [ʃ]: *hoped* [hoʊpt], *looked* [lʊkt], *washed* [wɒʃt];

[ɪd] after [t] or [d]: *wanted* [wɒntɪd], *crowded* [kraʊdɪd];

[d] in all other cases: *received* [rɪsiˑvd], *died* [daɪd], *opened* [oʊpn̩d].

Rule 27. The regular inflection written *ing* in traditional spelling is transcribed phonetically as [ɪŋ]: *coming* [kʌmɪŋ], *going* [goʊɪŋ], *being* [biˑɪŋ], *flying* [flaɪɪŋ].

In the case of such words ending in *ring* the inflectional ending is transcribed as [rɪŋ]:

remembering [rɪmɛmbərɪŋ].

Rule 28. The inflection of the comparative (written *r* or *er* in traditional spelling) is transcribed phoneti-

[102]

cally as [ə] (with susceptibility of becoming [ər] when the following word begins with a vowel sound): *larger* [lɑˑdʒə], *higher* [haɪə].

In the case of adjectives ending in *nger* (traditional spelling), the inflection is transcribed phonetically as [gə] (with susceptibility of becoming [gər] when the following word begins with a vowel): *longer* [lɒŋgə], *younger* [jʌŋgə].

In the case of adjectives ending in *rer* (traditional spelling), the inflection is transcribed phonetically as [rə] (with susceptibility of becoming [rər] when the following word begins with a vowel): *nearer* [nɪərə], *rarer* [rɛərə].

Rule 29. The inflection of the superlative (written *st* or *est* in traditional spelling) is transcribed phonetically as [ɪst]:

largest [lɑˑdʒɪst], *highest* [haɪst].

In the case of adjectives ending in *ngest* (traditional spelling), the inflection is transcribed phonetically as [gɪst]:

longest [lɒŋgɪst], *youngest* [jʌŋgɪst].

In the case of adjectives ending in *rest* (traditional spelling), the inflection is transcribed phonetically as [rɪst]:

nearest [nɪərɪst], *rarest* [rɛərɪst].

[103]

SUFFIXES.

Rule 30. With comparatively few exceptions, the chief English suffixes are usually transcribed as follows:

—a	—ə	America	əˈmɛrɪkə
—able	—əbl̩	probable	ˈprɒbəbl̩
—ably	—əblɪ	probably	ˈprɒbəblɪ
—ace	—ɪs	preface	ˈprɛfɪs
—age	—ɪdʒ	damage	ˈdæmɪdʒ
—al	—l̩	capital	ˈkæpɪtl̩
—ally	—əlɪ	generally	ˈdʒɛnərəlɪ
—an	—ən	American	əˈmɛrɪkən
—ance	—əns	distance	ˈdɪstəns
—ancy	—ənsɪ	constancy	ˈkɒnstənsɪ
—ant	—ənt	instant	ˈɪnstənt
—ar	—ə(r)	similar	ˈsɪmɪlə(r)
—arity	—ærɪtɪ	similarity	sɪmɪˈlærɪtɪ
—ary	—ərɪ	dictionary	ˈdɪkʃənərɪ
—arily	—ərɪlɪ	necessarily	ˈnɛsɪsərɪlɪ
—ate (verb suffix)	—eɪt	imitate	ˈɪmɪteɪt
—ate (noun and adj. suffix)	—ɪt	accurate	ˈækjurɪt
—ately	—ɪtlɪ	accurately	ˈækjurɪtlɪ
—cy	—sɪ	accuracy	ˈækjurəsɪ
—day	—dɪ	Sunday	ˈsʌndɪ

[104]

—en	—ən	*happen*	ˈhæpən
—ence	—əns	*sentence*	ˈsɛntəns
—ency	—ənsɪ	*tendency*	ˈtɛndənsɪ
—ent	—ənt	*accident*	ˈæksɪdənt
—ently	—əntlɪ	*evidently*	ˈɛvɪdəntlɪ
—er	—ə(r)	*teacher*	ˈtiˑtʃə(r)
—ery	—ərɪ	*discovery*	dɪsˈkʌvərɪ
—ess	—ɪs	*actress*	ˈæktrɪs
—et	—ɪt	*ticket*	ˈtɪkɪt
—ey	—ɪ	*money*	ˈmʌnɪ
—ful	—fʊl	*useful*	ˈjuˑsfʊl
—fully	—fʊlɪ or —fəlɪ	*carefully*	ˈkɛəfʊlɪ or ˈkɛəfəlɪ
—fy	—faɪ	*satisfy*	ˈsætɪsfaɪ
—ia	—jə	*India*	ˈɪndjə
—sia	—ʃə	*Asia*	ˈeɪʃə
—ial	—ɪəl	*material*	məˈtɪərɪəl
—cial	—ʃəl	*special*	ˈspɛʃəl
—ially	—ɪəlɪ	*materially*	məˈtɪərɪəlɪ
—cially	—ʃəlɪ	*specially*	ˈspɛʃəlɪ
—ible	—əbl̩ or —ɪbl̩	*terrible*	ˈtɛrəbl̩ or ˈtɛrɪbl̩
—ibly	—əblɪ or —ɪblɪ	*terribly*	ˈtɛrəblɪ or ˈtɛrɪblɪ
—ic	—ɪk	*public*	ˈpʌblɪk
—ical	—ɪkəl	*practical*	ˈpræktɪkəl

[105]

—ically	—ıkəlı	practically	ˈpræktıkəlı
—ice	—ıs	office	ˈɒfıs
—ics	—ıks	phonetics	fəˈnetıks
—id	—ıd	solid	ˈsɒlıd
—ieth	—ııθ	twentieth	ˈtwentııθ
—ine	—ın	examine	ıgˈzæmın
—ion			
—cion	—ʃən	suspicion	səˈspıʃən
—gion	—dʒən	region	ˈriˑdʒən
—nion	—njən	opinion	əˈpınjən
—sion	—ʒən	confusion	kənˈfjuˑʒən
—ssion	—ʃən	mission	ˈmıʃən
—tion	—ʃən	station	ˈsteıʃən
—xion	—kʃən	complexion	kəmˈplekʃən
—ional			
—gional	—dʒən̩l	regional	riˈdʒən̩l
—sional	—ʒən̩l	occasional	əˈkeıʒən̩l
—ssional	—ʃən̩l	professional	prəˈfeʃən̩l
—tional	—ʃən̩l	national	ˈnæʃən̩l
—ionally			
—sionally	—ʃənəlı	professionally	prəˈfeʃənəlı
—tionally	—ʃənəlı	intentionally	ınˈtenʃənəlı
—ish	—ıʃ	finish	ˈfınıʃ
—ist	—ıst	chemist	ˈkemıst
—istic	—ıstık	optimistic	ɒptıˈmıstık
—istically	—ıstıkəlı	optimistically	ɒptıˈmıstıkəlı

[106]

—ite	—ɪt	definite	ˈdefɪnɪt

(Note however *finite* [ˈfaɪnaɪt], and verbs in *ite*, such as invite, unite, recite, etc., all pronounced with [ˈaɪt].)

—ity	—ɪtɪ	quality	ˈkwɒlɪtɪ
—ive	—ɪv	active	ˈæktɪv
—ively	—ɪvlɪ	actively	ˈæktɪvlɪ
—ize (or —ise)	—aɪz	realize	ˈrɪəlaɪz
—land	—lənd	England	ˈɪŋglənd
—less	—lɪs	careless	ˈkɛəlɪs
—lessness	—lɪsnɪs	carelessness	ˈkɛəlɪsnɪs
—ly	—lɪ	badly	ˈbædlɪ
—man	—mən	workman	ˈwɜːkmən
—ment	—mənt	moment	ˈmoʊmənt
—mental	—mentl̩	experimental	ɪkspɛrɪˈmentl̩
—mentally	—mentəlɪ	experimentally	ɪkspɛrɪˈmentəlɪ
—ness	—nɪs	goodness	ˈgʊdnɪs
—o	—oʊ	potato	pəˈteɪtoʊ
—or	—ə(r)	tailor	ˈteɪlə(r)
—ory	—ərɪ	history	ˈhɪstərɪ
—orily	—ərɪlɪ	satisfactorily	sætɪsˈfæktərɪlɪ
—our	—ə(r)	colour	ˈkʌlə(r)
—ourable	—ərəbl̩	favourable	ˈfeɪvərəbl̩
—ourably	—ərəblɪ	favourably	ˈfeɪvərəblɪ
—ous	—əs	famous	ˈfeɪməs
—ously	—əslɪ	seriously	ˈsɪərɪəslɪ
—ow	—oʊ	window	ˈwɪndoʊ

[107]

—sion	(see —ion)		
—tion	(see —ion)		
—ty	—tɪ	pity	ˈpɪtɪ
—th	—θ	breadth	ˈbrɛtθ
—ual	—juəl	actual	ˈæktjuəl

(Note equal [iˑkwəl])

—ually	—juəlɪ	actually	ˈæktjuəlɪ

(Note equally [iˑkwəlɪ])

—ure

—gure	—gə(r)	figure	ˈfɪgə(r)
—lure	—ljə(r)	failure	ˈfeɪljə(r)
—sure	—ʒə(r)	measure	ˈmɛʒə(r)
—ture	—tʃə(r)	lecture	ˈlɛktʃə(r)
—zure	—ʒə(r)	seizure	ˈsiˑʒə(r)
—ute	—jut	absolute	ˈæbsəljut
—utely	—jutlɪ	absolutely	ˈæbsəljutlɪ
—ude	—jud	attitude	ˈætɪtjud
—ward	—wəd	forward	ˈfɔˑwəd
—wards	—wədz	forwards	ˈfɔˑwədz

(Note towards [tɔˑdz] and such plural nouns as rewards [rɪˈwɔˑdz])

—y	—ɪ	happy	ˈhæpɪ

PREFIXES.

Rule 31. With comparatively few exceptions, the

[108]

chief English unstressed prefixes are usually transcribed as follows:

a—	ə—	awake	əˈweɪk
ab—	əb—	abstain	əbˈsteɪn
ac—	ək—	account	əˈkaʊnt
ad—	əd—	admire	ədˈmaɪə(r)
af—	əf—	afford	əˈfɔːd
ag—	əg—	agree	əˈgriː
al—	əl—	allude	əˈljuːd
am—	əm—	among	əˈmʌŋ
an—	ən—	annoy	əˈnɔɪ
ap—	əp—	appeal	əˈpiːl
ar—	ər—	arrange	əˈreɪndʒ
as—	əs—	assist	əˈsɪst
at—	ət—	attract	əˈtrækt
be—	bɪ—	behave	bɪˈheɪv
col—	kəl—	collect	kəˈlekt
com—	kəm—	complain	kəmˈpleɪn
con—	kən—	connect	kəˈnekt
cor—	kər—	correct	kəˈrekt
de—	dɪ—	decide	dɪˈsaɪd
di—	{dɪ— / daɪ—}	direct	{dɪˈrekt / daɪˈrekt}
dis—	dɪs—	disturb	dɪsˈtəːb
e—	ɪ—	edition	ɪˈdɪʃn
ef—	ɪf—	effect	ɪˈfekt

[109]

el—	ɪl—	*elect*	ɪˈlekt
em—	ɪm—	*employ*	ɪmˈplɔɪ
en—	{ɪn— ɪŋ—	*entire* *encourage*	ɪnˈtaɪə(r) ɪŋˈkʌrɪdʒ
es—	ɪs—	*escape*	ɪˈskeɪp
ex—	{ɪks— ɪgz—	*excuse* *examine*	ɪkˈskjuːz ɪgˈzæmɪn
for—	fə—	*forget*	fəˈget
il—	ɪl—	*illusion*	ɪˈljuːʒən
im—	ɪm—	*immense*	ɪˈmens
in—	{ɪn— ɪŋ—	*invite* *include*	ɪnˈvaɪt ɪŋˈkluːd
inter—	ɪntə—	*international*	ɪntəˈnæʃnəl
ir—	ɪr—	*irregular*	ɪˈregjulə
mis—	mɪs—	*misfortune*	mɪsˈfɔːtʃən
o—	{ə— oʊ—	*omit*	əˈmɪt oʊˈmɪt
ob—	əb—	*oblige*	əˈblaɪdʒ
oc—	ək—	*occur*	əˈkɜː(r)
of—	əf—	*offend*	əˈfend
op—	əp—	*oppress*	əˈpres
out—	aʊt—	*outwit*	aʊtˈwɪt
over—	oʊvə—	*overtake*	oʊvəˈteɪk
par—	pə—	*particular*	pəˈtɪkjulə(r)
per—	pə—	*perform*	pəˈfɔːm
pre—	prɪ—	*prefer*	prɪˈfɜː(r)
pro—	prə—	*produce*	prəˈdjuːs

[110]

re—	rɪ—	*receive*	rɪˈsiˑv

(Occasionally however re— rɛkəˈlɛkt)

re— (meaning "again")	riˑ—	*re-write*	riˑˈraɪt
sub—	səb—	*submit*	səbˈmɪt
suc—	sək—	*succeed*	səkˈsiˑd
sup—	səp—	*suppose*	səˈpoʊz
sur—	sə—	*surprise*	səˈpraɪz
sus—	səs—	*suspect*	səˈspɛkt
trans—	træns—	*transcribe*	trænsˈkraɪb

(*Translate*, however, is usually transˈleɪt)

un—	ʌn—	*undo*	ʌnˈduˑ
under—	ʌndə—	*understand*	ʌndəˈstænd

[111]

THE 70 WEAKENABLE WORDS.

THE 70 WEAKENABLE WORDS.

About seventy of the commonest English words possess strong and weak forms. The strong forms are used when the words are isolated or stressed, in other cases the weak forms are generally more normal.

It is convenient to divide these words into four groups:

Group 1 contains 18 "anomalous finites."
Group 2 contains 21 pronouns and determinatives.
Group 3 contains 10 prepositions.
Group 4 contains 21 miscellaneous words.

Group 1. Eighteen of the "Anomalous Finites."[1]

am	æm	əm, m
is	ɪz	ɪz, z, s
are	ɑːˑ	ɑː, ə
was	wɒz	wəz, wz
were	wəˑ	wə, wə
have	hæv	həv, v

[1] The small figures 1 to 23 refer to the various "Notes."

has	hæz	həz, z
had	hæd	həd, d
do	duˑ	du, də, d
does	dʌz	dəz, dz
did	dɪd	dɪd, dd
shall	ʃæl	ʃəl, ʃl
should	ʃʊd	ʃəd, ʃd
will	wɪl	wɪl, əl, l
would	wʊd	əd, d
can	kæn	kən, kn, kŋ
could	kʊd	kəd, kd
must	mʌst	məst, məs, mst, ms.

Note 1.

The strong form is used when the word is isolated, stressed, or at the end of a sentence or of a more or less complete word-group. At the beginning of a sentence the strong form is frequently used. In most other cases the weak forms are used.

Group 2. Twenty-one Pronouns and Determinatives.[2]

you	juˑ	ju[4]

[116]

he	hiˑ	hi, hʊ³
she	ʃiˑ	ʃi, ʃɪ
we	wiˑ	wi, wɪ
me	miˑ	mi, mɪ
him	hɪm	hɪm³
*her*⁵	hɜˑ	hə, hə³
it	ɪt	ɪt
us	ʌs	əs, s⁷
them	ðɛm	ðəm, ðm, əm⁸
my	maɪ	mɪ
your	jɔə	jɔ, jə
*his*⁶	hɪz	hɪz²
who	huˑ	hu³
whose	huˑz	huz³
myself	maɪˈsɛlf	məˈsɛlf, msɛlf
yourself	jɔəˈsɛlf	jɔˈsɛlf, jəˈsɛlf
himself	hɪmˈsɛlf	hɪmˈsɛlf³
herself	hɜˈsɛlf	həˈsɛlf, hɜˈsɛlf³
yourselves	jɔəˈsɛlvz	jɔˈsɛlvz, jəˈsɛlvz
themselves	ðɛmˈsɛlvz	ðəmˈsɛlvz, ðmˈsɛlvz

[117]

Note 2.

The strong form is used when the word is isolated or stressed. In all other cases the weak forms are used.

Note 3.

The weak forms of *he, him, her, his, who, whose, himself* and *herself* are aspirated when the word stands at the beginning of a sentence or breath-group. In other cases the aspiration is generally inaudible, especially in rapid speech.

Note 4.

You are. The weak form of this collocation [ju ə] is generally pronounced [jɔə] or [jə], and is therefore often indistinguishable from the pronunciation of *your*.

Note 5.

Her. This is both the personal pronoun and the possessive determinative.

Note 6.

His, when used pronominally (e. g. this book is his) invariably takes the strong form.

[118]

Note 7.

Us. This word is pronounced [s] in the collocation *let us* when used in the sense of *shall we?* In all other cases, the weak form is [əs].

Note 8.

Them. The pronunciation [əm], a survival of the Middle English *hem*, is occasionally used in familiar and facetious speech. Note in this connection the legendary "Up Guards and at 'em!" of Wellington at Waterloo.

Group 3. Ten Prepositions.⁹

at	æt	ət
by	baɪ	bə
for	fɔˑ	fə, fə, f
from	frʊm	frəm, frm
in	ɪn	ɪn
into	ɪntuˑ	ɪntu, ɪntə
of	ɒv	əv, v, ə, əf, f
till	tɪl	tɪl
to	tuˑ	tu, tə
with	wɪð	wɪð

[119]

Note 9.

The strong forms are used

(a) when the preposition is isolated or stressed,

(b) when at the end of a sentence or breath-group, or when not followed immediately by an object. E. g. hwɒt ə ju ˈlukɪŋ æt? hwɒt wə ju ˈlukɪŋ æt dʒʌst naʊ?

(c) generally when followed by an unstressed pronoun. E. g.

hi wəz ˈlukɪŋ æt ju (but hi wəz lukɪŋ ət ˈjuˑ), ðə z ə ˈletə fɔˑ ðəm (but ðə z ə letə fə ˈðem).

Group 4. Twenty-one Miscellaneous Words.[10]

the	ðiˑ	ði, ðə[11]
a	eı	ə
an	æn	ən
than	ðæn	ðen, ðn
that[12]	ðæt	ðət, ðt

Note 10.

The strong form is used only when the words are isolated or in those rare cases in which they are stressed.

[120]

Note 11.

The. When followed by a vowel, the weak pronunciation is [ði]; in all other cases it is [ðə]. *E. g.* ðə bɪˈgɪnɪŋ ənd ði ˈɛnd.

Note 12.

That. This is the conjunction and relative pronoun. In all other cases the strong form alone is used. *E. g.*
I think that that is the one that I left here on that day.
aɪ θɪŋk ðət ðæt s ðə wʌn ðət aɪ lɛft hɪər ɒn ðæt deɪ.

Note 13.

and	ænd	ənd, nd, m, ŋ
or	ɔːr	ɔ, ə
nor	nɔːr	nɔ, nə
but	bʌt	bət
be	biː	bi
such	sʌtʃ	sətʃ, stʃ
which	hwɪtʃ	hwɪtʃ

Both the strong and the weak forms of the above 8 words are in frequent use, the weak forms however predominating.

[121]

Note 14.

as   æz   əz, z

The strong or weak form is used according to the function of the word in the sentence. The strong form is generally heard in the collocations *as for, as to* and *as such*. The weak form is almost invariably used in such expressions as *as long as, as soon as, such things as,* etc. In other cases usage is variable.

Note 15.

some   sʌm,   səm, sm

When used pronominally this word always takes the strong form (aɪ ˈhæv sʌm). This is also the case when the word means *certain, not all,* etc., (sʌm piˑpl prɪfəˑ ðɪs sɔˑt). In other cases the weak form is generally used. The collocation *some more* is usually pronounced [smɔə].

Note 16.

this   ðɪs   ðɪs, ðəs

The weak form apparently occurs only in the collocation *this morning, this afternoon* and *this evening,* in the senses respectively of *the morning, the afternoon* and *the evening of to-day.*

Note 17.

there ðɛə ðə

The weak form occurs only in cases where *there* together with a member of the verb *to be* have the meaning of *il y a, es gibt,* 有ル, etc. *E. g.*

There are some books = Some books are there
(ðɛər ə səm bʊks).

There are some books = Some books exist
(ðər ə səm bʊks).

Note 18.

not nɒt nt

The weak form is generally used after an anomalous finite, but in no other cases. Note that *do, will, shall* and *can* each become fused with *not* in one word = [dəʊnt], [wəʊnt], [ʃɑˑnt], [kɑˑnt].

Note 19.

saint seɪnt sənt, snt

The weak form is used when the word serves as an honorific prefix, but in no other cases. *E. g.* [snt dʒɒn], [snt pɔˑl].

Note 20.

sir səˑ sə, sə

The weak form is used when the word serves as

[123]

an honorific prefix or when not used at the beginning of a sentence. E. g. [sə dʒɒn braun], [sər ɑ·θə sʌlıvən], [jɛs sə].

Note 21.

so   sou   sə

In rapid speech the weak form, or an intermediate form which might be transcribed [so], is occasionally heard.

Note 22.

any   ɛnı   nı

In rapid speech the weak form, or an intermediate form which might be transcribed [nnı], is occasionally heard.

Note 23.

A few other words are occasionally weakened by most British speakers, notably the group of words ending in —*body*, which then becomes [bədı]. American speakers also tend to weaken certain words not figuring in the above list (notably *go* and *come* which are often heard as [gə] and [kəm] and *too*, which is often heard as [tə]).

[124]

A MODEL ENGLISH PHONETIC TEXT.

A MODEL ENGLISH PHONETIC TEXT.

Those who have at times found it necessary, for one reason or another, to produce a specimen text in phonetic transcription will have experienced a difficulty in selecting a suitable passage. To be ideally suitable it should fulfil four requirements. It should

(1) contain all the symbols,

(2) exemplify the chief phenomena of weakening, shortening, stress, word-linking, etc.,

(3) make sense,

(4) be as short as possible.

Now if we select a passage at random from any book, before our conditions (1), (2) and (3) are fulfilled, the text does not fulfil condition (4). On the other hand, if we restrict our passage in order for it to conform to condition (4) it will not fulfil conditions (1), (2) and (3).

The following passage is an essay towards finding a text which the most nearly fulfils the four requirements. It contains all the symbols, including the long and short forms of [i], [ɑ], [ɔ], [u] and [ə].

[127]

Examples are given of [w] and [hw], [ɔ·] and [ɔə], of *r*-linking, of consonant-doubling, of syllabic [n] and [l], and of other phonetic phenomena.

Among the weakenable words figure

    at   [ət].
    you   [ju].
    the   [ðə], [ði].
    your   [jɔ].
    this   [ðɪs].
    us   [əs].
    but   [bət].
    am   [m].
    and   [ənd].
    is   [s].
    will   [l].
    be   [bi].
    are   [ə], (contrasted with [ɑ]).
    to   [tə], [tu] (contrasted with *too* [tu·]).
    that   [ðət], (contrasted with [ðæt]).
    must [məst], (contrasted with [mʌst]).
    can   [kən], (contrasted with [kæn]).

As this text contains examples of the chief tones and tone-sequences, tone-marks have been added for the purpose of reference.

ət ⁻hwɒt taɪm ə ju gouɪŋ tə ði eksɪ˰bɪʃn̩? aɪ \θɔ˙t aɪ həˑd ju tel jə /brʌðə ðɪs mɔ˙nɪŋ ðət ju ɪkspektɪd tə \miˑt hɪm ðɛər ət əbaʊt \tuˑ.

\jes. wʊd ⁻juˑ laɪk tə /dʒɔɪn əs ðɛə?

aɪ ˰wʊd, wɪð ˰pleʒə, bət aɪ m ⁻nɒt ˰ʃʊə hweðər aɪ \kæn. ɪn \enɪ keɪs aɪ məst ⁻liˑv ˰əˑlɪ tə kætʃ ðə fɔə \treɪn. aɪ doʊnt \liˑv həˑ /naʊ; aɪ liˑv ɪn ðə \sʌbəbz, ənd aɪ ⁻wɒnt tə get hoʊm bɪfɔər ɪt s ˰daˑk.

⁻a ju /rɪəlɪ ɪn sətʃ ə hʌrɪ tə get hoʊm? /mʌst ju? ⁻ɪf ɪt s soʊllɪ ɒn ˰ðæt əkaʊnt, wi kən teɪk ju bæk ɪn aʊə \kaˑ.

/kæn ju? ðæt l̩ bi ˰splendɪd! ⁻ɔˑl˰raɪt.

[129]

THE SAME TEXT IN CONVENTIONAL SPELLING.

At what time are you going to the exhibition? I thought I heard you tell your brother this morning that you expected to meet him there at about two.

Yes. Would you like to join us there?

I would, with pleasure, but I am not sure whether I can. In any case I must leave early to catch the four train. I do not live here now; I live in the suburbs and I want to get home before it is dark.

Are you really in such a hurry to get home? Must you? If it is solely on that account, we can take you back in our car.

Can you? That will be splendid! All right.

[130]

SPECIMENS OF ENGLISH PHONETIC TRANSCRIPTION.

SPECIMENS OF ENGLISH PHONETIC TRANSCRIPTION.

Passage from Wyld's "The Growth of English."

Language, of course, existed and was handed on for ages before writing was invented, and there are plenty of races at the present day who have fully developed languages in which they can express everything that is in their mind, but who have no system of writing. Even in England and other highly civilized countries there are still old people who never learned in their youth either to read or to write. For such people as these it is clear that language only exists as something which is spoken. We see, then, that the life of language may be quite independent of writing and spelling.

What is writing? It is simply a clever and convenient device by which certain symbols, which we call letters, are used to represent the sounds of speech. Words are built up of a collection of several sounds, and so when we write we are supposed to use a letter for each sound of which the word is

[133]

composed. Letters in themselves are not language, but merely symbols which are used for the sounds of which language is composed. There is no life or meaning in written symbols by themselves; but they must be translated, as it were, into the sounds for which they stand before they become languages or have any meaning. We become so accustomed to the look of letters, in groups to represent words, that we learn to read them off quite rapidly into the sounds for which they stand. Even when we read silently, without pronouncing the words aloud, we carry out the process mentally, and often unconsciously, of turning the letters into the sounds which each represents, and in this way we get at the meaning of what is written.

[134]

The same passage in the present phonetic notation, transcribed according to the conventions now proposed of writing Received Standard English.

læŋgwiʤ, əv kɔ·s, ɪgzɪstɪd ənd wəz hændɪd ɒn fər eiʤɪz bɪfɔə ratɪŋ wəz ɪnvɛntɪd, ənd ðər ə plɛntɪ əv reɪsɪz ət ðə prɛznt deɪ hu hæv fulɪ dɪvɛləpt læŋgwɪʤɪz in hwɪʧ ðeɪ kən ɪksprɛs ɛvrɪθɪŋ ðət s ɪn ðɛə maɪnd, bət hu hæv nou sɪstəm əv ratɪŋ. i·vn ɪn ɪŋglənd ənd ʌðə halɪ sɪvɪlaɪzd kʌntrɪz ðər ə stɪl ould pi·pl hu nɛvə lə·nd ɪn ðɛə ju·θ aɪðə tə ri·d ɔ tə raɪt. fə sʌʧ pi·pl əz ði·z ɪt s klɪə ðət læŋgwɪʤ ounlɪ ɪgzɪsts əz sʌmθɪŋ hwɪʧ ɪz spoukn. wi si·, ðɛn, ðət ðə laɪf əv læŋgwɪʤ meɪ bɪ kwaɪt ɪndɪpɛndənt əv ratɪŋ ənd spɛlɪŋ.

hwɒt ɪz ratɪŋ? ɪt s sɪmplɪ ə klɛvə ənd kənvi·njənt dɪvaɪs baɪ hwɪʧ sə·tn sɪmblz, hwɪʧ wi kɔ·l lɛtəz, ə ju·zd tə rɛprɪzɛnt ðə saundz əv spi·ʧ. wə·dz ə bɪlt ʌp əv ə kəlɛkʃn əv sɛvərəl saundz, ənd sou hwɛn wi raɪt wi ə səpouzd tə ju·z ə lɛtə fər i·ʧ saund əv hwɪʧ ðə wə·d z kəmpouzd. lɛtəz ɪn ðəmsɛlvz ə nɒt læŋgwɪʤ, bət mɪəlɪ sɪmblz hwɪʧ ə ju·zd fə ðə saundz əv hwɪʧ læŋgwɪʤ ɪz kəmpouzd. ðeɪ z nou laɪf ɔ mi·nɪŋ ɪn rɪtn sɪmblz baɪ ðəmsɛlvz; bət ðeɪ məst bi· trænslaɪtɪd, æz ɪt wə·, ɪntə ðə saundz fə hwɪʧ ðeɪ

[135]

stænd bıfɔə ðeı bıkʌm læŋgwıʤ ɔ hæv enı mi·nıŋ. wi bıkʌm sou əkʌstəmd tə ðə luk əv letəz, ın gru·ps tə reprızent wɜ·dz, ðət wi lɜ·n tə ri·d ðəm ɔ·f kwaıt ræpıdlı ıntə ðə saundz fə hwıʧ ðeı stænd. i·vn hwen wi· ri·d saıləntlı, wıðaut prənaunsıŋ ðə wɜ·dz əlaud, wi kærı aut ðə prouses mentəlı, ənd ɔ·fn ʌnkɔnʃəslı, əv tɜ·nıŋ ðə letəz ıntə ðə saundz hwıʧ ıʧ re-prızents, ənd ın ðıs weı wi get ət ðə mi·nıŋ əv hwɒt s rıtn.

[136]

The same passage, in the 1908 notation, transcribed according to the usual conventions of writing Received Standard English.

læŋgwidʒ, əv kɔːs, igzistid ənd wəz hændid on fər eidʒiz bifɔː raitiŋ wəz inventid, ənd ðər ə plenti əv reisiz ət ðə preznt dei huː hæv fuli divelapt læŋgwidʒiz in witʃ ðei kən ikspres evriθiŋ ðət s in ðɛə maind bət huː hæv nou sistəm əv raitiŋ. iːvn in iŋglənd ənd ʌðə haili sivilaizd kʌntriz ðər ə stil ould piːpl huː nevə ləːnd in ðɛə juːθ aiðə tə riːd ɔː tə rait. fə sʌtʃ piːpl əz ðiːz it s kliə ðət læŋgwidʒ ounli igzists əz sʌmθiŋ witʃ iz spoukn. wiː siː, ðen, ðət ðə laif əv læŋgwidʒ mei biː kwait indipendənt əv raitiŋ ənd speliŋ.

wɒt iz raitiŋ? it s simpli ə klevə ənd kənviːniənt divais bai witʃ səːtn simblz, witʃ wiː kɔːl letəz, ə juːzd tə reprizent ðə saundz əv spiːtʃ. wəːdz ə bilt ʌp əv ə kəlekʃn əv sevərəl saundz, ənd sou wen wiː rait wiː ə səpouzd tə juːz ə letə fər iːtʃ saund əv witʃ ðə wəːd z kəmpouzd. letəz in ðəmselvz ə nɒt læŋgwidʒ, bət miəli simblz witʃ ə juːzd fə ðə saundz əv witʃ læŋgwidʒ iz kəmpouzd. ðə z nou laif ɔː miːniŋ in ritn simblz bai ðəmselvz; bət ðei məst biː trɑːnsleitid, æz it wəː, intə ðə saundz fə witʃ ðei

[137]

stænd bifɔː ðei bikʌm læŋgwidʒ ɔː hæv eni miːniŋ. wiː bikʌm sou əkʌstəmd tə ðə luk əv letəz, in gruːps tə reprizent wəːdz, ðət wiː ləːn tə riːd ðəm ɔːf kwait ræpidli intə ðə saundz fə witʃ ðei stænd. iːvn wen wiː riːd sailəntli, wiðaut prənaunsiŋ ðə wəːdz əlaud, wiː kæri aut ðə prouses mentəli, ənd ɔːfn ʌnkɔnʃəsli, əv təːniŋ ðə letəz intə ðə saundz witʃ iːtʃ reprizents, ənd in ðis wei wiː get ət ðə miːniŋ əv wɔt s ritn.

[138]

The same Passage

transcribed in Mid-West American Pronounciation.

By J. Victor Martin.

NOTES

[ɔ̣], [ə̣] and [ạ] are varieties respectively of [ɔ], [ə] and [ɑ] with the tongue in the "retroflex" position. They are slightly suggestive of [ɔr], [ər], [ɑr] (or, more precisely, of [ɔɹ], [əɹ], [ɑɹ]).

[ɚ], also, is always of the retroflex variety, slightly suggesting [ər] or [əɹ].

[eɪ] and [oʊ] although diphthongal are less so than in Received Standard; in rapid speech they suggest respectively [eˑ] and [oˑ].

[ɪ], in certain cases, is suggestive of [ə], notably in slow and careful speech; this is particularly the case when it stands for orthographic *e*. Thus [hændɪd] and [eɪdʒɪz] tend to resemble [hændəd], [eɪdʒəz].

[ɛə] tends towards [eə].

───◆───

læŋgwɪdʒ, əv kɔ̣əs, ɪgzɪstɪd ənd wəz hændɪd ɒn fɚ eɪdʒɪz bɪfoə raɪtɪŋ wəz ɪnvɛntɪd, ənd ðɛər ə plɛntɪ əv reɪsɪz ət ðə prɛznt deɪ hu hæv fulɪ dɪvɛləpt læŋgwɪdʒɪz ɪn hwɪtʃ ðeɪ kən ɪkspres ɛvrɪθɪŋ ðət s ɪn ðɛə maɪnd,

[139]

bət hu hæv nou sistəm əv raitiŋ. iˑvn in iŋglənd ənd ʌðə haili sivilaizd kʌntriz ðɛə ə stil ould piˑpl hu nevə lərnd in ðɛə juθ iˑðə tə riˑd ə tə rait. fə sʌtʃ piˑpl əz ðiˑz it s kliə ðət læŋgwidʒ ounli igzists əz sʌmθiŋ hwitʃ iz spoukn. wi siˑ, ðen, ðət ðə laif əv læŋgwidʒ mei bi kwait indipendənt əv raitiŋ ənd speliŋ.

hwat iz raitiŋ? it s simpli ə klevər ənd kənviˑnjənt divais bai hwitʃ sərtn simblz, hwitʃ wi kɔˑl letəz, ə juˑzd tə reprizent ðə saundz əv spiˑtʃ. wərdz ə bilt ʌp əv ə kəlekʃn əv sevərəl saundz, ənd sou hwen wi rait wi ə səpouzd tə juˑz ə letə fər iˑtʃ saund əv hwitʃ ðə wəˑd z kəmpouzd. letəz in ðəmselvz ə nat læŋgwidʒ, bət mieli simblz hwitʃ ə juˑzd fə ðə saundz əv hwitʃ læŋgwidʒ iz kəmpouzd. ðɛə z nou laif ə miˑniŋ in ritn simblz bai ðəmselvz; bət ðei məst bi trænsleitid, æz it wər, intə ðə saundz fə hwitʃ ðei stænd bifoə ðei bikʌm læŋgwidʒ ə hæv eni miˑniŋ. wi bikʌm sou əkʌstəmd tə ðə luk əv letəz, in gruˑps tə reprizent wəˑdz, ðət wi lərn tə riˑd ðəm ɔˑf kwait ræpidli intə ðə saundz fə hwitʃ ðei stænd. iˑvn hwen wi riˑd sailəntli, wiðaut prənaunsiŋ ðə wəˑdz əlaud, wi kæri aut ðə prases mentəli, ənd ɔˑfn ʌnkanʃəsli, əv tərniŋ ðə letəz intə ðə saund hwitʃ iˑtʃ reprizents, ənd in ðis wei wi get ət ðə miˑniŋ əv hwat s ritn.

[140]

THE PRINCIPLES OF ENGLISH
PHONETIC NOTATION

大正十四年八月　十　日印　　刷
大正十四年八月十四日發　　行
昭和　三　年四月　十　日再版發行

不許複製

東京市赤坂區臺町廿四番地
著　者　　　ハロルド・イー・パーマ

東京・文部省内
版權所有　　　英語教授研究所

東京市神田區表猿樂町十番地
　　　株式會社開拓社
發行者　　　代表者　伊藤一隆

東京市麴町區内幸町一丁目四番地
印刷者　　　秋　本　宗　市

東京市麴町區内幸町一丁目四番地
印刷所　　　ヘラルド社印刷部

東京・文部省内
發行所　英語教授研究所

東京市神田區表猿樂町十番地
發賣元　　株式會社　開　拓　社
電話神田二〇〇一・二〇〇二番
振替東京三九五八七番

Agents:
THE KAITAKUSHA (The Japanese Y.M.C.A. Press)
10 Omote-Sarugakucho, Kanda, Tokyo, Japan

定價金壹圓　　　PRICE: ￥1.00

14

LE MAÎTRE PHONÉTIQUE

DIALECTS/VARIETIES

ə′mɛrɪkən ɪŋglɪʃ

ae ev ɔːfən bɪn tɛmtɪd tə sɛnd **mf** ə spɛsɪmən əv ði ɪŋglɪʃ spooken ɪn ðə riidʒən əv ðə greet leeks, ə nao ae m gooɪŋ tə sɛnd ə træn′skrɪpʃən əv "ðə bæt" gɪvən an pɛedʒ θəːrtɪ′fɔːr əv ðə læːst nʌmbər.

əv kɔːrs, ae əv ɪgˈnɔːrd ə gud menɪ faen dɪˈstɪŋkʃənz; fər ɪgˈzæːmpəl, ðə vauəl ɪn *bird* ɪz nat ðə lɔːŋ əv ðæt ɪn wiik *thz, are,* ən sɔo aːn. ɪt wɪl nat bi aot əv plɛes tə kɔːl əˈtɛntʃən tu ə fjuu əv ðə tʃɪif pɔents əv dɪˈvəːrdʒəns frəm ðɪ ɪŋglɪʃ ʃɔon an pɛedʒ 34.

mae (r) ɪz præktɪkəlɪ ðə seem, nɔo mætər ʍat ɪts pəˈzɪʃən. bɪˈfɔːr frʌnt vauəlz, (ʍ) həz bɪˈkʌm (f); hɛnts "fɪtʃ" *which,* bət "ʍat" *what.* ʃɔːrt (ɔ) ɪz ɔːfən ʌnˈrɔondɪd, ən sʌmtaemz lɛŋθənd; hɛnts "nat/ˈnaːt" *not,* "an/ˈaːn" *on,* "ˈhatər/ˈhaːt" *hotter/hot.* ɔold (æ) ɪn *last, path, aunt,* &c. həz nat jɛt bɪˈkʌm (aː) ər (ɑː), bət ɪt ɪz mɔːr ɔopən ðən ðə ʃɔːrt (æ) ɪn *bat.* strɛst (ns), (nθ) &c., həv bɪˈkʌm (nts), (ntθ) &c., hɛnts "wʌnts" *once,* "mʌntθ" *month.* ae raet uu, ii, ɔo, ɛe, ɔe, ae, ao, əz ðə rɛgjulər fɔːrmz əv ðə dɪfθɔŋz, ræðər ðən uw, ij, ou, ɑi &c., bət aor spiitʃ ɪz nat pɪˈkçuuljər ɪn ðɪs. ae əv nɛvər həːrd Pɛnɪbadɪ sɛe uw, ij, ou, &c., ɪkˈsɛpt bɪˈfɔːr ə vauəl. ət əˈnʌðər taem ae ʃəl gɔo ɪntə ðɪs mætər mɔr fulɪ. wi juuz ðə glatəl stap ɪˈnɪʃəlɪ bɪˈfɔːr ðə hɛvɪlɪ strɛst vauəl əv ən əmˈfætɪk wəːrd.

Ann Arbor, Michigan,   GEORGE HEMPL.
[ænˈɑːrbər, mɪʃɪgən]   [dʒɔːrdʒ hɛmpəl]
 Feb. 6th, 1900.
[fɛbjuwɛrɪ sɪksθ, naentɪnˈhʌndrɪd]

ðə bæt

ðə bæt həz wɪŋz, ən ɪt flaez laek ə bəːrd. ɪts hɛd, iːrz, skɪn, ən triθ ər laek ðɔoz əv ə mɑos.

ɪt hæz ə sɔːft kɔot ə fəːr. ɪts aez ər smɔːl, ən ɪt kæːnt bəːr ðə strɔːŋ laet əv ðə sʌn.

ɪn ðə deetaem ɪt haedz əˈwɛe ɪn sʌm ɔold bɑːrn ər ʃɛd, ɔr ɪn ə halo triː.

fɛn ðə sʌn ə sɛt, ən ɪt bɪˈgɪnz tə grɔo daːrk, ðɛn ðə bæt kʌm zaot frəm ɪts haedɪŋ-plɛes, ən flaez əˈbaot, tə kætʃ mɔːðz, ən ʌðər ɪnsɛkts, an fɪtʃ ɪt fiidz.

fɛn wɪntər kʌmz, ðə bæt faendz ə snʌg haedɪŋ-plɛes, hæŋz ɪtˈsɛlf ʌp bae ɪts haend klɔːz, kʌvərz ɪtˈsɛlf klɔos wɪð ɪts wɪŋz, ən gɔoz tə sliip tɪl ðə wɔːrm wɛðər kʌmz əˈgɛn.

spesimɛn
ekɔsɛ

ðə fɔlouiŋ iz ə welnoun skɔtʃ pouem bai Burns, æz red tə miː bai Miss B. Robson M. A., əv Edinburgh. ai sʌbdʒɔin ə trænskripʃən in ɔːdənri sʌðən iŋgliʃ fə kəmparisən.

vɔislis plousivz hæv vɔist ɔːfglaidz bifɔː vauels. ɪ = ɪr, ɔːlmoust è. u iz ɔːlweiz tens.

sʌmbʌdɪ.

ma hɛrt is seːr, a darnə tɛl;
ma hɛrt is seːr fər sʌmbʌdɪ;
a kud weːk ə wɪntər nɛxt
fər ðə seːk o sʌmbʌdɪ.
ɔx hoːn! fər sʌmbʌdɪ!
oː heː! fər sʌmbʌdɪ!
a kud reːndʒ ðə wʌrl ərun
fər ðə seːk o sʌmbʌdɪ.

ji purz ðət smaıl ɔn vʌrtjuəs lʌv,
oː! switlı smaıl ɔn sʌmbʌdı!
frɐ ılkə deːndʒər kip ım friː,
ən sɛn mı seːf ma sʌmbʌdı.
   ɔx hoːn! fər sʌmbʌdı!
   oː heı! fər sʌmbʌdı!
a wəd deː — ʍɔt 'wʌd a noː
fər ðə seːk ɔ sʌmbʌdı?

in sʌðən ıŋglıʃ

sʌmbədi.

mai haːt iz sɔː, ai dɛə nɔt tel;
mai haːt iz sɔː fə sʌmbədi;
ai kəd weik ə wintə nait
fə ðə seik əv sʌmbədi.
   ou houn! fə sʌmbədi!
   ou hei! fə sʌmbədi!
ai kəd reindʒ ðə wəːld əraund
fə ðə seik əv sʌmbədi.

jiː pauəz ðət rein ɔn veːtjuəs lʌv,
ou! swiːtli smail ɔn sʌmbədi!
frəm evri deindʒə kiːp him friː,
ənd send miː seif mai sʌmbədi.
   ou houn! fə sʌmbədi!
   ou hei! fə sʌmbədi!
ai wəd duː — wɔt wud ai nɔt
fə ðə seik əv sʌmbədi?

ai əm indetid tə Miss Robson fə kaindli helpiŋ miː in ðə prepəreiʃən əv ðə skɔtʃ trænskripʃən.   D. Jones.

ereitəm

in ðə laːst nʌmbər əv ðə **mf**, peidʒ 119, in ðə fəːst lain əv ðə sekənd vəːs əv ðə skɔtʃ pouem (sʌðən iŋgliʃ trænskripʃən) ðə wəːd **rein** ʃud riːd **smail**.   D. Jones.

ereitəm

in ðə lɑːst nʌmbər əv ðə mf, peidʒ 119, in ðə fəːst lain əv ðə sekənd vəːs əv ðə skɔtʃ pouem (sʌðən iŋgliʃ trænskripʃən) ðə weːd **rein** ʃud riːd **smail**. D. JONES.

daiəlekt əv whitby (jɔːkʃiə)

nout. a in ʃoːt siləblz əproutʃiz æ, ɔ in dipθɔŋz iz njeːli œ ɔr iːvn ø. 1 iz njeːli ʎ hwen nɔt fainl ər iniʃl, r iz ɹ. ði ʌðə simblz hæv ðɛər ɔːdinəri iŋgliʃ væljuːz.

ðə prənʌnsjeiʃn veiriz in difrənt paːts əv ðə taun, bʌt ði spesimən givn bilou mei bi teikn əz tipikl; in sʌm paːts aː (reprizentətiv əv ðə sʌðən dipθɔŋ ai) iz slaitli dipθɔŋgaizd, aⁱ.

ðə hwitbi daiəlekt iz spouken veri dilibəreitli ənd wið ə slait drɔːl.

---

kɔnvəseiʃn heːd in ə hwitbi striːt.

meiri an. ðu wiljəm ɛnəri, kum ði wɛəz jam; ði miðə z bin ə lɛətn ɔ ðə sɛn faːv əklɔk. ʍi əstə bin?

wiljəm ɛnəri. aːv bin gaŋin wi dʒak duːn trɔəd tə t fauwə jakə fijəld, t jan wi t stjən jatpɔəsts, ðə nɔəz. ɛː! but wi jəd

---

1. Premier paragraphe seulement du texte.

ə fɑːn tɑːm. wi siːd sum bɔni bədz ðiə. ðə wəz jan wi blijuw ən rɛd wiŋz, but əfəə a kəd siː ət prɔpə t git fjəl dʒak ʃɑːd ə stjən ət it, ən frɑːtnd ət. so a skɛlpt iz lugz fr im; i bunʃt mi bak ən wi ɛd ə bit əv ə fɑːt, but wi sjən mɛəd it up ən kumd jam təgeðə. ɔn t wɛə wi siːd ə vɛminus rat; dʒak smaʃt iz ə ɛd; iːz fjəd ɔn əm.

meiri an. wɛl, kum in tə ði tiə. — lɔːks ə mɐsi! ʍɐt ɛst ðə dun tə ði briːks? it s ði bɛst kljəz ə ðu st rjuind əm.

wiljəm ɛnəri. ʍɑː, əz ə wəz gɛtn auwər ə jat a slipt ən kɛtʃt ɔn t snɛk ən t rɑːvd t sjət ut ən əm.

meiri an. ɛə! but ðu l kɔp it ʍɛn ði miðə siːz ðə.

(ænd hi did).

trɑnsleiʃn.

meiri æn: — ðau wiljəm hɛnri, kʌm houm: ðai məðə z biːn lukiŋ fə ði sins faiv əklɔk. hwɛə hæst ðau biːn?

wiljəm hɛnri: — ai v biːn goiŋ wið dʒæk daun ðə roud tə ðə fɔːər eikə fiːld, ðə wʌn wið ðə stoun geit poust, ðau nouwest. iːl bʌt wi hæd ə fain taim. wi sɔː sʌm priti bəːdz ðɛə. ðə wəz wʌn wið bluw ən red wiŋz, bʌt bifɔr ai kəd sij it prɔpəli ðə greit fuːl dʒæk θruː ə stoun ət it ən fraitənd it. sou ai bɔkst iz jəːz fər im; hi hit mi bæk ənd wi hæd ə bit əv ə fait, bʌt wi suːn meid it ʌp ən keim houm təgeðə. ɔn ðə wei wi sɔː ə venəməs ræt (æŋglisi "toud"). dʒæk smæʃt iz hed: hiːz əfreid ɔv əm.

meiri æn: — wel, kʌm in tə ðai tiː. — lɔːd əv məːsi! hwɔt əst ðau dʌn tə ðai trauzəz? its ðai best klouðz ən ðau st ruwind ðəm.

wiljəm hɛnri: — hwai! əz ai wəz gɛtiŋ ouvər ə geit ai slipt ən kɔːt ɔn ðə lætʃ ənd it tɔːə ðə siːt aut əv ðm.

meiri æn: — ih! bʌt ðau l kætʃ it hwen ðai məðə siːz ði.

G. Noël-Armfield.

sʌm iːst lʌndən striːt kraiz.

veri fjuː əv ði ould mjuːzikl lʌndən striːt kraiz səvaiv, ən ðɛə pleis hæz, fə ðə moust paːt, biːn teikn bai rɔːkəs ənd ʌnmjuːzikl ʃauts. djuːriŋ ðə paːst tuː jəːz ai v mænidʒd tə meik ə kəlekʃn əv sʌm əv ðə moust tipikl kraiz həːd in ðə nɔːθ iːst əv lʌndən, ənd ai ɔfə sʌm əv ðəm hiə, in ðə houp ðət kəliːgz, bouθ in mai oun lænd ənd əbrɔːd, mei bi led tə put ən pəːmənənt rekɔːd hwɔt mʌst, ʌndə mjuːnisipl ristrikʃnz, suːn disəpiəː.

ðə mjuːzikl nouteiʃn ai giv hiə wud bi betə ripleist bai intəneiʃn kəːvz sʌtʃ əz auə frend *dʒounz juːziz in iz buk[1]), bʌt fə ðə seik əv ikɔnəmi in printiŋ ai kəntent maiself wið staːf nouteiʃn. ðə riːdər iz aːskt tə rimembə ðət ðər iz nou ʃaːp ən difaind pæsidʒ frəm nout tə nout, ənd kɔnsikwentli 'portamenti' mʌst bi sʌplaid in ðə medʒɔriti əv keisiz. ðə voisiz ə dʒenrli lækiŋ in louə haːməniks, ən ðə "toːnfarbə" iz kɔnsikwentli sʌmhwɔt straidənt ənd metælik.

wʌn wud nætʃrəli sʌpouz ðət ə mæn hu hæz eniθiŋ fə seil wud meik it noun in ðə kliərist mænə pɔsibl, bʌt kliənəs iz faː frəm biːiŋ ə maːkt kærəktristik əv ðə striːt seilzmən. tu ði ʌniniʃjeitid ðə kraiz ə mɔər ɔ les inaːtikjulət, ənd it iz ounli bai kɛəfl stʌdi ɔː bai kʌstəm ðət wʌn ləːnz ðə miːniŋ əv ðə hɔːkəz krai. hwɔt fər igzaːmpl kud ə streindʒə, tə sei nʌθiŋ əv ə fərinə, meik əv "ˈækniŋˌkiːzlaːˈkiːzla"? jet ðouz hu hiə ðə krai regjələli nou ət wʌns ðət ði ounər əv ðə vɔis iz kɔːliŋ ðə njuː iʃjuː əv ðə "hækni ənd kiŋzlənd gəzet". ðə riːzn fə ðis læk əv distiŋktnəs iznt faː tə siːk : ə mæn hu hæz tə wɔːk θruː 10 ɔ 15 mailz əv driəri striːts ə dei, puʃiŋ ə hevili leidn hændkaːt ənd ripiːtiŋ ðə seim fjuː wəːdz ət intəvəlz əv ə minit ɔ sou, nætʃərli bikʌmz kɛələs in iz inʌnsjeiʃn. let ðouz hu daut it trai ði iksperimənt.

iniʃl kɔnsənənts ə fɛəli kliəli inʌnʃjeitid bʌt miːdjəl ənd fainl wʌnz ə juːʒwəli "swɔloud" ɔː niglektid. sʌmtaimz fainl plousivz ər ʌnfiniʃt ənd miːdjəlz ə ripleist bai ðə glɔtl stɔp[2]), hwitʃ ɔːlsou əkəːz əkeiʒnli "ʔim ʔauslaut".

in ðə fɔlouiŋ spesimənz pitʃ ənd intəvəl əv biːn tʃekt wið ə tjuːniŋ fɔːk ənd in meni keisiz wið ðə piaːnou.

---

1) "Intonation Curves", B. G. Teubner, Leipzig.
2) ðis iz bai nou miːnz ən ʌnkɔmən spiːtʃ saund in ði iːst ənd. iz it djuː tu ði imigreiʃn əv ðə dʒəːmən dʒuː?

wʌn əv ðə fəːst kraiz tə bi həːd iz ðæt əv ðə milkmən huːz ædvənt iz hereldid bai ə kaind əv "joudl", givn, ɔr ət eni reit endiŋ in ə hai fɔlsetou vɔis. əmʌŋst ʌðəz ai v noutid

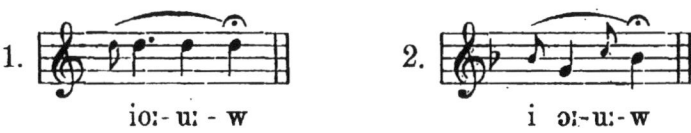

ðər ə meni veərjənts ənd ði ikstriːmz ə reprizentid bai

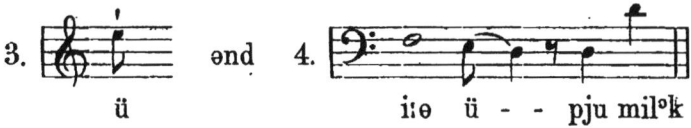

nʌmbəz 1, 2 ənd 3 ə sʌpouzd tə bi reliks əv ðə dʒenuin kʌntri milk diːləz krai, "milk bilou"; nʌmbə 4 iz iksepʃnl.
ðiːz kɔːlz hæv ə seːtn mjuːzikl vælju in moust keisiz, bʌt ðæt əv ðə swiːp, hu iz ɔːlsou ən eːli mɔːniŋ vizitə, iz mɔər ɔ les əv ən iːəspliiŋ ʃriːk, əz fɔlouz

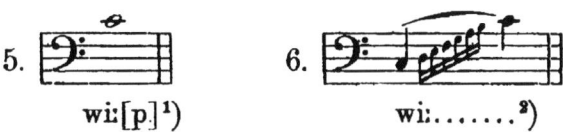

əmʌŋ ðə moust friːkwənt ənd nɔizjəst distəːbəz əv ðə piːs ə ðə hɔːkəz əv koul, huːz kɔːl, sʌpouzd tə bi "koul mæn", iz sʌbdʒikt tə meni veərjeiʃnz əz rigaːdz bouθ intouneiʃn ənd prənʌnsjeiʃn. əmʌŋst ðiːz ai v noutid

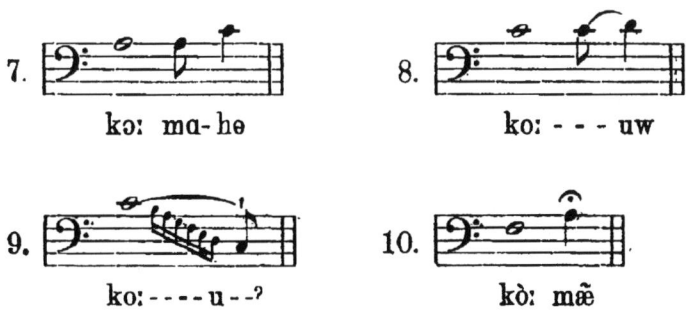

1) [ ] indikeits inkəmpliːt aːtikjuleiʃn.
2) wyː iz sʌmtaimz həːd.

bifɔə lɔŋ ðə peripətetik griːngrouse iz strɔŋli in evidəns, hiz krai tʃeindʒiŋ əkɔːdiŋ tə ðə siːzn. ai v biːn eibl tə teik daun ðə fɔlouiŋ əmʌŋ ʌðəz: —

11. mː baː (h)rai·θriː-ɛ pə bʌː hə də¹)

12. mː-bə θrjə ba-hə-də.²)

13. ʋɛː (ˀ)ə mæˀ rə ˀə raiː iˀ

sʌndei aːftənuːn ɔftn prədjusiz

14. θriː (h)ə ˀə paː laː ʃriː[mp] ə hə hə³)

fə nain jəːz ai v həːd ɔːlmoust deːli ðə fɔlouiŋ frəm ə wumən seliŋ wɔːtəkrɛs

15. mnŋ ə kriːɐθ - - iz

finiʃiŋ wið ə kætʃ in ðə vois ðə pitʃ əv hwitʃ it iz veri difiklt tu aidentifai. **mnŋə** iz prɔbəbli ə veri wɔːn aut fɔːm əv wɔːtə. əbaut tiːtaim wi hiə ðə mʌfin mæn huːz toun iz θrouti ənd əz if ə hɔt ənd flauəri pətətou həd lɔdʒd in sʌtʃ ə pəziʃn əz tə intəfiə wið ðə kliər imiʃn əv iz vois. hiː siŋz

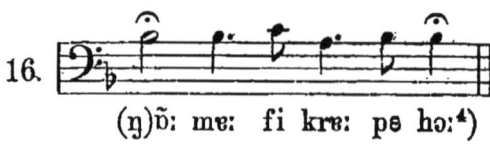

16. (ŋ)õː mʋː fi krʋː pə hɔː⁴)

1) ruːbaːb raip, θriːheipns ə bʌndl.
2) ruːbaːb, θriːheipns ə bʌndl.
3) θriː (pəns) ə paint, laːdʒ ʃrimps, ohou!
4) ou! mʌfinz, krʌmpəts hɔt. nout ɐ iz ʌ╫ʟ.

in wʌn distrikt ðə skævindʒər ənaunsiz iz wikli vizit wið

dʌs mæ̃læ̃īm jə

ə diːlər in faiəwud, leitli ded, əlas!, juːst tə prəkleim iz wɛəz wið

fɑː wud o-oɪ-uː,tʃʌm[p]wud ouw

əz ə ruːl ðə laːst krai əv ðə nait iz ðæt əv ən aitinrnt ɔistə selə, huːz mənətound krai iz rimɑːkəbl fə ðə proulɔŋgeiʃn əv ðə fainl s

fain oissss frɛːʃ oissss

sins ai v livd in ði iːst end əv lʌndən ai əv hɛːd bʌt wʌn riəli mjuːzikl kɔːl, hwitʃ ai giv əz ðə bɔn buʃ əv mai silekʃn. it iz sʌmtaimz suŋ in ə ritʃ bæritoun bai ə trævliŋ ɔilmən

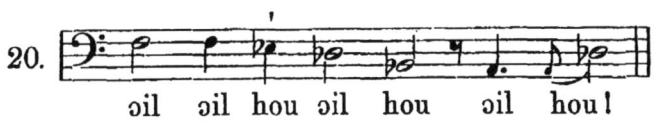
ɔil   ɔil hou   ɔil hou   ɔil hou!

G. Noël-Armfield.

iŋgliʃ

*tainsaid daielekt (*nɔːθʌmbelend)

kom *dʒɔːdi haːd¹) ðe been²)
as ʃuːɐʀ a winiet³) bi læŋ
ad tjɛk⁴) ðe dʒuːl mi′sɛl⁵)
bot ʀiːeli aːz⁶) net stʀæŋ.
ðɔːz fluːwɐʀ⁷) end koːulz te gɛt
ðe huːs-tɔːnz⁸) ðɔː nɔt djon⁹),
sou haːd ðe been fe feez¹⁰),
jev ɔften djond¹¹) fe fon.

siː¹²) *dʒɔːdi hɛld ðe been
ðou seɐʀ¹³) egjɛn¹⁴) hiz wil.
ðe puːe bit θiŋ wæz gud
bot *dʒɔːdi hæd niː¹⁵) skil.
hiː hædnt its moðez weːiz,
hiː sæt bjeθ¹⁶) stif en nom;
efɔː faiv minits wæz paːst
hiː wiʃt its moðe wæd¹⁷) kom.

    teikn daun bai D. J. frem ðe dikteiʃn
      ev Mr. S. G. HORSLEY.

---

1) hould. 2) tʃaild. 3) wil nɔt. 4) teik. 5) mai′self. 6) aim.
7) ðɛez flauɐr. 8) hauswɐːk. 9) dʌn. 10) sieriesli. 11) dʌn it.
12) sou. 13) sɔː (sore). 14) egeinst. 15) nou. 16) bouθ. 17) wud.

sʌm æbedi:nʃə vauelz

ðə nɔ:θwest dʒə:mən ʃɔ:t i (menʃnd in ðə **mf** 1911, 170) iz prɔbəbli ðə vauel əv skɔtʃ *it*, æz prənaunst bai ðə wə:kiŋ kla:siz in æbədi:nʃə.

ðɛr iz ə houl si:rjiz əv ði:z vauelz, reindʒiŋ frəm ðə fə:st vauel əv *mither* ('*mother*'), θru: ðə vauel əv ʌnəksentid *yer* ('*your*'), daun tə ðə vauel əv *fir*. ði:z θri: ar əv əbaut ðə seim hait æz iŋgliʃ ì, è, ɛ (in *it get there*). ðei ar intəmi:djit in saund bitwi:n ì, è, ɛ ənd nɔ:ml mikst ï, ö, ë, pəhæps ni:rə tə ðə fɔ:mə, fə hwitʃ ðei ar i:zili misteikn bai pə:snz tə hu:m ðei ar ʌnfəmiljə. ðei mei bi reprizentid bai ï, ö, ë, æz skɔtʃ dʌz nɔt pəzes ðə nɔ:məl mikst saundz. in ðɛə prədʌkʃn ðə fɔ: pa:t əv ðə tʌŋ ki:ps əbaut ðə seim sloup æz in ì, è, ɛ, bʌt ðə midl iz les reizd. ðei a felt æz prədju:st ə litl wei bihaind ðə tip əv ðə tʌŋ, nɔt æt ɔ: klous tu ðə tip, æz iz ðə keis wið ì, è, ɛ.

ï iz ɔfn hə:d in iŋgliʃ *prince*, ï̆ (ðə seknd vauel əv *mither*) in iŋgliʃ *different* [**difrïnt**], *terrible* [**terïbl**].

ö æz in *yer* saundz nɔt veri difrïnt frəm è əv iŋgliʃ *yet*.

ë æz in *girl* iz nɔt veri ʌnlaik iŋgliʃ ɛ, bʌt bouθ saundz a ju:zd, æz **fɛrm** ('*farm*'), **gërl** ('*girl*').

igza:mplz: —

ï — **mïdï·r**, **hïz** ('*has*'), **gïn** ('*if*').

ö ounli ʌnstrest — '**fa:rz jër 'dòg** ('*Where is your dog*').

ë — **fët** ('*foot*'), **nëxt** ('*night*'), **fër** ('*fir*'), **gërl** ('*girl*'), ənd strɔŋ **ët** ('*it*'), **hër** ('*her*').

---

wið æptitju:d fə fonetiks wil prənauns ði iŋgliʃ ʃɔ:t læks ì kərektli i:vn ðou it bi ritn **ì**, wail ə frenʃmən wið bət litl æptitju:d fə ðə sʌbdʒikt wil kəntinju: tə prənauns tens ì, weðə ðə saund bi ritn i ɔ: ɪ ɔ: ì ɔ: i̯! — D. J.]

ʹgis jër ʹïðï⁓r ʹfët (ʹ*give us* [= *me*] *your other foot*ʹ).

ëts ë ʹrëxt ʹbrëxt ʹnëxt ðë ʹnëxt, mɛstrë⸗s ʹrëxt (ʹ*it's a right bright night tonight, Mrs. Wright*ʹ).

hï ʹwïdnë⸗ bï ʹòn ʹfòxn wï z ʹbrïdï⸗r ën ïz ʹsëstë⸗r (ʹ*he would not be without* [= *keep from*] *fighting with his brother and sister*ʹ).

J. L. WILSON.

spesimɛn

lʌndən daiəlɛkt

(kɔkni)

ðə noːθ win n ðə san ɛd ə kwɔrl. ðə noːθ wind sez: "ɔi bet ʃə ɔim strɔŋgə ðn jïü;" n ðə san iː sez: "gaːn, jïü aint." sau ðə win sez: "weŏ, dʒə sei ðis iːə blauk kamin əlɔŋ wið ə hauvəkaut. ɔi vau⁹ wei əgrei ðəd ueve maiks im taig id oːf fəːst ʃə bi ðə strɔŋgist". "ɔː rɔit", sez ðə san. ðen ðə noːθ win bigɛn də blau əz aːd z i kud, bə⁹ wen i blïü aːdə ðə mɛn aunli rɛpt iz kaut raund im oːl ðə moːwə. sau ə⁹ laːst ðə noːθ win sez: "weŏ, ɔim sik ə ðis iːə fïüln əbaːt; jïü gŋ ɛv ə trɔi f jə lɔik, bəd jïü waun dïü id əni bedə". "joːl sei", sez ðə san. sau i ʃon aːt əz ɔt əz i kud, n ə koːs in aːf ə minit ðə mɛn wəz aːf baikt lɔik, n ɛd tə taig oːf iz kaut. sau ðə noːθ win ɛd tə kənfɛs, weðr i lɔikt it ə nɔt, ðət ðə san wəz strɔŋgə ðn 'im.   D. J.

kɛntiʃ daiəlɛkt

(Hythe)

də nɔːf wınd ən də sʌn wz ɛvın ə reu beut wıtʃ wz də strɔŋgıst wen dei sʌi ə tʃɛp kʌm lɔŋ də rʌud weɹn ə ʌʊvəkʌʊt. den də θɔːt ıt d bʌı ə laɹk tə sʌı wıtʃ wʌn ɔv əm kd mæık ım tæık ıt ɔːf, ən də wʌn wɔt əd mæık ım tæık ıt ɔːf fəɹst əd bʌı də wınɹ. sʌʊ də nɔːf wınd bıˈgɛn tə blʌʊ lɔɛk enıfıŋ bət ıt waɹnt nʌʊ jïüs kɔz d tʃɛp ʌʊnlı rɛpt ız kʌʊt tɔıtɹ. d læːst dı ʌʊ nɔːf wɪnd ɛd tə gɪv ɪt ʌp z ə bɛd dʒɔb. ðen ðə sʌn ɛd ə gʌu ɒn ɪ? gɔt sʌu dʒɔlɪ ɔt t ðə mɛn ɛd tə tæɪk ɔːf ɪz kʌut. sʌu ðə nɔːf wɪnd ɛd t ʌuɒ ʌp t ðə sʌn wz ðə strɒŋgɪst æːftr̩ ɔːl.

Harold E. Palmer.

daiəlɛkt əv nɔːθ wɛst læŋkəʃiə

[ɑ tɛndz tɔːdz a, ɛksɛpt in ðə difθɔŋ ɑu. o, e = oͬ, eͬ.
i, u ɑː tɛns hwɛn lɔŋ, ənd in ðə difθɔŋz iə, uə. u iz tɛns in ɑu.
l iz rɑːðə "kliə". ɹ iz hɑːdli mɔː ðən ən invəːtid mədifikeiʃn əv
ðə priːsiːdiŋ vauel. d̪ iz ə dɛntl d; it iz ɔ distiŋktiv saund.]

blɑːn²) t kɑnl³) aut

ðə wəz ə ɑːd tʃap liːvd up ətʰ tɔp ənd ə *siəθət ət ðə kɔːd
dʒɔɹdi dʒuənsn. i wəz reːdəɹ ə kəmikl liəken soəɹt əv ə fɛlə.
iz gɔb⁴) wəz ɔ ətʰ teə hə̃⁵). t fəɹst taim ət i sɑ ə kɑnl (ðəd
ɔːləs iuzd reiʃliːts əfuəɹ), i traid ət blɑ it aut ən kudnt. t waif
kəm in ən teək t wiːk ətwiːn əɹ fiŋəɹ ən θaum ən nipt it aut,
ən sɛd: "ðau gəɹt⁶) gɔːmləs⁷) ðau, wɔt s t ius ə sik əz ðiː traiən
tə blɑ aut⁸) aut⁹).

prənʌnsieiʃn əv ðə Rev. R. D. Ellwood
(əv Torver niə Coniston)
noutid bai D. J.

---

1) ɔː θïəːlo.   2) = blouiŋ.   3) = kændl.
4) = mauθ.   5) = ɔn wʌn ʼsaid.   6) = greit.
7) = fuːl.   8) = ɛniθiŋ.   9) = aut.

daiəlɛkt əv nɔːθ-wɛst læŋkəʃiə

(Torver, niə Coniston)

[wɛn ðə dɛfinit ɑːtikl t əkɛːz nɛkst tu ðə saund t, ðə tuː tugɛðə fɔːm miəli wʌn slaitli prəlɔŋd t.]

feibl əv ðə nɔːθ wind ənd ðə sʌn

t nɔːɹθ wind ən t sun wər əvən ə fratʃ jɑː dæːː[1]) wɛððəɹ ɔ ðəm wəz t straŋəɹ, wɛn ə tʃap kɔm up wi ə gət[2]) tɔp kuət ɔn.

---

1) hæviŋ ə fræːtʃ (dispjuːt) wʌn dei.
2) greit.

suə ðə beəθ meəd it in ət wɛdðəɹ ivəɹ¹) ɔ ðəm kud meək t tʃap dɔf²) iz kuət ɔf wɔd bə rakənd straŋəɹ nəɹ³) t tudðəɹ. ðɛn t nɔːɹθ wind staɹtʰ⁴) ən bleu əz aɹd əz ivəɹ it kud blɑː, but t aɹdəɹ it bleu t kluəsəɹ t tʃap lapt iz kuət raund əm, tlə eftəɹ ə bit t nɔːɹθ wind gɛv in. ðɛn t sun kəm aut riːl jat⁵) ən t tʃap teək iz kuət ɔf t fiɹst θiŋ. ən suə t nɔːɹθ wind əd tə lɛt wiːt⁶) əz t sun wəz straŋəɹ nəɹ wat 'it wɔz.

R. D. Ellwood
kəmjuːnikeitid bai D. Jones.

kɔːnɪʃ daɪəlɛkt

[i, u, o stænd fɔˑ iʳ, uʳ, oʳ⁻. ə ɪz əbaʊt kɑːdɪnl. a stændz fɔˑ a⊥ ; ɑ fɔˑ a+ ; ɛ fɔˑ ɛ⊥.]

ðə tuː pæsɪdʒɪz ə teɪkn frəm ðə "Cornish Almanac", 1905, 1907. ðə prənʌnsɪeɪʃn ɪz ðæt əv ə neɪtɪv əv saʊθ kɔːnwəl, noʊtɪd baɪ D. J.

    ɑˑm viːlɪn pɜɹdɪn weʃt ən lɛmp,
        noʊ hɑɹt tə ɛɪt əɹ wɜɹk ;
    ɑˑv gʊd maɪn goʊ tə taʊn tə wans
        ən ziː aʊld dɒktəɹ bɜɹk.

    maɪ stɒmɛk düː siːm ɒpsaɪd daʊn,
        ən ɔːl ðə taɪm ðɛɹz peɪn ;
    aɪ θɛŋk təz aʊld taɪm fəɹ mɪ tüː
        bɪ pʌt tə ɹaɪts əgeɪn.

    ðeɪ zeɪ, an üː nɔː bʌt təz tɹɪŭ,
        təz gɛːnən zetʃ ə ɹɛːət,
    ðət ɛf wɪ dɔːnt sʊn ɹuːl ðə dɹɛŋk,
        ðə dɹɛŋk l ɹuːl ðə stɛːət.

əmɛrɪkən ɪŋglɪʃ

ðə θri most dʒenr̩əl taɪps əv kʌltəvetɪd ɪŋglɪʃ ɪn əmɛrɪkə həv kɑmənlɪ bɪn kɔld istr̩n, sʌðr̩n, ən mɪdl-wɛstr̩n. ðə læst dɛsɪgneʃən ɪz, hauɛvr̩, kwaɪt mɪslidɪŋ. prəfɛsr̩ Krapp, ɪn hɪz *History of the English Language in America,* kɔlz ðɪs læst taɪp "dʒenr̩əl əmɛrɪkən." ðət ðɪs ɪz ə mor ækjurɪt neɪm wɪl bɪ ʃoun bɪlou.

ðə prɛznt trænskrɪpʃən rɛprɪzɛnts maɪ ɪndɪvɪdʒuəl pr(ə)nʌntsɪeʃ(ə)n əv ðɪs taɪp spokən ɪn ən ævr̥ɪdʒ kəlokwɪəl staɪl. kwantɪtɪ əv vauəlz ɪz nɑt mɑrkt, əz ə rul. sɪmblz ɪn raund brækɪts mɪn ðət ðə saund rɛprɪzɛntɪd meɪ r̥ me nɑt bɪ hə̣d, əkɔrdɪŋ tə staɪl əv ʌtr̥ənts.

ðə sɪmbl r hɪ·r rɛprɪzɛnts, ɪn strɛst sɪləblz, ðí ɪnɪʃ(ə)l, mɪdrəl, ən faɪnl kɑnsənæntl tʌŋ-glaɪd, nɪðr̥ trɪld nr̥ frɪkətɪv (ɛksɛpt æftr̥ sʌm kɑnsənənts, əz t, d), æz dɪskraɪbd ɪn *American Pronunciation*, §§ 84–86, ænd ɪn *American Speech* fr̥ mɑrtʃ, 1926. ɪn ʌnstrɛst sɪləblz ðə sɪmbl r̥ ɪz juzd tə rɛprɪzɛnt ðɪ ʌnstrɛst ɪnvə̣tɪd vauəl ə, æz ɪn bɛtr̥. ɝ stæn(d)z fr̥ ðə strɛst ɪnvə̣tɪd vauəl ɪn *hurt* [hɝt]. fɔr ðɪs saund ənʌðr̥ sɪmbl ɪz prəpouzd bɪlou. ðə saund ɝ ɪz nɑt faund ɪn dʒɛnr̥əl əmɛrɪkən.

ðɪ e(ɪ) ənd o(ʊ) saun(d)z vɛ·rɪ frəm vətʃuəlɪ pjur vauəlz tə dɪfθɔŋz. ðə dɪfθɔŋgl kwɑlətɪ ɪz juʒ(ʊ)əlɪ lɛs mɑrkt bɪfor vɔɪslɪs kɑnsənənts ðən bɪfor vɔɪst, r̥ hwɛn faɪnl; bət wɪk strɛs ən(d) ræpɪd ʌtr̥ənts ɑr stɪl grɛtr̥ fæktr̥z ɪn ílɪmənetɪŋ ðə sɛkənd ɛləmənt. ɪn ðɪs trænskrɪpʃən ðə sɪmblz e, o mɪn ðət ðə saund əproutʃɪz ə pjur vauəl, ənd eɪ, oʊ ðət ɪt ɪz mɔr ɔr lɛs notɪsəblɪ dɪfθɔŋgl. ðə fɝst ɛləmənt ɪz nɪr̥ tə kɑrdn̩l e ənd o ðən ɪt juʒ(ʊ)əlɪ ɪz ɪn sʌðr̥n brɪtɪʃ.

maɪ vauəl ɪn wə̣dz laɪk *pair, there*, ɪz ən æ slaɪtlɪ haɪr̥ ðən æ ɪn mæn, ənd əv vɛríɪŋ lɛŋkθ; bət ɪn sʌm wə̣dz əv ðɪs klæs maɪ vauəl ɪz ɛ, əz ɪn **vɛríɪŋ**: ə vɛrɪ kɑmən əmɛrɪkən vauəl ɪn ðɪz wə̣dz ɪz ɛ̀.

ðə frʌnt vauəlz ɪ, ɛ, æ, r̥ lour ɪn əmɛrɪkən ðən ɪn sʌðr̥n brɪtɪʃ. tʊ ən əmɛrɪkən ɪ·r ðə wə̣d **bæk** prənaun(t)st baɪ ən ɛdʒəkɛtɪd lʌndənr̥ səgdʒɛsts **bɛk**, **gɛt** rɪzɛmblz **get**, ən **sɪt**, **sit**.

maɪ ʌ ɪz mɔr rɪtræktɪd ðən ðæt, fr̥ ɪgzæmpl, əv prəfɛsr̥ JONES. ðɪ ʌ aɪ hɪ·r ɪn lʌndən ɔfn̩ səgdʒɛsts ɑ. ðɪs ɪz nɑt tru əv əmɛrɪkən ʌ.

əmɛrɪkən ɔ laɪz əkustɪkəlɪ bɪtwin sʌðr̥n brɪtɪʃ ɒ ənd ɔ. hɛnts mɛnɪ əmɛrɪkən wə̣dz ðət wʌn̞ts hæd ɒ nau həv gɔn ouvr̥ ɪðr̥ tʊ ɔ, sʌtʃ əz lɔg, ɔr tʊ ɑ, sʌtʃ əz **stɑp**.

ɪn wə̣dz laɪk *except* ðɪ ɪnɪʃ(ə)l vauəl əproutʃɪz ɪ ɪn ræpɪd spitʃ, bət ɪz saundɪd ɛ ɔfnr̥ ðən ɪn sʌðr̥n brɪtɪʃ. maɪ faɪnl ɪ ɪn wə̣dz laɪk sɪtɪ ɪz juʒ(ʊ)əlɪ *í*; ðɪs vəraɪətɪ ɪz waɪdsprɛd ɪn əmɛrɪkə. mɪdrəl ʌnstrɛst vauəlz spɛlt wɪð *i* weɪvr̥ ɪn maɪ spitʃ bɪtwin ɪ ənd ə; ðə lætr̥ ɪz æpt tʊ əkə̣ nɛkst tʊ l, r, m, n; bət maɪ mɪdrəl ə ɪz ɔfn vɛrɪ nɪ·r tʊ ɪ.

ɪn ðə dɪfθɒŋ ĭu ðə gretr̩ stres ɪz ɑn ðə bɪgɪnɪŋ, bət ðə glaɪd ɪntə ði u ɪz so ræpɪd ðət ðɪs pɑrt prɪdɑmənets tə ði ɪ·r. ðə bɪgɪnɪŋ ɪz ə rɪtræktɪd ɪ ən(d) ði ɛnd ən ədvæn(t)st u. ĭu ʃeɪdz ɪmpr̩sɛptəblɪ ɪntə ju. ɪnɪʃ(ə)lɪ ĭu bɪkʌmz ju, ɪn maɪ spɪtʃ ɔfn jĭu.

hw ɪz w wɪð ɪnkrɪst ɪnɪʃ(ə)l fɔrs, ən(d) lɪtl, ɪf ɛnɪ, æspr̩eʃən. ɪt ɪz nɑt vɔɪslɪs w, hwɪtʃ wəd bi saɪlənt, fɔr maɪ w, laɪk maɪ j, ɪz ə vokl glaɪd wɪðaʊt sɪgnɪfəkənt frɪkətɪv ɛləmənt.

maɪ ɪnɪʃ(ə)l l ɪz dɑrk, ðo juʒ(ʊ)əlɪ lɛs so ðən æftr̩ vaʊlz r̩ hwɛn sɪlæbɪk.

bɪtwin wr̩dz laɪk əmɛrɪkə ənd, ɔr əmɛrɪkə ɔlwɪz, aɪ ɔfn ɪnsr̩t ə slaɪt ʔ əz ə haɪetəsfɪlr̩.

ðət Krapp's tr̩m, "dʒɛnr̩əl əmɛrɪkən," ɪz æmplɪ dʒʌstɪfaɪd, ɪz ʃoʊn baɪ ə kɑmpjuteʃən əv ðə nʌmbr̩ əv pipl spikɪŋ ðə θri taɪps. ɪn mekɪŋ ðɪs, aɪ həv kənsɪdr̩d ɛvrɪ daʊtfl erɪə[1] tə ði ɪstr̩n ɔr tə ðə sʌðr̩n, əz əgɛn(t)st ðə dʒɛnr̩əl taɪp. aɪ həv gɪvən tə ði ɪstr̩n ɔl əv *nĭu ɪŋglənd ən *nĭu jɔrk sɪtɪ, ən tə ðə sʌðr̩n, bɪsaɪdz ðə stets juʒ(ʊ)əlɪ so klæst, ɔl əv *mɛrɪlənd, ðə dɪstrɪkt əv *kəlʌmbɪə, ənd ɔl əv *tɛksəs. ðə rɪzʌlt, best ɑn ði əfɪʃ(ə)l sɛnsəs estəmɪts fr̩ naɪntin twɛntɪ-fɔr, ʃoʊz əbaʊt θr̩tin ənd ə hæf mɪljən spikɪŋ ði ɪstr̩n taɪp, θr̩tɪ ənd ə hæf mɪljən ðə sʌðr̩n, ən sɪkstɪ-sɪks ənd ə hæf mɪljən ðə dʒɛnr̩əl. aɪ hæv ði əpɪnjən əv ə brɪtɪʃ fonɪtɪʃ(ə)n naʊ rɛzɪdənt ɪn *kænədə ðət ə vɛrɪ lɑrdʒ mədʒɔrɪtɪ əv kənedɪənz spik ðə seɪm taɪp, ən(d) ðɪs əgriz wɪð maɪ oʊn ɑbzr̩veʃ(ə)n, so fɑr əz ɪt ɪkstɛn(d)z. ɪn naɪntin twɛntɪ-wʌn ðə pɑpjəleʃ(ə)n əv *kænədə wəz nɪrlɪ naɪn mɪljən. nɑt kaʊntɪŋ tu mɪljən hu r̩ əv frɛntʃ ɛkstrækʃ(ə)n, wi meɪ, aɪ θɪŋk, seflɪ əsĭum ðət ət list fɔr mɪljən kənedɪənz spik dʒɛnr̩əl əmɛrɪkən. ðɪs brɪŋz ðə totl tu oʊvr̩ sɛvəntɪ mɪljən.

ɪn kənsɪdr̩ɪŋ ðɪs rɪzʌlt, ɪt ʃəd bi rɪmɛmbr̩d ðət ɪn ðə dʒɛnr̩əl taɪp pr̩tɪkjəlr̩lɪ, noʊ sʌtʃ waɪd dɪfrəntsɪz ɪn pr(ə)naʊntsɪeʃ(ə)n ɪgzɪst bɪtwin ðə spɪtʃ əv ði ʌŋkʌltəvetɪd ənd əv ðə kʌltəvetɪd əz ɪgzɪst, fr̩ ɪgzæmpl, bɪtwin ðə spɪtʃ əv ðə loʊr̩ ənd ʌpr̩ klæsɪz ɪn ɪŋglənd. ðə dɪfrəntsɪz r̩ lɑrdʒlɪ ɪn sɪntæks, vo'kæbjəˌlɛrɪ, ən grəmætɪkl fɔrmz.

ðɛr[2] ɪz noʊ dɪspəzɪʃ(ə)n, so fɑr əz aɪ noʊ, tu ædvəket ði ədapʃən ɪn əmɛrɪkə əv ɪðr̩ əv ðə taɪps spokən baɪ θr̩tɪ mɪljən ɔr

---

[1] ɔr, ɛ·rɪə.

[2] hwɛn ɪt ɪz fʊlɪ strɛst aɪ prənaʊnts ðɪs wr̩d ðær; hwɛn ɪt ɪz ʌnstrɛst, ðr̩; hɪ·r ɪt ɪz laɪtlɪ strɛst.

baɪ sev(ə)ntɪ mɪljən æz ə stændɪ̯rd fɪ̯ ðə houl kʌntrɪ ; ðou ðɪ̯ hæv bɪn sʌm efɪ̯ts tu ədʒ ðɪ ədɑpʃən əv ðɪ istɪ̯n taɪp, pɑrtlɪ an ðə graund ðət ɪt əgrɪz ɪn sʌm əv ɪts most straɪkɪŋ fitʃɪ̯z, ðou baɪ nou mɪnz ɔl, wɪð ðə so-kɔld rɪsivd pr(ə)nʌntsɪeʃ(ə)n əv ɪŋglənd. əmerɪkən fonɪtɪʃ(ə)nz ɪ̯ nɑt, aɪ θɪŋk, ət preznt mʌtʃ kənsə̯nd wɪð ðɪs kwestʃən. ðeɪ ɪ̯ dʒʌst nau tʃɪflɪ kənsə̯nd ɪn establɪʃɪŋ ðɪ (h)ɪstərɪkl ən kə̯rənt fækts əv əmerɪkən pr(ə)nʌntsɪeʃ(ə)n, hwɪtʃ ɪ̯ tu lɪtl noun, ivən ɪn əmerɪkə.

ɪn fəðɪ̯ənts əv ðɪs əbdʒɪkt ðer həz letlɪ bɪn ən ɪnkrist efɪ̯t baɪ sevɪ̯əl əmerɪkən fonɪtɪʃ(ə)nz tə kɑnsəntret əpɑn ðə jus əv ðɪ ælfəbet əv ðɪ a.f. ɪn fonetɪk pʌblɪkeʃ(ə)nz ənd ɪn titʃɪŋ.

ðouz əmerɪkən skɑlɪ̯s aɪ həv kənsʌltɪd bɪliv ðət ɪndɪkeʃənz əv kwɑntɪtɪ ən kwɑlətɪ ʃud bɪ kept strɪktlɪ sepɪ̯ɪt. aɪ əm grætɪfaɪd tə si ðə seɪm prɪntsəpl ædvəketɪd ɪn rɪsnt nʌmbɪ̯z əv m.f.

tu əmerɪkən fonɪtɪʃ(ə)nz həv kəmiunɪketɪd tə mi ðer [1] əpruv(ə)l əv Palmer's prəpouzd sɪmbl fɪ̯ ʌnstrest ɪ. olðou aɪ du nɑt nid ə sepɪ̯ɪt sɪmbl ɪn elementɪ̯ɪ titʃɪŋ ənd 'ɔrdɪ̯ˌerɪ trænskrɪpʃ(ə)nz, aɪ əgri wɪθ sʌm əv maɪ əmerɪkən kɑligz ðət ɪt ʃəd bɪ pɑsəbl tu ɪkspres ðə dɪstɪŋkʃ(ə)n ɪf dɪzaɪrd, ən fɪ̯ ðɪs ðə niu sɪmbl simz tə mi ə gud wən. tə dɪstɪŋgwɪʃ ðə louɪ̯ ʌnstrest ɪ frəm ðə haɪɪ̯ (hwɪtʃ ɪz kɑmən ɪn əmerɪkə) ðɪ æksent mɑrks meɪ bɪ juzd ouvɪ̯ ðə sɪmbl ðʌs : ì, í.

for əmerɪkən trænskrɪpʃ(ə)n ɪt əpɪ̯ɪrz dɪzaɪrəbl tə hæv sepɪ̯ɪt sɪmblz fɪ̯ ðə vauəlz əv *pen* ənd əv *pair*, æz wəz ðə præktɪs ɪn ðɪ ouldɪ̯ staɪl əv brɪtɪʃ trænskrɪpʃ(ə)n. ðer ɪz, aɪ bɪliv, nou dɪsəgrɪmənt ðət ðə vauəlz ɪ̯ nɑt aɪdentɪkl; bət fɪ̯ dʒenɪ̯əl əmerɪkən wi hævnt ðɪ ədvæntɪdʒ əv ðə glaɪd bɪfor r hwɪtʃ kips ɛ dɪstɪŋkt frəm ɛə. ðə glaɪd ɪz iðɪ̯ nɑt so mɑrkt, or ɪz æbsɪ̯nt ɔltəgeðɪ̯. əmerɪkənz əz ə rul du nɑt seɪ ʃɛərɪŋ, bət ʃèrɪŋ; nɑt fɛərɪ, bət fèrɪ; nɑt vɛərɪəs, bət vèrɪəs; hents ɪf ðə sɪmbl ɛ ɪz juzd ɔlsou ɪn *very*, ðer rɪzʌlts ə kənfiuʒ(ə)n ɪn trænskrɪpʃ(ə)n bɪtwin *very* ən *vary*, *merry* ən *Mary*, *ferry* ən *fairy*, *terror* ən *tearer*, əz ðeɪ ɪ̯ pr(ə)naunst baɪ lɑrdʒ nʌmbɪ̯z əv əmerɪkənz.[2] ɔl əmerɪkən fonɪtɪʃ(ə)nz, so fɑr əz aɪ nou, ən sʌm brɪtɪʃ, juz sepɪ̯ɪt sɪmblz fɪ̯ ðə vauəlz ɪn *pen* ən *pair*. tu əbvɪet ðə dɪfɪkʌltɪ ðə sɪmbl ɛ həz bɪn juzd fɪ̯ ðə vauəl ɪn *pen*, ɛ bɪŋ kept fɪ̯

---

[1] nɑt ðɪ juʒ(u)əl pr(ə)nʌntsɪeʃ(ə)n.

[2] maɪ oun pr(ə)nʌntsɪeʃ(ə)n əv ðə sekənd wə̯d ɪn ɪtʃ əv ðɪz pærz ɪz **vèˑrɪ, mɛˑrɪ, færɪ, tærɪ̯**.

ðæt ɪn *pair*. ðə sɪmbl həz faʊnd kənsɪdrəbl feɪvr̩. ɪt meɪ, ɪf wʌn tʃuzɪz, bi rɪgɑrdɪd əz ə mɑdɪfaɪd fɔrm əv ɛ, hwɪtʃ wɪl kɔz no riəl kənfɪuʒ(ə)n fr̩ ðouz hu prɪfr̩ tə juz ounlɪ ɛ.

fɔr ðə dʒenr̩əl əmerɪkən vauəl ɪn *hurt* ðə sɪmbl ɚ həz bɪn juzd.[1] ðɪs vauəl ɪz ðɪ ounlɪ junəvr̩səlɪ ɪnvr̩tɪd vauəl ɪn dʒenr̩əl əmerɪkən ɪn strɛst pəzɪʃ(ə)n. Grandgent, Krapp, Palmer, Kurath, Moore, ðə raɪtr̩, ənd ʌðr̩z hæv fɛlt ðə nid fr̩ ə defɪnɪt sɪmbl ʌðr̩ ðən ɝ fr̩ ðɪs saund. ðə prəpouzd sɪmbl, səgdʒɛstɪŋ ə saɪmltənɪəs kɑmbəneʃ(ə)n əv ə ənd r, həz bɪn faund præktɪkəlɪ jusfl. ɪt ɪz ɪmpɔrtnt tə dɪstɪŋgwɪʃ ðɪs ɪnvr̩tɪd saund entaɪrlɪ frəm ɝ; hwɛn fulɪ ɪnvr̩tɪd, ɪt ɪz ə sɪmpl vauəl, æz ɪn hɚt; hwɛn ounlɪ ðə læst part ɪz ɪnvr̩tɪd, ə wɝd laɪk *hurt* me bɪ spɛlt hɚrt. ðɪs ɪz nɑt kwaɪt ɪkspresd baɪ hɝt ɔr hɝət.

ɪntr̩ɪst ɪn ðə saɪəntɪfɪk ən præktɪkl stʌdɪ əv brɪtɪʃ ənd əmerɪkən spitʃ həz ræpɪdlɪ ɪnkrɪst ɪn əmerɪkə əv let. ðə fonetɪks sɛkʃən ən(d) ðə preznt-ɪŋglɪʃ sɛkʃən əv ðə mɑdr̩n læŋgwɪdʒ əsoʃɪeʃ(ə)n əv əmerɪkə ɑr æktɪvlɪ ɪntr̩ɪstɪd ɪn ðə sʌbdʒɪkt, ænd r̩ kənsɪdr̩ɪŋ ðə kwɛstʃən əv ə junəfɔrm ælfəbet. ɪf ðɪ ælfəbet əv ðɪ a.f. kən bɪ ədæptɪd tə ðə rɪkwaɪrmənts əv əmerɪkən pr(ə)nʌntsɪeʃ(ə)n, ɪt wɪl bɪ mɔr dʒenr̩əlɪ juzd, ən(d) wɪl gretlɪ əsɪst nɑt ounlɪ ɪn ðə prɑgres əv saundr̩ titʃɪŋ əv ɪŋglɪʃ ɪn əmerɪkə, bət ɪn ə betr̩ mɪutʃuəl ʌndr̩stændɪŋ əv brɪtɪʃ ənd əmerɪkən spitʃ.

John S. Kenyon.

[wi faɪnd ɪt dɪfɪklt tə bɪliːv ðət tuː kaɪndz əv ɛ ənd ən æ kən ɪgzɪst əz θriː sɛprɪt founiːmz ɪn enɪ læŋgwɪdʒ; ənd wi səspekt ðət ðouz əmerɪkənz hu meɪk ə dɪfrəns ɪn prənʌnsɪeɪʃn bɪtwin *very* ənd *vary* meɪk leŋθ ðə tʃiːf dɪstɪŋgwɪʃɪŋ fiːtʃə. ə sɛprɪt sɪmbl fə ðə klousə ɛ ɪz ðeəfɔ nɒt rɪkwaɪəd.—D. J.]

---

[1] ðɪz tu sɪmblz wr̩ juzd ɪn ðə raɪtr̩z *American Pronunciation*.

ə'merikn̩ 'iŋgliʃ¹

ðe 'midl̩ 'westr̩n ('dʒenr̩l̩ ə'merikn̩) 'tajp ov 'spijtʃ, 'ɛz 'hr̩d, for 'instn̩s, in *ʃi'kɔgow, 'difr̩z sow 'marktlij from *'soðr̩n *'britiʃ ðet it wud bij kon'fjuwziŋ tuw ə'tempt tr̩nskripʃn̩ wið ðe 'simbl̩z ðet hev be'kom kon'venʃn̩l̩ for ðe 'lɛtr̩.² in'sted, aj 'fɑlow ðe "'prinsipl̩z" ov ðij *'aj *'pij *'ej.

ðe 'simpl̩ 'strest 'vawl̩z ar 'najn, 'ɔl 'lɛks end 'on-'rawnded:—

    i   'pin *pin*, 'spirit *spirit*.
    e   'pen *pen*, 'merij *merry*, 'verij *very*.
    ɛ   'pɛn *pan*, 'mɛrij *marry*, 'kɛrij *carry*.
    a   'faðr̩ *father*, 'far *far*, 'bam *balm*.

---

¹ ɪn spaɪt əv ðɪ ʌnfəmɪljər əpɪərəns ov ðe trænskrɪpʃn juˑzd ɪn ðɪs aˑtɪkl, wi ɑ pʌblɪʃɪŋ ɪt æz sent tʊ ʌs baɪ ðə raɪtə, ɪksɛpt ðət wi hev prɪntɪd tʃ, dʒ wɛə hi həz juˑzd č, ǰ, sɪmblz wɪtʃ ɑ nɒt rɛkəgnaɪzd baɪ ðɪ **a.f.** wi ɑ nɒt kwaɪt klɪər æz tə ðə vælju·z əv sʌm əv ðe sɪmblz, pətɪkjʊləlɪ o ənd ʌnstrɛst e. prɪzjuˑməblɪ, ʌnstrɛst e rɛprɪzɛnts ə saʊnd əprɒksɪmeɪtɪŋ tu ə, wɪtʃ ðə raɪtə rɪgɑˑdz əz bɪlɒŋɪŋ tə ðə seɪm fɑuniˑm əz e ɪn hɪz spiˑtʃ. wi hoʊp hi wɪl ɪkspleɪn ðə vælju·z əv hɪz vauəl sɪmblz mɔˑ fʊlɪ ɪn ə fjuˑtʃə nʌmbər əv **m.f.**

² kom'pejr ðij edi'towrijl̩ 'nowt, *'em *'ef, 'dʒenjuwrij-'martʃ, 'najntijn-'twentij-'sevn̩, 'pejdʒ 'fajv; ðe 'difikl̩tij ðejr iz 'djuw 'ɔlsow tu kon'fjuwʒn̩ ov dis'tiŋktiv wið 'nɑn-dis'tiŋktiv 'fijtʃr̩z.

ɑ 'gɑt *got*, 'bɑrow *borrow*, 'bɑm *bomb*.
ɔ 'sɔft *soft*, 'sɔ *saw*, 'wɔʃ *wash*, 'wɔr *war*.
o 'son *son, sun*, 'hors *horse*, 'korn *corn*, 'morniŋ, *morning*.
u 'fut *foot*, 'puʃ *push*.
r̩ 'ʃr̩t *shirt*, 'fr̩ *fur, fir*, 'hr̩ij *hurry*.

i, e, u, end 'prɑbəblij o ar 'lowr̩ ðen in *'britiʃ, ɛnd ,o iz 'farðr̩ 'bɛk. r̩ hɛz ðe 'tip ov ðe 'toŋ 'tr̩nd 'op, 'nɑt 'totʃiŋ. ɛ, a, ɑ, ɔ ar 'lɔŋgr̩ ðn̩ ðij 'oðr̩z. in "'fajnl̩ po'ziʃn̩ en be'fowr 'vɔjst 'sɑwndz 'vawlz n̩ 'difθɔŋz ar 'lɔŋgr̩ ðn̩ befowr 'onvɔjst, end hɛv 'rajziŋ-'fɔliŋ 'stres. in 'menij 'distrikts ('sentr̩l *'ili'nɔj) a end ɑ kowin'sajd. som 'spijkr̩z dis'tiŋgwiʃ 'tuw 'kwɔnitijz ov a befowr r : 'fa:r *far*, 'ha:rd *hard*, 'ha:rdn̩ *harden*, bot 'arm *arm*, 'ʃarp *sharp*, 'gardn̩ *garden*.

ðe 'difθɔŋz hɛv ðe 'seknd 'elemn̩t 'rɛðr̩ 'tens, w wið 'lip-'rawndiŋ. ðe 'seknd 'elemn̩t iz 'lowr̩d if ðe 'fr̩st iz 'low, bot ðis ɔltr̩'nejʃn̩ iz 'nɑt dis'tinktiv. ðe di'vr̩dʒn̩s betwijn ðij 'elemn̩ts iz 'les ðn̩ in *'soðr̩n *'britiʃ, bot ðe difθɔŋgl̩ 'kɛrektr̩ iz 'wel 'markt, e'speʃlij hwen e 'vawl̩ 'fɑlowz :—

ij 'sij *see*, 'sijiŋ *seeing*.
ej 'sej *say*, 'sejiŋ *saying*.
aj 'haj *high*, 'hajr̩ *higher*.
ɔj 'bɔj *boy*, 'bɔjiʃ *boyish*.
uw 'duw *do*, 'duwiŋ *doing*.
ow 'gow *go*, 'gowiŋ *going*.
aw 'baw *bow, bough*, 'bawiŋ *bawing*.

befowr r ðe 'seknd 'elemn̩t ov 'difθɔŋz iz ijvn̩ 'mowr e'similejted tu ðe 'fr̩st, bot ðe 'tensnes 'ɛnd, in ðe 'kejs ov w, ðe 'lip-'rawndiŋ, ar 'kept. hwajl ij, ej, uw, ow befowr r hɛv ðos 'ɛktʃuwl̩ij ðe 'kɛrektr̩ ov 'lɔŋ 'tens 'vawl̩z (i:, ɛ:, u: ɔ:, 'motʃ ez in *'frentʃ), jet ðej ar ðe 'sejm 'fownijmz, end o'kejʒn̩lij (" 'kejrfl̩ 'spijtʃ ") en pr̩heps dajl'lektl̩ij, ar 'spowkn̩ wi'ðawt ðis esimi'lejʃn̩, ez 'rijl̩ 'difθɔŋz. 'sepr̩t 'simbl̩z for ðijz 'vejrjn̩ts ar nɑt 'ownlij on-'nesesr̩ij bot kon'fjuwziŋ ; ðe 'fɑlowiŋ r so'fajsez tuw 'indikejt ðe 'mɑnofθɔŋgajzd 'vɛljuw.

ijr 'stijr *steer*.
ejr 'tʃejr *chair*, 'vejrij *vary*, 'mejrij *Mary*.
ajr 'hajr *hire*.
uwr puwr *poor*.

owr　'powr *pore, pour*, 'howrs *hoarse*, 'mowrniŋ *mourning*,
　　　'wowr *wore*.

awr　'awr *our, hour*.

in 'nɛrow trn̩'skripʃn̩ :

'mɪɛɹıĭ *merry*.　　　　k'ɤʌɪn *corn*.
'mɛ́ːɹıĭ *Mary*.　　　　wɔ́ːɹ *wore*.
'mæ̀ːɹıĭ *marry*.　　　　wɒ́ːɹ *war*.

in 'menij 'onstrest si'lɛbiks ðe 'difθoŋz re'tejn ðe 'seknd 'elemn̩t : 'pitij *pity*, 'felow *fellow*, 'intuw *into*. ijvn̩ ðe 'wijkest 'silebl̩z 'prɑbeblij in 'norml̩ 'spijtʃ ('nɑt e'legrow) dis'tiŋgwiʃ 'ejt 'difrn̩t si'lɛbiks :—

i　'finiʃ *finish*, i'mr̩s *immerse*.
e　'fiʃez *fishes*, e'gow *ago*.
u　gud-'najt *good-night*.
o　on'til *until*, 'ɛno *Anna*.
r̩　'dɑktr̩ *doctor*, 'terr̩ *terror*.
l̩　'bɑtl̩ *bottle*, 'pikr̩l̩ *pickerel*.
n̩　'botn̩ *button*, 'onjn̩ *onion*.
m̩　'bɑtm̩ *bottom*.

e'moŋ ðe 'nɑn-si'lɛbiks, r iz ðe 'sejm 'sawnd ez r̩. be'twijn si'lɛbiks, e'speʃlij befowr r̩, t iz 'ofn̩ re'plejst baj e 'vojst 'flipiŋ iv ðe 'toŋ e'genst ðe 'suwpro-ɛl'vijl̩r̩ 'ridʒ (ɾ) —'nɑt dis'tiŋktiv.

'tekst

ðe 'norθ-wind n̩ ðe 'son wr̩ dis'pjuwtiŋ ez tu 'hwitʃ woz ðe 'stroŋgr̩, hwen e 'trɛvlr̩ kejm e'loŋ, 'rɛpt in e 'wɔrm 'klowk. ðej e'grijd ðet ðe 'won huw 'fr̩st mejd ðe 'trɛvlr̩ tejk 'ɔf iz 'klowk ʃud bij kn̩'sidr̩d 'stroŋgr̩ ðn̩ ðij 'oðr̩. ðen ðe 'norθ-wind 'bluw wið 'ɔl-iz 'majt, bot ðe 'mowr ij 'bluw, ðe mowr 'klowslij did ðe 'trɛvlr̩ 'fowld iz 'klowk e'rawnd im ; n̩ et 'lɛst ðe 'norθ-wind gejv 'op ðij e'temt. ðen ðe 'son 'ʃown 'awt 'wɔrmlij, end i'mijdjetlij ðe 'trɛvlr̩ tuk 'ɔf iz 'klowk ; n̩ 'sow ðe 'norθ-wind woz o'blajdʒd tu kn̩'fes ðet ðe 'son woz ðe stroŋgr̩ ov ðe 'tuw.

LEONARD. BLOOMFIELD.

ðə sʌðən əmɛrəkən drɔl

(ɑːtɪkl̩ trænskraɪbd ɪn stændəd sʌðən əmɛrəkən ɪŋglɪʃ)

sʌðən əmɛrəkən ɪŋglɪʃ ɪz kærɪktəraɪzd baɪ ʍat ɪz kɔld ðə sʌðən drɔl. oʊnlɪ ə rɛlətɪvlɪ smɔl nʌmbər əv sʌðənəz juz ðə drɔl, bət sɪmts nʌθɪŋ prɪsaɪslɪ laɪk ɪt ɪz noʊn ɛlsʍɛə, ɪt ɪz pɑpjʊləlɪ rɪgɑːdɪd əz tɪpɪkəl sʌðən spitʃ. ðə drɔl ɪz nɑt mɪəlɪ ə mænərɪzm̩ əv ʌtərənts ʍɛəbaɪ æksɛntɪd vauəlz ɑ gɪvən ʌnjuʒuəl djureɪʃən, æz sʌm tokɪŋ pɪktʃər æktəz əpɪə tə θɪŋk; ɪt ɪz ræðər ə sɪstəm əv dɪfθoŋaɪzeɪʃən, trɪfθoŋaɪzeɪʃən ænd:ʌbəl dɪfθoŋaɪzeɪʃən, æfɛktɪŋ vauəlz ɪn ə weɪ prɛzn̩tlɪ tə bi dɪskraɪbd.

tʊ(w) ʌndəstænd ðɪz fɪnɑmənə, wi mʌst rɪkɔl ðæt ɪn ɔl ɪŋglɪʃ spitʃ ɛnɪ vauəl əv kənsɪdərəbl̩ djureɪʃən tɛndz tə dɪfθoŋaɪz, æt list:ə ðɪ ɪkstɛnt əv ən ɔn-glaɪd ɔr ən ɔf-glaɪd. eɪ ænd oʊ ɑr autstændɪŋ ɪgzæmpl̩z, bət ðɛr ɑr ɔlso ɪu, ju, jɜ, ɑɛ, ɪə, oə, ɔə, iː, uʊ, ænd mɛnɪ ʌðəz. ðə sʌðən spitʃ, sɔft, loʊ-pɪtʃt, læŋgwɪd, spoʊkən wɪð lɪps, tʌŋ ænd toʊtl̩ voʊkl̩ mʌskjulətjuə lækɪŋ ɪn toʊnəs, ɪz pətɪkjuləlɪ laɪklɪ tʊ(w) ɪgzɪbɪt ðɪz ænd ivən moə fæntæstɪk fɪnɑmənə. ivən so stɛɪbl̩ ə vauəl æz ɔ ɪz, ɪn ðə spitʃ əv mɛnɪ sʌðənəz, oo, æz ɪn hɔok (*hawk*).

ɪn ðɪ ʌltəmət vəgeɪrɪz əv ðə sʌðən drɔl, ðə frʌnt vauəlz dəvɛləp ðə sɛmɪ-vauəl glaɪd j ɪn ðə sɛntər əv ðɛə prolɪfɪk grʊps, ænd ðə bæk vauəlz ðə sɛmɪ-vauəl glaɪd w. ðɪs ɪz, əv kɔəs, ðə fonɛtɪk kɑnsɪkwɛnts əv ðə frʌnt vauəlz ɪn ɪŋglɪʃ bɪɪŋ ʌnraʊnd, ænd moʊst əv ðə bæk vauəlz æt list:ə sʌm dɪgri raʊnd.

    æ, ðɛn, dəvɛləps j ænd bɪkʌmz æjə ɔr æɪjə, æz ɪn **klæjəs** ɔ **klæɪjəs** (*class*).

    ɛ dəvɛləps j ænd bɪkʌmz ɛjə ɔr ɛɪjə æz ɪn **gɛjəs** ɔ **gɛɪjəs** (*guess*).

    ɪ dəvɛləps j ænd bɪkʌmz ɪjə, æz ɪn **bɪjət** (*bit*).

    ɔ dəvɛləps w ænd bɪkʌmz ɔwə, æz ɪn **ɔwət** (*ought*).

    ʊ dəvɛləps w ænd bɪkʌmz ʊwə, æz ɪn **gʊwəd** (*good*).

    u dəvɛləps w ænd bɪkʌmz uwə, æz ɪn **kjuwət** (*cute*).

ðə fɑlo(w)ɪŋ sɛntənts ʃoʊz, ɪn sʌmʍɑt ɪgzædʒəreɪtɪd fɔːm, ðə dɪgri tʊ ʍɪtʃ ə sɪŋgəl vauəl me dəvɛləp wʌn, tu ɔ θri sætəlaɪts: ɪz ðæɪjət kjuət lɪtəl flɜɪt ɪn ðɪjəs klæɪjəs?[1]

eɪ ænd oʊ, bɪɪŋ ɔlrɛdɪ dɪfθoŋz, du nɑt dʒoɪn ɪn ðɪs founoladʒɪkl̩ fɛkʌndətrɪ, bʌt ðə sɛntrəl vauəlz du, ʌ bɪkʌmɪŋ ʌə ænd ɜ bɪkʌmɪŋ ɜɪ, æzɪn kʌət (*cut*) ænd bɜɪd (*bird*). ɑ goʊz noʊ fɑːðə ðæn tə bɪkʌm ɑə.

---

[1] *Is that cute little flirt in this class?*

71

ɪt mʌst nɑt bi θɔt ðæt ðiz ɪkstrim fɔːmz me bi hɜːd ɪn ðə spitʃ əv ɛvrɪ sʌðənə hu drɔlz, ɔ ðæt ɛnɪ pɜːsən əv drɔlɪŋ spitʃ juzɪz ðəm kənsɪstəntlɪ. bʌt ɔl ðiz fɔːmz ɑr ɛkstənt, ænd ðe me bi sɛd tə kɑnstətjut kəlɛktɪvlɪ ðə *sɪnɛ kwɑ nɔn* əv ðə sʌðən drɔl.

C. M. WISE.

spesimen

daɪəlɛkt əv *'mɔbætl

(*Morebattle*, nɔθ ist *rɒksbərəʃaɪə, skɒtlənd)

[i ɪz vɛrɪ klous, bʌt ʌnstrɛst i = i̯.

ɪ ɪz kənsɪdrəblɪ louəd. ɑ meɪ bi ɑ (əbaut kɑdŋəl) ɔr ɒ. u ɪz slaɪtlɪ ədvɑnst. ə bɪfɔr r ɪz ədvɑnst, bɪkʌmɪŋ ə rɪtræktɪd ɪ̯.

i̇ ɪz ə læks klous sɛntrəl vauəl. ë hæz ə slaɪtlɪ louə tʌŋ pəzɪʃn ðən i̇.

brɛθt plousɪvz ər ʌnæspɪreɪtɪd. t ənd d bɪfɔr r ɔr ər ɑ dɛntl. l ɪz dɑk. x ɪz əkʌmpənɪd baɪ strɒŋ prougrɛsɪv leɪbjəlaɪzeɪʃn, sou ðət ɪt saundz rɑðə laɪk xʍ.]

ðə nɔrθ wʌnd ən ðə sʌn

'jæː 'deː, əz ə 'trɛvlər wəz 'gɑːn ə'lʌŋ ðə 'rod, ðə 'nɔrθ wʌnd n ðə 'sʌn kɪ̇st 'ut [1] əz tə 'ʍʌtʃ ə ðə 'pæːr wəz ðə 'strɒŋəst, ən æftər

---

[1] fɛl aut.

ə 'lɑːŋ 'ɑrgi ðə 'griːd ðət ðə 'jɪn ðət 'gɑːrd¹ ðə 'trevlər tek 'of ɪz 'kot ðə 'sɪnəst wəd bi ðə 'stroŋəst. ðə 'wʌnd 'tʃasit² θə 'fʌrst 'ʃot; ən əz ðə 'norθ wʌnd z ðə mest 'bʌustrəs o 'ɑː ðə 'wʌndz ɪt 'θʌut ɪt 'wʌdnə bɪ laŋ ə 'strɪpn ðə 'mɑn o ɪz 'kot. so ɪt brɪ'gud tə 'blɑː, bət θo ɪt 'bliu, ən 'bliu, ən 'bætər 'bliu, ɪt 'wʌzni ə bɪt ə 'jës, fər ðə 'ludər ɪt 'huld, ən ðə 'kɑːldər ɪt 'tʌrnt, ðə 'tәitər ðə 'trevlər pud ɪz 'kot rund ə'but ɪm, ən ðə 'klosər i 'kuːrd 'ɪntɪlt.³ so ʍæn ɪt əd 'blɑːn ɪtsæl 'klin ut ə 'breθ, ðə 'wʌnd həd tə 'giː ɪn ðət ɪt wəz 'feːr 'bet.⁴ ðæn ðə 'sʌn krap 'ut frə 'hɪnt ə 'klʌd,⁵ ən ɪt 'bikɪt⁶ ən 'bikɪt, 'stræit dun ən ðə 'trevlər so ðət ɪn ə 'wiː ʍәili hi 'hɑd tə 'lʌuz ðə 'bʌtnz o ɪz 'dʒækɪt. or 'laŋ, hi wəz 'swɪtn ləik ə 'pʌuni,⁷ ən ðə 'hætər ðə sʌn 'blizd dun, hi 'swɑt ðə 'seːrər. ənd ɪ ðə 'finɪʃ hi wəz 'glæd ɪ'njux tə 'kɑst ɪz 'kot 'ɑːðəgɪðər, ən 'hoɪ⁸ ə'laŋ ɪn ɪz 'særk⁹ sliːvz. so ðər wəz 'neθɪŋ æls 'for ɪ̯, bət fər ðə 'wʌnd tə 'ʌun ʌp ðət ðə 'sʌn wəz ðə 'stroŋəst ə ðə 'tweː.

trænskrɑɪbd bɑɪ J. C. Catford.

¹ meɪd.   ² tʃouz ə kleɪmd.   ³ kɑuəd ɪntʉ ɪt.
⁴ kwɑɪt bɪtn.   ⁵ krɛpt ɑut frəm bɪhɑɪnd ə klɑud.
⁶ beɪkt.   ⁷ swɛtɪŋ lɑɪk ə pounɪ.   ⁸ gou.   ⁹ ʃət.

spesimɛn

iˑst dɛvn daɪəlɛkt

ðə fɒloɪŋ spɛsɪmən ɪz ə rɛkɔd əv ə riːdɪŋ baɪ ə rɛzɪdnt əv *ɛksɪtə (ɛksëd̥əɪ).

ɹ ɪz fulɪ rɪtroʊflɛkst ; e ənd ɛ ə mɔˑr oʊpən ðən kɑːdɪnl ; æ ɪz mɔˑr oʊpən ðən ɪn saʊθ-iˑstən ɪŋglɪʃ ; a ɪz rɑːðə rɪtræktɪd ; ɑː hæz ɪts nɔːml pəzɪʃn ɪn saʊθ-iˑstən ɪŋglɪʃ ; ɒ ɪz ədvɑˑnst ən reɪzd ; ø ənd ʏ ər rɪtræktɪd.

ðə ˈnoˑɹɠ ˈwiːnd ən ðə ˈz̥ɒn wəɹ dës'pøɪtën 'wëtʃ wëz ðə ˈstrɑːŋgəɪ wɛn ə ˈtræːvləɪ ɠeːm əˈlaːŋ ˈɹæˑpt iːn ə ˈwoːɪm ˈklok. ðeː əˈɡɹëɪd ðət ðə ˈwɒːn øʏ ˈvɜɪst ˈmeːd ðə ˈtræːvləɪ teˑɠ ˈɑˑʏ iːz ˈklok, ʒøˑd bi kənˈzëdəɹd ˈstrɑːŋgəɪ ðən ð ˈɒðəɪ. ˈðeːn ðə ˈnoˑɹɠ ˈwiːnd ˈbløʏ wëð ˈɔˑl iːz ˈmæːët, bət ðə ˈmoəɹ iː ˈbløʏ ðə ˈmoəɹ ˈklosllë dëd ðə ˈtræːvləɪ ˈfoˑld iːz ˈklok əˈrɛʏnd ëm, ənd ət ˈlaːst ðə ˈnoˑɹɠ ˈwiːnd ɡeˑv ˈɒp ð əˈtɛmt. ˈðɛn ðə ˈz̥ɒn ˈʒaːn ˈɛʏt ˈwoːɪmlë, ənd ëˈmiːdʒətlë ðə ˈtræːvləɪ tøɠ ˈɑˑʏ iːz ˈklok. ən ˈz̥oː ðə ˈnoˑɹɠ ˈwiːnd wëz əˈblæːëdʒd tə ɠənˈfɛs ðət ðə ˌz̥ɒn wëz ðə ˈstrɑːŋgəɹ əv ðə ˈtøʏ.

R. KINGDON.

ʌ ənd ə in britiʃ iŋgliʃ

it dʌznt siːm tə bi dʒenrəli noun ðət ə greit meni piːpl in ðə noːθ əv iŋglənd duː not meik eni distiŋkʃən korispondiŋ tə ðat meid in ðə sauθ bitwiːn ʌ ənd ə. weər ə lʌndənə wud sei ˈkʌm ˈʌp ət ˈwʌns, meni (pəhaps moust) noːðənəz wud sei ˈkəm ˈəp ət ˈwəns.

auə koliːg G. H. Richardson əv Newcastle-on-Tyne, həz riːsntli ritn tə miː əz folouz (hiː rout in simplifaid speliŋ, ənd ai hiə transkraib hiz wəːdz intu auə nouteiʃn, juːziŋ haueve ə weər ai ʃud prənauns ʌ). "rifəːriŋ tu m.f., nəmbə 84, p. 24, 25 ' broːd tranˈskripʃn ənd ðə 'taip-raitər', ai həv nevə jet bin eibl tu pəsiːv eni difrəns bitwiːn ðə tuː vauəlz in, fər instəns, *udher*, *uter*,[1] iksept ðət ðə fəːst iz strest ənd ðə sekənd ˈənstrest. if wiː aː tu maːk ðə stres, ðən ðeər iz nou niːd tu juːz difrənt vauəl letəz ; wiː kən ridjuːs ði alfəbet bai ˈwən. hens ai wud rait ðiːz' wəːdz on ðə taip-raitə *cdhc*, *ctc*, ənd əvoid ðə *q*."

ðə fakt ðət miljənz əv iŋgliʃ spiːkəz duː not distiŋgwiʃ ʌ from ə dizəːvz moː noutis ðən it həz hiðətuː risiːvd. it iz temptiŋ tə θiŋk ðət bai ignoːriŋ ðis distiŋkʃən ðə forin ləːnə wud bi riliːvd əv wʌn əv hiz meidʒə difikəltiz wiðaut impeəriŋ ði intelidʒəbiliti əv hiz prənʌnsieiʃn.

it wud bi intristiŋ if ʌðə koliːgz huː meik nou distiŋkʃən bitwiːn ʌ ənd ə, oː huː ə fəmiljə wið ðis wei əv spiːkiŋ, wud giv ðeə vjuːz on ðə sʌbdʒikt.

D. J.

---

[1] ðə " njuː speliŋ " foːmz əv *other*, *utter*.

kɔrɛspɔ̃dã:s
ʌ ənd ə in iŋgliʃ [1]

əz ə nɔːðənə, ai əm əweər əv ðə juːs əv ə weə sʌðən iŋgliʃ piːpl sei ʌ. ai dount duː ðis maiself, ðou sevrəl membəz əv mai fæmili duː. in mai ikspiəriəns, ai həv faund ðət nɔːðənəz wið ə prənaunst daiəlekt spiːtʃ, hu əv biːn əkʌstəmd tə juːziŋ u in wəːdz laik *but*, wen ðei trai tə " kərekt " ðis tɔːdz ðə sʌðən ʌ, feil tə riːtʃ ði oupən pəziʃn əv ʌ əz ðis prənʌnsieiʃn *fiːlz* ən saundz tə ðeər iəz tuː mʌtʃ laik ɑː. kɔnsikwəntli ðei gou tɔːdz ə sentrəl vauəl pəziʃn, i.e. sʌm kaind əv ə. ðis gets rid əv ðə " brɔːd " u ənd iz inʌf tə meik ə kliə difrəns bitwiːn ðə vauəlz in *but* ənd *put*.

IDA C. WARD.

ai əm 'veri fə'miljə wið 'taips əv 'nɔːðən 'iŋgliʃ witʃ 'duː not dis'tiŋgwiʃ ə ənd ʌ, ənd ai həv 'həːd 'taips əv ə'merikən 'iŋgliʃ witʃ 'duː not 'duː sou. ðə dis'tiŋkʃn iz 'not 'meid, in 'fakt, in 'sevrəl 'sistəmz əv fə'netik trans'kripʃn, ə pə'tikjuləli 'intrəstiŋ ig'zaːmpl biːŋ ðə nou'teiʃn 'pʌbliʃt in Philadelphia, in 1793, bai WILLIAM THORNTON (1759-1828). hiː trans'kraibd, fər 'instəns, *sun* **sən**, *come* **kəm**, *majesty* **madʒəsti**, *seizure* **siiʒər** (ai ri'tein hiz 'simblz). it iz 'difiklt tə 'ges 'wot 'taip əv 'iŋgliʃ THORNTON 'spouk, fə hiː wəz 'bɔːn in ðə West Indies əv 'iŋgliʃ 'peərənts, 'tuk iz di'griː (in 'medsən) ət Aberdeen, ənd aːftə 'travliŋ in Europe 'setld in America, weər iː 'livd 'moust əv iz 'laif. hi 'woz, insi'dentli, ə 'moust ri'maːkəbl 'man — hiː wəz 'dɔktə, 'aːkitekt, 'taun-'planə, 'peintər, ənd in'ventə, əz 'wel əz ə 'gud founə'tiʃn ənd ðə 'fəːst in America tə 'rait on ðə tek'niːk əv 'tiːtʃiŋ ðə 'def tə 'spiːk. ə kən'tempərəri dis'kraibd im əz " ə 'skolər ənd ə 'dʒentlmən, 'ful əv 'talənt ənd eksən'trisiti ".

HENRY SWEET sez (*Handbook of Phonetics*, p. 175) ðət it wəz J. A. SCHMELLER huː 'fəːst 'juːzd ə in ðə 'sens 'nau sou fə'miljə tu 'ɔːl fi'lɔlədʒists ən founə'tiʃnz. SCHMELLER, hau'evə, 'rout in 1821, ən THORNTON iz kən'sidrəbli 'əːliə ðən 'ðat. 'probəbli ðə 'fəːst ə'piərəns əv ðə 'simbl in England wəz in 1814, in ə 'hostail ən 'fuːliʃ 'noutis əv THORNTON'z 'wəːk in ðə *Quarterly Review*, in witʃ 'meni 'diːteilz əv iz trans'kripʃn aː 'rɔŋli 'givn, bət ə iz pri'zəːvd.

D. ABERCROMBIE.

---

[1] siː **m.f.** dʒanjuəri 1946, p. 2.

ðə fənetik sistəm əv ə daːəlekt əv Newcastle-upon-Tyne.

ðə spiːtʃ hiə rikoːdid iz ðat əv boiz bitwiːn ði eidʒiz əv twelv n̩ eitiːn jiəz in ðə distrikts əv Benwell ən Elswick (elzik), Newcastle-upon-Tyne. it oːlmous səːtnli haz ə waidə kʌrn̩si ɔn ðis, bət az ðiːz nouts wə meid əʔ ðə Grainger Park Boys' Club, ən ðeər ounli, ai m not in ə pəziʃn tə pontifikeit əbaut its probəbḷ ekstent. praps ʌðə membəz əd keə tə giv ðeə vjuːz on ðis point.

ðər əpiə tə bi twenti wʌn vaːəl founiːmz in ðə spiːtʃ əv ðiːz boiz. twelv pjuə vaːəlz—i ɩ e: ɛ a(ː) ɑː ɔ ɔː ɷ u ə ɐ, ən nain difθoŋz— ei ɛi ɔi ou əu eə ɛə iɐ uɐ.

i ən ɑː ər əproksimətli kaːdnḷ.

ɩ iz ə ritraktid frʌnʔ vaːəl midwei bitwiːn ouʔmn ən tlous.

eː iz ə frʌnʔ vaːəl midwei bitwiːn ouʔmn ən tlous.

ɛ ənd ɔː ə slaitli moːr ouʔm ðən kaːdnḷ.

a(ː) iz niərə tə kaːdnḷ a ðn kaːdnḷ ɑ.

ɔ iz frʌntid n̩ moːr ouʔm ðən kaːdnḷ.

ɷ iz frʌntid n̩ ə litl moːr ouʔm ðən haːf tlous, wið feəli tlous lip raundiŋ.

u iz distiŋtli frʌntid, sʌmtaimz kwait sentrəl.

ə iz haːf tlous oː slaitli əbʌv.

ɐ iz ə veri ritraktid ʌnraundid vaːəl, midwei bitwiːn ouʔmn ən haːf ouʔm.

oːl ðə difθoŋz ə foːliŋ difθoŋz—

ei, frəm kaːdnl ə tu i.

əu, ðə fəːst eləmənt iz moːr ouʔm ðən ðə pjuə vaːəl.

eə, frəm tlousə ðn kaːdnl ə tu ə.

ɛə, meinli ə lip difθoŋ, wið ə slait louəriŋ əv ðə tʌŋ fə ðə seknd eləmənt ; dʒenrəli ridjuːst tu ə in ʌnstrest pəziʃnz.

ðə rimeiniŋ difθoŋz ə self-eksplanətri.

vaːəl leŋθ iz ekstriːmli veəriəbl. ounli eː, ɑː ənd ɔː ər oːlwiz loŋ, bət eni vaːəl mei bi meid fuḷi loŋ in ə strest pəziʃn foloud bai ə voist konsənənt.

oːlðou ðər ə twenti wʌn vaːəl founiːmz, ðə rileiʃn bitwiːn ðiːz n ðouz əv edjəkeitid sʌðn̩ iŋgliʃ iz natʃərəli not on ə wʌn tə wʌn beisis ; fər egzaːmpl, sʌðn̩ iŋgliʃ oː mei bi *tainsaid oː, ou oːr aː, əz in koːn, θout, waːk ; weəraz *tainsaid oː mei bi sʌðn̩ iŋgliʃ oː, əː oːr oə, əz in pəː, poː, poə (*pore*), ən sou on.

ðə konsənənts biheiv laik ðeə sʌðn̩ iŋgliʃ kauntəpaːts wið ðə folouiŋ eksepʃnz—

ʔ mei bi sʌbstitjuːtid fər ʌnstrest p, t ən k (mous komənli fə t) ;

ʔ veri ofn priːsiːdz ðiːz saunz, noutəbli bitwiːn vaːəlz, ənd in ðis ivent p, t, k aː veri wiːk b̥, d̥, ɡ̊.

tʃ, dʒ ə truː afrikəts in oːl pəziʃnz.

l iz moːr ə les kliər in oːl pəziʃnz.

m, n, ŋ ər veri ʃoːt, eksept wen leŋθnd signifikəntli. kp. kɔm (kʌm), kɔmm (kʌmiŋ). ai v həːd gann nʔ ðə klɔːb, wið ə tripl leŋθ n, miːniŋ "gouiŋ intə ðə klʌb".

ðə folouiŋ iz ə spesimən traːnskripʃn.

ðə wəz ə 'fɛlɐ keəm 'ɔp tə njəˈkasəl ə 'kɔʔpəl ə 'jeːz bak, ən i 'θɔut ðə 'tɛinsɛid 'taːk wəz 'riʔ 'kani, sɐ i 'staːʔs 'trɛiən ʔtə 'taːʔk əd̥ ɪsˈsɛːl. i 'gaːnz əˈbuʔt ɔn 'bɔsəz n̩ 'kaːz ən i 'hiɐz piːʔpəl 'askən ʔfə 'sɔmɪk kaːld ə 'pɛni 'haːf. i θɪŋʔs 'ðɪs əz ðə weə ʔtə 'ask fər ə θriˈhaʔpni 'feː, sɐ i 'rɛiʔs əʔ 'dun ɪn ɪz 'lɪʔl 'buk ən 'gɪz ɪssəl ə 'paʔt ɔn ðə 'bak fə 'biˑən sɐ 'klɛvɐ. 'woːn ˌfrɛidn̩'it i wəz 'gann ʔ ðə 'pɪtʃɐz wɪð ɪz 'anʔti ðəʔt i z 'stɛˑən wɪð, ən 'wen ðə 'las kɔmz fə ðə 'feːz i asks fə 'təu 'pɛni 'haːvz ɪn ɪz 'bɛs 'tɛinsɛid 'stɛil. ðə 'las 'lɔʔks ad̥ 'əm, ən ɪz 'anʔti lɔʔks ad̥ əm, ən ðə 'beəð 'boːst uʔ 'lafn. 'əʔ ðə 'funəʃ ðə las 'seəz tu əm — "'weː z jɐ ʃoːt 'truzɐz, hɪni?" "a dɪvn naˑ woʔ jɐ 'taːʔkn əbut," i seəz. "'wɛi, man," ʃə seəz, "jə v gɔd̥ ə bi 'ɔndɐ 'twɛˑlv ʔtə hav ə 'haːf 'feː." ət 'toːnz 'uʔ, jə sei, ðəd̥ ə 'pɛni 'haːf s 'haːf ə 'tɔʔpni feː, sɐ i 'gaːnz 'bak tu ɪz 'kɔlər ən 'kɔfs taːʔk ən 'liːvz 'tɛinsɛid ʔtə ðə 'dʒɔːdiz.

J. D. O'Connor.

ə skotiʃ vauəl

in ðə spiːtʃ əv meni spiːkəz əv " edjukeitid " oː " pəlait " skots, ə vauəl founiːm iz tə bi faund witʃ dʌznt siːm tu əv bin noutist ʌp tə nau bai founitiʃnz (mai ətenʃən wəz fəːst droːn tu it bai Mr. A. J. AITKEN, əsistnt editər əv ðə *Dictionary of the Older Scottish Tongue*). ðis vauəl mei moust tipikəli bi həːd in ðə fəːst siləbl əv ðə wəːd *never*, bət it əkəːz in ə nʌmbər əv ʌðə wəːdz oːlsou. it iz not iksplikəbl əz ən aləfoun əv eni ʌðə vauəl founiːm in edjukeitid skots. its distribjuːʃn iz, nevəðəles, kjuəriəsli ristriktid (witʃ mei bi wai it həz iskeipt noutis fə sou loŋ).

ðə kwoliti əv ðis vauəl is juːʒuəli əbaut haːf wei bitwiːn kaːdnəl vauəlz 2 ən 3, ənd its kənsidrəbli sentrəlaizd. ðə lips ə njuːtrəl. it veəriz, əv koːs, frəm spiːkə tə spiːkə, əz duː oːl ðə vauəlz əv edjukeitid skots ; it s ofn indistiŋgwiʃəbl frəm ðə saund juːzd bai meni iŋgliʃ piːpl— maiself, fər instəns—in ðis seim wəːd *never* (witʃ iz posəbli ənʌðə riːzn wai it əz iskeipt noutis). it iz, hauevə, kept distiŋkt bai skots spiːkəz frəm ðə vauəl in ðə fəːst siləbl ov, fər igzaːmpl, *sever*, witʃ iz ə fuli frʌnt vauəl ən klous tə kaːdnəl 3. *never* ən *sever* duː not, ðeəfoː, prəvaid ə raim. its oːlsou kept distiŋkt frəm ðə vauəl in ðə fəːst siləbl əv *shiver*, witʃ ðou iːkwəli sentrəlaizd iz oːlwiz mʌtʃ haiə. ðə praktis ət preznt in ðə fənetiks dipaːtmənt ət Edinburgh iz tə transkraib ðis " njuː " vauəl founiːm bai ðə simbl ɛ̈. it həz sou faː bin aidentifaid ounli in strest siləblz.

ðə folouiŋ ə sʌm əv ðə wəːdz in witʃ ðə vauəl iz komənli həːd : *seven, seventy, eleven, twenty, ever, never, every, heaven, devil, next, together, shepherd, earth, McKenzie*. it s faund spəradikli in ə laːdʒ nʌmbər əv ʌðə wəːdz (in meni əv witʃ, əz in meni əv ðə prisiːdiŋ list, it s foloud bai ðə konsnənt v). its distribjuːʃn veəriz wið difrənt spiːkəz, ənd it s posəbl ðət ðis həz ə riːdʒnəl beisis. ði ːziːist wei əv testiŋ fər its əkʌrns in ə givn wəːd iz bai miːnz əv posəbl raimiŋ peəz ; ðʌs *heaven* kən bi testid bai *leaven*, *next* bai *vexed*, *shepherd* bai *leopard*, *earth* bai *berth*, ən sou on. if ðə wəːdz in iːtʃ peə duː not raim, ɛ̈ mei bi prizjuːmd tu əkəːr in ðə fəːst wəːd, sins *leaven, vexed, leopard, berth* siːm oːlwiz tə hav ɛ. (it s wəːθ noutiŋ ðət ə spiːkə huː həz ɛ̈ in *earth* veri probəbli ðeəfoː həz foːr ikwivələnts for R.P. əː—*birth, earth, berth, worth* mei oːl kəntein difrənt vauəlz.) ə " miniml peə " iz prəvaidid, fə sʌm spiːkəz, bai ðə wəːdz *bury* bɛ̈re ənd *berry* bɛre.

it iz not sou faː noun wot prəpoːʃn əv edjukeitid skots spiːkəz hav ðis fouɲiːm in ðeə vauəl sistəm ; səːtnli ə laːdʒ nʌmbər, ən pəhaps ə mədʒorəti, hav. it s intrəstiŋ ðət, oːlðou it s not əparntli bin menʃənd bifoːr in diskripʃənz əv skots, meni spiːkəz ər əweər əv its igzistns. ðʌs ə koliːg əv main, on biːŋ aːskt hau iː prənaunst ðə wəːd *never* (wiðaut biːŋ tould ðə pəːpəs əv ðə kwestʃən), aːnsəd "n**ĕ**vər", ənd adid "bət wiː had ə boi ət skuːl huː juːst tə sei n**ɛ**vər". ʌðə piːpl əv tould mi ðət ðei wə tould ət skuːl tə stop juːziŋ **ɛ̈**. stil ʌðəz əv sed ðət ðei faind ðə juːs əv ɛ fə ɛ̈ əfensiv ənd əfektid.

David Abercrombie.

ðə glɔtḷaizeiʃn əv vɔislis plousivz in * lʌndən spiːtʃ

ðə siŋkrɔnik ɑːtikjuleiʃn əv ðə glɔtḷ plousiv, ʔ, wið ði ʌðə vɔislis plousivz, **p, t, k,** wen ðei əkəːr in səːtn pəziʃnz, iz dʒenrəl in kɔkni spiːtʃ. ðə siŋkrɔnik ɑːtikjuleiʃn iz rifəːd tuː əz ðə "glɔtḷaizeiʃn əv ðə **p, t** ɔː **k**", ənd iz ritn **p̣ʔ, ṭʔ** ɔː **ḳʔ**. ðə "səːtn pəziʃnz" kən bi diskraibd dʒenrəli əz "siləbl-fainḷ" pəziʃnz.

in sʌm fənetik kɔnteksts ði ifekt əv ðə glɔtḷ plousiv iz ɔbviəs, iː dʒiː ˈpep̣ʔə, ˈbeṭʔə, ˈpeḳʔə (*pepper, better, pecker*). in ʌðə kɔnteksts it iz les noutisəbl; ənd in sʌm kɔnteksts ði ifekt iz sou slait əz tu əv ɔːlmoust iskeipt rekəgniʃn ɔːltəgeðə. in kɔnteksts əv ðə lɑːst kætigri ðə glɔtḷaizd plousiv iz juːzd bai meni huː mait bi sed tə spiːk wið RP iː dʒiː ˈðæṭʔ ˈtaim, ˈskræp̣ʔpeipə, ˈheip̣ʔni, ˈkʌp̣ʔtai ˈfuṭʔbɔːl mæṭʔʃ (*that time, scrap-paper, halfpenny, cuptie football match*).

in intəvoukælik pəziʃnz, if ðə prisiːdiŋ vauəl iz nɔt ounli strɔŋli strest bət ɔːlsou lɔŋ ɔː difθɔŋgəl, ðə stɔp əv ðə glɔtḷ plousiv iz leŋθnd bai sʌm kɔkniz tə prədjuːs ði ifekt əv ə dʌbld plousiv. iː dʒiː, ə mæn huː sez ˈkɔp̣ʔə (*copper*) mei sei ˈkeip̣ʔʔə (*caper*), ˈkeiṭʔʔə (*cater*), beiḳʔʔə (*baker*), ˈθəːṭʔʔi (*thirty*).

in wəːdz weər RP hæz **p̣r, ṭr, ḳr** ɑːftər ə strɔŋli strest vauəl ðə stɔp əv **p, t** ɔː **k** iz ɔfn leŋθnd tə prədjuːs ði ifekt əv ə dʌbld plousiv:— ˈeip̣ʔp̣rən (*apron*), ˈpæṭʔṭriəṭʔ (*patriot*), ˈsæḳʔḳrifais (*sacrifice*). it kən bi sed ðət hiə wʌn siləbl endz wið **p̣ʔ, ṭʔ** ɔː **ḳʔ** ən ðə nekst biginz wið **p̣r, ṭr** ɔː **ḳr**, ði r biːiŋ ʌnvɔist. if ðə **p, t** ɔː **k** stɔp iz nɔt leŋθnd ði r iz fuli vɔist; ənd in ðis keis it kən bi sed ðət wʌn siləbl endz wið **p̣ʔ, ṭʔ** ɔː **ḳʔ** ən ðə nekst biginz wið fuli vɔist r. ðʌs, if ði RP əv *sacrifice* bi ritn ˈsækrifais, ðə kɔkni prənʌnsieiʃn iz aiðə ˈsæḳʔrifais ɔː ˈsæḳʔḳrifais. ðə lɑːst prənʌnsieiʃn iz ɔfn həːd in ðə spiːtʃ əv weledjukeitid pəːsnz.

in sʌm wəːdz bouθ ðə dʌbliŋ ən ðə glɔtḷaizeiʃn ə juːzd bifɔːr r bitwiːn tuː wiːkli strest siləblz:— ˈlævəṭʔṭri (*lavatory*), ˈmimiḳʔḳri (*mimicry*). wen ə neizl kɔnsənənt ɔːr l intəviːnz bitwiːn ðə vauəl ən ðə plousiv ðə glɔtḷaizeiʃn ən ðə dʌbliŋ ər ɔfn bouθ riteind:— ˈpænṭʔṭri (*pantry*), ˈkʌlp̣ʔp̣riṭʔ (*culprit*).

wen **p** ɔː **k** iz fɔloud bai l ði ifekt iz similə tə ðæt prədjuːst bai ə fɔlouiŋ r, iː dʒiː *Poplar, buckler* kən bi ˈpɔp̣ʔpḷə, ˈbʌḳʔkḷə ɔː ˈpɔp̣ʔlə, ˈbʌḳʔlə. bət wen t iz fɔloud bai l nou dʌbliŋ əkəːz, iː dʒiː *settler, butler,* ə ˈseṭʔlə, ˈbʌṭʔlə, ən seldəm prənaunst wið **ṭʔṭḷ**. ðə difrəns bitwiːn kʌp̣ʔpḷə, bʌḳʔkḷə ɔn ðə wʌn hænd ən bʌṭʔlə ɔn ði ʌðə hænd iz prizjuːməbli rileitid tə ðə fækt ðət wail iniʃl pḷ ən kḷ ə fəmiljər in iŋgliʃ iniʃl tḷ iz nɔt.

similə glɔtḷaizeiʃn ən dʌbliŋ ə həːd bifɔː w ən j :—ˈmɑːkʔkwis (*marquis*), ˈpɔpʔpjələ (*popular*). wen t iz fɔloud bai j ə similər ifekt iz prədjuːst; bət ðə tʃ bikʌmz tʃ ən ðə tʔ, frəm biːiŋ ə glɔtḷaizd ælvioulə t, bikʌmz ðə glɔtḷaizd fɔːm əv ðə stɔp əv ði æfrikit tʃ :— *spatula* (ˈspætʔtjələ), ˈspætʔtʃələ. similə prənʌnsieiʃnz ə həːd in ʌðə wəːdz weər RP hæz tʃ, iː dʒi: ˈbætʔtʃələ (*bachelor*), ˈtiːtʔtʃə (*teacher*).

in wəːdz weər RP hæz ðə siːkwəns neizl kɔnsənənt, vɔislis frikətiv, fɔlouiŋ ə strɔŋli ɔː wiːkli strest vauəl, bət nɔt prisiːdiŋ ə strɔŋli strest vauəl, ə glɔtḷaizd plousiv iz insəːtid bitwiːn ðə neizl kɔnsənənt ən ðə frikətiv :—wʌntʔs (*once*), ˈkɔntʔstəntʔs (*Constance*), ˈplimpʔsəlz (*plimsolls*), ˈjʌŋkʔstə (*youngster*), ˈsevəntʔθ (*seventh*), ˈkæmpʔfə (*camphor*), ˈleŋkʔθ (*length*). in *twopence, threepence, fourpence*, ði ntʔs ɔfn bikʌmz mpʔs bai əsimileiʃn :—ˈtʌpʔmpʔs, ˈθrupʔmpʔs, ˈfɔːpʔmpʔs.

ən iksepʃənəl keis əv dʌbliŋ əv ðə p stɔp əkəːz in ðə wəːdz *ninepence, tenpence*, witʃ ə prənaunst bai meni əz ˈnaimpʔpəntʔs, ˈtempʔpəntʔs. ðis dʌbliŋ dəz nɔt əkəː, fər igzɑːmpl, in *ninepins*, ˈnaimpinz, ənd iz prizjuːməbli djuː tu ənælədʒi wið, ɔːr imiteiʃn əv, ðə prənʌnsieiʃn əv *eightpence* :—ˈeipʔpəntʔs. wen ðiːz wəːdz ə prənaunst widaut əsimileiʃn əv ði ælvioulə tə ðə baileibiəl kɔnsənənt ðei bikʌm ˈeitʔpəntʔs, ˈnaintʔpəntʔs, ˈtentʔpəntʔs, prənʌnsieiʃnz witʃ ə kwait ɔfn həːd.

fainl vɔislis plousivz, ai iː ðouz witʃ əkəːr ət ði end əv ən ʌtrəns ɔːr ət ði end əv ə wəːd spoukn in aisəleiʃn, ə dʒenrəli glɔtḷaizd ņ iŋkəmpliːt, ai iː wiðaut plouʒn.

L. A. ILES.

səm æspɛkts əv ðə fənɛtɪks əv vaʊəlz ɪn saʊθ æfrɪkən ɪŋglɪʃ

mɒnəfθɒŋz

ɪn saʊθ æfrɪkə, weər ɪn moʊst pɑːts əv ðə kʌntrɪ piːpl ɑː baɪlɪŋgwəl ɪn ɪŋglɪʃ ənd æfrɪkɑːns, ɪt ɪz nætʃərəl ðət ðə saʊndz əv ðə wʌn læŋgwɪdʒ ɪnflwəns ðoʊz əv ðiː ʌðə læŋgwɪdʒ. ɔːlðoʊ mɛnɪ saʊθ æfrɪkənz spiːk ə kaɪnd əv stændəd ɪŋglɪʃ, moʊst əv ðəm, huː weə bɔːn ɪn saʊθ æfrɪkə, ətɛndɪd loʊkəl skuːlz, ɔː həv lɪvd ɪn ðə kʌntrɪ fər ə lɒŋ taɪm, hæv ə tɛndənsɪ mɔːr ɔː lɛs prənaʊnst tə juːz saʊndz wɪtʃ ɑː tɪpɪkəl əv tədeɪz saʊθ æfrɪkən ɪŋglɪʃ. ðɪs miːnz ðət ɪn sʌm spiːkəz oʊnlɪ wʌn ɔː tuː kærəktərɪstɪk tʃeɪndʒɪz meɪ biː noʊtɪsəbl, wəræz ɪn ʌðəz ə greɪtə nʌmbə meɪ biː faʊnd.

ə stʌdɪ əv ðə vaʊəl sɪstɪm əv ðə stændəd prənʌnsɪeɪʃən əv ɪŋglɪʃ ənd æfrɪkɑːns ʃoʊz ðæt :—

    I. sɜːtn vaʊəlz (sʌm mɔːr ɔː lɛs mɒdɪfaɪd) əkɜːr ɪn boʊθ læŋgwɪdʒɪz.

II. sʌm vaʊəlz əkɜːr ɪn ɪŋglɪʃ bət nɒt ɪn æfrɪkɑːns.

III. ʌðə vaʊəlz ə faʊnd ɪn æfrɪkɑːns bət nɒt ɪn ɪŋglɪʃ.
ðə fɒloʊɪŋ daɪəgræm ʃoʊz ðiː æfrɪkɑːns vaʊəlz [1] :—

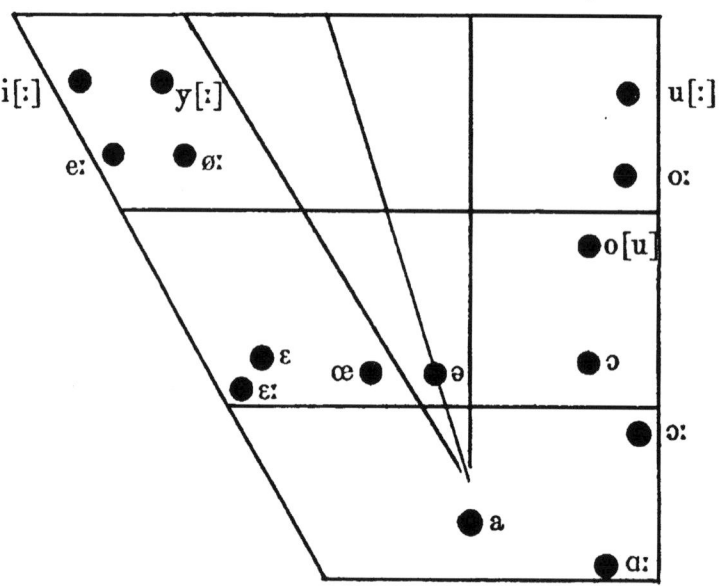

æfrɪkɑːns vaʊəlz

kəmpɛərɪŋ ðiː æfrɪkɑːns ənd ðə stændəd ɪŋglɪʃ vaʊəlz wʌn faɪndz :—

I. vaʊəlz əkɜːrɪŋ boʊθ ɪn stændəd ɪŋglɪʃ ənd ɪn æfrɪkɑːns—
i(ː), ɛ(ː), ɑ(ː), ɔː, uː, ə

II. vaʊəlz əkɜːrɪŋ ɪn stændəd ɪŋglɪʃ oʊnlɪ—
ɪ, æ, ɒ, ʌ, ʊ, ɜː

III. vaʊəlz əkɜːrɪŋ ɪn stændəd æfrɪkɑːns oʊnlɪ—
y(ː), eː, øː, œ, oː

ɪn ðə keɪs əv I, vaʊəlz əkɜːrɪŋ ɪn ðə stændəd fɔːm əv boʊθ læŋgwɪdʒɪz, baɪlɪŋgwəl spiːkəz friːkwəntlɪ ʃoʊ ðə fənetɪk diːvɪeɪʃənz ɪn saʊθ æfrɪkən ɪŋglɪʃ prənʌnsɪeɪʃən əz ɪləstreɪtɪd baɪ ðə fɒloʊɪŋ wɜːd ɪgzɑːmplz :—

---

[1] kəmpɛə ðə daɪəgræm əv æfrɪkɑːns vaʊəlz baɪ PIENAAR and HOOPER, *An Afrikaans-English Phonetic Reader*, Johannesburg, 1948, p. viii, ðiː [ɑː] ɪn ðiː ərɪdʒɪnəl həz biːn riːpleɪst baɪ [ɑː].

(1) iː > eː
    fiːl > feːl
    riːd > reːd
    diːl > deːl

(2) ɛ > e
    ɛ > ĕ
    ɛ > ɩ
    bɛd > bed
    pɛn > pën
    jɛs > jɩs

(3) ɑː > ɒ
    ɑː > ɔː
    pɑːk > pɒ(r)k
    gɑːdn > gɒ(r)dn
    ɑːnt > ɔːnt
    ɑːnsə > ɔːnsə(r)

(4) ɔː > oː
    ɔː > ɷ
    kɔːt > koːt
    kɔːt > kɷːt
    sɔː > soː
    sɔː > sɷː

(5) uː > ɷ
    uː > ÿ
    kuːl > kɷl
    ruːd > rɷd
    tuːduː > tÿdÿ
    ʃuː > ʃÿ

(6) ə > ---
    --- > ə
    pəliːs > pliːs
    poɷəm > poɷm
    mɩlk > mələk (miːlək)
    ʌmbrɛlə > œmbərɛlə

ɩt ɩz ɩntrɛstɩŋ ðət ðə tʃeɩndʒɩz (dɩskʌst ʌndə nʌmbəz 1–6) əkɜː, ɔːlðoɷ ðə vaɷəlz rɩkwaɩəd fɔː ðə stændəd ɩŋglɩʃ prənʌnsɩeɩʃən ɑːr əveɩləbl ɩn æfrɩkɑːns.

ðə moɷst friːkwənt tʃeɩndʒɩz faɷnd ɩn II, ðə stændəd ɩŋglɩʃ vaɷəlz wɩtʃ duː nɒt əkɜːr ɩn ðiː æfrɩkɑːns læŋgwɩdʒ, ɑː ðə fɒloɷɩŋ :—

(7) ɩ > ə
    ɩ > iː
    pɩn > pən
    pɩn > piːn
    wɩʃ > wəʃ
    wɩʃ > wiːʃ

(8) æ > ɛ
    blæk > blɛk
    hæt > hɛt

(9) ɒ > ɔ
    ɒ > oː

(10) ɷ > uː

                pʊt > pɔt   bɒk > buːk
                pʊt > poːt   fʊt > fuːt
                mɒdən > mədə(r)n
                mɒdən > moːdə(r)n
     (11) ʌ > œ   (12) ɜː > œ
           ʌ > ɩ
           ʌ > ɔ   bɜːd > bœ(r)d̥
           bʌt > bœt   lɜːn > lœ(r)n
           dʒʌst > dʒɩst
           kʌvə > kɔvə(r)

ɩn ðə priːvɩəs sɛkʃənz (I ənd II), wiː faɩnd sʌm tʃeɩndʒɩz əv ðə
stændəd ɩŋglɩʃ vaωəlz tuː, (III), vaωəlz wɩtʃ ər ʌðəwaɩz oωnlɩ juːzd
ɩn æfrɩkaːns — wɩð ði: ɩksɛpʃən əv [ø] wɩtʃ həz nɒt ɛntəd saωθ æfrɩkən
ɩŋglɩʃ prənʌnsɩeɩʃən — neɩmlɩ [e], [œ], [o] ənd ə mɒdɩfaɩd [ÿ]
(kəmpɛə ɩgzaːmplz 1 ; 11, 12 ; 4, 9 ; 5 rɩspɛktɩvlɩ).

ɔːl ðə saωθ æfrɩkən ɩŋglɩʃ vaωəlz lɩstɩd əbʌv ʌndəgoω mɔːr ɔː
lɛs prənaωnst fənɛtɩk tʃeɩndʒɩz ɩn dɩfərənt saωnd ɩnvaɩərənmənts.
ðə fɒloωɩŋ tuː vaωəl mɒdɩfɩkeɩʃənz, kɔːzd baɩ kɒnsənæntl kɒntækt,
aː tɩpɩkl əv saωθ æfrɩkən ɩŋglɩʃ :—

   (a) ði æfrɩkaːns hæbɩt əv ʌnvɔɩsɩŋ faɩnəl vɔɩst kɒnsənənts həz
       ɛntəd ɩntə saωθ æfrɩkən ɩŋglɩʃ prənʌnsɩeɩʃən ənd kɔːzd ə tʃeɩndʒ
       ɩn ðə kwɒntɩtɩ əv ðə priːsiːdɩŋ vaωəl, fər ɩgzaːmpl :—
       bæːd > bɛ·d̥ > bɛt
       pruːv > prω·y̥ > prωf

   (b) ɩn æfrɩkaːns wʌn neɩzəlaɩzɩz ɔːl vaωəlz wɩtʃ ə fɒloωd baɩ ə
       neɩzl plʌs frɩkətɩv, ðɩs hæbɩt ɩz friːkwəntlɩ kærɩd oωvə ɩntə
       ði: ɩŋglɩʃ əv spiːkəz huːz hoωm læŋgwɩdʒ ɩz æfrɩkaːns. ɛnɩ əv
       ðə saωθ æfrɩkən ɩŋglɩʃ vaωəlz meɩ biːkʌm neɩzəlaɩzd ɩn ðæt
       keɩs, fər ɩgzaːmpl :—

       hænsəm > hɛ̃ːsəm
       daːns > dãːs
       biːnz > bĩːs
       nɒnsəns > nɔ̃ːsɛ̃ːs (nɔ̃ːsœ̃ːs), ɩtsɛtrə.

moωst əv ðə fənɛtɩk daɩvɜːsɩfɩkeɩʃn əv vaωəlz ɩn saωθ æfrɩkən
ɩŋglɩʃ ɩz ɒbvɩəslɩ djuː tə ði: ɩnflwəns əv ði: æfrɩkaːns læŋgwɩdʒ. ðə
moωst rɩmaːkəbl fɩnɒmɩnən, haωɛvə, ɩn ðə vɛərɩəs vaωəl tʃeɩndʒɩz

frəm stændəd ɪŋglɪʃ tə saʊθ æfrɪkən ɪŋglɪʃ ɪz ðə *reɪzɪŋ əv vaʊəlz*. ðə fɒloʊɪŋ θriː daɪəgræmz wɪl klærɪfaɪ ðɪs :—

1. vaʊəlz reɪzd fɔːwəd

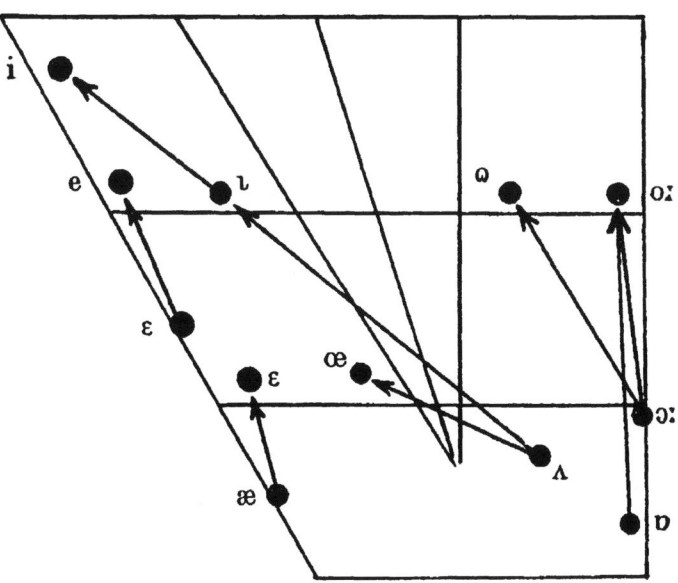

2. vaʊəlz reɪzd bækwəd

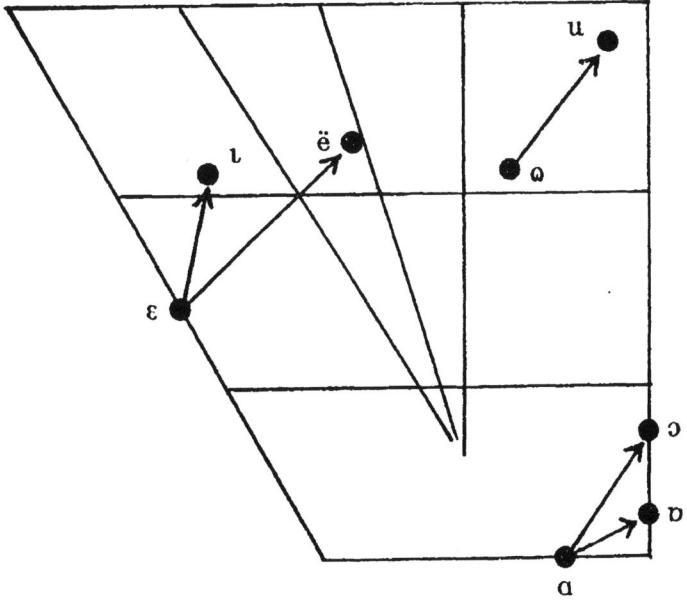

3. vaʊəlz reɪzd vɜːtɪkəlɪ

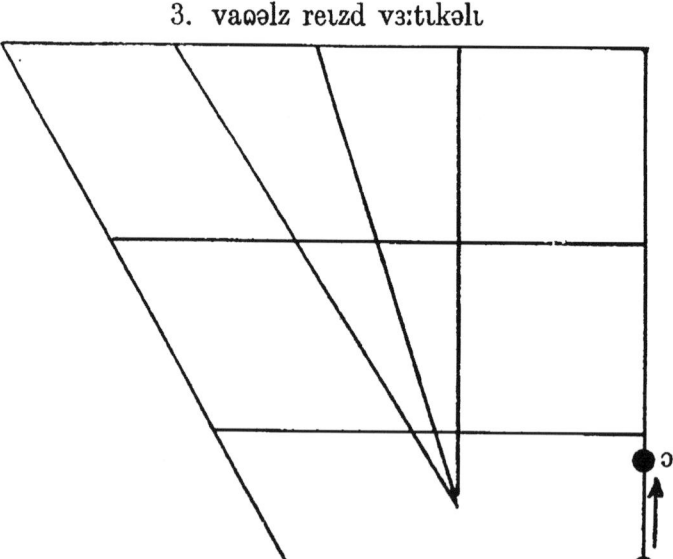

ə kəmpærətɪvlɪ smɔːl nʌmbər əv saʊθ æfrɪkən vaʊəlz duː nɒt ʌndəɡoʊ ən ɑːtɪkjʊleɪtrɪ reɪzɪŋ. ɪn ðə keɪs əv [i] ənd [u] ðə riːzən fə ðɪs laɪz ɪn ðə mɪə fækt ðət ðiːz saʊndz kænət biː reɪzd bɪjɒnd ðeə pɔɪnt əv ɑːtɪkjʊleɪʃn. ðə fɒloʊɪŋ tuː daɪəɡræmz ɪləstreɪt ðə dɪsɛndɪŋ ənd lɛvəl vaʊəl muːvmənts :—

4. vaʊəlz loʊəd fɔːwəd ɔː bækwəd

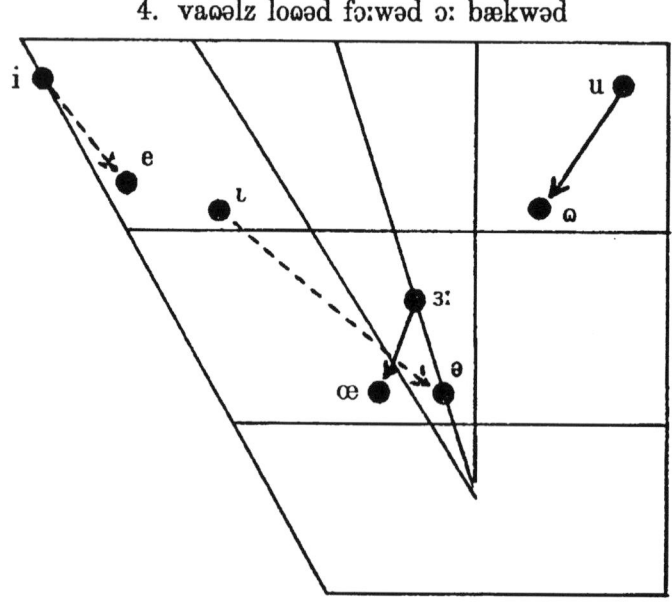

5. vaʊəlz muːvd hɒrɪzɒntəlɪ fɔːwəd ɔː bækwəd

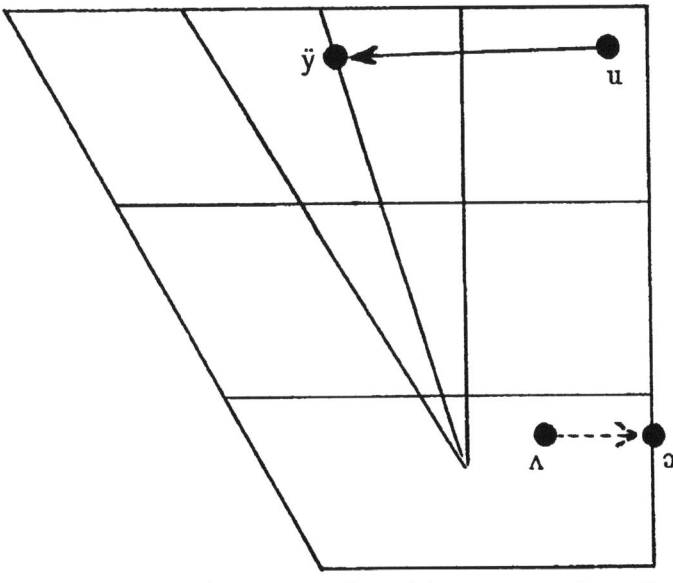

ðə priːsiːdɪŋ faɪv daɪəgræmz kən biː sʌməraɪzd ɪn ðə fɒloʊɪŋ tæbjuːleɪʃn :—

muːvmənt	daɪrɛkʃən			toʊtəl
	fɔːwəd	bækwəd	vɜːtɪkl	
reɪzd	8	5	1	14
loʊəd	2	2	0	4
lɛvəl	1	1	—	2
				20

ðə vaʊəl reɪzɪŋ (ɪn 14 ɪnstənsɪz aʊt əv 20) əpɪəz tə biː sɪgnɪfɪkənt, ənd ə stʌdɪ əv ðə saɪkoʊ- (ənd soʊʃɪoʊ-) fənɛtɪk bækgraʊnd əv ðɪs fɪnɒmɪnən meɪ rɪviːl kɔːzɪz bɪjɒnd ðiː ɒbvɪəs ɪkɒnəmɪ əv ɛfət. saʊθ æfrɪkən ɪŋglɪʃ dəz nɒt oʊnlɪ lɪv ʌndə ðə seɪm ruːf wɪð ənʌðə əfɪʃəl læŋgwɪdʒ, bət ɪz səraʊndɪd baɪ ə greɪt nʌmbər əv æfrɪkən læŋgwɪdʒɪz wɪtʃ ɔːlsoʊ ɪgzɜːt ðɛər ɪnflwəns ɒn saʊθ æfrɪkən ɪŋglɪʃ.[1]

[1] pətɪkjələlɪ jʌŋ tʃɪldrən huɪ ə lɛft ə greɪt diːl tə ðə kɛər əv æfrɪkən nænɪz ɒfn pɪk ʌp ən ɪŋglɪʃ prənʌnsɪeɪʃən kənteɪnɪŋ fənɛtɪk ɛləmənts əv æfrɪkən læŋgwɪdʒɪz. ət skuːl ðeɪ juːʒwəlɪ groʊ aʊt əv ðɪs ɜːlɪ hæbɪt.

sʌmɪŋ ʌp aʊər ɪnvɛstɪgeɪʃən, wiː faɪnd ðət saʊθ æfrɪkən ɪŋglɪʃ vaʊəlz əv tədeɪ ʃoʊ ðə fʊloʊɪŋ kærəktərɪstɪks :—

(a) daɪvɜːsɪfɪkeɪʃn (θruː kɒntækt wɪð ðiː æfrɪkɑːns læŋgwɪdʒ) ;

(b) pəzɪʃənəl reɪzɪŋ.

G. H. Breckwoldt,
University of the Witwatersrand.

ə spesəmin əv britiʃ iŋgliʃ

ðə folowiŋ iz ə diskripʃən əv səʜtən ¹ fəwnəlodʒikəl fijtʃəz əv maj idijəlekt. aj wəz boʜn ən broʜt ap in *laŋkəʃə, bət bitwijn ðij ejdʒiz əv najn ən ejtijn wəz edʒukejtid ət boʜdiŋ skuwlz (fəʜs pripərətri, ðen pablik) in ðə sawθ əv *iŋglənd. maj faʜðə spijks RP, bət in maj maðəz spijtʃ ðər ə səʜtən slajt fijtʃəz əv ə *west rajdiŋ joʜkʃə daʜlekt. aj wəz boʜn in 1939 ; maj prənansijejʃən majt bi dezignejtid RP wið slajt rijdʒənəl influwəns.

konsənənts

maj prənansijejʃən əv konsənənts iz səbstanʃəli ðat diskrajbd baj JONES, wið ðə folowiŋ iksepʃənz. /p t k/ ə glotəlajzd in meni siləbəl-fajnəl konteksts. ðis finominən iz veri wajdspred in karənt RP.²

/r/, iksept in ðə klastəz /tr dr/ (weʜr it iz ən alvijəwlə frikətiv) iz ən "ɹ-kaləd" kəntinjuwənt aʜtikjulejtid baj banʃiŋ ðə taŋ təwoʜdz ðə vijləm, ðə sajdz əv ðə taŋ bijiŋ prest əgejnst ðə məwləz bət əlawiŋ ðij eʜ tuw iskejp latrəli rawnd ðəm, waʜl ðə taŋ tip pojnts dawn. it haz kəŋkomitənt lip-rawndiŋ, pətikjuləlij in iniʃəl pəziʃən. aj kastəmərəli juwz liŋkiŋ /r/, ənd oʜlsəw intruwsiv /r/ aʜftə /ə,

---

¹ ðə simbəl ʜ iz juwzd tə dinəwt ðə sekənd elimənt əv loŋ monəfθoŋz oʜ sentriŋ difθoŋz az in GLEASONZ *Introduction to Descriptive Linguistics*.

² sij rijsənt aʜtikəlz baj L. A. ILES (**m.f.** 113), I. THOMPSON (**m.f.** 116).

iʜ, aʜ/ (bət nɒt ɑʜftə /oʜ/), weðə bitwijn wəʜdz oʜ wiðin ðəm, ðas *polkaing* (" dɑʜnsiŋ ðə polkə ") /'polkəriŋ/, *Ma isn't here* /'mɑʜr izənt 'hiʜ/.

ðə klɑstəz /ntʃ, ndʒ/ tend tə bij əvojdid in fejvər əv /nʃ, nʒ/, ðas *inch* /inʃ/, *orange* /'orinʒ/.

in sɑm wəʜdz, weʜ mɑws spijkəz hav /s/ bifoʜ strest /əʜ oʜ/, aj hav /s/ əwnlij əz ən eligənt veʜrijejʃən fə /z/. ðas *research* /ri'zəʜtʃ/, *absurd* /əb'zəʜd/, similəli *discern, insert, absorb, resource*.

ɑnlajk menij RP spijkəz, aj duw nɒt dijvojs /r, l/ ɑʜftə vojsləs konsənənts ət ðə biginiŋ əv strest siləbəlz.

vawlz ən difθoŋz

silabik njuwklijij ər əv θrij tajps — ʃoʜt vawlz, loŋ vawlz, ən kləwziŋ difθoŋz. ðər ə sevən ʃoʜt vawlz (distribjuwʃənəli difajnəbəl əz nevər əkəʜriŋ strest imijdʒətli bifoʜ poʜz); dej əkəʜr in ðə wəʜdz *bid, bed, bad, bud, bod, Bud(dha), (slum)bered.* in əkoʜdəns wið IPA prinsipəlz aj rajt ðəm /i e a ɑ o u ə/. ðeʜ tipikəl aləfəwnz ə ʃəwn in figə wan. /ɑ/ kəntrɑʜsts wið /ə/ ɑnstrest, ənd əkejʒənəli strest. /'gɑnə/ *gunner* iz difrənt frəm /'gənə/ *gonna* (" gəwiŋ tu "); ðər iz ə difrəns bitwijn ðə fajnəl siləbəlz əv *humdrum* /'hɑmdrəm/ ənd *conundrum* /kə'nɑndrəm/. /ə/ iz ofən riʜlajzd əz siləbisitij əv /l, r, m, n, ŋ/. aj hav /ə/ in ə grejt meni plejsiz weʜ menij RP spijkəz hav /i/. ðas aj prənawns *carelessness* /'keʜləsnəs/, *possibility* /'posə'bilǝti/, *pirate* /'paʜrǝt/; bət *linen* /'linin/, *remember* /ri'membǝ/, *element* /'elimǝnt/.

ðər ə sevən korispondiŋ loŋ vawlz, /iʜ, eʜ, aʜ, ɑʜ, oʜ, uʜ, əʜ/, əkəʜriŋ in *beard, bared, tired, bard, board, toured, bird*; sij figə tuw. /iʜ, eʜ, aʜ, uʜ/ juwʒəli hav sentəriŋ difθoŋ aləfəwnz wen in ə siləbəl beʜriŋ njuwklijə təwn, bət ər aðəwajz praktikli monəfθoŋgəl; bifoʜ /r/ ðej ə priti monəfθoŋgəl ijvən wen njuwklijə. wəʜdz trədiʃənəli transkrajbd wið aiə juwʒəli hav /aʜ/, bət sɑmtajmz /ajə/, pətikjuləlij if ðat segmənt kəntejnz ə moʜfijm bawndri. ðas *hire* iz /'haʜ/, bət *higher* mej bi /'haʜ/ oʜ /'hajə/. wəʜdz trədiʃənəli transkrajbd wið auə ə lajkwajz prənawnst wið /aʜ/ oʜ /awə/, iksept fər *our*, witʃ iz /ɑʜ/. *Towering* iz ðeʜfoʜ juwʒəli həmofənəs wið *tiring* /'taʜriŋ/; in səʜtən stajlz əv spijtʃ, hawevə, ðej ɑʜ pəhaps distiŋgwiʃt, if sɑmwot iratikli, əz [tʼɑ:ɚɪŋ], [tʼɑ:ɚɪŋ] (bəwθ difrənt frəm *tarring* /'tɑʜriŋ/ [tʼɑ:ɚɪŋ].) bət if ə sitjuwejʃən ərajziz weʜr it iz nesəseri tə kliʜli

distiŋgwiʃ bitwijn ðəm, ðə sijkwənsiz /awə, ajə/ ə juwzd. frenʃ
ləwnwəнdz wið speliŋ *oir* ə prənawnst wið /aн/. *Memoirs* /ˈmemwaнz/
endz ajdentikəli wið *tripwires* /ˈtripwaнz/; ðə fəнs paнt əv *soirée*
/ˈswaнrej/ iz prənawnst lajk ðə səнnejm *Swire*. satʃ wədz nevər
evə hav /ajə/; it iz ðis ðət mejks it imposəbəl tuw anəlajz [aː] əz
/ajə/, ənd foнsiz ðə setiŋ ap əv ə seprət loŋ vawl /aн/.

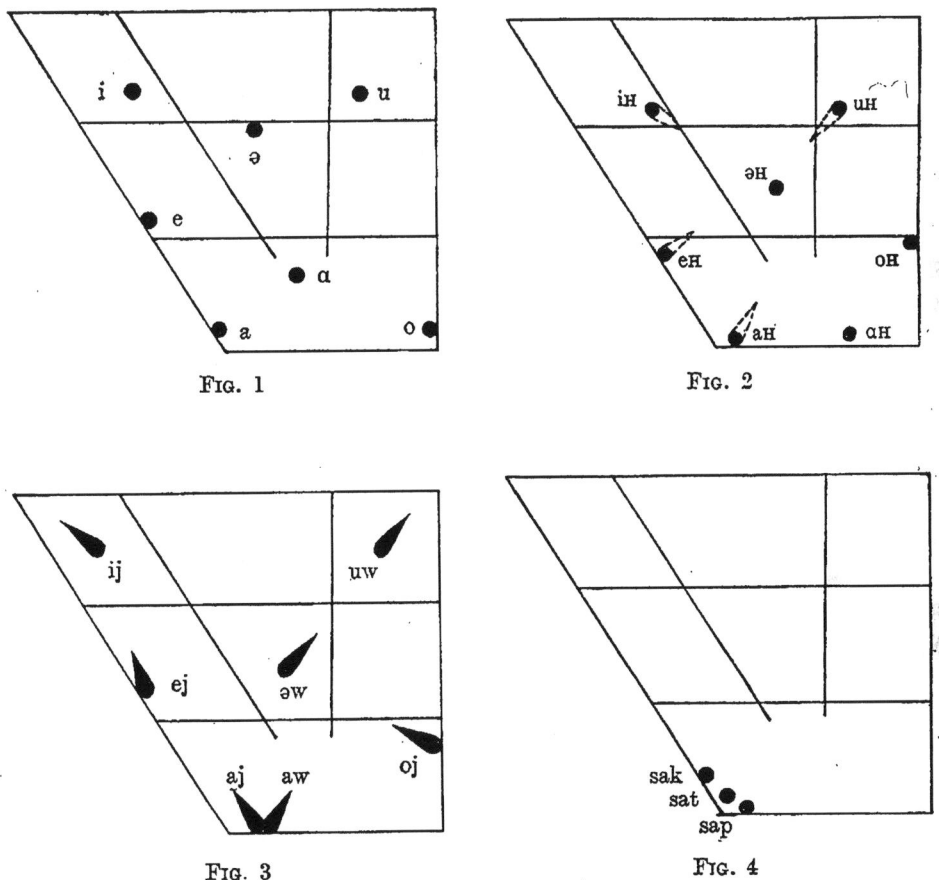

FIG. 1   FIG. 2

FIG. 3   FIG. 4

ðər ə sevən kləwziŋ difθoŋz, /ij, ej, aj, aw, oj, uw, əw/, əkəнriŋ
in *bead, bayed, bide, boughed*,[1] *Boyd, booed, bode* (figə θrij). /ij, uw/
tend tuw əkəн tə ðij iksklūwʒən əv /i, u/ bifoн vawlz. aj hav nəw
monəfθoŋgəl aləfəwn əv /əw/ in wəнdz lajk *November*, witʃ iz ajðə

---

[1] trijtiŋ *boughed* əz /ˈbawd/ raнðə ðən /ˈbawd/ — witʃ kud bi dən əwnlij on
pjuнli strakʃərəl grawndz — wud jijld ə veri nijt θrij-baj-sevən vawl sistəm, wið
pəwstvəkalik /j/ ənd /w/ in komplimentri distribjuwʃən.

/nəwˈvembə/ oʜ /nəˈvembə/. latin pluʜrəlz in *-i* ə prənawnst wið /ij/, ðas *stimuli* /ˈstimjulij/. ðis prənansijejʃən həz veri dʒenrəlij awstid ðə foʜmə prənansijejʃən /aj/ əmaŋ pijpəl əv maj ejdʒ. *Deity, deify, spontaneity* aʜ /ˈdejəti/, /ˈdejifaj/, /spontəˈnejəti/, wið /ej/ not /ij/ — ðis tuw iz naw veri komən.

/i, e, a, ɑ/ ən difθoŋz in /-j/ hav slajtli kləwsər aləfəwnz bifoʜ vijləz, ən slajtlij əwpənər aləfəwnz bifoʜ lejbjəlz. igzɑʜmpəlz fər /a/ ə ʃəwn in figə foʜ.

it wil bij əbzəʜvd ðət maj vawl sistəm fits wel intə ðij "əwvəroʜl patən" fər *ingliʃ fəʜs diskrajbd baj Trager ən Smith. wot aj əv ritən /a, ɑ, o/ iz ðeʜ /æ, a, ɔ/, ənd aj lak ðeʜ /ɨ, o/.

J. C. Wells.

spesimεn
* blæk kʌntrɪ spitʃ

1. ðə deɪtə wə rɪkɔdɪd ət ə dɑts geɪm ət ðə *rεd laɪən pʌb ɪn *raʊlɪ rɪdʒɪs (ROWLEY REGIS), *saʊθ stæfədʃɪə. ðə haɪ dɪgri əv fri veərɪeɪʃn̩ ənd loʊkl̩ dɪfərənsɪz noʊtɪd ɪn ðə θri spikəz rɪkɔdɪd lɪv ðɪ ɪntəprɪteɪʃn̩ əv sɜtən fæks ɪn daʊt (i.dʒi. [ü] ənd [əü], ənd ðə slaɪt pælətəlaɪzeɪʃn̩ əv kɒnsənənts). *blæk kʌntrɪ ənd əsoʊsɪeɪtɪd daɪəlεkts ə spoʊkn̩ baɪ 3–4 mɪljən pipl̩.

2a. ðə vaʊəlz — ʃoʊɪŋ tʃeɪndʒɪz əv foʊnim vɪz-æ-vi *RP*.

	blæk kʌntrɪ foʊnimz	blæk kʌntrɪ fənεtɪk rɪəlaɪzeɪʃn̩	RP foʊnimz		
1	ɪ	i– (strεst) ɪ+ (ʌnstrεst)	ɪ		
2	e	ẹ–	ε	ɔ	eɪ
3	a	kɑdməl	æ	ɔ	ɑ
4	ɑː	ɑː+	ɑ		
5	ɔ	kɑdməl	ɒ		
6	ɔː	ǫː	ɔ		
7	o	o+	ʌ		
8	ʊ	ʊ–	ʊ		
9	ü	uː+	u	(si 22)	
10	ə	ẹ / ə̣	ə		
11	ɪə	ɪ → ə	iə	ɔ	eə
12	ëə	ẹ+ → ə̣	ɜ		
13	ëə	ε– → ə	eə		
14	oə	o+ → ə	ɔ	ɔ	ɔə
15	üə	u+ → ə	ɔ	ɔ	uə
16	əɪ	ə̣ → ɪ	i		
17	æɪ	ạ– → ɪ	eɪ		
18	ɑɪ	ɑ+ → ɪ	aɪ		
19	oɪ	ǫ+ → ɪ	oɪ		
20	ëʊ	ε– → ʊ	aʊ		
21	ɔʊ	ǫ+ → ʊ	oʊ	ɔ	u
22	əü	ə̣ → u+	u	ɔ	oʊ (si 9)

2b. *fri veərɪənts faʊnd ɪn ðə fʊl tɛkst ənælɪsɪs*

1	ɪ	—	[ëɪ] (strɛst), [ë] (ʌnstrɛst)
2	e	—	[ɛ], sʌmtaɪmz [e] ɔ [ɛ̞]
7	o	—	[ü] (reə)
11	ɪə	—	[ëə]
12	ëə	—	spikəz juzɪŋ [ëə] fə /ɪə/ du nɒt ɔlsoʊ juz ðə kɒmən fri veərɪənt [ëə] fə /ëə/ = [ə̝+ → ə̞]
13	ëə	—	[ɛə]
15	üə	—	[əwə]
16	əɪ	—	[ɪ] ɔ [ëɪ] wɛn ʌnstrɛst
18	ɑɪ	—	[ɑː+] ʌnstrɛst
20	ëʊ	—	[ëü], [ëː], [ëə], [ɐː]
21	ɔʊ	—	[ɐʊ], [ɐü]
22	əü	—	[ü], (si 9), [əwə] ɔ [ëü] (reə)

2c. *noʊts ɒn ðə vaʊəlz ənd dɪfθɒŋz*

1) ðə kloʊzɪŋ dɪfθɒŋz muv kwaɪt kloʊs (kʊ́ntrɑst RP) ənd ðə fɔːmz [pëʊwə], [bloʊwə], [ɪmplɔɪjə], [bɑɪjə], [sæɪjə] kɒrɪspɒnd tə ðɪ RP tu dərɛkʃənəl dɪfθɒŋz.

2) /ëə/ ɪz kwaɪt raʊndɪd.

3) ðə foʊnimz /ɑɪ/, /ëʊ/ ənd /ɔʊ/ (18, 20, 21) ʃoʊ oʊvəlæp əv ðə fɜst ɛlɪmənt ən mɛnɪ fri veərɪənts, prɒbəblɪ bɪkʌz rɪəlaɪzeɪʃn̩z əv ðɪz foʊnimz muv ɪn dɪfərənt dərɛkʃn̩z.

4) ðə tu ʃwɑz ʃoʊ ə vaʊəl hɑməni : [ə] wɛn fɒloʊɪŋ ə kloʊs ɔ hɑf kloʊs vaʊəl, [ɐ] wɛn fɒloʊɪŋ ən oʊpn̩ ɔ hɑf oʊpn̩ vaʊəl. faɪnəlɪ wi faɪnd [ɐ].

3. *ðə kɒnsənənts*

1) *leɪbɪəlaɪzeɪʃn̩.* kɒnsənənts ə slaɪtlɪ leɪbɪəlaɪzd bɪfɔ ə strɛst /ɔ/, /oː/, /o/ ɔ /ɔʊ/.

2) *pælətəlaɪzeɪʃn̩.* kɒnsənənts ə slaɪtlɪ pælətəlaɪzd bɪfɔ ə strɛst [i] ɔ /ü/.

3) *vɔɪsɪŋ.* mɪʃl̩ ənd faɪnl̩ vɔɪst kɒnsənənts ə juʒʊəlɪ fʊlɪ vɔɪst.

4) *ploʊzɪvz.* faɪnl̩ vɔɪslɪs stɒps ər ɪdʒɛktɪv ; faɪnl̩ vɔɪst stɒps ə fʊlɪ ɪksploʊdɪd ənd fʊlɪ vɔɪst.

5) "*—ing*". freɪz faɪnl̩ [—ɪn] kʊntrɑsts wɪð ðə *bɜmɪŋəm [—ɪŋg].

6) *flæps*. ɪntəvoʊkælɪk /r/ = [ɾ]. mɛnɪ RP wɜdz wɪð /t/ meɪ fɔl ɪntʊ ðɪs foʊnim əz [ɾ]. ðə "lɪŋkɪŋ" /r/ ɪz juʒʊəl. [ɹ] ɪz reə.

7) [ʔ] dʌz nɒt əkɜ.

4. *spɛsɪmɪn tɛkst*

A: a+ɪ o+p ë:t ðə̣ ɾə̣+ʊd. wɛ̣–l, *baɾə̣t sta:+tɪ̣+d tə̣ mə̣+ʊn əbë:ɾɪ̣+t, jə nə̣+ʊ; sɛ̣–d: "jə̣+ʊ æɪ ə bad lɔt o+p ðɪə", sə̣+ʊ ɛnɪ̣+ẹ̈ʊ a+tëənd ɹə̣ʊnd ən tə̣+ʊld ɪ̣+m, a+ sɛd: "wɔd də̣ jə̣+ʊ nə̣+ʊ əbẹ̈ʊt ɪ̣+t; ɔn ðə̣ ka:+d ðə̣ wəz sɛ̣vən no+θɪ̣+n"; a+ sɛz: "nə̣+ʊ plæɪjə̣z tëənd o+p fə̣ ðə̣ matʃ". frə̣m wɔɾa+ kn̩ mɛk ë:t ɔn ɪ̣+t, ɪ̣+ts ə lɔt ə̣ bʊ̣-nkʊ̣-m. a+ tə̣+ʊld əm wɪ̣+ gɔɾə̣ plæj ɪ̣+t əgɛ̣n.

B: ðas safnɪ̣+s.

C: ðæɪ sɛd ət ðə̣ məɪtɪ̣+n, dʒanjʊ-ɛɾɪ̣+ ðɪ̣+ ɪ̣+lɛ̣vn̩ (ðə̣ wəz ə̣+ʊnlɪ̣+ fa+ɪv ðɪə, wə̣: ðə̣?), ðæɪ ə̣:l və̣+ʊtɪd fɔɾə̣: ... ðə̣ sɛ̣vən tə̣ ɾəɪplæɪj ɪ̣+t. ɪ̣+ts ɪ̣+n ðə̣ ɾə̣ʊwəlz.

B: wɛ̣l, a+ɪ æɪ ɾɛd ɪ̣+t ɛnɪ̣+jẹ̈ʊ.

C: ɪ̣+s ðə̣ last ɹəwəl ɪ̣+n ðə̣ bʊ̣-k.

B: a+ɪ æɪ gɔt ma+ɪn wɪ̣+ mɪ̣+.

C: a+v dʒüst ad ə̣ lʊ̣-k.

A: twɛnɪ̣+ tʲü:. ë: mnɪ̣+ dəz ðat ləɪv, mæɪt? tʊ: ə̣+ʊvə tʲüw. wɔnt tə̣ ɾo+b ðə̣ bowəd ɔf? na+ɪn — sɛ̣vn̩ — tʲüw. a+ kɔ̣: gɛ̣ɾə̣wæɪ.

B: a+ jat tə̣ sɛnd ðə̣ ka:+d ɪ̣+n; a+ kʊ̣-dnt dʲüw no+θɪ̣+n əbẹ̈ʊt ɪ̣+t.

C: dɪ̣+d ðæɪ fa+ɪn ð o+ðə̣ klo+b fə̣ nɔt tëənɪ̣+n o+p? ðəz ə̣ fa+ɪnɪ̣+n əz ə̣ klo+b nɔt tëənɪ̣+n o+p ... fa+ɪv ʃi–lən.

B: ðæɪ fo+n ðə̣ klo+b a:+f ə̣ krẹ̈ən ə mɛ̣mbə̣.

A: ðæɪ ɔ:+tə̣ fa+ɪn əm tʲü pẹ̈ʊn. a+ ʃl̩ atə̣ g̣üw.

5. *ə fjü dɪstɪŋktɪv lɛksɪkəl aɪtəmz*

1) a+ kɔ: (aɪ kɑnt).
2) aɪ æɪ gɔɾɪt (aɪ hævnt gɒt ɪt).
3) jəʊ bæɪ (ju ɑnt).
4) a+ ʃɔ: (aɪ ʃɑnt).
5) a+ wəʊ (aɪ woʊnt).

6) joʊm (ju ɑ).
7) wɪm (wi ɑ).
8) ðæɪm (ðeɪ ɑ).
9) ɑ+ dëəsn̩t (aɪ deənt).
10) wɔtn̩ jə don (wɒt əv jə dʌn).
11) wɔtn̩ jə d̪üwɪm (wɒt əjə duɪŋ).
12) wɔs i don (wɒts hi dʌn).
13) ɑ+ v ad ɪt g̪id mɪ (aɪv hæd ɪt gɪvn̩ tʊ mɪ).

C. PAINTER.

spesimɛn

ðə fɒlwɪŋ vəːʒn əv "ðə nɔθ wɪnd ən ðə sʌn" reprəzents ən ʌnsəfɪstɪkeɪtɪd *kɑdɪf (CARDIFF) prənʌnsɪeɪʃn.

ʌ ɪz sentrl, ə hɑf klɔʊs, a(ː) = ä, u = ü‹, aɤ = äɤ, w = w‹, ö = ö̟‹, i = ï, ɔɷ = ö̟ɷ, ö = ö̟‹, aɪ = äɪ, l = lə..., ...lʳ, r = alvjələ ɹ ɔ ɾ, eː = eᴛ, ɛɪ = ɛᴧɪ ; ʌðə valjuz ər ɔl əbaʊt kɑdnl.

ə 'nɒːθ 'wɪn(d) ən nə 'sʌn wəz avɪn 'aːg(ju)mənt baɣ 'wɪtʃ 'wʌn əv əm wəz ə 'strɒŋŋəs. ɛn ʌp kʌmz ɪs 'travlər 'ɒːl 'rapt 'ʌp ɪn ə 'wɔːm 'klɔ̈k. sɔ̈ ðɛɪ ə'griz əʔ ðə'wʌn ək kəg 'gɛr ɪm tə 'tɛɪk ɪr' ɒːf 'fəːs əb bi 'rɛkŋ 'strɒŋŋər ən ni 'ʌðə. ɛn ðə'nɒːθ 'wɪm blɔωz 'aːdz i 'kan. bəʔ ðə 'mɔːr i 'blɔωz (ð)ə'taɪtə ðə'travlə pɣlz ɪz 'kö̈ω ʔ 'raɣn(d) ɪm, ən ɪn i ɛn(d) ðə 'nɒːθ 'wɪŋ gɪvz ʌp 'traɪɪn. ɛn ə 'sʌn 'ʃãĩz 'aɣʔ 'wɒːm ən 'strɛːrəwɛɪ ðə'travlə tɛɪs 'ɒːf ɪz köt. sɔ(ω) ðə 'nɒːθ 'wɪŋ 'gɒr əb'mɪt ðəʔ ðə 'sʌm wəz ə 'strɒŋŋəs.

dʒak wɪnzə lɯɪs.
(JACK WINDSOR LEWIS.)

spesimɛn

spesimən pæsɪdʒɪz əv ðə spiːtʃ əv geɪtshed-ən-taɪn
(Gateshead-on-Tyne)

ðɪ fɒlouɪŋ pæsɪdʒɪz¹—tʃouzn aut əv ðə spiːtʃ əv mɛnɪ ɪnfɔːmənts—rɛprɪzɛnt dʒɛnjuɪn daɪəlɛkt əz rɪkɔːdɪd baɪ maɪsɛlf. əz ɪt ɪz kəntɪnjuəs spiːtʃ, tɪpɪkḷ fɔːmz ən rɛpɪtɪʃnz həv bɪn prɪzəːvd. sɪmblz ən daɪəkrɪtɪkḷ mɑːks koɪnsaɪd ɪgzæklɪ wɪð aɪ piː eɪ kənvɛnʃnz. strɛs ɪz ʌnmɑːkt.

1. dʒɔːdi wəz kʌmɪn hoŏm fʀəm *lʏndən ən hiz sɪtən ɪn ə tʀeŏn—ɪn kʌmz ə leːdi dʀɛst ɪn ə spɑːtŋ̩ manə. ðə jʏŋ leːdi lʊks ʀuːnd ən siːz ðə wɪndəz kləːzd ən ʃi əmiːdɪətli oːpənz ðə wɪndəz. dʒɔːdi aˑftə e moŏmənts hɛzɪteːʃn dʒʏmps ɒp ən kləːzəz ðə wɪndəz. ðə jʏŋ leːdi əgɛn oːpənz ðə wɪndəz, dʒɔːdi əgɛn dʒʏmps ɒp ən kləːzəz ðə wɪndəz.

¹ kəmpɛə Daniel Jones, *taɪnsaɪd daɪəlɛkt (*nɔɪθʌmbələnd), **m.f.**, Nov.–Dec., 1911, p. 184.

ðə jʏŋ leːdi ɪn fʏʀstʀeːʃn toːnz ʀuːnd tə dʒɔːdi ən seˑz, " jɷu kad! "
hi seˑz, " aˑi, aˑm kad, aˑm staːvɪn."

2. ðə dʒɔːdi hɔːts hɪz nei ən hi gans tə ðə dʊktəz. ðə dʊktə haz ə lʏk ət ðə nei ən seˑz, " aˑi, jɷu gʊt ə nasti nei ðɛə̌, lad." seˑ aftə gɪvən dʒɔːdi ðə tʀiːtmənt, bandədʒɪn hɪm ɷp, hi seˑz tə dʒɔːdi, " naɷ, dɷu jɷu θɪŋk jɷu kən wɔːk? " dʒɔːdi lʏks ət hɪm ən hi seˑz " wɔːk? " hi seˑz, " aˑ kən haːdli wɑːk! "

3. ðə stɔːʀi əv tɷɷ bɷə̌ts ɒn ðə ʀɪvʀ ɪn ə fɒg. ðɛə̌z ən iːstən bɷə̌t kaːld " ana ", ən kɷstəm ɪz ðə kaptənz kaːl " əhɒi, hɷuz ðɛə̌? " ə tainsɛid kaptən kaːlɪn fɔːst " əhɒi, hɷuz ðɛə̌? " gʊt ðɪ ansə " ana ", ðə neːm əv ðɪ iːstən bɷə̌t. ə sɛkənd taim hi kaːld " hɷuz ðɛə̌? " ən hi gɛts ðɪ ansə " aːnaː ". ɪn ɪmpeːʃəns hi kaːld ə θɔːd taim " aː naː, jiː naː, bʏt hɷu əm aː tə naː? "

WOLFGANG VIERECK.

ɪŋglɪʃ: RP

ðə fʊloʊɪŋ spɛsɪmən ɪz ə kərɛktɪd vɜːʃn əv ðə kəmpærətɪv æləfɒnɪk trænskrɪpʃn əv ðə "nɔːθ wɪnd ənd ðə sʌn" wɪtʃ əpɪəd ɪn **m.f.** 124 (dʒʊlaɪ-dɪsɛmbə, 1965), p. 28. ðə prənʌnsɪeɪʃn ɪz ðæt əv David Abercrombie ənd ðə trænskrɪpʃn baɪ Elizabeth Uldall.

ðə fʊloʊɪŋ saɪnz ən sɪmblz, ədɪʃnl tʊ IPA juːsɪdʒ, ʃʊd bɪ noʊtɪd:

| — bɪgɪnɪŋ əv fʊt (strɛst sɪləbl).

ˌ — saɪlənt strɛs.

c — frɪkʃnlɪs (ɒn ənælədʒɪ əv "oʊpənə" fə vaʊəlz).

° — ɪnədɪblɪ rɪliːst.

ɾˢ — vɔɪslɪs flap tʊ ə frɪkətɪv pəzɪʃn.

1 |ˌ ðə |nɔ̃θ |wɪnːd̥ʰ |ˌ ən ðə |sʌn:
2 |ˌ wə dɪs|pçuɾˢɪŋ |wɪtʃ wəz ðə |stɪ̰ɒŋɡə:
3 |ˌ wɛn ə |t̬ɹavlə kʰeɪm ə|lɒːŋ: |ɹapˀtʰ ɪn ə |wɔːm |klɔʊkʰ |ˌ
4 |ˌ ðeɪ ə|ɡɹiːd ðət ðə |wʌn fiu |fɜst sək|sidɪd
5 |ˌ ɪn |meɪxɪ̰ŋ ðə |t̬ɹavlə |tʰeɪk ɪz |klɔʊk̬ʰ ɒːf |ˌ
6 |ʃʊd°bi kʰən|sɪdəd |stɪ̰ɒŋɡə ðən ðɪ |ʌð̥ə: |ˌ|ˌ
7 |ðɛn̩ ðə |nɔ̃θ wɪnd° |blu: əz |hɑːd əz i |kʰʊdə
8 |ˌ bət ðə |mɔ̃ː fiɪ |blu:
9 |ˌ ðə mɔ |klɔʊslɪ dɪd̬ ðə |t̬ɹaɾə |foʊ̯ld ɪz |klɔʊkʰ ə|ɾaʊnd hɪm:
10 |ˌ and ət |lɑːstʰ |ˌ ðə |nɔ̃θ |wɪnd |ɡeɪv ʌp ðɪ ə|tʰɛmtʰˈ |ˌ|ˌ
11 |ðɛn̩ ðə |sʌn |ʃɒn aʊt |wɔmlɪ:
12 |ˌ ənd ɪ|mɪdjɪtlɪ̰ ðə |t̬ɹaɾə |tʰʊk̬ʰ ɒf ɪz |klɔʊkʰ
13 |ˌ ən |soʊ ðə |nɔ̃θ |wɪnd wəz ə|blaɪdʒd° tʰə kʰən|fɛs:
14 |ˌ ðət ðə |sʌn wəz ðə |stɪ̰ɒŋɡəɾ əv ðə |tʰuː |ˌ|ˌ|

ðə *stɒkpɔt daɪəlekt

(1) ðə daɪəlekt əv *stɒkpɔt ɪz ən ɪndʌstrɪəl wʌn. əmʌŋst əʊldə pipl ðər ɪz mɔ vɛərɪeɪʃn ɪn ðə vɛərɪəs ləʊkælɪtɪz wɛə ðə daɪəlekt ɪz spəʊkn. jʌŋgə pipl spik ə mɔ levəld aʊt fɔm, tə sʌm ɪkstent ʌndə ðɪ ɪnflʊəns əv stændəd prənʌnsɪeɪʃn. ðɪs daɪəlekt ɪz spəʊkn əʊvə məʊst əv nɔθ ist *tʃeʃə ənd ɪt kæn bɪ hɜd ɪn pɑts əv *mæntʃestə.

(2) *ðə fəʊnimz—vaʊəlz*

fəʊnim sɪmbl	fənetɪk rɪəlaɪzeɪʃn	RP
1. /ë/	[ë]	/ɪ/
2. /ɛ/	[ɛ-]	/e/
3. /a/	[a-]	/æ/, /ɑ/
4. /ɑ/	[ɑ+]	/ɒ/
5. /ö/	[ö]	/ʊ/, /ʌ/
6. /ə/	[ə]	/ə/
7. /eː/	[ẹː]	/eɪ/
8. /ɛː/	[ɛː]	/ɛə/
9. /aː/	[aː-]	/ɑ/
10. /äː/	[äː]	/aɪ/
11. /ʌː/	[ʌː]	/ɔ/
12. /oː/	[ǫː]	/əʊ/
13. /ɵː/	[ɵː]	/ɜ/
14. /ɪi/	[ɪi]	/i/
15. /ëə/	[ëə]	/ɪə/
16. /æʊ/	[æö]	/aʊ/
17. /ɑɪ/	[ɑ+ë]	/ɔɪ/
18. /ɔə/	[ɔə]	/ɔə/
19. /öə/	[öə]	/ʊə/
20. /ʊu/	[ʊu]	/u/

9 & 10. } si nəʊts

nəʊts ɒn vɛərɪənts ənd dɪstrɪbjuʃn.

fəʊnim 1. ɪz əkeɪʒənlɪ [ë] ɪn æksentɪd sɪləblz.

    6. ɪz əkeɪʒənlɪ juzd fə RP [ʌ] ɪn wɜdz " bɒrəʊd " frm RP æz /bərə/.

    7. vɛərɪz bɪtwin kɑdmɫz 2 ənd 3.

9 & 10. ðɪz prɪzent ə prɒbləm. ðeɪ ə nɒt ɔlwɪz kept strɪktlɪ əpɑt. fəʊnim 9 tendz tə bɪ prənaʊnst [äː] ðʌs meɪkɪŋ ɪt aɪdentɪkl

27

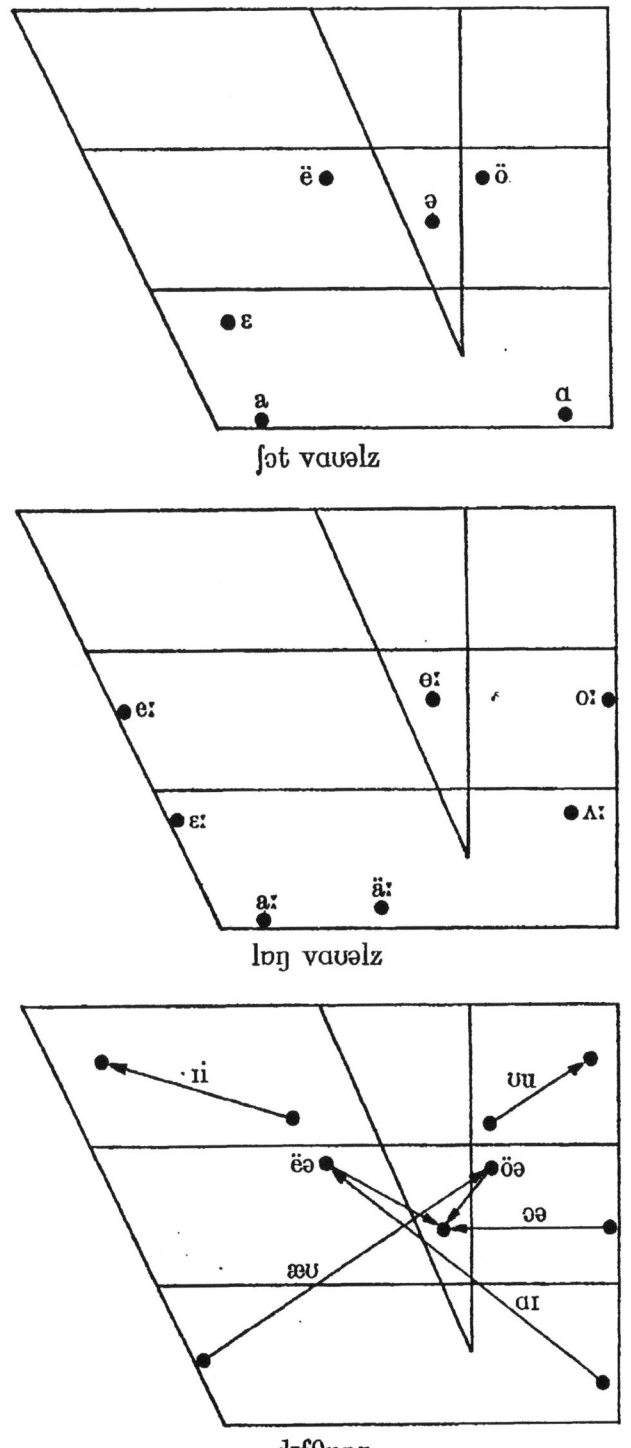

wıð fəʊnim 10. bʌt, ʌndə ði ınflʊəns əv stændəd prənʌnsıeıʃn bəʊθ 9 ənd 10 kæn bi əkeıʒnlı həd əz dıfθɒŋz, [ä·ë] fə fəʊnim 10 ənd [ä·ə] ɔ [ää] fə fəʊnim 9. ın ðız ınflʊənst fɔmz ðeı ə nevə kənfjuzd. ðız tu fəʊnimz kɒnstıtjut ə preʃə pɔınt ın ðə sıstəm. nəʊ daʊt, sʌm tʃeındʒ ın ðə sıstəm wʊd teık pleıs ıvn ıf ðə daıəlekt wə left tʊ ıtself, bət əmʌŋ jʌŋgə spikəz ðə dıstıŋkʃn həz rıəsətıd ıtself prɒbəblı ın əkɔdəns wıð ðə tendənsı tə levl aʊt tʊ ə mɔ stændəd prənʌnsıeıʃn ıvn ðəʊ ə rıdʒənəl wʌn. ðə fəʊnimz əv ðə jʌŋgə dʒenəreıʃn a /aː/ ənd /aı/ (= RP /a/ ənd /aı/).

11. veərıəs dıgriz əv raʊndıŋ kən bı həd—[ɔ̞ː], [ɔː] ɔr ıvn [ʌɔ̞].
12. veərız bıtwin kɑdməlz 6 ənd 7.
14. fri veərıeıʃn wıð [ëı] ðəʊ [ii] ız mɔ frikwənt. dʌz nɒt əkɜ bıfɔ /ı/.
15. bıfɔ /ı/ ız [e̞ːə].
19. bıfɔ /ı/ ız [ö̞ːə]. ðıs sikwəns ɔlsəʊ əkɜz əkrɒs mɔfim baʊndrız æz ın [dö̞ə] = *doer*.
20. əkeıʒnl fri veərıənts—[ɵʊ], [əʊ] ɔ [ëʊ]. dʌz nɒt əkɜ bıfɔ /ı/. əkeıʒənlı vaʊəlz ə slaıtlı neızlaızd bıfɔ /m/ ənd /n/. ðə sikwəns /Vm/ ɔ /Vn/ meı = [Ṽ].

kɒnsənənts.

ðə kɒnsənənts ɑr əz ın RP wıð ðə fɒləʊıŋ ıksepʃnz :—
/t/ meı ɔ meı nɒt bi æspıreıtıd ənd ıt ız verı əkeıʒənlı æfrıkeıtıd.
/k/ ız əkeıʒənlı æspıreıtıd.
/p/ ız nevə æspıreıtıd bət ə fɒləʊıŋ /l/, /ı/ ɔ /j/ ız pɑʃəlı dıvɔıst.
/t/, /k/ ənd /p/ (æz ın [kɑːmʔ meːk] = *can't make*) ər ɒftən rıəlaızd əz [ʔ]. ɔl ɒftən hæv glɒtl rıınfɔsmənt ın faınl pəzıʃn.
[ŋ] ız nɒt fənimık bʌt ən æləfəʊn əv /n/ bıfɔ /k/ ənd /g/. /ng/ + stɒp meı = [ŋ] + stɒp.
dıstıŋkʃn əv neızlz ız njutrəlaızd bıfɔ /f/ ənd /v/ ın [ɱ].
/h/ ız nɒt ə fəʊnim bət meı əkeıʒənlı bi juzd, ın verı keəfəl spitʃ.
/b/, /d/, /g/ ə juʒʊəlı prənaʊnst əz vɔıslıs leımeız ın æbsəlut faınl pəzıʃn ənd bıfɔ vɔıslıs saʊndz. laıkwaız /v/, /ð/, /z/, /d͡ʒ/ ənd /ʒ/.

(3) *spesımın tekst.*

ın ðə tekst ðə trənskrıpʃn ız meınlı fənimık, bʌt æləfɒnık veərıənts ə ʃəʊn ın ıntrəstıŋ keısız. /p/, /t/, /k/ ə mɑkt əkɔdıŋ əz ðeı ər æspıreıtıd, æfrıkeıtıd, glɒtəlı rıınfɔst ɔ nɒt. ðə leımıs saʊndz ə mɑkt wen ðeı ə vɔıslıs. dɒts (....) ındıkeıt ə pɔz ın ði ınfɔmənts spitʃ.

dæʃɪz (——) ɪndɪkeɪt ənʌðə spikə tɔkɪŋ, ɒn ði ərɪdʒɪnəl teɪp. ði ʌðə spikəz həv bin əmɪtɪd. ði əuvəlæp əv /a:/ ənd /ä:/ ɪz ʃəun. ðə fɒləuɪŋ reprɪzents ðə spitʃ əv ðə prɪnsɪpl ɪnfəmənt, ə wumən əv 68.

ðë avʌmp brin'æut tə'de: ðë 'wo:nk go: 'æu? jə 'no: n̥les .... ðḷ 'go: 'æut ëf *'malëz ëa bə²t ðë 'wo:nk go: 'æu? wä:l 'ä:m luukën 'aftə ðəm. sɪim tə'stap 'ën, a 'ka:nk gɛʔ ðəm tə go: 'æu²t. wë wɛɹe ëntə *'luuësëz an .... 'mʊndë and wë wɛnt ëntu ə 'k'afë aë avʌmp 'brɪn ëm bë'fəa, 'nëa *luuësëz. ay fə'ga?n̥ 'wat ëts 'kʌ:ld. ə vɛɹë 'nä:s 'ple:s, *'d͡ʒakë.——

k'ən juu 'ëɛɹ 'ʌ:l ðə θëŋĝz̥ lä:? 'ða? an ë?.——

*'k'ɛnəθ 't'uuk ðə 'plan̥dz̥, tə sɪi ðə 'bəɹe sə've:ɹə, jëstə'de:.——

wɛl, ʊu az̥ 'fä:ɹ əz ɹi köd 't'ɛl ëm, ë? wöd bë 'ʌɹ 'ɹä:t' ëf wë gat' .... ðə 'be:s 'ʌ:l 'bɹëk'. wë 'kä:nt av ə 'sɹidə wöd 'be:s.——

'wɛl, ë?s 'tuu 'de:nd͡ʒəɹəs ə 'sömθëën. nat' ən'lɛs ë? wəz me:d 'faëə 'pɹɹuuf. n̥ jə 'me:k ðəm 'faëə 'pɹɹɹd͡ ðë 'kast ə 'lat əv 'mönë. 'kas kwä:t ə bët' əz ðë 'ä:.——

'no:, ɹi 'gat tˢʊu av ëz̥ 'planz 'dɹʌ:n̥ næu n̥ söb'më²t ðəm t'uu ðɹi 'k'æunsḷ an 'o:p ðë 'pas ë?, 'sɹi. so: *'k'ɛnəθ ad 'pä:t əv ðë aftə'nuun af.

'θank 'gödnës, ë? 'wo:nt t'e:k më 'laŋ t'ə 'dɹä: ë?, 'wɛl ë? ðën.——

av ðë 'fënëʃ jə 'baθɹuum?——

ë?s ðə dɛkə'ɹe:tën ðət 'kan bɪi ə 'bögbɛː. *kɛəθs 'fënëʃt ....
*'nʌ:mənz lëtḷ 'ɹuum. ë? 'luuks vɛɹë 'nä:s 'tʊu.——

n̥ ɹiz 'pöt 'ðat' .... 'peɪpɹ an jə 'no: ðət 'ɹits ðə 'wʌ:lz. so: 'ða? ɹuum ʃödn̥t bë 'damp næu. kös ë? .... 'ʌ:l ða? 'sä:d əv ðë 'æus wants 'paɪntën. njə 'fa:ðə wəz 't'ɛlën *'k'ɛnəθ las 'nä:t', ë sɛ, a 'θɛnk wä:l jəɹ 'avën ðës 'wʌ:l 'dön, ðə 'se:m 'bɹɛksɛɹə kən 'duu ðɹi 'pəetʃ ət ðə ''fɹont' ən 'lɛʔɹ gɛʔ 'ɹɛd ə ðo:z 'bɹɛks ɹɛː ɹɛe ən 'ä: sɔə.——

wɛl jə 'sɹi, *'k'ɛnəθ 't'e:ks söt͡ʃ ə 'lat' əv 'd͡ʒabz an an ɹi 'nɛvə siimz̥ t'ə gɛʔ wan 'fënëʃ bë'fəɹ ɹi 'stä:ts ə'nöðə wan. jə 'no: ðəz söt͡ʃ ə 'laʔ ðə²t 'wants 'duuën ðət' ɹi 'tɹɹä:z̥ t'ə duu 't'uu 'möt͡ʃ əʔ 'wöns. a wəz go:ën 't ask jəz̥ æʊ .... köʃ jə 'wo:n²t a:dlë 'no: 'æʊ jə go:ën 'an wë 'ða²t. böt 'sömwan ðət 'wəːk wëd 'fa:ðə, 'ɹiz ad 'wan pöt 'ën. o: ɹi 'pɹɹe:zəz̥ ëʔt. ë?s 'ɹɹilë 'wöndəföl. ë k'ən av 'aʔ 'baθs ʌ:l de: 'o:ɹeɹ a bə'lɹiv.

(4) *ɹidɪŋ pis ɪn ʃənimɪk tɹənskɹɪpʃn̥ wið ði ədɪʃn əv [ʔ]*

ðə 'nʌ:θ 'wënd and ðə 'sön

ðə 'nʌ:θ 'wënd an ðə 'sön wə dës'pjuutëm wët͡ʃ wəz ðə 'stɹaŋə wɛn ə

ˈtɹavlə keːm əˈlɑŋ ˈɹapt ën ə ˈwʌːm ˈkloːk. ðəː əˈgɹɹid ðət ðə ˈwɑn ʊʊ ˈfəːs sökˈsɹɪdëd ën ˈmeːkën ðə ˈtɹavlə ˈteːk ëz ˈkloːk af ʃəd bɹi kənˈsëdəd ˈstɹɑŋə ðən ðë ˈöðə. ðən ðə ˈnʌːθ ˈwënd ˈblʊu wëð ˈʌːl ëz ˈmäːt, böt ðə ˈmɔəɹ ɪi ˈblʊu ðə mɔə ˈkloːslë dëd ðə ˈtɹavlə ˈfoːld ëz ˈkloːk əˈɹæʊnd ëm. ənd ət ˈlas ðə ˈnʌːθ ˈwënd geːv ˈöp ðë əˈtɛmt. ˈðɛn ðə ˈsön ˈʃɑn æʊʔ ˈwʌːmlë ənd ëˈmɹɪdjətlë ðə ˈtɹavlə tʊʊk ˈaf ëz ˈkloːk ənd ˈsoː ðə ˈnʌːθ ˈwënd wəz əˈbläːd͡ʒd tə kənˈfɛs ðət ðə ˈsön wəz ðə ˈstɹɑŋəɹ əv ðə ˈtʊʊ.

K. R. LODGE.

spesimɛn

*dʒə'meikən 'kriːoul

'wɔt 'fɔlouz iz ðə 'stɔːri əv *'sində'relə (CINDERELLA), 'æz 'tould bai ə 'wumən 'eidʒd əbaut 'θəːti huː əz 'livd 'ɔːl hə 'laif in ə 'smɔːl 'vilidʒ in WESTMORELAND, JAMAICA. it wəz ri'kɔːdid bai ðə 'raitə in 'sʌmə 'naintiːn 'siksti 'siks, ənd iz 'hiə træn'skraibd frəm 'teip.

ðə træn'skripʃn̩ iz fə'niːmik. it 'difəz frəm 'ðæt juːzd in BAILEYZ *Jamaican Creole Syntax* 'fəːstli in ðət 'mɔːfiːm 'ɔːltənənts ə 'hiə di'stiŋgwiʃt, ən 'sekəndli in ðət ðə 'simbl̩z iː eː aː oː uː ʃ tʃ dʒ j ŋ ə 'juːzd in'sted əv həː *ii, ie, aa, uo, uu, sh, ch, j, y, ng*. 'skwɛə 'brækits iŋ'klouz 'hezi'teiʃn̩z, mi'steiks, ən 'sou ɔn. ðər ə 'njuːmərəs 'stændəd iŋgliʃ 'fɔːmz in ðə 'pæsidʒ ri'pleisiŋ 'kriːoul fɔːmz. ðə 'riːdə ʃud pə'hæps bi 'wɔːnd ðət /madarinlaː/ miːnz 'stepmʌðə, ən /oːbin/ 'ʌvn̩, ən ðət 'ɔːl 'kriːoul 'naunz, iŋ'kluːdiŋ /slipaz ∼ sliporz/, ɑːr in'difrənt 'æz tə 'nʌmbə.

sindirila 'mada 'dai, an hor 'faːda 'marid a 'njuː 'waif. di 'waif [briŋ] 'baːt hoːm 'tuː 'tʃildrin wid 'hor, 'tuː 'gorlz. 'sindi'rila 'madarin'laː 'put hor 'out'said in di 'kitʃin tu duː 'aːl di 'kukin, di 'waʃin, an di 'kliːnin, an di 'tuː 'gorl dat ʃi 'baːt 'hoːm 'wid hor, ʃi 'dres dem 'op 'evri 'deː. 'wan 'deː di 'kiŋ 'giv 'out dat 'hiː iz 'goin tu 'hav a 'daːns. 'sindi'rila 'madarin'laː 'drest op fi hor 'tuː 'daːta an 'sen dem 'aːf tu di 'daːns, 'liːv sindi'rila at 'hoːm. 'sindi'rila 'krai. a 'feːri 'kom an 'dres sindi'rila, 'put hor intu 'goːlen 'sliporz, 'glitorin 'dres, an 'giv or a 'bogi [tu 'raid] tu 'draiv 'aːn. 'wen sindi'rila 'riːtʃ di 'baːl [di di] di 'kiŋ 'son 'kom 'out an 'eks'kaːt hor 'in. an di 'kiŋ son 'neva waːnt 'eniwan 'els tu 'daːns wid bot 'sindi'rila. bot di 'feːri 'tel sindi'rila dat i mos bi 'ʃoːr dat wen di 'klak straik 'wan ʃi 'mos bi at 'hoːm 'bak. an 'wen di 'oua woz 'komin [di] di 'kiŋ 'son did nat 'waːn tu 'let or 'goː. sindirila 'haz tu ri'zis an 'pul a'weː. an ʃi 'luːz 'wan av hor 'sliporz. an in di 'maːrnin di 'kiŋ 'son 'sen 'out 'men tu 'sortʃ for di 'gorl dat 'luːz di 'sliporz. 'evri'weːr deː 'goː deː 'trai di 'sliporz. it 'kudn fit 'noː'wan. 'wen dem 'riːtʃ fi 'sindi'rila 'madarin'laː 'jaːd, 'sindi'rila 'madarin'laː 'kjar 'out di 'tuː 'gorlz dat ʃi 'teːk fi or 'aidal an ʃi [ʃi] 'trai it. an 'aːl dat dem 'duː it 'kudn 'fit dem. dem 'heːr a 'likl 'bord 'siŋin, ju kud 'peːr ju 'hiːl, ju kud 'peːr ju 'toː, di 'wan av di 'ʃuːz iz in di 'oːbin. bai 'dat taim 'sindi'rila woz 'in di 'oːbin, for [i de d] di 'madarin'laː 'hid or a'weː. di 'man 'aːks if 'deːr iz 'eniwan 'els in di 'jaːd. 'dem sed 'noː. its 'oːnli a 'likl 'dorti 'gorl 'outsaid di 'doːr. di 'man se 'fetʃ or. an 'wen dem 'briŋ sindi'rila, a 'sindirila 'dʒos put hor 'toː tu di 'slipaz, it 'slip rait 'in. an sindi'rila 'dʒos torn or 'han bi'hain or an 'tek di 'ada wan. an di 'feːri 'dres 'aːf sindi'rila a'geːn. an [di] di 'man 'tek 'hoːm sindi'rila, an di 'kiŋ son 'marid tu sindi'rila an 'liːv di 'tuː 'gorlz at 'hoːm 'stil.

J. C. WELLS.

ɪŋglɪʃ: kɒkni

fɒlʌʘɪŋ ðə spɛsɪmən əv ðə spiːtʃ əv *bɛn ɪn mɛtʀ fonetik nʌmbər
130, hiːr aːr tuː mɔːr kɒkni transkrɪpʃənz. wʌn ɪz əv *nan, rilɛɪtɪd tə
*bɛn baɪ ðə marɪdʒ əv hər dɔːtər tə hɪz sʌn. ði ʌðər spɛsɪmən ɪz əv
*stiːvi, *nanz sʌn. sʌm ʌnjuːʒəl sɪmblz mɛi niːd ɛksplənɛɪʃən.

ɹ̺—pʌʘst alviʌʘlər vɔɪst frɪkʃənləs kəntɪnjuənt.
d̺—alviʌʘlər vɔɪst frɪkʃənləs kəntɪnjuənt.
n̺—nɛɪzəlaɪzd alviʌʘlər vɔɪst frɪkʃənləs kəntɪnjuənt.
ʂ—vɔɪsləs frɪkətɪv vɛri sɪmɪlər tə [s] jɛt lʌʘər ɪn pɪtʃ—mɔːr
    "hʌʃɪŋ", nɒt alviʌʘlʌʘ-palətəl, palətʌʘ-alviʌʘlər ɔr
    rɛtrəflɛks.
ʻ—slaɪt aspərɛɪʃən.
f̬—vɔɪst dɛntəl flap.

ði "ʌnjuːʒəl" saʘndz sɪmbəlaɪzd ðʌs aːr dɪskʌst ɪn dɪtɛɪl ɪn maɪ
aːrtɪkəl, "The Range of Contoidal Articulations in a Dialect," *Orbis*
XVII, 2, disɛmbər, 1968. ðə valjuz əv ðə vaʘl sɪmbəlz juːzd ər ʃʘn
ɪn ə tʃaːrt ɪn ði əbʌv mɛtʀ fonetik (dʒulaɪ–disɛmbər, 1968). ə lɒŋ daʃ
ɪndɪkɛɪts ə pɔːz ɔr hɛzɪtɛɪʃən baɪ ðə spiːkər. spɛɪsɪz hav bɪɪn lɛft at
ɔr əz klɒʘs əz pɒsɪbəl tu wəːrd baʘndəriz bət ðiːz hav nʌʘ fənetɪk valju.

*nan wəz sɛvənti sɛvən wɛn ðɪs tɛɪp rikɔːrdɪŋ wəz mɛɪd. ʃi həz
lɪvd hər hʌʘl laɪf wɪðɪn ə maɪl ər sʌʘ əv hər bəːrθplɛɪs ɪn *bɛθnəl
griːn, *lʌndən, ɪksɛpt fər ʃɔːrt hɒlɪdɛɪz ənd ivakjuɛɪʃən tə *wɪtstəbəl
djuːrɪŋ ðə sɛkənd wəːrld wɔːr. ʃi həz wəːrkt ɪn ə təbakʌʘ faktəri, əz
ə siːmstrɪs ənd əz ə haʘswaɪf. ʃi wəz ðə jʌŋgɪst əv twɛnti tuː tʃɪldrən.

ðə fɒlʌɑɩŋ mɒnəlɒg ɩz hər riplɑɩ tə ðə kwɛstʃən, " ɑːr mɛni əv jər brʌðərz ən sɩstərz stɩl əlɑɩv ? "

ə fjuː wəːrdz ənd frɛɩzɩz mɛɩ niːd trænzlɛɩʃən ɩntu ɩŋglɩʃ ɔːrθɒgrəfi. ðə fəːrst wəːrd əv lɑɩn 7 ɩz " Well ". ðə sɛkənd ənd θəːrd wəːrdz əv lɑɩn 7 ənd ɔːlsʌɒ əv lɑɩn 16 ɑːr " don't know ". ðə fəːrst " wəːrd " ɒn lɑɩn 15 ɩz " I haven't ". ðə sɩksθ ən sɛvənθ wəːrdz ɒn lɑɩn 18 ɑːr " saucy answer ".

    1. ˈnɐɑ ə?—
    2. z̩ ˈɛɒnẽ
    3. ˈtˢʏ ʔə—
    4. ˈt̪θɹɛː v əs əˈlɑɪf ˈnɑɩ̯ ˈɑː?—
    5. ɛ s ˈmɛɐ
    6. æ ˈsɩsd̪8 ˈflɔɹɛ əm—
    7. ˈb8ɑ ˈdɛ3 næ f ðə ˈbɹɑðə z̩ əˈlɑɛɣ
    8. ˈtʃɕɑlɛɛ ðə ˈjəŋgɛs ˈwʌn
    9. ˈeː ˈmœɒɣd̪ð əˈwʌɛ wə mɛ̩ ˈsɩst'ɹ̩ ɩn ˈlɔː tʰə ˈdægŋəm b̪ə̊?—
   10. ˈbwɛm me ˈbɹɑðə ˈd̪ɑɐ̯d̪ ən ˈɑ—
   11. d̪ˢe ˈʌðə ˈlɑɐ̯? ˈmɛɛ̩ ə—
   12. ˈbɹavəs—
   13. ˈɩː wəz̩ ˈlɩvɩm wɛ̩ me ˈbɹɑðɐ
   14. am ˈbwɛn ɛ̩ː ˈd̪ɑːd̪ ɛz̩ ˈwɑːf ˈmøɹɣ tʰɛ ˈdægŋnəm
   15. ˈʌɪvə̃ ˈsɩn ˈkʰʌl8ɹ ˈɒv ẽm fə ˈjəːs
   16. ɕ ˈd̪ɛɑ ˈnɛə f eː z əˈlɑːɪv ɔː—
   17. ˈdɛɛd̪
   18. æ ˈnɔ? ˈg̊ɩvẽ jə ə ˈsɔːsɩ ˈɑ̃ːsɹ̩ ˈɑː ˈd̪æɒm ˈb̪ɔðʌ
   19. ˈb̪ə? ɕ ˈwɑd ˈlɑɐ̯? tˢə̃ ˈnæɐ f mẽ ˈsɩsd̪ə z ɛˈlɑːɪv ʃeː z əˈbɑː?—
                                       k
   20. ˈɩf ʃɩ z əl—
   21. ɛˈlɔɐv ˈʃe z əˈbɑːtˢ—
   22. ˈaɛtˢe tˢɑ ˈʌɛtˢɩ ˈwʌn
   23. æn̩ ˈɛn̩ ɛː z ˈmɛɛ
   24. ˈsɛʔmtˢɩ ˈaɛ? əː—
   25. ˈsɛvntˢɩ ˈsɛvn
   26. ˈjɛː
   27. ɕ ˈb̪eː ˈsɛvntʰe ˈaɛ? ˈðɩs ˈb̪əːθˈd̪æɛ f ɕ ˈlev

*stiːvi wəz fɔːrti fɔːr ət ðə tɑɩm əv rikɔːrdɩŋ. hi tuː həz spɛnt ɔːlmʌɒst ɔːl hɩz lɑɩf wɩðɩn ə fjuː " təːnɩŋz " əv hɩz bəːrθplɛɩs ɩn *bɛθnəl griːn. ðə mɛɪdʒər absənsɪz hav biːn sɪks mʌnθs ɪn ðə nɛɪvi djuːrɪŋ ðə sɛkənd wɔːr and sʌm mʌnθs ɪn ə hɒspɪtəl ɪn *bɛɪzɪŋstʌɒk. hi həz weːrkt əz ə lɒri draɪvər fər ðə *lʌndən kaɒnti kaɒnsəl, əz ə striːt trɛɪdər ɒn hɪz faːðər-ɪn-lɔːz vɛdʒətəbəl barʌɒ and mʌɒst risəntli əz ə pɔːrter ət ðə *bɪlɪŋzgɛɪt fɪʃ maːrkɪt. ɪn ðə pasɪdʒ transkraɪbd hi ɪkspleɪnz haɒ ənd waɪ ðə tiːtʃərz ət hɪz dɔːtərz skuːl həd dɪsweɪdɪd hər frəm eɪmɪŋ fər ə kərɪːr ɪn ðə liːgəl prəfɛʃən.

ðə θɜːrd weːrd ɪn laɪn 4 ɪz " mistress ".

1. 'nɛː ɪn 'ɔɒ 'fɛɛnəs 8 'mɛɪn̯ ɛɪ—
2. ðə 'pʰɒd̯ ɪʔ—
3. 'fɛəlɪ 'pɨlvɪn
4. ðɪ 'ɛ̯d 'mɪsɪs 'ɔːsəɒ də—
5. kʰə'ɹɪə 'wɒmən̯ ɪ 'ɕ—
6. bɪ'tʰwɪin̯ ə 'laðz ɛ 'nɛvə 'sɛd ɪʔ ʌː̯ʔɹɑəʔ bət ʃ 'dɕɒn æf də 'æv ɪʔ 'sb̯ɛɒʔ 'æː ʔ 'tˢɤ jɤ
7. 'mɔː lɛs ɪʔ s ə 'faːmləɪ—
8. ə'fɛː 'lɔə
9. jɪ 'nɐɒ lɒɪk—
10. 'dɛd z ə 'bʌɹɪsd̯ə̯ ən—
11. ɪɪʒ 'faːɤ bɛ'fɔɹ əm wəz ə 'bʌɹɪsd̯ə̯ ən—
12. 'gɹaɱ'fɒːvə wəz ə 'bæɹɪsd̯ə̯
13. 'ɔːsəɒ ðɪɪ ə—
14. 'mɛnɪɪ 'kʰɐmz 'ɪntɕɒ əʔ ə'gen 'lɑɪkʰ
15. jɨ 'n̯ɒʔ—
16. 'bɔːn on̯ 'ɛʔ 'saːɪd ə ðə 'fɛnʔs
17. 'ɔːsɐɒ—
18. 'bɪːn ə 'gɒːɒ—
19. 'wɛːɹ ə 'fələ 'sɛɪ—
20. 'g̊ɒʔ ɤ gɪʔ 'naɒ̃tʰɪ pə 'sɛnʔ—
21. ə:—
22. 'sɛvənti pə 'sɛnʔ ə 'gɒə z gɒʔ ə gɛʔ 'naɒ̃tʰɪ pə 'sɛnt ʃi 'nɐɒ
23. 'fɒːvə'mɔː ɹɛɪ 'dɕɒ̃ wɒn əm 'ʔɪn ðæʔ pʰə'fɛsən 'ji nɐɒ lɒʔ ɪʔ s ə—
24. 'kɨlɐɒʒ 'ʃɒpˈ 'tˢɕəpʰ ə 'fɪŋ

J. R. HURFORD.

ɪŋglɪʃ : kokni

ɑːftər ðə transkrɪpʃənz əv *bɛn, *nan, ənd *stiːvi ɪn priːviəs ɪʃuːz əv ðɪs dʒɜːrnəl, hiːr ɑːr spɛsɪmənz əv ðə spiːtʃ əv ðɛːr rɛlətɪvz, *fʊl ənd *ɛɪdə. *fʊl ɪz *bɛnz sʌn, marid tu *ɛɪdə. *ɛɪdə ɪz *nanz dɔːtər ənd *stiːviz sɪstər. sʌm ʌnjuːʒəl sɪmbəlz ɑːr ɛksplɛɪnd bɪlʌꚙ.

ð̪—dɛntəl vɔɪst frɪkʃənləs kəntɪnjuənt.
ɹ̠—pʌꚙst-alvɪʌꚙlər vɔɪst frɪkʃənləs kəntɪnjuənt.
ʔ—viːləraɪzd glɒtəl stɒp.
m̥—nɛɪzəlaɪzd baɪlɛɪbiəl vɔɪst frɪkʃənləs kəntɪnjuənt.
'—slaɪt aspərɛɪʃən.

ðiːz and ʌðər "ʌnjuːʒəl" saꙍndz ɑːr dɪskraɪbd ɪn mɔːr ditɛɪl ɪn maɪ ɑːrtɪkəl, "The Range of Contoidal Articulations in a Dialect," *Orbis*, xvii, 2, dɪsɛmbər, 1968. aɪ hav dɪskraɪbd ðə mɛθəd əv transkraɪbɪŋ vaꙍlz juːzd hiːr ɪn "The Judgment of Vowel Quality", *Language and Speech*, 12, 4, dɪsɛmbər, 1969, and ə tʃɑːrt ʃʌꙍɪŋ ðə valjuz əv ðə vaꙍl sɪmbəlz juːzd hiːr ɔːlsʌꙍ əpiːrz ɪn ði **m.f.**, 130. ɪn ðə transkrɪpʃənz iːtʃ ʌtərəns baꙍndɪd baɪ pɔːzɪz ɪz rɪtən ɒn ə sɛpərət nʌmbərd laɪn. ə lɒŋ daʃ sɪgnɪfaɪz ə hɛzɪtɛɪʃən ɔːr ə brɛɪk ɪn ði ɪkspɛktɪd grəmatɪkəl patərn. spɛɪsɪz hav biːn lɛft at, or əz klʌꙍs əz pɒsɪbəl tu, wərd baꙍndəriz, bət ðiːz hav nʌꙍ fənɛtɪk valju.

*fʊl wəz fɔːrti tuː wɛn ðɪs tɛɪp rikɔːrdɪŋ wəz mɛɪd. hi wəz bɔːrn ɪn *stɛpni ənd lɪvd ɔːl hɪz priː-marɪtəl laɪf ðɛːr. sɪns marɪɪŋ *ɛɪdə, hiː həz lɪvd ɪn *bɛθnəl *griːn. hɪz ʌꙍnli absənsɪz frəm ði *iːst *ɛnd əv *lʌndən hav biːn fər sɜːrvɪs wɪθ ðə nɛɪvi ɪn *skɒtlənd fər mʌꙍst əv ðə sɛkənd wɜːrld wɔːr and fər briːf hɒlɪdɛɪz, juːʒəli ɒn ðə saꙍθ kʌꙍst. hi həz wɜːrkt əz ə bʊkmɛɪkər ənd striːt mɜːrtʃənt. ɪn ðə pasɪdʒ bɪlʌꙍ hi kəmplɛɪnz, ɪn ðə prɛzəns əv sɛvərəl əv hɪz brʌðərz and əv *bɛn, hɪz fɑːðər, əv ði ɪmpɒsɪbɪlɪti əv wɪnɪŋ mʌni gamblɪŋ ɒn hɔːrsɪz. ɪn laɪnz 13 tu 20 hi lɪsts ðə kəntɪndʒənsiz wɪtʃ ə pʌntər mʌst kənsɪdər wɛn bakɪŋ ə hɔːrs.

1. ð̪ɛt s 'wɐe je ɣ8ʔ 'nɐɤ 'tʃɔ̃ːs 'bækʰɪn 'ɔːsɪʑ
2. 'bɛɪd 'n̪ɐf d̪ʒ 'd8ɣz bə ð̪ɛm 'ꙍɔsɪz jɤ ɣ8ʔ 'nɐꙍ 'tʃɑːnts
3. ð̪ɛ 'sʌɛv 'ꙍɔsɪz—
4. d̪ð̪ə 'kʰɯː?p̬ 'gəː—
5. 'ð̪ɛ gɔ̃ 'ɹ̠ɛn 'fɒæf 'tʰɹ̠ɛmʑ
6. bəʔ ð̪æɛ 'nɐuː əː?—

7. ðə 'sṷk̯s̭ 'tʰɑɛm
8. 'bæŋ
9. 'kʰɹæʃ
10. 'wɒl8p
11. ɔ̃:—n 'dɛt s wən æɛ 'pʰɐɹ ɩʔ—ðə 'mʌnɩ 'dɐ:
12. 'jœ gɜʔ—'jɐ g8ʔ 'sɩʔk ən 'tʰɑːəd ɜ 'bakʰɩn ɩʔ 'fɒæv 'tʰᵥɐmz ɔ̃ 'sɐks 'tˢaːm jɛ̭ 'nɒɪ̭ 'ɒn
13. 'sɯ: ðɛ̭ 'gɐɑ̃ wəẑ 'tˢəʘ 'ɑːd
14. ðɛ 'gÆɪ̃ wəẑ 'tˢʏɐ 'sof
15. ɔ: ḓœ 'dʒɔʔkˈɩ 'kʰɐm 'tˢɜʘ 'sœun
16. e 'ɛod ʏm 'ʌp 'tˢœʘ 'beʔtʃ
17. ɩ 'nɛvə 'kʰʌm 'kʰwɛʔ ɩ'nɛf
18. jɩ 'sɯ: ðɛ̭ 'pʰɐd ɛm ɔ̃m 'bleŋk̯əzs
19. ḓɛɳ ɛ 'fʌːnd 'ɑːʔ e 'wɛns 'tˢœʘben
20. ðɛn ɛɛ 'feːɾ 'ʌːʔ ɩ 'wɒ̃ts 'gɛɵden

*ɛɩðə wəz θɜːrti faɩv wɛn ðə tɛɩl bilʌʘ wəz rikɔːrdɩd. ʃi həz lɩvd ɔːl hər laɩf wɩðɩn ə fjuː hʌndrɩd jɑːrdz əv hər bəːrθpleɩs ɩn *bɜθnəl *griːn, ɩksɛpt djuːrɩŋ ðə sɛkənd wəːrld wɔːr, wɛn ʃi wəẑ ivakjuɛɩtɩd tə *wɩtstəbəl, ənd fər ʃɔːrt hɒlɩdeɩz. ʃi ɩz ə haʘswaɩf. hiːr ʃi tɛlz hər tuː tʃɩldrən ənd miː ə stɔːri əbaʘt *nan, hər mʌðər.

1. ʃəl ɐ 'tʰɛl əm ə'bæʔ 'nanɩ wɐ̃ 'ʃɩ fəs gɒʔ 'mæɹɩḓ·
2. ɒ 'wɛm mɐ 'mɐvə fəs gɒʔ 'mæɹɪd ʒ̊ɨ 'sɛɩ
3. wɩθ—
4. 'sɒɔʔ əv 'nɒlɩẑ ðɨt 'ʃɔː 'tʰɔokʰən ə'bæɛʔ
5. ðɛɩ 'dɩʔɳ 'nʌʘ—
6. 'wɛʘ ʃɩ z̭ 'sɛvəntʰɨ 'sṷk̯s 'nɯːlɩ 'næɛ bœʔ ʃi ɒz baʔ 'ɛɩ'tʰəɩn 'ðɛn
7. əm 'wɛ̃ ʃɩ 'fəs gɒʔ 'maɹɩd ðɛɩʔ—
8. ʃ—
9. 'ðɛː 'səd—
10. ³jɩ 'nɛʘ wɛ̃ ʃ 'wɛ̃ʔ—
11. tʰ 'pʰɐʔ əː 'bæːnz 'ɐːʔpˈ jɛ 'nɛʘ ðə 'vɩkʰɹ 'ɑːst ɐ
12. 'ɩf ʃʏ wɨz i 'spɩnstɐ
13. ɛ̃ ʃː sɛd 'nʌ ːm ə 'tˡɹæːzɨẑ 'fənɩʃɐ
14. ʃɩ 'wɒz 'aktʃələɩ

J. R. HURFORD.

PHONETIC TRANSCRIPTION/SPELLING

nɔːməlaizd founetik speliŋ

founetik speliŋz mei bi kritisaizd frəm tuw distiŋkt points əv vjuw. wij mei aːsk, fəːst, dʌz ðis təkst əfoːd ə feiθfl rəprəznteiʃən əv ðə prənʌnsieiʃən əv its raitə? sekəndli, wij mei aːsk, iz it ijzi tə rijd? ðijz tuw points əv vjuw aː nɔt ounli distiŋkt, bət ðei aː, if kærid tu ən ikstrijm ijtʃ wei, æbsəljuwtli æntægənistik. if it wə pɔsəbl tə giv ən iŋzɔːstivli, minjuwtli ækjərit reprəznteiʃən əv ðə prənʌnsieiʃən əv eni wʌn spijkə bai mijnz əv ælfəbetik sainz, sʌtʃ ə trænskripʃən wud nɔt bi ledʒəbl in ðə præktikl sens əv ðə wəːd: it wud ounli bij, ət ðə best, disaifrəbl.

bət founetik teksts ə nɔt ritn soulli əz spesimənz əv prənʌnsieiʃən; ðei mei bi ritn simpli tə kənvei infəmeiʃən. moust əv ðə teksts in ði **mf** ər əv ðis kærikte — ijvn hwen ðei dijl wið pjuəli founetik kwestʃənz. ən hwen wi ə rijdiŋ əbaut ə sʌbdʒikt in hwitʃ wi ər intristid, wij nætʃərəli prifəː tə hæv ði ekspəziʃən ritn in ðæt speliŋ hwitʃ ineiblz əs moust ijzili ən ræpidli tə rekəgnaiz ðə wəːdz əv hwitʃ it s kəmpouzd.

rəpiditi əv rekəgniʃən dipendz ɔn juwnifɔːmiti: ðə mɔə ðə speliŋ əv ðə njuw tekst difəz frəm ðæt tə hwitʃ wijv hiðətuw bijn əkʌstəmd, ðə mɔə difiklti wij hæv in rijdiŋ it. ðʌs, if wij v bijn juwst tə 'mai litl haus', wi ər æpt tə stʌmbl ouvə 'mɔĕ lĭtl̆ hæŏs'; ənd if wij v wʌns əkʌstəmd auəselvz tə sʌtʃ dʒəːmən speliŋz əz 'viːr baidə' ən 'veːgən dər ainfaxhait unt leːzbarkait', wij kən haːdli bi bleimd fə heziteitiŋ ouvə 'viă paĭdə' ən 'veːŋ da ăĭnfaxhaĭt ŭnt leːspaʀkhaĭt' (**mf** '95. 1, p. 116).

ai əbdʒekt tə sʌtʃ speliŋz əz 'mai, maĕ, məiʳ' etsetrə bikɔz ðɛə nɔt ounli præktikəli inkənvijnjənt ənd ə sɔːs əv kənfjuwʒən, bət bikɔz ðɛə sjuwpəːfluəs, ən ðɛəfɔə tə sʌm ikstent ijvn mislijdiŋ.

hwen ə fɔrinə kəmpɛəz 'ai' wið ði ʌðə spelinz, hijʒ æpt tu əsjuwm ə difrəns əv prənʌnsieiʃən hwitʃ præps dəz nət igzist.

mai əbdʒekʃən tə ðə laːst trænskripʃən kwoutid əbʌv iz nət ðə rizʌlt əv eni dislaik tə ðə vjenə daiəlekt. ənd ijvn if it wəː, ai ʃəd stil hæv tu ədmit ðət fə ðə raitə tə trænslitəreit iz nætʃərəl prənʌnsieiʃən intə ðæt əv nɔːθ dʒəːməni wud bi ə vaiəleiʃən əv founetik prinsiplz.

bət ði æksepteiʃən əv ðə dʒenrəl prinsipl ðət ijtʃ iz tə rait iz oun prənʌnsieiʃən stil lijvz oupn ðə kwestʃən, hau faːr iz ij tə gou in rijprədjuwsiŋ its naisitiz?

ðə mein əbdʒekʃən frəm ðis point əv ˈvjuw tə sʌtʃ ə speliŋ əz 'lɪtḷ' kəmpɛəd wið 'litl' iz ðət ðə speʃl infəmeiʃən it kənveiz iz wəːθlis: evriwʌn nouz ðət ði iŋgliʃ i iz waid; ən ðə maːk ʌndə ði l wud bi sjuwpəːflɵəs ijvn in ə minjuwtli saiəntifik nouteiʃən, fə ði l ʌndə ðə ˈsəːkəmstənsiz kænət bi eniθiŋ els ðən silæbik.

sou ɔlsou ðə z litl geind bai maːkiŋ ðə nəzæliti in dʒəːmən ˈünt': wij ɔːl nou ðət dʒəːmən vauəlz tend tə bikʌm neizl bifɔə neizl kənsənənts.

ðen əz rigaːdz ðə dipθɔŋz, wij ɔːl nou ðət ðɛə sekənd elimənts bouθ in iŋgliʃ ən dʒəːmən ə nət pjuər i ənd u, ən ðət ðɛə fəːst elimənts vɛəri ɔːlmoust frəm mauθ tə mauθ ijvn in ðə seim daiəlekt, ən ðət it s ɔːlmoust impəsəbl tu ikspres ðijz minjuwt distiŋkʃənz ædikwitli, sou ðət it s nət ounli məə præktikl bət ɔlsou les mislijdiŋ tə rait 'mai haus' in ɔːl keisiz hwɛə ðijz spelinz ə nət æbsəljuwtli ʌnfounetik. əv kɔːs, hwen ðə fəːst elimənt əv ai z distiŋkli raundid, wij məst ðen rait 'moi'.

sou ɔlsou ai θiŋk it s ə misteik ˈin ə præktikl ælfəbit tə trai tə distiŋgwiʃ ðə difrənt r-saundz, ən ðət it s betə tə rait simpl r əlaik in iŋgliʃ, frenʃ, ən dʒəːmən. hwen ai faind ʀ insted əv r in ə frenʃ tekst it simpli iriteits mij wiðaut kənveiiŋ eni infəmeiʃən; fər ai nou ɔːlredi ðət ði ɔːdinri frenʃ *r* iz nət ə point kənsənənt. sou ɔlsou in dʒəːmən.

in ʃɔːt, hwen ai m traiiŋ tə get ət ə raitəz mijniŋ aim nət ət ɔːl intristid tə nou hwɛər ij fɔːmz iz ʀ, ɔ hweðər ə nət ij neizəlaiziz iz vauəlz bifɔə neizl kənsənənts. if ij wiʃiz tə kɔːl mai ətenʃən tə pikjuwliæritiz əv iz prənʌnsieiʃən, let im duw sou in ən iniʃl nout — 'vauəlz neizəlaizd bifɔə neizl kənsənənts, *r* = ʀ' etsetrə. ɔ let im giv ə fjuw sentensiz in ə minjuwtli ækjərit nouteiʃən, ən ðen lijv mij tə wei iz aːgjumənts wiðaut hæviŋ mai ətenʃən distræktid bai ʌnnesisərili ʌnkuwθ eksintrisitiz əv speliŋ.

hwɔt ai sədʒest ðɛəfɔr iz ðət ði af ʃəd set ʌp ə stændəd əv præktikl founetik speliŋ fər ijtʃ læŋgwidʒ ɔn ðə lainz indikeitid, frəm hwitʃ sʌtʃ dijvieiʃənz ounli wud bi əlaud hwitʃ ə nesisri tə prizəːv ðə founetik prinsipl.

ðis kud nɔt, əv kɔːs, bi kærid aut wið ijkwəl səːtnti in ɔːl dijteilz: sʌm points wəd hæv tə bi left oupn; fə ðə founetik prinsipl itself əlauz əv sʌm lætitjuwd.

bət ijvn ə limitid juwnifɔːmiti wud bi betə ðən ðə preznt keiəs. ənd it wəd səːtnli tend tə meik founetik teksts ijziə tə rait, print, ən rijd, ən tə meik founetik speliŋ les ripelənt tə ðə dʒenrəl pʌblik.

Henry Sweet.

simplifaid founetik speliŋ(¹)

in ətemtiŋ tə popjuləraiz founetik speliŋ wi ər æpt tə fəɡet ðət ðə dʒenrəl pablik wil ɔːlwiz prifəː ðæt sistim əv raitiŋ whitʃ iz moust kənvijnjənt. nou əmaunt əv propəɡændə wil ɡet ouvə ðis. ijvn inθjuwziæsts when raitiŋ in ə hari wil insensibli slip bæk intə ðə trədiʃənəl ɔːθoɡrəfi if ðə lætər iz ijziə tə rait on ðə houl.

ðə trədiʃənəl ɔːθoɡrəfiz hæv θrij points in ðeə feivəː 1) ðeə fəmiljə, 2) ðeə juwnifɔːm, ən 3) ðeə kəmpærətivli ijzi tə rait. ðə fəːst əv ðijz əloun ɡivz ðəm satʃ ən ədvaːntidʒ ðət wij kaːnt əfɔːd tə let auə founetik ælfəbit fɔːl bihaind ðəm əz riɡaːdz 2) ən 3), if wij kən əvoid it.

auər ælfəbit iz olsou ə roumən wan. it s beist on ði iɡzistiŋ roumən letəz, saplimentid bai təːnd, daiəkritik, ən njuw letəz, ən bai ðə juwtilaizeiʃən əv iɡzistiŋ sjupəːflues letəz satʃ əz c. tu ijtʃ letə wij ɡiv ə mɔːr o les definit vælju — əz faːr əz posibl its əridʒinəl lætin or els its moust dʒenrəl juərəpiən vælju — bət wij əlau ijtʃ læŋɡwidʒ in its præktikl nouteiʃən tə juwz ijtʃ letə fə ðə niərist saund in ðæt læŋɡwidʒ, juwziŋ ap ɔːl ði ould letəz bifɔə hæviŋ rikɔːs tə njuw fɔːmz.

auər ælfəbit in its preznt steit iz, əz əz bijn ripijtidli pointid aut, ə komprəmaiz bitwijn ə præktikl ənd ə saiəntifik ælfəbit, ə saiəntifik ælfəbit bijiŋ wan in whitʃ ðə væljuz əv ðə simblz ə fikst, ən dount veəri frəm læŋɡwidʒ tə læŋɡwidʒ. ai prəpouz nau tə dijl ounli wið ðə fɔːmə.

frəm ðis point əv vjuw meni əv auə simblz ən distiŋkʃənz ə sjupəːflues. ðas ai kaːnt imædʒin eni læŋɡwidʒ rikwaiəriŋ ʊː ðæt iz, ai dount nou eni in whitʃ ʊ, v, b, w ər ɔːl rikwaiəd ət wans, ɔːr, in aðə wəːdz, in whitʃ ʊ kaːnt bi ripleist bai wan əv ði aðə θrij. sou olsou wan r-simbl iz inaf — ət lijst in iŋɡliʃ, frenʃ, ən dʒəːmən.

meni əv auə njuw letəz ə wel sjuwtid fər ə saiəntifik ælfəbit, wheə ðə letəz kən bi ritn o drɔːn ditætʃt, bət ər aut əv pleis in ə præktikl sistim, wheər ɔːl ðə letəz məs bij əz ijzi tə rait ən dʒoin əz posibl. naθiŋ iz məə difiklt ðən tu invent ə ɡud skript letə. ən ðə nambər əv əveiləbl wanz iz limitid. ðə folouiŋ ər

---

1. eksɛpsjɔnɛlmã, e pur mjø mõːtre pratikmã lə saːs dez ɔpsɛrvaːsjõ isi prezãːte, nuz avõ rɛspɛkte l ɔrtɔɡraf də l ɔːtœːr, mɛːm kãt ɛl ɛt ã kõːtradiksjõ avɛk no prɛ̃ːsip alfabetik. k õ n aj pa fɛːr də la ʃoːz œ presedã! — red.

əz gud əz eni əv ði ould letəz: ŋ, ɲ, ʃ, ʒ, ð (in its skript fɔːm), ɥ, θ, ɛ. meni əv ðəm, indijd, ə rieli ould letəz. ə ənd ɒ kam nekst. ən jet ai faind ðət ijvn ðijz kɔːz sam difiklti tə ðə mədʒoriti əv mai pjuwplz. nieli ɔːl auer aðə njuw letəz ai ʃəd ridʒekt frəm eni præktikl sistim əv raitiŋ, aiðə loŋ o ʃɔːt hænd. satʃ distiŋkʃənz əz ɪn ən m ər ɔːlmoust impræktikəbl ijvn in print.

sam əv ðə skript fɔːmz, tuw, ə difiklt tə rimembə bikoz əv ðeə wont əv rizemblens tə ðə printid wanz. ənaðə θiŋ whitʃ pijpl ə ʃuə tə qrambl æt iz hæviŋ tə rait ould letəz in ə not ounli anfəmiljə bət inkənvijnjənt wei; whitʃ iz ðə rizalt əv satʃ diferenʃieiʃənz əz ʋ, v ən ɑ, a.

ðə lætə, it iz tə bi əbzəːvd, iz meid soulli in ði intərests əv frenʃ. ðə rizʌlt iz ðət nou wan kən juwz ðijz simblz wiðaut θiŋkiŋ founetikəli in frenʃ, ən ðət ðə z nou præktikəbl simbl fə ðə nɔːml itæljən ənd iŋgliʃ saund.

ðə frenʃ, əz əpouzd tə ði intənæʃənəl beisis, is olsou sijn in ði juws əv ði æntikweitid (') əz ə maːk əv stres: it s kwait inædikwit fər eni aðə læŋgwidʒ; ənd iz, bisaidz, rikwaied fə intəneiʃən.

it iz, ai θiŋk, dʒenrəli ədmitid ðət auə nouteiʃən əv kwontiti, stres, ənd intəneiʃən iz ansætisfæktəri. whai not ðen lijv ðijz ənd aðə dautfl points oupn? dabliŋ əv loŋ vauəlz ɔːt tə bi opʃənəl.

əz rigaːdz iŋgliʃ ai sij nou nijd fə ði anmijniŋ ənd anraitəbl ʌ fər ə vauəl — o raːðər ə vəraiiti əv vauəlz — whitʃ iz præktikəli ðə ʃɔːt əv ɑː. if wij peər i, ii, wi ə baund tə peə ʌ, ɑː. sou olsou e, ei involvz o, ou. ə iz ounli rikwaied fə ðə loŋ saund in ɔːl, wheə ðə maːk əv leŋθ iz sjupəːflues. ə fəːðə simplifikeiʃən wəd bij tu əboliʃ ɔ ən rait ɔːl or ool; bət ai dount ædvəkeit ðis fər obvies rijznz. it sijmz kliə ðət ə ʃəd bi sabstitjuwtid fə ði agli ənd anraitəbl ø, ən ðət þ ʃəd teik its pleis. ðə laːst iz ritn əz ə luwpt ap p: ðə z nou difiklti in kijpiŋ ðə tuw əpaːt. ai olsou prifəː wh tə ði anfəmiljər ənd æmbigjues hw ən ði anraitəbl ʍ. ai teik ði opətjuwniti əv rimaːkiŋ ðət ɔːl sistimz əv raitiŋ, wheðə præktikl o saiəntifik, mast inkluwd daigræfs; olsou ðət ə rieli præktikl ælfəbit ɔːt tə giv daigræf oltəːnətivz fər ɔːl njuw letəz, satʃ əz sh = ʃ, th = θ (æspərits kən bi distiŋgwiʃt əz t-h etsetrə), tə bi juwzd in raitiŋ tə njuwspeipəz ən fə similə pəːpəsiz.

in frenʃ ai d sabstitjuwt ə fə ø, ən æ fər a, ðas getiŋ rid əv ən imposibl skript fɔːm, ənd juwtilaiziŋ ən ijzili ritn ould letə.

ðə maːk əv nəzæliti mait bi meid intu ən aprait modifaiə folouiŋ ðə vauəl. ðə fəmiljə ñ mait bi səbstitjuwtid fə ɲ, whitʃ iz laiəbl tə bi kənfjuwzd wið ŋ.

fə ði oupn dʒəːmən ɡ in *sagen* it sijmz moust præktikl tə juwtilaiz ɋ, insted əv weistiŋ it on ə vəraiiti əv k ən lijviŋ ðə korispondiŋ vəraiiti əv ɡ ənprəvaidid fɔə. c iz ðə nætʃərəl simbl əv ðə konsənənt in *ich*.

əv kɔːs ai mijn ɔːl ðijz sədʒestʃənz miəli əz igzaːmplz əv ðə wei in whitʃ ai θiŋk wij ɔːt tə feis ðə problim əv popjuləraiziŋ founətik speliŋ not əmaŋ inθjuwziæsts, bət əmaŋ ðə leizi ən predʒudist mədʒoriti.

HENRY SWEET.

ðə træn'skrìpʃn əv ìŋglìʃ vaɔəlz.

əbaɔt faèv jəːz əgɔo, a(è) kəmenst jùuzìŋ ə fənètìk træn'skrìpʃn fə tìitʃìŋ ìŋglìʃ tə maè pjùuplz, ɔ́l ə'dʌlts, mɔost ɔv ðm bìznìsmèn, fjùu ɔv ðm stjùudjəslì ìŋ'klaènd, ɔ́l ɔv ðm ìn ə gɾèét hʌrì tə leːn əz mʌtʃ ìŋglìʃ əz pɔ̀sìbl ìn ðə ʃɔ́tìst pɔ̀sìbl taèm ən wìð ðə lìist pɔ̀sìbl èfət. wìð ə fjùu rèər ən prèézwəː ðì ìk'sèpʃnz, it wz ìm'pɔ̀sìbl tu ìn'djùus ðə pjùuplz tə tèék tə ðə sìmblz sìirìəslì. wèn rìidìŋ, ðèər aèz wùd bi glùud tə ði ɔ́θə'græfìk træn'skrìpʃn ən ðèə hɔol ətènʃn tèékn ʌp bə ðə nɔ́ml spèlìŋ. æz tu ìk'spèktìŋ ðm tə *raèt* ìn fənètìk kærìktəz — ðè maèt dʒʌst əz wèl bi ìk'spèktìd tə raèt ìn tʃaènìiz kærìktəz.

haʊˈevə, maè inˈtènʃn ət prèznt iz nɔt tə rìlèét ðə lɔŋ tʃæptər əv dìfìkltìz ən strɑɡlz in kənèkʃn wið maè èfəts tu imˈplɑːnt fənètìks ɔn ʌnˈkʌltivèétìd ən nʌn tùu frùutfl ɡraʊnd, bət tu inˈvaèt əpìnjn ɔn sʌm əv ðə mènì θɔ́nì kwèstʃnz ət pəːˈplèks ðə tèkst-raètə.

sìns a(è) ɔɔ maè inìˈʃjèéʃn intə fənètìks tə ði **af**, it s ɔonlì nætʃərl ət a(è) ədɔ́ptìd ði **af** ælfəbìt. djùurìŋ ə pìrìed əv əbaʊt θrìi jəːz a(è) jùuzd fənètìks mɔ́ər ɔ́ lès ìkspèrìˈmèntəli, ðə pjùuplz wəːkìŋ frm mænjuskrìpt ʃìits. a(è) wz ðèəfɔ́ frùu tu intrədjùus ènì mɔdìfìˈkèéʃn wìtʃ a(è) maèt knsìdə jùusfl ɔ́ nèsəsèrì. frm taèm tə taèm a(è) *dìd* mɔdìfaè ə fjùu dìitèélz ən əkɔ́dìŋ tə ðə rìˈzʌlts əbtèénd, aèðə rìˈdʒèktìd ɔ́ pəːmənəntlì ədɔ́ptìd ðə mɔdìfìˈkèéʃn.

ət lèŋθ it bìˈkèém nèsəsèrì tə hæv rìˈkɔ́s tə ðə prìntə. bə ðìs taèm a(è) d dìˈsaèdìd in prìnsəpl nɔt ɔonlì tə brèék ɔ́f frm ðə staèl əv trænˈskrìpʃn a(è) d bin jùuzìŋ hìðəˈtùu, bət ɔ́lso, if nèsəsèrì, tə dìˈvəːdʒ frm ði **af** ælfəbìt itˈsèlf. ɔn ðə fèéṣ ɔv it, it wz ə sʌmwɔ̀t ræʃ stèp tə kɔntəmplèét. nɔt ɔonlì wùd it bi ən əˈtèmt əɡènst ði *ynite fɔnetist*, kælkjulèétìd tə sæden ðə hɑːts əv a(ɔ)ə wəːðì èdìtəz; nɔt ɔonlì wùd it bi ə tæsit əvaɔel ət a(è) faʊnd maè knklùuznz səpìi(ə)rìə tə ðɔɔz əv maè əθɔ̀rətìz; it əd mìin ɔlso ət maè pjùuplz əd bi dìˈbɑːd frm jùuzìŋ wið fəsìlìtì ʌðə tèksts ðn ðɔɔz rìtn ɔ́ prìntìd bə ma(è)ˈsèlf. haʊˈevə a(è) kʌmfətìd məsèlf wið ði əʃɔ́rəns ət "it iz bètə . . . tə lììv dìsˈpjùu- "tìd ən daʊtfl pɔènts tə bi sètld ba(è) ikˈspìirìəns, tə trʌst tə "ðə səvaèvl əv ðə fìtìst, rɑːðə ɔn mèék ðə vèén ətèmt tu infɔ́s "wʌn jùunìfɔ́m sìstem əv nətèéʃn waèl ðə vèrì faʊnˈdèéʃuz əv "fənètìks ə stìl ʌndə dìsˈkʌʃn." (*Sweet, The Sounds of English*, § 315.)

ðè(ə)rəpɔ́n a(è) rɔot aʊt ðə wəːk in əkɔ́dns wið maè lèétìst knklùuznz n wènt tə près. maè inˈtènʃn wɔ̀z, n stìl iz, tə jùuz ðìs prìntìd mætə (in ðə fɔ́m əv ʃìits əv sìˈnɔ́ptìk tèéblz) fə maè ɔon pjùuplz, wìðaʊt pʌblìʃìŋ it brɔ́dkɑːst. a(è) prìˈfəː tə ɡìv ðə trænˈskrìpʃn (n ðə mèθəd itˈsèlf) ə fùl n fèə traèl, rìˈzəːvìŋ fər ə fjùutʃə dèét ðə pʌblìˈkèéʃn əv ðə wəːk in əkɔ́dns wið wɔt mé bi maè faènl knklùuznz, wìtʃ l bi dìˈtəːmìnd in pɑːt bə ðə vjùuz əv pɔ̀sìbl krìtìks əz wèl əz baè ə raèpər ikˈspìirìəns.

rìˈvjùuəz haʊevə ər iŋˈklaènd tə kndèm ði inəvèétə: vèərìəs kntrìbjutəz tə ðə **mf** dìsəˈprùuv mɔ́(ə)r ɔ́ lès strɔ̀ŋlì əv ènì trænˈskrìpʃn nɔt in knfɔ́mətì wið ði **af** ælfəbìt. ʌðəz, əɡèén, sìim tə jùuz ði **af** ælfəbìt fə ðə sèék əv jùunìˈfɔ́mətì, frm ə sèns əv djùutì (ɔ́ wɔt èspəˈræntìsts ər in ðə hæbìt əv kɔ́lìŋ *fideleco*).

wi kŋ haːdlì ìg'nɔə ðə fækt, haəèvə, ðt "l ynite fɔnetist" ìz ən æspə'rèéʃn raːðə ðn ə ri'æletì. *Tot homines tot—træn'skrìpʃnz* ìz ðə dʒènr(ə)l rùul ʌp tə ðə prèznt. ði **af** ælfəbìt ìt'sèlf əlaɔz sɔo mèni dìfr(ə)nt ìntəːprì'tèéʃnz ðt tùu tèksts rèprì'zèntìŋ ðə sèém prɔnʌnsjèéʃn mé gìv tùu rì'zʌlts dìfrìŋ vìzjuəlì sɔo grèétlì əz tə gìv ði ìm'prèʃn əv tùu dìfr(ə)nt ælfəbìts. ìz ðə jèt nɔɔ pɔsə-'bìlətì əv ə kɔmən əgrùiment ɔn ə brɔd jèt k(ə)nsìstnt ənd ìg'zækt nɔɔ'tèéʃn əv sʌð(ə)n ìŋglìʃ?

wɔ̀t a(è) pətìkjuləlì dì'zaèə tə nɔo ət prèznt ìz, fəːst, dʒʌst haɔ faːr a(è) *hæv* dì'vəːdʒd frm ði **af** ælfəbìt, ənd, sèkndlì, haɔ faːr a(è) m dʒʌstìfaèd ìn jùuzìŋ ðə fənètìk sìmblz ìn ə mænə ʌðə ðn ðæt əv ðə mèdʒɔrətì əv raètəz əv sʌð(ə)n ìŋglìʃ. ðə staèl əv træn'skrìpʃn a(è) jùuz ìz *ræpìd kɔlɔokwìəl* ədæptìd fə frèntʃ stjùudnts. a(è) v ədɔ̀ptìd ðìs staèl (a.) bì'kɔz ðə wəːk ìn kwèstʃn trìits ðə kɔlɔokwìəl læŋgwìdʒ ɔonlì, ənd (b.) bì'kɔz a(è) v faond ðt ìt s lìzìə fər ə frèntʃ-spìikìŋ pjùupl sʌbsìkwentlì tə træns'fɔm, ìf nèsəsèrì, wìik sìləblz ìntə strɔŋ wʌnz ðn fər ìm tə dùu ðə rì'vəːs. bì'saèdz ðìs, a(è) v ɔ́lwéz faond ðt ðə sʌbsìkwent nɔ̀lìdʒ əv ði ɔ́θə'græfìk spèlìŋ kərèkts ènì pɔ̀sìbl tèndənsì tɔ́dʒ ə tùu slʌvnlì prɔnʌnsì'èéʃn.

ðə sèntənsìz ə nɔ̀t dì'vaèdìd ìntə wəːdz. ðìs bì'kɔz ðə mèθəd ìt'sèlf ìz bèést fʌndə'mèntəlì ɔn ə sìstəm əv "*traːn'slèéʃn-jùuìnìts*" ìn'stèd əv ɔn "*wəːd-jùuìnìts*".

a(è) ə'pènd ə lìst əv dì'vəːdʒənsìz nd ìn'vaèt krìtìsìzm ɔn ìitʃ.

1. å ìn'stèd əv ɔː (ɔ́ əv ðə prèznt aːtìkl).

a(è) v faond ìt nèsəsèrì tə dì'stìŋgwìʃ ɔ ìn *naught* frm ɔ ìn *not*, əz ðə dìfrəns ìz nɔ̀t ɔonlì wʌn əv lèŋθ bət ɔ́lso əv saond-vælju. ɔ ìn *naught* ìz tèns; ɔ ìn *not* ìz læks. a(è) v nèvə bìn èébl tə rèkŋsaèl məsèlf tə jùuzìŋ ðə lèŋθ mɔ̀dìfaèə əz ə saèn əv tènsnìs nɔ́(ə), mɔ́(ə)r ìs'pèʃəlì, tə jùuzìŋ ðə maːk əv lèŋθ ìn ən ʌnstrèst sìləbl. ìn wəːdz sətʃ əz *although* ənd *already*, ði ɔ ìz ɔ́lwéz ʌnstrèst. ìn wìik fɔmz sətʃ əz *for, your, or* ənd *nor*, ðə ɔ ìz dʒènrəlì ʌnstrèst. waè nɔ̀t, ðèn, jùuz ðə grèév nd əkjùut æksènts æz ìn ðə prèznt aːtìkl? pəhæps ðìs wùd bi ðə bèst sə'lùuʃn, lìivìŋ ʌnæksèntìd ɔ fə ðæt smɔ́l klaːs əv wəːdz: *cloth, soft, god, because, loss, lost, gone* ənd ə fjùu ʌðəz. ðə vaɔəl ìn ðìiz wəːdz sìimz tə bi ìntə'mìidjìt bì'twìin ɔ̀ nd ɔ́ (sìi *Phonetic Transcription of English Prose*. pèédʒ VII).[1]

ðə saèn ɒ əz bìn rìisntlì prəpɔozd ən jùuzd baè mìstə *Jones* ìn tùu rìisnt wəːks. ðìs ìz ədìʃənl èvìdəns ðt ə sèprìt saèn ìz

---

[1] sìː ɔːlsou p. 43 ənd 107 əv ðìs **mf** [D. J.].

nèsəsèrì. a(è) rèd wìð grèét ìntrèst ìn ðə nəvèmbə-dìsèmbə nʌmbər əv ðə **mf** ðə rì'maːks əv mìstə *Tuttle* ɔ̀n ðìs pòènt, ən wìð hìm kwèstʃn ðɪ ìm'plæèd stèétmənt əv dɔ̀ktə *P. Passy* ðt ìt ìz "rɑːrmɑ̃ nesəsəːr".

a(è) hæv fɔ́(ə) rìiznz fə tʃùuzìŋ å ìn prèfrns tu ènì ʌðə sìmbl:

(1). ìt sədʒèsts vìzjuèlì ə saond ìntəmìidjət bì'twìin ɑ nd ɐ, bət ìz mɔ́ə knvìinìent ðn ɑᵒ.

(2). ðɪ å ìg'zìsts ìn swìidìʃ. ìt mé bi əv ìntrèst ɔ́lso tə noot ðt ðis sìmbl ìz jùuzd ìn ə njùu ælfəbìt əv *Liégeois* wɔ̀'lùun. ìn booθ ðìiz kèésìz å hæz præktìklì ðɪ ìgzækt vælju əv ɔ́.

(3). ìt s ìizìlì rìtn ən rèkəgnaèzəbl ìn kəːsìv kærìktəz.

(4). ìt s əbtèénəbl frm ènì ìm'pɔ́tnt taèpfaondə ən rì'kwaèz nɔɔ spèʃl kɑːstìŋ.

2. **aa** ənd **ɵɵ** ìn'stèd əv **ɑː** ənd **əː**.

a(è) mèék ðìs tʃèéndʒ pɑːtlì ìn ɔ́də tə fəsìlìtèét ðə raètìŋ əv ə kəːsìv træn'skrìpʃn baè pjùuplz ən pɑːtlì ìn əkɔ́dns wìð ðə prìnsìpl əv "ì'mìidjìt ìntèlìdʒə'bìlìtì" (tə bɔ̀ro ə təːm frm ðɪ nèébərìŋ saèəns əv ìntə'næʃ(ə)nl læŋgwìdʒ). ðə dʒènərl æspèkt əv *Sweet's* "brɔ́d rɔɔmìk" lùks mɔ́(ə)r ìn'vaètìŋ tə nɔ̀n-fɔɔnì'tìʃnz ɔ̀n ðɪ **af** nɔɔ'tèéʃn. a(è) v nèvə nɔɔtìst ðt ðə dʌbl lètə tèmpts pjùuplz tə prənaons ən èkstrə sìləbl.

3. **ʌ** ìn'stèd əv **ʌ**.

ə mìiə dìfrəns əv ə hɔ̀rì'zɔ̀ntl strɔok. ðìs əgèén, fə ðə sèék əv ìiz ìn ì'mìidjìt rèkəg'nìʃn. a(è) d θɔ́t əv jùuzìŋ ə sìmpl **a**, bət faènəlì dì'saèdìd ɔ̀n **ʌ** ìn ɔ́də tu əvɔèd knfjùuzn bì'twìin ðìs saond ən ɑː.

4. **ɵ** ənd **è** ìn'stèd əv **ə** ənd **ɛ** rìs'pèktìvlì.

ðə fəːst rìizn wz tu əvɔèd ðɪ ʌnnɔon lètə ɛ, ðə saond əv wìtʃ ìz sədʒèstìd tu èvrì frentʃmən ba(è) ðə nɔon kærìktə ð. ðə grèév æksènt bìiìŋ ðə saèn əv læksnìs, wi hæv ən ədìʃ(ə)nl rìizn fə jùuzìŋ è. ðɪ è wʌns bìiìŋ tʃɔozn, ðə sʌbstì'tjùuʃn əv ɔ́ fə ə ət wʌns sədʒèsts ìtsèlf nɔ̀t ɔonlì fə ðə sèék əv jùunì'fɔ́mətì bət ɔ́lso bì'kɔz ə wìl ɔ́lwéz sədʒèst ɵ tu ə frèntʃmən ən tu ə dʒəːmən.

ìt s ɔonlì, a(è) θìŋk, ɔ̀n ðìiz fɔ́ə pòènts ðt ðɪ ælfəbìt ìt'sèlf dìfəz frm ðæt əv ðɪ **af**. a(è) nɔot haəvèə ðə fɔ̀loìŋ kèésìz wè(ə)r a(è) dìfər ìn ðə *jùus* əv ðə fənètìk sìmblz frm ðə mədʒɔ̀rətì əv raètəz əv sʌð(ə)n ìŋglìʃ. ɔ́l ðìiz pòènts mé bi rì'zɔ́lvd ìntə ðə wʌn kwèstʃn: "haɔ ʃl wi træn'skraèb ðɪ 'ìŋglìʃ dìpθɔ̀ŋz?"

a(è) naɔ jùuz

ìi ìn'stèd əv	**ij**, **rì**, **iː** ɔ́r **ii**	ùu ìn'stèd əv	**uw**, **ʊu**, **uː** ɔ́r **uu**,
èé „	„ **ei**,	ɔo	„ „ **ou**,
aè „	„ **ai**,	aɔ	„ „ **au**,
ɔè „	„ **ɔi**.		

5. **ìi** in'stèd əv **ij, ıi, i:** ór **ii**.

ðìs ìz wʌn əv ðə pɔènts əpɔ̀n witʃ a(è) rì'zə:v ə pə:fìk(t)lì ɔopm maènd. ìt s sə:tnlì nèsəsèrì tə dì'stìŋgwìʃ læks ì ìn *live* frm tèns **i:** ìn *leave*. hìiər əgèén ìz ðə saèn əv lèŋθ ə səfìʃnt dì'stìŋkʃn? frèntʃ pìipl hæ'bìtjuəlì knfjùuz pèəz əv wə:dz sətʃ əz *live* ən *leave*, dʒʌst əz ðè dùu bì'twìin ðə pèəz *let* ən *late* ó *not* ən *note*. əgèén a(è) kæn nɔ̀t rèknsaèl məsèlf tə raètìŋ wìik *he, she, we, be* ən *the* wìð ðə saèn əv lèŋθ. *He's (he is)* ən *his* ə bɔoθ prənaɔnst wìð ɔ́lmoost ðə sèém ræ'pìdìtì wèn ʌnstrèst, ən jèt ðè z ə vèrì əprìiʃjəbl dìfrəns bìtwìin ðm. a(è) v sɔ̀lvd ðə pɔènt tə maè prəvìʒənl sætìs'fækʃn baè jùuzìŋ **ì** fə **i** ìn *live* (nɔ̀t dìs'tìŋgwìʃìŋ ðə tùu vaɔəlz ìn *pity*) ən rì'zə:vìŋ **i** fə jùus ìn ðə dìpθɔ̀ŋ(?) **ìi** ìn *leave*, witʃ mé bì wìiknd tu **i** ìn ðə kèés əv ʌnstrèst *he, she, we, be* ən prìi-vɔɔ'kælìk *the*.

6. **ùu** in'stèd əv **uw, ʊu, u:** ór **uu**.

ðə sèém prɔ̀bləm əkə:z hìiə, ən məs bì sɔ̀lvd ìn ə sìmìlə mænə fə knsìstnsìz sèék. a(è) jùuz **ù** fə **u** ìn *book*, ən rì'zə:v **u** fə ðə dìpθɔ̀ŋ(?) **ùu** ìn *hoot*, witʃ mé bì wìiknd tu **u** ìn ʌnstrèst *you, who, do* ən prìi-vɔɔ'kælìk *to*.

7. **èé** in'stèd əv **ei**.

a(è) raèt **èé** bì'kɔz ðæt s wɔ̀t a(è) sə:tnlì prənaɔns ma(è)'sèlf ən wɔ̀t (əz fa:r əz aè kn dʒʌdʒ) a(è) ìn'vèərìəblì hìiə prənaɔnst baè ɔ́l ìŋglìʃmən. pɔ̀sìblì **ei** mé bì prənaɔnst wèn ðə wə:d kntèénìŋ ìt ìz aèzəlèótìd ən strèst, bət sʌtʃ əbnɔ́ml kèésìz ka:n(t) bì əksèptìd əz ə kraè'tìirìən. ìf wi raèt ðə wə:d *pay* əz **pei**, ðə frèntʃmən əl prənaɔns sʌmθìŋ wìð ə səspìʃəs rì'zèmbləns tə ðə frèntʃ wə:dz *paie* ó *pays*. ðə wɔ̀'lùun daèəlèkt əv *Verviers* kntèénz ðə dìpθɔ̀ŋ ìn kwèstʃn, ənd èvrìbɔ̀dì tə hùum a(è) v pùt ðə kwèstʃn əgrìiz ðt ìt s rèndəd fèéθfəlì ìn frèntʃ baè **èé**.

ʌnstrèst *they* a(è) raèt **ðè**, ɔ́lðoo, ìn ɔ́də tə bì knsìstənt, ìt ɔ́t tə bì **ðé**. wìik *may*, haɔevə, a(è) raèt **mé**.

8. **ɔo** in'stèd əv **ou**.

ə prì'saèslì sìmìlə kèés tə ðə prì'sìidìŋ wʌn. ìn ʌnstrèst sìləblz a(è) jùuz **o** (**wìndo**, ɔ́lso).

9. **aè** in'stèd əv **ai** ənd **aɔ** in'stèd əv **au**.

ìn *Phonetic Transcriptions of English Prose*, mìstə *Jones* rì'ma:ks (pèédʒ ix):

"ìn mènì kèésìz ðə træns'krìpʃn dʌz nɔ̀t rèprì'zènt ìg'zæktlì
"wɔ̀t ìz prə'naɔnst bət ra:ðə wɔ̀t ìz èémd æt. ðʌs, ðə dìpθɔ̀ŋ
"ìn *side* ìz gìvn əz **aì**; ðə tʌŋ, haɔevə, dʌz nɔ̀t jùuzuəlì ətèén
"ðə fùl **ì** pəzìʃn, bət stɔ̀ps ʃɔ́t ɔ̀v ìt, soo ðt **aì** ór **aè** wùd bì
"mɔ́(ə)r ækjurìt."

prì'saèslì; ðèn waè ʃəl wì nɔ̀t bìi "mɔ́(ə)r ækjurìt" sìns sətʃ ækjurəsì dʌz nɔ̀t rèndə ðə træn'skrìpʃn ènì ðə lès klìiə?

a(è) v nɔotìd ìn *Meyer's "Deutsche Gespräche"* ði ìk'strìim faè'dèlìtì əv **ae** ənd **ao** (**hɛ'raeⁿ, zaen; aof, ɹ'laobm,** ètsètrə) əz kmpèəd wìð ði **ai** ənd **au** əv ði af pæmflìt.

ìn ðə wìik prɔonaɔn *I* ðə faènl è mé bi drɔ̀pt, ənd wìik *our* mé bì'kʌm aə.

10. ɔè ìn'stèd əv ɔi.

ðə sèém tʃèéndʒ, nɔ̀t ɔonlì ìn knfɔ́mətì wìð ði ʌðəz, bət ɔ́lso əgèén ɔ̀n əkaont əv ìts ìk'strìim ækjurəsì. ìn **ao** ənd **ɔi** wi hæv ðə trùu ɔ æz dìstìŋkt frm ðə ɔ əv *not* ənd *naught*.

wèn fɔ́məlì aè jùuzd **ij, uw, ei, ou,** ètsètrə, ðə rìzʌlts we rèəlì mɔ́ə ɔ̀n əprɔ̀ksìmìt, ìk'sèpt ìn ðə kèés əv ðɔoz pjùuplz (h)u pèéd mɔ́(ə)r ətènʃn ɔn rìs'pèkt tə maè vɔès ɔ̀n tə ðə træn'skrìpʃn ìt'sèlf. Harold E. Palmer [pɑːmə].

[ði əbʌv ɑːtìkl reìzìz sevrəl ìntrìstìŋ pɔìnts əpən wìtʃ wiː houp tu əfər ə fjuː rìmɑːks ìn ðə nekst nʌmbər əv ðə **mf**. wiː ʃəl bi glæd tə rìsiːv kəmjuːnìkeìʃnz ɔn ðə sʌbdʒìkt frəm auə membəz. D. J.]

ðə trænskripʃən əv iŋgliʃ vauelz

mistə *hærəld *pɑːmə in ðə lɑːst nʌmbər əv ðə mf səbmits səm prəpouzlz fə mɔdifaiiŋ ðə juːʒuəl trænskripʃən əv iŋgliʃ vauelz. hiz ɑːqjumənt in səpɔːt əv ðə tʃeindʒiz iz ðət hiː faindz hiz mɔdifaid trænskripʃən betər ədæptid tə ðə niːdz əv frenʃ stjuːdənts ðən ðə fɔːm əv trænskripʃən kɔmənli implɔid. hiː iz nɔt ði ounli tiːtʃə huː əz sədʒestid mɔdifikeiʃnz əv ðis diskripʃən fə ðə seim pəːpəs. auə frend məsjø G. Camerlynck hæz liːniŋz in ðə seim direkʃən, if wiː rimembə raitli, ənd ðɛər ɑː dautlis ʌðəz huː ʃɛə ðiːz əpinjənz.

ðɛər iz mʌtʃ tə bi sed in feivər əv sʌm əv mistə *pɑːməz sədʒəstʃənz, bət ət ðə seim taim wiː haːdli fiːl eibl tə rekəmend ðəm. ðə tʃiːf riːzn iz ðis. mistə *pɑːməz fɔːm əv trænskripʃən iz dizaind tə sjuːt *wʌn* əv ðə meni klɑːsiz əv stjuːdənts huː rikwaiər ə fonetik trænskripʃən əv iŋgliʃ, bət it iz nɔt wel sjuːtid tu ʌðə klɑːsiz əv stjuːdənts. it mei giv sætisfæktəri rizʌlts in ðə keis əv frenʃ stjuːdənts əv iŋgliʃ, bət it wud nɔt bi veri sjuːtəbl, fər instəns, fər iŋgliʃ piːpl stʌdiiŋ fonetiks fə ðə pəːpəs əv tiːtʃiŋ kərekt iŋgliʃ prənʌnsieiʃn tə tʃildrən in *lʌndən skuːlz.

ðə riəl pɔint ət isjuː iz nɔt sou mʌtʃ ðə diːteilz əv mistə *pɑːməz sistim əz ðə mɔː dʒenərəl kwestʃən weðə wiː ə tə juːz əz faːr əz pɔsəbl *wʌn* sistim fər ɔːl brɑːntʃiz əv præktikəl wəːk, ɔː weðə wiː ə tə hæv wʌn fɔːm əv trænskripʃən fə frenʃ stjuːdənts, ənʌðə fər ingliʃ stjuːdənts, ə θəːd fə dʒəːmənz, ənd sou ɔn.

ði ætitjuːd əv moust membəz əv ði af iz ðət wʌn sistim fər ɔːl pəːpəsiz iz tə biː prifəːd, wenevə præktikəbl. ənd in ðə keis ʌndə diskʌʃn wiː səbmit ðət sʌtʃ juːnifɔːmiti *iz* præktikəbl.

meni jəːz ikspiəriəns həz ʃoun ðət ðə juːʒuəl fɔːm əv trænskripʃən əv iŋgliʃ givz eksələnt rizʌlts bouθ wið frenʃ stjuːdənts ənd wið ʌðə fɔrinəz, əz wel əz wið iŋgliʃ piːpl stʌdiiŋ iŋgliʃ prənʌnsieiʃn wiðaut refərəns tə fɔrin læŋgwidʒiz. iz it wəːθ wail daivəːdʒiŋ tə sou greit ən ikstənt frəm ðis juːʒuəl fɔːm əv trænskripʃən in ɔːdə tu ifekt tʃeindʒiz witʃ kən ounli biː əv juːs tə wʌn klɑːs əv stjuːdənts, ənd wen ðə benifit diraivd bai ðis klɑːs əv stjuːdənts frəm ðə prəpouzd tʃeindʒiz iz ɑːftər ɔːl kəmpærətivli insiqnifikənt?

D. J.

stænded iŋgliʃ spiːtʃ ənd skript

in severəl buks pʌbliʃt in riːsnt jəːz ai hev noutist ə tendənsi tə rait səːtən iŋgliʃ difθɔŋz æz ɛə (nɔt ei), ɔo (nɔt ou), ets.; ænd sʌm olsou juːz ɛ fə ðə vauəl in *pen*.

riːdəz əv ðə **mf** mei bi əwɛə ðət wi a nau əproutʃiŋ ə kritikl steidʒ in ðə divelopment əv ði iŋgliʃ læŋgwidʒ. əːnist ətemts a biiŋ meid tə simplifai ðə speliŋ; tə ðouz hu a intrəstid in ðə mætə ai ʃəl bi hæpi tə send ə kɔpi əv ðə leitist pæmflit iʃud bai ðə *Simplified Spelling Society* (Secretary: Mr. William Archer, 44 Great Russell Street, London, W. C.), in witʃ ðə muːvmənt iz diskraibd. ðə kənsidəreiʃən əv efəts tə simplifai ðə speliŋ nesesərili drɔːz ətenʃn tə ðə kwestʃən əv stænded spiːtʃ. Dr. EDWARDS, in ən ədres ɔn ðə sʌbdʒikt tə ði impiəriəl edjukeiʃn ˏkɔnfərəns (in eiprəl) iksprest ði əpinjən ðət mʌtʃ fənetik wəːk rimeinz tə bi dʌn bifɔː ðə simplifikeiʃən əv ðə speliŋ kən bi teikən in hænd. if ðə simplifaid speliŋ iz tə bi ridʒidli fənetik, ai əgriː wið im; bət ai ʃəd bi sɔri if simplifaid speliŋ hæd tə weit ʌntil junifɔːmiti əv spiːtʃ iz sikjued θruaut ðə britiʃ empaiə. ai biliːv ðət ə rifɔːm əv ðə speliŋ ɔn ðə lainz indikeitid in ði əbʌv menʃnd pæmflit wil li:d tə kwait iksepʃənəl intərist bii̯ŋ teikən in ðə saundz əv ðə livii̯ŋ læŋgwidʒ. speli̯ŋ rifɔːm ənd spiːkii̯ŋ rifɔːm gou hænd in hænd.

nau wɔt, in præktis, iz auə stændəd spiːtʃ? it iz ʌndautədli ðə spiːtʃ əv wɔt, fə wɔnt əv ə betə təːm, wi məst kɔːl ði ʌpə midl klɑːs in sʌðən iŋglənd. ðis iz ðə spiːtʃ wi trai tə tiːtʃ in auə skuːlz, — kənʃəsli ɔ (mɔːr ɔːfn) ʌnkənʃəsli it iz ðə mɔdl. it iz ðə spiːtʃ əv ðə steidʒ, if wi ouvəluk ðə pikjuːljæritiz əv individjuəlz. in ðə prənʌnsieiʃən əv səːtn wəːdz ðɛr iz daivəːdʒəns əmʌŋ spiːkəz əv stændəd iŋgliʃ, bət əz fɑːr əz ðə difθɔŋz tə witʃ ai həv rifəːd ɑ kənsəːnd, ðɛr iz litl daivəːdʒəns. ðə trænskripʃn **ei, ou** reprizents ðə vauəl saundz in *lay, low* fɑː mɔr ækjurətli ðən **εθ, ɔo,** — if ðə juːʒuəl væljuz (in ðə "brɔːd" noteiʃən əv iŋgliʃ) ɑ givn tə ðiːz sainz. ðɛr iz ə veri greit difərəns bitwiːn ði ə in *egg* ənd *aim* (fəːst saund) ænd ði ɛ in *air*; ænd bitwiːn ði ɔ in *hot* ænd ði o in *old* (fəːst saund). auə ɛ iz nɔt fɑː frəm æ, ənd auə e iz əbaut midwei bitwiːn ðə frenʃ ɛ ənd e; ðə kɔmbineiʃən əv auə ɛ ənd e prədjuːsiz ə difθɔŋ witʃ əpiəz tə miːkæriktəristik əv louə midl klɑːs spiːtʃ, æz dʌz ðə kɔmbineiʃn əv auə ɔ ənd o. in louə midl klɑːs spiːtʃ (ɔːlsou in sʌm fɔːmz əv əmerikən ənd kəlounjəl spiːtʃ) ðɛr iz ə mɑːkt tendənsi tə louə ðə haiə vauəlz; ənʌðər igzɑːmpl iz ði e witʃ iz ɔːfn həːd fər **i**, in strest siləblz. ðiːz mɔdifikeiʃnz ɑ nɔt tɔːt in auə skuːlz, ænd wið gud riːzn, — ʌnles indiːd ðə spiːtʃ əv ðə njumerikl mədʒɔriti iz tə bi ədɔptid əz ðə stændəd. ðis, hauevə, ʃouz veri ikstensiv daivəːdʒənsiz ənd wəd bi difiklt tu æsətein. ði ʌpə midl klɑːs in sʌðən iŋglənd is prɔbəbli ði lɑːdʒist gruːp əv iŋgliʃ spiːkəz wið sʌmθiŋ laik juːnifɔːm spiːtʃ.

ə stændəd spiːtʃ iz, in ðə veri neitʃər əv θiŋz, ɑːtifiʃl; ðis biii̯ŋ sou, wi duː wel tə siːk auə mɔdlz əmʌŋ ðouz huːz spiːtʃ iz dʒenərəli rigɑːdid əz gud. in præktis wi hæv litl difiklti in meikii̯ŋ ʌp auə maind weðər ə mænz spiːtʃ iz gud ɔ bæd; ænd wi redili noutis eniθiŋ in his spiːtʃ ðət iz ɔd, i. e. ðət daivəːdʒiz frəm ðə stændəd. ðə fonetiʃn kænɔt rest kəntent wið ðə rikɔːdiŋ əv spiːtʃ; fə tiːtʃiŋ pəːpəsiz wi rikwaiə sʌmθiŋ mɔː. it iz nɔt ounli ðə fɔrinə hu hæz ə rait tu ɑːsk: wɔt iz stændəd iŋgliʃ? in auər oun skuːlz ðɛr is grouiŋ intərist in ðə kwestʃn. ðis meiks it ɔːl ðə mɔːr impɔːtnt ðət in auə trænskripʃnz fə ðə juːs əv ləːnəz ðɛə ʃəd bi əgriːmənt. ðə tʃiːf riːzn wai ði æplikeiʃən əv fonetiks hæz meid sʌtʃ ræpid prougres in iŋglənd iz ðət ði **af** ælfəbit reinz præktikəli ʌntʃælənʒd. let ʌs nɔt impiːd prougres bai intrədjuːsing ʌnnesəsəri vɛərieiʃnz.

wɔltə ripmən.

fonɛtik spɛliŋ ɔv iŋgliʃ

intərɛst in ðə mɛθəd ɔv tiːtʃiŋ riːdiŋ tu tʃildrən bai startiŋ wið fonɛtik transkripʃən — ðə sʌbdʒɛkt dɛlt wið bai M. Passy in ðə last nʌmbər ɔv ðə **mf** — iz rapidli groːiŋ, and an impɔrtənt kwɛstjən iz kʌmiŋ tu ðə frʌnt neːmli hwɔt fɔrm ɔv transkripʃən ɔv iŋgliʃ iz bɛst sjuːtid fɔr əplaiiŋ ðis mɛθəd səksɛsfuli ɔn ə lardʒ skeːl.

ðə difikəltiz konɛktid wið ðə prɛpəreːʃən ɔv ə gud skiːm ar konsidərəbl, ɔn əkaunt ɔv ðə wɛlnoːn fakt ðat noː tuː piːpl pronauns in ɛgzaktli ðə seːm weː. ðʌs ə transkripʃən rɛprizɛntiŋ akjuritli ðə pronʌnsieːʃən ɔv ɛdjukeːtid sʌðərnərz wud nɔt bi sjuːtəbl fər ði əbdʒɛkt in vjuː. ðə greːt mədʒəriti əv britiʃ tʃildrən duː nɔt juːz ðis prɔnʌnsieːʃən. iːvən in ðə sauθ ðə greːt mədʒəriti əv tʃildrən duː nɔt juːz it; ðə mədʒəriti spiːk kɔkni ər sʌmθiŋ əproːtʃiŋ it. wiː meː diplɔr ðə waidsprɛd juːs əv kɔkni əmʌŋ skuːl-tʃildrən and wiː meː ɛndɛvər tu tiːtʃ ðɛm tu spiːk ʌðərwaiz, bʌt wiː kanɔt tʃeːndʒ ðə fakts. wiː hav tu feːs ðə fakt ðat ði avəridʒ ɛlimɛntəri skuːl tʃaild dʌz nɔt juːz ðə prɔnʌnsieːʃən əv ɛdjukeːtid piːpl, and if hiː ɛvər sɛksiːdʒ in əkwairiŋ it, it iz oːnli aftər mɛni jirz əv kərful tiːtʃiŋ; hiː sərtinli kanɔt biː ɛkspɛktid tu hav əkwaird it bifɔr ði eːdʒ at hwitʃ hiː lərnz tu riːd.

ðə striktli fɔnɛtik mɛθəd əv tiːtʃiŋ sʌðərn ɛlimɛntəri skuːl tʃildrən tu riːd wud ðɛrfɔr siːm tu implai startiŋ ðɛm wið tɛksts rɛprizɛntiŋ akjuritli ðɛr oːn prɔnʌnsieːʃn, neːmli kɔkni! sʌtʃ ə proːpoːzəl wud, hauɛvər, fil ɛvri tiːtʃər and ɛdjukeːtid pərsən wið hɔrər. iːvən if ðə nɛsisəri tɛksts wər pripɛrd, it wud hardli bi pɔsibl tu faind tiːtʃərz huː wud juːz ðɛm.

əgeːn, riːdiŋbuks in ɛdjukeːtid sʌðərn prɔnʌnsieːʃən kud nɔt pɔsibli bi juːzd in skɔtlənd and mɛni parts əv ðə nərθ əv iŋglənd. ðə spɛliŋ wud bi kwait ʌnfɔnɛtik in mɛni rispɛkts fər boːθ tiːtʃərz and tʃildrən in ðiːz lokalitiz.

and jɛt juːnifɔrmiti ər ə kloːs əprɔksimeːʃən tu juːnifɔrmiti in ɔːl parts əv ðə kʌntri iz ɛvidɛntli ə nisɛsiti fər ɛni sistim əv fɔnɛtik spɛliŋ hwitʃ iz tu bi sjuːtəbl fər ʌltimit juːnivərsəl ədɔpʃən.

in ðə feːs əv ðiːz kɔnfliktiŋ kɔndiʃənz ði oːnli θiŋ tu bi dʌn iz tu divaiz ə *kɔnvɛnʃənəl* sistim əv fɔnɛtik spɛliŋ — ə sistim hwitʃ wið sərtin kɔnvɛnʃənz meː bi rigardid az praktikəli fɔnɛtik fər spiːkərz əv ðə moːst impɔrtənt daiəlɛkts. sʌtʃ ə sistim wud hav tu bi beːst ɔn nərðərn prɔnʌnsieːʃən, ɔn əkaunt əv ðə vɛri lardʒ nʌmbər əv wərdz hwitʃ ar aidɛntikəl in saund in ðə sauθ bʌt distiŋkt in ðə nərθ (*way* and *whey*, *laud* and *lord*, ɛts.).

an aidiə əv ðə kaind əv sistim rikwaird iz fɔːn bai ðə spɛliŋ juːzd in ðis artikl. ði issɛnʃəl fiːtjurz əv it ar az fɔloːz.

(1). ðə vauɛlz in *day*, *go*, ɛts., ar ritən eː, oː, wið ðə kɔnvɛnʃən ðat ðə saundz meː biː difθɔŋgaizd.

(2). r iz ritən fainəli and bifɔr kɔnsonɛnts, wið ðə kɔnvɛnʃən ðat sʌðərnərz duː nɔt saund ðis lɛtər (ɛksɛpt in **ir**, **ɛr**, **ur**, hwɛr ðeː saund it az ə).

(3). strɔŋ fɔrmz əv ʌnimpɔrtənt wərdz sʌtʃ **az əv, hav, bʌt, ðɛm**, ar juːzd θruaut (it wud siːm, hauɛvər, dizairəbl tu ədmit ðə wiːk fɔrmz ɔv *the* and *a*, az ðeː ar soː inkɔmpərəbli mɔr friːkwənt ðan ðə strɔŋ fɔrmz).

(4). a iz ritən fɔr ðə saund in *man* fɔr ðə seːk ɔv simplisitiː az ə kɔnsikwəns it wud siːm dizairəbl tu juːz ðə simbəl ɑ in prefərəns tu a in ðə difθɔŋz **ai, au**.

mɛni diːteːlz wud hav tu bi sɛtld bai kɔmən kɔnsɛnt, ɛ. g.

(1) hwɛðər ðə distiŋkʃən in prɔnʌnsieːʃən bitwiːn sʌtʃ wərdz az *good* and *food* ʃud bi riteːnd (it iz nɔnɛgzistənt wið mɛni nɔrðərnərz);

(2) hwɛðər ə simplifikeːʃən kud bi ifɛktid (az iz dʌn in ðis artikl) bai ɔmitiŋ ðə lɛŋθmark in wərdz laik *form, sort;* and if soː, hau wərdz laik *more, store* ʃud bi triːtid (it wud siːm dizairəbl tu kiːp ðə lɛŋθmark hir ɔn əkaunt ɔv dirivətiv fɔrmz sʌtʃ az *storing,* hwitʃ ar distiŋkt in prɔnʌnsieːʃən frɔm wərdz laik *forest, sorry);*

(3). hwɛðər wiː ʃud rait *hear* az **hiːər, hiər, hiːr** ɔr **hir**, *poor* az **puːər, puər, puːr** ɔr **pur**, *air* az **ɛər, ɛːr** ɔr **ɛr**, *fire* az **faiər** ɔr **fair**, *hour* az **auər** ɔr **aur**; and if ðə simplər fɔrmz **hir, pur, ɛr, fair, aur** ar ədɔptid, hwɛðər ə ʃud bi introdjuːst in diraivd fɔrmz sʌtʃ az *hearing* (**hiəriŋ** ɔr **hiriŋ**, kɔmpɛr **spirit**), *poorer* (**puərər** ɔr **purər**), *airy* (**ɛəri** ɔr **ɛri**, kp. **vɛri**), *fiery* (**faiəri** ɔr **fairi**), *flowery* (**flauəri** ɔr **flauri**, kp. *cowrie* **kauri**);

(4) hwɛðər ʌnstrɛst priːfiksiz and tərmineːʃənz sʌtʃ az *ad-, -tion, -ment,* ʃud bi ritən wið ə, az mɔr juːʒuəli prɔnaunst, ɔr hwɛðər ðə strɔŋ vauɛlz juːzd bai sʌm (**ad-, -ʃən** ɔr **-tjɔn, -mɛnt**) ʃud bi ədɔptid; hwɛðər ʌnstrɛst priːfiksiz and tərmineːʃənz sʌtʃ az *ex-, -ness* ʃud bi ritn wið **i, ɛ, ə** ɔr ə, and hwɛðər ðə difərəns in ðə prɔnʌnsieːʃən ɔv ðə fainəl siləblz ɔv *object* (naun) and *prospect* (naun) and similər keːsiz ʃud bi indikeːtid.

it meː bi az wɛl tu pɔint aut hir ðə fakt, hwitʃ meː pərhaps nɔt bi nɔːn tu ɔːl auər mɛmbərz, ðat ðə kwɛstjən ɔv ðə rifɔrm ɔv iŋgliʃ spɛliŋ iz rapidli kʌmiŋ intu ðə fɔrfrʌnt ɔv ɛdjukeːʃənəl prɔblɛmz. ðə wərk ɔv ði iŋgliʃ *simplifaid spɛliŋ sosaiiti (S.S.S., 44 Great Russell St., London, W.C.) haz biːn ətɛndid wið finɔminəl sɛksɛs, and mɛni ɔv aur liːdiŋ ɛdjukeːʃənists hav nau teːkən ʌp ðə sʌbdʒɛkt. ðə taim wil kʌm (and wiː hav riːzən tu biliːv ðat ðat taim iz nɔt far distənt) hwɛn ə rifɔrmd spɛliŋ ɔv iŋgliʃ wil risiːv ɔfiʃəl saŋkʃən; and fɔːnɛtiʃənz wil dautlis biː kɔːld in tu ditərmin hwɔt ðat sistim ʃal biː. ðɛr ar ɔːlrɛdi sɛvərəl sistimz in ɛgzistəns, and it bihɔːvz ði **af** nɔt tu bi bihaindhand in ənaunsiŋ its vjuːz ɔn ðis mɔːst impɔrtənt kwɛstjən.

wiː ðɛrfɔr invait ði opinjənz ɔv aur mɛmbərz ɔn ðə vɛries points reːzd boːθ bai ðə sʌbstəns ɔv ðis artikl and ðə sistim ɔv transkripʃən juːzd. wiː wɔnt mətiriəlz hwitʃ meː ineːbl ʌs tu konstrʌkt ə dɛfinit skiːm tu pleːs bifɔr ði ɛdjukeːʃənəl ɔːθɔritiz hwɛn ðə taim ɔv rifɔrm əraivz.

DANIEL JONES.

ə nærouə trænskripʃn fər ɪŋglɪʃ

menɪ riˑdəz həv aˑskt waɪ ɛkstrə vauəl sɪmblz əv biˑn ɪntrədjuˑst ɪn trænskraɪbɪŋ ɪŋglɪʃ ɪn *Le Maître Phonétique* ənd ɪn *Textes pour nos Elèves*. sʌm əv ðɪ ədvaˑntɪdʒɪz əv ðɪ ədɪʃənl sɪmblz a gɪvn hɪə.

fonɛtɪk tɛksts kən bɪ rɛd wɪð iːz ounlɪ baɪ ðouz hu ə kwaɪt

fəmɪljə wɪð ðə saʊndʑ reprɪzentɪd. ði eɪm əv ðə trænskrɪpʃn ɪz tə rɪmaɪnd ðə stjuˑdnt əv ðə saʊndʑ hi ʃəd juːz. ɪn trænskraɪbɪŋ ɛnɪ læŋgwɪdʑ, haʊɛvə, ɪt ɪz ɪmpɒsɪbl tə juːz ə sɪmbl fər ɛvrɪ seprət saʊnd. ɪt ɪz nesəsrɪ, əz ə dʑenrˑl ruːl, tə lɪmɪt ðə nʌmbər əv sɪmblz tə ðə nʌmbər əv ɪsenʃl saʊndʑ, ðæt ɪz, foʊnˑmz, ɪn ðə læŋgwɪdʑ. ðɪs lɪmɪtɪd lɪst əv sɪmblz ɪz səfɪʃntlɪ helpfʊl ɪf ðə riˑdə lɜːnz sɜˑtn iˑzɪ ruːlz ənd kənvenʃnz ɪn rɪgɑˑd tʊ ðəm; fər ɪgzɑˑmpl, ðət ðə sɪmbl l dʌz djuˑtɪ fə boʊθ " klɪər " ənd " dɑˑk " vəraɪətɪz wɪtʃ ə juːzd ɪn defɪnɪt pəzɪʃnz; ðət t ənd d iˑtʃ reprɪzent naɪn ɔ ten dɪfrənt vəraɪətɪz əv ðə t ənd d fæmɪlɪ ɪn ɪŋglɪʃ; ðət b, d, g, v, ð, z, ʒ, r ɒfn miːn ƀ, ḋ, g̊, v̊, etc.; ðət iˑtʃ vaʊəl sɪmbl dʌz nɒt ɔˑlweɪz reprɪzent ɪgzæktlɪ ðə seɪm ʃeɪd əv saʊnd. ən ɪŋglɪʃmən nætʃrəlɪ əbzɜːvz ðiːz θɪŋz, wɪtʃ, ðoʊ nɒt sɪgnɪfɪkənt, ɑr ɪsenʃl tʊ ə gʊd prənʌnsɪeɪʃn. bʌt ə fonetɪk tekst wɪtʃ ətemtɪd tə ʃoʊ ɔːl ðiːz mɒdɪfɪkeɪʃnz wʊd rɪkwaɪə sʌtʃ ən ɪnɔˑməs nʌmbər əv sɪmblz ðət ɪt wʊd bi noʊ mɔə ðən ə pʌzl tə ðə mədʑɒrɪtɪ əv riˑdəz.

ɪkɒnəmɪ əv sɪmblz ɪz nesəsrɪ, bət ðɛər ɪz noʊ riˑzn waɪ ɪt ʃʊd bi soʊ dræstɪk ðət ɪsenʃl saʊndʑ hæv noʊ letəz ət ɔːl əsaɪnd tʊ ðəm. ɪn ðə "brɔːd" trænskrɪpʃn, wɪð wɪtʃ riˑdəz ɑ fəmɪljə, twelv pjʊə vaʊəl saʊndʑ ɑ reprɪzentɪd baɪ eɪt sɪmblz, ənd tə meɪk ʌp fə ðɪs dɪfɪʃnsɪ, leŋθ mɑˑks ɑ kɔːld əpɒn tʊ ɪndɪkeɪt kwɒlɪtɪ, ɒfn kɒmplɪˑtlɪ neglektɪŋ ðɛər oʊn wɜˑk tə duː ðɪs. ðʌs, " hi kʊdnt du ɪt iˑzɪlɪ " ɪz rɪtn ɪn ðə " brɔːd " trænskrɪpʃn " hiː kʊdnt duː ɪt iːzɪli ". ðə leŋθ mɑˑks ɪn hiː ənd duː duː nɒt miːn ðət i ənd u ɑ lɒŋ ɪn ðiːz pəzɪʃnz, fə ðeɪ ə nɒt, bʌt ðət ðə vaʊəlz prɪsiˑdɪŋ ðə leŋθ mɑˑks ɑ dɪfrənt ɪn væljuː frəm ðoʊz ɪn it ənd **kudnt**.

wɪð fɔər ədɪʃənl sɪmblz fə fɔər ɪsenʃl vaʊəl saʊndʑ, wɪtʃ ɑː, mɔərouvə, ɪkstrɔˑdnərɪlɪ dɪfɪklt fə ðə mədʑɒrɪtɪ əv fɒrən stjuˑdnt tʊ əkwaɪər ənd tə juːz, ðə bɪgɪnər ɪz rɪmaɪndɪd tə meɪk ðə dɪfrəns bɪtwin ðə vaʊəl ɪn *eat*, iˑt, ənd ðæt ɪn *it*, ɪt ; ðæt ɪn *ought*, ɔˑt, ənd ðæt ɪn *hot*, hɒt ; ðæt ɪn *pool*, puːl, ənd ðæt ɪn *pull*, pʊl. ɜ rɪpleɪsɪz əː ɪn reprɪzentɪŋ ðə vaʊəl saʊnd ɪn *bird*, bɜːd ənd *pert*, pɜˑt.

ənd leŋθ mɑˑks ɑ naʊ friː tə duː ðɛər oʊn wɜˑk, ðæt ɪz tə ʃoʊ veərɪeɪʃnz ɪn ðə leŋθs əv boʊθ " lɒŋ " ənd " ʃɔˑt " vaʊəlz, fə " lɒŋ " vaʊəlz ər ɒfn ʃɔˑt, ənd " ʃɔˑt " wʌnz meɪ bɪ lɒŋ.

ðə lɪgətjʊə fɔːmz, **tθ, dð, ts, dz, tʃ, dʑ, tr, dr** ɑ juˑsfl tə ðə fɒrən stjuˑdnt, fə ðeɪ sədʒest ðə klousnəs əv ðə pleɪs əv atɪkjuleɪʃn əv ðə plousɪv ənd frɪkətɪv elɪmənt ɪn i·tʃ əv ðiˑz gruˑps.

stjuˑdnts ənd tiˑtʃəz hu ar ətætʃt tə ðə brɔːd trænskrɪpʃn ənd θiŋk ðət ɪt gɪvz ɔːl ðə help ðeɪ niːd, ar ət lɪbəti tə rɪteɪn ɪt; ənd aˑtɪklz, rɪvjuːz, letəz fə *Le Maître Phonétique* meɪ stɪl bɪ rɪtn ɪn ðɪ ould staɪl. bʌt ɪt ɪz houpt ðət membəz əv ðɪ **a.f.** wɪl rɪəlaɪz ðə juˑsflnəs əv ðɪ ekstrə sɪmblz, ənd wɪl teɪk ðə trʌbl tə ləːn ðəm. menɪ riˑdəz nou ðəm ɔˑlredɪ, fə ðeɪ həv biˑn juːzd baɪ sevrl raɪtəz ɒn fonetɪks.

LILIAS E. ARMSTRONG.

ʌnstrɛst ɪ

ɪn maɪ kəpæsɪtɪ əz ədvaɪzə tə ðə dʒæpəniːz mɪnɪstrɪ əv ɛdjukeɪʃn, aɪ m rɛkəmɛndɪŋ ofɪʃəlɪ ðət ðə fənɛtɪk nouteɪʃn tə bi juːzd ɪn dʒæpəniːz skuːlz ʃəd bi ðæt əv ði a.f. aɪ m pətɪkjuləlɪ spɛsɪfaɪɪŋ ðət ðə fɔˑm əv nouteɪʃn̩ ʃəd bi ðæt wɪtʃ əz fɪɡəd ɔˑlmoust ɪksklu·sɪvlɪ ɪn ði ɪŋglɪʃ kɒntrɪbjuˑʃn̩z tə ðə m.f. sɪns ðə rɪvaɪvl̩ əv auər ɔˑgn̩ ɪn 1923. ðə riːzn fə maɪ rɛkəmɛndeɪʃn̩ ɪz ðət ɪt siːmz tə bi ðə moust præktɪkl̩ staɪl əv nouteɪʃn fə ðə pɜˑpəsɪz əv tiˑtʃɪŋ ɪŋglɪʃ tə fɔrɪn stjuˑdn̩ts. ðɪs ɪz mɔˑr ɪspɛʃəlɪ də keɪs ɪn dʒəpæn, weər eɪtɪ pə sent əv ðə nɒn-dʒæpəniˑz tiˑtʃəz juˑz prənʌnsɪeɪʃnz dɪfərɪŋ kənsɪdərəblɪ frəm "rɪsiˑvd stændəd".

bət aɪ m gouɪŋ ə step fəˑðə, ənd əm rekəmendɪŋ ðət, iˑvṇ əz ði əbskjuə vauəl əv *ago, china, better,* ɪtsetrə, hæz ɪts oun speʃḷ əbskjuə sɪmbḷ (dɪfərenʃɪeɪtɪd frəm ɜ, ʌ, ɒ, ɪtsetrə) sou ʃəd ði əbskjuə vauəl əv *happy, houses, enough,* ɪtsetrə, hæv ɪts oun speʃḷ əbskjuə sɪmbḷ.

aɪ v prəpouzd fə ðɪs ðə sɪmbḷ ɪ. *Busy* wɪl ðeəfoə bi rɪtṇ **bɪzɪ**.

ðə fɒlouɪŋ ə maɪ riˑzṇz fə ðɪs dɪfərenʃɪeɪʃn:

(1) fəsɪlɪtɪ fə ðə fɒrɪn prənaunsə. ðə saundz ə founiˑmɪklɪ dɪfrənt ɪn ðə fɒlouɪŋ sens.

ðə vauəl əv *give* (ɪ) hæz ə fɪkst atɪkjuleɪʃn; ɪt s prənaunst ɪn ə səˑtn weɪ, ənd ɪn nou ʌðə; tə menɪ fɒrɪn stjuˑdnts (*e.g.* frentʃ, dʒæpəniˑz) ɪt s ən ʌnfəmɪljə saund. ðə vauəl əv *happy* (ɪ) hæz nou fɪkst atɪkjuleɪʃn; ɪt meɪ reɪndʒ bɪtwiˑn ðə tuˑ ɪkstriˑmz əv ðə vauəl əv *give* (ɪ) ənd ðæt əv *pen* (ɛ); ɪts maˑdʒɪn əv dɪtəmɪneɪʃn ɪz laˑdʒə, ənd ɪts dɪgriˑ əv dɪfɪkḷtɪ fə də fɒrɪn stjuˑdnt ɪz ðeəfoə lesṇd. ɪn ʌðə təˑmz, ɪ ɪz ə smɒˑl taˑgɪt, ənd kən iˑzɪlɪ bi mɪst; ɪ ɪz sʌtʃ ə laˑdʒ taˑgɪt ðət wʌn kən haˑdlɪ feɪl tə mɪs ɪt. ðə saɪn ɪ wɪl ðeəfoər ənauns tə ðə fɒrɪn stjuˑdnt: "dount wʌrɪ tuˑ mʌtʃ əbaut ðə tʌŋ pəzɪʃn əv ðɪs vauəl; meɪk ɪt səfɪʃṇtlɪ əbskjuə, ənd nʌθɪŋ æbnɒˑmḷ wɪl bi noutɪsəbḷ ɪn jə prənʌnsɪeɪʃṇ. rɪzəˑv jər efəts fə ðə (juˑʒuəl) məə dɪfɪkḷt ɪ."

(2) kəsɪstənsɪ. ðə rɪleɪʃṇʃɪp əv ɪ təˑdʒ ɪ ɪz sɪmɪlə tə ðæt səbsɪstɪŋ bɪtwiˑn ə ənd ʌ. dʒʌst əz ə ɪz nɒt ði əbskjuə kauntəpaˑt əv ʌ əloun, bət ɪz ɒˑlsou ðæt əv ɜ, ɛ ənd ʌðə fulɪ-atɪkjuleɪtɪd saundz, sou ɪz ɪ nɒt ðə kauntəpaˑt əv ɪ əloun, bət ɪz ɒˑlsou ðæt əv ɛ, eɪ ənd ʌðə fulɪ-atɪkjuleɪtɪd saundz. ə nouteɪʃn ðət raɪts *busy* əz **bɪzɪ** ʃud, ɪn maɪ əpɪnjən, raɪt *London* əz **lʌndʌn**.

(3) kənsɪstənsɪ bɪtwiˑn θɪərɪ ənd præktɪs. ɪ klɪəlɪ bɪlɒŋz tə ðə gruˑp əv vauəlz dezɪgneɪtɪd baɪ KRUISINGA əz "tʃekt", neɪmlɪ ɪ, e, æ, ɒ, ʊ, ʌ. wʌn əv ðə moust kærɪktərɪstɪk lɔˑz əv ɪŋglɪʃ prənʌnsɪeɪʃṇ-juˑzɪdʒ ɪz ðə fækt ðət ðiˑz sɪks vauəlz ər ʌnprənaunsəbḷ (baɪ ði ʌnfənetɪkḷɪ-treɪnd neɪtɪv ɪŋglɪʃ spiˑkə) ənles fɒloud baɪ ə kɒnsənənt. ðə fɒrɪn stjuˑdnt məst kʌm tə "sens" ðɪs fækt. hi məst fiˑl ðət sʌtʃ kɒmbɪneɪʃṇz əz bɪ, bɛ, bæ, bɒ, bʊ, ənd bʌ, ə dʒʌst əz ʌn-ɪŋglɪʃ əz ə ɑr, ɫɛ, ŋɑ, ɑh or ɛj. hi məst ðeəfoə bi tould rɪpiˑtɪdlɪ: "ðə vauəlz əv *give, get, cat, cot, book* ənd *cut,* nevər əkɜˑr ɪn faɪṇḷ pəzɪʃṇ.

ðə seɪm ɪndʒʌŋkʃn̩ məst bi gɪvn̩ tu ɔ·l (ɪŋglɪʃ ə fɒrɪn) hu ə lə·nɪŋ tə raɪt ɪŋglɪʃ trænskrɪpʃn̩. "wɒtɛvə ju du·, nɛvə raɪt ɪ, ɛ, æ, ɒ, ʊ, or ʌ ət ði ɛnd əv ə wə·d.

bət ɪf ðə sɪmbl̩ ɪ ɪz ju·zd fə ðə tu· dɪstɪŋkt pə·pəsɪz (*i.e.* ðə tu· vauəlz əv *busy*), wi hæv-frəm ði autsɛt ən ɪksɛpʃn tu aυə vɛrɪ fɑ·-rɪ·tʃɪŋ ru·l. wi ʃəl ðɛn hæv tə seɪ "ɪ, haʊɛvə, meɪ əkə·r ɪn faɪnl̩ pəzɪʃn̩ wɛn ðɪs sɪmbl̩ stændz fə ði əbskjυə vauəl əv *happy*."

ðə ju·s əv ðɪs sɪmbl̩ ɪ, ðɛəfɔə, ɪneɪblz əs tə gɪv ə væljυəbl̩ ru·l wɪðaut ɛnɪ ɪksɛpʃn, ə ru·l wɪtʃ rekənsaɪlz ðə θɪərɪ əv ði ɪŋglɪʃ vauəl dɪstrɪbju·ʃn̩ wɪð ðə præktɪs əv prənaunsɪŋ ɔr əv trænskraɪbɪŋ.

H. E. PALMER.

ʌnstrest ɪŋglɪʃ ɪ

maɪ fiˑlɪŋ ət preznt ɪz ðət ɪt ə nɒt dɪzaɪərəbl ɪn præktɪkl fonetɪk teksts tə juːz seprɪt sɪmblz fə ðə tuː vauəlz əv *city* ənd sɪmɪlə wəːdz. ðə fɒloɪŋ ɑ maɪ riˑznz.

(1) ɪn ðə spiˑtʃ əv ðouz huˑ juːz ə "louəd" ɪ ɪn ʌnstrest sɪləblz ðɪs saund ənd ði ɔˑdnrɪ ɪ ɑˑ membəz əv ðə seɪm founiːm. ðə sʌbstɪtjuˑʃn əv wʌn fə ði ʌðə wud nevər ɔˑltə ðə miˑnɪŋ əv ə wəːd.

(2) ðə dɪstɪŋkʃən ɪz əv nou ɪmpɔˑtns fə fɔrnəz ləˑnɪŋ ɪŋglɪʃ. ðeər ər ɪŋglɪʃ piˑpl huˑ dount meɪk ɪt, ənd ʌðəz huˑ meɪk ðə sekənd vauəlˊ əv *city* haɪə ðən ðə fəːst.

bouθ PASSY ənd PALMER siˑm tə rɪgɑːd ðə faɪnl vauəl əv *city* əz aɪdentɪkl wɪð ði ʌnstrest vauəl ɪn wəːdz laɪk *goodness, begin, distinct*. bət ɪn ðə prənʌnsɪeɪʃn tu wɪtʃ aɪ m əkʌstəmd ə faɪnl ɪ ɪz ə dɪstɪŋktlɪ louə vauəl ðən enɪ ʌðər ʌnstrest ɪ. ɪn menɪ wəːdz (fər ɪgzɑˑmpl *attitude*) aɪ m ʌneɪbl tə dɪtekt enɪ dɪfrəns bɪtwiˑn ði ʌnstrest ɪ ənd ən ɔˑdnrɪ strest ɪ. mɔˑrouvə wen ə wəːd endɪŋ ɪn -ɪ ɪz ɪmiˑdjətlɪ fɒloud baɪ ənʌðə wəːd ɪn ðə seɪm sens-gruˑp, ði ɪ ɪz nɒt louəd (ɪn maɪ prənʌnsɪeɪʃn); ðʌs *city* endz wɪð ən ɔˑdnrɪ ɪ ɪn *the city wall, the City of London*. sou wəːdz endɪŋ ɪn -*y* hæv tuː prənʌnsɪeɪʃnz əkɔˑdɪŋ tə ðeə sɪtjueɪʃn ɪn ðə sentəns.

wen PASSY ədvɑˑnsɪz ɑˑgjumənts ɪn feɪvər əv juːzɪŋ e tə reprɪzent ðə louəd ɪ, hiˑ siˑmz tə kwout əz ɪgzɑˑmplz ounlɪ ðə wəːdz endɪŋ ɪn -*y* ənd ðouz rɪtn wɪð e ɪn ɔˑθɒgrəfɪ. hiˑ dʌznt siˑm tə teɪk ɪntə kənsɪdəreɪʃn ðə fɑː mɔː njuˑmrəs keɪsɪz weər ʌnstrest ɪ ɪz rɪtn wɪð *i* ɪn ɔˑθɒgrəfɪ. ɪf PASSY'z vjuːz ɒn "spelɪŋ-prənʌnsɪeɪʃnz" wə nɒt sou wel noun, wʌn wud bɪ temptɪd tu θɪŋk ðət ði ɔˑθɒgrəfɪ həd ɪnfluənst hɪz trænskrɪpʃn. ɪn ðə prənʌnsɪeɪʃn tu wɪtʃ aɪ m əkʌstəmd *destroy* ənd *distress* hæv ðə seɪm saund ɪn ðə fəːst sɪləbl; sɪmɪləlɪ wɪð *endeavour, indeed, employ, imply*, ənd wɪð ðə faɪnl sɪləblz əv *limpet, limit, honest, florist*, ɪtsetrə. ɪf *goodness, begin* ɑˑ tə bɪ rɪtn **gudnes, begɪn**, ðen kənsɪstənsɪ rɪkwaɪəz ðət wiˑ ʃəd raɪt **destres, endiːd, emplaɪ, lɪmet, flɒrest, noutes** (*notice*), **pʌbleʃ, ɪŋgleʃ, kʌmeŋ** (*coming*), **empɔˑtnt, endevɪdjuəl, ɪndevɪzebɪlete**. fəːðə, ɪt wud bɪ nesɪsrɪ tə raɪt ðə wiˑk fɔːmz əv *it, his, him, this, with, in,* ɪtsetrə, wɪð e—'get et, 'gɪv em ez 'mʌne, hiˑ z 'kʌmeŋ weð 'miː

ðes mɔˑneŋ. aɪ θɪŋk mɛmbəz wʊd bi ɪntrɪstɪd ɪf Pᴀssʏ wʊd ɪkspleɪn mɔː fʊlɪ hɪz vjuːz ɒn ðə sʌbdʒɪkt.

D. J.

kɔrɛspõdã:s

ɛkstrə brɔd trænskrɪpʃn̩

ɪn ði ɒk'toubə-dɪ'sɛmbə nʌmbər əv ði m.f. əpɪəz ə spɛsɪmɪn əv "ɛkstrə brɔd trænskrɪpʃn̩" ɪn wɪtʃ a = æ, a: = ɑ:, e = ɛ (ɪn ɛə). wɪ meɪ ðɛəfɔr æntɪsɪpeɪt wɒt maɪt bɪ kɔld ə "sjupə-ɛkstrə brɔd trænskrɪpʃn̩" ɪn wɪtʃ o: = ou, e: = eɪ, sh = ʃ, zh = ʒ, th = θ, dh = ð, ng = ŋ, ngg = ŋg, ɪts.

wʌn mɔ stɛp ɪn ðɪs dərɛkʃn̩, ənd wɪ ʃl̩ bi eɪbl̩ tə trænskraɪb ɪn sʌtʃ ə fæʃn̩ ðət nou spɛʃl̩ taɪps wud bɪ rɪkwaɪəd. bət wud ɪt bɪ fɔunɛtɪk trænskrɪpʃn̩ ət ɔl ? ənd tə wɒt ɪkstɛnt wud ɪt bi "ɪntənæʃn̩l̩" ?

HAROLD E. PALMER.

[ðɛər ɪz mʌtʃ tə bi sed ɪn feɪvər əv rɛprɪzɛntɪŋ ði ɪŋglɪʃ eɪ ənd ou baɪ e: ənd o: wɪð kənvɛnʃn̩z æz tə ðɛə dɪfθɔŋgl̩ kærɪktə. aɪ θɪŋk, hauevə, ðət ɪn brɔ:dɪst trænskrɪpʃn̩ ɪt l bi faund prɛfrəbl̩ tə ju:z o: fər ɔ:.

ðə ju:s əv kɔnsnənt daɪgræfs kən bɪ dʒʌstɪfaɪd ɪn mɛni keɪsɪz. wi: ju:z ðɛm fə ði æfrɪkɪts, ənd wi ər əkʌstəmd tə raɪt kw fə leɪbjəlaɪzd k, ənd hw fə vɔɪslɪs w. bət tə ju:z sh, zh, th, dh, ng fə ʃ, ʒ, θ, ð, ŋ, wud bi kæriɪŋ ðə daɪgræf aɪdɪə tu: fɑ:. æmbɪgjuɪtɪz wud əraɪz fri:kwəntli, sɪns ðə gru:ps s + h, z + h, ɪtsetrə, ə fɛəli kɔmən ɪn ɪŋglɪʃ (æz ɪn *bekshil, ədhiə, ɪngeɪdʒ). mɔ:rouvə sh, zh, th, dh ə nɔt gud daɪgræfs, sɪns ðeɪ ɪmplɔɪ h ɪn sensɪz wɪtʃ hæv nou rɪleɪʃn̩ tə ði ɔ:dnrɪ sens əv ðæt lɛtə.

ai biliːv ði ekstrə brɔːd spesimin̩ givn bai miː in ðə lɑːst m.f. (p. 12) tə bi ðə veri brɔːdist pəsəbl. it iz striktli fonetik, ənd ai dount θiŋk it s pəsəbl tə meik eni fəːðə ridʌkʃn in ðə nʌmbər əv letəz wiðaut liːdiŋ tə siəriəs æmbigjuiti.—D. J.].

kɔrɛspõdã:s

ekstrə brɔ:d transkripʃən

ai laik juər ekstrə brɔ:d transkripʃən əv ingliʃ. it si:mz tə mi: tə bi ə step in ðə rait direkʃən, bət ai kən kwait ʌndəstand ðət meni əv auə koli:gz wil bi ʃokt. wot ju həv dʌn iz tu prəvaid ðə miniməm nesisəri fər intelidʒibiliti, ənd tu lei ðə faundeiʃən əv ə " ju:nivə:səl " ingliʃ prənʌnsieiʃən, əz distiŋkt frəm ə " standəd " ingliʃ prənʌnsieiʃən. ingliʃ prənaunst əkɔ:diŋ tu ðis nju: ski:m əv juəz wil bi ʌndəstud weərevər ingliʃ iz spoukən; ənd ðat ət eni reit iz sʌmθiŋ. wi: hav Ogden'z " beisik " vokabjuləri ənd Zachrisson'z " aŋglik " speliŋ, ɔ:l wə:kiŋ tɔ:dz simplifikeiʃən ənd intənaʃənəl ju:s. nau ju: kʌm əloŋ wið ə simplifaid prənʌnsieiʃən, witʃ iz wot wi: həv ɔ:l bi:n weitiŋ fɔ:. ai kleim nou gifts əv profisi, bət wen ai sed wot ai did in Michael West's " Bilingualism in Bengal " (1926), ai had in maind ðis veri

kwestʃən—ə prənʌnsieiʃən əv iŋgliʃ ðət wəz " adikwət " wiðaut
haviŋ o:l ði idiosiŋkrəsiz əv eni wʌn rekəgnaizd daiəlekt.

ju: mei, ai θiŋk, fə:ðə simplifai, fər instəns e: fər ei. in eni
keis, ai əm o:l in feivər əv ðis nju: ventʃər əv juəz.

A. Lloyd James.

[in propouziŋ ði " ekstrə bro:d " nouteiʃn ai didnt mi:n tə
" simplifai prənʌnsieiʃn ". mai obdʒikt woz miəli tə reprizent
o:dnri edjukeitid sʌðən iŋgliʃ wið ðə miniməm nʌmbər əv letəz. if,
hauevə, sʌtʃ ə sistim kud bi əplaid tu ə simplifaid prənʌnsieiʃn fə
ju:nivə:sl ju:s, it wud bi o:l tə ðə gud.

it iz tə bi houpt ðət bifo: loŋ sʌmwʌn wil ʌndəteik ən igzo:stiv
investigeiʃn intə ðə kwestʃən əv hau fa:r ə spi:kə mei daivə:dʒ
frəm ə fo:m əv " waidli ʌndəstud " iŋgliʃ wiðaut bikʌmiŋ
ʌnintelidʒəbl in eni pa:t əv ði iŋgliʃ-spi:kiŋ wə:ld. wen ðouz
limits həv bin asəteind, wi: ʃl nou betə wot ðə " moust waidli
ʌndəstud prənʌnsieiʃn " iz, ənd bi eibl tə transkraib it (aiðə
bro:dli o: narouli). it wil o:lsou bi posəbl tə prəpouz ə simplifaid
prənʌnsieiʃn əv iŋgliʃ, witʃ, wail bi:iŋ intelidʒəbl evriweə, wud
bi i:ziə fə ðə forinə tə lə:n ðən eni igzistiŋ fo:m əv prənʌnsieiʃn.

let əs not fəget ðət ðə houl kwestʃən əv fonetik transkripʃn
ənd rifo:md o:θogrəfi iz stil ounli in ən iksperimentl steidʒ.—D. J.]

kõtrãdy

H. E. Palmer, *The Principles of Romanization* (Maruzen Company, Tokyo, 1930).

ði ɔbdʒikt əv ðis buk iz tə set fɔːθ ðə dʒenərəl prinsəplz invɔlvd in raitiŋ daun laŋgwidʒiz bai miːnz əv roumanik sistimz, ənd tə diskʌs ði aplikeiʃn əv ðiːz prinsəplz tə ðə dʒapəniːz laŋgwidʒ in pətikjulə. it fulfilz ðiːz fʌŋkʃənz wið rimaːkəbl ifiʃənsi. ðə prinsəplz ə triːtid in greit diːteil, ənd ər ilərestitid bai ə welθ əv wel-tʃouzn igzaːmplz. ðə rizʌlt iz ə buk əv pəːmənənt valjuː tu ɔːl hu ər intristid in sʌtʃ matəz.

ðə buk iz divaidid intə fɔː paːts : (1) " ðə roumən alfəbit ənd ðə pəːpəsiz it səːvz " (21 peidʒiz), (2) " saundz ənd speliŋz " (48 peidʒiz), (3) " ðə dʒapəniːz founiːmz " (48 peidʒiz), ənd (4) " ðə prɔbləm əv dʒapəniːz roumənaizeiʃn " (31 peidʒiz) ; ðeər ər ɔːlsou sevrəl əpendisiːz.

ai m glaːd tə faind ðət in paːt 1, ənd indiːd θruaut ðə buk, Palmer leiz stres ɔn ðə fakt ðət difrənt kaindz əv roumanik raitiŋ aː rikwaiəd fə difrənt pəːpəsiz—ðət ðə kaind əv raitiŋ witʃ ə fɔrinə mei faind tə bi kənviːnjənt fə hiz oun juːs niːd nɔt bi aidentikl wið ðə simplist " ɔːθəgrəfi " fə kʌrənt juːs əmʌŋ neitivz, ənd ðət ðis əgein kanɔt bi aidentikl wið ən akjurit fonetik transkripʃən. in paːt 1 tuː Palmer rifəːz in sʌm diːteil tə ðə " fiːliŋ "

ðət piːpl hav tɔːdz ðə fonetik juːnits əv ðeə mʌðə tʌŋ. ðis iz ə
matə witʃ nou ʌðə raitə iksept Sapir əpiəz tu əv investigeitid ;
jet it iz wʌn əpən witʃ ði adikwit transkraibiŋ əv ə laŋgwidʒ məst
laːdʒli dipend.

paːt 2 iz ə ʃɔːt triːtiz ɔn dʒenərəl fonetiks. it inkluːdz ə
triːtmənt əv sevrəl matəz hiðətuː inadikwitli delt wið. ai nout
fə speʃl menʃən ðə sekʃənz ɔn ðə neitʃər əv " founz " ənd ɔn " ðə
kɔnkriːt ənd abstrakt neitʃər əv saundz " (in witʃ Palmer kwouts
ikstensivli frəm prəfesə K. Jimbo'z wəːk ɔn ðis sʌbdʒikt). ðə θiəri
əv abstrakt saundz luks kɔmplikeitid, bət ɔn igzamineiʃn it pruːvz
tu bi akjurit.[1]

paːt 3 iz ən eksələnt əkaunt əv ðə dʒapəniːz saundz iləstreitid
bai njuːmərəs igzaːmplz. iːtʃ igzaːmpl iz ʃoun in brɔːd ənd in
narou fonetik transkripʃən, əz wel əz in dʒapəniːz *kanə, tʃainiːz
kariktə, " Nihonshiki Rōmaji " ənd " Hepburnian Rōmaji ". ði
igzaːmplz əv wəːdz bɔroud frəm juərəpiən laŋgwidʒiz ə pətikjuləli
iluːmineitiŋ. wiː ləːn, fər instəns, ðət ðə fɔlouiŋ ə ðə dʒapəniːz
ikwivələnts fər iŋgliʃ ənd frenʃ wəːdz [2] :

peipa (*paper*)   purattohoomu (*platform*)
saadi (*serge*)   kirisuto (*Christ*)
hooku (*fork*)   ruuburu (*Louvre*, ɔːlsou *rouble*)
zentoruman (*gentleman*)   berudan (*Verdun*)
                           rutan (*Le Temps*)

---

[1] wʌn mei pəhaps daut weðə sou hai ə digriː əv akjurəsi in wəːdiŋ iz riəli
nesisəri. pəːsnəli ai hav ə fiːliŋ ðət if wʌn wə tu investigeit kwestʃənz əv fonetik
təːminolədʒi stil mɔː mainjuːtli, wʌn wud faind ðət Palmer'z ənd Jimbo'z akjurit
steitmənts kud bi meid stil mɔː akjurit (ənd mɔː kɔmplikeitid), ənd sou
ad infinaitəm. in eni keis ai hould ðə vjuː ðət nou kɔnsepʃən kən bi adikwitli
iksprest bai miːnz əv wəːdz—ðət wəːdz miəli giv hints əv ðə spiːkəz miːniŋ, witʃ
mei ɔː mei nɔt bi prɔpəli ʌndəstud bai ðə hiərə. (moust saikɔlədʒists ənd
liŋgwists əparəntli duː nɔt ʃeə ðis vjuː:) ai əm inklaind tə θiŋk ðeəfɔː ðət ðə
təːminolədʒi juːʒuəli imploid in rifəːriŋ tə fonetik finɔmina iz səfiʃəntli niə ðə
maːk fər ɔːl ɔːdnri praktikl pəːpəsiz.

[2] ai rait ðə wəːdz in ə brɔːd transkripʃən. r dinouts ə saund veəriiŋ bitwiːn
iŋgliʃ r ənd l. fainl n reprizents ə neizl saund wið inkɔmpliːt klouʒər in ðə
mauθ. d iz palətəlaizd bifɔː i; in ðət pəziʃn it reprizents ə saund intəmiːdjət
bitwiːn ɔːdnri d ənd z. u haz haːdli eni lip-raundiŋ.

pɑːt 4 biginz wið ə ʃɔːt histəri əv dʒapəniːz raitiŋ ənd əv ði aplikeiʃn əv roumən letəz tə dʒapəniːz. PALMER ðen injuːməreits sʌm əv ðə difikltiz witʃ biset ðə roumənɑizəz, ənd noutəbli ði igzistəns əv inɔːməs nʌmbəz əv homəfounz, ði əkʌrəns əv tounz ənd ʌnsəːtntiz in rigɑːd tu wəːd-diviʒn. hiː diskʌsiz meθədz əv ridjuːsiŋ ambigjuitiz in roumanik raitiŋ tu ə miniməm; pətikjuləli noutwəːði əmʌŋ ðəm iz ðə sədʒestʃən ðət səːtn distiŋkʃənz menteind in impɔːtnt daiəlekts ʃud bi ʃoun in raitiŋ iːvn ðou nou lɔŋgə prizəːvd in ðə standəd laŋgwidʒ.

in ðis pɑːt PALMER ɔːlsou diskʌsiz wið admərəbl impɑːʃialiti ðə mʌtʃ dispjuːtid relətiv merits əv ðə " Nihonshiki Rōmaji " (dʒapəniːz naʃnl sistim) ənd ðə mɔː kəmənli juːzd " Hepburnian Rōmaji ". hiː ʃouz ðət ðə tuː sistimz hav difrənt fʌŋkʃənz, ðə fəːst biːiŋ ən " ɔːθogrəfi " ənd ðə sekənd ə " translitəreiʃn ", ənd ðət iːtʃ sistim pəzesiz səːtn ədvɑːntidʒiz renderiŋ it speʃəli sjuːtəbl fər its ɔbdʒikt.

əv ði əpendisiːz, ðə θəːd, intɑitld " mʌltipl aidentiti ", mei bi siŋgld aut az əv speʃl intrist. PALMER points aut ðət keisiz duː əkeiʒnəli əraiz weər ə saund mei bi əsɑind tu aiðər əv tuː founiːmz, ənd ðət fə historikl ɔːr ʌðə riːznz it mei pruːv kənviːnjənt in kənstrʌktiŋ ən ɔːθogrəfi tə rigɑːd it əz bilɔŋiŋ tu wʌn founiːm in sʌm wəːdz ənd tə ði ʌðə founiːm in ʌðə wəːdz. ðə dʒapəniːz palətəlaizd d,[1] fər igzɑːmpl, haz iːkwəl kleimz tə bilɔŋ tə ðə d ənd ðə z founiːmz; bət PALMER ʃouz ðət in ən *ɔːθogrəfi* it mei bi dizɑiərəbl tə rait it d in sʌm wəːdz ənd z in ʌðəz.

it wil bi siːn ðen ðət ðis buk iz nɔt miəli wʌn tə bi red bɑi stjuːdnts əv dʒapəniːz, bət it fɔːmz ən impɔːtnt kəntribjuːʃn tə ðə litritʃə ɔn dʒenərəl fonetiks, ənd wil bi faund ispeʃəli valjuəbl tə ðouz kənsəːnd wið ðə kənstrʌkʃən əv ɔːθogrəfiz fə nɔn-juərəpiən tʌŋz in eni pɑːt əv ðə wəːld.

D. J.

---

[1] ðə saund intəmiːdjət bitwiːn d ənd z, witʃ əkəiz ounli bifɔir i. it s reprizentid in " Hepburnian Rōmaji " bai j; it mait bi reprizentid in feəli narou fonetik transkripʃən bai dz ɔi dʒ. PALMER həz sədʒestid ə speʃl sɑin ź fə juːs in narou transkrɪpʃən.

bɹɔd tɹæn'skɹɪpʃn əv ʤenɹəl ə'mɛɹɪkn

ɪn ði m.f. fɹ ʤun, 1934, mɪstr Joos pɹə'zents ə bɹɔd tɹæn'skɹɪpʃn əv ʤenɹəl ə'mɛɹɪkn best, hi sɛz, ɔn ðə Jones θiɹɪ. ðə pɹɪnsəpl ɔn ʍɪtʃ ɪt æktʃuəlɪ simz tə ɹest, hau'ɛvr—ðə də'vɪʒn əv vauəlz ɪntə fɹi, tʃɛkt ən əb'skuɹ (ʍaɪl ðr ɪz no kaɹə'spɑndɪŋ ə'næləsɪs əv ðə kɑnsn̩ənts)—baɪ fɔɹsɪŋ ɪm tə də'faɪn ðə vælju əv ɪtʃ sɪmbl tu næɹoɪɪ ən tə ɹə'gɑɹd tu meni ʃedz əv wikn̩ɪŋ əz fo'nimɪk, meks hɪz no'teʃn ɪm'pɑsəblɪ maɪ'nut n kəmbɹsəm. ɪntɹɛstɪŋ əz ɪt ɪz, ɪt kænɑt bi ə'dɑptəd fr ɔɹdn̩ɛɹɪ jus.

ə stɹɪktlɪ fo'nimɪk tɹæn'skɹɪpʃn əv ʤenɹəl ə'mɛɹɪkn hæz θɹi ɹə'kwaɪrmənts. ɪt ʃud bi æplɪkəbl, wɪθ ðə smɔləst pɑsəbl nəmbr əv tʃenʤəz, tu ɛvɹɪ taɪp əv kəltəvetəd ə'mɛɹɪkn ɪŋglɪʃ ɛk'sɛpt ðə ʃɑɹplɪ də'vɹʤnt daɪəlɛkts əv nu ɪŋglənd ən ðə sauθ; ɪt ʃud mek klɪɹ, bət wɪθ'aut əg'zæʤretɪŋ, ðə dɪfɹənsəz bə'twin ʤenɹəl ə'mɛɹɪkn ənd əðr fɔɹmz əv ɪŋglɪʃ; ənd ɪt ʃud bi əz izɪ tə ɹid n ɹaɪt əz ðə tɹæn'skɹɪpʃn əv səðrn ɪŋglɪʃ, fɹɛntʃ n ʤrmən tə ʍɪtʃ wi r ə'kəstəmd. wɪθ ðiz kənsɪdr'eʃnz ɪn maɪnd, aɪ ʃl tɹaɪ tə stet ðə pɹɪnsəplz ðət əv gaɪdəd mi ɪn wrkɪŋ aut ðə tɹæn'skɹɪpʃn juzd ɪn ðɪs ɑɹtɪkl.

1. ði æksɪəm "wən fonim wən saɪn" məst bi ɹɪgrəslɪ pɹə'zrvd.[1] (ðə dɪfθɔŋz r onlɪ ə'pæɹənt vaɪə'leʃnz əv ðɪs ɹul.) səb'sɪdɪɛɹɪ membrz əv fonimz kænɑt bi ɹɛkəgnaɪzd; bət æktʃuəl səbstə'tuʃnz, ə'dɪʃnz ənd o'mɪʃnz əv fonimz me bi ɪndəketəd.

---

[1] aɪ juz ðə trm "fonim" tə min ə sɪg'nɪfəknt junət ɪn ðə fo'nɛtɪk pætrn əv ə daɪəlɛkt, fəŋkʃn̩ɪŋ əz ən ɪntəgɹəl ən kɑnstətutɪv pɑɹt ɪn ðə fo'nɛtɪk mek-əp əv ə sɛntn̩s, ənd ə'pɪɹɪŋ ɪn ðə spitʃ əv ə gɪvn ɪndə'vɪʤuəl ɔz ə gɹup əv saundz r fonz (moɹ r lɛs ɹə'letəd ɪn ɑɹtɪkjə'leʃn ənd ə'kustɪk ə'fɛkt) æpɹəhɛndəd baɪ ðə spikr əz wən, ðə dɪfɹənsəz wɪθ'ɪn ðə gɹup ən ði æltr'neʃn əv ðə vɛɹɪənts biɪŋ gəvrnd baɪ ðə fo'nɛtɪk kɑntɛkst (pə'zɪʃn ɪn ðə wrd r fɹez, nebrɪŋ saundz, ɹɛlətɪv stɹɛs, tempo ən ðə laɪk), ən so ɹɛgjəletəd baɪ ðə spitʃ hæbəts əv ði ɪndə'vɪʤuəl ðət no tu membrz əv ə sɪŋgl fonim ɛvr ə'kr əndr ðə sem fo'nɛtɪk kən'dɪʃnz.

2. sıns aʊr kɑnsn̩ənt fonimz kɑɹəˈspɑnd ɔlmost pɔınt fr pɔınt tə ðoz əv səðrn ıŋglıʃ (ðo prˈtıkjəlr wrdz ɔfn ʃo dıfɹənt fonimz ın ðə tu daıəlekts) ðe me bi ɹıtn, wıθ wən əkˈsepʃn tɹıtəd bəˈlo, ın ðə sem we. ðı onlı kɑnsn̩ənt fonim əv ʤenɹəl əˈmeɹıkn no lɔŋgr waıdlı krənt ın səðrn ıŋglıʃ ız ʍ, æz ın *white*: ðıs ız ɹıtn baı menı fonəˈtıʃnz əz hw, bət ın əˈkɔɹdn̩z wıθ aʊr frst pɹınsəpl ə sıŋgl saın ız betr.

3. ðı əkˈsepʃn ʤəst ɹəˈfrd tu ız ðə frst fonim ın *red*. sıns aı v tʃozn ðə letr r fr ðə vaʊəl ın *bird*, ðə kɑnsn̩ənt məst bi ɹıtn ɹ. ə ɹul-əv-θəm fr dəˈstıŋgwıʃıŋ ðə jus əv ðiz tu saınz ız tə ɹaıt r ʍen ðə saʊnd ın kwestʃn ız səˈlæbık, əðrwaız ɹ. ðəs wi hæv ɑn ðə wən hænd ðə taıps *bird, labored, burr, labor, hour, fire* (brd, lebrd, br, lebr, aʊr, faıɹ); ɑn ðı əðr, *red, bread, carry, corrode, far, fear, farce, fierce, far away, fearing* (ɹed, bɹed, kæɹı, kəˈɹod, fɑɹ, fiɹ, fɑɹs, fiɹs, fɑɹ əˈwe, fiɹıŋ).[1]

4. laık r, ðı əðr vaʊəlz ʃʊd bi ɹıtn veɹı sımplı, wıθ ðə fɑnık væljuz əv ıtʃ sımbl əz bɹɔdlı dəˈfaınd əz pɑsəbl. ðəs aı ɹaıt e, o, i, u, ɔlðo ðə saʊndz ɹepɹəˈzentıŋ ðiz fonimz r juʒʊəlı dıfˈθɔŋgl. dıfɹənsəz ın leŋθ, ðo səmtaımz pɹezn̩t, aı nɑt sıgˈnıfəknt—ðæt ız, ðe dont srv tə dəˈstıŋgwıʃ fonimz.[2]

5. ðə ɹəˈdəkʃn əv vaʊəlz ın ənstɹest sıləblz ız prˈhæps les əksˈtɹim ın əˈmeɹıkn spitʃ ðn ın bɹıtıʃ: ət list hæf ðə vaʊəlz n dıfθɔŋz kən əˈkr wıθ ɹeləˈtıvlı wık stɹes. ðə θɹi most kɑmən kəl fr speʃl kɑmənt: ə, ı, r. maı ı əˈpıɹz tʃıflı ın srtn pɹıfıksəz (ın-, ım-, ıl-, dıs-, sım-) ən səfıksəz (-ıŋ, -ık, -ıʃ, -ıʤ, -lı, -ı), ın wrdz laık *him, iz*, ənd ın ðə wık fɔɹmz əv *be, he, she, me, we* ; r ız ðə ɹəˈdəkʃn

---

[1] ɑn fɑnık kənsıdrˈeʃnz ıt maıt sim plɔzəbl tə gɹup ðə vaʊəl əv *bird* ən ðı r əv *farce* əndr wən fonim, ɑn tə ɹəˈgɑɹd ðə kɑmbəˈneʃn ɑɹ (ɑr) əz ə dıfθɔŋ. bət æz wi si ʍen ðıs r ız fɑlod baı ə vaʊəl (*far away, fearing*), ıt ız ɹæðr ə səbˈsıdıeɹı membr əv ðə fonim ın *red*. ɑn ðı əðr hænd, ðə faınl saʊnd ın *burr, labor*, ʍen fɑlod baı ə vaʊəl hæz juʒʊəlı ən əf-glaıd ɹəˈzemblıŋ ɹ; bət sıns rɹ ız miɹlı ə səbˈsıdıeɹı membr əv r, ıt ʃʊd nɑt bi ɹıtn ın ə bɹɔd tɹænˈskɹıpʃn. ðıs əˈplaız nɑt onlı tə fɹezəz laık *fur is soft, labor on*, bət olso tə wrdz laık *worry, bury, occurrence, syrup* (wrı, brı, əˈkrəns, srəp, les kɑmənlı wəɹı, ət'setɹə).

[2] maı ɑn spitʃ hæz fıftin vaʊəl fonımz: (1) i *beat*, (2) ı *bit*, (3) e *bait*, (4) ɛ *bet*, (5) æ *bat*, (6) ɑ *pot*, (7) ɔ *bought*, (8) o *boat*, (9) ʊ *put*, (10) u *boot*, (11) ə *but*, (12) r *bird*, (13) aı *bite*, (14) aʊ *bout*, (15) ɔı *boil*.

əv ðə kʌmbə'neʃn vauəl + ɹ, ɔɹ əv stɹɛst r (kaɹə'spandɪŋ tə səðrn ɪŋgliʃ ə ʍɛn ɪt ɹɛpɹə'zɛnts ə spɛlɪŋ wɪθ r); ɪn ɔl əðr kesəz ðɪ ənstɹɛst vauəl ɪz ə.

6. hau ʃl ðɪz ənstɹɛst vauəlz bi ɹɪtn? baɪ maɪ dɛfə'nɪʃn əv ðə trm "fonim" ðə tu vauəlz ɪn *city*, sɪns ðə dɪfɹəns bə'twin ðəm ɪz gəvrnd ən'taɪrli baɪ pə'zɪʃn ənd ɹɛlətɪvɹ stɹɛs, aɪ mɛmbrz əv ðə sem fonim ən məst bi ɹɪtn ə'laɪk. so faɹ maɪ pɹæktɪs ə'gɹiz wɪθ ðæt əv Jones ən Kenyon. bət əg'zæktli ðə sem kənsɪdr'eʃnz ə'plaɪ tə ðə tu vauəlz ɪn *above*, ən tə ðə tu ɪn *further*: hiɹ ɔlso wi r dilɪŋ ɪn ɪtʃ kes wɪθ stɹɛst n ənstɹɛst mɛmbrz əv ə sɪŋgl fonim. aɪ si no ɹizn (ək'sɛpt ɪn titʃɪŋ bə'gɪnrz) fr juzɪŋ dɪfɹənt sɪmblz tə ɹaɪt ðɛm; ən so aɪ gɪv ðə wrdz ɪn kwɛstʃn onli wʌn vauəl-sain ə'pis: sɪtɪ, ə'bʌv, frðr.¹

7. ðɛɹ ɪz wʌn əd'væntɪdʒ ɪn juzɪŋ dɪfɹənt lɛtrz fr ðiz vauəlz, ʍɪtʃ aɪ fɔɹ'go ɪn ɹaɪtɪŋ ðɛm ə'laɪk: ɪt ɪndəkets, fr ðə wrdz ɪn ʍɪtʃ ðe ə'kr, ðə pə'zɪʃn əv ðə stɹɛs. sɪns wrd stɹɛs ɪz sɪg'nɪfəknt ɪn ɪŋgliʃ (kəm'pɛɹ naunz n vrbz laɪk *insult, import, transfer*) ɪt məst bi ɹɛkəgnaɪzd ɪn ə fo'nimɪk tɹæn'skɹɪpʃn. sɛntns stɹɛs, ɔn ðɪ əðr hænd, ɪz nat sɪg'nɪfəknt ɪn ðə sem we. fr ðə sek əv i'kanəmi, aɪ v ɪndəketəd wrd stɹɛs baɪ maɹkɪŋ ɪt onli ɪn wrdz əv tu r mɔɹ sɪləblz nat stɹɛst ɔn ðə frst.

aɪ bə'liv ðə tɹæn'skɹɪpʃn juzd hiɹ, best ɔn ə fo'nimɪk ə'næləsɪs əv maɪ on spitʃ ɪn ə'kɔɹdns wɪθ ðə pɹɪnsəplz ə'bʌv sɛt fɔɹθ, wl bi faund ædəkwət fr most taɪps əv dʒɛnɹəl ə'mɛɹɪkn, bət wɪθ sɪks ɹɛzr'veʃnz. ðiz r bɹɪfli stetəd bə'lo, ən ʃud pɹə'vaɪd fr ɔl tʃendʒəz ðət məst bi med ɪn ðɪs tɹæn'skɹɪpʃn tə fɪt ɹɪdʒənl pəkjul'jæɹətɪz.

(a) aɪ pɹə'naunts ju ɪn *beauty, few, pure, cute*, ænd u (ɹɛrlɪ ju ɪn kɛɹfl spitʃ) ɪn wrdz laɪk *new, tune, due*. bət ə gɹet mɛnɪ spikrz hæv ɪn ɔl ðiz wrdz ə dɪfθɔŋ ɹu.—(b) ɪn maɪ spitʃ *merry* ən *Mary, ferry* ən *fairy, very* ən *vary* aɹ homəfonz (mɛɹɪ, fɛɹɪ, vɛɹɪ). sʌm spikrz də'stɪŋgwɪʃ ðə tu sɛts, pɹə'naunsɪŋ *Mary*, ət'sɛtrə, wɪθ ðə fonim əv *make*.—(c) ʍɛɹ aɪ hæv æ bə'fɔɹ ɹ, əz ɪn *marry, barren*, mɛnɪ spikrz hæv ɛ, mekɪŋ homəfonz əv *marry* ən *merry*, *carry* ən

---

¹ ɪf wi ɹɪ'gaɹd ðə vauəlz ɪn *above* ən ðoz ɪn *further* əz sɛpɹət fonimz, ɪt simz tə mi nɛsəsɛɹɪ tə mek ðə sem də'stɪŋkʃn ɪn *city*, ən fr ðæt mætr ɪn *endeavor*. wi kud ðɛn ɹaɪt əbʌv, frðr (ɔɹ səmθɪŋ laɪk ðæt), sɪtɪ, ɛndɛvr.

Kerry.—(d) ɑɪ əv onlɪ wən fonim ɪn *father, calm* ənd ɪn *not, pond, fodder*. (ðəs *father* ən *bother*, *calm* ən *bomb* r prfɪkt ɹɑɪmz fr mi.) səm vəˈɹɑɪətɪz əv ðə dɑɪəlɛkt sim tə hæv tu fonɪmz hɪɹ. pɹəˈfɛsr Bloomfield ɹɑɪts *palm* **pɑm** bət *not* **nɑt**.—(e) ɑɪ dont dəˈstɪŋgwɪʃ *horse* fɹəm *hoarse*, *for* fɹəm *four*, *morn* fɹəm *mourn*, spikɪŋ ɔl ðiz wrdz wɪθ ɔ. pɹɑbəblɪ ə məˈʤɑɹətɪ əv mɪdˈwɛstrnrz hæv o ɪn ðə sɛknd wrd əv ɪʧ pɛɹ.—(f) ðə dɪstɹəˈbjuʃn əv ə, ɪ, r, ɹəflɪ dəˈskɹɑɪbd əˈbəv (si 5.) dəznt hold fr ɔl tɑɪps əv ʤɛnɹəl əˈmɛɹɪkn. pɹəˈfɛsr Kenyon fɹikwəntlɪ ɹɑɪts ɪ ʍɛɹ ɑɪ hæv ə (fr ɪnstns ɪn bɪgæn, ɹɪpitɪd, fɔɹtʃənɪt). fɹðr, mɑɪ ə ɪn səm pəˈzɪʃnz, əˈspɛʃlɪ ɪn səfɪksəz lɑɪk *-et, -est, -ess, -less* ən ðɪ ɪnˈflɛkʃənl ɛndɪŋz *-es, -ed*, ɪz ɔfn ɹəˈplɛst bɑɪ ɛ. fɑɪnl̩ɪ, ɪt ɪz pɑsəbl ðət səm spikrz hæv ə ɪnˈstɛd əv r ɪn wrdz lɑɪk jɛstrdɪ, pr'ten, ðo ɪn stɹɛst pəˈzɪʃn ðe ɔlwez hæv r.

fɔɹ ə dəˈskɹɪpʃn əv ðɪ ɪndəˈvɪʤuəl fonɪmz əv ʤɛnɹəl əˈmɛɹɪkn ðə ɹidr ʃʊd kənˈsəlt J. S. Kenyon, *American Pronunciation* (fɪfθ əˈdɪʃn 1932). ðə dɪfɹənsəz bəˈtwin mɑɪ dɑɪəlɛkt ən ðə tɑɪp dəˈskɹɑɪbd ɪn ðæt vɑljum wɪl bi əˈpæɹənt fɹəm ðə fɔɹgoɪŋ dɪsˈkəʃn.

Bernard Bloch.

ðə trɛnskripʃən əv iŋgliʃ

in ðis 'artikəl aj prə'powz tu sɛt forθ ə trɛnskripʃən əv iŋgliʃ 'formjulejtəd frəm ðə pojnt əv vjuw əv ðə kəmpɛrətiv liŋgwist huw wiʃəz tu di'tərmin ði ig'zɛkt 'strəkcər əv ðə lɛŋgwiɟ, bət iz nɑt 'intərestəd in ðə fajn minjuwʃiij əv prə‚nɑnsi'ejʃən, wic kən best bij rikordəd, in enij kejs, nɑt baj ə fownɛtik 'ɛlfəbət, bət baj instrumentəl mijnz. aj ɛm kən'sərnd, in 'əðər wərdz wið ðə 'relətivlij nuw sajəns wic hɛz bin kɔld fow'nolə ɟij, ənd wic aj bilijv mej pər'hɛps betər bij tərmd, tu əvojd kənfjuwʒən, "fownijmiks."

ə trɛnskripʃən wic wil ʃow ðə 'strəkcər əv iŋgliʃ məst bij simpəl, tajpə'grɛfikəlij ənd 'əðərwajz, sow ðət it mej bij 'ijzilij hɛndəld baj ðowz huw ar nɑt trejnd fownətiʃənz, ənd ijzilij printəd in wərks dijliŋ wið 'əðər fejzəz əz liŋgwistiks ðən prə‚nɑnsi'ejʃən.

fər ðə bejsis əv ðə trɛnskripʃən wic aj prəpowz ənd juwz hijr, aj hɛv ədɑptəd ðɛt juwzd baj prəfesəɹ BLOOMFIELD in hiz buk *Language* (nu 'jork, 1933), pejɟ 90–1, ənd wic hij hɛz diskrajbd ənd difɛndəd in m.f. ðowz əv bluwmfijldz simbəlz fər vawəlz ədɑptəd baj mij wiðawt cejnɉ ar : **ij, i, ej, e, ɛ** (fər **æ**), **aj, aw, a** (fər **ɑː**), **ɑ** (əmerikən ikwivələnt əv britiʃ ɔ), **ow, u, uw,** ənd ðə gruwps **ju, juw, ijr, ejr** (fər **ɛːr**), **ajr, awr, uwr, juwr.** aj bəlijv ðət **ij** ənd **uw** ar dizajrəbəl, bi'koz in ingliʃ leŋθ iz nat fownijmik, ənd ðə tuw sawndz ar ofən i'nəf difθɑŋgəl tu bij betər reprizentəd in ðis wej ðən baj iː, uː. hawevər, ðejr kud bij now əbɉekʃən tu ðə juwz əv ðə lɛtər simbəlz baj ðowz huw pri'fər ðem. in ðə difθɑŋz **ej, aj, aw, ow, aj** juwz **j** ənd **w** fər kənsistənsi wið **ij** ənd **uw**, bət **ei, ai, au, ou,** kud bij juwzd 'ɉəst əz wel. sins **a** iz juwzd fər ðə vawəlz əv **kart, kam** (*calm*), ənd sow forθ, ənd sins **æ** ənd **e** ar ði ownlij tuw 'mid-'frənt vawəlz, it iz kənsistənt wið a.f. prinsipəlz tu juwz **ɛ** fər **æ** (fər it məst bij rimembərd ðət in fownijmiks ðə 'strəkcər əv ðə lɛŋgwiɉ iz ig'zɛmind əpart frəm eni kən͵sidə'rejʃənz əv wat mej bij truw in ə'nəðər lɛŋgwiɉ). **ɛ** iz nat nijdəd ɛlswejr, bi'koz ðə sawnd gruwp **ejr** (prə'nawnst **ɛːr**) iz nat ə 'seperət fownijm in əmerikən ingliʃ ; nor ar ði 'əðər gruwps wið **r** seperət fownijmz.

fər ði 'əðər vawəl sawndz aj hɛv mejd səm cejnɉəz frəm bluwmfijldz simbəlz. fər hiz θrij gruwps **or, ɔr, owr** (əz in *fort, nor, store*), aj juwz **or** fər ðə fərst tuw—sins aj now əv now əmerikən prənənsiejʃən in wic ðə tuw sawnd gruwps difər in enij wej ik'sept in leŋθ, ənd ðej 'sərtənlij kəntejn ðə sejm vawəl fownijm ; ənd fər ðə θərd aj ʃud juwz **owr**, ðow in maj own spijc ðis gruwp hɛz ðə sejm sawnd əz maj **or** (ðɛt iz, *nor* ənd *store* ar igzɛkt rajmz). bluwmfijld juwzəz **o** fər **ʌ** (ə juwsiɉ wic hij 'ɉəstifajz baj ðə prinsipəlz əv ði a.f.), ənd hij dəz nat juwz **ə**, wic hij kənsidərz ə part əv ijðər ði **e** ər **ʌ** fownijmz. hawevər, aj bilijv hiz ə'nɛlisis iz mistejkən an ðis pojnt. ðə sawndz **ʌ** ənd **ə** in ol tajps əv ingliʃ [1] ə'pijr fər ijc 'əðər in strest ənd 'ən'strest pəziʃənz, rispektivlij, ənd ar tuw membərz əv ðə sejm fownijm (fər ðis məc əv ðis ajdijə aj ɛm indetəd tu dɑktər M. SWADESH əv jejl juni'vərsitij) ; 'fərðərmor, ðə vawəl əv ðə wərd *bird* bi'loŋz tu ðə

---

[1] [it wud bi betə tə sei "mɔni" (ɔː pɔsəbli "moust") taips əv ingliʃ. it dʌznt əplai, fər instəns, tə mai prənʌnsieiʃn. wið miː **ʌ** əkəːz ʌnstrest in **'hikʌp**, ənd ðə naun **'pikʌp** (kəmpeə **'biʃəp, 'gʌləp, 'sirəp** ənd ðə pleisneim *Bacup* **'beikəp**). in mai spiːtʃ **səm** ənd ʌnstrest **sʌm** ə difrənt wəːdz ; siː mai *Outline of English Phonetics*, 3rd ed., p. 124, futnout 20).—D.J.]

sejm fownijm olsow, in ðis kejs wen in kambinejʃən wið ə falowiŋ
r—bərd ; ðɛt iz, ðə sawnd (ər iz it ə sawnd gruwp?) dinowtəd in
nɛrow trɛnskripʃən baj r: ər ɚ (ən 'eksələnt simbəl, it sijmz tu mij),
iz fownijmikəlij simplij ər. tu gow stil 'fərðər, ði 'ən'strest
'siləbəlz 'juwʒuəlij reprizentəd əz vejrijiŋ frəm əl, əm, ən, ər, tu l̩,
m̩, n̩, r̩, 'prapərlij kəntejn ðə sejm fownijm ə, wic in ðijz kejsəz
mej bij riduwst tu zijrow. ðə siŋgəl fownijm ə, ðen, hɛz, in
əmerikən iŋgliʃ, ðə sawndz ʌ wen strest, ə wen 'ən'strest, ɚ wen
strest in kambinejʃən wið r, r̩ wen 'ən'strest in kambinejʃən wið
'siləbəl-klowziŋ r, ənd zijrow wen 'ən'strest bifor fajnəl l, m, n.
wið awr juws əv ə in ðis wej, ðə simbəl o iz frij tu bij juwzd fər
ðə sawnd juwʒuəlij ritən ɔ:, ənd in ðə gruwp or ; ðis kənformz tu
ðə prinsipəlz əv ði a.f., sins ðejr iz now 'əðər **ow**-sawnd in iŋgliʃ ;
wij rajt, ðen, **kol, nor, stor**, et'setərə. wij olsow rajt **oj**,
insted əv **oj**.

fər ðə 'kansənənts, aj juwz **p, b, t, d, k, g, m, n, ŋ, l, r, w, f, v,
θ, ð, s, z, ʃ, ʒ, j, h**, ənd **c** fər **tʃ**, **ɟ** fər **dʒ**. ðis lest juwsiɟ, ðow
'ən'juwʒuəl, iz 'sərtənlij əz 'ɟəstifajd fər iŋgliʃ ɛz it iz fər 'sərtən
leŋgwiɟəz əv indiə, sins **c** and **ɟ** in iŋgliʃ ar historikəlij ənd
'strəkcərəlij siŋgəl sawndz. in fɛkt, aj bilijv ðət **c** ənd **ɟ** ʃud bij
juwzd fər **tʃ** ənd **dʒ** wejrevər ðə sawndz ar fawnd, ispeʃəlij in
fownijmik trɛnskripʃənz, ən'les, əv kors, ðə truw 'pɛlətəl staps
igzist ɛz seperət fownijmz. ðowz huw hɛv **hw** in ðejr spijc (aj hɛv
nat) wud, əv kors, juwz it in ədiʃən tu **w**.

ðə trɛnskripʃən prəpowzd juwzəz, fər əmerikən iŋgliʃ, ðə fiftijn
fownijmik vawəl simbəlz **ij, i, ej, e, ɛ, aj, aw, a, ɑ, ə, oj, o, ow, u,
uw**, ənd ðə stres mark ', wið ðə frijkwənt kambinejʃənz **ju, juw,
juwr, ijr, ejr, ajr, awr, ar, or** (ənd **owr**), **uwr, ər** ; ənd ðə twentij-
for (ər -fajv) kansənənt simbəlz givən. if wən wiʃəz tu trɛnskrajb
" risijvd stɛndərd " (britiʃ) iŋgliʃ in ðis wej, ðə 'falowiŋ cejnɟəz ar
'nesəserij : **ijr, ejr, ajr, awr, ar, or, owr, uwr, juwr,** ənd strest **ər**
bi'kəm seperət fownijmz, ənd kən bij ritən **iə, eə** (**ɛə** iz ə nijdləs
rifajnmənt), **ajə, awə, a, o, o** (ər **oə**), **uə, juə, ɜ**, rispektivlij ; **ɑ** iz
riplejst baj **ɔ** ; 'ən'strest **ər** iz riplejst baj **ə** ; ðə kansənənts rimejn
ðə sejm. ði ownlij 'əðər difrənsəz wud bij ðowz duw tu difrənt
distribjuwʃən əv 'sərtən fownijmz, səc əz **ɛ** ənd **a**, or 'ən'strest
ə ənd **i**.

if ingliʃ wər kənsistəntlij trænskrajbd in ə sistəm lajk ðɛt prəpowzd, instɛd əv wið ol kajndz əv kwijr simbəlz, its 'strəkcər wud bij məc betər əndər'stud. bisajdz, it wud bij əpɛrənt frəm ðə pejjəz əv ðə m.f. ðət ði a.f. wəz rijlij 'fɑlowiŋ its prinsipəlz, ənd nɑt wərkiŋ, əz it sijmz tu bij naw, 'əndər ðə hɛndikɛp əv ðə fɛkt ðət its ɛlfəbət wəz fərst kənsistəntlij əplajd tu lɛŋgwijəz wið simplər sawnd sistəmz ðən ingliʃ, ənd wəz əplajd ijvən tu ðijz bifor ðə prinsipəl əv fownijmz wəz wɛl əndər'stud.

əv kors, fər dijtejld dajəlɛkt 'stədijz, spɛʃəl, nɛrow trænskripʃənz ar nijdəd; bət fər ə sajəntifik əprowc tu ɛni lɛŋgwij, səc trænskripʃənz ɛz, fər igzɛmpəl, ðowz əv M. Joos ənd B. Bloch in m.f. jɛnjuɛrij, 1934, ar mislijdiŋ ənd 'ən'suwtəbəl. ənd ijvən ðə simplifajd trænskripʃənz juwzd baj prəfɛsər jownz ənd 'əðərz dijviejt, in ə fjuw majnər pojnts, it sijmz tu mij, frəm ðə bejsik prinsipəlz əv ði a.f.

George L. Trager
(trejgər).

ðə letəz ɪ ənd ʊ

ðə riːsnt muːvmənt in feivər əv printiŋ in **sanserif taip,** ənd ispeʃəli əv printiŋ buks in ðə taip dizaind bai Eric Gill, meiks it əːdʒənt ðət ði a.f. ʃud kəmpliːt its sistim bai siːiŋ tu it ðət oːl ðə rekəmendid intənaʃnl letəz ə sʌtʃ əz kən bi printid in eni stail əv taip. ðə ʃeips əv auə letəz həv nevə bin propəli kənsidəd frəm ðis point əv vjuː, wið ðə rizʌlt ðət ə fjuː əv ðəm ə difektiv in not pəzesiŋ sjuːtəbl sanserif oːr italik foːmz.

foːmoust əmʌŋ ðiːz ər ɪ ənd ʊ. ə sanserif ɪ wud bi simpli ə ʃoːt vəːtikl lain, ɩ, difəriŋ frəm ðə sanserif i soulli bai ði absns əv ðə dot. ðə sjuːpəskript dot wud ðʌs kʌm tə bi juːzd əz ə daiəkritik distiŋgwiʃiŋ saundz witʃ ə keipəbl əv əkəːriŋ əz səpərit founiːmz.[1] sʌtʃ ə divais iz kontrəri tu auə prinsəplz, ənd it iz isenʃl ðət sʌmθiŋ ʃud bi dʌn tə remidi ðə difekt.

əgein ən ʊ dipraivd əv its serifs rizʌlts in ə veri ʌnsatisfaktəri foːm ʋ, ə foːm witʃ iz difiklt tə distiŋgwiʃ frəm o, ispeʃəli in smoːl print. if ðə letə wə riːdizaind wið vəːtikl saidz, əz həz bin sədʒestid bai Grant Brown ənd ʌðəz, it wud ðen bikʌm beəli distiŋgwiʃəbl frəm u in sanserif taip. ðə difrəns bitwiːn ðə tuː wud səːtnli biː inadikwit fə difərenʃieitiŋ saundz witʃ mei əkəːr əz səpərit founiːmz.

ai səbmit ðət ðə propə səluːʃn fər ɪ iz ðət fəːst sədʒestid bai auə leit koliːg Spieser (**m.f.** eiprəl 1904, p. 72) ənd sʌbsikwəntli prəpaundid indipendəntli bai Palmer ənd ʌðəz, neimli ðət ðə letə ʃud bi modifaid bai haviŋ ə huk tə ðə rait ət ðə botəm. in sanserif ðə foːm wud bi ı ; in roumən it wud bi ɩ (əz juːzd bai Palmer) or pəhaps betə ᴛ. ə leŋθənd ɩ mait wið ədvaːntidʒ bi ədmitid əz ən oːltəːnətiv (in sanserif ɭ).

it s nesisəri oːlsou tə dizain ə korispondiŋ italik letə, sins ə sloupiŋ ɪ dʌz not haːmənaiz wið ʌðər italik letəz. ðə komən italik *i* oːlredi həz ə huk ət ðə botəm, sou ðət ðə foːm ı (i.e. *i* wið ðə dot rimuːvd) iz not adikwitli difərenʃieitid frəm *i*. ai prəpouz ðeəfoː ðət ði italik foːm əv ɩ ʃud həv ðə huk kəːvd raund sou əz tə meik ə kəmpliːt luːp, ðʌs ι. ðə loŋ foːm ɭ mait bi juːzd əz ən oːltəːnətiv.

əz fə ðə letə ʊ, it ʃud ai θiŋk bi riːpleist bai ən impruːvd foːm əv ö,[2]

---

[1] əz ðei duː in səːtn taips əv iŋgliʃ ənd in meni afrikən laŋgwidʒiz.

[2] naroυə ðən ðis spesimin.

witʃ iz imploid in ðə Lundell alfəbit tə dinout ə saund intəmiːdjət bitwiːn o ənd u. ðis kariktə iz satisfaktəri in oːl faunts əv taip.

ai dount θiŋk ðə juːs əv sanserif taip liːdz tə difikəltiz wið eni ʌðər əv auə letəz. ðeər ər ə fjuː fə witʃ italik foːmz niːd riːkənsidəreiʃn, bət ai θiŋk ðət in evri keis satisfaktəri səluːʃnz foː ðəm kən bi əraivd at wiðaut eni oːltəreiʃn əv ðə beisik roumən foːmz.

ai houp auə membəz wil giv siəriəs kənsidəreiʃn tə ðiːz points, sins auər alfəbit kən nevə bi ikspektid tu ətein ðə wəːld-waid popjulariti witʃ wiː houp foː, əntil oːl its letəz hav sjuːtəbl dizainz in oːl faunts əv taip.

ai hav ə fiːliŋ tuː ðət in diskʌʃnz on points əv transkripʃn involviŋ ðə juːs əv ɪ ənd ʊ, ðeər iz ə baiəs əgeinst ðiːz letəz on əkaunt əv ðeə puə dizainz. ði ədopʃn əv gud letəz tə ripleis ðəm wud, ai biliːv, help tə klarifai sʌtʃ isjuːz.

D. J.

fənetik transkripʃənz

it wəz pointid aut bai L. Sprague de Camp in 1946 in ðiː m.f. (nʌmbər 86) ðət ðə təːmz " broːd " ən " narou ", əplaid tə difrənt kaindz əv fənetik transkripʃən, ər ambigjuəs. ai ventʃə hiə tə put foːwəd ən oltəːnətiv set əv təːmz, witʃ ai həv juːzd fə sʌm wail in tiːtʃiŋ biginəz in fənetiks. ðə təːmz ə not pətikjələli əridʒinl, bət ai houp ðət wið ðə definiʃnz ai həv givn ðəm ðei ə les kənfjuːziŋ.

ðə fəːst distiŋkʃən tə bi meid iz bitwiːn *sistimatik* transkripʃənz, ən non-sistimatik oːr *impreʃnistik* transkripʃənz.

ə sistimatik transkripʃən iz meid bai droːiŋ on ə limitid stok əv simblz, əsembld in ədvaːns fə ðə pətikjələ pəːpəs əv reprizentiŋ ðə foːm əv spiːtʃ tə bi transkraibd. ðis stok, oː sistim, əv simblz məs bi beist on nolidʒ əv ðə strʌktʃər əv ðə laŋgwidʒ.

ðər ə sevrəl kaindz əv sistimatik transkripʃən. ðei veəri (i) əkoːdiŋ tə ðə nʌmbər əv difrənt simblz juːzd ; (ii) əkoːdiŋ tə ðə ʃeips əv ðə simblz juːzd. ə transkripʃən witʃ droːz on ðə miniməm nʌmbər əv difrənt simblz, əv ðə simplist posəbl ən moust fəmiljə ʃeips, iz ə *simpl founiːmik* transkripʃən. it s kənviːnjənt tə diskraib ʌðə taips in təːmz əv dipaːtʃəz frəm ðis.

if ðə nʌmbər əv difrənt simblz iz moː ðən ðə miniməm, ðə transkripʃən iz ən *aloufonik* wʌn : sʌm əv ðə founiːmz wil hav moː ðən wʌn simbl iːtʃ. sʌtʃ wud biː ə transkripʃən əv r.p. (risiːvd iŋgliʃ prənʌnsieiʃn) juːziŋ ɫ ənd l, insted əv l əloun ; oː wʌn əv rʌʃn juːziŋ æ, a ənd ɑ insted əv simpli a. transkripʃənz mei biː aloufonik in difrənt digriːz.

if oːl ðə simblz ə not əv ðə moust simpl ən fəmiljə ʃeips, ðə transkripʃən iz ə *kəmparətiv* wʌn. sʌtʃ wud biː ə transkripʃən əv pəriʒiən frenʃ witʃ juːzd ʁ insted əv r. transkripʃənz mei bi kəmparətiv in difrənt digriːz. it iz tə bi noutid ðət simpl ʃeips hav, bai trədiʃn, əkwaiəd ə moː dʒenrəl fənetik valju ðən " iksotik " ʃeips ; fər igzaːmpl f iz moː dʒenrəl ðan, bikoz it kən inkluːd, ɸ. sou p iz moː dʒenrəl ðən pʻ, t ðən t̪. ə kəmparətiv transkripʃən, ðeəfoː, juːziz simblz sʌm əv witʃ, kənsidəd in aisəleiʃn, ə moː spisifik in ðeə refrəns ðən ðouz əv ə simpl transkripʃən. (ðə təːm " kəmparətiv " iz tʃouzn bikoz ðiː ounli riːzn fə prifəːriŋ ən iksotik tu ə simpl simbl iz ðət tuː foːmz əv spiːtʃ aː, implisitli oːr iksplisitli, biːiŋ kəmpeəd.)

dipaːtʃəz in ðiːz tuː difrənt daimenʃənz frəm ə simpl founiːmik transkripʃən ər indipendənt əv iːtʃ ʌðə ən kən əkəːr ət ðə seim taim. hens ðər ə foː dʒenrəl taips əv sistimatik transkripʃən :

    simpl founiːmik

    (simpl) aloufonik

    kəmparətiv (founiːmik)

    kəmparətiv aloufonik.

ðə wəːdz bitwiːn brakits kən juːʒuəli biː oumitid wiðaut misʌndəstandiŋz insjuːiŋ. ən igzaːmpl əv ðə laːst taip wud biː ə transkripʃən əv dʒapəniːz in witʃ ðə " simpl founiːmik " simblz a ; u ; i ; s ; z ; r ; g ; h wə ripleist bai ɑ ; ɯ, ɰ ; i, i̞ ; s, ʃ ; z, ʒ ; ɹ ; g, ŋ ; h, ç, ɸ rispektivli.

evri sistimatik transkripʃən riəli kənsists əv tuː paːts, ðə *tekst* ən ðə *kənvenʃənz*. ðə kənvenʃənz mei bi tasit oːr iksprest, bət ðə tekst iz not propəli intəpritəbl wiðaut ðəm. kənvenʃənz foːl intə tuː gruːps : (a) ðouz witʃ aidentifai ðə valjuː əv ðə simblz, weə ðis iz difrənt frəm dʒenrəl fənetik juːsidʒ ; (b) ðouz kənsəːnd wið ðə kəntekstjuəl modifikeiʃnz əv ðiːz valjuːz. it wil bi noutist ðət ə dipaːtʃə frəm ə simpl founiːmik transkripʃən meiks iksplisit in ðə tekst distiŋkʃənz witʃ wə priːvjəsli kənfaind tə ðə kənvenʃənz.

ðʌs ə tʃeindʒ frəm founiːmik tuː aloufonik transkripʃən traːnsfəːz infəmeiʃn frəm gruːp (b) əv ðə kənvenʃənz tə ðə tekst : it meiks *intəːnl* distiŋkʃənz iksplisit, distiŋkʃənz witʃ əkəː wiðin ðə foːm əv spiːtʃ biːiŋ transkráibd. ə tʃeindʒ frəm simpl tə kəmparətiv transkripʃən, on ðiː ʌðə hand, traːnsfəːz infəmeiʃn frəm gruːp (a) əv ðə kənvenʃənz tə ðə tekst : it mei bi sed tə meik *ikstəːnl* distiŋkʃənz iksplisit, distiŋkʃənz bitwiːn fiːtʃəz əv ðat foːm əv spiːtʃ ən sʌm ʌðə laŋgwidʒ, daiəlekt, oːr aksənt.

ðə veəriəs taips əv sistimatik transkripʃən difə, ðeəfoː, in ðə relətiv əmaunt əv infəmeiʃn kənteind in ðə kənvenʃənz əz kəmpeəd wið ðə tekst. weðər it s prefrəbl tə hav ðiː infəmeiʃn in ðə wʌn raːðə ðən in ðiː ʌðə məs dipend on ðə pəːpəs fə witʃ ðə transkripʃən iz biːiŋ meid. its misliːdiŋ tə sei ðət ðə veəriəs taips əv sistimatik transkripʃən difər in igzaktnəs; ðei ər oːl iːkwəli akjərət, wen kərektli juːzd: siː N. C. Scott, m.f. nʌmbər 76, 1941.

non-sistimatik, oːr impreʃn̞istik, transkripʃənz ə meid on ə dʒenrəl fənetik beisis raːðə ðən ə strʌktʃərl wʌn: ðei ə meid bai droːiŋ on ə θiəretikli ʌnlimitid nʌmbər əv simblz, witʃ ə difaind wið refrəns tə ðə toutl reindʒ əv hjuːmən spiːtʃ saundz, ən not wið refrəns tə ðə strʌktʃər əv ə pətikjələ laŋgwidʒ. nou kənvenʃənz əkʌmpəni ðəm, fə ðei ə meid on ðə seim beisis fər evri laŋgwidʒ. ən impreʃn̞istik transkripʃən iz juːzd aiðə wen ðə strʌktʃər əv ðə laŋgwidʒ iz not noun (it məst ðeəfoː bi ðə prəliminri tuː ə sistimatik transkripʃən əv ən ʌnanəlaizd laŋgwidʒ); oː wen it iz kənviːnjənt fə sʌm riːzn tuː ignoː ðə strʌktʃə. daiəlekt fiːldwəːkəz, fər instəns, ofn imploi ən impreʃn̞istik transkripʃən wen kəlektiŋ (ðou it s seldəm ə suːtəbl foːm fə prizentiŋ mətiəriəl tə ðə pʌblik). tə meik impreʃn̞istik transkripʃənz rikwaiəz kənsidrəbl skil ənd ikspiəriəns, ən ðə tekniːk iz ə veri pəːsn̩əl wʌn.

ðə təːmz " broːd " ən " narou " hav ət taimz bin juːzd foː, rispektivli: (i) sistimatik əz kəmpeəd wið impreʃn̞istik; (ii) founiːmik əz kəmpeəd wið aloufonik; (iii) simpl əz kəmpeəd wið kəmparətiv. ai əm not prəpouziŋ ðət " broːd " ən " narou " ʃəd bi dispenst wið. it s kənviːnjənt, wen prisiʒn iz not rikwaiəd ən wen ðəz ə moː prisais set əv təːmz tə foːl bak on if nesəsri, tə juːz *broːd* əz ən ikwivl̩ənt əv *simpl founiːmik*, ən *narou* fər eni kaind əv dipaːtʃə frəm ðis.

fənetik nouteiʃn haz, əv koːs, ʌðə pəːpəsiz bisaidz prəvaidiŋ kənektid transkripʃənz. ə ful ʌndəstandiŋ əv its veərid juːsiz iz not əkwaiəd iːzl̩i, bət ai v faund ðə təːminolədʒi set aut hiər ə juːsfl freimwəːk fə getiŋ stjuːdnts tə staːt θiŋkiŋ əbaut its poutenʃialitiz ən limiteiʃnz.

D. ABERCROMBIE.

PHONETIC/PHONOLOGICAL THEORY

kɔrɛspɔ̃ːdɑ̃ːs

hwɔt iz ə siləbl?

kæn ɛniwʌn səplai ən ækjurit dɛfiniʃn əv ə "siləbl"? ðouz juːʒuəli figəriŋ in tɛkstbuks siːm tu miː vɛri ʌnsætisfæktəri. wi ə tould ðət siləbl diviʒn əkɔːz ət ðə pɔints əv liːst sɔnɔriti (ɔː "laudnis" ɔːr "intɛnsiti"). əkɔːdiŋ tu ðis dɛfiniʃn ðə wəːd *sketched* skɛtʃt kənsists əv 4 siləblz, ðɛə biːiŋ nou sɔnɔriti ət ɔːl djuəriŋ ðə "stɔps" əv k, t ənd t, hwail ðɛər iz sʌm sɔnɔriti in ðə saundz s, ʃ ænd in ði ɔːf-glaid əv ðə fainl t.

D. J.

hwɔt iz ə siləbl?

in riplai tə ðə kwestʃən reizd in **mf** 1914, p. 12, ai mei pəhæps rifəː riːdəz tə ðə lɔŋ diskʌʃn əv ðə kwestʃən in mai Lehrbuch der Phonetik, tʃ. XIII. in 13·41 ai həv met ði əbdʒekʃən wið rigɑːd tə sʌtʃ gruːps əz **sketʃt**. it iz, ai θiŋk, kwait impɔsəbl tə giv ə definiʃn in tuː ɔː θriː lainz; ənd "siləbl diviʒn" dʌz nɔt implai ði igzistəns ət definit pɔints əv riəl diːmɑːkəiʃn

---

[1] ʒə n ã sᴉi pɑ syːr. ʒ ə tuʒur vy k lə lɛtr ãn italik sõ ly rəgyljɛrmã, apsœlymã kɔm lez ɔːtr. — P. P.]

(kf. 13.7). in sʌtʃ difiklt prɔbləmz wiː ʃud nɔt ɑːsk fə hɑːdnfɑːst definiʃnz, bət trai tu ʌndəstænd ðə fækts æz ðei rieli əpiər in ðə spoukn læŋgwidʒ.[1])

OTTO JESPERSEN.

ði æfrikits in iŋgliʃ

it siːmz ə piti ðət founitiʃənz kænot wʌns ənd fər ɔːl solv ðə kwestʃən æz tə weðə ði iŋgliʃ æfrikits aː simpl ɔː kompaund saundz. ai wud not ounli aːgjuː ðət tʃ ənd dʒ aː kompaund saundz bət gou sou faːr əz tə sei ðət θriː ʌðə similə pɛəz əv æfrikits igzist in ðə nɔːməl prənʌnsieiʃn əv iŋgliʃ, meikiŋ in ɔːl ðə fɔː pɛəz, tθ, dð, ts, dz, tʃ, dʒ, ænd tɹ, dɹ, ðə fəːst ənd sekənd pɛəz biːiŋ faund əz fainəl ounli, ðə θəːd æz iniʃəl ænd fainəl, ənd ðə fɔːθ æz iniʃəl ounli. (ðə wəːdz iniʃəl ənd fainəl əplai tə siləblz.)

iːtʃ t ənd d iz distiŋkt ənd kərispondz igzæktli tu ðə frikətiv witʃ fəlouz.

ai səpouz ðət ðə t (d), kərispondiŋ tə s ɔː ʃ (z ɔː ʒ) iz ðə komənist prənʌnsieiʃn əv t (d) bifɔːr ə vauəl ɔː wen fainəl; ðæt iz, s ɔː ʃ (z ɔː ʒ) iz ðə juːʒuəl trænzitəri saund. if, ðɛəfɔː, wiː sei ti (di) wiː prənauns t[s]i ɔː t[ʃ]i (d[z]i ɔː d[ʒ]i). if wiː sei tʃi (dʒi) ðə trænzitəri saund, æz sʌtʃ, disəpiəz, bət ə sepərit saund iz prənaunst insted. in ðə seim wei, if wiː sei hot (hod) ði iksplouʒən əv ðə t (d) iz kliəli həːd; if wiː sei hotʃ (hodʒ) ði iksplouʒən iz nou loŋgə noutist. ðis iz bikəz əz suːn əz ðə tʌŋ liːvz ðə point əv kontækt, ðə trænzitəri saund iz imiːdjətli həːd in ðə fɔːm əv ə frikətiv fuli prənaunst wið ðə seim fɔːs ənd intensiti əz iz juːzd in prənaunsiŋ ðə plousiv. ðis trænzitəri saund witʃ ðʌs kəmensiz əz suːn əz ðə tʌŋ liːvz ðə point əv kontækt, kəntinjuːz ʌntil ðə tʌŋ iz in ðə nɔːməl pəziʃn fə ðə frikətiv. it iz, ðen, obviəs ðət ðə sekənd elimənt əv ən æfrikit difəz frəm ən ɔːdinəri frikətiv in tuː weiz: fəːstli, ðə fækt əv its biːiŋ prənaunst wið ðə seim fɔːs ənd intensiti əz ə plousiv givz it ə ʃaːpə, tensə saund; sekəndli, ðə pæsidʒ əv ɛə biːiŋ nærouə tə bigin wið, ðɛər iz mɔː frikʃən.

it iz dʒenrəli ədmitid ðət dʒ iniʃəl iz not aidentikəl wið dʒ fainəl. ðis difrəns dʌz not əfekt ðə rileiʃn əv ðə wʌn elimənt əv ði æfrikit tu ði ʌðə. ðə difrəns iz ðət ðə fəːst paːt əv ðə plousiv wen iniʃəl iz sailənt, ənd ðət ðə frikətiv wen fainəl iz ləŋgə ənd paːʃəli ɔː houli ʌnvɔist; ðʌs *judge* iz prənaunst d͡dʒʌd͡dʒ̣. siməli in fainəl tʃ ðə frikətiv iz ləŋgə ðən in iniʃəl tʃ.

wiː hæv ðɛəfɔː æfrikits in sʌtʃ wəːdz æz: e͡ɪtθ, w͡iḍθ, æk͡ts, hed͡z̦, t͡ɹ̥iː, d͡ɹaɪ.

it iz sʌmtaimz əːdʒd ðət tʃ iz ə simpl saund ənd ə kaind əv c. ai wud əpouz ðæt bai kleimiŋ ðət c æz friːkwəntli prənaunst iz ən æfrikit raːðə, ənd ʃud biː ritn cç ɔː c͡j. tə səpɔːt ðis ai wud kwout məsjø Passy'z Petite Phonétique § 279, wɛər hiː sez ðət cç, ɟj ɑː distiŋgwiʃt wið difikʌlti frəm c, ɟ. əgein hiː sez in §§ 194, 199 ðət ɲ iz ɔːfn prənaunst ɲj ɔː nj, ənd ʎ æz ʎj ɔː lj. wiː nou fəːðə ðət fɔːmə ʎ həz bikʌm lj ɔː j in ðə nɔːθ əv frɑːns. ðʌs it əpiəz ðət əni pæləṭəl kɔnsənənt iz hɑːd tə prənauns wiðaut its kɔrespɔndiŋ frikətiv.

P. H. Dannatt.

breθt kɒnsənənts [1]

ɪt əz bɪn pɔɪntɪd aʊt tə mi mɔə ðən wʌns baɪ rɪdəz əv maɪ buks ɒn fə'netɪks [2], ənd ɔlsoʊ baɪ ə rɪ'vjuə [3], ðæt ðə prɒpə tɜm ɪz "brɪðd" kɒnsənənts, əz ɔθəraɪzd baɪ ðə lidɪŋ lʌndən titʃəz əv fə'netɪks. ɪt ɪz ðɪ ɒbdʒɪkt əv ðɪs noʊt tə ʃoʊ ðət "breθt" ɪz dɪ oʊnlɪ wɜd ðət kæn bi əpruvd, ɒn hɪ'stɒrɪkəl, lɪŋ'gwɪstɪk, ən fɪzɪoʊ'lɒdʒɪkəl graʊndz.

1. ðɪ ɪn'ventər əv ðə tɜm, æz əv ɔlmoʊst ɔl ðə moʊst jusfʊl tɜmz ɪn ðɪs sʌbdʒɪkt əv stʌdɪ, ɪz Sweet. hi kən'trɑstɪd "breθt" ən "vɔɪst" kɒnsənənts; ðə fɔmər əz ə sʌbstɪtjut fə ðə ðen kʌrənt "'ʌn'vɔɪst". ðɪ oʊldɪst əv ðə tu tɜmz, "vɔɪst," kən oʊnlɪ bi ɪn'təprətɪd əz "fɔmd wɪð vɔɪs"; ɪt kænɒt bi ə pɑtɪsɪpl. ðɪ ʌðə tɜm wəz evɪdəntlɪ ɪn'ventɪd baɪ weɪ əv pærəlel tə "vɔɪst", hens frəm ðə sʌbstəntɪv "breθ". ðər ɪz ən ɪndɪrekt pruf ðət Sweet lʊkt əpɒn ðə wɜdz əz kə'nektɪd wɪð ðə sʌbstəntɪvz; hi ɔlsoʊ juzɪz ðɪ ɔl'tɜnətɪvz "vɔɪs saʊndz" ən "breθ saʊndz" [4].

2. ɪf wi seɪ "breθt" wi kənekt ðə wɜd, sɪ'mæntɪkəlɪ əz wel əz fɔməlɪ, wɪð ðə sʌbstəntɪv "breθ"; ɪf "brɪðd" wi əsjum ə kənekʃən wɪð "tə brɪð". ðə fɔmər ɪz rizənəbl, fə "breθ" ɪz juzd əz ə teknɪkəl tɜm əv fə'netɪks, ɪn ə mɔə speʃəl sens ðən ɪn fɪzɪ'ɒlədʒɪ. "tə brɪð," ɒn ðɪ ʌðə hænd, ɪz nɒt ə fə'netɪk tɜm ət ɔl; ɪt ɪz ə pjʊəlɪ fɪzɪoʊ'lɒdʒɪkəl wɜd, ən kæn bi əplaɪd tu enɪ spɪtʃ saʊndz hwɒt'evə.

3. wi noʊ naʊ frəm ðɪ ɪk'sperɪmənts risəntlɪ meɪd baɪ ʔeɪkman [5] ðət ðə glɒtɪs ɪz verɪ slaɪtlɪ oʊpən fə breθt kɒnsənənts, ə greɪt dɪl waɪdə fə brɪðɪŋ. kɒnsɪkwəntlɪ, ɪt wəd sɪmplɪ bi ə mɪs'teɪk tə mɪks ʌp ðə tu tɜmz.

maɪ kənkluʒən ɪz, ðɛəfɔə, ðæt wi kən oʊnlɪ ədmɪt "breθt" əz ən əkseptəbl tɜm ɪn fə'netɪks.

E. Kruisinga.

---

[1] ɪn ðɪs ɑtɪkl ðə kwɒntɪtɪ əv vaʊəlz ən kɒnsənənts ɪz nɒt mɑkt.
[2] *Handbook*, i⁴, p. 13; *Introduction to the Study of English Sounds*, p. 8.
[3] Dunstan, *Englische Studien*, 66, p. 74.
[4] *Primer of Spoken English*, p. 16.
[5] L. P. H. Eykman, ɒn hɪz ɪksperɪmənts wɪð Russell'z foʊnoʊlæ'rɪŋgəskoʊp, ɪ *Tydschrift v. Logopaedie en Phoniatrie*, v, 45–56.

p.s.—sıns raitıŋ ði əbʌv, ai v faund ðət MURRAY ın ðə *New English Dictionary* gıvz ðə teknıkl tɜm əz " breθt ", wi'ðaut eni ɔl'tɜnətıv.—E. K.

[wiː ər inklaind tə θiŋk ðət KRUISINGA'z vjuː iz rait. wɔt du ʌðə kɔliːgz θiŋk əbaut it ?—D. J.]

ðə wiːk fɔːm əv *this*

əz evri stjuːdənt əv ingliʃ fənetiks nouz, ðər ɑː in ingliʃ əbaut 70 "wiːkənəbl wəːdz", ðæt iz: wəːdz pəzesiŋ wʌn strɔŋ fɔːm ənd wʌn ɔː moə wiːk fɔːmz. ðə list əv ðiːz wiːkənəbl wəːdz iz set fɔːθ in mɔː ðən wʌn buk diːliŋ wið ðə fənetiks əv spoukn ingliʃ.

in moust əv ðiːz lists haueva (ənd ɔːlsou in Jones'iz *English Pronouncing Dictionary*) ðə wiːk fɔːm əv wʌn pətikjulə wəːd siːmz tu əv bin ignɔːd. it iz ðə wiːk fɔːm əv ðə wəːd *this* in ðə θriː ædvəːb-kɔləkeiʃnz *this morning, this afternoon, this evening*). in ðiːz θriː keisiz ðə wəːd siːmz tə biː invɛəriəbli prənaunst ðəs. let əs kəmpɛə, iː dʒiː, "hiː hæznt bin hiə ðəs mɔːniŋ (ðəs ɑːftənuːn, ðəs iːvniŋ)" wið "nau 'ðis mɔːniŋ ('ðis ɑːftənuːn, 'ðis iːvniŋ) wəz difrənt frəm ɔːl ʌðə mɔːniŋz (ɑːftənuːnz, iːvniŋz)" ɔː wið "did ju sei 'ðis mɔːniŋ ɔː 'jestədi mɔːniŋ?"

(wen ai spel ðis wiːk fɔːm əz ðəs, ai riəli miːn ðɪs, ɪ biːiŋ ðə simbl ai əm əkʌstəmd tə juːz tə dinout ðæt founiːm witʃ hæz membəz laiiŋ bitwiːn ə vəraiəti əv ɪ, ə, ənd e.)

HAROLD E. PALMER.

ən iksperimənt on stres pəsepʃn

n ə fju: peəz əv ɪŋgliʃ wəːdz, wʌn membər əv ðə peər iz distiŋgwiʃt frəm ði ʌðə, not bai ə difrənt distribjuːʃn əv saundz bət bai ə difrəns in ði insidns əv stres. sʌtʃ peəz ə siːn in *import* (naun) ˈimpoːt, *import* (vəːb) imˈpoːt; *increase* (naun) ˈinkriːs, *increase* (vəːb) inˈkriːs. wen ðiːz ə spoukən in aisouleiʃn, intouneiʃn givz ən adid kluː tə ðeər aidentiti, az wen wiː faind ˈimpoːt [\.] oːr [— ·], ənd imˈpoːt [· \ ] oːr [. /]. on sʌm əkeiʒnz, hauevə, intouneiʃn givz nou help, ənd ədvɑːntidʒ mei bi teikən əv ðis fakt in testiŋ ðiː ifiʃnsi əv stres in distiŋgwiʃiŋ wəːdz.

ə klɑːs əv ilevn stjuːdnts wəz ɑːskt tə rait daun in trədiʃnl ɔːθogrəfi wot wəz həːd wen ðə sentəns ɑː ju ʃuə wud ˈimpɔːts wud? wəz sed wið ən imfatik fɔːliŋ toun on ʃuə, sou ðət ðiː intouneiʃn fɔːm əv ðə sentəns wəz [·· \....]. in ɔːdə tə minimaiz ðiː ifɛkt əv ikspiəriəns, witʃ mait əv led tu ə prefrəns, it wəz pointid aut bifɔːhand ðət ðə sentənsiz *Are you sure Wood imports wood?* ənd *Are you sure wood-imports would?* ə similə sou faːr əz saundz ə kənsəːnd.

eit stjuːdnts həːd ðə sentəns əz it wəz intendid bai ðə spiːkə, θriː rout daun ði ʌðə fɔːm. on ənʌðər əkeiʒn ə siŋgl stjuːdnt wəz ɑːskt tə sei witʃ əv ðə tuː sentənsiz wəz biːiŋ prənaunst, ənd in twenti-fɔː traiəlz fiftiːn ɑːnsəz korispondid wið ðə spiːkəz intenʃn.

nou prisais signifikəns kən bi ətatʃt tə ði aktjuəl figəz, bət ðə siːmz tə biː ə stroŋ indikeiʃn ðət stres, ʌneidid, iz not veri ifiʃnt əz ə distiŋgwiʃiŋ fiːtʃər in iŋgliʃ.

N. C. Scott.

kontekst in iŋliʃ intəneiʃn tiːtʃiŋ

pəhaps ðə bigist difiklti, ʌltimətli kənfrʌntiŋ ðə tiːtʃər əv iŋliʃ intəneiʃn, iz ðat əv getiŋ iz forin stjuːdnt tu əplai in iz evridei spiːtʃ ðə pitʃ patnz, oːlredi akjurətli prədjuːst in klaːs ruːm wəːk. ðis difiklti iz, in ðə vjuː əv ðə preznt raitə, friːkwəntli əksentjueitid bai ðə taip əv mətiəriəl juːzd in intəneiʃn tiːtʃiŋ. ðə juːʒl praktis iz tə dril ði individjuəl patnz in aisəleitid freiziz oː sentənsiz, ən tə raʃnəlaiz ðeə distribjuːʃn bai rileitiŋ ðəm tə spəsifik strʌktʃrəl foːmz. wen ə digriː əv prəfiʃnsi həz bin əkwaiəd in ðiːz tuː rispekts, sʌm ətemt iz ðen meid tə bridʒ ðə gʌlf, sepəreitiŋ ði aisəleitid sentəns frm konvəseiʃnl spiːtʃ; kənektid pasidʒiz ə red, ən ðə patnz involvd ər anəlaizd. it iz ʌndautidli truː ðət nou matə wot mətiəriəl iz juːzd in ðə klaːsruːm, ðeə məst oːlwiz biː ə saikəlodʒikl dʒʌmp, wen ðə trənziʃn iz meid frm kəntrould dril tə friː konvəseiʃnl spiːtʃ; bət it wəd siːm fiːzəbl, ən dizaiərəbl, tə minimaiz ðis dʒʌmp bai divaiziŋ drilz moː klousli rileitid tə konvəseiʃn ðən iz ði aisəleitid sentəns.

moust raitəz on iŋliʃ intəneiʃn əv rekəgnaizd ðət ðə spesimən sentəns iz ʌnnatʃrəl, bət fjuː, fə wʌn riːzn ər ənʌðə, həv ədmitid its pozitiv deinʒəz. in ðə fəːs pleis, it aktivli prəmouts ðə difiklti əv trənziʃn frm drilz tə spiːtʃ, bai riːzn əv its veri aisəleiʃn. it iz kʌt of frm oːl foːm əv kontekst, aiðə leksikl oːr imoutiv, ən ði ounli miːniŋ witʃ ðə stjuːdnt kən əskraib tuː it iz its dikʃnri miːniŋ. ən ðis, əv koːs, mei ofn biː ət veəriəns wið its riəl signifikəns in sʌm spəsifik kontekst. kəmpeə, fr igzaːmpl, ðə kənfjuːʒn witʃ wəd bi koːzd in ðə stjuːdnts maind, if ə sentəns əv ðə taip hiː dʌznt lend iz buks tuː enibodi wə praktist, wiðaut refrəns tu eni givn sitjueiʃn, fəːst wið ə foːliŋ toun

---

[1] reprizentiŋ **asau**.

ən ðen wið ə fɔːliŋ raiziŋ toun. iːvn ARMSTRONG *and* WARD, huːz manjuəl on iŋliʃ intəneiʃn iz beist, fə ðə mous paːt, on sentənsiz aut əv kontekst, ər əblaidʒd tə sei ðət ə fɔːl raiz hiə indikeits ə steitmənt wið ən implikeiʃn, ðat iz, prizjuːməbli, niːdiŋ ə speʃl kontekst.

iːvn moː trʌblsəm fə ðə stjuːdnt iz iz inəbiliti tə disaid witʃ siləblz in ði aisəleitid sentəns ə tə biː ðə kiː points in ðə pitʃ patn, ən, moːr ispeʃli, witʃ siləbl iz tə kouinsaid wið ðə toun (fɔːl, raiz oː fɔːl raiz). tə sei, wið ARMSTRONG *and* WARD, ðət ðə strest siləblz konstitjuːt ðiːz kiː points iz tə riːsteit ðə problem in ʌðə təːmz wiðaut iːvn paːʃəli solviŋ it ; foː ðə stjuːdnt haz nou miːnz əv ditəːminiŋ witʃ aː ðə strest siləblz. hiː iz tould, in moust fənetik teksbuks, ðət sentəns stres (witʃ ʃɔːli implaiz intəneiʃnl prominəns əz wel əz breθ fɔːs) fɔːlz on ðə strest siləblz əv ðə wəːdz, impoːtnt fə ðə miːniŋ əv ðə sentəns. bət hau kən iː nou its riəl signifikəns if its kontekst iz wiðheld ? ðə truːθ iz ðət, iːvn wið ə prəskraibd toun, ðə pitʃ patn əv ɔːlməst eni sentəns iz keipəbl əv kənsidrəbl veərieiʃn, if teikən əz ən aisəleitid entiti.

ə θəːd deinʒər əv ðə spesimən sentəns iz ðət it inveəriəbli ouvəremfəsaiziz ðə kənekʃn bitwiːn grəmatikl strʌktʃər ən pitʃ patn distribjuːʃn. it iz bouθ ilodʒikl ən kənfjuːziŋ, fr igzaːmpl, tə tiːtʃ ðət ə kwestʃn ikspektiŋ ði aːnsə jes oː nou involvz ə lou raiziŋ toun, wen it kən iːkwəli wel bi sed wið ə fɔːliŋ toun əv sʌm kaind. laikwaiz ðə difrəns bitwiːn ðə riːəʃɔːriŋ it ' dʌznt ˌ matə ən ðə kaʒjuəl ənd iːvn ruːd it ˌ dʌznt ˌ matə kən skeəsli biː kənveid bai refrəns tə ðə strʌktʃər əv ðə sentəns. ðis dəz not miːn ðət strʌktʃə ʃəd biː əbandənd əz ə miːnz əv klasifaiiŋ ðə juːsiz əv iŋliʃ pitʃ patnz ; ðə veri simplisiti əv ðis meθəd meiks it difiklt tə ripleis. bət it dʌz miːn, fr igzaːmpl, ðət jes/nou kwestʃnz oːt tə figər ʌndə bouθ ðə fɔːliŋ ən lou raiziŋ tounz, and wið ði əproupriət imoutiv kontekst indikeitid in bouθ keisiz.

it siːmz, ðen, ðət if ðə meidʒə problem set fɔːwəd ət ðə biginiŋ əv ðis aːtikl iz tə bi takld ət oːl sistəmatikli, oːl klaːsruːm məteəriəl ʃəd bi givn in kontekst. ði aidiəl, əv koːs, wəd biː tə kənfain wʌnself tə kənektid kəloukwiəl pasidʒiz, bət sʌtʃ ə prəsiːdʒə wəd pruːv tuː kʌmbəsm, ispeʃli in ði iniʃl steidʒiz, wen məkanikl repitiʃn əv simpl patnz iz isenʃl. spesimən sentənsiz mʌst, ðen, rimein, bət ʃəd bi givn wið ðə konteksts, əproupriət fə wʌn oː moːr əv ðə veərieiʃnz əv ðə patn involvd. it wəd bi aidl tə pritend ðət oːl posibl sitjueiʃnz fər ə komprihensiv set əv dril sentənsiz kəd oːlwiz biː givn oː toːt, mʌtʃ les ðət ðə stjuːdnt kəd kari ouvə tu iz evridei konvəseiʃn ðə mentl əsousieiʃn bitwiːn diːteild patn ən kontekst, wið kəmpliːt akjərəsi. bət tiːtʃiŋ intəneiʃn frm ðis taip əv mətiəriəl dʌz ət liːst put ðə stjuːdnt on ðə rait roud.

ðə spesimən sentəns, set in kontekst, haz ðiːz θriː disaidid ədvaːntidʒiz. fəːstli, it konstitjuːts ə wəːkəbl komprəmaiz bitwiːn ðə deinʒərəs, aut əv kontekst sentəns ən ðə kʌmbəsm kənektid pəsidʒ; əv ðə foːmə it riteinz ðə breviti, dimaːndid bai iːzi patn driliŋ, əv ðə latə, ðə konstənt əsousieiʃn əv patn wið kontekst, aiðə leksikl, imoutiv oː bouθ. sekndli, it iz ən evə preznt rimaində ðət ðə juːs əv sʌm pətikjulə toun in ə givn sentəns iz friːkwəntli ditəːmind, not bai grəmatikl oː strʌktʃrəl kənsidəreiʃnz, bət raːðə bai ðə sitjueiʃn in witʃ ðə sentəns iz sed. θəːdli, ən moust impoːtnt, it ineiblz ðə stjuːdnt in sʌm meʒə tə disaid wot wəːdz in ðə sentəns ər impoːtnt fər its miːniŋ, ən ðʌs, witʃ siləblz ə tə biː ðə kiː points in ði intəneiʃn patn. kwait ofn ðiːz kiː points kouinsaid wið wəːdz witʃ ə kəntraːstiv, oː pətenʃəli kəntraːstiv, wið ʌðə wəːdz in ðə vəːbl kontekst; on ʌðər əkeiʒnz, ðei əkəːr on wəːdz, huːz imoutiv kənəteiʃnz kəntraːst wið sʌm imouʃn, iksprest oːr implaid bai wot prisiːdz oː folouz ðə spesimən sentəns. it siːmz səːtn ðət ði aidiə əv kontraːst, limitid bai ARMSTRONG *and* WARD tə ðə juːs əv ðə hai foːliŋ toun, iz implisit in oːl tounz, ənd it iz laikli ðət fəːðə risəːtʃ wil ʃou ðə seim tə bi truː, in sʌm kənsidrəbl meʒə if not intaiəli, əv ðə non tounl (ðat iz, relətivli hai, levl) prominənt pitʃiz əv eni givn patn.

G. F. ARNOLD.

stroŋ ən wiːk fɔːmz in sʌðən britiʃ iŋliʃ

ðə triːtmənt əv stroŋ ən wiːk fɔːmz in moust kʌrənt teksbuks ɔn iŋliʃ fənetiks kɔːlz fə kɔment ʌndə fɔː mein hedz.

1. **ðɛə rileiʃn tə stres.** ðə wəːdz listid in moust buks əz relivənt tə ðis sʌbdʒikt ʃou kənsidrəbl ʌniːvnnis in ðɛə fɔːm/stres kərileiʃn. sʌm, ðiː ɔːgziljəri *have*, fər instəns, ɔfr ə kənsistənt rileiʃnʃip bitwiːn fɔːm ən stres ; ʌðəz, sʌtʃ əz *me*, fr igzɑːmpl, wailst dʒenrəli riteiniŋ ðə stroŋ fɔːm in stroŋli strest pəziʃnz, əlau ðə stroŋ ɔː ðə wiːk fɔːm indifrəntli wen wiːkli strest ; jet ʌðəz, *been* iz ən igzɑːmpl, siːm tu əkəː wið aiðə fɔːm irispektiv əv stres. nau frəm ə θiəretikl stænpoint it kən bi ɑːgjuːd ðət stroŋ fɔːm ən wiːk fɔːm, təːmz witʃ diraiv frəm ðə fɔːm/stres kərileiʃn, ʃud biː əplaid ounli tə ðouz wəːdz in witʃ ðis kərileiʃn iz kənsistənt, ðæt iz, tu wəːdz əv ðə *have*-taip. frəm ðə fɔrən ləːnəz point əv vjuː tuː, ðis rigə hæz mʌtʃ tə kəmend it. if ounli ðə *have*-taip wəːdz ə listid, ðə fɔrən stjuːdənts ətenʃn iz kɔnsntreitid ɔn ðə wəːdz in witʃ ðə stroŋ ən wiːk fɔːmz ən ðɛə rileiʃn tə stres riəli mætə ; wəːdz əv ðə *me*- ən *been*-taips hiː kən disrigɑːd in ðis kənekʃn, sins ðɛə stroŋ fɔːm iz pɔsibl in eni kɔntekst, irispektiv əv stres. if hauevə wəːdz əv ɔːl θriː kætigəriz ə listid, ðə klousnis əv ðə fɔːm/stres rileiʃnʃip ʃud bi kliəli indikeitid fər iːtʃ wəːd. ðis kud præps best bi dʌn bai klæsifaiiŋ ðə wəːd list intə ðə θriː kætigəriz əbʌv, bət fə præktikl pəːpəsiz, ðə raitər əz faund tuː kætigəriz səfiʃnt, ðə *have*-taip wəːdz in wʌn, ðə rest in ði ʌðə. fə ðə raitə ðə fəːst kætigəri kənteinz : *a, an, and, as, at, for, from, he, her, him, his, of, saint* (wið ə fɔlouiŋ prɔpə neim ounli), *some* (pɑːtətiv ædʒəktiv ounli), *them, us, who,* ði ɔːgziljəriz *am, are, can, do, does, had, has, have, is, must, shall, was* ən *will,* ən *the* ən *to* (bouθ wen fɔloud bai ə kɔnsənənt). nou daut ðə diːteil əv ðis diviʒn wil nɔt miːt wið juːnæniməs əpruːvl — fə ðə raitə sʌm əv ði əbʌv wəːdz, *he* ən *who,* fr igzɑːmpl, ə mɑːdʒinl — bət it iz kliə ðət sʌm sʌtʃ diviʒn kæn bi meid. iŋliʃ spiːkəz ə dʒenrəli mʌtʃ mɔː sensitiv tə ðə fɔrən ləːnəz misteiks wið moust wəːdz əv ðə fəːst kætigəri ðən wið ðouz əv ðə sekənd.

sʌtʃ ə diviʒn wil nɔt hauevər əkaunt fər ɔːl əkʌrənsiz əv stroŋ fɔːmz wið əledʒədli wiːk stres. wɔt, fr igzɑːmpl, əv /fɔː/ ən /frɔm/ in /ˈwɔt də juː ˈteik miː fɔː?/[1] ən /ˈtel miː ˈwɛə juː ˈgɔt it frɔm/? in ðiːz n similə keisiz it iz isenʃl fəːstli tə distiŋgwiʃ bitwiːn stres ən wɔt iz

---

[1] ðə toun-mɑːks juːzd in ðis peipə hæv KINGDON væljuːz.

best tə:md æksnt, ən ðen tə rileit wə:d-fɔ:m striktli tə ðə fɔ:mə. æksnt iz ðə mi:nz wεəbai ə spi:kər indikeits ðə wə:d ɔ: wə:dz in ən ʌtrəns tu witʃ i: ətætʃiz impɔ:tns ; it iz ju:ʒwəli ətʃi:vd bai ə kəmbineiʃn əv strɔŋ stres ən pitʃ prəminəns ɔn ət li:st wʌn siləbl əv i:tʃ əksentid wə:d ; *what, take, tell, where, got*, in ði əbʌv ʌtrənsiz, ər ɔ:l əksentid. bət ə wə:d ni:d nɔt bi: əksentid fə wʌn ər ʌðər əv its siləblz tə bi strɔŋli strest. refrəns tə ðə riðm əv ðə tu: ʌtrənsiz [1] ʃouz ðət in ədiʃn tə ðə faiv wə:dz kwoutid, *for* ən *from* ər ɔ:lsou strɔŋli strest sins ðei kouinsaid wið strɔŋ bi:ts in ðə riðm. it si:mz kliə ðət in ðə pa:st ðei həv bin teikn tə bi: wi:kli strest simpli bikəz ðei læk ðə pitʃ prəminəns əv ði əksentid, ən ðεəfɔ: mɔ:r ɔbvjəsli strɔŋli strest, wə:dz. laikwaiz, wʌns stres n æksnt ə kliəli difərenʃieitid, ðə vεəriiŋ fɔ:mz əv *to* ən *me* in *Give it to me* (ounli ðə fə:st wə:d əksentid) ər iksplikəbl in tə:mz əv stres : kəmpεə /ˈgiv it ˌtu: mi/ ən /ˈgiv it tə ˌmi:/.

2. **ðεə rileiʃn tu æksnt.** ðou ði: isenʃl kərileiʃn iz ðæt bitwi:n fɔ:m ən stres, ə klous rileiʃnʃip kwait ɔfn igzists bitwi:n fɔ:m ən æksnt ; ən ðə wə:d, moust ɔbvjəsli kwɔlifaiiŋ fə ðə fə:st əv ðə tu: kætigəriz əbʌv, iz wʌn witʃ, in ə givn wə:d si:kwəns, hæz difrənt fɔ:mz wen əksentid ən ʌnəksentid. gud igza:mplz ə *was* in /ai ˈwɔz ˌrait/ ən /ai wəz ˈrait/ ən *does* in /hau ˈdʌz ʃi: ˌdu: it?/ ən /ˈhau dəz ʃi: ˌdu: it?/. nɔt ɔ:l ðə wə:dz in ðə fə:st kætigəri ɔfə miniml pεəz əv ðis kaind, bət ɔ:l məs bi ri:znəbli i:zili əksentid in evridei kənvəseiʃnl iŋliʃ. nau it iz pɔsibl tu əksent ɔ:l iŋliʃ wə:dz ; bət eni wə:d, witʃ kən bi əksentid ounli in sʌtʃ kɔnteksts əz "hau iz ðə wə:d spelt... prənaunst?" ɔ: "wɔt də ðə letəz... spel?", ʃud nɔt bi kənsidəd in tə:mz əv strɔŋ ən wi:k fɔ:mz. ðʌs ðə raitə wud iksklu:d ɔ:ltəgeðə *that* (kəndʒʌŋʃn ɔ: relətiv prounaun), *there* (indefinit ædvə:b) ən *than*. ðεə difrənt fɔ:mz kən nɔt bi rileitid tə difrənsiz əv stres, sins, iksept in kɔntekst əv ði əbʌv speʃəlaizd kaind, ði:z wə:dz, wotevə ðεə fɔ:m, ər ɔ:lwiz wi:kli strest. /ðæt/, /ðεə/ ən /ðæn/ ə best riga:did əz fri: vεəriənts, əkə:riŋ mʌtʃ les kəmənli ðən ðə fɔ:mz wið /ə/.

3. **ðεə fəni:mik strʌktʃə.** ðou moust əv ðə relivənt wə:dz ə mɔnousilæbik, it iz nɔt ðə nʌmbər əv siləblz witʃ iz impɔ:tnt, bət ðə neitʃər əv ðə vauəl founi:mz əkə:riŋ in ðouz siləblz. ounli wə:dz ðə vauəl founi:mz əv witʃ kənfɔ:m tə ðə fɔlouiŋ distribju:ʃn kən bi sed tə hæv strɔŋ ən wi:k fɔ:mz :

---

[1] fər ə fulə diskʌʃn əv ðis meθəd əv ditə:miniŋ stres kætigəriz, si : G. F. ARNOLD, "Stress in English Words," North Holland Publishing Company, 1957.

əksentəbl siləbl wen strɔŋli strest: dʒenrəli ə fɔːtis [1] vauəl, bət liːnis [1] /i/ ənd /u/ ə pɔsibl, ðə lætər əpærəntli ounli in mɔnəsiləblz.

əksentəbl siləbl wen wiːkli strest: ziərou vauəl ɔː liːnis vauəl, juːʒwəli /ə/. /i/ iz pɔsibl wen ðə strɔŋ fɔːm hæz /iː/ ɔ /i/ fəlouiŋ /h/, ðə lætə biːiŋ ilaidid in ðə wiːk fɔːm. similəli /u/ ənd /o/ əkə: wen ðə strɔŋ fɔːm ʃouz /uː/ ɔː /ou/.

ɔːl ʌðə siləblz: liːnis vauəl ɔː ziərou vauəl. ðis fɔːmjuleiʃn, insistiŋ əz it dʌz ɔn ðə distribjuːʃn əv vauəl founiːmz in strɔŋ ən wiːk fɔːmz, əvɔidz ði ouvəremfəsis ɔfn leid ɔn ðə fʌʃn əv kɔnsənæntl iliʒn in ðə fɔːmeiʃn əv wiːk fɔːmz. iksept in ðə rɑːðə speʃl keis əv /h/, ðis kɔnsənæntl iliʒn iz insidentl ən nɔt nesəsrili rileitid tə wiːk stres.

4. **ðə strʌktʃər əv ðə wəːdz hæviŋ strɔŋ ən wiːk fɔːmz.** ðə miniməm juːnit tə witʃ ðiːz təːmz kən bi əplaid, iz ðə wəːd: fɔːm ən æksnt ə klousli rileitid ənd æksnt iz ə fiːtʃər əv ðə wəːd. ðət ðə wəːdz, dʒenrəli listid in ðis kənekʃn, ɔːlsou hæv ən ɔbvjəsli mɔːfiːmik steitəs iz irelivənt; ən ðou ðei ɑːr in fækt ɔːl mɔnoumɔːfiːmik, ðər iz nou ei praiɔːrai riːzn wai ə pɔlimɔːfiːmik wəːd ʃəd nɔt bi kærəktəraizd bai ðə seim fɔːm/stres kɔrileiʃn. ði: isenʃl founiːmik difrəns bitwiːn its fɔːmz mʌst hauevə lai in ðæt siləbl əv ðə houl wəːd witʃ nɔːməli kæriz ðə strɔŋ stres ən pitʃ prɔminəns wen ðə wəːd iz əksentid. ðʌs, wail ðεə baimɔːfiːmik strʌktʃə krieits nou difikltiz, wəːdz sʌtʃ əz *Scotland* ən *fivepence*, ɔfn kwoutid əz igzemplifaiiŋ ðə wiːk fɔːmz əv *land* ən *pence*, məs nʌnðəles biː iksklːuːdid: ðei ʃou nou founiːmik ɔːltəneiʃn in ðεər əksentəbl (fəːst) siləbl ðət kən biː rileitid tə difrənsiz əv stres. bisaidz ði iŋkənsistənsi invɔlvd in kəmpεəriŋ, fər igzɑːmpl, ðə wəːd *land*/lænd/ wið ðə baund mɔːfiːm *-land*/-lənd/, ðεər iz ɔːlsou ðə difiklti ðət ðə wəːd *land* kən əkə: strɔŋli ɔː wiːkli strest wiðaut tʃeinʒ əv fɔːm.

G. F. ARNOLD.

ði instəbiliti əv iŋgliʃ alviəulər aːtikjuleiʃnz

it iz nəutisəbl ðət in intəːnl dʒʌŋktʃərl sitjueiʃnz ði iŋgliʃ alviəulər aːtikjuleiʃnz ə pətikjuləli sʌbdʒikt tə ðat kaind əv əsimileiʃn witʃ involvz ə modifikeiʃn əv ðə pleis əv aːtikjuleiʃn. not əunli aː ðə modifikeiʃnz witʃ ʃəu ə straikiŋ fənetik, aləfonik, tʃeindʒ frəm ði

---

[1] fɔi bouθ ðiiz təimz, əgein si: "Stress in English Words," fɔitis = vauəl nɔiməli əsouʃieitid wið stroŋ wəid stres, iː dʒiː /iː/, /æ/, /ou/; liinis = vauəl nɔiməli əsouʃieitid wið wiik wəid stres, /i/, /u/, /ə/, /o/.

aisələt wəːd foːm (similitjuːd), iː dʒiː [t] > [t̪], ets., bət ðər ə oːlsəu tʃeindʒiz witʃ ə friːkwəntli əv ə fəniːmik taip, iː dʒiː, /t/ > /k/ oː /p/ ənd /n/ > /m/ oː /ŋ/. in ðə keis əv sʌtʃ tʃeindʒiz əv fəuniːm, it siːmz kliə ðət ðə ridʌndənsi əv iŋgliʃ pəmits kənsidrəbl njuːtrəlaizeiʃn əv fəuniːmz θruː əsimileiʃn wiðaut lisnəz biːiŋ əweər əv eni distəːbəns əv iːz əv kəmjuːnikeiʃn. ðʌs, [ˈraŋ ˌkwikli] mei signl *ran* oː *rang*, ðə bəːdn əv miːniŋ restiŋ on ðə kontekst; oːr əgen, ðə kʌrənt ədvəːtismənt *Have a good rum for your money* dipendz fər its impakt əpon ðə kəuəlesns əv /n/ ənd /m/ in [m̩]. in ðiːz keisiz, ðə taip əv oːrl kləuʒə biːiŋ not səu mʌtʃ kəntraːstiv əz kəndiʃnd bai ðə kontekst, ðə neizaliti fiːtʃər əunli rimeinz əz distiŋktiv.

oːdnri spiːkəz əv RP ə not juːʒəli əweər əv ði əsimileiʃnz əv ðis kaind witʃ ðei meik; if iksplisit kwestʃnz kənsəːniŋ sʌtʃ tʃeindʒiz ə put tə ðəm, ðeər aːnsəz wil not ʌnnatʃrəli bi kʌləd bai predʒudisiz diraiviŋ frəm ðə ritn foːm əv ðə laŋgwidʒ. jet it siːmz tə bi truː ðət ðəu ə greit nʌm̩bər əv əsimileitəri tʃeindʒiz wil bi əkseptid wiðaut ðə lisnəz biːiŋ əweər əv ðəm, ʌðəz wil bi nəutist ən karəktəraizd bai sʌm sʌtʃ təːm əz "slipʃod" oːr "ʌnedjukeitid". ðʌs, ði /n/ əv *ten* in *ten men, ten girls*, mei bi friːli riəlaizd əz /m/ ənd /ŋ/ rispektivli, ðə tʃeindʒiz riflektiŋ noːml juːsidʒ. bət ə prəgresiv əsimileiʃn sʌtʃ əz iz igzemplifaid bai ðə lʌndən daiəlekt vəːʃn əv *down the road* əz [ˈdaun nə ˌrəud] iz ridʒektid əz ə vʌlgərizm.

fəniːmik tʃeindʒiz involviŋ /t, d, n, s, z/ (prəvaidiŋ ðət ðei rimein in ði əprəupiət "manə" oːdə) ər ispeʃəli laikli tə paːs ʌnnəutist. if ðə dʒʌnktʃərəl posibilitiz əv wəːd fainl /p, t, k, b, d, g, m, n, ŋ, f, v, θ, ð, s, z, ʃ, ʒ/ wið wəːd iniʃl /p, t, k, b, d, g, m, n, f, v, θ, ð, s, z, ʃ, h, j, w/ ər igzamind, it iz kliə ðət ði alviəulər aːtikjuleiʃnz ə məust laiəbl tə tʃeindʒ :—

/t/ redili əsimileits tə /p/ oː /k/ bifoː /p, b, k, g, m/ (ðə stop fiːtʃə rimeiniŋ əz distiŋktiv), iː dʒiː, [ˈðap ˌpen, ˈðap ˌboi, ˈðap ˌman, ˈðak ˌkʌp, ˈðak ˌgəːl] *that pen, boy, man*, ets. bət /p/ dəz not noːməli tʃeindʒ tə /t/ oː /k/ bifoː /t, d, n, k, g/ — [ˈtot ˌtaun, ˈpaik ˌkliːnə] wud bi ʌnjuːʒl fət *top town, pipe cleaner*; noː dəz /k/ noːməli modifai tə /t/ oː /p/ bifoː /t, d, n, p, b, m/ — [ˈblat ˌdog, ˈblap ˌpig] biːiŋ abnoːml fə *black dog, black pig*.

/d/ oːlsəu əsimileits redili bifoː /p, b, m, k, g/, weərəz /b, g/ əpiə tə bi moː steibl.

(it iz tə bi nəutid ðət RP /p, t, k/ ə fri:kwəntli riəlaizd əz [ʔ] in wəːd fainl pəziʃnz wiðaut ə mauθ kləuzə. opəziʃnz mei in ðis wei bi nju:trəlaizd :—['raiʔ bəˌnɑːnəz] əz ə riəlaizeiʃn əv *right* oː *ripe bananas*, ənd ['toːʔ ˌpəuliʃ] əz *talk* oː *taught Polish*.)

/n/ əsimileits redili tə /m/ oː /ŋ/ bifoː (ənd sʌmtaimz ɑːftə) p, b, m, k, g/, iː dʒiː ['tem ˌpleiəz, 'ram ˌbak, 'θim ˌman, 'teŋ ˌkʌps, 'teŋ ˌgəːlz, ˌtʌpms, ˌsekŋ] *ten players, ran back, thin man, ten cups, ten girls, tuppence, second*; bət /m/ əsimileiʃnz tə /n/ oː /ŋ/ ər abnoːml, əz ɑː tʃeindʒiz əv /ŋ/ tə /n/ oː /m/ — sʌtʃ prənʌnsieiʃnz əz ['θʌn ˌneil, səŋ 'keik, 'θin tə ˌduː, 'rim mi ˌʌp] wud bi ʌnjuːʒl fə *thumb nail, some cake, thing to do, ring me up*. (nəut, hauevə, səm speʃl keisiz sʌtʃ əz [lenθ, strenθ] *length, strength*, ənd oːlsəu ðə fakt ðət ði *-ing* təːmineiʃn [-iŋ] mei əsimileit, iː dʒiː, ['nʌθin ˌduiŋ, 'teikim ˌmoː] *nothing doing, taking more*. ði instəbiliti əv ðis təːmineiʃn mei bi djuː paːtli tu its dʒenrəl prənʌnsieiʃn əz [-in] witʃ wəz waidspred in ðə 17θ-18θ sentʃəriz ənd witʃ igzists tədei əz ə səuʃl veəriənt.)

/s/ əsimileits fəniːmikli tə /ʃ/ (ðə frikʃn rimeiniŋ əz distiŋktiv) əunli bifoː /ʃ, j/, iː dʒiː, ['ðiʃ ˌʃop, 'ðiʃ jəː oː 'ðiʃ ˌʃəː] *this shop, this year*. bət fainl /f, v, ʃ, ʒ/ ə not influənst in ðis wei bai ðə konsənantl invaiərənmənt. /θ, ð/, tuː, rimein steibl in RP, iksept in rapid spiːtʃ, wen ə priːsiːdiŋ /s/ oː /z/ mei ritrakt ðə dentl aːtikjuleiʃn tu ən alviəulə wʌn, iː dʒiː, [wots zə ˌtaim, 'haz zə 'pəust ˌkʌm] *What's the time, Has the post come*. ðə siːmz tə bi nəu keis əv /s, z/ bikʌmiŋ dentl in ðə visiniti əv /θ, ð/.

it iz difiklt tu əkaunt fə ðis əpərənt alviəulər instəbiliti on aːtikjulətri oː sistimatik graundz. it iz posibl ðət ðə tʌŋ aːtikjuleiʃn əv, fər instəns, /t, d, n/ iz moː redili ədʒʌstəbl ðən ðə baileibiəl kləuzə karaktəristik əv /p, b, m/; bət wʌn mait iːkwəli ikspekt tʃeindʒiz əv /k, g, ŋ/ tə /t, d, n/. ði alviəulə stop siəriz iz, əv koːs, biːiŋ miːdiəl, ikspəuzd tu ə dʌbl ətrakʃn frəm ðə baileibiəl ənd viːlə siəriːz. (ðə stroŋ vəukalik tranziʃn karaktəristik əv ðə viːləz mei oːlsəu bi ə faktər in inhibitiŋ ðeə modifikeiʃn.) /s, z/, hauevə, əkəːriŋ midwei bitwiːn ðə dentl ənd palətəu-alviəulə siəriːz, əsimileit əunli in ðə dərekʃn əv /ʃ, ʒ/. frəm ə fʌŋkʃənl standpoint, it iz truː ðət ði alviəulə fəuniːmz okjupai ə hai pleis in ði oːdər əv friːkwənsi əv əkʌrəns in iŋgliʃ, səu ðət ðeə "fʌŋkʃənl ləud" mei bi sed tə bi relətivli greit ət ðə wəːd levl. bət ðis hai friːkwənsi əv əkʌrəns mei, in fakt, kəntribjuːt tə ðeər instəbiliti in wəːd fainl pəziʃnz wiðin ðə kəntinjuəm, əz kəmpeəd wið ðə les komən təːminl konsənənts, wen it iz ə kwestʃn əv ðə njuːtrəlaizeiʃn əv ridʌndənt opəziʃnz.

 it wud bi intrəstiŋ tə nəu membəz vjuːz əz rigaːdz bəuθ ðə fakts iləstreitid əbʌv — in iŋgliʃ ənd ʌðə laŋgwidʒiz — ənd oːlsəu posibl ekspləneiʃnz ov ðəm.

A. C. G.

diskraibiŋ əsimileiʃn̩

əsimileiʃn̩ həz trədiʃn̩li biːn ə təːm əplaid tu meni taips əv igzaːmpl̩z. ðiːz igzaːmpl̩z kʌvə fənetikli kəndiʃn̩d nuːtrəlaizeiʃn̩, /siŋk/ ; fənetikli kəndiʃn̩d aləfəunz, [t̺ɹäï] ; moːfəufəniːmik oːltəneiʃn̩z, /kats/ v. /dogz/ ; historikl̩ tʃeindʒ, /meʒə/ ([ʒ] < [zj]) ; ənd kəntekstʃuəl veəriːeiʃn̩, bəuθ aləfonik, [wän̥ θin̬], n̩d fəniːmik, /hagŋk got/. ðiː əunli komən graund witʃ kən biː ikstraktid frəm ðə teksbuks (bəuθ ingliʃ and əmerikən) iz əz folauz : wen wʌn saund in ə wəːd oː tekst əpiəz fənetikli similə tə sʌm ʌðə saund in ðat wəːd oː tekst n̩d sʌm soːt əv koːzl̩ rileiʃn̩ʃip iz əsjuːmd, ðis iz sed tə biː ə keis əv əsimileiʃn̩. ət liːst θriː faktəz ər invəulvd :

(1) ðə dəmein əv ðə rileiʃn̩ʃip :

 (a) intrə-wəːd,   (b) intə-wəːd (" dʒʌkstəpəziʃn̩l ",
                                              " kəntekstʃuəl ")
 /meʒə/, [t̺ɹäï]   /hagŋk got/, [wän̥ θin̬]

(2) ə veəriːeiʃn̩ in wəːd-fɔːm implaid oː not :

 (a) veəriːeiʃn̩ *not* implaid,   (b) veəriːeiʃn̩ implaid,
     [t̺ɹäï], /siŋk/   [wän̥ θin̬], /meʒə/

(3) ðə rileiʃn̩ʃip bitwiːn ðiː əsimileitid saund n̩d ðə saund witʃ it in sʌm sens " ripleisiz " oː " iksluːdz "

 (a) aləfonik,   (b) fəniːmik,
     [wän̥ θin̬], [t̺ɹäï]   /siŋk/, /hagŋk got/

fəːðə diskʌʃn̩ wil nau biː iksluːdid on historikl̩ əsimileiʃn̩z witʃ ər intrə-wəːd, weə veəriːeiʃn̩ (= prəuses əv tʃeindʒ) iz oːlweiz implaid n̩d weə (3) wil əunli biː steitəbl̩ əz paːt əv sʌm moː təutl̩ strʌktʃurəl kəmparisn̩. ðə rimeində əv ðis nəut kənsəːnz əunli sinkronik diskripʃn̩z weə ðə diviʒn̩ (1) (a)/(b) igzakli korisponz wið (2) (a)/(b).

folauiŋ *dʒəunz ə nʌmbər əv raitəz distiŋgwiʃ (3) (a) frəm (3) (b) bai ðə juːs əv ðə təːm " similitjuːd " bət ðə meidʒə riːzn̩ fə ðiː intrədʌkʃn̩ əv ðis təːm iz əparəntli tu diskraib ðəuz igzaːmpl̩z weə veəriːeiʃn̩ in wəːd-fɔːm iz *not* tə biː infəːd. ðʌs igzaːmpl̩z ə juːʒuəli limitid tə ðəuz satisfaiiŋ (2) (a) əz wel əz (3) (a) (e.g. [t̺ɹäï]). fəːðəmoː buks imploiiŋ ðis təːm ofən iləstreit " əsimileiʃn̩ " səuli bai fəniːmik igzaːmpl̩z. ðis implaiz ðiː əbligətri kʌpliŋ əv fəniːmik n̩d veəriːeiʃn̩, n̩d əv aləfonik n̩d nəu veəriːeiʃn̩. bət it mei ɔːlsəu biː dizaiərəbl̩ tə kʌpl̩, fə səːtn̩ diskriptiv pəːpəsiz, fəniːmik n̩d nəu veəriːeiʃn̩ (az in /siŋk/) ɔː aləfonik n̩d veərieiʃn̩ (az in [wän̩ θi̩ŋ]). raitəz juːziŋ ðə similitjuːd/əsimileiʃn̩ diviʒn̩ hæv nəu pleis ət ɔːl fə ðə fɔːmə wail ðə latə həz biːn diskraibd ʌndə similitjuːd wið ət best ə futnəut seiiŋ ðət similitjuːd həz biːn brɔːt əbaut bai kəntekstʃuəl əsimileiʃn̩.

it dʌz siːm juːsful tu distiŋgwiʃ bitwiːn ðəuz similaritiz weə ə veəriːeiʃn̩ in wəːd-fɔːm iz implaid n̩d ðəuz weə it iz not implaid. bət ðə təːm " similitjuːd " mait bi mɔː helpful if it wə divɔːst frəm its aləfonik liŋks. ðə foləuiŋ leiblz wud ðen biː əveiləbl̩ əz rikwaiəd: aləfonik similitjuːd, [tɟäi̩]; fəniːmik similitjuːd, /siŋk/ (ðis təːm kud biː juːzd tə leibl̩ səːtn̩ taips əv nuːtrəlaizeiʃn̩ ənd mɔːfəufəniːmik ɔːltəneiʃn̩z); aləfonik əsimileiʃn̩, [wän̩ θi̩ŋ]; ənd fəniːmik əsimileiʃn̩, /hagŋk got/. ðə latə tuː wud ɔːtəmatikli implai ðə fɔːmə tuː bət ðis wud not əplai in rivəːs.

A. CRUTTENDEN.
University of Manchester.

kõtrãdy

BJØRN STÅLHANE ANDRÉSEN, *Pre-glottalization in English Standard Pronunciation* (Norwegian Universities Press, 1968. 187 pp.).

ə greɪt diːl əv fənetɪk θɪŋkɪŋ ɪn rɪleɪʃn̩ tə trendz ɪn prənʌnsɪeɪʃn̩ ɪz ɪmpreʃn̩ɪstɪk ənd spekjələtɪv : ðɛər ɪz ɒfn̩ ə rɪlʌktəns tə kaʊnt hedz. ə bʊk laɪk ðɪs wʌn, ðɛəfɔː, ʃʊd bɪ ɔːl ðə mɔː welkəm əz ɪt sets aʊt tə duː ɪgzæktlɪ ðæt : tə gɪv əs səm fɪgəz ɒn ðə fiːtʃər əv ɪŋglɪʃ prənʌnsɪeɪʃn̩ menʃn̩d ɪn ðə taɪtl̩. enɪ sʌtʃ kwɒntɪfɪkeɪʃn̩ ɪn wɒtevər ɛərɪə mʌst bɪ əv væljuː.

ðiː ɪnvestɪgeɪʃn̩ wəz beɪst ɒn rɪkɔːdɪŋz əv ə kɔːpəs əv 509 speʃlɪ kənstrʌktɪd sentənsɪz prɪzentɪŋ /p t k tʃ/ ɪn ə vəraɪətɪ əv fənetɪk kɒntekstʃ. ðə rɪkɔːdɪŋz wə meɪd baɪ 45 neɪtɪv ɪnfɔːmənts bɪtwiːn 16 ənd 30 jɪəz əv eɪdʒ, ɔːl əv huːm wə dʒʌdʒd baɪ ðɪ ɔːθə tə hæv æksn̩ts fɔːlɪŋ wɪðɪn ðə lɪmɪts əv *ɪŋglɪʃ *stændəd, ðæt ɪz, wɪð nəʊ grəʊs riːdʒən̩l̩ fiːtʃəz. sɪns ðə mətɪərɪəl wəz red baɪ ðiː ɪnfɔːmənts wʌn ʃʊd bɪwɛər əv ɪkstræpəleɪtɪŋ tuː laɪt-hɑːtɪdlɪ tʊ ɪmprɒmptjuː prənʌnsɪeɪʃn̩, bət iːkwəlɪ sɪns ðɪs ɪz ðɪ əʊnlɪ præktɪkəbl̩ weɪ əv getɪŋ ðə mæksɪməm əv reləvənt deɪtə ɪn kəndenst fɔːm wʌn məst greɪtfəlɪ əksept ðə kəndɪʃn̩z əv ðiː ɪksperɪmənt.

ðə deɪtə wər ænəlaɪzd ɪn rɪleɪʃn̩ tʊ ə nʌmbər əv fæktəz wɪtʃ maɪt pɒsɪblɪ bɪ kɔːzəlɪ kənektɪd wɪð priː-glɒtl̩aɪzeɪʃn̩ : seks, edjʊkeɪʃən̩l ænd riːdʒənl̩ bækgraʊnd, priːvɪəs spiːtʃ-treinɪŋ, ɪntəneɪʃn̩, stres, kwɒntəti/ kwɒləti əv priːsiːdɪŋ vaʊəl, kləʊzd/əʊpən sɪləbl̩, wɜːd-faɪnl̩ pəzɪʃn̩, ænd taɪp əv fɒləʊɪŋ kɒnsənənt.

əmʌŋst ðə dʒenrəl fæktəz, seks ənd riːdʒənl̩ bækgraʊnd ə ʃəʊn tə hæv lɪtl̩ ɔː nəʊ ɪfekt ; pʌblɪk-skuːl edjʊkeɪʃn̩ ənd praɪə spiːtʃ-treinɪŋ bəʊθ siːm slaɪtlɪ tʊ ɪnhɪbɪt priː-glɒtl̩aɪzeɪʃn̩. ðə fənetɪk kəndɪʃnz məʊst feɪvərɪŋ ðə fɪnɒmɪnən ɑː bɪfɔː pləʊsɪvz (55% əv ɔːl sʌtʃ əkʌrənsɪz), nɒn-sɪlæbɪk neɪzl̩z (54%) ənd /r/ (43%). bɪfɔː frɪkətɪvz ðə pəsentɪdʒ ɪz 39%, bɪfɔː semɪ-vaʊəlz 30%, ənd bɪfɔː /l/ 33%. bɪfɔː vaʊəlz ɔː sɪlæbɪk kɒnsənənts verɪ lɪtl̩ priː-glɒtl̩aɪzeɪʃn̩ əkɜːz ət ɔːl. stres ʃəʊz nəʊ ɪfekt ənd ɪntəneɪʃn̩ hɑːdlɪ enɪ, bət əʊpənnəs əv ðə priːsiːdɪŋ vaʊəl dʌz hæv ən ɪfekt waɪlst ðə kwɒntəti əv ðə vaʊəl dəz nɒt. wɜːd baʊndrɪz slaɪtlɪ feɪvə priː-glɒtl̩aɪzeɪʃn̩ əv ðə priːsiːdɪŋ stɒps. əʊvər ɔːl ðə mətɪərɪəl ðə pəsentɪdʒ əv priː-glɒtl̩aɪzeɪʃn̩ ɪz 36%, bət ðə reɪndʒ ɪz verɪ waɪd, frəm 0% fə 2 sʌbdʒɪkts tʊ 84% fə wʌn.

səʊ briːf ə sʌmərɪ gɪvz ə pʊər aɪdɪə əv ðə menɪ eksələnt teɪblz ɪn wɪtʃ ðɪ ɔːθə prɪzents hɪz faɪndɪŋz ənd wɪtʃ ə wel wɜːθ diːteɪld stʌdɪ. wʌn mʌst, haʊevə, vjuː ðəm ɪn ðə laɪt əv tuː kjʊərɪəs dɪsɪʒn̩z əv meθəd. fɜːst, nəʊ dɪstɪŋkʃən ɪz meɪd bɪtwiːn ə glɒtl̩ ɑːtɪkjələreɪʃn̩ ædɪd tʊ ən ɔːrl̩ wʌn (iː.dʒiː. **mæʔtrəs**) ənd ə glɒtl̩ ɑːtɪkjələreɪʃn̩ ələʊn (iː.dʒiː. **mæʔrəs**), ðæt ɪz tə seɪ bɪtwiːn ðə riːɪnfɔːsɪŋ ənd ðə riːpleɪsɪŋ glɒtl̩ stɒp. naʊ ɪt ɪz nəʊ daʊt truː, əz ðɪ ɔːθə sez (p. 43), ðət " kɒŋkriːt saʊndz ɪndɪspjuːtəblɪ əv ðɪs taɪp [riːpleɪsɪŋ glɒtl̩ stɒp] ɑː verɪ skɛəs ɪn maɪ mətɪərɪəl ," bət ɪt wʊd bɪ verɪ ɪntrəstɪŋ tə nəʊ dʒʌst wɛə ðɪ əkʌrənsɪz wɜː ænd ðɛər ɪgzækt friːkwənsɪ ; ɪndiːd sʌtʃ nɒlɪdʒ maɪt bɪ krɪtɪkl̩, sɪns ðɪ əkʌrəns əv riːpleɪsɪŋ glɒtl̩ stɒp priː-pɔːzəlɪ ɔːr ə fɔːm sʌtʃ əz **mæʔrəs** wʊd miːdjətlɪ kɔːl ɪntə kwestʃən ðə relətɪv hɒməʊdʒəneɪətɪ əv prənʌnsɪeɪʃn̩ wɪtʃ ðɪ ɔːθə kleɪmz fə hɪz ɪnfɔːmənts. ɔːlðəʊ, əz hiː ɔːlsəʊ sez, ɪt ɪz nɒt ɔːlwɪz iːzɪ tə dɪstɪŋgwɪʃ ʔ frəm, seɪ ʔt, ɪt ɪz baɪ nəʊ miːnz ɪmpɒsəbl̩ iːvən ɔːdɪtrəlɪ ənd ɪt ɪz sɜːtn̩lɪ wɜːθ ətemptɪŋ, tə rɪliːv aʊər ʌnsɜːtn̩tɪ ənd sætɪsfaɪ lɪdʒɪtɪmət kjʊərɪɒsətɪ.

ðə sekənd kjʊərɪəs, ðəʊ nɒt dɪseɪbl̩ɪŋ, dɪsɪʒn̩ ɪz tə kaʊnt ðɪ ɪnevɪtəbl̩ ɪrelɪvənt riːdɪŋz əz pətenʃəlɪ priː-glɒtl̩aɪzd ənd ðʌs tə prɪzent tuː nʌmbəz əz ən ɪndeks əv priː-glɒtl̩aɪzeɪʃn̩, ə fɜːm fɪgə frəm ðə deɪtə, seɪ 36·8%, ænd ə pətenʃl̩ mæksɪməm ɪŋkluːdɪŋ ðiː ɪrelɪvənt riːdɪŋz, seɪ 39·5%. aɪ kən siː nəʊ ədvɑːntɪdʒ ɪn ðɪs ænd aɪ həv juːzd əʊnlɪ ðə fɜːm fɪgə ɪn ðɪs rɪvjuː.

ə məʊst mɪtɪkjələs sɜːveɪ əv priːvɪəs refrənsɪz tə ðə sʌbdʒɪkt

liːdz tʊ ə kwaɪt njuː ənd ʌnɪkspektɪd vjuː əv ðə ɡlɒtl̩ stɒp spredɪŋ
sauθwəd frəm *skɒtlənd frəm əbaʊt ðə jɪə 1860 tə riːtʃ *lʌndən əbaʊt
1910. waɪlst ðɪ evɪdəns ədjuːst ɪz kwaɪt ʌnɪmpiːtʃəbl̩, ðə kəŋkluːʒn̩ ɪz
nevəðəles nɒt həʊlɪ əkseptəbl̩, bɪkɒz ðɪ ɔːθər ɪksplɪsɪtlɪ rɪdʒekts ʌðər
evɪdəns, wɪtʃ enɪ neɪtɪv fəʊnɪtɪʃn̩ wʊd ɔːlməʊst sɜːtn̩lɪ əksept, fə ðɪ
əkʌrəns əv ɡlɒtl̩ stɒp ɪn *lʌndən spiːtʃ ət mʌtʃ ɜːlɪə deɪts. spelɪŋz sʌtʃ
əz " Woostreet ", " statues ", " fonstone ", " uprigh ", (fə *Wood
Street, statutes, fontstone, upright*), ɔːl kwəʊtɪd ɪn ðɪs bʊk (p. 12),
prɪsaɪslɪ pærəlel trænskrɪpʃn̩z wɪtʃ kwaɪt pəseptɪv stjuːdn̩ts meɪk ət
ðə prezn̩t taɪm. aɪ hæv lɪtl̩ daʊt ðət [ʔ] fə /t/ ət enɪ reɪt ɪz ət liːst θriː
sentʃərɪz əʊld ɪn lʌndən. bət ə fæsɪneɪtɪŋ kwestʃən rɪmeɪnz : wɒz ðɛə
nʌnðəles ə saʊθwəd drɪft frəm *skɒtlənd ɔː duː ðɪ ɒbzəveɪʃn̩z əv ɜːlɪə
fəʊnɪtɪʃn̩z ɡɪv ðɪs ɪmpreʃn̩ fɔːtjʊɪtəslɪ ? maɪ ɡes ɪz ðə lætə, bət wɒt
Dr. ANDRÉSEN ʃəʊz ɪn hɪz ædmərəbl̩ bʊk ɪz nɒt ɪnʌf, pətɪkjələlɪ ɪn
ɒpəzɪʃn̩ tə sʌtʃ rɪdaʊtəbl̩ əbzɜːvəz əz BELL, ELLIS ənd SWEET. wiː niːd
hɑːd fɪɡəz, iːvən ɪf ðeɪ əʊnlɪ sɜːv tə kənfɔːm aʊər ɪmpreʃn̩z, ənd wiː
məst bɪ ɡreɪtfl̩ tə ðɪs ɔːθə fə hɪz kɒntrɪbjuːʃn̩.

J. D. O'CONNOR.

PHONETICS IN THE WIDER WORLD

rɛmi'nisənsez əv Melville Bell

[ðə foloiŋ nouts əɹ frəm ən aɹtikl bai pastəɹ D. Macrae ə pʌɹsənl frɛnd əv Bell'z, pʌbliʃt in ði *Edinburgh Evening News* ən kaindle sɛnt tu əs bai auɹ kəli:g H. Drummond].

..... ɔːlðo Bell wəz bɛst noun in skɔtlənd əz ə pʌblik riːdər, ənd in skuːlz θruː hiz feiməs 'standəɹd ɛlokjuːʃənist', hiː wəz eˈsɛnʃəle ə man əv saiəns, ən devouted imsɛlf laɹdzle tə ðə moːr abstruːs stʌdez kənɛkted wið iz profɛʃən. hwail ɔlwez disˈtiŋgwiʃt az ə tiːtʃər ənd ɛlokjuːʃənist, hi stud supriːm in iz profɛʃən az ə saiəntifik ɛkspounənt əv ðə prinsiplz əv spiːtʃ ən ðə mɛkənizm əv ðə vɔis. it wəz hiz stʌdez in ðis dirɛkʃən ðət lɛd im tu inˈvɛnt ðə sistəm əv "vizibl spiːtʃ" hwitʃ mei bi regaɹded əz ðə krauniŋ ətʃiːvmənt əv iz laif. ai hapnd tə biː ət iz haus ɔn ðə mɛmərəbl nait hwɛn ðəɹ flaʃt əpɔn im ði aidiə əv ə fizjoˈlɔdzikl alfəbet hwitʃ wəd fʌɹniʃ tə ði ai ə kompliːt gaid tə ðə proˈdʌkʃən əv ɛne ɔrəl saund, bai ʃouiŋ in ðə vɛre fɔɹm əv ðə lɛtəɹ ðə poziʃən ənd akʃən əv ði ɔɹgənz əv spiːtʃ hwitʃ its prodʌkʃən rekwaiɹd. it wəz ði ɛnd tɔɹdz hwitʃ mɛne jiɹz əv θɔːt ən stʌde həd bin briŋiŋ im, bət ɔːl ðə seim it keim əpɔn im laik ə sʌdn ɹeveleiʃən, az ə landskep mait flaʃ əpɔn ðə viʒən əv ə man sʌdnle emʌɹdʒiŋ frəm ə fɔrest....

hwɛn i gɔt iz sistem elaboreited, hi tɔːt it tə hiz bɔiz, ən wəz eneibld wið ðɛr əsistəns tə giv dəmənstreiʃənz əv its valju. hi keim tə mai faːðəɹz haus, ən geiv ə praivet dəmənstreiʃən ðɛɹ, hwitʃ greitle əstɔniʃt əs ɔːl. wi had ə fjuː frɛndz wið əs ðat aftəɹnuːn; ən hwɛn bɛlz sʌnz əd bin sɛnt əwei, wi geiv bɛl ðə moust pəkjuːljər ən difiklt saundz wi kəd θiŋk əv, iŋkluːdiŋ wʌɹdz fɹəm ðə frɛnʃ ən galik — fəloiŋ ðiːz wið inaɹtikjulet saundz, az əv kisiŋ, tʃʌkliŋ, etsɛtrə. ɔːl ðiːz bɛl rout daun in iz vizibl spiːtʃ, ənd iz bɔiz wəɹ kɔːld in. ai stil rɛmɛmbər auɹ kiːn intrɛst, ən baiənbai əstɔniʃmənt, az ðə ladz stud said bai said lukiŋ ʌmɛstle ət ðə peipəɹ, ən sloule riːprɔdjuːsiŋ saund aftəɹ saund, dʒʌst əz wiː d ʌtəɹd ðem. wʌn frɛnd in ðə kʌmpənə həd givn əz hiz kəntribjuːʃən ə lɔŋ jɔːniŋ saund, ʌtəɹd əz i stɹɛtʃt iz aɹmz ən sloule twisted iz bɔdə laik wʌn in ðə last steidʒ əv wiːrenes. əvkɔɹs, vizibl spiːtʃ kəd ounle rəprezɛnt ðə saund, nɔt ðə fizikl muːvmənt; ənd ai wɛl rɛmɛmbəɹ ðə ʃauts əv laftəɹ ðət fɔlod, hwɛn ðə ladz, aftəɹ stʌdeiŋ ʌmestle ðə simbəlz befɔːɹ ðem, riːprɔdjuːst ðə saund feiθfəle, bət laik ðə goust əv its fɔɹməɹ self, in its detatʃmənt frəm ðə stretʃiŋ ən bɔdə twistiŋ wið hwitʃ it əd ɔridʒinəle bin kəmbaind.

bɛlz buk ɔn vizibl spiːtʃ wəz pʌbliʃt in djuː taim; ən hwɛn suːn aftəɹ, hi lɛft ðis kʌntre ən sɛtld in kanədə, ðə sistem began tu əweikn intrɛst ɔn ðat said əv ði atlantik. ɔn ði inviteiʃən əv ðə prɛzidənt əv Harvard juːnivʌɹsite, hi wɛnt ðɛɹ tu eksplein it tu ən ɔːdjəns əv spɛʃəle invaited gɛsts. əmʌŋst ðouz prɛznt wəz ə mistəɹ Hubbard, huːz dɔːtəɹ wəz ə dɛf-mjuːt; ɔlso ə mis Fullar, huː həd tʃaɹdʒ əv ðə Horace Mann skuːl fəɹ ðə dɛf ən dʌm. bouθ əv ðəm wəɹ stɹʌk bai ðə pɔsibilitez oupnd ʌp bai vizibl spiːtʃ fəɹ tiːtʃiŋ ðə dʌm tə spiːk; ən profesəɹ bɛl wəz invaited tə kʌm tə Boston ənd ʌndəɹteik eksperimentl wʌɹk ðɛɹ. ðis i wəz nɔt eibl tə duː; bət iz sʌn Graham Bell akseptiŋ ði inviteiʃən, hi wəz suːn sɛtld in bɔstn, hwɛːr i treind ouvəɹ 2000 dɛf-mjuːts tə spiːk, əz wɛl əz tə nou hwət ʌðəɹz wəɹ seiiŋ bai riːdiŋ ðɛɹ lips. miːntaim i kared ɔn ðə siːrez əv eksperiments ðət iʃud in ði invɛnʃən əv ðə telefoun..... hwɛn, aftəɹ ə taim, hiz faːðəɹ retaiɹd frəm iz pʌblik wʌɹk in kanədə, ðə sʌn indjuːst im tə kʌm ən sɛtl in Washington, hwɛːr iz oun houm nau wəz.

hwɛn ai wɛnt tə riːvizit emɛrikə in 1898-1899, ai had ə wɔɹm inviteiʃən frɔm im tə gou ən stei wið im fər ə hwail.

ai ʃl nɛvəɹ fəɹgɛt ðə delaitfl fɔɹtnait ai had wið im ðɛn. ðou ai faund im wiːkər in bɔdele hɛlθ ən vigəɹ, hi wəz ritʃ əz ɛvər in ðə wɔɹmθ əv iz əfɛkʃənz, ənd in ɔːl ðə bjuːtefl fiːtʃəɹz əv karɛktəɹ bai hwitʃ iː d bin distiŋgwiʃt θruaut iz laif . . . . .

bɛl wəz ɔlso noun əz ə dʒɛnrəs filanθrəpist. hi juːst tə gou wið iz haushould tə Colonial Beach fəɹ ðə sʌməɹ mʌnθs; ən ðɛɹ hi had erɛkted ə siːsaid houm fəɹ puːr ən dɛliket tʃildrən.

ən nau, after ə lɔŋ, strɛnjuəs, fruːtfl, ən bjuːtefl laif, Melville Bell əz past əwei, liːviŋ behaind im nɔt ounle wʌɹks əv pʌɹmənent valju, bət delaitfl mɛmərez in ðə haɹts əv ɔːl hu njuː him.

brɔ·dka·stɪŋ ənd fonɛtɪks

ɪt meɪ ɪntrəst ri·dəz əv ðɪ m.f. tə nou ðət djuərɪŋ ðə pɑ·st jə: rɛgjʊlə tɔ·ks əpɒn fonɛtɪks həv bin brɔ·dka·st frəm ðə lʌndən steɪʃn. ðə sʌbdʒɪkts həv bin vɛərɪəs, reɪndʒɪŋ frəm ə tɔ·k ɒn ðə læŋgwɪdʒɪz əv ðə brɪtɪʃ ɛmpaɪə, wɪð ʃɔ·t ɪləstreɪʃnz baɪ neɪtɪv spi·kəz, tʊ ɪkspɛrɪmənts əpɒn ðə rɛkəgnɪʃən əv saʊndz; bət aɪ prəpoʊz tə kənfaɪn ðɪs a·tɪkl tə ðə moʊst ri·snt ɪkspɛrɪmənt.

ɪt ɪz, əv kɔ·s, ə mætər əv kɒmən ɪkspɪərɪəns naʊədeɪz, ðət sɜ·tn saʊndz ɑ nɒt wɛl ri·prədjuːst baɪ ɛnɪ əv ðɪ a·tɪfɪʃl mɛθədz əv spi·tʃ ri·prədʌkʃn. ðə tɛlɪfoʊn ɪz ə noʊtɔ·rɪəs əfɛndə, ənd lɪŋgwɪstɪk wɜ·k baɪ mi:nz əv ðə græməfoʊn ɪz la·dʒlɪ hæmpəd baɪ ðɪs lɪmɪteɪʃn. ðə saʊndz moʊst fri·kwəntlɪ mɪst ɑ ðə vɔɪsləs frɪkətɪvz, əv wɪtʃ ðɪ ɪŋglɪʃ læŋgwɪdʒ hæz faɪv: f, θ, s, ʃ, h. wɛn ðɛər ɪz noʊ a·tɪfɪʃl mi·dɪəm bɪtwin ðə spi·kər ənd ðə lɪsnə, ðɛəɹ ɪz noʊ dɪfɪkltɪ ət ɔːl ɪn ɹekəgnaɪzɪŋ iˑʧ əv ðiˑz saʊndz ɪn aɪsoleɪʃn, əz hæz bɪn ɹɪpiˑtɪdlɪ pɹuːvd baɪ ɪə-treɪnɪŋ tɛsts ət juˑnɪvɜˑsɪtɪ kɒlɪʤ.

ði ɒbʤɪkt əv ðə brɔˑdkɑˑstɪŋ ɪkspɛɹɪmənt wəz tʊ æsəteɪn tə wɒt ɪkstɛnt ðə saʊndz kʊd bɪ aɪdɛntɪfaɪd wɛn hɜːd θɹu ðə miˑdɪəm əv waɪəlɛs trænsmɪʃn.

ði ɔˑdɪəns, kənfaɪnd ɒn ðɪs əkeɪʒn meɪnlɪ tə lʌndən, əz ðə tɔˑk wəz nɒt riːleɪd, wə toʊld ɪgzæktlɪ wɒt wəz tə teɪk pleɪs. ðə saʊndz ðət wə tə bɪ juːzd wəɹ ɪnjuˑməreɪtɪd, dɪskɹaɪbd, gɪvn wɪð ɪgzɑˑmplz, ənd ɛvɹɪ ɛfət meɪd tə meɪk ðə tɛst əz iˑzɪ ənd friː fɹəm kɒmplɪkeɪʃnz əz pɒsəbl. h wəz omɪtɪd, ənd ɪn ədɪʃn tə ðə fɔː rɪneɪnɪŋ ɪŋglɪʃ saʊndz, tuː ʌðəz wə juːzd : **x**, kɒmən ɪn skɒtlənd, ənd ɫ, kɒmən ɪn weɪlz. ðiːz wə dɪskɹaɪbd ɪn diˑteɪl.

naʊ, fɹəm ðiˑz sɪks saʊndz, ə lɪst əv tɛn wəz meɪd, ɪn wɪʧ iˑʧ əv ði ɪŋglɪʃ saʊndz əpɪəd twaɪs, ənd ðə lɪst wəz dɪkteɪtɪd, iˑʧ saʊnd fɔː taɪmz :

f, ɫ, f, θ, s, ʃ, x, θ, ʃ, s. ðə lɪst wəz kɔːld oʊvəɹ əgeɪn fə ðə lɑˑst taɪm.

lɪsnəz siːm tʊ əv fɔˑt ʃaɪ əv ðə tɛst, əz oʊnlɪ 35 ɹɪplaɪz keɪm ɪn, ɪn kɒntɹɑˑst tʊ oʊvə 900 ɹɪplaɪz tə ðə pɹiˑvɪəs tɛst. əmʌŋst ðə ɹɪplaɪz wə tuː fɹəm vɛɹɪ ɛmɪnənt foʊnətɪʃnz, wʌn ɪn lʌndən ənd wʌn ɪn ɛdɪmbɹə. hɪəɹ ɪz ə sʌməɹɪ əv ðə ɹɪzʌlts :

ʃ	wəz ɹɛkəgnaɪzd	50	taɪmz	aʊt əv ə pɒsəbl	70.
x	,,	,,	18	,, ,,	35.
f	,,	,,	12	,, ,,	70.
θ	,,	,,	7	,, ,,	70.
ɫ	,,	,,	3	,, ,,	35.
s	,,	,,	3	,, ,,	70.

ʃ	wəz ɹɛkəgnaɪzd ɒn boʊθ əkeɪʒnz baɪ	22	lɪsnəz.
f	,, ,, ,, ,,	1	lɪsnə.
θ	,, ,, ,, ,,	1	,,
s	,, ,, ,, ,,	0	,,

f	wəz gɪvn əz	h, ʃ, θ, wh, ənd ɫ.
θ	,, ,,	h, f, x.
s	,, ,,	θ, ɫ, x, h.

fɹɒm wɪʧ wi meɪ səmaɪz ðət ði oʊnlɪ ɪŋglɪʃ saʊnd ðət pɹɪzɜːvz ɪts aɪdɛntɪtɪ ɪz ʃ ; ði ʌðəz əpɪə tə bɪ kwaɪt ʌnɹɛkəgnaɪzəbl.

ðə bɛəɹɪŋ əv ðɪs tɛst əpɒn ðə lɑːʤ kwɛsʧn əv ði ɪntɛlɪʤəbɪlɪtɪ əv spiˑʧ mʌst bɪ ɒbvɪəs : ðɛəɹ ɪz oʊnlɪ ɹum tə tʌʧ əpɒn ɪt hɪə.

haʊ ɪz ɪt ðət wi ʌndəstænd wɒt ɪz brɔˑdkɑˑst wɛn aʊər æpəreɪtəs ɪz ɔˑtəmætɪkəlɪ rɒbɪŋ sɜˑtn saʊndz əv ði ɛlɪmənt nɛsəsrɪ fə ðɛə rɛkəgnɪʃn? ɪf ɪt ɪz nɒt nɛsəsrɪ tə hɪər ɔːl ðə saʊndz ə spiˑkə juˑzɪz ɪn ɔˑdə tʊ ʌndəstænd hɪm, haʊ fɑː kən ðɪs proʊsɛs əv ɪlɪmɪneɪʃn bɪ kærɪd bɪfɔˑ ðə spiˑkə bɪkʌmz ʌnɪntɛlɪʤəbl? ɪz ðɛə, ɪn ɪfɛkt, ən əkaʊstɪk mɪnɪməm nɛsəsrɪ fər ɪntɛlɪʤəbɪlɪtɪ, ənd wɒt dʌz ɪt kənsɪst ɒv?

ɪf ðə foʊnətɪʃn ənd ðə saɪkɒləʤɪst kʊd dɪtɜˑmɪn ðə kɒnstɪtjuˑʃn əv ðɪs əkaʊstɪk mɪnɪməm—fə wi kænɒt daʊt ðət ðɛər ɪz sʌtʃ ə θɪŋ—ðɛn pɒsəblɪ wi meɪ hæv njuː laɪt əpɒn ðə neɪtʃər əv lɪŋgwɪstɪk tʃeɪnʤɪz, wɪtʃ meɪ pruːv tə bi nʌθɪŋ bət ə pəpɛtjʊəl riˑəʤʌstmənt əv ðɪs əkaʊstɪk mɪnɪməm.

A. LLOYD JAMES.

ðə biː biː siː kəmɪtɪ ɒn prənʌnsɪeɪʃn

ðə British Broadcasting Company həz biˑn bould ɪnʌf tu əpɔɪnt ən ədvaɪzərɪ kəmɪtɪ ɒn spoukən ɪŋglɪʃ. ðə dɪsɪʒnz əv ðɪs kəmɪtɪ həv ərauzd waɪdspred ɪntrəst, fə menɪ əv ɪts mɛmbəz ɑ skɒləz huz əpɪnjənz kærɪ weɪt. Dr. Robert Bridges (ðə pɔɪt lɔːrɪeɪt) ɪz ðə tʃɛəmən. ʌðə mɛmbəz ɑ Sir Johnston Forbes-Robertson, Professor Daniel Jones, Mr. Bernard Shaw, Mr. Logan Pearsall-Smith (səsaɪətɪ fə pjʊər ɪŋglɪʃ), Mr. Lloyd James, Mr. J. C. W. Reith (mænɪdʒɪŋ dɪrɛktə, brɪtɪʃ brɔˑdkɑˑstɪŋ kʌmpənɪ), Mr. J. C. Stobart (biː biː siː), Mr. B. E. Nicholls (biː biː siː) ənd Miss Somerville (biː biː siː).

ðə praɪmərɪ ɒbdʒɪkt əv ðə kəmɪtɪ ɪz tə dɪskʌs ðə prənʌnsɪeɪʃn əv "dautful wɜːdz", ənd ɑˑftə djuː "kənsɪdəreɪʃn əv derɪveɪʃnz ənd trədɪʃənl juˑzɪdʒɪz" tu ɪstæblɪʃ ə juˑnɪfɔˑm prənʌnsɪeɪʃn fə ðə juˑs əv waɪələs ənaunsəz ənd ʌðər əfɪʃlz əv ðə kʌmpənɪ ɪn ðeə wɜˑk. prəzjuˑməblɪ ðə kəmɪtɪ wɪl ɪsju ɪts ɪˑdɪkts frəm taɪm tə taɪm.

35

əmʌŋ ðə dısıznz ri·tʃt ət ðə fəːst ful miːtıŋ əv ðə kəmıtı ɒn dʒulaı ðə fıfθ wə ðə fɒlɒıŋ :

acoustics	ə'kuːstıks
humour	hjuːmə
often	ɒfn, ɔːfn
idyll	'ıdıl
precedence	prı'siːdns
allies	ə'laız
condolence	kən'douləns
despicable	'dɛspıkəbl
hospitable	'hɒspıtəbl
indisputably	ındıs'pjuːtəblı
obligatory	ob'lıgətərı
garage	'gæraːʒ
char-a-banc	'ʃærəbæŋ

ın ðə keıs əv pleıs neımz, ðə kəmıtı dısaıdıd ðət nou dɛfınıt prınsıpl kud bı leıd daun, bət ðət iːtʃ ʃud bı kənsıdəd əz niːd ərouz. ðə fɒlɒıŋ wər əgriːd əpɒn :

Boulogne	bu'loun
Lyons	'laıənz
Marseilles	maː'seılz]
Rheims	riːmz

ıt wəz ɔːlsou dısaıdıd ðət ðə tɛndənsı tu ınkriːs ðə nʌmbər əv hɒməfounz ın ðə læŋgwıdʒ ʃud bı əpouzd : iː dʒiː, ðət ənaunsəz ʃud meık ə dıstıŋʃn bıtwiːn wəːdz laık *Shaw, shore,* ənd *sure*; bıtwiːn *your* ənd *yore,* ıtsɛtrə; ðət ənaunsəz ʃud ətɛmpt tə gıv tu ɔːl vauəlz ın ʌnæksɛntıd sıləblz ə "fleıvər əv ðɛər ɒrıdʒınl kærəktə". hau faːr ız ðıs laːst rɛkəmɛndeıʃn sədʒɛstıd baı ðə spɛʃl rıkwaıəmənts əv reıdıou ? .

ðə biː biː siː hæz ðʌs ıstæblıʃt ə faınl kɒət əv prənʌnsıeıʃn tə huz əθɒrıtıː ɔːl ıts ənaunsəz mʌst ın taım səbmıːt. hau wıl ıts dısıznz əfɛkt ıŋglıʃ prənʌnsıeıʃn əv ıŋglıʃ? ız ıt ɛvə laıklı tə bıkʌm fə ðə dʒɛnrl pʌblık wɒt ıt ız fə ðə brıtıʃ brɔːdkaːstıŋ kʌmpənı ? ðı əpınjənz əv mɛmbəz əv ðı a.f. ɒn ðə sʌbdʒɪkt wıl bı wɛlkəmd.

L. E. A.

ə test fə ˈtɛlɪfoun ˈɒpəreɪtəz

ðə ˈnæʃnəl ˈɪnstɪtjut əv ɪnˈdʌstrɪəl saɪˈkɒlədʒɪ həz ˈbiːn fə ˈsʌm ˈtaɪm ɪŋˈgeɪdʒd əpɒn rɪˈsɜ·tʃ ɪntu ðə ˈmenɪ ˈkwestʃənz ðət əˈraɪz ɪn ðə ˈwɜ·k əv ˈtɛlɪfoun ˈɒpəreɪtəz, ənd ˈæz ˈsʌm əv ˈðiːz ˈkwestʃənz ə kənˈsɜːnd wɪð ˈspiːtʃ, aɪ həv bɪn ˈɑ·skt tu ˈhelp ɪn dɪˈvaɪzɪŋ ˈtests.

'mɛni prəs'pɛktɪv 'tɛlɪfoun 'ɒpəreɪtəz 'feɪl tə gɛt 'θru: ðɛə
'pɪərjəd əv prə'beɪʃn bɪ'kɔ:z ðeɪ 'kænɒt ə'teɪn ðə 'nɛsɪsrɪ 'stændəd
əv ə'kjuːtɪ ɪn 'hɪərɪŋ. ɪt bɪ'keɪm 'nɛsɪsrɪ 'ðɛəfɔ, tə 'tɛst ðə
'kændɪdeɪts ə'kjuːtɪ bɪ'fɔːr əd'mɪtɪŋ ðəm tu prə'beɪʃn, ɪn 'ɔːdə tu
ɪ'lɪmɪneɪt ət 'wʌns ðə dɪ'fɛktɪv wʌnz. tu ɪn'vɛnt ə 'tɛst ðət ʃud
rɪ'zɛmbl ði 'ɔːdɪnəri 'wɜ·kɪŋ kən'dɪʃnz əv ði 'ɒpəreɪtəz 'deɪlɪ
'tɑ·sk, wəz 'nɒt ən 'iːzɪ 'mætə, ənd ɪn 'ɔːdə tu ɪn'vɛstɪgeɪt ðə
'neɪtʃər əv 'ðiːz kən'dɪʃnz, aɪ 'spɛnt ən 'auər ɪn ə 'sɪti 'tɛlɪfoun
ɪks'tʃeɪndʒ 'lɪsnɪŋ 'ɪn ə'lɒŋ'saɪd ən 'ɒpəreɪtə, ənd 'hɪərɪŋ 'ɪn'kʌmɪŋ
'kɔːlz ʌndər 'ɔːdɪnəri kən'dɪʃnz. aɪ 'lɛft ðə 'swɪtʃbɔ·d wɪð ə 'vɛri
'haɪlɪ ɪŋ'krɪ·st rɪ'gɑːd fə ði 'ɒpəreɪtəz ɪ'fɪʃnsɪ, fɔ ʃi 'hɑːd 'kɔːlz ðət
ɪs'keɪpt mi kəm'plɪ·tlɪ, ənd ɪt wəz 'vɛri 'iːzɪ tə 'siː ðət ðə 'stændəd
əv 'əkjuɪtɪ əv hɪərɪŋ 'mʌst əv nɪ'sɛsɪtɪ bi 'haɪ. bət tə rɪprə'djuˑs
'ðiːz kən'dɪʃnz atɪ'fɪʃəlɪ fə ðə 'pɜ·pəsɪz əv ə 'tɛst ðət wud bɪ 'keɪpəbl
əv rɛpɪ'tɪʃn wɪð'aʊt vɛərɪ'eɪʃn wəz 'noʊ 'iːzɪ 'mætə. ɪt wəz 'ɒbvɪəs
ðət ə 'græməfoʊn 'rɛkɔd 'maɪt bi 'sjutəbl ɪf ɪt kud bi 'meɪd tə
rɪprə'djuˑs ɪn 'ɛni 'weɪ ðə 'sɔ·ts əv 'θɪŋ ðət ði 'ɒpəreɪtə hæz tu 'wɜ·k
əpɒn. ʌn'fɔ·tʃənətlɪ, ðə 'mɒdən 'prousəs əv rɪ'kɔːdɪŋ ɪz 'soʊ 'gud
ðət wi kud gɛt 'noʊ 'rɛkɔd ' bæd ɪnʌf: 'ɛvrɪ 'kændɪdeɪt wud
həv gɒt 100%! ət 'lɑ·st, wi 'meɪd ə 'rɛkɔd əv ðə 'vɔɪs træns'mɪtɪd
θru ən 'ɔːdɪnəri 'tɛlɪfoun, ənd 'ðɪs wəz 'mɔː sætɪs'fæktrɪ.
ɪn 'ɔːdə tə gɪv 'ɛvrɪ 'kændɪdeɪt ə 'fɛə tʃɑːns əv bɪɪŋ fə'mɪljə
wɪð ðə 'neɪmz 'kɔːld 'aʊt, ði 'ɪŋglɪʃ 'kaʊntɪ 'neɪmz ə 'juːzd ɪnstɛd
əv 'lʌndən 'ɪkstʃeɪndʒ neɪmz, ənd 'ðɛn 'nʌmbəz 'fɒloʊ ɪn ði
'ɔ·θədɒks 'weɪ. 'taɪm ɪz ə'laud bɪ'twiːn ðə 'kɔːlz fə 'kændɪdeɪts tə
'raɪt 'daun wɒt ðeɪ 'hɪə.
ə 'fɜːðə kɒmplɪ'keɪʃn ə'raɪzɪz, bɪkɒz ðə 'tɛlɪfoun 'ɒpəreɪtə ɪn hə
'deɪlɪ 'laɪf hɪəz 'ɔːl 'sɔ·ts əv 'vɔɪsɪz ɪn 'ɔːl 'sɔ·ts əv 'æksənts, 'spoʊkn
ət 'ɔːl 'sɔ·ts əv 'spiːd wɪð 'ɔːl və'raɪtɪz əv ɪ'moʊʃn. soʊ wi brɔ·t
'ðɪs 'fɪ·tʃə ɪntu ðə 'rɛkɔd: aɪ 'juːzd 'ɛvrɪ və'raɪtɪ əv 'vɔɪs, 'pɪtʃ,
ɪnto'neɪʃn ənd 'æksənt ðət aɪ wəz fə'mɪljə wɪð, frɒm ði ædə'nɔɪdl
'drɔːl əv ðə 'kɒknɪ tu ðə 'faɪərɪ 'spiˑd əv ði aɪ'reɪt 'wɛlʃmən hu həz
bɪn 'gɪvn ðə 'rɒŋ 'nʌmbə. 'tuː 'fiːmeɪl 'vɔɪsɪz—əv ðə saɪkə'lɒdʒɪkəl
'stɑ·f— ər ɪntə'spɜ·st, ənd ðə rɪ'zʌlt ɪz ə 'fɛəlɪ 'dʒʌst rɪprə'dʌkʃn
əv wɒt ði 'ɒpəreɪtə 'hæz tu ɪn'djuə.
æt ðə 'moʊmənt, ðə 'rɛkɔd ɪz bɪɪŋ 'juːzd ɪkspɛrɪ'mɛntəlɪ, bət ɪt
ɪz 'laɪklɪ tu bi ə'dɒptɪd 'faɪnəlɪ, ənd wɪl bɪ'kʌm ə 'pɑ·t əv ði
ə'fɪʃl 'tɛst.

əˈnʌðər ˈæspɛkt əv ˈðɪs ˈwɜ·k ðət ɪz əv ˈɪntrəst tʊ foʊnɛˈtɪʃnz ɪz ðə ˈtɛstɪŋ əv ˈkændɪdeɪts prənʌnsɪˈeɪʃn, ənd ˈhɪər əˈgɛn ðə ˈstændəd ɪz ˈhaɪ. ðɛər ɪz ˈɛvɪdəntlɪ ə kəˈrɪə ˈhɪə fə ˈsʌm ˈfjutʃə foʊnɛˈtɪʃn, hu wɪl hæv tə ˈmeɪk ði əˈfɪʃl ˈstændəd prənʌnsɪˈeɪʃn əv ˈɪŋglɪʃ tʊ bi əˈdɒptɪd baɪ ðə ˈpoʊst ɒfɪs.

ˈkændɪdeɪts hu ˈkænɒt ˈtrɪl ði " ɑːr " ər əv ˈkɔ·s rɪˈdʒɛktɪd wɪðaʊt ˈfɜ·ðə ˈtraɪəl. bət ðɛr ə ˈsʌtl vəˈraɪɪtɪz əv ˈvaʊəl ən ˈdɪfθɒŋ prənʌnsɪˈeɪʃn ðət ˈmʌst ˈkɔːz ði əˈfɪʃl ɪgˈzæmɪnəz ˈmʌtʃ æŋˈzaɪətɪ, ənd aɪ əm ˈɔ·fn ˈtɛmtɪd tʊ ˈwʌndə ˈhuː dɪˈsaɪdz ˈhaʊ ˈmʌtʃ æfrɪˈkeɪʃn of ðə " t " ɪn " ˈtuː " ənd ɪn " ˈtɛn " ʃəl bi əˈlaʊd.

əˈpɑ·t frəm ðə ˈspɛʃl ˈɪntrəst əv ˈðiːz ˈtɛsts, ɪt ɪz ˈgrætɪfaɪɪŋ tʊ əbˈzɜːv ðət ðə ˈfiːld əv foˈnɛtɪk ɪŋˈkwaɪərɪ ənd ækˈtɪvɪtɪ ɪz ˈwaɪdnɪŋ ɪntʊ ði ɪnˈdʌstrɪəl ˈɛərɪə, ənd aɪ ɪksˈpɛkt ðət ðɛə wɪl bi ˈfɜːðə saɪkəˈlɒdʒɪkl ɪnvɛstɪˈgeɪʃn ɪntʊ ˈvɛərjəs ˈʌðər ˈæspɛkts əv ˈlæŋgwɪdʒ.

·A. LLOYD JAMES.

ðə lɑːst m.f.

əz mɛmbəz wil nəu, ðis iz ðə lɑːst nʌmbər əv ði **m.f.** in its preznt fɔːm. ɑː dʒɜːnl wəz pʌbliʃt fə ðə fɜːst taim in 1889, ðəu priːvjəsli, frəm 1886, it əd əpiəd əz " ðə fənetik tiːtʃə ". in 1889, ɑːr əsəusieiʃn hæd 321 membəz in 18 kʌntriz, ðə mədʒɒrəti kʌmiŋ frəm *swiːdn, *dʒɜːməni ən *frɑːns. tədei, wiː hæv mɔː ðn 800 membəz in əuvə 40 kʌntriz, ðə greit mədʒɒrəti kʌmiŋ frəm ðə *jʊnaitid steits ən *greit britn.

nɑu ðət wiː əv disaidid tə print ɑː njuː *Journal* in ɔːθɒgrəfi, fə ðə fɜːst taim in dʒuːn 1971, it iz həupt ðət ðə riːdəʃip wil bi inlɑːdʒd ən ðət kɒntribjuːʃnz wil bi risiːvd frəm ə waidə sɜːkl əv fəunitiʃnz ən tiːtʃəz. məust əv ɑː membəz huː əv riplaid tə ðə sɜːkjələr in ðə lɑːst **m.f.** həv signifaid ðət ðei wiʃ tə kəntinjuː tə səbskraib tə ðə njuː *Journal*. ðəuz huː əv nɒt jet infɔːmd əs əv ðɛər intenʃnz ər ɜːdʒd tə duː səu wiðaut dilei, sins ɑː fainænsiz wil nɒt əlɑu əs tə send ðə *Journal* tə fɔːmə membəz huːz səbskripʃnz ə nɒt rinjuːd.

wi ikspekt ðə njuː *Journal* tə kəntein əbaut 50 peidʒiz ət ði autset. fə ðis riːzn, in ðə fɜːst nʌmbəz ət liːst, wiː wil limit ðə leŋkθ əv kɒntribjuːʃnz tuː ə mæksiməm əv əbaut 3,000 wɜːdz. ðə fɒləuiŋ nəuts fə kəntribjutəz giv ən indikeiʃn əv ðə rikwaiəments əv prezenteiʃn fə ðə *Journal*; ðei wil in fjuːtʃə bi printid ɒn ðə *Journalz* kʌvə.